GENEALOGICAL ABSTRACTS
FROM

The

Mirror

1880-1890
LOUDOUN COUNTY
VIRGINIA

Patricia B. Duncan

HERITAGE BOOKS
2008

HERITAGE BOOKS
AN IMPRINT OF HERITAGE BOOKS, INC.

Books, CDs, and more—Worldwide

For our listing of thousands of titles see our website
at
www.HeritageBooks.com

Published 2008 by
HERITAGE BOOKS, INC.
Publishing Division
100 Railroad Ave. #104
Westminster, Maryland 21157

Copyright © 2008 Patricia B. Duncan

All rights reserved. No part of this book may be reproduced or transmitted in any form or by any means, electronic or mechanical, including photocopying, recording or by any information storage and retrieval system without written permission from the author, except for the inclusion of brief quotations in a review.

International Standard Book Numbers
Paperbound: 978-0-7884-4578-1
Clothbound: 978-0-7884-7659-4

INTRODUCTION

This book provides abstracts of articles containing genealogical or other historical information from *The Mirror* newspapers of Loudoun County, Virginia. The *Democratic Mirror* newspapers were published 1857-1861, with later issues titled *The Mirror*.

Microfilms of the following Loudoun County newspapers are available through the Interlibrary Loan service of the Library of Virginia.

The Democratic Mirror and *The Mirror* newspapers:
(Library of Virginia Reel Series 284)

17 Jun 1857 - 4 Dec 1861
14 Jun 1865 - 31 Dec 1874
12 Jul 1865 – 31 Oct 1878
7 Jan 1875 - 25 Feb 1879
6 Feb 1879 - 15 Nov 1883
1 Jan 1880 - 27 Dec 1883
24 Jan 1884 - 27 Dec 1888
3 Jan 1889 - 31 Dec 1891
7 Jan 1892 - 20 Dec 1894
3 Jan 1895 - 16 Dec 1897
6 Jan 1898 - 27 Dec 1900
3 Jan 1884 - 31 Oct 1901
1 Jan 1901 - 7 Aug 1902
4 Jun 1908 - 24 Dec 1919
4 Jul 1913 - 22 Dec 1916

The Loudoun Telephone newspapers:
(Library of Virginia Reel Series 363)

7 Jan 1881 - 26 Dec 1884
2 Jan 1885 - 21 Dec 1888
4 Jan 1889 - 25 Dec 1891
1 Jan 1892 - 28 Apr 1893
4 May 1894 - 11 Sep 1896

Some of the above reels show overlapping dates. Although some issues appeared on both reels, most reels contain mainly issues that do not appear in the other reels. There are also a number of missing issues in each series.

The front page of each issue usually consisted of business cards and general entertainment articles. Subsequent pages contained advertisements and legal notices, local general and personal news, obituaries, marriage announcements, and some national and international news.

Although some entries in this book are the complete article, many are shortened abstracts. Marriage announcements and obituaries were sometimes long and flowery, and parts have been omitted here.

Abbreviations may have been used in these abstracts. Administrator/Administratrix may be abbreviated as Admr. and Executor/Executrix as Exor. Ages are often shortened to year month day (y m d.) Months are sometimes abbreviated and dau. might be used as an abbreviation for daughter.

As with any transcription of records, it is advisable to obtain a copy of the original document to verify the accuracy. Although every effort is made to transcribe accurately, mistakes are inevitable.

Special thanks to the Library of Virginia and the Special Collections Library of Albuquerque, New Mexico.

The Mirror
Published at Leesburg, Loudoun County, Virginia

Thursday, 1 January 1880   Vol. XXIV, No. 29

Married: In Washington City on the 17th of Dec 1879, by the Rev. Mr. ___, Mr. James M. HEAD, formerly of Leesburg, and Miss Annie ROTCHFORD, of Vienna, Fairfax Co.

Married: Near Upperville, Fauquier Co, on Tues., Dec 23rd 1879, by the Rev. I. B. LAKE, Mr. James W. MORIARTY and Miss Lizzie LANHAM, both of Loudoun Co.

Married: On the afternoon of Christmas eve, at the Baptist Church, in Warrenton, by Rev. H. H. WYER, Mr. A. Cornelius WYCKOFF, formerly of Loudoun Co, to Miss Barbara L. BOOTH, dau. of Mr. Geo. G. BOOTH, of Warrenton.

Married: In Christ Church, Winchester by Rev. Dr. HUBARD, on the 16th instant, at 1 p.m., George Barksdale ANDERSON, Esq., of Texas to Miss Maria Burwell CARTER, daughter of A. B. CARTER, of Winchester, Va.

Married: In Washington city, on Sunday evening, Dec. 28th 1879, by Rev. Dr. HARRISON, John J. TYLER, Esq. and Marietta F., dau. of the late Joseph P. MEGEATH, both of Loudoun Co.

Died: At Avon, Fairfax Co, Thurs. Dec. 25th, 1879, after a protracted illness, Nannie Lee, dau. of Judge R. H. COCKERILLE, and wife of Richard Moncure CHICHESTER.

Died: At his residence near Lovettsville, in this county, on Wed. morning, Dec. 11th, 1879, Noah COOPER, in his 46th year.

Mr. Robert B. FILLER, son of Col. A. T. M. FILLER, of Leesburg, and brother of Dr. C. W. FILLER, of Baltimore, died at St. Louis on Monday, of typhoid fever. He was cashier in the wholesale grocery house of F. Mitchell & Bro.

Thursday, 8 January 1880   Vol. XXIV, No. 30

Married: on the 30th ult., at the Methodist Parsonage in Hamilton, by A. A. P. NEEL, Mr. J. Isaac BROWN, to Miss Sarah W. TAVENNER, both of this county.

Married: On the 18th ult, in Alexandria, by Rev. W. K. BOYLE, A. A. P. NEEL, of the Balto. Conf., to Miss Ida C. PAYNE, of this county, formerly of Baltimore.

Married: By Rev. J. A. HAYNES, Nov. 26, 1879, Mr. Campbell MIDDLETON and Miss Julia A. McDONALD, both of Fauquier County.

Married: By the same, Dec. 11, Mr. Chas. S. GRAY and Miss Augusta M. SMALLWOOD, both of Fauquier County.

Married: By the same on the same day, Mr. A. J. YOUELL and Miss Sallie C. MILBURN, of Loudoun County.

Married: By the same on Dec. 23d, at Long Branch Church, Mr. Chas. E. DAVIS, of Loudoun, and Miss California CROUCH, of Fauquier County.

Married: At the residence of the bride's parents, Dec. 18, 1879, Mr. Burr O. COMPHER and Miss Floretta D. KALB, Rev. P. H. MILLER officiating.

Married: Dec. 24, 1879, by the same, at the Parsonage, Mr. Tilghman EVERHART and Miss Margaret O. SNOOTS.

Married: On the 18th ulto., at the Lutheran Parsonage, in Jefferson, Md, by the Rev. W. H. SETTLEMYER, Benj. L. REX to Miss Lavinia J. SMITH, both of the vicinity of Lovettsville.

Married: At the Lutheran Church, Neersville, on Tuesday evening, Dec. 30th, by the Rev. Isaac W. BOBST, Mr. John H. REED and Miss Clara J. ROBEY, both of Loudoun.

Married: At the residence of Mr. A. CONRAD Sr., on Tuesday morning Dec 30, by the Rev. Isaac W. BOBST, Mr. Jos. H. JONES and Miss Mollie HARTMAN, both of Loudoun.

Married: [creased] In this town, Dec. 31, by Rev. J. F. CANNON, Mr. T. H. ROSE and Miss Sarah F. SOLOMON, all of Loudoun.

Died: At her residence, near Goresville, on Monday morning, Dec. 22d, 1879, Mrs. Sallie LOY, aged 68 years.

Died: Of diphtheria, in Leesburg, at the residence of her grandfather, John W. HAMMERLY, Ridie, daughter of Thomas F. and Helen A. BURCH, in the 6th year of her age.

Died: Repps B. CRENSHAW, second son of Rev. L. H. and Annie CRENSHAW, aged 15y 1m 21d, died at the Parsonage in Upperville, Dec. 27th, 1879. Disease, scarlet fever.

Died: Annie HUGHES, youngest daughter of Elias and Virginia HUGHES, died early in the morning of the 30th ult, of scarlet fever, aged 12 years.

Mr. F. M. HENDERSON a few weeks ago lapsed into such a fit of melancholy as to incapacitate him for the duties of his office. On Monday morning he was conveyed to the Asylum at Staunton.

Thursday, 15 January 1880 Vol. XXIV, No. 31

Married on the 23d ultimo, by the Rev. E. BUHRMAN, in Montgomery Co, Md, at the residence of the bride's brother, Dr. B. F. LANSDALE, W. Edmund OSBURN, of Jefferson Co, W. Va. to Alice, dau. of H. N. LANSDALE, of Washington DC.

Married: On the evening of the 1st instant at the Reformed Parsonage near Lovettsville, by the Rev. H. St. Jno. RINKER, Mr. J. Jared ATWELL to Miss Gertrude JOHNSON, all of Loudoun County.

Married: On the 30th of Dec 1879, at the residence of Mr. George F. MILLER, of Frederick City, Geo. W. KAUFMAN to Miss Ella V. MILLER, both of Loudoun County.

Married: At the residence of the bride's mother, Dec. 3d, 1879, by the Rev. L. C. MILLER, Mr. J. A. HAMPTON and Miss Jennie D. RILEY, all of Loudoun.

Married: At the residence of Mr. G. W. SUMMERS, near Middleburg, Jan. 8th, 1880, by Rev. L. C. MILLER, David J. COLEMAN and Sallie B. CHICHESTER, all of Fauquier Co.

Died: In Leesburg, on Tuesday morning, Jan. 6, 1880, Mrs. Ann RYON, consort of the late John RYON, in the 50th year of her age. Member of the M. E. Church.

Died: Rebecca FRANCIS, widow of the late Henry FRANCIS, died on Sunday, the 4th inst., aged 87.

Died: Near Mountsville, Dec. 27th, 1879, Annie, infant dau. of Wm. J. and Mary F. COCHRAN, aged 9d.

Samuel BALL died at his home, near Waterford, on the 7th inst., aged 67 years.

Hannah J. PIGGOTT died at her residence, near Philomont, of pneumonia, on Monday, the 5th inst., in the 66th year of her age. Her last illness was short and severe. Member of Society of Friends. Interred on the 7th in Friend's burial ground at Goose Creek Meeting House.

Died: In Leesburg, on Friday afternoon, Jan. 9th, 1880, at the home of her nephew, Mr. L. W. S. HOUGH, Miss Fanny SHEPHERD, in the 76th year of her age. For more than half a century a member of M. E. Church.

January Ct.: Administration granted on estates of Armistead MAGAHA dec'd., Hannah J. PIGGOTT and Susan A. RYAN dec'd. Estates of Claiborne BARLEY and John RYAN committed to Sheriff. Jno. MILTON qualified as Committee of Rachel A. BEAMER. Will of John EVERHART dec'd. admitted to probate. Henry REED's estate – account recommitted to Commissioner R. H. TEBBS.

A letter has been received in the city from the Deputy Sheriff of Loudoun Co., Mr. Wm. S. SUMMERS, asking information in regard to an old man named Wm. P. McGUIRE. McGUIRE came to his house a short time ago and stated that he was from Alexandria, and owned a house and lot near Hunting Creek. He was taken sick shortly after arriving, died on the 13th of Dec. and was buried by Mr. SUMMERS at Belmont Church some five miles from Guilford Station. People living in the neighborhood of Hunting Creek have no knowledge of such a man ever living in that neighborhood. *Alexandria Gazette.*

Thursday, 22 January 1880   Vol. XXIV, No. 32

Married: On Tuesday, 6th of Jan, 1880, by Elder Benjamin BRIDGES, Mr. J. W. CARSON to Miss Martha A. HORSEMAN, both of Loudoun County.

Married: On Thursday, 9th of January, by the same, Mr. William TRICKETT to America, eldest daughter of H. W. and Lucinda COCKERILLE, of Fairfax County.

Married: On the 8th of January 1880 at the residence of the bride's parents, by Rev. W. R. STRINGER, Mr. E. V. JENKINS and Miss Mary F. WORKS, all of Loudoun County.

Married: On the 30th ulto., at the rectory of the Cathedral, in Baltimore, by Rev. Father CURTIS, John R. BARNHOUSE, of Loudoun County, to Miss Genevieve BOTELER, of Frederick County, Md.

Married: On the 7th instant, at the residence of the bride's father, near Buckeystown, by the Rev. Dr. TRAPNELL, Maurice DADE, of Jefferson, to Miss Rachie, daughter of Capt. Joseph N. CHISWELL, both of Frederick County, Maryland.

Married: January 14th 1880, at the residence of the bride's mother, by the Rev. John WOOLF, Mr. Washington BEAVERS to Miss Fannie BEAVERS, all of Loudoun County.

Died: At the residence of her son-in-law, Mr. G. W. WEADON, near Woodburn, on the 1st day of January 1880, Mrs. Elizabeth LOVELESS, in the 74th year of her age.

Died: [creased] October 28th? 1879, in Snickersville, Meshach, son of Joseph F. and Sallie M. ALDER, in his 4th year.

Died: Of pneumonia, at Sugarland View, Loudoun Co, January 14th, James Coleman COCKERILLE, in his 56th year.

Mr. James COCKERILLE, of Loudoun, brother of Judge R. H. COCKERILLE, of Fairfax, died at his residence in this county last week.

Winchester – An investigation brought out the fact that the negro, Arthur GORDON, a married man with two or three children, from Fauquier Co., eloped with a white woman, a Miss CORDER. The latter is said to be of one of the first families in Fauquier co but of weak intellect. Seven men, citizens of the county, had followed the negro over into Maryland, near Clear Spring, where they arrested him and brought him through here on their way to their own county. J. B. STRIBLING, as special constable, let them proceed on their way. It is understood that after the pair eloped they proceeded to the house of Chas. SHUPP, about four miles from Williamsport, Md, where they had been living for the past ten days. [second article] – Negro JORDAN, as above, was taken to Warrenton and remained in jail until Sunday night when a party of masked men surrounded the building, seized the prisoner, and hung him to a tree.

Warrenton, Jan. 19 – Near the little village of Markham, a station on the Manassas Gap railroad, in Fauquier Co, there lives a family named CORDER, consisting of an old man, his wife, two sons and a daughter. The daughter is a fine looking buxom girl, but very simple in intellect. A negro man named Arthur JORDAN has been employed by Mr. CORDERS for three years. He was about 30 years old and had a wife and two children. Last summer he violated the girl and threatened to kill her if she informed the family of the fact, and by the same threats made her submit to his wishes during the late summer and fall. Some days ago Miss CORDER became *enceinte*, and the negro persuaded her to run off with him. .... Arthur JORDAN was a large bull-necked, thick-lipped negro, very black and forbidding looking.

Thursday, 29 January 1880   Vol. XXIV, No. 33

Married: At the residence of Mr. WALKER, near Guilford, on the 20th inst., by Rev. W. R. STRINGER, Mr. John W. DARNES and Miss Martha E. NICHOLS, all of Loudoun County.

Married: On the 21st inst., by the Rev. B. A. SHREVE, at the residence of the bride's parents, Mr. Chas. F. MUSE, to Miss Ida J. HAVENNER, all of Loudoun.

Married: January 22d, at the Parsonage of the M. E. Church, in Leesburg, by Rev. W. H. FORSYTH, L. Neal HOUGH, to Miss Ada E. BENNETT, both of Loudoun.

Married: At the Lutheran Parsonage, Lovettsville, Jan. 8th, by Rev. P. H. MILLER, Mr. Wm. L. SLATER and Miss Flora E. COLLINS, both of Loudoun.

Married: In Alexandria, January 25th, at the parsonage of the Baptist Church, by Rev. Mr. PENICK, Mr. Albert D. BEACH, of Leesburg, to Miss Katie D. RUDD, of that city.

Died: Hannah TAYLOR, relict of the late Yardley TAYLOR, departed this life at her residence, near Lincoln, at 5 o'clock, on the morning of the 24d inst., in the 87th year of her age.

Died: On Monday morning, Dec. 22d, 1879, Mrs. Sarah LOY, consort of Adam LOY. She was in her 68th year. Faithful wife and mother. For two weeks her suffering was great.

Died: In Hillsboro, on the night of January 19th, Mrs. Estell TAVENNER, wife of Dr. W. W. TAVENNER, and daughter of William HOUGH, Esq.

Thursday, 5 February 1880   Vol. XXIV, No. 34

Early on the morning of Oct. 23rd, '79, the body of Edward THOMAS, a colored man, was found lying in the public road a short distance from Snickersville with a gunshot wound in the back of the neck. He died during the next day. A feud was known to exist with Saml. ROBINSON, another colored man. Trial held, sentenced to death on Friday the 9th of April between 6 and 8 in the morning. ROBINSON is a bright mulatto, about 5' 8", of slender build, and about 30 years of age. He has a wife and six children. He makes the 4th man hung in Loudoun Co since its formation. The first unknown, the second was "Roger's Dick" hung on gallows hill about 1 mile south of Leesburg, somewhere about the year 1830, and the third, "Ramey's Lewis," hung about 1 mile east of Leesburg, near what is now known as Fort Beauregard, in 1848. All three were negroes, all hung for the crime of rape.

Married: By the Rev. B. A. SHREVE, on the 26th inst., Mr. Lemuel W. BRECKENRIDGE to Miss Alberta SHRY, all of Loudoun.

Married: On the 28th inst., by Elder E. V. WHITE, at New Valley Meeting House, Mr. Thomas J. LOY to Miss Mary E. UMBAUGH, all of Loudoun.

Married: January 28th 1880, at Round Hill, by the Rev. Saml. BROWN, Mr. Wm. H. FRAME, to Miss Virginia B. PANGLE, all of this county.

Mary C. FRERE departed this life at her residence in Mt. Gilead, 10 minutes of twelve, Friday night, January 30th 1880, in the 45th year of her age.

Mr. Samuel MULLEN, for many years a citizen of Leesburg, died at Bethel, in this county, Thursday night last.

Last week the escape of Page WALLACE, colored, who awaited trial for attempted rape. News received that on Thursday night he assaulted another white woman, Miss Mary MORMAN, on this side of the river opposite Pt. of Rocks, then escaped into Maryland. The victim was badly bruised, one eye being entirely closed. He was captured on Monday.

Thursday, 12 February 1880   Vol. XXIV, No. 35

Married: February 5th 1880, at the Parsonage of the M. E. Church, South, Leesburg, by Rev. H. H. KENNEDY, Mr. Herbert GRAHAM and Miss Sallie J. JOHNSTON.

Married: February 5th, at the Parsonage of the M. E. Church, Leesburg, by Rev. W. H. FORSYTH, Isaac H. MOCK and Miss Mary V. VIRTZ, both of Loudoun.

Married: At the residence of Mr. James ROBERTS, February 5th, by Rev. John WOOLF, Mrs. Ruthanna ARNETT and Mr. John ARNETT, all of Loudoun.

Married: At the residence of the bride's father, John S. GLASCOCK, February 5th 1880, by Rev. I. B. LAKE, Miss Agnes GLASCOCK to Henry V. GLASCOCK.

Married: February 5, 1880, at Paris, Va., Mr. Milton J. HOPPER, of Fauquier, to Miss Emma A. GREENE, daughter of J. Frank

GREENE, Esq. of Clarke Co, Rev. L. H. CRENSHAW officiating.

Died: At his residence in Baltimore, Md, on the 4th inst., John J. OSBURN, elder son of Mortimer and Mary OSBURN, and formerly a residence of this county, in the 38th year of his age.

Died: Mrs. S. E. PRICE, wife of Russell PRICE, Esq., of Neersville, and eldest dau. of the late Col. John CHURCHILL, of Warren Co. Va, died at the former place Jan. 12th 1880, aged 33 years.

Remains of Mr. John JANNEY, son of the late George W. JANNEY, of Hamilton, were brought to this town, on Tuesday, and buried in Union Cemetery. He took cold and ran into pneumonia, from which he died on Sunday night. He was in about the 27th year of his age.

Rev. Henry CLEMENTS, of the Va Conference, M. E. Church, died last Tuesday in Baltimore, after a brief illness. At one time pastor of the M. E. Church at Leesburg.

Frederick H. FRITTS, of Purcellville, has been assailed on account of testimony given by him before us, upon the commitment of Wm. BIRKETT as a lunatic on the 6th of July 1875.

Thursday, 19 February 1880   Vol. XXIV, No. 36

Page WALLACE, arrested on suspicion of rape [see previous issues] was lynched by a mob who overcame the deputy, about 7 o'clock on Tuesday last, Feb 17th.

Married: February 5th 1880, at St. Mark's Church, by Rev. A. Floridus STEEL, Lucius E. GRIDLEY, of Michigan to Edith A. WALKER, of Washington DC.

Married: On Thursday evening, February 12th at the residence of the bride's father, by Elder Joseph L. FURR, Mr. Frank N. FURR to Miss Fannie B, second dau. of Henry VIRTS, Esq.

Died: At her home in Loudoun County, on February 12th 1880, Ella, daughter of Maj. Geo. W. and Ruth H. NOLAND.

Betsy HOPKINS (colored), died in Waterford last Sunday night, at the advanced age, according to most reliable data, of 106 years.

Round Hill, February 16: A negro named David CALVERT, froze to death in the woods near Mr. Norval SILLCOTT's in the neighborhood of Snickersville, on Saturday night, the 7th inst. He had been to a raffle and become so intoxicated that he could not travel.

Thursday, 26 February 1880   Vol. XXIV, No. 37

Married: At Christ Church, near Goresville, on Tuesday morning, February 24th 1880, by Rev. S. S. WARE, Mr. George A. BALL and Miss Annie, second daughter of Mr. John H. WHITMORE, all of Loudoun.

Married: February 17, 1880, at the residence of Mr. N. T. ASHBY, by Rev. W. G. HAMMOND, Mr. Henry C. BROWN, of Rappahannock, and Miss L. T. ASHBY, of Fauquier.

Married: By Rev. Mr. LEONARD, on the 10th inst., at the Trinity Episcopal Church, Hannibal, Mo, W. R. CHINN, son of R. S. CHINN, of Loudoun Co, to Miss Libbie S. CORBETT, of Hannibal, Mo.

Died: In Baltimore, on Sunday, Feb. 15th, 1880, Annie Eubank, in her 21st year, wife of Samuel REGESTER Jr., of Baltimore, and daughter of the late Dr. Thomas P. EUBANK.

Died: At his residence in Columbus, Texas, on the morning of the 9th instant, of acute bronchitis, James Hendley SIMPSON, formerly of Fairfax Co., aged 60y 10m 27d.

Died: Suddenly, at his mother's residence, Hamilton, February 8th 1880, of consumption, J. C. JANNEY, in his 29th year. Funeral took place at his home, Tuesday, at 11 a.m., Rev. P. H. MILLER, who was his college and class-mate for five years, officiated. Interred in Union Cemetery, Leesburg.

Died: Mary F. DAVIS, after a lingering illness between 3 and 4 years, on the 7th of February, in the 21st year of her age.

Mr. Peter Edmunds HOFFMAN died at "Raspberry Plains," near Leesburg, on Tuesday morning, the 24th of Feb., after a brief illness. For many years an officer in the Bank of the Old Dominion at Alexandria, but for the last 15 years a resident of Loudoun. Member of Episcopal Church. If he had lived until the next day (Wed., his birthday) he would have been 82 years old.

Mr. POWERS, owner of the "Wheatland Mills" was paralyzed on Sat. evening and died on Monday morning. Buried at Lovettsville on Tuesday.

Rev. J. F. CANNON, pastor of the Presbyterian Church, Leesburg, left here last week, for Clarksville, Tenn, where he was to have been married on Tuesday to Miss Mary LUPTON, eldest daughter of Rev. J. W. LUPTON, formerly of this town.

Thursday, 4 March 1880   Vol. XXIV, No. 38

Married: At the Baptist Church, Middleburg, by Rev. Dr. HAYNES, on Wednesday, 25th inst., W. F. CARRINGTON, M.D., of Halifax Co., Va, and Miss Georgie B. ADAMS, of Middleburg.

Married: At Paris, February 25th 1880, Mr. John Quincy ADAMS to Mary E. PIERCE, both of Paris, Fauquier Co, Rev. L. H. CRENSHAW officiating.

Married: In Harrisonburg, Va, at the parsonage of Rockingham Circuit, on Thursday the 26th inst., by Rev. Andrew ROBEY, Mr. Thornton MOUNTJOY, of Stafford Co, Va, to Julia A. ROBEY, daughter of the officiating minister.

Married: By Rev. G. W. POPKINS, on the 29th of February, in Alexandria, Mr. Vanderbilt QUICK to Miss Susie KEIM, all of Loudoun.

Died: William Martin PRESTON, in Baltimore city, on the 26th of January 1880, in the 65th year of his age.

Died: George Washington, infant son of M. M. and Kate RODEFFER, February 20th 1880, of diphtheria.

George ROBINSON, brother of the colored man now in jail under sentence of death, has made serious threats against the witnesses who testified against his brother.

Mr. H. C. SLAYMAKER, for several years engaged in mercantile business in Alexandria, died in that city Friday night, in the 37th year of his age.

Last Tuesday evening at 5 o'clock at the Presbyterian church the marriage of Miss Mary H. LUPTON, of this city [Clarkesville, Tenn] to Rev. John F. CANNON of Leesburg. She is the dau. of Rev. J. W. LUPTON, pastor of the Presbyterian Church. ...

Thursday, 11 March 1880   Vol. XXIV, No. 39

Married: At the M. E. Parsonage, South, Leesburg, on the 26th of February, by the Rev. H. H. KENNEDY, Mr. James A. STEVENS to Miss Catharine T. LOWE, all of Loudoun County.

Married: On the 26th February, at the Reformed Church, Lovettsville, by the Rev. H. St. J. RINKER, assisted by the Rev. P. H. MILLER, Mr. Saml. S. ARNOLD to Miss Carrie V. WENNER, all of Loudoun County

Married: By the Rev. G. W. POPKINS, on the 29th of February, in Alexandria, Va, Mr. Vanderbuilt QUICK to Miss Susie KEIM, all of Loudoun.

Joseph Addison HAINES departed this life at his residence, at Hughesville, on Sun. evening, Feb. 29th 1880, in his 59th year.

Died: Near Long Branch, Fauquier Co, February 17, 1880, Edmonia, daughter of Samuel and Sarah V. FIELD, in his 25th year. Leaves parents, sisters and young brothers.

Lot HOLMES, a native of Loudoun County, died at his home in Marshalltown, Iowa, on the 11th of February, in his 74th year. Fifty years ago he gave to the present village of Hamilton, the name of "Harmony."

Co. Ct.: Rev. J. T. SKINNER and W. S. O. THOMAS licensed to celebrate rites of matrimony. Administration of estates of Jno. E. FULTON, Noah COOPER, Edward HARRIS, John C. JANNEY, Edward C. OSBURN, granted. Wills of Jno. H. BOWERS and Jas. COCKERILLE admitted to probate. J. W. WENNER qualified as Guardian of Clara STOUTSENBERGER.

In memoriam: Poem for Robert B. FILLER.

Thursday, 18 March 1880   Vol. XXIV, No. 40

Married: March 4th 1880, by Rev. John WOOLF, at his residence, Mr. Thomas CUMMINS and Miss Mollie RUTTER, all of Loudoun County.

Married: At the Lutheran Church, Lovettsville, February 25th, by Rev. P. H. MILLER, Mr. C. N. DIVINE and Miss Annie E. ALEXANDER, both of Loudoun.

Married: Near Paris, on the 11th inst., by Elder A. T. M. HANDY, Chas. E. MOUNT, Esq., of Loudoun, and Miss Maria Louisa OREAR, of Clarke County, Va.

Married; At the residence of the bride's brother, on the 11th of March, 1880, by Elder E. V. WHITE, Wm. Thos. SAFFER and Elizabeth T. BYRNES, all of Loudoun.

Died: Of heart disease, in Missouri, February 28, 1880, Judith W. MORROW, wife of B. J. MORROW, and daughter of Abraham and Isabella HEWETT, formerly of Leesburg.

Died: On the 25th of February 1880, Elizabeth C. MARSHALL, of consumption, the only daughter of W. B. MARSHALL.

Died: On consumption, March 3d, 1880, near Bloomfield, Miss Sallie J. ADAMS, in the 26th year of her age.

Joseph Addison HAINES departed this life at his residence, at Hughesville, on Sunday evening, February 29th, 1880, in the 59th year of his age. Native of Loudoun Co. Funeral on Tuesday by his old friend and neighbor, Elder Joseph FURR, interred at North Fork cemetery. He leaves a childless companion. He was the last of a family of 8 children.

Thursday, 25 March 1880   Vol. XXIV, No. 41

Married: March 4th 1880 by Rev. John WOOLF, at his residence, Mr. Thomas CUMMINS and Miss Mollie BUTLER, all of Loudoun County.

Died: At the residence of her husband, near Leesburg, on Friday, the 12th of March, Mrs. Sallie E. DOVE, wife of Mr. Thomas DOVE, in the 27th year of her age.

Died: March 13th of consumption, at Mt. Pleasant, Md., Mr. Samuel S. STONE, in his 70th year., from dyspepsia and consumption.

Interred in the cemetery at the Lutheran Church, where he had been a member for many years.

Death of William D. DRISH, a son of the late Wm. D. DRISH, of Leesburg, suddenly in Pickens co, Alabama, on Sunday evening the 7th inst., evidently paralysis of the heart.

Mr. William FOLEY, for many years constable in Broad Run District, died at his home near Gum Spring, on the 17th instant, in about the 78th year of his age.

Thursday, 1 April 1880   Vol. XXIV, No. 42

Married: At the house of John CONRAD, Loudoun County, on Tuesday evening, March 16th, by the Rev. Isaac W. ROBERT, Mr. Bartholomew MOORE and Miss Ophilia F. DEMORY, both of Loudoun County.

Married: March 4th 1880, by Rev. John WOOLF, at his residence, Mr. Thomas CUMMINS and Miss Millie BUTLER, all of Loudoun County.

Married: March 21st 1880, by the same at his residence, Mr. William S. BELL and Miss Gertrude STICKLES, both of Clarke County.

Married: At the parsonage in Leesburg, on Tuesday the 29th March, by the Rev. W. H. FORSYTH, Mr. Edgar P. HOUGH, to Miss Ida RUSSELL, all of Loudoun County.

Died: At the residence of her father, Mr. J. H. WILEY, in Hamilton, on Sunday, the 21st inst., Miss Florence M. WILEY, after a protracted attack of paralysis, in the 21st year of her age.

Died: At the residence of A. G. CHAMBLIN, near Bloomfield, on 13 March 1880, Mrs. Sarah T. CHAMBLIN, in her 74th year.

Death of Rev. Dr. J. A. HAYNES at his home in Middleburg, on Tuesday morning about 11 o'clock, of an affection of the heart. He was a minister in the Baptist Church.

Mr. William BURGESS died on Monday last, at his home 2 miles east of Leesburg, of pneumonia, in about his 65th year.

Samuel ROBINSON, colored, confined in jail under sentence of death for the murder in October last of Edward THOMAS, also colored, will be executed between 6 and 8 on Friday morning, April 9.

Mr. Alexander NEWTON, of this county, died at the residence of his son-in-law, Michael COGLIN, on [torn] of March, in the 67th year of his age. Member of Presbyterian Church.

Thursday, 8 April 1880   Vol. XXIV, No. 43

Collins DIXON, formerly of Fauquier County, was killed recently in Colorado in a personal encounter. His father was killed several years ago in a street fight in Alexandria, Va and his brother was killed last year in Yazoo City, Miss., by Barksdale.

Married: On the afternoon of 3rd month, 30th 1880, at No. 1733 Filbert St., Philadelphia, by Friends' cemetery, Elisha H. WALKER, formerly of Loudoun County, to Lucy COOPER.

Married: On the 25th ultimo, in the Lutheran Church, in Lovettsville, by the Rev. P. H. MILLER, C. N. DIVINE, of Waterford, to Miss Anna E. ALEXANDER, of Lovettsville.

Married: At Salem Church, March 31st 1880, by Rev. Samuel BROWN, Mr. Robert W. GRUBB and Miss Sallie M. B. THOMPSON, all of Loudoun County.

Died: On the morning of April 5, 1880, in Washington city, after a lingering illness, Samuel L. GOUVERNEUR, in his 53d year.

Mr. Burr P. CHAMBLIN died at his home near Round Hill on Monday night in the 72d year of his age. His health for several year had been quite infirm.

Thursday, 15 April 1880   Vol. XXIV, No. 44

At 1 o'clock Thursday, April 15th at the residence of Senator THURMAN, in Washington City, Rev. J. S. LINDSEY, officiating, Capt. J. W. FOSTER, Commonwealth's Attorney for Loudoun County, is to marry Miss Mamie MITCHELL, granddaughter of Gen. Leslie COMBS, of Lexington, Ky.

Miss Mary J. DAVIS, daughter of Rev. Dr. DAVIS, Rector of the Episcopal church of Leesburg, died at the residence of her uncle in Charlottesville, last Sunday afternoon after a short illness.

Mr. N. J. SKINNER, formerly of this county, died at his home in Fauquier County, last Sunday.

Mr. Newton KEENE died at his residence near Guilford, on Thursday morning last. For many year was Magistrate.

April Ct.: Wills of Edward HAINES, Geo. FIELDS, Burr P. CHAMBLIN, Hannah TAYLOR and Joseph A. HAINES admitted to probate. Administrations granted on estates of Jane TILLETT dec'd., and Wm. BURGESS dec'd.

Married: At "Glebeland," on Tues. April 6th 1880, by Rev. Henry BRANCH, R. M. PRESTON, of Washington County, Va, and Hattie, daughter of John ALDRIDGE, Esq. of Loudoun.

Married; April 6th at the residence of the bride's mother, near Aldie, by Elder BADGER, Mr. J. S. FERGUSON, and Miss Lelia A. MEGEATH.

Married: At the same time and place, by the same, Mr. Johnson FURR and Miss Blanch MEGEATH, all of Loudoun County.

Married: March 31st, near Mechanicsville, by Rev. P. H. MILLER, Mr. Fayette FUNK, and Miss Emma L. DERRY, both of Loudoun.

Died: Of cancer, March 16, 1880, near Farmwell Station, Josephine FLING, eldest daughter of Edward and Alice FLING, aged 5y 9m.

Died: April 1st, 1880, after a lingering illness from a combination of diseases, Miss Lucinda FRY.

Died: April 10, 1880, at the residence of Harriet NICHOLS, near Silcott's Springs, Saml. THOMPSON in his 34th year.

Died: Of whooping cough, April 4th, John Eddie, infant son of John E. and Eliza BENEDUM, aged 3m 3w.

Thursday, 22 April 1880   Vol. XXIV, No. 45

Married: At the Parsonage of the M. E. Church, April 6th 1880, by Rev. A. J. PORTER, Mr. John ATHEY to Miss Margaret A. SHRY, both of Loudoun County.

Married: On Wed. April 14th 1880, at Trinity (Episcopal) Church, Shepherdstown, by the Rev. Dr. J. P. HUBBARD, Lt. W. A. SIMPSON, of the 2d U. S. Artillery, to Miss Laura Morgan LEE, only daughter of Mrs. Lily P. LEE, of Shepherdstown.

Died: April 10, 1880, at the residence of Harriet NICHOLS, near Silcott's Springs, Samuel THOMPSON, in his 34th year.

On Saturday, the 10th inst., young man named Samuel THOMPSON, son of John THOMPSON, living near Silcotts Springs, died from a terrible wound inflicted by an infuriated Alderney cow. Her horn in the groin tore upward in his bowels.

Marriage of Capt. J. W. FOSTER, of this town, with Miss Mary MITCHELL, of Lexington, Ky, was consummated at the residence of Senator THURMAN, in Washington on Thursday last at 1 p.m., performed by Rev. Mr. LINDSEY, rector of St. John's Episcopal Church, Georgetown. Bride's mother gave her daughter away in marriage. They will reside in Leesburg.

Mr. Thos. B. ATHEY (brother of W. W. ATHEY) for several years a resident of Leesburg, died at his home in Alexandria, on Tuesday night of consumption. Today he will be buried in that city with Masonic honors.

Hanging of the first person who suffered the death penalty in Loudoun. It must have taken place after 1800, some short time, as Dr. Thomas SMITH obtained the body (after death) by purchase of the condemned man, for $10 and ginger bread until executed. The culprit's name was HAMMON, and his crime rape. Dr. SMITH was located at Green Garden, Loudoun County, 1 mile north of Upperville in the year of 1810. My father and other neighbors were at the execution. They all reported him to be a mulatto, upwards of 6' high. Dr. SMITH shortly after my father and myself were there, moved into Upperville, and died there. I was born in the year 1800. Signed Thos. L. HUMPHREY.

On Thursday evening, April 12, at residence of the Misses PAXSON, of Waterford, marriage of Mr. Addison VANDEVANTER and Miss Lillian PAXSON, both of this county. Ceremony of Episcopal Church by Rev. S. S. WARE, assisted by the Rev. Henry BRANCH. Bride was attired in white tarleton dress, trimmed with white satin bows, long veil studded at the top by orange blossoms, clematis and white roses. ... Groom's mother is Mrs. Patience VANDEVANTER.

Thursday, 29 April 1880   Vol. XXIV, No. 46

Married: At Bewdley, King and Queen Co, Va, the residence of the bride's father, on Wed. evening, the 7th inst., by the Rev. Jas. RAWLINGS, of Lynchburg, Claggett B. JONES (second son of Judge J. H. C. JONES) to Miss Julia, eldest daughter of Bishop James A. LATANE, of the Reform Episcopal church.

Died: At the residence of her husband, near Philomont, on the 17th inst., Sallie B. NICHOLS, wife of John NICHOLS, in the 75th year of her age.

Mr. John COCKERILLE died at his home near North Fork on Sat. last, in about the 75th year of his age. He had been paralyzed several days previous to his death.

Married on Wednesday evening last, at the M. E. Church of this place, by Rev. Dr. ROGERS, P. E., assisted by Rev. George TYLER, pastor, Rev. L. R. GREEN, formerly a minister at this place, but at present located at Middleburg, and Miss M. Addie STONESTREET, daughter of Dr. E. E. STONESTREET, of Rockville. *Rockville Md Sentinel of the 24th.*

Died on Sunday, April 25th near Unison, Silas MERCER, a colored man aged 100 or more years. He lived in this county all his life. I have known him myself upwards of 65 years. By Jno. M. MORAN.

The marriage of Miss Violet L. PACE and Rev. H. Melville JACKSON took place yesterday afternoon at 2 o'clock at the residence of the bride's father, Mr. James B. PACE, corner of Franklin and Adams streets, performed by Bishop F. M. WHITTLE, of the Episcopal Church. *Richmond Whig.*

Thursday, 6 May 1880   Vol. XXIV, No. 47

Married: At the Lutheran Parsonage, Lovettsville, April 27th 1880, by Rev. P. H. MILLER, Mr. O. A. HAMILTON and Miss Mary A. MASON, both of Loudoun.

Married: In the Presbyterian Manse, Leesburg, April 28th, by Rev. J. F. CANNON, Mr. Chas. D. FRANKLIN and Miss Alice C. GOVER, both of Loudoun County.

Died: At her mother's residence, near Grove Church, April 10th, Ann Amanda WYNKOOP, aged 25y 7m 1d. She joined the

Methodist in Sept. 1872. For nearly five years she suffered from lung disease.

Died: At his residence, near North Fork, April 24, 1880, Jno. COCKERILLE, in his 79th year. Interred at North Fork, service by his pastor, P. P. WARREN. Member of North Fork Baptist Church, baptised by Rev. Thaddeus HERNDON in 1858.

Died: At the residence of her son-in-law, Mr. M. RODEFFER, near Lovettsville, April 18th 1880, Mrs. Mary M. SOUDER, in the last month of her 66th year. Member of Lutheran Church.

Yesterday the train arriving here at 3:25 p.m. with the W. & O railroad connection, brought into the B. & P. depot a young lady of Loudoun County. She was taken sick in the depot and in a short time increased the population of Washington – a boy. she with her child was sent to Columbia Lying-in Asylum. *Washington Star, May* 1.

Death of Saml. M. JANNEY: Eminent minister of Society of Friends, died at his home at Lincoln, in this county, on the afternoon of the 30th ulto, in his 80th year. The principal modern Historian and Biographer of the Society, and for over 40 years a minister among Friends. Funeral took place from the Goose Creek Meeting House, on Monday afternoon. Son of Abijah JANNEY, born in or near Hamilton, in 1800. In about 1826 or probably earlier he came to this city from his native county and engaged in shipping and commission business. After the close of business here he went to Occoquan, Va, where, in connection with Samuel H. JANNEY, Esq. of this city, he established a cotton factory, which he conducted until 1888, when he retired to Loudoun and engaged in teaching as principal of Springdale Female Seminary. ...

Mrs. Laura STANSBURY (nee WILEY, formerly of Loudoun Co) wife of Mr. C. F. STANSBURY, died at the residence of her husband, in this city, this morning, of consumption, after an illness of a few months, in her 20th year, having been married but little more than a year. *Alex. Gazett[e] of 4th inst.*

Thursday, 13 May 1880   Vol. XXIV, No. 48

Married: On the 29th ulto, at the residence of J. C. LUCKETT, Esq., of Frederick County. Md, by Rev. Dr. TRAPNELL, Rector of St. Marks, Alfred HARDEN, Esqr. of Morrow County, Ohio, and Miss Mollie F. LUCKETT, of Loudoun County.

Married: At the home of the bride on Wed. the 28th ult., by the Rev. S. S. WARE, Mr. Joseph CROWN to Miss Fannie GRUBB.

Married: In Washington DC, April 29th, by the Rev. RICHARDS of the M. E. C. N., Miss Alice V. PALMER to Mr. Benj. BRIDGES Jr., all of Loudoun County.

Married: On the 27th ultimo, at the M. E. Parsonage in Frederick City, Md, by the Rev. S. V. LEECH, James A. BAKER of Green Co, Ohio, to Miss Annie M. COMPHER, of Loudoun County.

Married: At Grace (Episcopal) Church, in Berryville, on Thursday, April 29th 1880, by the Rev. P. P. PHILLIPS, Mr. Samuel Scolly MOORE to Miss Elvira McCORMICK, daughter of the late Edward McCORMICK, Esq., all of Clarke County, Va.

Dead body of a white male infant was found at "Laurel Hill," on the farm of C. Boyd BARRETT, near Waterford, last Friday evening. Child was fully developed and came to its death by violence at the hands of some person – bonds on left side of the head fractured and depressed.

B. Frank CARPENTER died on Monday night, at the residence of Mr. L. F. CARPENTER, 14 miles east of St. Joseph, of typhoid pneumonia. He was 23 years of age and unmarried. Leaves parents, one sister and nine brothers. He was a nephew of Mr. M. B. CARPENTER, of this county, and son of Mr. L. F. CARPENTER, who moved from Loudoun about 45 years ago.

May Ct.: Will of Rebecca N. HOGE admitted to probate with J. M. HOGE as Exor. Samuel KIDWELL qualified as Admr. of Zedekiah KIDWELL dec'd. Estate of M. H. LACEY committed to Sheriff.

Thursday, 20 May 1880   Vol. XXIV, No. 49

Married: At the Reamer House, Leesburg, on the 12th inst., by the Rev. J. S. GARDNER, Mr. Jonathan B. RAMSAY and Miss Emma L. THOMAS, all of Loudoun.

Married: At the residence of the bride's father, Leesburg, on Tuesday, the 13th inst., by the Rev. J. S. GARDNER, Mr. Michael T. WHITMORE and Miss Emma V. SHAFER, all of Leesburg.

Married: at the Friends' Meeting House at Waterford by Friends ceremony, May 13th 1880, Yardly T. BROWN, of Hamilton, editor of the *Telephone* to Miss Eleanor E. HOLLINGSWORTH, of Waterford.

Married: In Woburn, Mass., May 6th, by Rev. V. M. SIMONS, Fred. W. VYE, of Woburn and Miss Lizzie S. WALLACE, of Leesburg.

Died: At the residence of its father at Americus, Georgia, on the 8th inst., Beverly Lomax, infant son of the Rev. Theodore REED.

Died: At the residence of Mahlon TAVENNER, near Hamilton, John McDANIEL, in the 59th year of his age.

Mr. Geo. W. WENNER died at his home near the Point of Rocks, on Monday night. A strange horse kicked him in the stomach, and he survived the injury but a short time.

Mr. Wm. P. EASTERDAY, of this place, aged 77 years, who was attacked with paralysis a few days ago, died on Tuesday night last. Father of our townsman, Mr. Wm. D. EASTERDAY.

Rev. Ezra F. BUSY, minister of the M. E. Church, South, died at the residence of Rev. S. K. COX, in Baltimore last Thursday evening, in the 63d year of his age.

Mr. Solomon STOVER, wood and coal dealer, who came to this city from Frederick Co, Md, some years before the war and established his business at the West End, died at his residence, 2025 H. St, NW, this morning about 7:30 in his 57th year. Shortly after his arrival here he married Hester, dau. of Capt. TRAVERS, who was then a well known riverman. She died some years ago, leaving no children. Funeral from Western Presbyterian church, at 10 o'clock. *Washington Star.*

Mr. Chauncey BROOKS, of Baltimore, died on Tuesday in the 82nd year of his age.

Hugh J. JEWETT, President of the Erie Railroad has been associated with a possible candidacy for Pres. of the U.S. by the Democratic Convention, has directed public attention to the reminscences of the JEWETT family, of which Jos. H. JEWETT, of this county, and at present Pres. of the Purcellville Manu. Co., was an elder member, and the Exor. of his father's will. In Hartford Co. Md – Deer creek, on which Hugh J. JEWETT passed his youth. Between this and the next mill above Wilson's, on the heights N of Deer Creek is a very old Quaker settlement called Darlington. There the parents of the JEWETT boys are buried in the ancient Quaker graveyard by the meeting house, dating back to 1727. Susannah, wife of John JEWETT died 9th month 1853, aged 71 years. John JEWETT died 1st month 28, 1854, aged 77 years. James J. JEWETT, 5th month 9th, 1839, aged 23. The latter was a brother of Pres. JEWETT, over whose body his mother, Susannah, a Quaker preacher, preached the funeral sermon. Will of John JEWETT, father of Hugh J. JEWETT, is recorded at Belair, dated 16th of 4th month 1850 – lists wife Susanna JEWET, farm where he resides on road from Deer creek ironworks to Dublin, Joseph H. JEWETT, dau. Annie W. JOHNS, sons John, Joshua, Isaac and Hugh J. JEWETT, sons Thomas L. JEWETT and Edward H. JEWETT. The Exor. of will was probably a son who remained a Quaker and removed from Md to Loudoun County and is a farmer there. John JEWETT, the eldest son, also remained around Maryland and is now in Baltimore. Another son, Dr. James, was in practice in Baltimore and died near the age of 26 and was brought home to Darlington to be buried. Only girl Annie, married Stephen S. JOHN, of Harford Co, Md. who made his home at Donald Station, Pa. She became an Episcopalian. Thos. L. JEWETT was Judge JEWETT, who went to New York as a boy. He later went into business with his brother, probably Edward H., and they failed due to the business depression. Joshua JEWETT emigrated by his brother Hugh's advise, to Kentucky, became a land lawyer and was sent to Congress. Isaac W. JEWETT is president of a fire insurance company in Baltimore City. Hugh J. JEWETT married the sister of a governor of the State of Md. He is of English Quaker, English Episcopal and New England types intermixed.

Thursday, 27 May 1880   Vol. XXIV, No. 50

Died: On the 14th inst., Willie, 3rd son of Mr. John J. COCHRAN, of Fauquier County.

The dead body of an unknown white man was found in a small strip of woods adjoining the village of Paris, Va, Monday evening. He is supposed to have been a tramp, and claimed to have been a native of Westmoreland Co, Va, and a member of the Masonic Order.

Thursday, 3 June 1880   Vol. XXIV, No. 51

Married: May 31st, at Grace P. E. Church, Baltimore, by Rev. Dr. LEEDS, Dr. T. Clay MADDUX, of Baltimore, to Miss Isabel O. BETTS, formerly of England, and recently of Albemarle County, Virginia.

Mr. Louis H. POWELL, of Leesburg, is to be married on the 2d of June at Genesee, New York, to Miss Jane L. YOUNG, of that place.

Thursday, 10 June 1880   Vol. XXIV, No. 52

Married: In the M. E. Church, South, Leesburg, on Tuesday evening, June 8th 1880, by Rev. Dr. HEAD, Mr. Wm. H. JOHNSON and Miss Rosa, daughter of Capt. Geo. R. HEAD, all of this town.

Died: On Sunday, May 30th, at the residence of her brother-in-law, Mr. Rodney BEALES, in Leesburg, Miss Lucy RUSSELL, after a long and painful illness.

Died: On the 4th inst., at his residence, near Chantilly, Fairfax County, Mr. Alexander HAIGHT, in about his 60th year.

Mr. Asher W. GRAY, of Baltimore, a former merchant of Leesburg, is recovering from a recent severe sickness.

Marriage of Mr. Louis H. POWELL (of law firm of Harrison & Powell, of Leesburg) and Miss Jane Lee YOUNG, of Geneseo, New York, daughter of ex-Gov. YOUNG, on Wednesday last, at St. Michael's Church, at Geneseo at 2 o'clock. Reception by the bride's sister, Mrs. T. C. T. BUCKLEY. Performed by rector,

Rev. Mr. COLE, assisted by Rev. Dr. INGERSOL. Bride was given away by her brother, Gen. Campbell H. YOUNG.

Thursday, 17 June 1880   Vol. XXV, No. 1

Married: On June 3d, 1880, at the residence of John W. BEAVERS, near Frankford, Mo, by the Rev. R. F. BEAVERS, Mr. Thomas B. BEAVERS (late of Clarke County, Va) to Miss Mary L. SMITH, both of Pike County, Va.

Married: In Clarke County, on the 6th last, at the residence of the bride's father, by Elder A. T. M. HANDY, Mr. William LONG to Miss Sarah THELL, daughter of Stephen D. THELL, formerly of Loudoun.

Died: On the 12th inst., at "Whitehall," her residence, Loudoun Co., after a long and painful illness, Mrs. Frances HAWLING in her 87th year, consort of the late Isaac HAWLING.

In memoriam – Nathaniel Jackson SKINNER was born in Loudoun Co, in 1821? and died April 12th 1880, in Fauquier County. United with M. E. Church, South, 25 years ago. Twice married, and leaves a widow and five children.

Co. Ct.: Wills of Jane E. KEYS, John COCKERILLE, John McDANIEL, Benj. BRIDGES Sr. admitted to probate. John J. DILLON appointed Committee of Anna E. DILLON. Estates of Samuel NUTT (col'd) and Edward OREM committed to Sheriff. Wm. B. LYNCH qualified as Admr. dbn of Jared CHAMBLIN dec'd.

Death of Mrs. Frances HAWLING, widow of the late Isaac HAWLING, of this county, at age 87 years. Member of Episcopal Church. Interred in Union Cemetery on Sunday afternoon, Revs. Drs. DAVIS and GARDNER officiating.

Araminta JOHNSON, an old colored woman, formerly owned by the late Tilghman GORE, of this county, died in Leesburg on Wednesday, June 9th 1880, aged 101 years.

Thursday, 24 June 1880   Vol. XXV, No. 2

Died: At her husband's residence, in Hampton, Va, at 15 minutes to 8 a.m. Saturday, June 12th 1880, after a painful illness of 13 weeks and 3 days, Mrs. Heloise Eubank DONOHOE, wife of S. R. DONOHOE, Esq., Editor of the "*Hampton Monitor.*" She was the daughter of Joseph C. EUBANK, Esq., of "Nestling," Middlesex Co, Va, and was born 18 Feb 1854.

Death of Bernard HOUGH, Esq. at his home in Hamilton, on Monday last, in about his 65th year. At one time was engaged in the wholesale commission business in Baltimore city.

Thursday, 1 July 1880　Vol. XXV, No. 3

Married: In Warrenton, at the residence of the bride's father, by Father DONOHO, on the 23d of June, Dr. T. Marshall JONES and Miss Bessie, daughter of Major Rice W. PAYNE.

Died: On the 13th inst., at her residence at Lovettsville, Mrs. Hannah W. CLAPHAM, widow of the Rev. Josiah CLAPHAM of the P. E. Church who died 32 years ago.

Mr. Wm. C. SHAWEN died very suddenly at his home near Waterford on Monday evening last. When he entered his house after receiving some friends at the door, he fell and expired in a few minutes.

Mr. Julian A. HUTCHISON, of Atlanta, Ga (formerly of the Drug firm of Edwards & Hutchison, of this town) accompanied by his wife, passed through Leesburg on Tuesday.

The same day, Mr. J. Will. DEAR, formerly of Loudoun, but for several years past a sojourner of the far off frontier, Front Robinson, Nebraska, being his present headquarters, visited.

Richard T. M. BALL, of Fauquier, son of Mr. Geo. W. BALL, formerly of this county, has been appointed Asst. Paymaster in the U. S. Navy.

Thursday, 8 July 1880　Vol. XXV, No. 4

Married: At the Lutheran Church, Myersville, Md, June 17th 1880, Rev. Martin Luther BEARD pastor of the Lutheran Church at Mt. Joy, Md, and Miss Mattie S. BOWERS, daughter of Rev. H. G. BOWERS, pastor of the Myersville Lutheran Church. Father of the bride, assisted by Rev. P. H. MILLER, performed the ceremony.

Died: On June 29th 1880, little Willie, only child of Richard H. and Martha HENDERSON.

Mrs. Fannie BEVERLEY, widow of the late Wm. BEVERLEY, on morning of her death rode in from "Selma," about 4 miles from Leesburg, to the cars to visit her son near Upperville. In Leesburg she stopped at her relative's Mrs. R. W. GRAY. She died there.

Nimrod GUIDER, a colored man living near Round Hill, died very suddenly last Saturday morning of heart disease. He was about in the 65th year of his age.

Thursday, 15 July 1880   Vol. XXV, No. 5

Married: At Rokeby, May 18th 1880, by Rev. Mr. BUTTE, J. J. WENNER, of Lovettsville, to Miss Gennie L. ASHTON, dau. of Mr. Geo. D. ASHTON, of King George County, Virginia.

Died: On Friday, 2nd instant, at 5 o'clock, Gertrude Avery, infant dau. of George T. and Alice V. BEUCHLER, aged 2m 5d.

Died: On the 11th inst., in the 22d year of age, Llewellyn, son of Edward B. and Cordelia S. POWELL, of this place.

July Ct.: Wills of Wm. C. SHAWEN and Jane TAYLOR admitted to probate. Administrations granted on estates of Jas. H. FILLER, Geo. W. WENNER, Alexander NEWTON and John E. STOTT.

Thursday, 22 July 1880   Vol. XXV, No. 6

Died: On Friday, July 16th 1880, at her house near Hamilton, Mrs. Carrie E., wife of G. V. BRADEN, and daughter of Washington VANDEVANTER, in the 54th year of her age.

Died: At "Morven," near Leesburg, on Thursday, July 15, 1880, Louise Sherlock, dau. of Dr. Shirley CARTER, in her 5th year.

Died: In Leesburg, on Friday night, July 16, 1880, after a protracted illness and much suffering, Mrs. Mary E. EVARD, wife of Mr. Chas. E. Evart, in the 58th year of age.

At his residence near Hillsboro, July 14th, 1880, of paralysis, Charles BASCUE, Esq., aged about 92 years. He was a soldier of war of 1812.

Thursday, 29 July 1880   Vol. XXV, No. 7

Died: Mr. John SAUNDERS died at his home in Leesburg in the 84th year of his age. Born and raised in this immediate vicinity, member of the M. E. Church.

Died: On Monday July 14th 1880, in Leesburg, Mary, youngest daughter of Joseph and Mary E. ABBOTT, aged 3m 3d.

Thursday, 5 August 1880   Vol. XXV, No. 8

Married: In the Presbyterian Church, on the 3rd inst., by Rev. J. F. CANNON, Mr. James L. HIGDON and Miss Martha A. NEWTON, both of Loudoun County.

Mr. H. Clay MILLER, a native of Loudoun County, but for a number of years a resident of Baltimore, died in that city last week. He was only 39 years of age, for some time head of firm of Miller & Co, wholesale dry goods dealers.

Thursday, 12 August 1880   Vol. XXV, No. 9

Died: In Leesburg, July 26th 1880, after a painful illness, Mrs. Lydia A. MULLEN, wife of Saml. MULLEN, aged 47y 5m 17d.

Died: At Salome, Loudoun Co, Friday afternoon, July 16th 1880, Mrs. G. V. Braden, daughter of Mr. Washington VANDEVANTER of this county.

Elijah JAMES died at his residence, near Waterford, in this county, on Saturday last, in his 91st year.

On Sunday, Mr. John SNOOTS died at his home near Morrisonville, in about the 82d year of his age.

August Ct.: Wills of Lucinda FRY, Hannah W. CLAPHAM and John SAUNDERS admitted to probate. A. T. M. RUST qualified as Guardian of A. R. YELLOTT, R. E. L. YELLOTT and Florence YELLOTT. Wm. G. BEVERLEY qualified as Admr. of Fannie W. BEVERLEY dec'd.

D. C. FULTON, hardware merchant of Baltimore, and a native of Loudoun, died at his country seat, near Ellicott city, Md, on Sunday, August 1st, of Bright's Disease of the kidneys. Born near Leesburg, September 19th 1827, entered the hardware trade in Baltimore a short time before the war as clerk. Leaves an estate worth $75,000. Nephew of Mr. David CARR of this county, and a brother-in-law of W. F. MERCIER, of Hamilton.

Thursday, 19 August 1880   Vol. XXV, No. 10

Died: In Leesburg, August 3d 1880, Mrs. Mary J. GREEN, wife of Mr. John E. GREEN, in the 66th year of her age. Member of the M. E. Church for more than 50 years.

Died: At Tennallytown, July 29th 1880, Mrs. Jane P. DAVIS, wife of Henry J. DAVIS, formerly of Loudoun.

Died: In Leesburg, on August 8th, 1880, Miss Rebecca THOMPSON, in the 69th year of her age.

Thursday, 26 August 1880   Vol. XXV, No. 11

Married: At the residence of the bride's father, on Wednesday morning, Aug. 18th 1880, by Rev. Father JANSSENS, of Richmond, Mr. Roberdean ANNAN, of Baltimore, and Lizzie P., daughter of Col. Lorman CHANCELLOR, of Middleburg.

Died: At Leesburg, after a long and wasting sickness, on Monday, Aug. 16, 1880, Mrs. Elizabeth WALLACE, aged 27y 4m. Member of Episcopal church.

Died: Near Waterford, on Saturday, June 26th 1880, Edgar T. WOODARD, aged 20 years.

In Middleton, on the morning of the 18th inst., marriage of Miss Lizzie P. CHANCELLOR to Mr. Roberdean ANNAN, of Baltimore, at residence of bride's father, Col. Lorman CHANCELLOR, by Rev. Father JANSSENS of Richmond. In wedding party was Miss Hattie ANNAN, sister of the groom. Bride wore white musline trimmed with valenciennes lace and white satin bows. .... [long article]. They will reside in monumental city.

Thursday, 3 September 1880   Vol. XXV, No. 12

Married: On the 11th inst., at the bride's father's, in Logansport, by the Rev. J. J. SHAFFEREY, Mr. Jos. H. STOCKS, of Loudoun County, to Miss Armilda HALLAN, of Cass County, Indiana.

Married: At the parsonage of the Metropolitan Church, Washington City, on August 25th, by Rev. Dr. BAER, Mr. Benjamin F. HEAD to Miss Arabella F. McINTOSH, all of Loudoun.

Married: Near Leesburg, August 31st by Rev. J. F. CANNON, Mr. George W. JACKSON and Miss Indiana HARDY, both of Loudoun County.

Died: At Berkeley Springs, W. Va. on the morning of the 19th of August 1880, Mrs. Ellen BOWLEN, formerly of Loudoun County, aged about 74 years.

Thursday, 9 September 1880   Vol. XXV, No. 13

Died: At her home in Leesburg, a few minutes after 9 o'clock, on the morning of Wednesday, September 8th, 1880, Mrs. Jane D. WILDMAN, age 84 years.

Wm. Busy RODGERS, eldest son of Rev. Samuel RODGERS, of Baltimore, died at his home in Toledo, Ohio, on the 22d of August, in his 27th year. He leaves a wife and two children.

Arthur GORUM, a colored boy about 14 years of age, living in the Taylortown neighborhood, went fishing last Thursday, and later his father found him lying in the Creek in Shafer's Meadow, face downward, dead. He was subject to epilepsy.

Thursday, 16 September 1880   Vol. XXV, No. 14

Married: On the 2d inst., at the Reformed Church, Lovettsville, by the Rev. H. St. J. RINKER, Mr. George D. BAKER, to Miss Son [?] R. BROWN, all of Loudoun.

Married: On Tuesday, September 7th 1880, at the M. E. Parsonage, by the Rev. Mr. GARDNER, Wm. F. FEASTER, to Miss Fannie MOSS, all of Loudoun.

Married: At Bethel, in this county on Wednesday the 8th of September by Elder E. V. WHITE, Mr. Samuel P. MULLEN and Miss Mary F. FRY, all of this county.

A fortnight ago, Enoch FARR, an industrious laborer, was engaged in walling up a well on the farm of Dr. J. F. MASON, the stone being lowered to him by a rope with a noose in the end. The noose slipped and the stone fell to the bottom, striking the man on the head and fracturing his skull, from which he died one day last week.

September Ct.: Will of Elijah JAMES dec'd. admitted to probate. Jonah NIXON qualified as committee of Danl. WHITE. Zachariah READ (col.) licensed to celebrate rites of matrimony.

On the W. & O. Railroad last Tuesday morning, as the early morning train was coming from Round Hill, when it cut just beyond Hamilton depot, the engineer discovered a man walking down the track a few hundred years in front; the brakes were put on and every signal sounded, but the train was upon the man. The dead, mutilated body was that of Mr. Jos. L. DAVIS, a deaf mute. He was about 50 years of age and leaves a wife, also a mute, but no children.

In Mountsville, last Tuesday evening at 7 o'clock, the marriage of Mr. Benj. F. GRIFFITH and Miss Mary B. GAINES.

Thursday, 23 September 1880   Vol. XXV, No. 15

Mrs. Mary Eleanor RANSON, wife of James M. RANSON, of Jefferson County, West Virginia, died last Thursday. Sister of the late Hon. John B. BALDWIN, of Staunton.

Married: Near Taylortown, September 16th 1880, by Rev. James McDONOUGH, Wm. SHOEMAKER and Elizabeth A. MYERS, both of Loudoun County.

Married: In Durham, N. C., Tuesday, September 7th, by Rev. Mr. CHESIRE, Charles H. BEATTY, of the firm of Barley, Beatty & Co., of Front Royal, Va, to Kate R., eldest daughter of the late Major J. Morris WAMPLER, C. S. A.

Died: On Thursday, the 3rd of September, after a short illness, Mrs. Mollie HAWKINS, wife of Mr. Charles HAWKINS and eldest daughter of Dr. James LEITH DEC'D. in her 30th year. Leaves a family of six small children, and a devoted husband.

Died: In Front Royal, Va, on Sunday, 12th September, after a long and painful illness, Carrie, in the 21st year of her age, wife of J. T. WAMPLER, formerly of this town.

Thursday, 30 September 1880   Vol. XXV, No. 16

Died: In Leesburg, on Sunday, September 26th 1880, after a protracted illness of typhoid fever, Mr. Benjamin SURVICK, in about the 28th year of his age.

Died: In Waterford, on the morning of August 17th 1880, Alice Carey, wife of C. D. FRANKLIN.

Died: On Thursday, 16th of September 1880, in the city of Washington, in his 74th year, Burgess D. BARTLETT. For many years a resident of Middleburg. Interred in Middleburg.

Mr. V. H. SURGHNOR, of Hannibal, died this morning at the residence of Henry McPHERSON, a few miles west of this city. Born Christmas day, 1813, at Middleburg, Loudoun County, and would have been 67 years old on the 25th of December. Leaves several children, all we believe, being grown.

Thursday, 7 October 1880   Vol. XXV, No. 17

Yesterday morning at Pleasant Valley, near Hamilton, the marriage of Mr. Clark NORRIS, of Illinois, and Maggie HOGE, by Rev. Henry BRANCH. They will reside in Illinois.

Married: In Lovettsville, at the M. E. Church, South, Sept. 29th 1880, by Rev. W. R. STRINGER, Mr. Henry G. WILES, of Hagerstown, Md, and Miss Mary E. CRUZEN, of Loudoun.

Married: At Pleasant Valley, Tuesday, September 28th, by the Rev. Henry BRANCH, Mr. Clark NORRIS, of Illinois, to Miss Margaretta R. HOGE, daughter of the late Isaac and Rachel N. HOGE, of Loudoun County.

Married: On the 24th inst., at Berlin Ferry, by the Rev. H. St. J. RINKER, Mr. William H. TARLETON to Miss Virginia SIMPSON, all of Loudoun County.

Married: On September 21, at Bishop Cummins Memorial Church, by Rev. H. H. KENNEDY, assisted by Bishop J. A. LAIANE, rector, Henry S. DULANEY to C. Estelle KENNEDY, both of Baltimore City.

Died: At the home of her parents, Somerfield and Sarah BOLYN, on the morning of the 27th of September, Mary BOLYN, in the 5th year of her age.

Died: At Hillsboro, Sunday, September 13th 1880, John E. JONES in the 31st year of age.

At the Plains, Fauquier Co, on Wed. last, the marriage at Grace Church, by Rev. C. C. PEARSON, of Mr. Edward P. TURNER, son of Admiral TURNER, U.S.N., and Miss Mary Beverley TURNER, dau. of Edward C. TURNER, Esq. of the Plains.

Thursday, 14 October 1880   Vol. XXV, No. 18

Died: At her home, near Guilford, on Sunday evening, Oct. 10th 1880, of cancer, Miss Bettie GIST, in the 59th year of her age. Member of M. E. Church, South. Interred in Union Cemetery, Leesburg, on Tuesday.

Died: At the residence of her father, on Oct. 3d, 1880, Martha E., daughter of J. M. HALL, aged 8y ?m 12d. [tear in paper]

Co. Ct.: Estate of W. F. BRADEN dec'd. committed to Sheriff. Henry HEATON qualified as Admr. of Chas. A. REED dec'd. W. A. MISKELL qualified as Admr. of Enoch FAIR dec'd.

Rev. H. S. KEPLER, clergyman of the Episcopal Church, died at his residence on 7th St. N or Leigh St (Richmond) yesterday at noon. Born in Maryland 8 January 1807 and in 1848 accepted a call to St. John's church in this city. ...

The Mirror
Thursday, 21 October 1880   Vol. XXV, No. 19

Thursday, 21 October 1880   Vol. XXV, No. 19

Mr. Joseph L. DISHMAN, of Loudoun County, after a protracted and painful illness of typhoid fever, died at the residence of Mrs. Ursula HUNSICKER, his boarding house, in Luray, Page County, Virginia, on last Saturday night. Funeral on last Sunday was preached in the Lutheran Church, by Rev. H. M. WHARTON, and buried in the Cemetery.

Died: At his home, in Georgetown, D.C., on the 8th of October 1880, of menengitis, Mr. William Corrie LIPSCOMB, in his 54th year. At one time he conducted a school in Leesburg.

Last week, James CROSS, colored man of Leesburg, was tried for stealing $8 from C. F. NICKENS, colored barber of this place, and sentenced to 5 years in the penitentiary.

Thursday, 28 October 1880   Vol. XXV, No. 20

Married: In the Episcopal Church, at Hamilton, on Tuesday evening, October 26th 1880, by Rev. Henry BRANCH, Mr. John R. SMITH, Agent W. & O. R. R. at Pursellville, and Miss Annie, daughter of James McDANIEL Esq., all of Loudoun County.

Married: At the residence of the bride's father, in this county, on Wednesday morning, October 20th 1880, by Rev. S. S. WARE, Robert W. WYSONG, of Jefferson County, W. Va, and Mary L., second daughter of Lewis HAWLING, Esq., of Loudoun.

On Thursday evening last in the Methodist Church at Hamilton, marriage of Dr. Adrian BALDWIN, physician of Purcellville, to Miss Lizzie, daughter of Asa M. JANNEY, Esq., of the same place. Groomsmen were Messrs. Julian BALDWIN, Samuel SIMPSON Jr., Fayette WELCH and Notley BALL. Bridesmaids were Misses Anna and Emma BALDWIN, Miss Lillie SAFFER, and Miss Ella HATCHER. Ceremony by Rev. A. A. P. NEEL.

Thursday, 4 November 1880   Vol. XXV, No. 21

Died: On the 26th of August, Lillie V. COE, aged 9 years, after an illness of nine days.

Marriage of Mr. Lucien POWELL, Loudoun's young artist, and Miss Nannie FITZHUGH, was celebrated on the 26th inst., Rev. Mr. GREEN of the Methodist Episcopal Church officiating. They will take the train for Philadelphia, where they contemplate spending the winter.

Brutal crime near Gum Spring on Tuesday the 26th of October. A colored man lived with his wife and his wife's sister near Gum Spring. On that morning a difficulty arose between him and his sister-in-law and he assaulted her with a large knife used for cutting off corn. He then shot her. The wife then hit the husband with a large stone.

Thursday, 11 November 1880   Vol. XXV, No. 22

Married: On Thursday at St. James Church, Leesburg, by Rev. Dr. DAVIS, Mr. Augustine LOUGHBOROUGH, and Miss Minnie FAUNTLEROY, daughter of Dr. J. H. FAUNTLEROY, of Loudoun, formerly of Clarke County.

Married: At St. James Church, Leesburg, on Oct. 28th, by Rev. R. T. DAVIS, Miss Sadie B. CHICHESTER, eldest dau. of A. M. CHICHESTER of Loudoun, to F. M. PAGE, of the Univ. of Va.

Died: At his home near Guilford, in this county, on Monday night, Nov. 8th, 1880, of asthma, Mr. R. L. BENTLY, in his 58th year.

Died: At her home near Farmwell Station, Loudoun County, on the 29th of October 1880, of old age, Mrs. Jane LYON, widow of Alexander LYON, in the 89th year of her age.

Death of Robt. L. BENTLY, Esq. occurred Monday night at his home near Guilford. He had for a long time been a great sufferer from asthma, which was the immediate cause of his death. For a number of years he was engaged in the mercantile business in Leesburg. He was in the 58th year of his age. Interred in Union Cemetery, Leesburg on Wednesday.

Mr. ___ LEE, grandfather of Mr. David I. LEE, of this county, became the owner of Clem CANADA, a negro man then in middle life. At the death of the elder LEE, provision was made by will for the manumission of Clem, but as the latter could not at that time accept his freedom and remain in Virginia, he removed to Pennsylvania; but soon returned to Loudoun and surrendering himself to the heirs of his late master. He was purchased by Mr. Matthew P. LEE, a son of his former master, for $100. A short time after LINCOLN's proclamation he again returned to the surviving members of the LEE family, where he remains as a "hired servant," but really as a pensioner upon their charity, until a few months ago when he went to live with some of his own race and family connection, near Guilford. Had he lived until next January, according to a record still preserved in the LEE family, he would have been 121 years old. For more than 70 years a member of Mt. Zion Baptist Church. Interred in Mt. Zion burying ground.

Marriage on Thursday of last week of Miss Minna FAUNTLEROY to Mr. Augustine LOUGHBOROUGH. She was not a native of Leesburg. .... They took the train at once for Philadelphia to visit her uncle, Admiral TURNER.

Dr. Lemuel Charles GORDON died at his residence, No. 311 North Broadway (Baltimore), on Saturday last. Born in Baltimore. Three years ago he married Miss M. Dora BIRD, formerly of Leesburg, Va., who survives him. They had no children. Funeral on Monday from Church of the Holy Innocents. Interred at Greenmount Cemetery.

Thursday, 18 November 1880   Vol. XXV, No. 23

Married: At the Parsonage in Hamilton on Wednesday, November 19th, by Rev. A. A. P. NEEL, Mr. John LOGAN, late of Loudoun County, to Miss Ann E. HOLMES, of the vicinity.

Married: November 16th, in the Presbyterian Manse, Leesburg, by Rev. J. P. CANNON, Mr. Benjamin F. CAMPBELL and Miss Sarah P. SHUMAKER, both of Loudoun County.

Mr. Harry S. BELT, of this city [Baltimore], was married on Wednesday to Miss Marietta DULANY, eldest daughter of Capt. Henry G. DULANY, of Fauquier Co. Wedding took place at Oakley, the old family residence in Fauquier Co. Bride is a lineal descendant of Daniel DULANY, one of Baltimore's greatest statesmen and lawyers and a contemporary of Charles CARROLL, of Carrollton. Niece of Col. R. H. DULANY, of Loudoun Co. They will reside in Baltimore.

Columbia, S. Carolina Register of Nov. 9th: The preceding evening, wedding of Mr. Wm. S. REAMER, formerly of Leesburg to Miss Cornelia M. YOUMANS, of Columbia, at Trinity (Episcopal) Church. She is the eldest daughter of Attorney Gen. YOUMANS. He a prominent railroad official of the Wilmington Columbia and Augusta Railroad, whose home has been in Carolina for the past 6 years. .....

Thursday, 25 November 1880   Vol. XXV, No. 24

Married: In this county, on the evening of the 17th inst., by Rev. J. F. CANNON, Mr. John W. MOFFETT and Miss Annie B. HENDERSON, daughter of Charles W. HENDERSON, Esq.

Married: On the 19th inst., at the residence of Mr. Jacob KINTZ near Rocky Springs, Maryland, by Rev. C. W. STINESPRING, Mr. John H. MYERS and Miss Florence MOORE, both of Loudoun County.

Died: At the residence of his father near Aldie, in this county, of brain fever, on November 1st, 1880, Hugh Adair, infant son of Wallace and Mollie TIFFANY, aged 2y 5m.

Died: At Oak Level, Loudoun Co, November 12, 1880, Mr. P. H. SMITH, in the 65th year of his age.

Died: Near Leesburg, November 7th 1880, Mrs. Ann ETCHER, wife of Peter ETCHER, in the 83rd year of her age.

Died: Near Philomont, on Saturday, November 20, 1880, Turner Ashby, son of Leven T. and Annie JACOBS, aged 5y 5d.

Thursday, 2 December 1880   Vol. XXV, No. 25

Married: In Alexandria, November 24, 1880, by Rev. O. C. BEALL, J. C. COLEMAN, of Loudoun County, and Florence S. ENGLISH, of that city.

Married: At the residence of the bride's father near Bethel, Loudoun County, November 16th, 1880, by Rev. A. J. PORTER, Mr. Luther R. MYERS and Miss Sarah E. HARPER, both of this county.

Married: On Sunday, November 21st, at Harper's Ferry, Mr. Thos. C. DONAHUE, formerly of Baltimore, Md, to Miss Jeffie JANNEY, both of Hamilton. Ceremony performed by W. C. CAMPBELL, of Harper's Ferry.

Married: November 23d, 1880, by Elder A. T. M. HANDY at the bride's residence in Prince William Co., Mr. John G. WILEY of Loudoun to Miss Amanda F. STEVENSON.

Died: In Hillsboro, at the home of his parents, Lee S. and Kate MOORE, on Monday, November 22d, 1880, of diphtheria, Walter S. MOORE, aged 10y 3m.

Death of Wm. B. CLAGETT (second son of the late Dr. Thos. H. CLAGETT, of this town) occurred at "Woodburn," on Sunday night last.

Kansas City (Mo.) Journal: Marriage on Thursday, November 18th of Maj. B. L. WOODSON, of that city and Miss Nora DELANEY, formerly of Leesburg, at father DOHERTY's house. Native of Va and became engaged to her husband some years ago. she comes of an old French family and nurtured in the refined atmosphere of a Va home; reverse of circumstances came which called the family to this city, where some three years ago she met her now husband. .... Among gifts, one set of delicate glass from the bride's brother, engraved with the coat of arms of the ancient French family from which Mrs. DELANEY, the bride's mother is descended. Also a rare piece of carving, "St. Nicholas Blessing Little Children." The exquisite heirloom was carved during the reign of Louis XVIth, of France, by Andre Joseph VILLARD, an ancestor, who manufactured his own tools and was 3 years in executing from a sea cow's tooth this carving. The carving has passed through three revolutions and is still in perfect state of preservation.

Thursday, 9 December 1880   Vol. XXV, No. 26

Died: At the house of Burr HAMILTON, in Loudoun County, on the 26th ultimo, John R. PIERPOINT, after a short sickness, in his 83rd year. Native of Loudoun. His early life was devoted to teaching. Afterward engaged in the drug business in Alexandria. Soon after he lost his eyesight and a little later his wife died. He then returned to his friends in Loudoun.

Death of Mr. Samuel CARR, farmer, at his home two miles west of Leesburg, on Sunday night last, in the 67th year of his age. Interred in Presbyterian burying ground on Tuesday.

Accident near Guilford, on Tuesday morning last, by which Mr. Casper LENT, son of Mr. Sam. LENT, died. While at work at a quarry belonging to his father, the rock above loosened and jarred by the picking fell on him. He was about 22 years of age.

Case of Mrs. Carrie B. ROBERTSON against Norville R. ROBERTSON. Divorce granted and her name changed to Carrie B. ROBERTS, her maiden name. *Winchester, Illinois, Times, Oct. 29th.*

Diphtheria in Brandy station, Culpeper Co, Rev. James McGILL, residing near the station, has lost one child and three others are ill. Mrs. McGILL is the daughter of Robert BEVERLY Esq., of Fauquier. Dr. Samuel McGILL, of Leesburg, who is the brother of Rev. Mr. McGILL, passed through Alexandria on Thursday. Another child, making the second, died on Thursday before Dr. M. arrived. Before its death his three surviving children were removed to their grandfather's in Fauquier.

Thursday, 16 December 1880   Vol. XXV, No. 27

Married: In Lovettsville, by the Rev. P. H. MILLER, Mr. J. Cost FREY to Miss Roberta GOODHEART.

Married: In Lovettsville, by the Rev. St. John RINKER, Mr. Robert CONNER to Miss Anna WRIGHT.

Died: Bessie VIRTS, aged 8 years, died at the residence of her parents, Abraham and Florida VIRTZ, on Tuesday, Nov. 30th 1880.

Died: At her residence in Hamilton, on Friday, Nov. 26th, in her 59th year, Mrs. Mary Elizabeth MUSE, wife of James H. MUSE.

Co. Ct.: Jas. L. GARDNER qualified as Committee of Ann M. SHRYOCK. Estates of P. H. and Edmonia SMITH committed to Sheriff. Silas W. WRIGHT qualified as Administrator dbn wwa of Alfred WRIGHT dec'd. Tazewell LOVETT qualified as guardian of Caroline LOVETT.

Mr. Wm. E. ELLISON, of this county, was one day last week summoned to the bedside of his father in Waltham, Massachusetts, but before he reached there his father was dead, and his aged mother died within three days after his arrival.

On Sat. night, the 11th inst., Mort. LAMBERT and Jas. PRESTON, both colored, became engaged in a quarrel while at a dance in Fauquier Co, near Coutett's. LAMBERT procured a shot gun and proceeded to PRESTON's home about daybreak and shot PRESTON through the head. He died in a few hours.

Thursday, 23 December 1880   Vol. XXV, No. 28

Married: On the 15th inst., by the Rev. G. W. POPKINS, near Farmwell, Mr. Marcellus MOFFETT to Miss Sarah E. FLING, all of Loudoun County.

Married: On December 21st 1880, at the residence of the bride's mother, by Rev. H. SUTER, Dr. Thos. M. LEWIS, of Clarke County, and Jennie, daughter of the late Edgar SNOWDEN.

Married: On Sunday the 12th at the residence of Mrs. Frances, by the Rev. H. H. WYER, E. G. EDMONDS, Treasurer of Fauquier County, and Miss Adaline EDMONDS, youngest daughter of the late Capt. Elias EDMONDS.

Married: On the 15th inst., by Elder Joseph N. BADGER, at the bride's residence, Wm. H. FRANCES, of Fauquier, and Mrs. E. C. LONG, of Manassas, Prince William County.

Married: On the 15th inst. at the residence of the bride's parents, by Rev. J. F. POULTON, Snowden W. TAYLOR and Miss Ella PIERSON, both of Fauquier.

Married: At the Lutheran Church, Lovettsville, December 14th 1880, by Rev. P. H. MILLER, Mr. C. W. DOWNEY, to Mrs. Laura V. DOWNEY, both of Loudoun.

Died: At his residence, near Martinsburg, Md, on the 27th of November, 1880, Mr. John REED, a native of Loudoun County, in the 81st year of his age.

Wash. Republican of Monday: Sudden death of Capt. Alfred GLASSCOCK, who but recently removed from Loudoun County to this city, yesterday of pleuro-pneumonia. He was 42 years of age. He leaves a wife and little ones. Interred in Union Cemetery, Leesburg.

A gentleman just here from Bealton, Fauquier Co, says that a day or two ago a young man named William SHUMATE, son of Mr. W. J. SHUMATE, of that place shot himself through the left lung while in the parlor of a neighbor, no one being present at the time, but himself and a young lady, who, it is supposed, had discarded him. It is feared his wound is mortal.

Thursday, 30 December 1880   Vol. XXV, No. 29

Married: In the M. E. Church, South, on Wednesday, December 22nd, 1880, by Rev. J. S. GARDNER, Mr. Joseph Randolph RHODES and Miss Amanda F. WALLACE, both of Loudoun.

Married: At Mt. Pleasant, Stafford Co, Va, on Thursday, December 16th, 1880, by Rev. Father TIERNAN, Dr. A. M. BRENT, of Northumberland County, to Bertie A., second daughter of J. Newton HARPER, formerly of Alexandria.

Died: At the residence of Asa H. RECTOR at Rector's X Roads, Fauquier County, on Sunday morning, December 12th 1880, Mrs. Sally WEEKS in the 83d year of her age.

Thursday, 6 January 1881 Vol. XXV, No. 30

Died: At her residence near the Pot House, on Monday, December 27th, Mrs. Chris. LEITH, widow of the late Wm. LEITH.

Mr. John T. GRIMES, of this town, died at the residence of his mother in Leesburg, on Sunday night, in the 41st year of his age. He was a soldier in the Loudoun Artillery during the war.

Mrs. Mary B. WHITING, relict of Mr. Frank WHITING, and daughter of Col. Nathaniel BURWELL, of "Carter Hall," died in Clarke County, last week, aged 82 years.

Thursday, 6 January 1881 Vol. XXV, No. 30

Married: On the 3d instant, at the Epiphany Church, by Rev. Dr. BALDWIN, Dr. Cyrus M. GINGRICH, of Leesburg, to Miss Lulie DOWELL of Washington.

Married: At the residence of the bride's uncle, Mr. E. G. CAUFMAN, at Goresville, on Wednesday December 29th 1880, by Rev. Father Van DeVIVER, Mr. Chester M. COLT, and Miss Rose, daughter of Col. C. W. PAXSON, all of Loudoun County.

Died: At Hope Grove, Loudoun County, December 18th 1880, of consumption, Miss Susan C. RUSK, 3rd daughter of Samuel and Marizee H. RUSK.

Marriage licenses issued in Washington city on Monday: John H. WILLIAMS, of Danville, Va, and Mattie L. BROWN, of Philomont; Dr. Cyrus M. GINGRICH, of Leesburg, and Lulah O. DOWELL.

Wm. PEARCE, well known in Fauquier County, was frozen to death on Thursday night near Rectortown.

Thursday, 13 January 1881 Vol. XXV, No. 31

Married: On the 23d of December, by the Rev. John WOOLF, at the residence of the bride's parents, Miss Sallie E. CARLISLE and Mr. Humphrey N. LATHAM.

Married: Near Round Hill, Dec. 30th, by Rev. Samuel BROWN, Mr. Smith REED to Miss Cebella A. COLLINS, all of Loudoun.

Married: On the 23d ulto., at the residence of the bride's father, by Rev. L. M. LYLE, Mr. Wm. E. FLETCHER and Miss Mary M. ALLISON, all of Fauquier.

Married: Dec. 29th, by Rev. T. W. NEWMAN, Mr. David S. KEMPER to Miss Lucy C. HARDING, all of Fauquier.

Married: On the 4th inst., in Warrenton, by Rev. Jno. F. POULTON, Mr. John W. DUNN and Miss Laura PAYNE, both of Prince William Co, Va.

Died: At Warrenton, Va, on December 26th, of inflammation of the brain after an illness of only nine days, Burgess, second son of Geo. W. and Mary Randolph BALL, aged 26 years.

Died: At the residence of her father, near Guilford, Loudoun County, on Thursday evening, December 16, 1880, Mary F.

JENKINS, wife of E. JENKINS, and daughter of Alfred and Betsy WORKS, in the 26th year of her age.

Died: On the 10th of December 1880, near Catocton Church, Loudoun, Mrs. Julia A. BROWN, wife of Geo. N. BROWN, in the 68th year of her age.

Henry THOMAS, colored, who was arrested a few weeks ago for a murderous assault upon Mr. Henry W. RUSSELL, living near Taylortown, was found guilty and sentenced to 7 years.

Co. Ct.: H. B. GLASSCOCK qualified as Admx. of Alfred GLASSCOCK dec'd.; Geo. W. GRIMES as Admr. of John T. GRIMES dec'd. Joseph and Chas. E. JAMES appointed committee for Sarah JAMES. Will of Mary B. THRIFT admitted to probate.

Thursday, 20 January 1881   Vol. XXV, No. 32

Mrs. Hannah Lee ALEXANDER, daughter of the late Bushrod C. WASHINGTON, died in Charlestown, W. Va., Wednesday, of paralysis.

Mrs. M. A. E. BARTON, wife of Mr. Benjamin BARTON, of Loudoun Co., died at the residence of Mr. Jos. BRODERS, in this city, yesterday, after a short illness. Interred in Ebenezer burying ground today. *Alex. Gazette of Tuesday.*

Married: In this town, on the evening of the 11th inst., by Rev. J. F. CANNON, Mr. John F. KIDWELL and Miss Susie B. THOMPSON.

Married: On Thursday evening, January 13th, at the residence of the bride's aunt, in Hamilton, by Rev. A. A. P. NEEL, Mr. Oscar N. MOORE, of Berryville, Va, to Miss Edmonia NESMITH, of Hamilton, Va.

Married: Thursday, January 6th 1881, at the residence of the bride's parents, near Short Hill, Mr. Robert WENNER and Miss Alice O. KALB, Rev. P. H. MILLER officiating.

Married: At North Fork Baptist Church, January 11th 1881, by Rev. P. F. WARREN, Mr. Wm. M. JAMES and Miss Rose CRAIG, all of Loudoun.

Married: January 13, 1881, at the residence of the bride's father, Taylortown, by the Rev. P. H. MILLER, Mr. John W. BITZER and Miss Leonoro GOODHART, all of Loudoun.

Died: At the residence of her son-in-law, Mr. D. T. FOUSCHE, at Newmansville, Illinois, on Thursday, January 6th 1881, Mrs. Mary HOUGH, mother of Mr. L. W. S. HOUGH, of this town, in the 88th year of her age.

Died: At the Dry Mill, near Leesburg, on Wednesday, the 12th of January, 1881, of consumption, Miss Martha A. DAVIS, aged 38y 10m 2d.

Mr. Abram LENT, of New York State, but who for the last few years had made his home with his son, Mr. Samuel E. LENT, near Guilford, died Monday morning, in the 97th year of his age, having been born 6 June 1784. He retained his faculties unimpaired. He was buried on Wednesday. It has only been a few weeks since that his grandson, Mr. Casper LENT, met his death by the caving in of an embankment.

John SCOTT, a native of Fauquier, and second son of the late Robert E. SCOTT, has recently gone from Baltimore where he practice law, to San Luis Obispo, California, to restore his health.

Thursday, 27 January 1881   Vol. XXV, No. 33

Married: On the 23d ultimo, in Brownsville, Washington Co, Md, by Elder D. AUSHERMAN, Henry C. TURNER, of Frederick Co, to Miss Hattie F. CASTLE, of Washington Co, Md, daughter of the late Dr. CASTLE of Leesburg.

Married: At the residence of the bride's father, near Middleburg, on Wed., January 19th 1881, by Rev. Mr. JOHNS, Mr. George O. FURGUSON, of Leesburg, and Miss Mattie T., daughter of Mr. William DODD, all of Loudoun.

Died: At the residence of her mother, near Leesburg, on Wed. morning, January 26th, 1881, Katie RHODES, youngest daughter of the late Joseph RHODES. Funeral will take place from her mother's residence at 10 o'clock Friday morning.

Died: On the 16th of Jan. 1881, at his home near Union, of consumption, Turner H. GALLEHER, in the 52nd year of his age. Leaves a wife and eight children.

Died: At her residence, near Little River Church, Loudoun Co., Mrs. Leeah HUTCHISON, in her 89th year, on Friday morning, Jan. 21st. Member of Little River Baptist Church.

Died: Near Fairfax Court House, January 6th 1881, Mary E. GARRISON, wife of B. T. GARRISON, in her 49th year.

Church property in Hamilton and Hillsborough, so long in litigation, was sold under decree of the court on Friday last. Mr. J. B. PEUGH bought the church at Hamilton, for the M. E. Church, South, for $1100; Mr. C. C. WENNER bought the parsonage at Hillsborough, for $1200.

Mrs. Alice JANNEY, widow of the late John JANNEY, of this county, died at the residence of her nephew, Mr. C. P. JANNEY, in Leesburg, on Wednesday morning last, in her 81st year. Daughter of the late Sampson MARMADUKE, and was born at Shepherdstown, W. Va., on the 20th of February 1800. Married to Mr. JANNEY on the 26th of January 1826, and died on the 55th anniversary of her wedding day. Removed with her husband to Leesburg immediately after her marriage. Oldest communicant on the registry of St. James Church, Leesburg. Funeral will take place from St. James (Episcopal) Church this (Thursday) morning, January 26th at 11½ o'clock.

Death of Chalkley GILLINGHAM, Esq. at his residence, Woodlawn, Fairfax County, on Saturday last, after a long illness, in his 74th year. He was a native of Frankford, Pa. and came to Fairfax County about 1852, where he established, in conjunction with Mr. John MASON, "Woodlawn Settlement," a short distance from Alexandria. ...

Thursday, 3 February 1881   Vol. XXV, No. 34

Married: January 18th 1881, at the residence of the bride's uncle, Mr. A. W. STROTHER, by the Rev. F. A. STROTHER, Mr. Charles W. JOHNSON of Loudoun, and Miss Nannie S. CONWAY, of Fauquier.

Married: On the 29th of December 1880, in Stafford Co, Va, by Rev. Mr. McBRYDE, Thomas WALLACE Esq. to Miss Hallie E., only remaining single child of Judge R. C. L. MONCURE and his wife, of said county, who now have living 11 sons and daus., the wives and husbands of all of whom are still living.

Died: Obed PIERPOINT, son of Jonathan PIERPOINT of Morgan County, Ohio, and grandson of Obed PIERPOINT of Loudoun County, died at his residence at Waynesville, Warren Co. Ohio, on November 1st 1880, aged 75 years

Died: In Washington City, on Friday, December 17th 1880, of pneumonia, Mary Lee, oldest child of Edward B. and Mary A. FADELY, aged 2y 3m.

Death of Mr. Wm. B. JACKSON died at his home near Goresville, on Saturday, in about the 67th year of his age.

Little child of Mr. Lewis C. HELM, near Hamilton, was buried in Leesburg on Monday, having died a day or two previous with diphtheria. An older child of Mr. H. is also quite ill.

At Upperville, Va, last Monday night Mr. B. F. CONRAD, merchant of that place, having returned from his store, he and his wife, Mrs. Lizzie CONRAD, who was carrying a lamp, were ascending the stairway preparing to retire. He had reached the landing when his wife screamed and he saw her at the foot of the stairs in a blaze, the lamp having exploded. Mr. CONRAD and his niece, Miss Fannie BRYNE, ran to her assistance, but he being a cripple and she being palsied with fright were scarcely able to do anything. Two men from a store nearby broke open the door and took her into the yard to bury her in the snow. She was almost roasted alive. A blanket was wrapped around her, and she walked up stairs to her room without assistance, begging them not to touch her. She suffered extreme pain until Thursday, when she died.

Thursday, 10 February 1881   Vol. XXV, No. 35

Died: In Leesburg, at the residence of her only son, on the 31st of January, Mrs. Mary ANDERSON, in her 75th year. For nearly 40 years a member of the Baptist Church.

Died: In Washington City, on Wednesday morning, February 9, 1881, at 6 a.m., Edward Ashton, aged 9m, only child of Edward B. and Mary Agnes FADELEY.

Died: At the residence of her mother, 403 G St., NW, Feb. 7th 1881, at 8:30 p.m. of diphtheria, Hattie B., third daughter of Hattie B. and the late Capt. Alfred GLASCOCK, aged 9y 7m. Remains brought to Leesburg on Wed. and laid beside her father in Union Cemetery.

Death in Washington city, of a daughter of the late Capt. Alfred GLASSCOCK and a little child of Mr. E. B. FADELY. Mrs. GLASSCOCK is the sister of Mr. E. B. FADELY, children of the late C. F. FADELY of this town. On the 17th of December last, Mr. FADELY lost a little daughter, in her 3rd year. Three days later, on the 20th of the same month, Capt. GLASSCOCK died. Last Monday night, February 7th, a daughter of Capt. G., in the 10th year of her age, followed her father to the tomb, and on Wednesday morning the 9th, the only surviving child of Mr. E. B. FADELY, joined her departed friends.

Thursday, 17 February 1881   Vol. XXV, No. 36

Married: On the 10th inst., in the M. E. Church, South, at Falls Church, by Rev. B. F. BALL, of Baltimore, Mr. J. Frank SHREVE, of Fairfax County, and Miss Annie FEBREY, of Alexandria County.

Married: At the residence of E. V. WHITE, on Wednesday, February 9, 1881, by Elder E. V. WHITE, Mr. John R. BARNHOUSE and Miss Mary A. FRY, all of Loudoun.

Married: At New Valley Meeting House, on Wednesday, February 9, 1881, by Elder E. V. WHITE, Mr. Geo. W. FAWLEY and Miss Ida V. CARNES, all of Loudoun.

Married: At the same place, by the same, on Tuesday, February 15, 1881, Mr. Isaac L. STOCKS and Miss Minerva WILLIAMS, daughter of the late John WILLIAMS, all of Loudoun.

Married: By Rev. A. J. PORTER, on the 23d of January, 1881, at the residence of the bride near Ebenezer M. E. Church, Mr. Edward W. RECTOR to Mrs. Emma R. MOORE.

Married: On the 14th instant, near Mt. Hope, by Rev. Geo. W. POPKINS, Mr. Joseph W. WORTMAN to Miss Linnie J. MAFFETT, eldest dau. of James MAFFETT, all of Loudoun.

Married: In the Protestant Episcopal Church in Charlottesville, by Rev. Dr. HANCKEL, Alex. B. MOORE, of Loudoun Co, to Lucy

B., daughter of Major Wm. N. BERKELEY, of Albemarle County, formerly of Loudoun.

Died: In Baltimore on Sunday morning, February 13 at 8 o'clock, James M., aged 38 years, son of Hiram and Mary E. McVEIGH.

Died: At his residence near Philomont, on Sunday, the 30th of January, Mr. Thomas BEAVERS, in the 76th year of his age. Member of Methodist Church.

Died: On the 31st of January 1881, at his residence in Philomont, John W. WALKER, in the 51st year of his age. Leaves a widow and three children.

Died: At his residence near Philomont, on Thursday, February 10th 1881, Mr. Fielding TAVENNER, in his 76th year. Injury of several months ago together with other diseases caused his death. Leaves several children, all are of mature years.

Died: Of consumption, at the residence of her husband, Charles D. WEADON, Esq., near Hamilton, February 1st 1881, Mrs. Mary M. WEADON, eldest daughter of Justice and Caroline KUHLMAN, in the 35th year of her age. Leaves a husband and five little children.

Philomont loses: On 30 January Mr. Thomas BEAVERS died in his 76th year. On Monday the 31st of January, Mr. John W. WALKER died in his 51st year, and on Thursday, February 10th Mr. Fielding TAVENNER died in the 76th year of his age. They lived within a few miles of each other.

Feb. Ct.: Wills of Catharine BARNHOUSE and Ellen BOLEN admitted to probate. Administration granted on estate of Wm. B. JACKSON dec'd., Saml. CARR dec'd., Christian LEITH dec'd., Mary TURNER dec'd., Geo. W. CHAMBLIN dec'd. Thos. BROWN qualified as Committee of Jas. GARDNER. Estates of Sallie WEEKS, Elizabeth HOUGH and P. H. SMITH committed to Sheriff.

Marriage license issued in Washington City on Tuesday to Westwood F. PAXSON, of Loudoun County, and Miss Carrie SKIRVING, of that city.

Thursday, 24 February 1881   Vol. XXV, No. 37

Married: In St. James Episcopal Church, Leesburg, February 23d 1881, by Rev. R. T. DAVIS, Mr. Frederick B. HAYES, of Barnesville, Frederick Co, Md, and Miss Ida L., daughter of C. T. HEMPSTONE, Esq., of Loudoun County.

Married: In Washington city, February 23, 1881, by Rev. C. C. MEADOR, Edward FURR, of Loudoun County, and Miss Dora E. ANDERSON, of Washington DC.

Married: Near Lovettsville, January 31st, at Mt. Olive M. E. Church, by Rev. A. J. PORTER, Mr. Samuel R. PAINTER to Miss Laura KENT.

Married: On Wednesday, the 16th of February by Rev. J. S. GARDNER, at the residence of Charles JENKINS, near Leesburg, Franklin E. SAFFER to Laura A. DODD.

Married: At the residence of the bride's father, February 9th 1881, by Rev. J. B. LAKE, Mr. F. Marion LAKE, of Fauquier, to Miss Lizzie HATCHER, of Loudoun County.

Died: In Baltimore, on the morning of the 16th instant, of typhoid fever, Miss Julia A. MORISSEY, aged 30? years.

Mr. Chas. O. VANDEVANTER, of this county, leaves today (Thursday) for Texas to work on a railroad survey in Mexico.

Washington Post of 16th inst.: Wedding of Mr. Westwood F. PAXSON, of Loudoun, to Miss Carrie T. SKIRVING, of that city took place at 6:30 last evening at the Metropolitan Baptist church, corner 6th and A St. NE, Rev. Dr. J. PARKER conducting. ...

Thursday, 3 March 1881   Vol. XXV, No. 38

Married: At the residence of the bride's father, between the Hills, Tuesday, February 22nd, by Rev. P. H. MILLER, Mr. E. Sheldon ARNOLD and Miss Lizzie M. MILLER.

Married: In the 3rd Presbyterian Church, Richmond, February 16th 1881, by Rev. W. R. SCOTT, H. Clay LYNN, of Snickersville, and Jennie H., dau. of Hon. R. E. GARDNER, of Richmond.

Died: At her uncle's residence, near Morrisonville, on Wednesday, February 16th 1881, Mary E. DARR, aged 15y 5m. She was the only daughter of E. W. and M. A. DARR.

Died: In Hillsboro, February 16th 1881, Miss Jane A. COCKRILL, in her 37th year.

Died: At Round Hill, Feb. 17th 1881, of consumption, Bettie L., dau. of Samuel and Parmelia BROWN, in her 23rd year. Member of Blue Ridge Lodge, I.O.O.G.T. United with M. E. Church when 10 years old. Leaves parents, 3 brothers and 1 sister.

Mr. John S. CLAIR, an inmate of Alexandria Infirmary for some time past, died at that institution yesterday morning, in the 83d year of his age. He came there from Loudoun Co, was a prosperous man before the war. Funeral services conducted by Rev. Mr. PENICK, yesterday afternoon, interred in St. Paul's cemetery.

Tribute of respect from Blue Ridge Lodge No. 64 for sister Bettie L. BROWN, eldest daughter of Rev. Samuel and Pamelia A. BROWN, who died Thurs. February 17th 1881, in her 23rd year.

Thursday, 10 March 1881   Vol. XXV, No. 39

Married: At the residence of the bride's father, Henry W. CASTLEMAN, Esq., by Rev. Mr. PHILLIPS, February 16th 1881, Mr. J. S. POWERS, to Miss Estelle S. CASTLEMAN, both of Jefferson County.

Married: In Washington, at the Epiphany Church, on Wednesday, the 23d inst., by Dr. PARET, Mr. Mahlon PURCELL to Miss Maud FILLER, daughter of A. T. M. FILLER, all of Loudoun Co.

Married: On the 2d of March 1881, by Rev. B. A. SHREVE, assisted by Rev. L. B. TURNBULL, Mr. Peyton S. WORTMAN and Miss Lucinda E. HAVENNER, all of Loudoun.

Married: At Lovettsville, February 24th 1881, by Rev. P. H. MILLER, Mr. Laban C. GRUBB to Miss Mary E. BOGER.

Married: At Lovettsville, March 2nd 1881, by Rev. P. H. MILLER, Mr. William J. STONE and Miss Emma J. FRY.

Died: At the residence of her dau., Mrs. Mary E. WATERS near Middleburg, on Thursday, Feb. 24th 1881, Mrs. Elizabeth SWART, relict of the late Wm. R. SWART, in her 86th year.

Telegram from Mr. C. O. VANDEVANTER announces his safe arrival at Galveston, Texas, on Tuesday. He is on the engineer corps bound for railroad work in Mexico.

Thursday, 17 March 1881   Vol. XXV, No. 40

Married: In Rectortown, Fauquier Co, on Wed. Feb. 23d, 1881, by Rev. Lee M. LYLE, Dr. J. E. COPELAND to Miss Fannie V. HALLEY, dau. of Dr. S. N. HALLEY, all of Fauquier Co.

Married: In this county, on the evening of the 10th inst., by Rev. J. F. CANNON, Mr. Aaron T. DAILY and Miss Margaret J. HARDING.

Married: March 3d 1881, at the Lutheran Church, near Lovettsville, by Rev. P. H. MILLER, Mr. George W. FRY, to Miss Clara E. BROWN.

Married; On Tuesday, February 22nd, 1881, at the residence of the bride's uncle, Mr. David McINTOSH, at Brian, Brazos County, Texas, Mr. J. Aldridge CHEW, of Jefferson County, W. Va, to Miss Mary J. McINTOSH, of the former place.

Died: At the residence of his parents, in Clinton, Mo., Rush Chamblin FRAZIER, infant son of J. W. FRAZIER, formerly of Loudoun.

Died: Lillian, youngest daughter of John E. and Jennie BRENNER, of Middleburg, died February 22d, 1881, of membranous croup, aged 2y 7m 3d.

A little colored girl, about 10 years of age, employed at the Pickett House in Upperville, Fauquier County, was so severely burned by her clothes taking fire, that she died in a few hours. She was in the sick room of Miss Lucelia PICKETT, waiting upon her, when the fire communicated to her clothing by a spark from an open grate.

March Ct.: Administration on estates of Fielding TAVENNER and Thos. BEANS, and Reuben HUTCHISON. Will of Leah HUTCHISON admitted to probate.

Thursday, 24 March 1881 Vol. XXV, No. 41

No deaths or marriages.

Thursday, 31 March 1881 Vol. XXV, No. 42

Married: At the Lutheran parsonage, near Lovettsville, Sunday, March 13th 1881, by Rev. P. H. MILLER, Mr. William F. BEAMER, to Miss Mary V. FIELDS.

Married: On the same day, at the same place, Mr. Isaac A. ORRISON, to Miss Annie J. SLENTZ, by the same clergyman.

Died: On the 1st of March, 1881, at Hot Springs, Arkansas, of typhoid pneumonia, Hampton E. JACOBS, formerly of this county, in the 48th year of his age.

Died: In Leesburg, on Monday evening, March 28th 1881, after a protracted illness, Miss Mary Ann NEWTON, daughter of the late John and Judith NEWTON, of Fredericksburg, Va. Born on the 17th of August 1801.

Thursday, 7 April 1881 Vol. XXV, No. 43

Jacob ISH, formerly of this county, died near Jacksonville, Oregon, March 4th 1881.

Married: In Charleston, W. Va., on the 21st of March 1881, by Rev. Dr. FOLLANSBEE, father of the bride, Mr. B. R. BERLIN, of Washington DC, and Miss Josie M. FOLLANSBEE, of Charleston.

Married; At the residence of the bride's father, on Wed. March 30, 1881, by Elder E. V. WHITE, Mr. Samuel L. CARNES and Miss Mary E., daughter of Mr. Julius F. FRY, all of Loudoun.

Died: At his residence at Farmwell, Joseph ZRUNDELLO, born September 6th 1808, and died March 13th 1881. When about 40 years old joined the M. E. Church, South.

Died: Near Gum Spring, March 29th, 1881, of capillary bronchitis, Willie Asdell, infant son of James W. and Irene M. WYCKOFF, aged 7m 4d.

Died: At Hope Grove, near Aldie, Loudoun County, on the 17th of March 1881, Mr. Samuel RUSK, aged 85y 6m 19d. Born in York Co, Pennsylvania, on August 29th 1795, the eldest son of the late Samuel RUSK, of Manchester, England, and the grandson of the late William McCARVIN, of York County, Penn. He has been a citizen of Loudoun for 85 year, had 12 children, only 5 of whom survive him, 29 grandchildren, and 9 great-grandchildren.

Thursday, 14 April 1881   Vol. XXV, No. 44

Married: March 31st 1881, at the residence of Mr. Wm. BEATY, by Rev. P. H. MILLER, Mr. John H. FANLEY to Miss Sarah J. WRIGHT.

Married: At Bethel Evangelical Lutheran Church, Tankerville, March 24th 1881, by Rev. P. H. MILLER, Mr. Wm. T. BROWN, to Miss Hannah A. COMPHER.

Died: Near Mt. Gilead on the 3d day of April, 1881, of congestion of the lungs, Harry E., son of Joseph P. and Mollie T. FURR, aged 3y 7m 13d.

Died: In Staunton, April 4th of whooping cough, Ida May, infant daughter of E. M. and N. E. PARKER, aged 1y 5m.

Died: March 22nd 1881, at the residence of his father-in-law, Mr. George HEFFNER, on Quaker Branch, Mr. Joseph J. WILLIAMS, in the 41st year of his age.

Died: Near Short Hill, March 24th 1881, Robert Clinton, infant son of James W. and Catharine A. JACOBS.

Died: March 25th 1881, near Taylortown, Evert MOCK in the 14th year of his age.

Died: On Wed. the 6th instant, at the house of her mother, Mrs. Thomas FRANCIS, of a lingering illness, Ella C. FRANCIS in her 25th year. Member of M. E. Church, South since young.

Died: In Waterford, at the residence of his father on the evening of 9th of April 1881, Cornelius O. VIRTS, of consumption, aged 23y 1m 21d.

Death of R. G. BOWIE: of this county, died at his home at Clark's Gap, on Monday afternoon, in his 73d year. He was by profession a civil engineer and performed much of the work in locating the present line of the W. & O. Railroad. He was a brother of the late Judge BOWIE, of Md, who died a short time ago. Interred in Union Cemetery, Leesburg, on Wednesday.

Death of Mr. Geo. D. SMITH occurred at his home near Waterford on Saturday night, the 10th inst., in the 77th year of his age. Buried in Leesburg on Wed.

April Ct.: Wills of Thos. E. DISHMOND dec'd. and Mary A. NEWTON dec'd. admitted to probate. Administration on estates of Joseph ARUNDELL dec'd. and Harriet ANKERS dec'd. Jas. S. SHUMAKER qualified as guardian of Maggie E. SHUMAKER.

Mr. Asher W. GRAY, after a somewhat protracted illness, died at his home in Baltimore, on the 7th instant, in his 63d year. Born in Leesburg, where in early manhood he engaged in mercantile pursuits. Subsequently he engaged in business in Alexandria and Baltimore. He leaves a large number of relatives in this county. Funeral took place from his late residence, North Eutaw St., Baltimore, at 4 o'clock Sat. afternoon.

Thursday, 21 April 1881   Vol. XXV, No. 45

Married: At "Oakley," in Fauquier Co., the residence of the bride's father, on Tuesday morning, April 19th 1881, by Rev. John JOHNS, Mr. J. H. C. BEVERLEY and Miss Rebecca, dau. of Henry G. DULANEY, Esq., all of Fauquier.

Died: In Warrenton, on Thursday morning at 4 o'clock, Mrs. Eva R. POULTON, wife of Rev. J. F. POULTON, in her 32d year.

Died: At her residence, in Alexandria, on Saturday, the 16th inst., between 11 and 12 p.m., Mrs. Elizabeth E. PARROTT, beloved wife of John A. PARROTT, in her 70th year. She has gone to four of her children gone before. She was the mother of Mrs. Robt. HARPER, of Loudoun.

Home of Col. Henry E. PEYTON, about 2 miles N of Waterford, was destroyed by fire Saturday last.

Rev. Jared L. ELLIOTT, of Washington, died in that city Sunday morning, in his 75th year. He was an old army chaplain, of Presbyterian church. In his will he bequeathed $10,000 to Mary A. MEAD of Leesburg in trust for her sisters and others.

Thursday, 28 April 1881   Vol. XXV, No. 46

Married: At Unison, on the 19th of April 1881, by Rev. J. H. LAKE, Mr. Samuel NICHOLS to Mrs. Mary C. McALISTER.

Married: In Leesburg, at the residence of the bride's father, April 26th 1881, by Rev. R. T. DAVIS, Mr. P. P. PERRY and Miss Lillian M. WALLACE.

Died: At the residence of her mother, 8th of March, 1881, Fanny C., daughter of Wm. and Ann DONAHUE, leaving mother, brother and sister.

Remains of Alfred DULIN were buried in Union Cemetery at Leesburg on Saturday. He died at his home in Fairfax County, on Thursday in the 79th year of his age.

Circuit Ct.: Wm. SMITH qualified as Admr. of John HEFFNER dec'd. H. O. CLAGGETT qualified as Admr. of W. B. CLAGETT dec'd. Will of Alice S. JANNEY dec'd. admitted to probate with C. P. JANNEY as Exor.

Thursday, 5 May 1881   Vol. XXV, No. 47

Died: In La Grange, Mo., Thursday morning, March 24th 1881, Hon. A. C. WALTMAN, in the 67th year of his age. Born in Loudoun County and at an early age removed to La Grange, and has resided there for 43 years.

Died: Near Aldie, April 24th 1881, Mattie, daughter of Amelia and David COOK, and granddaughter of Martha and Rev. Braxton BROWN. She was 8y 11m old.

Died: At her residence, Mt. Beniah, near Aldie, April 23, 1881, Mrs. Ann Elizabeth PALMER, wife of Johnson Sheridan PALMER, in the 59th year of her age. Married for 31 years.

Mr. Robt. A. BEVERLEY, of this county, youngest son of the late Wm. BEVERLEY, was married at Memorial P. E. Church, Baltimore last Thursday night, to Miss Julia DUVALL, of that city. Rev. Wm. DAME officiated.

Thursday, 12 May 1881   Vol. XXV, No. 48

Died: Near Philomont, April 26th, Willie C., son of T. J. and Phebe H. CARTER, aged 7m 6d.

Died: On Saturday morning, April 30, near Round Hill, at the residence of her grandson, J. A. LYNCH, Mrs. Mary V. CHAMBLIN, widow of the late B. A. CHAMBLIN, in the 87th year of age. Member of Baptist Church.

May Ct.: Wills of Elizabeth SWARTS and Geo. D. SMITH admitted to probate. Administration on estate of Edgar L. SMITH granted.

At 6 o'clock on Wednesday morning, May 11th 1881, Mrs. Mary LACK, consort of Wm. LACK, died at her home in Leesburg in her 77th year. Leaves aged husband. Born in Scotland, but was brought to this country when quite young. Member of Episcopal Church.

Thursday, 19 May 1881   Vol. XXV, No. 49

Married: On May 4th 1881, at the White House, the residence of the bride's mother, Hanover Co, Va, by the Rev. W. A. ALRICH, Dr. Wm. B. BARHAM, of Southampton Co, Va, to Fannie BERKELEY, daughter of the late Edmund BERKELEY, of Hanover Co.

Married: May 5, 1881, at Lovettsville, by Rev. P. H. MILLER, Mr. George S. WILLIAMS to Miss Ann Elizabeth BAKER.

Died: On Saturday evening May 7th near Round Hill, at the residence of her brother-in-law, Mahlon THOMAS Esqr., Miss Tamar CARTER, in the 51st year of her age. Member of Ebenezer Baptist church. Leaves brothers and sisters.

Died: At Green Valley, near Union, on Thursday morning, April 28th 1881, at sunrise Olivia C. CHAMBLIN, wife of Wm. CHAMBLIN.

Died: April 20th 1881, at South Fork, of consumption, Mrs. Richardetta, wife of Wm. TAVENNER, in the 45th year of her age. Member of Methodist Church for last 4 years. Leaves husband and children.

Death of Dr. M. K. BALDWIN at his home near North Fork, on Saturday last, of Bright's Disease, from which he had been a great sufferer for the past two years. He was in his 59th year. Interred at North Fork burying ground on Monday.

Henry TOPPIN, a blacksmith at Guilford station, on the W. & O. R. R., while attempting to prevent the flight of a flock of sheep scared by a passing train last Saturday, was struck in the lower part of the abdomen by a large ram, and injured so severely he died yesterday afternoon.

Miss Lucelia PICKETT, remembered by guests in former days of the old "Pickett House," in Leesburg, died at her brother's residence in Upperville, a few days ago, of consumption.

Thursday, 26 May 1881   Vol. XXV, No. 50

Died: Near Round Hill, on Sunday, May 22d 1881, Mrs. Elizabeth L. BRADFIELD, (mother of Mr. A. J. BRADFIELD, of this town) in the 89th year of her age.

Mr. William GRIGSBY, young merchant living at White Post, in Clarke Co., was in Berryville last Saturday and in attempting to board the train slipped, the train passing over his leg, from which effects he died in a few hours.

Thursday, 2 June 1881   Vol. XXV, No. 51

Married: At the Episcopal Rectory, in Leesburg, on Tuesday morning, May 31, 1881, by Rev. Dr. R. T. DAVIS, Frank A. ODEN, and Miss Constance, daughter of Capt. John R. CARTER, all of Loudoun.

Married: In the Episcopal Church at Hamilton, on Wednesday morning, June 1st 1881, by Rev. P. T. WARREN, Mr. Wm. H. OTLEY and Miss Jane M., daughter of Benj. F. TAYLOR, Esq., all of Loudoun.

Married: May 10th 1881, by Rev. J. H. TEMPLE, at Round Hill M. E. Church, South, Mr. James L. FLING and Miss Sarah Josephene HODGSON, daughter of Rev. William HODGSON.

Married: On the 19th inst., at the residence of the bride's father, by Elder Joseph FURR, Mr. W. L. RODERICK to Miss Mary F. HOUGH, all of Loudoun County.

Died: In Baltimore on Sunday, May 29th, Julius E., youngest son of the late Geo. KEPHART, of Belmont, in this county. Interred in the Cemetery at Leesburg on Tuesday.

Died: In Leesburg, on Wednesday night, May 25th 1881, Thomas Hawkins CLAGETT, youngest son of the late Dr. Thomas H. and Christiana H. CLAGETT, in his 43rd year.

Died: Near North Fork, March 14, at the residence of her husband, Philip VANSICKLER, Mahala VANSICKLER, in the 77th year of her age. Reared under influence of Society of Friends, she made no public profession of faith until after her marriage, when baptised and united with North Fork Baptist church.

Departed this life, May 5th, aged 61y 1m 27d, Elizabeth Frances, wife of David CONNER, of Wheatland, she had long suffered from a pulmonary affliction.

Death of Mr. Thos. H. CLAGETT, youngest son of the late Dr. Thos. H. CLAGETT, occurred at his home in Leesburg, on Wednesday night, May 25th, in his 43d year. He followed to the tomb an elder brother, leaving a wife and five little children. Interred in Union Cemetery at sunset on Friday evening.

Yesterday morning about 9 o'clock, Mr. W. H. ROGERS, of the house of J. P. Rogers & Co., was found in a dying condition in his room at the American Hotel, and expired in a few moments. He had been afflicted for some 15 years past with heart disease. He was in his 70th year. Native of Loudoun and engaged in mercantile business in Middleburg with Gen. Asa ROGERS, whose sister he married. From there he went to Alexandria, where he lived till the war came on when he moved to Richmond and became a member of the firm of Robinson, Adams & Co. The conflagration of April, 1865, destroyed a vast amount of their property, and they were ruined. He then went into business with his son, J. Pendleton ROGERS. Member of Baptist Church 50 years.

Thursday, 9 June 1881   Vol. XXV, No. 52

Married: At the residence of the bride's parents, near Waterford, May 25th 1881, by Rev. P. H. MILLER, Mr. Martin L. MANN to Miss Annie M. RIDGEWAY.

Died: At "The Grove," on Monday, June 6th, Annie R., wife of O. M. BUSSARD, in the 24th year of her age.

Died: Near the Trapp, on the 27th of May, Samuel D., youngest son of Robert KELLEY, age 18 months.

Died: At Bramilton, May 21st 1881, of diphtheria, Lucy Wood, aged 7 years, daughter of Cuthbert and Maria HUTCHISON.

Thursday, 16 June 1881   Vol. XXVI, No. 1

Married: On the 10th inst., in Richmond, by the Rev. A. G. BROWN, Geo. W. SCHLEIF of Leesburg, to Miss Laura L. GRAY, of Richmond, Va.

Married: On June the 8th 1881, at Galileo church, near Welltown, Frederick County, Va by John PIRKEY, Charles E. EVARD, of Loudoun County, and H. M. MARSTELLA.

Married: Sunday, June 5th 1881, at the River Mills, near Knoxville, Md, by Rev. P. H. MILLER, Mr. James B. FORTNEY to Miss Susan A. VIRTZ, both of Loudoun.

Died: At his home, in Leesburg, on June 15th, at 11½ a.m., Mr. Henry T. HARRISON, in his 85th year. Funeral will take place from his residence on Friday morning at 11½ o'clock.

Died: At Hamden Village, Baltimore Co, on Sunday, June 5, at 5 p.m., Johanah FITZGERALD, in the 45th year of her age, wife of Peter FITZGERALD.

Died: On Thursday, June 9th 1881, in Baltimore, Rodger Temple, aged 2y 9m 24d, son of R. T. and M. K. DAWSON, and grandson of James H. CHAMBLIN, Leesburg.

Death of Mr. Henry T. HARRISON occurred at his home in Leesburg, about noon, on Wednesday June 15th 1881, in his 85th year. For many years a Justice of the Peace for Loudoun; for 1 or 2 sessions her rep. in the State Legislature, and Pres. of the Loudoun Nat. Bank. Funeral will take place at 11½ tomorrow (Friday) morning June 17th.

June Ct.: Will of Elizabeth BEAMER admitted to probate. John TOPPING qualified as Admr. of Henry TOPPING dec'd.; John W. GARRETT as Admr. of M. K. BALDWIN dec'd.; Clinton M. HOSKINSON as Admr. of R. W. HOSKINSON dec'd.; Geo. W. BAGEANT as Admr. of Wm. BAGEANT dec'd.; Kemp B. FURR as Guardian of Ella FURR; Mary E. BALDWIN as Guardian of Orion BALDWIN; Samuel ORRISON as Guardian of V. G. L. ROLLINS and Margaret M. ROLLINS; C. C. BITZER as Guardian of Annie LOGAN.

Thursday, 23 June 1881   Vol. XXVI, No. 2

Mr. John B. MORTON, cashier of the Merchants Nat. Bank, died suddenly early this morning at his residence on Grace St, in the 73rd year of his age. *Richmond State of Friday.* He was a brother of the wife of Rev. Dr. HEAD, of this town.

Thursday, 30 June 1881   Vol. XXVI, No. 3

Married: On June 23d 1881, at the residence of the bride's father, Mr. G. W. DERRY, Loudoun County, by Rev. A. J. PORTER, Mr. W. R. HOSTLER, of Memphis, Tenn, to Miss Ida F. DERRY, of Loudoun County.

Married: On the 21st inst., at "Hartlands," the residence of the bride, by Rev. Mr. LEE, Mr. John H. FOSTER to Miss Lizzie, daughter of Mrs. M. C. STRIBLING.

Married: On the 23d inst., by Rev. W. G. HAMMOND, Mr. Harrison D. MOORE and Miss Ella FINCH, both of Fauquier.

Married: At "Evergreen," June 21st 1881, by the Rev. Arthur P. GRAY, assisted by the Rev. Henry T. SHARP, John Seymour McNELLY, of Greenville, Miss., and Mary M. BERKELEY, of Prince William County, Virginia.

Married: On sixth month, 20th 1881, at Friends' Meeting House, 15th and Race Sts, Philadelphia, Howard W. LIPPINCOT and Anna M. JANNEY, daughter of the late Jas. C. JANNEY of Loudoun.

Died: At "Carlheim," the residence of his grandfather, Chas. R. PAXTON, Esq., near Leesburg, on Saturday morning, June 25th 1881, Charles Paxton CHRISTIAN, in his 5th year, from diphtheria. Laid to rest Sunday evening in Union Cemetery.

Thursday, 7 July 1881   Vol. XXVI, No. 4

Married: June 29, 1881, at the Parsonage of the M. E. Church, South, by the Rev. W. K. BOYLE, Mr. E. M. HOUGH to Miss Sarah M. SAUNDERS, all of Leesburg.

Married: In Leesburg, on Tuesday evening, July 5th, by Elder A. T. M. HANDY, Mr. Marion F. SNIDER and Miss Elizabeth DAWSON, all of Loudoun.

Thursday, 14 July 1881   Vol. XXVI, No. 5

Died: April 21st 1881, at the residence of her husband, near Philomont, Lou, wife of John CRAIG, in the 29th year of age. Was in delicate health for several months. Leaves husband and an infant a few weeks old. Discourse by Elder YATES at North Fork Baptist Church will be on 4th Sunday in July.

Mr. Joseph SHUGART died at his home near Clark's Gap, on Saturday last, at 90 years of age. He retained his faculties to the last.

July Ct.: Will of Henry T. HARRISON admitted to probate. Estates of Richard PINKHAM, Mary A. NEWTON, Ella C. FRANCIS and Burgess D. BARTLETT dec'd. committed to sheriff. Julia A. BOWIE qualified as Admx. of Robt. G. BOWIE dec'd. J. E. CARUTHERS appointed Curator for the infant children of Wm. GREGG dec'd.

The family of Mr. Geo. WYNKOOP, who moved from Loudoun Co 8 or 10 months ago, to take possession of a farm he had bought near Shenandoah River, has been afflicted by diphtheria. On Sat. the 25th of June, he lost one child, and by the next Sat. three more of his children had died, all ranging in ages between 21½ and 15 years. He had moved from the Woodgrove neighborhood about 6 months ago. His wife was a daughter of the late Benj. SAUNDERS, near Leesburg.

Dedication of the New Baptist Church at Guilford was Sunday last, conducted by Rev. Dr. JOHNSON, Secretary of the Baptist Publication Society.

Thursday, 21 July 1881   Vol. XXVI, No. 6

Married: On Tuesday, 12th inst., at Guilford, by Elder A. T. M. HANDY, David W. LOVE and Missouri C. CRIDLER, all of Loudoun.

Died: At her home in Washington city, on Thursday morning, July 7th 1881, after a somewhat protracted illness, Miss Susan YERBY. Interred in Union Cemetery, Leesburg.

Died: Near Warrenton, on the 9th of July, in the 83d year of her age, Matilda W. FITZHUGH, relict of Wm. C. FITZHUGH, near Upperville. Christian of 63 years.

Mr. John H. DRISH, of this town, died on Tuesday morning last, after a protracted illness of much suffering. He was a son of late Wm. D. DRISH, and was in about the 60th year of his age.

Death of Mr. Fenton FURR occurred at his home near Bloomfield on the morning of Sat. last, of cholera-morbus. For many years a Justice of the Peace and manager of the public schools of his district. Member of M. E. Church, South. On Monday interred in the family burying ground at Ebenezer Church.

Thursday, 28 July 1881   Vol. XXVI, No. 7

Married: July 26th, 1881, at Hamilton, by Elder F. T. WARREN, Mr. Howard SILCOTT and Miss Helen E. WORKS, all of Loudoun County.

Died: At the residence of her father at Berlin, Md, on Thursday evening last, Bessie, daughter of John L. and Julia JORDAN, aged about 14 years.

Death of John L. ROGERS, youngest son of Col. Hamilton ROGERS, of Middleburg, occurred at Buchanan, in Botetourt Co, Va. last Friday night [22nd]. He was in the service of the Shenandoah Valley Railroad Co. and boarding at the Exchange Hotel. Leaves his aged parents. Buried in the Cemetery at Middleburg on Monday. He was his 35th year.

Mr. John WOLFORD, for many years Justice of the Peace in this county, died at his residence near Waterford on Monday morning last, in about the 82d year of age.

Thursday, 4 August 1881   Vol. XXVI, No. 8

Died: On the 25th of July 1881, in Baltimore City, Cornelia, in the 47th year of age, wife of M. M. BIGHAM, and daughter of the late S. H. T. [S. B. T.] CALDWELL of this county.

Died: On July 25th 1881, at the residence of her parents, near Purcellville, Hattie C., infant daughter and only child of Samuel E. and Mollie E. NICHOLS, aged 8m 27d.

Funeral sermon of Mr. Joseph T. POWER will be preached at Mt. Hope Church, Sunday morning, the 14th, at 11 o'clock, by Rev. B. P. DULIN.

I will be in Leesburg on August 8th to receive cash contributions for an artificial leg for Mr. A. L. SAUNDERS, who lost his by a painful accident while working on the W & O RR near Belmont Station. Signed G. W. FOUCHE, Farmwell.

Mr. Wm. BENTON, of this county, died on last Thursday, aged 92 years. Born in Lincolnshire, England, on December 25, 1788 and came to this country 1801.

Thursday, 11 August 1881   Vol. XXVI, No. 9

Died: July 25th 1881, at her home near Guilford, Miss Adeline BLINCOE, dau. of Albert and Mary BLINCOE, in her 27th year.

Died: At her home near Oatland, Annie M., wife of Jacob B. WATSON, in the 44th year of her age.

Died: At the residence of her son, T. B. HUTCHINSON, near the Plains, Fauquier Co., June 17, 1881, Mrs. Catharine HUTCHINSON, widow of the late Lemuel HUTCHINSON, in the 85th year of age.

After a long illness of consumption, George R. HEAD Jr., of this town, died on Wed. morning, August 10th 1881, in his 41st year. Leaves a wife and several young children. Funeral under direction of Olive Branch Lodge, A. F. & A. M. will take place from his late residence, at 5 o'clock Thursday evening.

Death of Mr. Wm. BENTON at his home in this county, on 28th of July, aged 92y 7m 3d. Born in Lincolnshire, England, on December 25, 1788, emigrated to America in 1801 and spent his early life in Spotsylvania Co, Va. At outbreak of war of 1812, he espoused the cause of his adopted country, and soon became quartermaster. At the close of the war he took charge of the WILLIS estate, bordering upon Fredericksburg. In 1818 he came to Loudoun Co to take charge of the estate of Pres. MONROE. Remaining there 6 years, he left in 1824 to take charge of his own purchase in the same county. His faith was that of the established church of England.

Thursday, 18 August 1881   Vol. XXVI, No. 10

Married: At Noland's Ferry, on the 10th of August, 1881, by the Rev. James McDONOUGH, John Lewis ROLLINS to Miss Kate Ellsworth FEASTER, both of Loudoun County.

Died: On the 3rd of August, 1881, Mrs. Elizabeth Ann TINSMAN, at the age of 58y 7m 10d. Wife of Enoch TINSMAN Esq., and dau. of the late James ALEXANDER, of Loudoun Co. In 1847 she left her native county and with her husband emigrated to Clarksburg, West Va., where she resided until her death.

Died: At Selma, on the 31st ult. Philip Hopkins, son of Henry W. and Fannie CHAMBLIN, aged 2 years.

On Sunday morning last, Wm. CARSON, living at Broad Run bridge, in this county, was probably fatally shot by Samuel JENKINS. CARSON had been employed by JENKINS for some time as a farm hand, and after his usual morning duties had left for his home a mile or 2 away, to spend Sunday. After reaching there he found JENKINS standing in the yard some 20 feet away, gun in hand, who accused him of having stolen his coat, and shot him just below the shoulder blade. JENKINS is at large.

At the residence of Mr. James CHATHAM on Wednesday evening last, the marriage of Miss Nannie D. HANNON, of this city, to Mr. John MILHOLLEN, of Loudoun County.

Thursday, 25 August 1881   Vol. XXVI, No. 11

Married: August 18th 1881, by Rev. P. T. WARREN at his residence near Hamilton, Mr. Chas. W. LEMON and Miss Maggie TALLY, all of Loudoun.

Died: On the morning of August 10th 1881, Geo. R. HEAD Jr., in the 41st year of his age.

Died: On the 20th of August 1881, Edgar T. BEALES, in the 9th year of age. On the 10th of August 1881, William R. BEALES in the 5th year of age. On the 12th of August 1881, Benjamin B. BEALES in the 2nd year of age. On the 17th of August 1881, John D. BEALES in the 7th year of age.

Died: At Waterford, on Saturday, the 20th inst., Silas F. HOUGH in the 39th year of age.

Mr. W. W. PRESGRAVES, one mile from Guilford station, on Wednesday evening last, had Mr. James BLADEN and Antoine SHELHORN engaged in digging or finishing a well in his yard he had commenced several years ago. They had the evening before fired two blasts in the well and just before this accident were drilling a hole in the rock, when Mr. BLADEN complained of feeling badly. SHELHORN also felt so. BLADEN climbed out, but while attempting to climb out, SHELHORN slipped back. He then tried to get in the bucket lowered to him, fell back and in the fall broke his neck and fractured his skull, killing him instantly. He was a son of Godfrey SHELHORN, who formerly lived near Leesburg.

We regret to learn that Col. Geo. T. RUST will shortly remove to Maryland, having purchased a farm in Montgomery County.

Thursday, 1 September 1881   Vol. XXVI, No. 12

Died: On Saturday, August 27th 1881, at 12½ p.m. at Spring Valley, the residence of her husband, David CARR, Mrs. Susan Brown CARR, eldest daughter of the late William BROWN, aged 79y 9m 14d.

Mrs. Hettie FOX, of Waterford, was baptized last Sunday by the Rev. Mr. WARREN. She is nearly 80 years of age.

Mr. Geo. W. DORSEY, a former resident of this town, but who left Leesburg in 1818, returned on a visit after a 63 year absence. He is in the 78th year of his age and at present resides at Canton, near Baltimore.

Thursday, 8 September 1881   Vol. XXVI, No. 13

Died: At the residence of his brother, Mr. Jos. S. REED, at Aldie, in this county, on Wednesday, the 24th of August, 1881, Mr. Andrew J. REDD, in the 62d year of age.

Died: After a lingering illness, from a cancerous tumor in the stomach, Mr. Armistead M. MILLER, at his residence near Neersville, on Thursday, Aug. 25, 1881, aged 60y 8m 24d.

Rev. Alpheus L. EDWARDS, formerly of this county, was married in Washington last evening to Miss Mamie LLOYD, of that city.

Thursday, 15 September 1881   Vol. XXVI, No. 14

Died: Near Daysville, Friday morning, September 9th 1881, about 5 o'clock, Mrs. Jennie REID (widow of Charley REID dec'd) aged 68 years, of subacute gastrites (gastric dyspepsia) with chronic hepsatitis, involving the hepsatic ducts (complicated with pelvic culular ovaritis. She had been sick some months. Member of Southern Methodist Church. Services in the old Dranesville Church on Liberty Hill.

Died: On Sunday Sept. 4th 1881, at the residence of he son-in-law, F. E. ROBEY Esq., Mrs. Euphemia GAINES in her 78th year.

Sept. Ct.: J. E. FRANCIS qualifies as Exor. of Ella C. FRANCIS dec'd.; Hattie GLASSCOCK as Guardian of infant children of Alfred GLASSCOCK dec'd.; Jos. C. CALVER as Admr. wwa. of O. J. C. CHAMBLIN. Mary A. WHALEY's estate committed to Sheriff. Wills of Armistead M. MILLER dec'd. and Wm. BENTON dec'd. admitted to probate. G. E. TRUITT qualified to celebrate the rites of matrimony.

Less than a year ago was the marriage of Mr. W. S. REAMER, formerly of this town, and Miss YOUMANS of Columbia, S.C. *Columbia Register of 10 Sept.* – death of Mrs. W. S. REAMER occurred last evening at the residence of her father, Attorney Gen. YOUMANS. She left an infant only a few days old.

A colored child, well-dressed, with a bundle of clothing by his side, was left in Mrs. GOVER's yard, in this town, on Thursday night last. If the heartless mother is not found it will be sent to the poor house.

Thursday, 22 September 1881   Vol. XXVI, No. 15

Married: In the Church at Gum Spring, on Wed., the 14th of Sept. 1881, by Elder E. V. WHITE, Mr. James F. COCKERILLE, of Fairfax Co, and Miss Emily V. WYCKOFF, of Loudoun.

Died: Near Guilford Station, Sat. morning last, September 17th 1881, of tubercular disease of the lungs (phthisis pulmonalle), consumption, Miss BEAVERS, daughter of Saml. BEAVERS, aged about 22 years.

Mrs. H. BARTELS, daughter of John M. FORBES, Esq., died at her husband's residence, near Warrenton, on the 12th inst.

Thursday, 29 September 1881   Vol. XXVI, No. 16

Married: On the morning of Wed., Sept. 21st 1881, at the residence of the bride's parents, at Volcano, Wood Co, W. Va, by the Rev. Robt. A. GIBSON, Rector of Trinity Church, Parkersburg, Harry W. WITMAN to Emma C., dau. of D. C. MUDGE, Esq.

Married: September 21st 1881, by Rev. P. T. WARREN, at his residence, near Hamilton, Mr. Philips V. SAUNDERS and Miss M. Virginia ROLLINS, all of Loudoun County.

Married: At Lovettsville, Sept. 13th 1881, by Rev. P. H. MILLER, Mr. Addison G. McKIMMY and Miss S. Alice McGAVACK.

Died: At Savannah, Ga, September 14th 1881, of typhoid fever, Ed S. McINTIRE, son of C. C. and Harriet E. McINTIRE, formerly of Clarke County, Va, aged 22y 6m.

Appointed by the French War Dept. to attend the Yorktown celebration is Capt. George MASON, a native of Va and son of the late John Y. MASON, who was at one time U. S. Minister to France. As a boy Capt. MASON fought in the Confederate war, and a short time afterwards obtained a commission in the French army as sub-Lt. He is now a citizen of France and Capt. in the army of the republic.

Thursday, 6 October 1881   Vol. XXVI, No. 17

Died: At the residence of its father, on Tuesday the 27th September, Matilda C., infant daughter of Rev. B. A. and S. N. SHREVE, aged 6 months.

Died: September 26th 1881, near Hoyesville, Oliver Dovan, son of Wm. E. and Caroline SCOTT, aged 16y 5m 26d.

Departed this life Sept. 7th 1881, of diphtheria, Daingerfield, 3rd child of William H. and Annie TAYLOR, aged 4y 4m 7d.

Departed this life, Sept. 20th 1881, of diphtheria, Mary Eva Newton, infant dau. of Wm. H. and Annie TAYLOR, 11m 16d.

Died: At the residence of her husband, Mr. W. F. BURGESS, near Mt. Hope, Mrs. Penelope BURGESS, in her 25th year. She was taken sick on the 12th and very critically held till the 15th, at which time she so much revived that all were high in hopes, but at 4:20 p.m. in the evening of the 22d she died. Buried at Mt. Hope Baptist Church, where she was a member, services by Rev. Geo. W. POPKINS.

Thursday, 13 October 1881   Vol. XXVI, No. 18

Married: September 28th 1881, in St. Stephen's church, Bedford County, by the Rev. E. W. HUBBARD, the Rev. A. P. GRAY, of Prince William County, to Miss Mina Myers, 4th daughter of Mrs. Annie N. RADFORD, and the late Capt. Winston RADFORD, of Bedford County, Va.

Died: At "Welbourne Mills," near Middleburg, September 21st 1881, Miss Bettie R., daughter of Mrs. Sarah A. and the late J. Milton REED, in the 22d year of her age.

Oct. Ct.: Will of Lydia WHALEY dec'd. admitted to probate. F. E. ROBEY qualified as Admr. of Euphemia GAINES dec'd. Estate of Alice MILBOURN and John BYRD committed to Sheriff.

Thursday, 20 October 1881   Vol. XXVI, No. 19

Married: At Montsylva, the residence of bride's parents, October 11th, by Rev. T. H. JAMES, Mr. Geo. T. FORD and Miss Mollie L. JAMES, all of Loudoun.

Married: In Leesburg, October 11th 1881, by Rev. A. J. PORTER, Mr. Smith McGILL to Miss Henrietta J. GRIMES, both of Loudoun County.

Married: On the 11th inst., at the Reformed Church, Lovettsville, by the Rev. H. St. J. RINKER, Mr. Wm. W. VIRTZ to Miss Alice SHUMAKER, all of Loudoun County.

Died: At "Dresden," his residence, near Aldie in this County, Friday October 14th, 1881, Mr. Samuel SKINNER, in his 79th year.

Marriage license issued in Washington, on Tuesday, were Wm. H. DAILY, of Baltimore, and Rosa BENTLEY, of Leesburg, Va.

Members of Broad Run Sunday School express esteem for the late Mrs. J. V. REED, their teacher, who died on the 9th of September last in her 51st year. Member of Methodist Church. Leaves parents, a brother and sister, and two sons.

Thursday, 27 October 1881   Vol. XXVI, No. 20

Married: Near Lovettsville, on the 17th inst., by the Rev. H. St. John RINKER, Mr. W. H. WIGGINGTON to Miss Mary F. GREEN, all of Loudoun County.

Married: On the 18th inst., at the residence of the bride's parents, by the Rev. B. A. SHREVE, Mr. Samuel BEAVERS to Miss Elizabeth DAYMUDE, all of Loudoun.

Died: In Washington city, on Friday, October 21, 1881, after a brief illness, Clara, daughter of Wm. BURKE, examiner U. S. Patent Office, and granddaughter of the late Wm. D. DRISH, of Leesburg, in the 23d year of her age.

Died at Pughtown, W. Va. on October 21st 1881, Samuel J. WHITACRE, after a short and severe illness, of typhoid pneumonia. Member of Baptist Church. Leaves mother and brother.

Diphtheria has been prevailing to an alarming extent in Frederick city, Md. Among the deaths are Richard Edwards, third son of Dr. Lloyd T. and Rachel MAGILL, and grandson of Dr. R. H. EDWARDS, of Leesburg, in the 10th year of his age. Another child of Dr. MAGILL, a little daughter is seriously ill.

Funeral of Rev. Samuel REGESTER, D.D., presiding elder of the east Baltimore district, Methodist Episcopal Church, South, who died on Monday of last week at "Greyfields," Prince George County, Md, took place 17th instant, from Trinity M. E. Church, South, Baltimore.

Mrs. Sarah HITAFFER, consort of the late John HITAFFER, died at the residence of her son-in-law, Mr. Jas. H. ROLLINS, near Leesburg, on Sunday last, at the age of 89y 2m. Her mental and physical powers were well preserved up to within a few weeks of her death. Member for more than half a century of Baptist Church.

Dr. R. W. WITHERS, father of Hon. Robt. E. WITHERS, died at the residence of his son-in-law, near Lynchburg, on Sunday last, in the 87th year of his age.

Thursday, 3 November 1881   Vol. XXVI, No. 21

Married: In Baltimore, Md, on October 27th 1881, at the residence of the bride's uncle, Rev. Wm. R. MONROE, Robert L. GARRETT, of Philomont, to Lizzie O. MONROE, of Alexandria, Va.

Married: Oct. 26th 1881, at "Walnut Hill," at the residence of the bride's parents, by Rev. S. K. COX, Rev. J. W. GRUBB, Pastor of St. James' M. E. Church, South, Baltimore, and Delma, daughter of Hon. Williard H. NEAL, of Queen Ann Co., Md.

Married: October 26th 1881, at the parsonage of the M. E. Church, South, by Rev. W. K. BOYLE, Mr. Obed COOKSIE to Miss Rosa SEIBER, both of Loudoun.

Married: October 20th 1881, at Bolington, by Rev. P. H. MILLER, Mr. Samuel W. BROOKS of Warrenton, to Miss Nettie M. KALB, of Bolington.

Married: At the Lutheran Parsonage, Lovettsville, October 20th 1881, by Rev. P. H. MILLER, Mr. Stephen P. SHIPMAN to Miss Hannah R. COOKSEY, both of Loudoun.

Married: At Christ Church, Goresville, on Tuesday morning, November 1st 1881, by Rev. S. S. WARE, Frank L. FRED, Esq. of Indian Territory (formerly of this county) and Miss Anna P., second daughter of the late Geo. D. SMITH, of Loudoun.

Married: October 27th 1881, by Rev. P. T. WARREN, at the residence of the bride's parents, Mr. Charles NICHOLS and Miss Laura J. FENTON, all of Loudoun County.

Died: At her residence in Washington city, on Friday, Oct. 28th 1881, after a brief illness of typhoid fever, Miss Dorcas H. HANVEY, dau. of the late Jas. D. HANVEY of Leesburg, in her 27th year. Interred in Union Cemetery, Leesburg on Saturday.

Died: Oct. 21st, of congestion of the lungs, at the residence of her father, near Middleburg, Mattie T., wife of George O. FERGUSON, (of the firm of Bassell & Ferguson) in the 27th year of age.

Died: On October 18th in Frederick City, Md, of diphtheria, Eddie, youngest son of Dr. L. T. and R. E. MACGILL, and grandson of Dr. R. H. EDWARDS, Leesburg, aged 9y 1m.

Died: At the residence of his parents, Leesburg, October 27th, Bradshaw, infant son of Wm. H. and Miranda GRIMES, aged 6 weeks.

Died: Oct. 23d, near Taylortown, Daisy Myrtle, infant daughter of John W. and Alice P. BARTLETT.

Died: Near Lovettsville, October 20th 1881, of heart disease, Mr. John WIRE, in the 69th year of age.

Died: At Burkettsville, Md, October 21st, 1881, Mrs. Martha E. AUSHERMAN, in her 48th year.

Thursday, 10 November 1881   Vol. XXVI, No. 22

Married: In Washington City, Oct. 27th 1881, Mr. Hugh WATERS, of Loudoun, to Miss Charlotte D. SESSON, of Washington.

Married: Nov. 2d, 1881, by Rev. John WOOLF, at his residence, M. T. BROWN to Miss Hannah E. SAFFLE, all of Loudoun.

Married: On the 25th of October, at the residence of the bride's parents, by Rev. B. A. SHREVE, Mr. James W. PEACOCK and Miss Margaret E. BODINE, all of Loudoun.

Married: On Thursday morning, November 3, 1881, at Richmond, by Rev. Prof. HUNTINGTON, Prof. A. P. MONTAGUE, of Columbian College, to May, daughter of Chief Justice CHRISTIAN, of the Court of Appeals of Va.

Married: In the Baptist Church, in Martinsburg, Thursday evening, October 27th 1881, by Rev. O. FLIPPO, Rev. A. E. ROGERS, pastor of the church, and Miss Mollie FIERY, daughter of B. F. FIERY, of Martinsburg.

Married: On the 25th ultimo, at the Lutheran Parsonage, in Frederick city, Md, by Rev. Dr. DIEHL, George O. EVERHART to Miss Fannie V. SPRING, both of Loudoun Co.

Died: In Leesburg, November 1st, after a brief illness, John R. LOVELESS, in the 18th year of his age, son of John W. and Alcinda LOVELESS.

Died: In Leesburg, Thursday night, November 3, 1881, Miss Margaret A. CLINE, after a lingering illness, in her 65th year.

Died: October 24th 1881, at his residence, near Farmwell, Robert POWER, aged 79y 10m 1d, leaving a wife and family.

Died: Near Snickersville, after a lingering illness, Eva Linwood, dau. of Isaac F. and Kesiah F. SANTMYER, aged 2y 1m 21d.

Died: In Washington Sunday afternoon, November 6, 1881, Wm. E. SMITH in the 73d year of his age, formerly of Loudoun Co, but for the last 30 years a resident of that city.

Tim DULANEY, long the baggage agent on the Washington and Ohio Railroad, died Saturday and was buried at Falls Church Sunday. He died from having one of his feet mashed on the train some months ago.

Thursday, 17 November 1881 Vol. XXVI, No. 23

Married: On Tuesday November 8th 1881, by Rev. Dr. NORTON, R. H. HAVENER to Agnes, daughter of Geo. McBURNEY, all of Alexandria.

Married; November 13th 1881, at the residence of Mr. Charles LLOYD, Clarke County, by Rev. P. T. WARREN, Mr. John T. SMALLWOOD and Miss Annie LANHAM.

Married: At Aldie on Wednesday, November 9th 1881, by Rev. W. F. DUNAWAY, Mr. George E. MUSE and Miss Sallie A. PALMER, all of Loudoun.

Died: Near Round Hill, on Tuesday, November 15th 1881, infant son of Will and Rose JAMES.

Died: At the residence of his nephew, in this county, on the 28th of Oct. 1881, of lockjaw, Mr. Westley BROOKS, in his 76th year.

Nov. Ct.: Wills of Margaret A. CLINE and John WIRE, admitted to probate. T. E. THRASHER qualified as Admr. of L. A. THRASHER dec'd. Chas. T. HERNDON licenced to celebrate rites of matrimony. Estates of C. STONEBURNER and Sarah A. ELKIN, committed to Sheriff.

Mr. A. M. CHAMBLIN, eldest son of the late Mason Chamblin, Loudoun Co, died at the residence of J. B. THROCMORTON, Snickersville, on Tuesday morning last, in his 52d year. He was engaged in Mr. Joseph Hall & Co's. Richmond Iron Works until his health failed. Buried at the Catoctin Baptist Church.

Dr. Heath DULANY, who returned from Alaska last Saturday, with his nephew, Col. M. D. BALL, died at an early hour this morning at the residence of his relative, Major John CHICHESTER, in Fairfax County, whither he went yesterday. He was for a time Asst. Surgeon of the 17th Va regiment during the war. His brother, Mr. W. T. DULENY, died only a week or two ago. *Alex. Gazette.*

Thursday, 24 November 1881   Vol. XXVI, No. 24

Married: At the residence of the bride's mother, at Guilford Station, on Wed. evening, Nov. 16, 1881, by Rev. J. T. WILLIAMS, Mr. Thos. HUTCHISON and Miss Fannie A. ADIE, all of Loudoun.

Married: At the residence of the bride's parents, in Leesburg, on Wed. morning, Nov. 23d, '81, by Rev. W. K. BOYLE, Lewis M. CARR and Jeannette, dau. of Mr. Wm. CLINE, all of Loudoun.

Married: At the residence of the bride' parents, at Dalton, Georgia, on Wed. the 16th of Nov. 1881, by Rev. ___, Mr. R. D. BRIDGES, of Loudoun Co, and Miss Mollie, daughter of Col. J. E. SHUMATE, formerly of Loudoun.

Sudden death of Mr. John HAMMERLY early Wednesday morning at 6 o'clock as he took his seat at the breakfast table, of heart disease. For a number of years in the butchering business in this town. He was in about the 62d year of his age. Funeral will take place this (Thursday) afternoon at 3 o'clock.

Thursday, 1 December 1881   Vol. XXVI, No. 25

Died Sunday, the 6th instant, near Ebenezer Church, between the hills, Miss Margaret STOUTSENBERGER, in her 69th year.

Died: On Tuesday, the 22d day of November 1881, Mr. John L. TOWNER, of this town, in the 51st year of his age.

Died: At "Locust Hill," near Berlin, Md, the residence of her niece, Mrs. Mary PHILIPS, on the morning of the 16th of November 1881, Miss Martha THRIFT, in about the 64th year of her age.

On Wednesday evening last, at the residence of Col. T. L. PRESTON, near the Univ. of Va, Miss Anna Preston DAVIS was married to Mr. Geo. Robertson LOCKWOOD, of St. Louis, Mo. Daughter of the Rev. Dr. Richard T. DAVIS, of Leesburg, who officiated in the ceremony, with Rev. Dr. J. C. HANCKEL, of Charlottesville.

Thursday, 8 December 1881   Vol. XXVI, No. 26

Mr. Marcus B. BUCK died at his residence near Warrenton, Wednesday, after a lingering illness. He was a native of Warren County. He established and conducted up to a few years ago the Belmont Vineyards near Front Royal.

Married: In the Episcopal church, Front Royal, December 1, 1881, by the Rev. Mr. JONES, Mr. E. M. JEFFRIES, of Fauquier, and Miss Mary, daughter of Judge J. T. LOVELL.

Married: November 20th, by Rev. T. W. NEWMAN, Mr. John N. JOHNSON to Miss Annie L. RHINES, all of Fauquier County.

Married: November 17th 1881, at the Lutheran Church, near Lovettsville, by Rev. P. H. MILLER, Mr. John W. AXLINE to Miss Margaret T. SHUMAKER.

Married: At the Lutheran parsonage near Lovettsville, Nov. 17th 1881, Mr. George H. T. BEAMER to Miss Ella E. COLLINS.

Died: At his home, in Fauquier County, near Delaplane, suddenly of heart disease, Mr. J. R. KERCHEVAL, in his 62d year.

Mr. James R. KERCHEVAL died very suddenly at his residence in upper Fauquier, on Friday last, of heart disease. He married a daughter of the latter, sister of Circuit Ct. Clerk.

Thursday, 15 December 1881 Vol. XXVI, No. 27

D. W. LEWIS, colored lawyer from Prince William County, was last week, admitted to practice in the Va Court of Appeals.

Dr. John H. STEVENS died suddenly in his room in Dallas, Texas, on Thursday week, after returning from a pleasant ride. He was a brother of Capt. Joseph M. STEPHENS, of Middleburg, formerly store-keeper of the Penitentiary.

Married: December 7th 1881, at the house of the bride's father, by Rev. C. F. JAMES, Dr. Luther L. CHAMBLIN and Miss Lillian CHAMBLIN, all of Loudoun.

Married: Also, at the same place and by the same on the 8th of December 1881, Mr. Edwin A. HANCOCK, of Lynchburg, and Miss Eva A. CHAMBLIN, of Loudoun, daughter of Levin P. CHAMBLIN of Loudoun.

Married: At the residence of the bride's parents on Wednesday evening, December 7th 1881, by Elder Joseph BADGER, James Clay JENKINS to Miss Emoretta H. GULICK, daughter of Francis and Nancey GULICK.

Married: At the residence of the bride's mother, Montgomery Co, Md, on the 7th instant, by the Rev. R. S. D. HEIRONIMUS, Wm. H. CLOWE, Esq., of Loudoun County, and Miss Agnes May, daughter of the late Nickolas R. DARBY, Esq.

Married: In Philadelphia, on December 8th by Rev. J. H. CHAMBERS, Eli LEATHERMAN, of Bucks Co, Pa, to Sarah R. SAUNDERS, of Leesburg.

Died: November 23d 1881, Armstead McGill, 7th son of S. G. and M. V. STONEBURNER, aged 2y 3m 26d.

Died: At his residence, near Ebenezer M. E. Church, in this county, on December 2d, 1881, Mr. Conard VIRTS, in the 91st year of his age. He was a soldier in the war of 1812 and honorably discharged. Member of M. E. Church for many years. Leaves a wife and children.

Obituary: Annie HUTCHISON was born on 19th of March 1853. In infancy, her mother having died, she was taken by her aunts, Mrs. CLARKE and Mrs. RUTTER. In Nov. 1871 baptised at Long Branch Church by the late Dr. J. A. HAYNES. She had entered her 22d year when strickened by consumption. She died Sept. 23d, 1881. Buried at cemetery at Middleburg.

Circuit Ct.: Wills of Nancy HOOE, Sarah HITAFFER and John HAMMERLY admitted to probate. Estate of Emeline COOPER and Susan BEATTY committed to Sheriff.

Maj. Edwin L. MOORE, who removed last October from Cumberland to Charlestown, W. Va., died in the latter place last Sunday, after a short illness. He was about 50 years old and a native of Charlestown. He was in the Confederate army during the civil war, and held positions on the staffs of JACKSON, LEE and HILL. He removed to Cumberland about 1867 and was connected with the Second Nat. Bank. He was a son of the late Cato MOORE, for many years cashier of the old Valley Bank at Charlestown.

Warrenton, Dec. 12 – Brutal murder occurred yesterday morning about 8 o'clock at Orleans, a small village 12 miles from here. Dispute between two young men, named Arthur DAVIS and Leonidas TRIPLETTS, in regard to some turkeys which belonged to DAVIS which strayed over to TRIPLETT's. A fight ensued. TRIPLETT's brother William, seeing the fight but DAVIS leveled his revolved at TRIPLETT and told him to stand off. He then placed the pistol to the head of Leonidas TRIPLETTS and blew out his brains. DAVIS escaped while being taken from a house in Orleans to jail, with the help of his brother and others.

Thursday, 22 December 1881   Vol. XXVI, No. 28

Married: At the M. E. Parsonage, South, Leesburg, on Tuesday morning, Dec. 20, 1881, by Rev. W. K. BOYLE, Hon, Jas. B . McCABE, Judge of the County Ct. of Loudoun, and Ella, eldest daughter of Jos. L. NORRIS, Esq., all of Loudoun.

Married: November 29th, by Elder T. W. NEWMAN, Mr. James R. EDWARDS, of Culpeper, to Miss Sarah E. JACOBS, of Fauquier county.

Married: By the same, November 30th, Mr. Douglas W. EMMONS, to Miss Susan A. OLIVER, all of Fauquier.

Married: On the 1st inst., by Elder J. B. LAKE, Mr. Charles R. LAKE to Miss Florence V. RIXEY, daughter of Hon. B. F. RIXEY, all of Fauquier.

Thursday, 29 December 1881   Vol. XXVI, No. 29

Married: On the 15th inst., at the residence of Robert WEEDON, by Rev. H. H. WYER, John H. KLIPSTEIN and Miss Margaret E., daughter of the late Rev. John OGILVIE.

Died: At the residence of her son-in-law, Mr. J. C. DONOHOE, in Leesburg, on Saturday morning, December 17th 1881, Mrs. Edith SAUNDERS, in the 86th year of her age.

Died: On December 15, 1881, at Fairfax Court House, Va, Hiram K. SEATON, aged 58 years.

Mr. Edward B. STEER died suddenly at his home in Waterford, on Monday last, of apoplexy. He was in the 88th year of his age.

Resolution by Rock Hill Church Sabbath School (a charge of Hamilton Circuit, M. E. Church, South) on the death of Miss Mary D. HALEY, member of the church.

Thursday, 29 December 1881   Vol. XXVI, No. 29

Harper's Ferry, W. Va., Dec. 25 – At noon yesterday, Dr. J. F. HARTGROVE shot and instantly killed Wilford C. CHAMBERS in the bar room of the Mountain View Hotel at this place.

Died: At the residence of her son, in Leesburg, at 12:05 Wednesday afternoon, December 28th 1881, Mrs. Emily J. OSBURN, wife of Mr. Joab OSBURN, in her 62d year, had for a long time been the victim of intense suffering.

Thursday, 5 January 1882   Vol. XXVI, No. 30

Married: December 21st by Elder Benjamin BRIDGES, Mr. Walter V. HUMMER, to Miss Mollie E. BRIDGES, daughter of Hardage BRIDGES dec'd., all of Loudoun.

Married: On December 22nd, 1881, by Rev. John [torn] his residence, Miss Susan A. CONNER to Mr. [torn] TAVENNER, all of Loudoun.

Married: At the Lutheran Parsonage, Lovettsville, December 15th 1881, by Rev. P. H. MILLER, Mr. Temple C. MASON, to Miss M. A. V. BEAMER.

Married: On December 26th 1881, on the bridge at Harper's Ferry, by the Rev. James M. STEPHENSON, Henry C. POTTS to Miss Lizzie BEANS, both of Loudoun County.

Married: On Wednesday evening last, at the residence of Mr. Geo. JACKSON, by the Rev. Mr. SMITH, Mr. Alvarrado HARDY and Miss Hattie ATWELL, daughter of Mr. Thos. ATWELL, all of Loudoun.

Married: On Wednesday evening last, in the Presbyterian Church, by Rev. Mr. SMITH, Mr. Geo. R. FORSYTH and Miss Theresa W. SCHLEIF, daughter of John V. SCHLEIF, all of Leesburg.

Died: John PRESTON, at his home near Hamilton, on Sunday morning, December 25th, aged 40 years.

Thursday, 12 January 1882   Vol. XXVI, No. 31

Died: On the 21st inst., at the residence of her aunt, near Middleburg, Bertha Thomas, infant child of Geo. O. and Hattie F. FERGUSON, of congestion of lungs.

Died: In Leesburg, on Saturday night, December 31st 1881, Mr. Wm. H. SAUNDERS, in the 72d year of his age.

Died: Martha S. SMITH, youngest daughter of Henry and Elizabeth SMITH, died of diphtheria, near Aldie, on the evening of December 13th 1881, in her 12th year.

Second son of Thomas E. and Mary P. TAYLOR, aged about 4 years, died of dyphtheria on Wednesday morning, and their oldest child, a boy 6 or 7 years of age is very sick with the same disease.

On Saturday night, just as the old year was dying, Mr. Wm. H. SAUNDERS departed this life in his 72d year.

Capt. H. H. GARRETT, of Guilford, has recently been appointed Paymaster's Clerk in the regular army, under Major ROBINSON, and will leave in a few days for his post at Fort Union, New Mexico.

Thursday, 12 January 1882   Vol. XXVI, No. 31

Died: At the residence of her husband Maurice OSBURN, in Woodgrove, on Wed. the 4th instant, Bertha, eldest dau. of Mrs. Jane PANCOAST, in the 29th year of her age.

Death of Jos. THOMAS, which occurred on Wednesday the 4th inst. at his residence after a somewhat protracted illness. He was the son of the late Herod Thomas.

January Ct.: Administrations granted on estate of Wm. H. SAUNDERS dec'd., Robt. POWERS dec'd., Andrew J. REDD dec'd. Estates of Caroline COX and Lydia J. HAMILTON committed to Sheriff. Cornelius SHAWEN qualified as Committee of Harriet B. TAYLOR. Geo. W. NICHOLS qualified as guardian of Wm. C. LAUCK. Virginia S. FRANCIS qualified as Guardian of Henry M., Thomas W., Uriah E., Ann L., Virginia M., Sydnor B., and George M. BYRNE. Will of Wm. B. STEER dec'd. admitted to probate.

Mr. DAVIS former Loudouner – Springfield, Illinois paper: At the residence of Mr. and Mrs. James GREEN, occurred on last Thursday evening at 7 o'clock, the marriage of their daughter Maggie to Mr. John DAVIS, who emigrated last summer to Vernon Co. Mo. Performed by Rev. A. M. DUNNAVON. ...

Thursday, 19 January 1882   Vol. XXVI, No. 32

Dr. Orland FAIRFAX died suddenly at his residence in Richmond on Friday in his 76th year. Born in 1806 in Alexandria, of a family long famous in the mother country, and perhaps still better known in colony of Va through a great Baron FAIRFAX of the Valley. At the beginning of the late civil war, Dr. FAIRFAX removed to Richmond.

Married: January 4th 1882, by the Rev. A. J. PORTER, at the residence of the bride's mother, near Taylortown, Mr. John T. MOCK and Miss Sarah GOODHART, both of Loudoun.

Married: On the 17th inst., at the residence of the bride's parents, in Waterford, by Friends Ceremony, Joseph M. DUNLAP, of Indiana, to Miss Lizzie S. DUTTON, daughter of John B. DUTTON, of this county.

Married: At the residence of the bride's mother, January 17th, 1882, by Rev. P. T. WARREN, Mr. Edgar W. WARNER and Miss Mary E. HAMPTON, all of Loudoun County.

Died: Charles I. LOWELL, aged 12y 1m 18d, of diphtheria at 5 p.m. on the 17th of January 1882. Son of Jas. P. and Kate LOWELL.

Thursday, 26 January 1882   Vol. XXVI, No. 33

Married: On December 21, 1881, by Rev. H. L. DERBY, E. Goldsborough HALL, of Northumberland (formerly of Loudoun Co.) to Louisa, dau. of the late Dr. E. A. CURRIE, of Lancaster Co., and grand-dau. of the late Horace LUCKETT, of Loudoun.

Married: At the home of the bride's mother at Buckeystown, Md, on Wed. Jan. 18th 1882, by Rev. Mr. ___, Mr. David J. LEE, of Loudoun Co., and Miss Ella A. CONDRY, of the former place.

Died: At his residence, near Leesburg, on Saturday morning, January 14th 1882, of rheumatism of the heart, Mr. William H. VANDERHOOF, in about the 28th year of age.

Died: At Frederick, the residence of her husband, Burr P. FRED on Sat. January 14th 1882, of congestion of the brain, Rebecca J. FRED, aged 42 years. Since a child, member of Baptist Church at Ketoctin.

Miss Fannie COLEMAN, sister of Mr. J. C. COLEMAN, of Guilford, on the line of the Washington and Ohio Railroad dropped dead yesterday morning at 11 o'clock at her home, at the above named place, from heart disease.

Mr. John J. ADAMS, of Fauquier County, died of pneumonia a few days since, aged 65. Leaves five daughters. He contracted the fatal disease by leaving a warm room at night to answer a professional call.

Mr. Joseph M. HOWELL, a young business man of Alexandria, died last week.

Frederick, Md: Rev. Mr. INGLE has lost another child with diphtheria, this makes four within the present month. Christian ALBAUGH lost two children, making three he has lost within the present month. Mr. MUSSELLEER has lost another child making two inside of two weeks, and Mr. Q. S. J. RECKLEY lost a little girl, making the 3rd child he has lost with diphtheria during the past few months. Miss Cora STALEY, of this city, about 20 years old, died of diphtheria on Monday last. Miss Ida STANLEY, the eldest sister, died on Wednesday morning. On Monday Dr. SMITH was called to see Neta, second daughter of Mr. and Mrs. Charles H. BAUGHMAN, and on Tuesday night at 7 o'clock she died, making the second little one in this family. Mr. Isaac HALLER, of this city, lost on Wednesday a little boy of 4 years. As we go to press, we are informed another of Rev. Mr. INGLE's children has died, the fifth of his children within the month.

Thursday, 2 February 1882   Vol. XXVI, No. 34

Marriage licenses issued in Washington city last week to Ira I. ANDERSON, of Loudoun County, and Georgietta MATTHEWS, of Prince William Co, Va, and Charles L. HUTCHISON and Mollie L. MANKIN, both of Loudoun County.

A man by the name of NORTON, from Waco, Texas, was married near Warrenton, on Friday – he is a widower living near Waco, Texas, and engaged in farming. He is also the father of five children. A few months ago he read a communication written by Miss Rosa BROOKHIZER of Fauquier County in the "Hard Shelled Baptists" (he is a member of this denomination). He wrote her, which resulted in their marriage today. They did not meet in person until Thursday.

Married: At Daysville, on the 24th inst., by Elder A. T. M. HANDY, Mr. Thomas ODEN and Miss Roxanna REEVES.

Married: January 26th 1882, at the parsonage of the M. E. Church, Leesburg, by the Rev. A. J. PORTER, Mr. Andrew F. SHRY to Miss Catherine Virginia UMBAUGH, both of Loudoun.

Married: On Jan. 25, 1882, at the residence of the bride's mother by the Rev. James H. SMITH, of Leesburg, Mr. Washington HEISS, of Philadelphia to Miss Mary MYERS, of Loudoun Co.

Died: Alexandria, January 27th, 1882, Nellie Wheeler, daughter of William and Elizabeth MURRAY, in her 5th year.

Died at Rockhill, the residence of Mr. A. G. CHAMBLIN, Miss Margaret A. HUMPHREY, aged 46 years. Born near Bloomfield, suffered from distortion of the spine.

Died: In Philadelphia, January 20th 1882, Mrs. Jane L. BOYNTON, wife of Henry S. BOYNTON, of Washington, in her 50th year.

Thursday, 9 February 1882   Vol. XXVI, No. 35

Married: At Harper's Ferry, W. Va. on Thursday the 26th of January, by Rev. Father J. B. O'REILY, Mr. Chas. A. ELLMORE, to Miss Sarah C. PEACOCK, all of Loudoun Co.

Married: On the 26th ult., in Lovettsville, at the house of the bride, by the Rev. H. St. J. RINKER, Mr. Samuel J. WRIGHT, to Miss Annie S. ARNOLD, all of Loudoun County.

Married: On the 1st inst., at the residence of the bride's father, Mr. H. W. SKINNER, by the Rev. Mr. HADDAWAY, Mr. J. E. DOUGLAS, to Miss Marion SKINNER, all of Loudoun.

Married: Near Mountain Gap on the 2d inst., by the Rev. Dr. HEAD, Mr. Benjamin TAVENNER to Miss Mary T. VERMILLION, all of Loudoun.

Married: On the 2nd inst., near Guilford, by the Rev. B. A. SHREVE, Mr. Alfred WILLINER to Miss Lulle KUHN.

Married: On February 2, 1882, at Trinity Church, Washington DC, by Douglas P. FORREST, D.D., Arthur Percy FAIRFAX, youngest son of the last Capt. Archibald Blair FAIRFAX, U.S.N., to Nancy Hunter, only daughter of Judge John Blair HOGE, of Martinsburg, W. Va.

Departed this life at her residence near the Valley Church, January 21st 1882, Mrs. Catherine UMBAUGH, wife of the late John W. UMBAUGH, in the 87th year of age.

Mr. Chas. O. VANDEVANTER who had been engaged for the last 12 months on a railroad survey in Mexico, has returned.

Mr. James F. PAYNE, formerly Mayor of Lynchburg, and descendant of Sir Alexander SPOTSWOOD, dropped dead at the Opera House in that city, Friday evening, during the performance of a charity concert. He was about 60 years of age. Heart disease was the supposed cause. He was a brother of Mrs. Isaac VANDEVANTER of this town.

Maj. A. E. RICHARDS, a native of Loudoun Co, and an officer in Mosby's command during the late war, has been elected chairman of the Ky Democratic State Central Committee.

Thursday, 16 February 1882   Vol. XXVI, No. 36

Married: February 7th 1882, by Elder P. T. WARREN, at the residence of the bride's uncle, W. H. ADAMS, at Mt. Gilead, Mr. John T. RUSK and Miss Rose B. VANSICKLER, dau. of Emanuel VANSICKLER, all of Loudoun County.

Married: On the same day, by the same, at the residence of the bride's mother, near Union, Mr. John W. KEPHART and Miss Carrie A. RUSK, all of Loudoun County.

Married: At the Lutheran Parsonage, Lovettsville, February 7th 1882, by Rev. P. H. MILLER, Mr. George F. WENNER to Miss Orra B. WENNER.

Married: On Thursday February 9th 1882, by Rev. W. F. DUNAWAY, Mr. J. W. SMITH, of Fauquier, and Miss Mary E. CARTER, of Loudoun.

Married: On Feb. 2, 1882, at Mt. Hope, by the Rev. G. W. POPKINS, Mr. B. T. ALEXANDER, and Miss Melvina BODINE, all of Loudoun county.

Died: On February 5th, at his residence near Union, of consumption, John KEEN, in the 67th year of his age.

Died: Near Lovettsville, on Monday, November 28th 1881, of croup, little Bessie May, daughter of G. L. H. and Rosie M. HICKMAN, aged 2y 1m 26d.

Died: After a long, continued and severe illness, on December 21st 1881, Hauer Chester ENGLISH, in his 10th year.

Died: At the residence of her daughter January 29th 1882, Mrs. Mary Jane HIBBS, in the 62nd year of her age. Sufferer form more than 17 years form the disease which proved fatal. Member of Methodist Church for 30 years.

Feb. Ct.: Jno. MORRIS (colored) found guilty of rape and sentenced to 10 years. Wills of Patrick McQUIN, John F. PRESTON and Geo. W. BOWMAN admitted to probate. Administrations granted on estates of Curtis GRUBB, John HAMMERLY and Wm. H. VANDERHOFF. E. G. CAUFMAN qualified as guardian of Clara PAXSON.

Jno. MORRIS (colored) already found guilty of the rape of a colored girl also found guilty of breaking into the house of Mr. Chas. E. MOUNT and given an additional 6 years.

Chas. GREENE (white) who was sentenced several years ago to five years for stealing a horse from Mr. Washington HAINES – escaped and returned to Loudoun and a few weeks ago stole two horses from Mr. HAINES, one of them the same that he had taken a year or two before. Pleaded guilty and given 15 years.

Memoriam from *Mobile, Ala. Chronicle*, Feb. 4th 1882: Tribute to respect from survivors of the Alabama Battalion of Artillery to their commander, Col. W. L. POWELL, who died while in command of Fort Morgan and now rests in the lot of Capt. Douglass VASS. Slate of Alabama stone 7' 6" long and 3' 6" wide reads: William L. POWELL, Born in Leesburg, Va, March 6th 1826; Entered U. S. Navy 1841, Resigned the same 1861. Died, Col. Com'g Confederate States forces at Fort Morgan, Alabama, Sept. 25th, 1863. He was a native of Leesburg and a younger brother of Capt. E. B. POWELL, of this town.

Thursday, 23 February 1882   Vol. XXVI, No. 37

Died: On Feb 14th at Leeland, near Shepherdstown, W. Va, Rebecca Lawrence Rust, wife of Edmund I. LEE, and dau. of A. T. M. RUST, of Loudoun Co, in her 27th year, of pneumonia.

Thursday, 2 March 1882   Vol. XXVI, No. 38

Married: On the 22nd inst., near Gum Spring, by Rev. B. A. SHREVE, Mr. M. W. CHICK to Miss Rose Emma POOL.

Married; At Leslie Hall, near Hillsborough, on Thursday, the 23rd, by Rev. W. R. STRINGER, Leslie R. MARTIN, of Missouri, to Ethel V. LESLIE, of Loudoun Co.

Married: On the 23rd inst., by Elder Benjamin BRIDGES, at his residence, Mr. Elijah V. JENKINS, of Loudoun, to Miss Rosa TRAMMELL, of Fairfax County, Virginia.

Married: At the Centenary Methodist Episcopal Church, of Richmond, by Rev. B. F. WOODWARD, on February 16, 1882, J. W. BRONAUGH Jr., of Manchester, and Bettie J. BRAUSFORD, of Richmond Va.

Died: At the residence of his father near Middleburg, of diphtheria, February 21st, 1882, Thomas LEITH, eldest son of B. F. and Mary S. LEITH, aged 11 years.

Died: December 25th 1881, of diphtheria, at "Woodside," Samuel J., son of Eli J. and Lydia NICHOLS, in the 8th year of age.

Died: At her home near Lovettsville, on Sunday, February 12th 1882, after a short and painful illness, Mrs. Alice M. VINCEL, aged 21y 20d.

Died: On the 8th of January 1882, at the residence of her sons, Mrs. Mary E. MYERS, in her 60th year. She was a long and painful sufferer.

Edward SANGSTER Esq., father of Judge James SANGSTER, died at the residence of his son-in-law, Rev. Dr. BENNETT, president of Randolph-Macon College, at Ashland, Va., last Thurs. night of paralysis. Born in Fairfax Co, 6th of April 1802.

Loudoun Representative: Henry HEATON, who represents the 11th Senatorial district, was born in Loudoun, unmarried. War experience – one year with the Loudoun Artillery, one with Early as a volunteer aide, and two with the cavaliers who guarded Mosby's realm.

Loudoun Representative: Dr. Geo. E. PLASTER, born in Loudoun Co 12 May 1826. During the war was a Capt. in the 6th Va Cavalry and served under STUART, JONES, LOMAS, and PAYNE.

Major Smith CRANE, of Jefferson Co W. Va, was found dead in his bed last Wednesday morning. He served in the Mexican morning, and was conspicuous for bravery at Vera Cruz, Chapultepec and Molina del Rey.

Thursday, 9 March 1882   Vol. XXVI, No. 39

Married: February 23rd 1882, by Rev. John WOOLF, at the residence of the bride's father, Mr. William RIPPON to Miss Lelia A. E. BROWN, all of Loudoun.

Married: On the 23rd inst., at the Reformed Church, Lovettsville, by the Rev. H. St. John RINKER, Mr. Curtis J. BAKER to Miss Marie E. SHUMAKER, all of this county.

Married: On Thursday, the 2nd inst., at the residence of the bride's mother, near North Fork, by Rev. S. S. WARE, Mr. Arthur B. SHREVE, of this county, to Miss Annie M., daughter of the late Dr. M. K. BALDWIN and Mary E. BALDWIN.

Married: On March 2, at the Presbyterian parsonage, Farmwell, by Rev. L. B. TURNBULL, H. C. ALEXANDER to Martha J. BODINE, all of Loudoun.

Died: At her residence near Leesburg, on Saturday morning, March 4th 1882, Mrs. Jane GOVER, widow of the late John B. GOVER, in about the 62d year of age.

Died: December 2nd 1881, near Farmwell, Mrs. Anna HOUGH, daughter of Jonah HOUGH, in the 45th year of age.

Died: In Alexandria, on the 2d inst., Willie H., wife of Mahlon H. JANNER, and grand-daughter of the late Commodore William JAMESSON, U.S.N.

Died: Wednesday morning, March 1st 1882, at her home near Leesburg, Mrs. Francis R. MILLS, wife of Mr. Harrison MILLS, in the 50th? year of age.

Death of Geo. L. MOORE, stricken with paralysis, on Wednesday morning, in the 74th year of age. He was riding from Wheatland to his home, the fatal stroke fell upon him, and he was carried to the residence of Mr. C. C. WENNER. Laid to rest on Thursday.

North Fork, March 6th: On Thursday morning last, Miss Anna BALDWIN married at the residence of her mother to Mr. Arthur SHREVE, near Leesburg, by Rev. S. S. WARE, of St. John's Episcopal Church, Hamilton.

North Fork, March 6th: Mrs. Hester FENTON, wife of Enoch FENTON, Esq. died on Sat. morning last, of a large tumor.

Thursday, 16 March 1882 Vol. XXVI, No. 40

Married: At Salem church in Loudoun Co, March 1st 1882, by Rev. W. R. STRINGER, John B. GOOD and Theresa A. BATTS.

Married: At the Lutheran church, near Lovettsville, February 28th, 1882, by Rev. P. H. MILLER, Mr. James W. FRY to Miss Mary V. BAKER.

Married: March 8th 1882, by Rev. John WOOLF, at the residence of the bride's father, Mr. Thomas MARLOW, of Jefferson, to Miss Sarah E. MARTS of Loudoun.

Married: At the residence of Rev. Saml. BROWN, near Round Hill, on the evening of Wednesday, March 8th, Mr. Jas. H. MUSE to Miss Edna J. BRADFIELD, both of Loudoun.

Married: On the 8th inst., at the residence of the bride's father, near Leesburg, by Rev. Henry BRANCH, Mr. R. F. REED of this county, to Miss Alice R., daughter of Jno. HOPE, Esq., and Lydia HOPE.

Died: December 2nd 1881, near Farmwell, Mrs. Anna HOUGH, daughter of Jonah HOUGH, in the 45th year of age.

Died: Ruth Esther, wife of Enoch FENTON, died at her home, near Philomont, on the morning of the 4th inst., in the 62d year of her age.

Died: At her home, near Hamilton, on the morning of Friday, March 3d, Emily HOLMES, in the 44th year of age.

Died: At the residence of her son-in-law, Mr. Benjamin BEAVERS, in Jefferson Co. W. Va, on Saturday March 11th 1882, Mrs. PORTER, wife of Rev. Jesse PORTER, of Loudoun Co, aged about 80 years.

March Ct.: Wills of Sarah T. HAMILTON, John KEEN, Julia FLETCHER and J. W. CUMMINS, admitted to probate. J. E. CARRUTHERS, Sheriff, appointed Committee of Geo. E. KERCHEVAL. Jos. A. HAMMERLY qualified as Committee of Mary E. HAMMERLY; Samuel L. MOORE as Admr. of Geo. L. MOORE dec'd.; Peter BUCKNER as guardian of Annie CURRY. Estates of Edmonia S. ROGERS and Alcinda R. HESSER committed to Sheriff.

Mr. William T. MOUNT has closed out his business and will soon leave for the far West, where his son has secured for him a lucrative position. His life of a half century has been useful.

Thursday, 23 March 1882   Vol. XXVI, No. 41

Married: In the Episcopal Church, at Chantilly, Fairfax County, on the 8th of March 1882, by Rev. R. SMITH, Mr. Romulus BRADSHAW, of Chantilly, to Miss Ida F. PRESGRAVES, of Loudoun County.

Married: On the 8th of March, by the Rev. Louis WALKER, T. W. HARRISON, of Winchester, (formerly of Loudoun) to Miss Julia KNIGHT, daughter of Wm. KNIGHT, Esq., of Cecil Co, Md.

Died: At his home in Washington, March 9th, after a long and painful illness, James H. POPKINS (father of the Rev. G. W. POPKINS, of this county) in the 66th year of age.

Died: Mrs. Emily E. CARLISLE, wife of Jas. CARLISLE, March 10th 1882, in her 58th year.

Died: At Farmwell, on the 11th inst., John MURRY, in the 27th year of his age.

Died: Near Morrisonville, Ella Jane BALL, daughter of Charles and Janie E. BALL, died Jan. 31st 1882, aged 1y 5m 29d, after a severe illness.

Died: At the residence of her father, Mr. J. L. VERTS, near Oatlands, on Thursday 15th of March, after a short illness of six days, Miss Oda Lucy VERTS, in the 15th year of her age, with membranous croup.

Dr. Nicholas MARMION, of Harper's Ferry died at his residence in that place last week, at an advanced age.

Thursday, 30 March 1882   Vol. XXVI, No. 42

Married: At the residence of the bride's father, near Wheatland, March 16th 1882, by Rev. P. H. MILLER, Mr. Hector PEACOCK and Miss Josephine, daughter of Mr. Joseph MOCK.

Died: In Middleburg, on Thursday, March 23d, Jos. M. STEVENS.

Died: Florence BEANS at the residence of her father, Amos BEANS, near Woodgrove on Monday night, March 20th, about 18 years of age.

Died: At his residence, near Hillsboro, on the morning of March 18th 1881, Eli H. C. HOUSE, in the 67th year of his age.

Died: Near Lovettsville, March 15th 1882, after a long and severe illness, Mrs. Maria WIARD, in her 73rd year.

Departed this life March 18th, Danny ___, an orphan, in the 31st year of his age.

Tribute of respect from Blue Ridge Lodge, No. 64, for death of Florence V. BEANS, who died Monday evening, March 20th 1882, aged 23.

Thursday, 6 April 1882   Vol. XXVI, No. 43

Married: At the Guilford Baptist Church, on Tuesday evening, April 4th 1882, by Elder A. T. M. HANDY, Charles W. JENKINS and Mollie A., daughter of the late William TAVENNER, all of Loudoun Co.

Married: On April 4th 1882, in Leesburg, by the Rev. James H. SMITH, Mr. Chas. T. GUNNELL, of Fairfax County, to Mrs. Amanda L. LANE, of Loudoun County.

Departed this life, at his residence near Spinks' Ferry, March 15th 1882, George W. CHICK, aged 63y 2m 19d.

Died: Of typhoid fever, at his residence in Waterford, on the 29th of March, Edgar P. HOUGH, about 30 years of age, leaving a wife and one child.

Died: January 29th 1882, at his residence in Culpeper County, near Fauquier W. S. Springs, of typhoid pneumonia, Mr. John BEATY, aged 65 years.

Died: On Tuesday, March 14th 1882, at 5½ a.m., after a lingering illness of weeks, Florence Estelle, daughter of Ellwood H. and Louisa BEANS, aged 10y 2m 1d.

Died: In Washington City, Monday, March 27th 1882, of consumption, Maugrate E. LAUMAN, in her 51st year.

Warrenton, April 2: Mrs. CARNEAL died yesterday, her symptoms indicating that she had been poisoned with strychnine by her husband, C. N. CARNEAL. He was arrested this afternoon at his house, about 4 miles from Warrenton. While bringing him to prison he fired upon Constable T. R. LUNSFORD and made his escape. He is the same person who several years ago attacked District Attorney LEWIS at Culpeper Court House with a hatchet.

Thursday, 13 April 1882   Vol. XXVI, No. 44

Married: In Washington City, Wed. evening, March 5th 1882, by Rev. Dr. POWERS, Mr. Bushrod W. TREW and Miss Virginia W., youngest daughter of Major Jas. F. DIVINE, of Leesburg.

April Ct.: Wills of Eli C. H. HOUSE, Margaret A. HUMPHREY and R. H. SUMMERS admitted to probate. C. E. AHALT qualified as Admr. of Geo. W. CHICK dec'd. Estate of Edgar P. HOUGH and H. C. HILLIARY committed to Sheriff.

Mr. Samuel PURCEL died at his home near Lincoln, on Wednesday last, in his 77th year, after a long and protracted illness. Interred on Saturday at the Short Hill burying ground.

On Saturday morning at his residence near Guilford, at the age 88 years, R. H. SUMMERS, Esq., for many years Sheriff of Loudoun.

Thursday, 20 April 1882   Vol. XXVI, No. 45

Married: On April 13th 1882, by Rev. Joseph T. KELLER, Fairfax C. MINOR, of Virginia, to Miss Roberta L. WEST, of Washington DC.

Married: At the residence of Richard WEBB, in Leesburg, on Wed. evening, April 5th, by the Rev. Dr. Samuel RODGERS, Mr. Henry J. FADELY, to Miss Mary E. JOHNSON, all of Leesburg.

Married: At the residence of Dr. PHILIP, Stockton California, on Thursday evening March 23d, by the Rev. M. SCHOFIELD, Thos. H. BOND, late of Loudoun County, to Sara, second daughter of Chas. W. HORNER, of Washington DC.

Died: At the residence of her father, April 6th 1882, Miss Elma HATCHER, youngest daughter of Joshua HATCHER, of this county.

Mr. John F. ELGIN, farmer of this county, died at his home near Oatland's on Wed. evening, April 12th, after a protracted sickness of much suffering.

Mr. Jesse POOLE, aged 82 years, died at his home near Farmwell on the 9th inst.

Mr. Jos. SHAFER, son of Mr. F. W. SHAFER, of this town, who for the past three years has been in the Drug store of Mott &

Pursel, left last week for Camden, N. J. where he will be engaged with his brother in the drug business.

Telegram received her Tuesday night, announcing the death of Mrs. Sophia STICKLEY, wife of E. E. STICKLY, Esq. of Woodstock, Shenandoah Co, Va, and daughter of Rev. Joseph HELM, of this county. She was in about her 34th year.

Mr. Hiram D. BROWN, a former resident of Loudoun Co, but who had been stopping at the Howard House in Baltimore for several years, was found dead in his bed, about 6 o'clock Monday morning, from a hemorrhage of the lungs. He was in the 71st year of age.

Thursday, 27 April 1882 Vol. XXVI, No. 46

Married: On the 13th, at Lovettsville, by the Rev. H. St. J. RINKER, Mr. Butler FRY to Miss Annie HARRISON, all of Loudoun Co.

Married: At the residence of the bride's father, near Lovettsville, April 18th 1882, by Rev. P. H. MILLER, Mr. Stephen WIARD and Miss Rachel EVERHART.

Married: April 25th, 1882, at the residence of the bride's father, John A. VANSICKLER, of North Fork, by Rev. P. T. WARREN, of Hamilton, Mr. Samuel C. TILLETT and Miss Orra L. VANSICKLER, all of Loudoun County.

Died: April 4th instant, near Mountsville, of congestion of the lungs, Miss Susan LAKE, aged 68y 6d.

Died: At Sunnyville, Loudoun Co., on April 5th, Mrs. Emily M., wife of Mr. John CARTER, and daughter of Mr. John J. YELLOTT dec'd., and Mrs. Sarah J. YELLOTT, of Baltimore Co., Md.

Dr. Town. HEATON, who for several years past in practice in Marquette Co, Michigan, has returned to his native heath, and settled at Hamilton.

Mr. Wm. A. DENNIS, residing South of Leesburg, died suddenly, from neuralgia of the heart, on Wednesday last. He was seized suddenly and died in a few minutes.

Mr. Alexander JOHNSON died at his home near Mt. Gilead, on Monday night last, in the 77th year of his age.

Co. Ct.: Letters of Administration granted to Edgar JACKSON, on the estate of John F. ELGIN dec'd., also to Mrs. Alvernon THOMAS, on the estate of Joseph THOMAS dec'd.

Mr. Samuel CAMPBELL, for many years a resident of this county (father of Mrs. Edgar LITTLETON) died at the residence of his son-in-law, Geo. A. NEWMAN, in Louisville, Ky, on Wednesday morning, April 19th in the 85th year of his age. He emigrated to that city about 35 years ago.

Thursday, 4 May 1882   Vol. XXVI, No. 47

Married: On the evening of 26th of April at Trinity M. E. Church, South, Baltimore, by Rev. Thomas E. CARSON, Theodore H. LEITH and Miss Ella FURR, youngest daughter of the late Fenton FURR, both of Loudoun Co.

Died: On the 20th of April 1882, at the residence of C. F. OTLEY, Esq., Elizabeth HESSER, in the 59th year of her age.

Died: On Friday morning, 28th inst., Matthew Harrison, infant son of Dr. W. R. And S. H. WINCHESTER, aged 1y 2m.

Died: At the residence of Guilford Craven, on Monday, May 1st, 1882, Mrs. Harriet B. TAYLOR, wife of the late Col. Timothy TAYLOR, in the 81st year of her age.

Died: At Guilford, on the 24th of April 1882, of typhoid pneumonia, Mr. John H. TOPPING, aged 61 years. Native of Ayshire, Scotland, came to this county in 1860 and had resided at Guilford about 12 years. Leaves a widow and three children, and two sisters who reside in Philadelphia. Member of M. E. Church, South.

Died: Mrs. Ann GULICK, at her residence near Aldie of consumption and heart disease. Member of New School Baptist Church.

Mrs. Huldah ODEN, relict of Nathaniel J. ODEN, died at her home in Aldie, on the evening of the 26th of April 1882. She was 4 score and 4 years old.

Died: Alexander JOHNSON, at his home near Mt. Gilead, on the 24th of April, in the 74th year of his age. Funeral conducted by Revs. P. T. WARREN and G. W. POPKINS, on the 26th. Baptised two years ago by Rev. W. S. PENICK at Baptist Church. Leaves a wife and five children.

Chas. H. READ, Jr., of Washington city (brother of Mrs. Chas. B. BALL, of this town) was married last Wednesday to Margaret C., eldest daughter of ex-senator D. L. YULEE, of Florida. Ceremony performed at the residence of the bride's father, at Fernandina, Florida.

Death of Rev. S. S. ROGERS, minister of the M. E. Church, at the residence of his son near Rectortown, Fauquier Co., on Thursday morning, April 27th in his 70th year. Born in Loudoun Co in 1813, the son of Stephen G. ROSZELL, a famous Methodist preacher. He entered the ministry at an early age, and when 26 years old married Mrs. DeBUTTS, a widow, and daughter of John P. DULANY, of Loudoun Co. Death caused by carbuncle on the neck. Leaves a widow and 5 or 6 children, all of whom are grown.

Mr. Jonathan BROWN living near Wheatland, (known as bachelor John) died on Tuesday last, after a few days illness, of pneumonia. He was in about the 60th year of his age.

Thursday, 11 May 1882   Vol. XXVI, No. 48

Died: Near Corner Hall, Loudoun County, Sat. April 29th 1882, about 7 o'clock, Mr. Wm. Norris Russell SMITH (son of Wm. H. and Rhoda SMITH) in his 24th year. He had been sick for sometime, having returned to his home from Arkansas, sick last summer.

Mrs. Margaret HEAD, wife of Rev. Dr. Nelson HEAD, died very suddenly at her home in this town on Sunday last. Well advanced in years and had been in delicate health for a long time. Funeral took place on Tuesday, Rev. Dr. COX, of Washington, officiating, assisted by Rev. Dr. DAVIS and Rev. J. H. SMITH.

Marshal B. STEADMAN, for several years town sergeant of Leesburg, died at his home in this town on Monday, in the 56th year of his age. Had been in bad health for some time, and a few weeks ago was paralyzed.

J. Monroe HEISKEL, formerly of Leesburg and at present Secretary to the Mayor of Baltimore, has recently taken to himself a wife.

May Ct.: Wills of Henry THOMAS and Elizabeth H. HESSER admitted to record. Administrations granted on estates of John TOPPING dec'd., Pleasant JANNEY dec'd., Jonathan BROWN dec'd. and Alexander JOHNSON dec'd. Estates of Emily LITTLETON and Sarah HAMILTON committed to Sheriff.

Thursday, 18 May 1882   Vol. XXVI, No. 49

James A. BAUGHMAN, brother of John W. BAUGHMAN, dec'd., late editor of the *Republican Citizen*, Frederick, Md, died near Lovettsville, in this county last week.

Died: Sophia Helm STICKLEY, born at Helmwood, Loudoun Co, September 19th 1842, and died at Woodstock, Shenandoah County, Va, April 18, 1882, at the age of 39y 6m 28d. Member of Methodist E. Church. since 1870. Married to Col. E. E. STICKLEY in spring 1870. Had four children, three of whom she has left with her husband.

Died at his own residence, near the Creek and Ball's Mill in Loudoun County, on Sunday at 12 o'clock m. May 7th 1882, Mr. L. Chris. MAFFETT, about 40 years of age, after an illness of just 8 days, of pleuro-pneumonia complicated with neuralgia of the muscles of the heart and plurodynia of the left pleura. Leaves a wife, 2 sons and 2 daughters. A native of this county. Married the daughter of Harmon BITZER.

Dr. Joseph D. BARNES, acting Asst. Surgeon, U.S.A., son of Surgeon General Joseph K. BARNES, U.S.A., died suddenly Sat. afternoon at his residence, in Washington, from dropsy of the heart. Born in 1844 at Fort Jesup, La. while his father was on duty at that post. ... Married in 1875 to Miss CHEW, dau. of Hon. Robert S. CHEW the former chief clerk of the Dept. of State. She survives with two sons and a little dau. He was a nephew of Capt. Chas. M. FAUNTLEROY, of this town.

Thursday, 25 May 1882   Vol. XXVI, No. 50

Married: On May 17, at Foundry Church, Washington DC, by Rev. W. F. WARD, T. C. DULIN and Irene D. STINEMETZ.

Died very suddenly, at his home near Dranesville, Fairfax County, Friday morning about 4 o'clock, May 19th 1882, Nelson VOORHEES, aged about 64, leaving a wife, 2 sons and 2 daughters.

Died: In Washington DC, on May 17th 1882, after a brief illness, Josephine, wife of Chas. F. JARVIS, in the 48th year of age.

Died: February 23d 1882, after a long illness, Mrs. Elizabeth JENKINS, wife of Chas. T. JENKINS, in the 44th year of age. Leaves a husband and 7 small children.

Died: At the home of his father, near Bloomfield, on Sunday, May 14th 1882, Willie S. KEEN, son of Jonathan and Amanda S. KEEN, aged 16y 6m.

Thursday, 1 June 1882   Vol. XXVII, No. 51

Died: May 16th, at Clifton, James, the infant son of O. J. and L. T. PIERPOINT, aged 1m 9d.

At the January term 1875, John W. GOULDIN, for the shooting and killing of Jos. W. McFARLAND, at Gum Spring, was convicted of murder in the second degree and sent to penitentiary for 18 years. Due to failing health, at the expiration of 7y 4m he received clemency, and on last Thursday returned to his old home at Gum Spring.

Thursday, 8 June 1882   Vol. XXVII, No. 52

Died: Wm. LONG, at his residence, northwest of Lovettsville, on Friday, at 10 a.m., May 19th 1882, about 70 years of age, husband of the late Mary LONG, who died some four weeks previous.

Died: At the residence of his son, near Waterford, April 26th 1882, Mr. Nelson FISHER, in the 84th year of his age.

Died: In Leesburg, on Monday, May 22, 1882, of whooping cough, Hattie A., daughter of Howard and Margaret HARDY, aged 3y 9m 21d.

Mr. Geo. W. McINTOSH, tinner and stove dealer, died at his home in Poolesville, Md, on the 25th of May, of consumption. He was a former residence of Leesburg, to which place his remains were brought for interment.

Mr. Jefferson MILBOURN, residence of Hamilton, died at his home on Wednesday afternoon, and was buried at Harmony Church, at 3 p.m. on Thursday. He was the father-in-law of Mr. Geo. H. NIXON, of this town.

Thursday, 15 June 1882 Vol. XXVII, No. 1

Married: By Rev. P. T. WARREN, at his residence near Hamilton, June 13th 1882, Mr. Benjamin DAVIS and Miss Sallie A. HIGDON, all of Loudoun Co.

Married: At the residence of the bride's father in Middleburg, on Wednesday, May 31st by Rev. W. F. HADAWAY, Mr. George W. BOPMER and Miss Mary M. DAVIS, all of Loudoun Co.

Married: On June 1st, by Rev. Hamilton W. KINZER, Mr. Fenton M. LOVE, of this county, to Miss Gertrude T. WOOLF, at the residence of the bride's father, Andrew WOOLF, Esq., Rosemont, Fauquier Co.

Married: At the residence of the bride's father, Geo. W. FLING, near Woodburn, on Thursday, June 8th 1882, Mr. Samuel LAYCOCK to Miss Susan FLING.

Married: At Washington City, D.C., on June 5th 1882, by Rev. R. N. BAER, Pastor, Metropolitan M. E. Church, Mr. Richard H. SUMMERS, to Miss Annie M. PANGLE, both of Loudoun Co.

Died: Mrs. Mary A. CARTER, at her residence near Mountsville, on Monday, the 5th inst., Interred in Middleburg on Wednesday.

Died: At "Groveton," on Monday, June 5th, 1882, Mrs. Ann CARTER, wife of Mr. Francis M. CARTER, of this county. Interred in Sharon cemetery. Member of Episcopal church.

Mrs. Mary BIRKBY, widow of the late Joseph W. BIRKBY, died at her home in this town on Tuesday morning last, in the 70th year of her age. Funeral will take place from her late residence this Thursday afternoon at 3 o'clock.

Co. Ct.: Wills of Huldah ODEN, Wm. TAVENNER, and Lucinda JONES admitted to probate. Administration granted on estates of Eliza J. LYON, Athelia HUTCHISON, Levin C. MAFFETT, Maria WIARD, Geo. KEEN, and Adelaide THOMAS.

Thursday, 22 June 1882 Vol. XXVII, No. 2

Married: On June 13th 1882, by Rev. John WOOLF, at the residence of the bride, Mr. Townsend C. FURR and Mary V. ARRNETT [ARNETT?].

Married: On June 15th 1882, by Rev. Dr. HEAD, Mr. James E. BEALES and Miss Ella BEALES, all of Loudoun County.

Died: In Georgetown, on Monday June 12th 1882, of bronchitis and pneumonia, Mrs. C. A. BUSSARD, in her 62d year.

Died: Near Morrisonville, May 5th 1882, after a brief illness, Alvery Ashton, infant son of Columbus and Cordelia J. COOPER, aged 1y 10m 13d.

Died: Near Goresville, on Thursday, the 15th of June 1882 at 2 a.m., in her 38th year, Mrs. Mary Esther KIDWELL, wife of Jas. KIDWELL, Esq. in this county. Member of P. E. Church.

Mr. R. I. FULTON, a native of this county, but for several years past a resident of Kansas City, Mo, where he teaches Elecution, was on Wednesday (yesterday) married to Miss Clara BUXTON, of Worcester, Mass.

Severe storm: Wheat field of Mr. James GEORGE, about 3 miles S of Aldie, was ruined. Residence of Mr. Richard CARTER, on the Sudley road, was completely denuded of window glass.

Thursday, 29 June 1882   Vol. XXVII, No. 3

Married: At the residence of the bride's brother, near Front Royal, on June 14th, 1882, by the Rev. Mr. SHEPHERD, Mr. H. G. MEGEATH, of Loudoun, to Miss Emma F. HICKS, of Warren.

Married: In the city of Worcester, Mass., June 21st, by F. N. CAIVIN, assisted by Rev. Jehiel CLAFLIN, Prof. Robert I. FULTON, of Leesburg, to Clara J. BUXTON, of Worcester, Mass.

Mr. Isaac CARR residing near Ball's Mill, died very suddenly in his harvest field on Tuesday afternoon. He was in about the 76th year of his age. Remains will be interred in the cemetery in Leesburg, about noon today (Thursday).

D. W. FEASTER, a native of Frederick Co., Md, was shot and killed in a street encounter in Leadville, Col., recently with Robert BARTAMOSS, who was also killed. The men fired simultaneously and both dropped dead.

Rev. John POISAL, oldest minister in the Baltimore Conference of the M. E. Church, South, died in Baltimore last Sunday evening, in the 75th year of age. Born in Martinsburg, W. Va, April 13, 1807, and entered the ministry when about 20 years old. ... He married a niece of the late Dr. BOND, and with her, last fall celebrated their golden wedding, in Baltimore.

Thursday, 6 July 1882   Vol. XXVII, No. 4

Married: At the residence of the bride's brother, near Front Royal, on June 14th, 1882, by the Rev. Mr. SHEPHERD, Mr. H. G. MEGEATH, of Loudoun, and Miss Emma F. HICKS, of Warren.

Married: In Aldie, at the church by the Rev. J. B. LAK[E?], on Thursday June 29th 1882, Mr. Thomas R. TILLETT Jr. to Miss Annie SOWERS, all of Loudoun County.

Died: In Snickersville, June 20, of cholera infantum, William Burnett, infant son of Mr. and Mrs. Walter C. OSBURN, aged 10 months.

Died: Louise Knight, infant daughter of Wm. and Carrie V. HUGHES, died at the residence of Mr. T. C. DUNAHUE, in Hamilton, on Thursday morning, June 29th.

Died: At Hillsboro, June 26th, suddenly, Roy, infant son of T. F. and Mamie W. GAVER, aged 5m 30d.

Died: Of consumption on the 30th of May, near the Trapp in this county, Addie THOMAS, daughter of the late Herod THOMAS, in the 43rd year of her age.

Died: At the residence of her mother, near Leesburg, on Saturday, June 3rd, Mrs. Martha E. TURNER, wife of Mr. Jno. TURNER, in the 29th year of her age.

On Thursday night last, at his home in this town, Mr. Jno. W. WOOD, passed away in his 80th year. He had lived his whole life in Leesburg. For more than 60 years he was engaged in teaching school in this town. Buried on Saturday evening in Union Cemetery, with the Odd fellow ceremonies.

Mrs. Mary E. KAIGHN, widow of the late Dr. John H. KAIGHN, of this town, died quite suddenly on Saturday last. She was in her 76th year. Member of M. E. Church, South. Buried in Union Cemetery at 4 o'clock Monday afternoon.

Thursday, 13 July 1882   Vol. XXVII, No. 5

Died: Suddenly of heart disease at her home, near Silcott's Springs, June 3rd 1882, Amanda C., wife of John BITZER, aged 56y 21d.

Died: Mr. Henry VIRTS, at his residence in Waterford, June 18th 1882, of consumption, in the 66th year of age.

Died: At the residence of her son, John H. MORIARTY, near Leesburg on the 29th of May 1882, Mrs. Jane E. MORIARTY, in the 49th year of age.

Died: At her residence, near Aldie, on Tuesday the 27th of June 1882, Miss Malinda RITICOR, in the 74th year of age.

Died: At Snickersville, Wm. Bernard OSBURN, son of Walter C. OSBURN, Esq. aged 10m 18d.

Mrs. Ann McILLHANY, widow of the late Milton McILLHANY, former citizen of this county, and for several years represented Loudoun in Va Legislature, died at the residence of her son-in-law, W. P. HILLEARY, in Warrenton, on 5th of July, in the 73rd year of her age. She was a sister of Gen. Asa and Col. Hamilton ROGERS, of this county.

July Ct.: A. M. HUTCHISON qualified as guardian of Mary E., Franklin, Maria L. and A. M. HUTCHISON. Wills of Wm. L. TIMMS, Malinda RITICOR, A. J. MILBOURN and Isaac CARR admitted to probate. J. C. LOVE and Samuel AGUILLA (colored) licensed to celebrate the rites of matrimony. C. C. GAVER qualified as Admr. of L. W. DERRY.

Near Warrenton, Sat. afternoon, Meredith ROBINSON, while loading a wagon with old iron, threw a piece on a jacket in the wagon, which struck a pistol in the pocket of the jacket, exploding it, the ball entering ROBINSON's stomach, killing him almost instantly.

Major A. E. RICHARDS, lawyer of Louisville, has been nominated for judge of the Superior Ct for the second district of Ky, embracing 87 counties. He is a native of Loudoun County.

Thursday, 20 July 1882   Vol. XXVII, No. 6

Mrs. Ann Mason TUTT, widow of Col. Charles Pendleton TUTT, of Loudoun County, died at the residence of her son-in-law, Philip PENDLETON, Berkeley Springs, W. Va, on the 11th inst., age 98 years. Lived to see her descendants to the 5th generation.

Death of Abram S. HEATON occurred on Sunday morning at 5 o'clock. after several months of intense suffering. Born Oct. 17th 1828 at Woodgrove, the third son of Dr. Jonathan HEATON. ... Leaves widow, 1 son and 1 daughter. He was a brother of State Senator Henry HEATON, of this town.

Cincinnati Commercial of July 13th: Early afternoon wedding yesterday at the residence of Mr. and Mrs. C. D. MEADER, of Mr. W. Yale MORALLEE (son of Mr. T. C. MORALLEE, formerly of this town) and Miss Miriam E. MEADER. His business affiliations are with Jeffras, Seeley & Co., of 4th Street. Only daughter of Mr. and Mrs. C. D. MEADER, the father being on of the firm of Meader furniture Co. .... Performed by Rev. Mr. Jonathan EDWARDS, pastor of the Seventh Presbyterian Church.

Mrs. Elizabeth HARDING died at her home near Hillsborough on Thursday, the 6th inst., in the 93rd year of age. Member of Methodist Church for 70 years.

Thursday, 27 July 1882   Vol. XXVII, No. 7

Married: In Leesburg, at the Parsonage of the M. E. Church, July 10th 1882, by the Rev. A. J. PORTER, Mr. J. C. HARPER to Miss Ida HARPER, both of Loudoun County.

Died: At the residence of her daughter-in-law, Mrs. Susan STEADMAN, in this town, on Wednesday, the 12th of July 1882, Mrs. Harriet THOMPSON, in the 62d year of her age.

Died: July 25th, James Henry son of Thos. T. and Mollie F. MUSE, aged 2y 9m 25d.

Accident about 1½ miles east of Leesburg on Sunday afternoon, by which Harrison K. HARDY, little 10 year old son (last and only child) of Mr. Howard HARDY, of this town, lost his life. He, in company with Robt. HARDY, his cousin, and Edward T. FEICHSTER, each a couple of years older than himself, had been in the woods gathering blackberries, each of them provided with a leather sling. On the way home about 4 o'clock, and when within a short distance of his grandfather's, Mr. Henry HARDY, the boys were amusing themselves throwing stones from their slings. Turning around, the older boys saw Harrison on his feet turning rapidly round and round, and suddenly fall. They supposed him dead and gave alarm. A colored woman, Jane COLEMAN, was the first to reach him, about ten minutes later he was dead. Believed that death was the result of a blow inflicted by a stone whilst in or thrown from a leather sling and purely accidental.

Thursday, 3 August 1882   Vol. XXVII, No. 8

Married: In Middleburg, on Thursday morning, July 27th 1882, by the Rev. S. W. HADDAWAY, Mr. Smith GERMAN, to Miss Annie O'BANNON.

Married: On Thursday, July 20th, 1882, at Christ's Episcopal Church, Winchester, by Rev. Dr. J. R. HUBARD, Mr. Alexander M. BAKER and Miss Jennie, daughter of J. Smith GILKESON, Esq., all of Winchester.

Married: By Rev. P. T. WARREN, at the residence of the bride's father, Mr. Eli T. RUSE, Mr. George H. HAMPTON and Miss Ella RUSE, all of Loudoun Co.

Died: At Guilford, on Thursday July 27th, John Cleveland, infant son of J. Cleveland and Florence S. COLEMAN, aged 7m 11d.

Died: Near Ellis, Vernon County, Missouri, July 15, 1882, of cholera infantum, Theodore Hoge, youngest child of J. C. and N. L. CRANE, 1y 5m 15d.

Died: At her residence in Charlestown, July 23d, of apoplexy, Mrs. Margaret AISQUITH, daughter of the late Cato MOORE, aged 62 years.

Died: Near Pt. Pleasant, Pa., July 26th 1882, after a lingering illness, Isabella M. LEIDY, widow of the late Amos LEIDY, formerly of Fairfax Co, Va, aged 56y 4m 21d.

Died: In Leesburg, on Sunday, July 23rd, 1882, Harrison K., son of Howard and Margaret HARDY, aged 9y 2m 11d.

Thursday, 10 August 1882   Vol. XXVII, No. 9

Married: In Grace Church, Plains Station, Fauquier Co, on Wed. morning, August 2, 1882, by Rev. Mr. GRAMMAR, Col. John SLOANE, of Columbia, South Carolina, and Jane, youngest daughter of Col. Robert BEVERLEY, of Fauquier.

Died: At Coton, the residence of her grandfather, Richard E. FURR, Esq., on the morning of Aug. 4th, 1882, Maude White, infant daughter of Frank and Fannie FURR, aged 1y 2m 12d.

Letter from Petersburg, Va, dated August 5th: Mr. Joseph COCKRILL, aged 72, died yesterday at his home in this city. He was one of our oldest merchants. He was a native of Loudoun Co, but moved here in 1839.

Thursday, 17 August 1882   Vol. XXVII, No. 10

Married: On July 27th 1882, at the city Hotel, in Frederick city, by Rev. B. F. BROWN, Jas. B. HICKMAN, of Montgomery Co., Md, to Miss Jennie McGARTER, of Loudoun County.

Married: On the 10th inst., at the Reamer House, Leesburg, by Rev. Andrew ROBEY, Mr. Luther A. LOVE to Miss Pocahontas D. SAFFER.

Died: On Monday, August 7th 1882, Sarah Ellen infant daughter of John and Sarah MORIARTY, aged 7m 7d.

Died: At her residence near Aldie, in this county, on the 6th instant, Mrs. Margaret TRIPLETT, in the 74th year of her age.

Died: At the residence of her husband, in this county, on Wednesday, the 26th of July, 1882, of heart disease, Mrs. Drucilla T. MOFFETT, wife of Benj. MOFFETT, aged 56y 6m.

Died: At Appleton, his residence in this county, on the evening of the 5th of August, James S. CARTER, in his 88th year.

Mr. James THOMAS died at his home about two miles west of Leesburg, on Sunday morning last, in the 83d year of his age.

Aug. Ct.: Wills of Ruth LUCAS, Elizabeth HARDING, Margaret TRIPLETT, Julia JORDAN, and Margaret SHUMAKER admitted to probate. Administrations granted on estates of Chas. ARNOLD and Timothy TAYLOR. Geo. H. NIXON qualified as guardian of Orra and Blanch MILBOURN; B. F. SAFFER as committee of Margaret J. FOLEY; J. T. GRUBB as committee of J. W. DILLON.

Mr. C. F. STANSBURY, of Alexandria, who was visiting relatives in Hamilton, died suddenly of a hemorrhage, about 2 o'clock Friday morning, at the residence of his uncle, W. W. THOMPSON. He retired but about 2 o'clock called three times to his cousin, Miss Belle THOMPSON, who found him sitting up in bed, with blood flowing profusely from his mouth. He gasped and expired before the Dr. (KEEN) could arrive. He was about 27 years of age. ... He was a nephew of Mr. J. J. STANSBURY, of Leesburg.

Thursday, 24 August 1882   Vol. XXVII, No. 11

Married: At the residence of the bride's parents on the 15th of Aug., 1882, by the Rev. J. T. WILLIAMS, M. T. HOUSER to Mary Virginia, only dau. of Jas. W. CONNER Esq., all of Loudoun.

Married: At the residence of the bride's parents, in Leesburg, on June 28th 1882, by the Rev. Dr. Samuel RODGERS, Mr. Herman OEHLRICH, of Baltimore, Md, to Miss Reta, daughter of John V. SCHLEIF, of this town.

Died: Friday morning, August 4th, at White Hall, the residence of her parents, Laura White, infant daughter of T. S. and Lovisa TITUS, aged 6m 14d.

Died: Near Round Hill, July 29th 1882, of lung disease, Miss Arabelia V. BEST, in the 33rd year of her age. For 12 months she had been a great sufferer.

Died: At Groveton, Loudoun Co, on Friday, August 11th, Emily M., infant daughter of John CARTER Jr., and Emily CARTER dec'd. aged 5m.

Death of Miss Annie FRIEND occurred here at 8 o'clock Tuesday night. Sister of the wife of Rev. Jas. H. SMITH, of this town. About two weeks ago she was taken with typhoid fever. She was only about 20 years of age. Remains were placed on the morning train Wed. and taken to Petersburg for interment.

Death of Col. Hamilton ROGERS occurred very unexpectedly Sunday morning at his residence, near Middleburg, age 87 years. He was a native of this county. Was a husband and father. Elder of Presbyterian Church. Funeral took place in Middleburg on Monday.

Tribute of respect from Anchor Lodge, No. 111, I.O.G.T. for death on 11th of this month of John H. POSTON.

Thursday, 31 August 1882   Vol. XXVII, No. 12

Died: At the residence of his sister, Mrs. M. E. SEXTON, at Guilford, after a protracted illness from paralysis, Mr. Samuel COCKERILL, aged 65 years.

Thursday, 7 September 1882   Vol. XXVII, No. 13

Died: On the 13th of August 1882, at Chantilly, Va, Mrs. Louisa Ellen, wife of Wm. L. H. KENDRICK, in her 59th year.

Died: Near Arlington, Alexandria Co, Va, August 24th, Jas. F. PALMER, in the 32d year of his age, from injuries received by a fall while walking in his sleep.

Wm. BEANER, a negro about 16 years old, is charged with having outraged a little 10 year old daughter of Mr. Geo. A. HUNT, living about 2 miles north of Purcellville. Trial on next Monday.

Thursday, 14 September 1882   Vol. XXVII, No. 14

Married: At the residence of the bride's father, Thos. A. SCHOOLEY, Esq., of Hamilton, on Wednesday evening, September 6th, Mr. Thos. M. BOLYN, of Purcellville, to Miss Emma N. SCHOOLEY, the Rev. W. T. SCHOOLEY, of Berryville, officiating.

Married: Thursday, August 3d, 1882, by Rev. Samuel RODGERS, at the residence of the bride's father, Mr. J. F. DUKE and Miss Martha S. ELLMORE.

Died: At the residence of his son, Mr. James WORKS, near Farmwell, on Monday evening, September 4th 1882, Mr. Alfred Peyton WORKS, Sr., aged 77y 6m. Native of Loudoun County. Leaves a widow only 3 years his junior with whom he lived in wedlock nearly 52 years. Four of his nine children survive him. Funeral by Elder HANDY, interred in old Rohobeth burying ground.

Died: On Thursday September 8th 1882, of remitting fever, Lillian Richards BROOKS, daughter of Philip and Annie E. BROOKS, aged 1y 13d.

Co. Ct.: Wills of Eli N. LOVE and Wm. FOX admitted to probate. Estates of Jas. BEST, Sarah A. PERKINS, Margaret VANSICKLER and Benjamin DAVIS admitted to Sheriff. Rev. C. F. BEALES licensed to celebrate the rites of matrimony. Margaret C. AMOS qualified as guardian of Annie R., Charlie N. and Wm. H. AMES.

Mr. Mahlon H. JANNEY, of Alexandria, died suddenly at the residence of his father, Samuel H. JANNEY, Esq., on Cameron Street. He was taken suddenly sick in his drug store, on King St., yesterday evening at 5 o'clock and was assisted to his home. This morning he left the house and went to the store. He then swallowed strychnine, and died at nearly 11 o'clock. He was only about 39 years of age. He leaves a wife.

Thursday, 21 September 1882   Vol. XXVII, No. 15

Mrs. Lucy WATSON died at the residence of her brother-in-law, Mr. G. W. RUPP (where she was spending a few days) last Friday evening. She was paralyzed on Thursday. Daughter of the late Rev. Thos. BIRKBY, and widow of the late Lemuel WATSON. She was in the 76th year of her age.

Adam HOUSEHOLDER died at his home near Lovettsville last week, in the 75th year of age.

Thursday, 28 September 1882   Vol. XXVII, No. 156

Married: In San Francisco, Ca, on Tuesday, September 12th 1882, by Rev. ___, Geo. F. DAVIS and Nannie D., youngest daughter of the late Benjamin D. RATHIE, of Leesburg.

Married: September 20th 1882, by Elder P. T. WARREN, at his residence near Hamilton, Mr. Amos A. BEALES and Miss Adeline WYNKOOP, all of Loudoun County.

Married: Near Mt. Hope on the 12th, Mr. Benjamin HAVENER to Miss Lucretia POOL, by Rev. G. W. POPKINS, assisted by Rev. A. T. M. HANDY, all of Loudoun.

Died: In Georgetown, D.C., on September 8th, 1882, at the residence of her brother, Hugh G. DIVINE, Mrs. Mary Ann WILSON, aged 74 years, formerly of Leesburg. A great sufferer for many years.

Deputy Sheriff H. H. RUSSELL and Asst. D. H. VANDEVANTER, of Loudoun County arrived here (Alexandria) this morning with Rachael BEAMER, an insane white woman from near Morrisonville, on their way to the Eastern Lunatic Asylum, at Williamsburg.

Charlestown W. Va. Free Press of last Saturday: Funeral of two children of Mr. LITTLEPAGE, son-in-law of Henry W. CASTLEMAN of this county. Little boy was 10 years of age, Henry Castleman LITTLEPAGE, and the other a girl about 7 years of age, Mary LITTLEPAGE. They both died on Tuesday at their grandfather's residence and were interred at "Edge Hill."

Harper's Ferry W. Va., Sept. 18: Armstead BUFFINGTON, of Loudoun County, was struck by the eastern bound freight train at 6 p.m., one mile east of this place. His left arm was cut off near the elbow, and he sustained severe bruises about the head. It is likely that he will not recover.

Another daughter. of Thomas MOORE Esq, at Fairfax Court House has died from diphtheria. On Saturday night of last week his youngest daughter died from diphtheria.

Thursday, 5 October 1882   Vol. XXVII, No. 17

Died: On the 20th of Sept. at "Arlosta," the residence of Geo. A. BALL, near Goresville, of cholera infantum, Wm. Thomas, infant child of Samuel H. and Virginia A. BALL, aged 6m 26d.

Died: On Saturday morning, Sept. 23d 1882, after a long and painful illness, Blanche Virginia, the fifth daughter of S. J. and Blanche E. NIXON, aged 2m 12d.

Died: Tues. Sept. 25th, Henry St. Lawrence HOGELAND, aged 52.

Died at his residence, near Pleasant Grove, Loudoun Co, September 20th 1882, Mr. Washington BEAVERS, in the 69th year of his age. Member of M. E. Church about 45 years. He was twice married. Married less than 3 short years to widow. Leaves three children.

Died: At the home of his son-in-law, Geo. HALLACK, west of town, on Sat. Sept. 19th 1882, Mr. Edwin R. GOVER, aged about 63 years, from typhoid fever. He moved to this place about 1865 and was for ten years a resident of town engaged in the lumber trade in this place and then grocery business as partner with Henry DODD, after which he removed to a farm near town. Member of M. E. Church at Harmony. Wife preceded him. Father of five children, two of whom have died, and three, two of whom are heads of families are left. *Kansas, Edgar Co. Ill Journal.* Mr. GOVER was a native of this county.

Thursday, 12 October 1882   Vol. XXVII, No. 18

Married: At the residence of the bride's father, Wm. WATERS, Esq., September 21st by Rev. S. A. BALL, Rev. H. A. SCOTT, P. E. of the Greenbrier District, Va. Conference, to Miss Mattie WATERS, of Fairfax County.

Married: In Washington DC, October 4, by Rev. Dr. D. W. FAUNCE, Mr. J. C. CARR, of Loudoun County and Miss Mollie T. BRAWNER, of Alexandria.

Died: In Baltimore, Md, on Tuesday, October 3, at 1:30 p.m., Teackle Wallis HEISKELL, eldest son of J. Monroe HEISKELL and Esther Fairfax HEISKELL, aged 14 years.

Died on the 27th ult., at 4 o'clock in the evening, John T. CONSTABLE, aged 30y 7m.

Died: Of diphtheria, Saturday October 7th 1882, at her father's residence in Loudoun County, Annie Lee, child of Lewis H. and Hattie L. FREEMAN, aged 18 months.

Departed this life at her late residence, near Daysville, after a brief illness, Mrs. Theodosia Simpson GREEN, wife of Henry GREEN, in her 73d year. Native of Prince William Co, but spent most of her life in Loudoun. Member of Methodist Church in Leesburg since 1834. Wedded more than half a century. Leaves widow and two children. Interred in Union Cemetery, Leesburg.

Willis HUGHES died suddenly on Friday night last, September 23d 1882, at his late home, about ½ a mile north of Hamilton Station, believed in his 85th year. Born a slave, the property of the late William CARR, Sr., father of David CARR, he was a trusted servant. Freed at the age of 27 (as were all the male servants and the females at 25).

Oct. Ct.: Will of Adam HOUSEHOLDER admitted to probate. Administrations granted on the estates of Jas. FIELDS, Washington BEAVERS and Delilah BEAVERS. Father J. B. O'REILLY licensed to celebrate the rites of matrimony.

Thursday, 19 October 1882   Vol. XXVII, No. 19

Married: In Leesburg, on Tuesday morning, Oct. 17th 1882, at the residence of the officiating clergyman, Rev. Dr. HEAD, Mr. Thos. J. DOWNS and Miss Sarah F. KINSER, all of Loudoun.

Died: At Soldier's Rest, near Gum Spring, Loudoun Co, Saturday night, October 7th, of diphtheria, Annie Lee, aged 18 months; on Wednesday night, October 12th, John McGill, aged 4y 2m, only children of Lewis H. and Hattie L. FREEMAN.

Died at her uncle's residence in Leesburg, October 11th 1882, Lillie WRIGHT, in the 14th year of her age. About 2 years ago Lillie came to her uncle and aunt to make their home here. Devoted scholar in St. James Sabbath School.

Last Wednesday night, Lillie WRIGHT, girl of 14 years, died at the residence of her uncle, Mr. Edwin WRIGHT, after an illness of little more than 24 hours, of diphtheria.

Circuit Ct.: Divorce from the bonis of matrimony between Ella D. MENARD and John B. MENARD.

Mr. John H. POWELL's son, Thomas Leigh, died from lockjaw during Tuesday night. It came from a splinter stuck under the toenails. He was in his 11th year. Services took place yesterday evening at Mr. POWELL's residence and remains were last night taken to Halifax for interment. He was a nephew of Mr. Louis H. POWELL, of this town.

Thursday, 26 October 1882   Vol. XXVII, No. 20

Married: October 18th 1882, at the residence of Messrs. Bushrod and Isaac PIGGOTT, near Silcott Springs, by Elder P. T. WARREN, Mr. Henry CRAIG and Miss Rosa E. NICHOLS, all of Loudoun.

Married: By Elder P. T. WARREN at his residence, near Hamilton, October 22d 1882, Mr. George W. TAVENER, of Ohio, and Miss Cora RUSE, of Hamilton, Loudoun County.

Married: At "Briery Knowe," Amherst Co, on Wednesday morning, October 18th by Rev. R. J. McBRYDE, assisted by Rev. Mr. LAWRENCE, Major John D. RODGERS (formerly of Loudoun) to Miss Kitty, daughter of Launcelot MINOR, Esq.

On Wednesday evening in the church of St. James, the Rector, Rev. G. W. NELSON, united Mr. Robert W. NELSON, late of Philadelphia, now of Fauquier, and Miss Margaret KEITH, eldest daughter of Isham KEITH, Esq. Judge KEITH, uncle of the bride, gave her away in the Episcopal service.

Thursday, 2 November 1882   Vol. XXVII, No. 21

Married: In Lovettsville, at the residence of the bride's mother, October 28th, by the Rev. Father J. B. O'REILLY, James HOGAN and Mary E. KELLEY, both of this county.

Married: At Hopeton, near Washington DC, by Rev. Samuel H. GREENE, Mr. Lewis Rodney TAYLOR of Purcellville, Va, to Miss Mary Kingsford STICKNEY, of Washington.

Died at his residence northwest of Lovettsville, Wednesday October 18, 1882, Joseph EVERHART, aged 81y 15d.

Died: On the 26th of September of whooping cough, Sarah Ellen, infant daughter of Lee. M. and Medora DADE, aged 2 months.

Died: In Alexandria on the night of October 27th 1882, Rebecca, wife of C. R. HOOFF, Esq., of that city.

Died of diphtheria, at 2 o'clock on Saturday the 21st of October, near Woodward, Luther BEALES, son of M. J. BEALE, aged 11y 8m.

Kanasha Station, Wood Co. W. Va. Oct 25th 1823 [83]: the subject of this notice, Lavenia ROSE, was born near Aldie, Loudoun Co, February 24th 1800, married Thompson C. BYARD, September 26th 1882 [1828?], of Fairfax County, who departed this life May 3d 1866, aged 72y 5d. They moved near the above named place in 1834 with their family, then quite a wilderness, she surviving until October 17, 1882. Aged 82y 7m 23d. Both were member of Regular Baptist Church.

Mr. John W. CONRAD died suddenly at his home, near Hillsborough, on Sat. night last. He went to bed as usual and was found dead in bed Sunday morning. He was 50 years old.

Mr. Henry HEATON, Agent for Miss Lizzie GOVER, has sold the brick dwelling and ground on the eastern suburbs of Leesburg, known as "Govers' Hill, to F. A. NICOL, recently from Germany.

Thursday, 9 November 1882   Vol. XXVII, No. 22

Married: At Hillsdale, Rappahannock Co, November 1st 1882, by Rev. S. M. ATHEY, Mr. J. S. CHINN, of Loudoun, and Miss Ida E. SETTLE, of Rappahannock County, Va.

Married: In Aldie, on the morning of Tuesday, Oct. 24th, 1882, by Rev. Mr. HOUGH, Capt. John R. HUTCHISON, and Miss Laura, dau. of the late Jas. W. BRAWNER, all of Loudoun.

Died: In this town, at 6 o'clock, on Wednesday, November 7th 1882, of diphtheria, Farian, youngest child of John Y. and Rebecca BASSELL, in the 3rd year of his age. Funeral will take place from his father's residence at 11½ o'clock this (Thursday) morning.

Died: At New Lisbon, Loudoun Co, the residence of her grandfather, James M. BENTON, on the 23rd inst., Margaret Benton, daughter of James W. and E. Virginia DISHMAN, aged 2y 1m.

Died: Near Gum Spring, October 10th, 1882, Mrs. Matilda SUMMERS, wife of the late Daniel SUMMERS, and mother of our Deputy Sheriff, in her 70th year. Member Methodist Church for many years.

Died: At Roseville, Oct. 20, 1882, Mrs. Annie McFARLAND, wife of Maurice McFARLAND, of consumption, aged 39y 1m 22d.

Thursday, 16 November 1882   Vol. XXVII, No. 23

Married: At Hillsdale, Rappahannock Co, November 1st, by the Rev. S. M. ATHEY, Mr. S. J. CHINN, of Loudoun, to Miss Ida E. SETTLE, of Rappahannock Co.

Married: At the residence of the bride's aunts, in Hamilton, on Thursday, Nov. 9th 1882, by Rev. P. T. WARREN, Mr. W. T. ROGERS and Miss Alice G. GREGG, all of Loudoun Co.

Died: Of diphtheria, on the 5th of November 1882, Virginia Louella, daughter of Thos. N. CARRUTHERS, aged 8y 9m 2d.

Mr. Otterbein HOFFMAN died at "Raspberry Plains," the family homestead, near Leesburg, on Sunday, November 12th, in the 73rd year of his age. He had been a great sufferer for several weeks. Interred in Union Cemetery on Tuesday.

In St. James Episcopal Church, at 12 m. today (Thursday), Mr. John A. BEAVER, of Penn., will wed Bessie, second daughter of the late R. M. BENTLEY, of Leesburg.

Mr. B. F. CONRAD, merchant of Upperville, Fauquier County, died on Monday from injuries received in a fall on Sunday.

Mrs. Mary E. TURNER, widow of the late Dr. Samuel TURNER, of Loudoun County, died suddenly of paralysis in Georgetown on the 28th of October.

Mr. John SCOTT, recently a member of the Baltimore bar, died in Sal Luis Obispy, California, on the 6th instant. Son of Robt. E. SCOTT, of Warrenton, Va. and brother of Major R. Taylor SCOTT.

Mr. Truman SKINNER, liquor dealer of Baltimore, died suddenly at his office in that city Tuesday, of heart disease. He was a native of Loudoun Co, and a son of the late Samuel SKINNER, who resided near Middleburg. He was in the 52d year age.

Nov. Ct.: George JOHNSTON sentenced to one year in penitentiary for assault with intent to kill. Wills of Washington BEAVERS, Willis HUGHES and Elizabeth SHRY admitted to probate.

Thursday, 23 November 1882   Vol. XXVII, No. 24

Married: At St. James' Episcopal Church, Leesburg, on Thursday, November 16th 1882, by the Rev. R. T. DAVIS, Mr. John A. BEAVER, of Penn., to Miss Bessie, second daughter of the late R. M. BENTLEY, of this town.

Married: At "Mountain View," the residence of the bride's mother, November 14th 1882, by Elder Joseph FURR, Mr. James R.

HOUSER and Mary Ellis, sixth daughter of the late John WILLIAMS.

Married: November 9th 1882, at the Lutheran church, near Lovettsville, by Rev. R. H. MILLER, Mr. Mahlon T. ARNETT and Miss Mollie L. SIMPSON.

Married: by the Rev. A. J. PORTER, November 15th 1882, at the residence of the bride's parents, Miss Janie STREAM to Mr. Thomas BRADY, all of Loudoun County.

Married: At the residence of the bride's parents, near Waterford, November 16, 1882, by Rev. P. T. WARREN, Mr. Oscar C. JAMES and Miss Sue F. BRABHAM, all of Loudoun.

Married: In the Methodist Church, Aldie, on Tuesday morning, Nov. 21, 1882, by Rev. Mr. HADDAWAY, Dr. R. D. LEITH and Miss Janie F., dau. of Romulus FURGUSON, all of Loudoun.

Died: October 22d, 1882, near Worton, Kent Co., Md, Mrs. Rose V. SNAPP, in the 28th year of her age, daughter of Mrs. Virginia L. VIRTS, formerly of this county.

Died: In Middleburg, on Wednesday, Nov. 8th 1882, Lula Moore, only daughter of Jno. and Marian BARKER, aged 2y 1m.

Thursday, 30 November 1882 Vol. XXVII, No. 25

Married: In St. James Episcopal Church, Leesburg, on Wednesday morning, November 29th 1882, by Rev. Dr. R. T. DAVIS, Capt. James S. STANDLEY, of Atoka Indian Territory, and Mrs. Lizzie C. HARRISON, of this county.

Married: At Waterford Baptist church, November 22d inst., by Rev. P. T. WARREN, Mr. Richard Henry BROWN, and Miss Margaret E. MYERS, all of Loudoun County.

Married: On Wednesday, November 22nd, 1882, in the Leesburg Presbyterian church, by the Rev. Jas. H. SMITH, Mr. T. Jefferson MYERS to Miss Katie CURRY, all of Loudoun Co.

Died: Luther WYNKOOP, eldest son of Samuel T. WYNKOOP, near Round Hill, of scarlet fever, on the 15th inst., aged about 10 years.

Died: Emma Florence SKINNER, youngest daughter of James and Mary E. SKINNER, died of malaria fever at Hughesville, November 3d, 1882, aged 9m 8d.

Mr. C. W. PAXSON, former merchant of this county, died at his home at Goresville on Wednesday of last week in about the 62d year of his age. Several years ago stricken with paralysis, and since almost dead to the world. Leaves large circle of relatives. Interred in Union Cemetery on Friday.

Mr. Thos. CARRUTHERS, Deputy Sheriff of this county, lost another child on Sunday – a little boy about 8 years old, of diphtheria. This is the third member of his family to fall victim.

Miss Willa BUCKNER, of Shelby Co., Ky, was married on Tuesday 14th inst., to Mr. James M. OSBURN, of Louisville, at the residence of her aunt. Rev. Dr. PRATT, of Lexington, officiated. They left for Cincinnati the same afternoon. *Courier Journal*. He is a son of Mr. Joab OSBURN, of this county, and was for some time engaged in business in this town.

Thursday, 7 December 1882   Vol. XXVII, No. 26

Died: At the residence of T. N. BROWN near Lincoln, on Wed. morning, Nov. 8th 1882, Elizabeth SHRY, in her 85th year.

Died: Near Purcellville, on Sunday morning, November 26th 1882, Annie J., infant daughter of Samuel E. and Mollie E. NICHOLS, aged 1m 10d.

Died: Of consumption, at Warton, Kent Co, Md, Mrs. Rose V. SNAPP, wife of Eugene D. SNAPP and daughter of Mrs. Virginia VIRTS.

One day last week, diphtheria entered the home of Rev. James H. SMITH, of this town, and seized the first born of the household, a fair haired child, Charlie, of scarce three summers.

Departed on Monday last for the far West, Thos. S. PURDIE. He goes to Helena, Montana. Has been a resident of this place for several years.

Mr. Oliver TAYLOR, a former citizen of this county, but for the past 16 years a resident of Alabama, died near Lincoln on Friday night, November 16th, of consumption.

The new Presbyterian church at Delaplane Station, Fauquier county, will be dedicated on Dec 57 [27?] by Rev. Moses HOGE D.D. of Richmond.

Fauquier Co.: John SOMERS, colored, was sentenced yesterday to five year in the penitentiary for an outrage committed on a colored woman.

Thursday, 14 December 1882   Vol. XXVII, No. 27

Married: In Leesburg, Dec. 5th 1882, by the Rev. J. H. SMITH, Mr. Wilfred L. COOPER, of Lancaster, Penn. to Miss Margaret L. LEWIS, daughter of the late Jas. LEWIS, of Loudoun Co.

Married: Wed., Dec. 6th, at the residence of the bride's father, James M. BENTON Esq. by the Rev. Mr. HADDAWAY, Mr. Oscar BEAVERS, to Miss Maggie BENTON, both of Loudoun.

Married: At the residence of the bride's father, on Tuesday, Dec. 5th, Mr. Wm. BENTON, son of James M. BENTON, Esq. of Loudoun Co., to Miss Annie B. GARDEN, of Clarke Co.

Married: By the same, December 6th 1882, at the residence of the bride's father, John S. JOHNSON, Mr. John W. PARKS to Miss Louisa JOHNSON.

Married: At the residence of Mr. John A. SPILMAN, of Warrenton, Dec. 6, 1882, by Rev John B. TURPIN, M. J. ALEXANDER, Esq., of Pulaski Co, to Miss Laura B. WHITE, of Loudoun Co.

Married: At the home of Mr. John T. RISLER, in Hunterdon Co, N. J., December 6th 1882, by Elder A. B. FRANCIS, Mr. F. S. TERRY, of Philadelphia, Penn. to Miss Susie E. FRANCIS, Fauquier Co.

Died: At her son's residence, near Point of Rocks, on Sat., the 2d of Dec, 1882, Mrs. Margaret MATHERS, aged 67y 11m 26d.

Died: In Washington DC, December 2nd 1882, of heart disease, Elizabeth, wife of A. B. CRUPPER, aged 65 years.

Died: On the 17th and 26th of November, Carrie May and Anne Gertrude, youngest daughters of Thos. N. CARRUTHERS in the 8th and 5th years of their age.

Died: Also on the 18th, Lizzie, youngest daughter of T. W. WEADON, in the 15th year of age.

Died: Mrs. ___ RUSK, wife of the late John RUSK, died on Friday, December 1st, at her residence near Unison, in her 53d year.

Co. Ct.: Estates of Huldah ODEN and Manly HAMPTON dec'd. committed to the Sheriff.

Sad accident in Aldie on Tuesday night of last week. Several gentlemen were seated around the stove in the store of Mr. John DOWNS, when a negro man under the influence of liquor came in and asked for a drink, which was denied him, becoming importunate. Mr. DOWNS picked up from behind the counter what he thought was an unloaded pistol. He snapped the pistol once or twice and it discharged, the ball striking Mr. Robt. WHITLOCK, one of the parties present, in the abdomen. He lingered until Sat. evening. He was unmarried and about 30 years of age.

Alexandria Gazette: On Tuesday morning at 11½ a.m. at the residence of George W. GORDON, Esq. of Clarke Co, some 100 guests witnessed the marriage by Rev. F. A. STROTHER, of Wm. Hyde BENTON to Miss Nannie Bently GORDON, youngest daughter of the gentleman above named.... They will reside in New Lisbon. She has relatives in Loudoun.

On Wednesday evening at 7 o'clock, Mr. Oscar BEAVERS and Miss Maggie Carlin BENTON, at New Lisbon, were married by Rev. Mr. HADDAWAY in the presence of 150 guests.

Thursday, 21 December 1882   Vol. XXVII, No. 28

Married: Dec. 12th 1882, by Rev. P. T. WARREN, of Hamilton, at Antioch Church, Prince William Co, Va., Mr. Cyrus W. BOWLEY and Miss Mary O. OWENS, of said county.

Married: In Presbyterian Church, Leesburg, on Wednesday morning, December 20, 1882, by Rev. Jas. H. SMITH, Mr. R.

C. VASS, of Culpeper C. H. and Miss Florence N., second daughter of Mr. Robert HARPER, of Loudoun.

Cards are out for the marriage of Mr. Rosslyn C. VASS, merchant of this town, and Miss Florence N. HARPER, daughter of Mr. Robert HARPER, of Leesburg. Ceremony will take place on Wed. next in the Presbyterian Church at Leesburg. *Culpeper Exponent of the 13th*.

Thursday, 28 December 1882 Vol. XXVII, No. 29

Married: At the residence in Pr. William Co. on Thursday, December 21st by Rev. W. F. DUNNAWAY, Mr. Barnett C. PEARSON, of Fauquier and Miss Ruth A. CAMPBELL.

Married: On the 21st by Rev. Geo. W. POPKINS, at the residence of Mr. Christopher HOUSER, Mr. W. H. W. MORAN to Miss Bettie ATWELL, all of Loudoun.

Married: December 21st 1882, by Rev. P. T. WARREN, at his residence near Hamilton, Mr. H. C. BENNETT and Miss Mary E. WHITE, all of Loudoun County.

Married: By the same, at the same place, and on the same day, Mr. Herbert JENKINS and Miss Mollie M. HIGDON, all of Loudoun.

Married: December 24th, at Rehobeth M. E. Church, Loudoun County, by Rev. A. J. PORTER, Mr. Henry M. NICEWARNER to Miss Rose A. VIRTS, both of Loudoun County.

Died of membranous croup, at Philomont, November 19, 1882, Minnie Josephine, daughter of William Alpheus and Mary Jane HAWS, in the 7th year of her age.

Mr. Thos. J. DELANY and wife, nee Evelyn LEE, arrived in Leesburg on a visit to Mrs. D's mother, Friday evening last, from their home in Kansas City, Mo., first visit since their departure about ten years ago. Mr. D. is in the cattle business in the west.

James SEWELL, colored man, sent to Md penitentiary on September 11th, died last week at that place of consumption. He was a brickmaker by trade and was sick when sent to the penitentiary. He was born in Leesburg and was 27 years old.

Mr. Jno. E. WRIGHT died at his home in Leesburg, on Tuesday night, after a brief illness of typhoid pneumonia, in about the 53d year of his age. Member of M. E. Church, South. For number of years Superintendent of Union Cemetery.

James F. TIMMS, native and for many years resident of this county, died at the home of his son-in-law, Mr. Joseph HOUGH, at Bethel, on Sunday last, in the 65th year of his age. Buried in Leesburg on Tuesday.

Mr. John T. NEWMAN, from Salem, Fauquier co, who has been canvassing this county during the past summer as Agent for the sale of fruit trees for Franklin Davis & Co.'s Nursery, Richmond, died suddenly at the Reamer House on Thursday evening about 10 o'clock, from heart disease. Interred in Union Cemetery on Saturday.

Thursday, 4 January 1883 Vol. XXVII, No. 30

Married: At the residence of Geo. W. SUMMERS in Frederick Co., Md, on December 20th 1882, by Rev. W. H. RETTLEMYER, Mr. Chas. C. KEPHART of Loudoun County and Miss Martha C. DEGRANGE, of Frederick County, Md.

Married: December 27th, in Richmond, Va, Miss Meta A. HANNEWINCLE to Joseph PACKARD Jr. of Baltimore, Md.

Married: On December 14th, 1882, at the Reformed Parsonage in Frederick city by Rev. D. ESCHBACH, Charles E. FOX to Miss Martha FRY, both of Loudoun County.

Married: December 26th, 1883, by Rev. John WOOLF, at his residence Mr. Robert HINDMAN and Miss Hannah F. TRENARY, all of Loudoun.

Married: At the Lutheran Church, near Lovettsville, December 21st, 1882, by Rev. P. H. MILLER, Mr. John H. BOWERS, to Miss Rosetta MOCK, both of Loudoun County.

Married: At the Presbyterian Parsonage, Leesburg, Va, December 21, 1882, by the Rev. Jas. H. SMITH, Mr. William H. HENDERSON to Miss Mollie E. REACH, both of Loudoun Co.

Married: At the Presbyterian Manse, Farmwell, by Rev. L. B. TURNBULL, December 28, John POOL to Theresa LEFEVRE, both of this county.

Died: Miss Catharine WOLFORD, at the residence of W. H. ADAMS, near Morrisonville, December 16, 1882, in the 63rd year of her age.

Died: December 28th 1882, at the residence of her husband, near Philomont, Anna, wife of Henry TAVENNER, Esq., in the 31st year of her age. Married but one year. Leaves husband and little babe.

Died: At his home on Wed. morning, of typhoid pneumonia, Mr. John E. WRIGHT, in the 58th year of his age.

Death of Mr. Jas. E. McCABE, a native and for many years of this town, died in Washington Wednesday, December 27th 1882, in his 54th year. A son of the late Dr. McCABE of this town. During the war he was a member of Richmond Howitzers. Interred in Union Cemetery, Leesburg Friday.

Dr. Jos. W. BRONAUGH, formerly of Loudoun County, died at the residence of his son, in Manchester, Va, on Saturday last, in the 77th year of his age.

Pro. Jessie LITTLETON, of Murfreesboro, N. C., son of the Rev. Oscar LITTLETON, was married on Tuesday last, in Farmville, to Miss Lulu ROSSER, daughter of Rev. Leo. ROSSER.

Thursday, 11 January 1883 Vol. XXVII, No. 31

Married: At Manassas in Trinity (Episcopal) Church on Thursday, the 21st of December 1882, by Rev. Arthur P. GRAY, rector, Jas. Warren ROBERTS, Esq. of Richmond, Va. to Mrs. Kate KENTER, dau. of Col. Wm. S. FEWELL, Mayor of Manassas.

Married: At the residence of the bride's mother, near Manassas, on Tuesday, the 26th? of December 1882, by Rev. Arthur P. GRAY, J. W. WILCOXEN, Esq., to Miss Ida E., only daughter of Mrs. Kate E. MARDERS.

Married: On January 3, 1883, at the residence of the Misses KIRKMAN, Culpeper, Va. by Rev. John McGILL, D.? I. JOHNSON, of Uniontown, Penna. and Estelle V., third daughter of the late Capt. Samuel T. ASHBY, of Culpeper.

Married: On January 3d 1883 by the Rev. Dr. SUNDERLAND, Mr. Marion I. HAVENER, of Springfield, Ohio, to Miss Lillie M. SLACK, of Washington DC.

Died: Suddenly, at the house of her cousin, Eugene W. MASON, of Providence, R. I., Josephine Eleanor HOPKINS, aged 17 years, daughter of Louis N. HOPKINS, of Baltimore, Md.

Jan. Ct.: Estates of Mary PINKETT, Thomas THORNTON and Patrick McQUINN dec'd. committed to Sheriff. Saml. CLENDENNING qualified as Committee of Emory J. FIELDS. Administrations on estates of Thomas KLICE, John SCIPIO, Phineas OSBORN and Jeff C. THOMAS granted.

Mahlon THOMAS, farmer, died at his home near Round Hill, on Monday last, in about the 72d year of his age. After breakfast, while moving about, he fell and expired in a few minutes. Buried at Short Hill on Wednesday.

A child of Mr. Geo. CORNELL, living a few miles from Leesburg, was very badly burned one day last week by its clothing catching fire. The mother was also badly burned about the hands.

Charles PERRY, junior member of the firm of Hempstone & Perry, dry goods merchants on Market space, Washington, committed suicide Sunday night, at his residence, 626 F. St. NW, by shooting himself through the right temple. He was 22 years old and youngest son of the late Augustus PERRY, and a brother of R. Ross PERRY, ex-asst. District attorney.

Thursday, 18 January 1883 Vol. XXVII, No. 32

Married: On December 20th 1882, by Rev. Mr. HADDAWAY, in the church at Aldie, Mr. Chas. E. NORMAN to Miss Georgie GULICK, both of this county.

Died: On the 23d of December 1882, at Lawnville, the residence of H. F. LYNN, Prince William Co. Va, Mrs. S. E. HOLMES, in the 63d year of age.

Died: In Middleburg, December 13, 1882, of pneumonia, Mr. Israel B. THOMPSON, in the 91st year of his age.

Died: Mrs. Catharine BALL was born April 9th 1803, and died at her home near Waterford, Jan. 10th 1883, aged 79y 8m 4d. Member of M. E. Church. Wife of late Samuel BALL, and mother of Revs. S. A. and C. W. BALL of the Va Conference of the M. E. Church.

Miss Rebecca GRAY, eldest daughter of the late John GRAY, of this town, died at her home in Leesburg, at 6 o'clock Monday morning, of paralysis, in the 71st year of her age. Member of Episcopal Church. Funeral took place from the Episcopal church on Wednesday afternoon.

Mr. Samuel SIMPSON died at his home near Mt. Gilead, on Saturday evening last, in about his 65th year. Several years ago he was partially paralyzed and since then "dead to the world." Interred in North Fork burying ground on Monday.

Married license issued in Washington on Tuesday, to Geo. A. DORRELL, of Loudoun Co, and Georgie L. FARR, of Fairfax.

Baltimore American: Mr. Edwin L. JANNEY, formerly a member of the firm of Janney & Cogden, dealers in rubber goods, No. 8 North Charles St., but who retired about 2 years ago due to health, died Thursday morning at Staunton, Va, after a long and severe illness. He was born in 1838 at Alexandria Va. When a youth he went to Louisville, Ky. ... Remains were brought here (Alexandria) last night and funeral took place this evening at 4 o'clock.

Afternoon of Sept. 5th 1882, two little children of Mr. Geo. A. HUNT, living near Purcellville, were playing a short distance from their father's house. The little 10 year old girl, quite deaf the result of scarlet fever was playing. Negro boy named Wm. BEANER, aged about 16 years and employed in the area, seized the eldest child, threw her to the ground, and threatened to take her life if she outcryed. The mother went searching for the children which alarmed the scoundrel, who jumped up and ran, pursued by the father of the child who captured him. When arrested he was almost entirely nude, his clothing found lying on the ground at the assault. Sentenced to death.

Thursday, 25 January 1883   Vol. XXVII, No. 33

Married: At the Episcopal Rectory, in Leesburg, on Tuesday morning, January 23, 1883, Mr. Maurice OSBURN and Miss Olivia, daughter of Mr. Bushrod OSBURN, all of Loudoun.

Died: January 9th 1883, Dora L., eldest daughter of Edgar B. and Annie E. HAVENER, near Belmont aged 9y 5m 6d.

Death of Willie BEVERLEY, who developed pneumonia Monday night and died on Sunday. Leaves a young widow and two little children. Interred in Union Cemetery on Tuesday.

Mr. William CLENDENNING, farmer of this county, died at his home near Hillsborough last week, in about 72d year of his age. He bequeathed $2000 to the Baptist Church at Short Hill.

Wm. BEANER, colored boy convicted last week for criminal assault will be hung on Friday the 30th of March 1883 between 6 and 8 a.m.

Mrs. G. W. TYLER, widow of the late Judge John Webb TYLER, died at her residence in Warrenton, on the 14th inst., of pneumonia, in her 74th year. Leaves 2 daughters and a son.

Dr. Samuel R. RIXEY, physician of Culpeper C. H., died at his home in that place last Wednesday of paralysis.

Thursday, 1 February 1883   Vol. XXVII, No. 34

Letter from Frederick city, Md January 28: Mrs. INGLE, wife of Rev. Osborne INGLE, pastor of All Saints' Episcopal Church of this city, died at her residence on Record st. at an early hour this morning, after a severe illness of a few days. Within the past 18 months, 6 children and a newly born babe of this family have died.

Married: At the Lutheran Church, near Lovettsville, January 11th 1883, by Rev. P. H. MILLER, Mr. John H. LEWIS and Annie J. FRY, both of Loudoun.

Died: January 19th 1883, at the residence of her son-in-law, Jos. M. CONRAD, Esq., Mrs. Nancy POTTS, wife of Ezekiel POTTS, in the 86th year of age.

Died: Florence Estel LOW, daughter of Joseph and Annie A. LOW, near Lincoln, aged 2y 10m 4d.

Died: January 27th 1883, at the residence of his grandfather, Armistead SILCOTT near Silcott Springs, of membranous croup, Johnnie Walter, son of James B. and Bertie CRISSEY of Leesburg, aged 2y 4m.

Lt. P. P. POWELL, of the Ninth Cavalry, U.S.A., is in Baltimore for a visit. Born in Loudoun County, when a boy served in the Confederate army, and at the close of the war returned to his native place to study law. Tiring of the profession, he enlisted in the Ninth Cavalry as a private. Three years ago he was appointed Lt. He is at present stationed at Fort Sale, Indian Territory.

Letter to *Blue Ridge Echo*, dated Woodville, Rappahannock Co., December 30, 1882: Bride is the daughter of F. M. HENDERSON Esq., formerly of Leesburg. At recently reopened Episcopal church in this place at 12 m. on Thursday, the marriage of Mrs. Annie Henderson MILLAN of our village, and Dr. Napoleon Bonaparte NEVITT, of Accotink, by Rev. Mr. WALLACE, of Accotink. Bride given away by her father-in-law, Dr. L. MILLAN. They will reside in Fairfax.

Thursday, 8 February 1883   Vol. XXVII, No. 35

Married: On Thurs., Jan. 25th 1883, at the residence of the bride's parents, by the Rev. Frank PAGE, of Herndon, Va, Richard COLEMAN, son of the late Maj. James COLEMAN, to Thehla, youngest daughter of Carl ROESER, Esq. of Washington DC.

Married: Wednesday January 24, 1883, at the residence of the bride's father, Mr. Mason JAMES, near Round Hill, by Rev. L. R. STEELE, Mr. Robert C. HARRIS, of Clarke County, to Miss Eliza JAMES, of Loudoun County.

Married: January 24th 1883, at the Lutheran Parsonage, near Lovettsville, by the Rev. P. H. MILLER, Mr. Alpheus R. L. DARR, to Miss Alice UNDERWOOD.

Died: On Sunday morning, February 4th 1883, of typhoid pneumonia, Lewis, second son of Lewis M. and Mary T. SHUMATE, in the 5th year of his age.

On Sunday, January 27th of Bright's Disease of the Kidneys, Mr. Bennett WRIGHT, died at his home near Round Hill, in the 64th year of age and on Wed. following, Mr. Daniel WHITE died at his home near Woodburn, in the 83^{d} year of age.

Marriage license issued in Washington last Thursday to John M. CARTER and Lena WILEY, of Loudoun County.

Death of Edwin T. "Ned" ASHBY, Esq., occurred at Delaplane in Fauquier County, last night.

Mrs. Kate HARRISON, wife of Rev. Dr. W. P. HARRISON, late chaplain of the House of Representatives, died a few days ago in Nashville, Tenn. She was a sister of Rev. John A. KERN, of the M. E. Church, South, and had only been married a little more than a year.

Thursday, 15 February 1883   Vol. XXVII, No. 36

Married: On Wednesday, February 7th, 1883, at the residence of Mr. Wm. H. PRITCHETT in Washington city, by Rev. J. A. MORGAN, Millard F. RYON to Miss Lillie SIMPSON, both of Leesburg.

Died: At the residence of R. M. LAWSON, Esq., near Upperville, February 7th 1883, Mrs. M. Florence LANE, wife of Beverly H. LANE, Esq., of Amelia Co., Va, and granddaughter of the late S. B. T. CALDWELL, of this county.

Feb. Ct.: Wills of Malinda MYERS, Samuel SIMPSON, and Ann COCHRAN, admitted to probate. Administration granted on estates of Walter NICHOLS and Bennett WRIGHT dec'd.

Mr. Richard E. FURR died at his home near Belmont, last Thursday, after a few days illness of pneumonia, in his 65th year. Interred in Union Cemetery in this town on Saturday.

Mr. Murphy SHUMATE died of pneumonia at the home of his son, Mr. Lewis M. SHUMATE, on Monday morning last, in his 85th year. Member of M. E. Church, South, and until recently was the only male survivor of a once large membership at Sycolin.

Death of David HIXSON at the residence of Mr. John W. NIXON, near Wheatland (where he had for several years made his home) on Tuesday last, February 13th 1883, of pneumonia, in about the 83d year of age. For nearly 40 years, was deputy Sheriff and Sheriff of this county, entered in service in about 1830. Interred in Union Cemetery, Leesburg, today (Thursday), at 10 o'clock.

Thursday, 22 February 1883 Vol. XXVII, No. 37

Married: In Staunton, Va, on 8th inst., at the residence of the bride's father, Rev. Jno. S. MARTIN, D.D., Presiding Elder of Rockingham District, Baltimore Conference, M. E. Church, South, by the father of the bride, Rev. O. W. HAMMOND and Miss Addie MARTIN, youngest dau. of the officiating minister.

Married: At the residence of the bride's father, in Snickersville, on February 13th, by the Rev. HENRY, Mr. WARE of Clarke County, to Miss Rose BRADFIELD.

Married: At the residence of the bride's father, James LAYCOCK, Esq., near Hughesville, on February 14th by Rev. Dr. HEAD, Mr. Geo. W. FLING to Miss Mary J. LAYCOCK.

Married: On Thursday, Feb. 15, 1883, at the residence of the bride's mother, in Hamilton, Rev. Dr. Nelson HEAD officiating. Mr. William Phillips CARR, of Carrara, near Leesburg, to Miss Georgie O., second daughter of Hon. Geo. W. CARTER, sometime Minister from the U.S. to Venezuela, South America.

Died: At her father's residence, in Fredericksburg, February 14th 1883, after a lingering illness, Miss Susie CHANCELLOR, daughter of Rev. Melzi CHANCELLOR.

Died Little Lillie M., daughter of B. F. & Harriet E. MORGAN, on 6th of February 1883, in the 11th year of her age.

Alexandria Gazette: Marriage of Lt. P. P. POWELL and Miss Catherine Woodruff HICKS, at the residence of the bride's parents, Mr. and Mrs. A. H. BRADNER's place, Dansville, Livingston Co., N.Y. yesterday, Wednesday, February 21st. She met Lt. POWELL, who is also attached to the Ninth, while a guest last year of Col. & Mrs. HENRY, of the Ninth Cavalry (colored) in Indian Territory.

Thursday, 1 March 1883   Vol. XXVII, No. 38

Married: February 21st 1883, at the parsonage in Leesburg, by Rev. Samuel RODGERS, Mr. Silas H. UMBAUGH and Miss Lydia E. FRY.

Married: At the home of the bride's parents, February 18th 1883, by Rev. A. J. PORTER, Mr. Peter SNIDER to Miss Mary A. WEBB, both of Loudoun.

Died: At her residence in Canton, Mo., Monday, January 29th 1883, Mrs. Matilda McDANIEL, widow of Wm. McDANIEL, dec'd., aged 65y? 6m 9d.

Died: At the residence of Samuel T. WYNKOOP, near Woodgrove, February 21st 1883, Hiram THAYER in the 83d year.

Died: In Washington DC, on Friday, February 23, 1883, at 11 a.m., John W. GROSS, after a short but painful illness, in the 62nd year of age.

Died: On Friday, February 23d, 1883 in the 54th year of age, Mary Peyton, wife of Townsend D. SEATON, of Loudoun, and daughter of the late J. Innes RANDOLPH.

Died: On Monday, Feb. 24, Frances, wife of William T. SMITH, in the 32d year of age. Member of Farmwell Presbyterian Church.

Article in *Hillsborough, Ohio Herald* gives an account of 100th birthday of Mrs. Katie HIXSON, a native of this county.

Unison: Mr. Redding HUTCHISON, died on the evening of the 14th inst., at the home of his son, L. E. HUTCHISON, in this town. Born in lower Loudoun, in 1807. Early life devoted to teaching. Laid to rest in old family burying ground at Gumspring on Friday last.

Richard LLOYD, Esq., of Alexandria, died of pneumonia, at the residence of his son-in-law, Mr. C. F. LEE, on Sat. last, in his 68th year. He was attacked on Thursday and died on Saturday.

Katie HIXSON, the subject of this sketch, was born in Loudoun Co, Va., February 5, 1783. On Monday, February 5, 1883 she was 100 years old. She was only married once, her husband was David HIXSON, who died in Fairfield Township, Highland Co., Ohio, on the 22d day of April, 1882. David HIXSON and Katie HIXSON, whose maiden name was Katie RUSE, was married in Loudoun Co. in 1806. Her parents were Michael and Elizabeth RUSE. They raised quite a family of children, all of whom have passed away long years ago, except Katie. She and her husband emigrated from Va to Ohio in 1811. They, with a small family of children, crossed the Alleghany Mountains on horseback, she carrying one before and one behind her, and her husband with the others in the same way. They stopped temporarily, a few months in Ross co, where one of her children, William HIXSON, was born. In 1812 they removed to Highland Co. and settled on the road running from Hillsboro in New Lexington, on a farm now owned by William ROADS and formerly owned by John STRETCH. They bought that farm, then in the woods, opened it up and resided there until her husband died, when it was bought by John STRETCH, who married Polly HIXSON, a daughter of Katie. Since the death of her husband in 1832 she has continued to reside with her children to the present time. Mother of 9 children, 8 of whom still live, and one, a young lady of 17 or 18 years, died many years ago. John HIXSON, her oldest son, about 76 years old, resides in Iowa and so do David HIXSON and Joseph HIXSON, two more of her children. Nancy JOHNSON, Polly STRETCH, Emily DONOHUE, William HIXSON and Samuel HIXSON, all reside in Ohio. Katie has 45 grand children living in different states, and 12 grandchildren dead. She has 88 great-grandchildren living and 20 dead. She has 19 great-great-grandchildren living. The following relatives were present at the anniversary: William HIXSON and Polly STRETCH, her children: Taylor HIXSON, Noah HIXSON, Samuel HIXSON, David HIXSON, Katie McWALKER, Emma STRETCH, Susannah TERRELL and Mrs. Dr. R. P. ELWOOD, grand-children. ....

Thursday, 8 March 1883   Vol. XXVII, No. 39

Married: At the Presbyterian Parsonage, Farmwell, on the 28th inst., by Rev. L. B. TURNBULL, Decatur W. COOKSEY to Mary V. SIMPSON.

Died: At her home, in La Salle Co., Illinois, on the morning of Feb. 27, 1883, of lung fever, Mrs. Pleasant FURR, in her 85th year. Native of this county and mother of the late R. E. FURR.

Last week we published an article taken from an Ohio paper of the celebration in Highland Co., Ohio, of the 100th birthday of Mrs. Katie HIXSON, formerly a Miss RUSE, of Loudoun Co., where the writer stated that she was the only survivor of a once large family of whom have passed away excepting. We have learned that she is a sister of our countyman, Mr. Solomon RUSE, living near Hamilton, who is himself in the 85th year and there is another sister, Mrs. Polly MORRISON, still living in Guersey Co. Ohio, at age 94 years. Another sister died about four years ago, who was in her 83d year at her death.

From San Antonio, Texas paper – Sudden death of Mr. George W. CALDWELL, native of Loudoun Co Va, a son of the late S. B. T. CALDWELL and a brother of Mrs. Wm. MATTHEW, of this place. Born in Va 14 Apr 1834. Came to San Antonio in 1855, and lived among us except time spent in Confederate army during the late war. Cause of death was heart disease. Interred yesterday afternoon in the city cemetery.

Death of Col. Harry GILMOR, cavalryman of Confederate fame, died at his home in Baltimore, about 1 o'clock Sunday morning.

Samuel T. WRIGHT a planter from Tarboro, N. C. shot himself in a hotel, in New York Friday last. He had gone there some time ago expecting to get into business, and was disappointed and shot himself. He was a major of artillery in Lee's army, and a native of Virginia.

Mrs. Anna HITZ died in Washington on Monday. She was born in Switzerland, in 1796, and the mother of Mr. Jno. HITZ.

Thursday, 15 March 1883   Vol. XXVII, No. 40

Died: In Washington, March 12th 1883, at 8:15 a.m., Hattie Lee, youngest daughter of Joseph and Martha J. PRATHER.

Died: Mrs. Eliza J. WILEY, wife of H. G. WILEY, and third daughter of John F. and Susan M. KIDWELL was born near Leesburg, and died at Herndon, Fairfax Co., Saturday, January 27th 1883.

Died: February 20th 1883, of consumption, Norah, daughter of Joshua and Mary Jan MORAN, in her 16th year.

Died: At his residence near Leesburg, on Tuesday 6th inst., Mr. Thomas CLARKSON, in the 74th year of age.

Died: At the residence of his son, Thos. A. CARTER, in Taylortown, in this county, on Friday, the 2nd day of March 1883, Mr. Henry CARTER in the 73d year of age.

Died: Feb. 2nd 1883, at her residence, Mrs. Minerva A. LYNN, aged 65 years, after a short and painful illness. Leaves four children. Funeral was preached by Rev. G. W. POPKINS.

March Ct.: Wills of Amanda SEITZ and M. C. SHUMATE admitted to probate. Administrations granted on estates of Malinda MYERS, Israel B. THOMSON, Richard E. FURR, David HIXSON, Sweringer BUTTS, Margaret HUMPHREY and Peter COLE dec'd. Chas. W. MYERS qualified as Guardian of Robt. L., Minnie M., Jno. F., Jonathan W. and Henry C. MYERS. John F. CRAIG; John F. CRAIG as Guardian of John A. CRAIG. John T. ALEXANDER licensed to celebrate rites of matrimony. Jos. L. NORRIS qualified as Guardian of Joseph E. and Beverley O. WRIGHT.

Last Thursday morning as Miss Annie, daughter of Mr. R. C. CHAMBLIN, living near Bloomfield, was standing in front of an open fire place, the flames communicated with her clothing and she was seriously burned. Slight hope of recovery.

Thursday, 22 March 1883   Vol. XXVII, No. 41

Died: Near Farmwell, on the 17th inst., Mrs. Sarah HANES, in her 79th year. For 30 years a member of the Methodist Church.

Death of Mrs. Annie SMITH, wife of Mr. John R. SMITH, occurred at her home in Purcellville, on Wednesday night, March 14th. Leave husband and a little bate 17 months old.

Miss Rebecca DONOHOE died at the residence of her relative, Joseph L. NORRIS, Esq., in this town, Saturday night, March 17th, in the 90th year of age. She never used glasses and to day of death could read the smallest print.

Mrs. Eliza INGRAM, wife of Dr. S. L. INGRAM, coroner of Manchester, died yesterday morning in that city after a long and painful illness. *Rich. Whig.* She was a daughter of the late John P. SMART of this town.

Death of Lloyd Walter SURGHNOR on Monday. Born in Leesburg 12 September 1833, where he spent his youth, leaving there at early manhood for Washington City. He was living in Texas at the beginning of the late war. He entered the army from Texas and was with Walker's division. At close of war he came to Monroe with his family to engage in keeping hotel, merchandising. ... Funeral services held at Methodist Church with Masonic and Pythian honors. Wife and 4 children survive.

Major James Pendleton ROGERS, of Richmond, son of the late Wm. H. ROGERS, of this county, died at his home in Richmond on Saturday after an illness of less than two weeks of paralysis. ... Leaves a wife and four children.

Thursday, 29 March 1883   Vol. XXVII, No. 42

Married: At the residence of the bride's parents in Leesburg, on Wed. morning, March 28th 1883, by Father FOLEY, of Baltimore, Harry S. JENKINS, of Baltimore, and Katie L., daughter of Dr. A. R. MOTT, of this town.

Died: At his residence near Leesburg, on Wednesday, March 14, 1883, Mr. George W. WYNKOOP.

Died: At Woodburn, March 17th 1883, Sarah Ruth C. GILL, infant daughter of Charles H. and Catharine L. GILL, aged 3m 17d.

From the formation of Loudon Co, in 1753 [1757], til spring of 1880, the death penalty had been inflicted but three times. On the 9th of April 1880, Sam. ROBINSON, colored was executed for the murder in vicinity of Lincoln of Edward THOMPSON, also colored; and tomorrow, Wm. BEANER, colored, convicted not of murder outright but of a crime the most despicable and hellish will share the same fate, that of assaulting a daughter of Mr. George A. HUNT. [long article about the trial]

Thursday, 5 April 1883 Vol. XXVII, No. 43

Married: March 28th 1883, at Purcellville, by Rev. I. B. LAKE, Miss Carrie TAYLOR, daughter of Lewis TAYLOR to Mr. John H. EMERICK, of Ohio.

Married: By the Rev. A. J. PORTER at the residence of the bride's father, in Loudoun county, near Harper's Ferry, March 25th 1883, Mr. Calvin L. EVERHART, to Miss Elizabeth C. SNYDER, both of Loudoun county.

Married: By the same minister, at the same time and place, Mr. John T. VIRTZ, to Miss Ellen V. EVERSON, both of Loudoun.

Died: Clara Virginia DIEDERICK, born July 20th, 1880, died March 22, 1883, aged 2y 8m 2d.

Died: At Hyndman, Bedford Co, Pa, March 29, 1883, Mrs. Laura J. FREY, daughter of Wm. and Ann E. HICKMAN and wife of Saml. L. FREY, aged 33y 4m 8d. Leaves 4 small children and husband. Body conveyed to Point of Rocks and interred in Lutheran Cemetery at Lovettsville.

Died: On Saturday, 24th of March 1883, at the residence of her son, of pneumonia, Mrs. Mary WYNKOOP, widow of the late John WYNKOOP in the 74th year of her age.

Death at his home near Woodgrove, of Mr. Jonah OSBURN, of congestion of the lungs, at 8 o'clock Saturday night, in his 75th year. Interred at Short Hill burying ground on Monday.

Thursday, 12 April 1883 Vol. XXVII, No. 44

Married: March 22d, 1883, at the residence of the bride's mother, near Lovettsville, by Rev. P. H. MILLER, Mr. John S. PAXSON, and Miss L. Virginia McNEALEY.

Died: Near Snickersville, on the 20th of March 1883, after a lingering illness, Mrs. Eliza P. JAMES, wife of Benton JAMES, aged 37 years.

Died: Mrs. Mary COOKSIE, near Taylortown, on March 29th, of pneumonia.

Died: In Loudoun Valley, March 22d, 1883, Blaine G., son of Geo. R. and Alice J. RUSSELL, aged 1y 4m 16d.

Died: Mrs. Joel BEALES, at her home, near Silcott's Springs, on Thursday, March 22d, of consumption.

Died: At her home in Pittsburg, on Wednesday, March 21st 1883, Mrs. Annie E. BeCRAFT. Native of this county, daughter of Mr. Oliver G. BUTTS.

Died: Near Bloomfield, April 2d, 1883, Anna L. CHAMBLIN, daughter of Richard C. CHAMBLIN, in the 20th year of age, from a severe burn received about 4 weeks previous. Leaves parents, brothers and sister.

Died: At her home on McDowell's Creek, in Davis Co., Kas., March 31, 1883 at 2 a.m., Susan Elizabeth, wife of W. W. PEPPER, age 28 years. Born in Jefferson Co, Va, came with her parents, Mr. and Mrs. ROSS, to Kansas, in 1873; married to Mr. PEPPER April 7, 1878, was connected with the M. E. Church, South. Leaves a boy 3 years of age.

Miss Willie PORTER, only daughter of Mrs. Mary E. PORTER, formerly of this town, died at "Brierley," her mother's residence, near Poolesville, Md, on Saturday last, of pneumonia.

Mr. Samuel J. STEER died at his home in Waterford on Saturday last, in the 76th year of his age. Interred in Friend's burying ground at that place Monday.

Landon C. SILCOTT, of Fauquier Co, died in Lynchburg last Saturday. He was on a visit to his brother, who lives in Lynchburg, and was sick by a few days. He was one of the largest dealers in live stock in the State.

April Ct.: Wills of Martina HUMMER and David HUMMER and David HIXSON were admitted to probate, A. J. BRADFIELD Exor. of the latter. Administrations on the estate of Chas. WOLFORD, Thos. MUNDAY and Saml. COMPHER. G. G. CRAVEN, qualified as committee of Giles T. CRAVEN; Sarah F. PAXSON as Guardian of her minor children; A. G. CHAMBLIN as Guardian of Jno. B. and Humphrey R. CHAMBLIN.

Thursday, 19 April 1883   Vol. XXVII, No. 45

Death of Judge Charles B. BALL, native of Loudoun, at the residence of his father-in-law, Rev. Dr. C. H. READ, in Richmond, about 10 o'clock Saturday night, after a brief illness... After he lost the position of county judge of Loudoun he removed with his family to Richmond. Leaves a wife and five sons. Funeral will take place from Dr. READ's church, corner 4th and Grace, at 4 o'clock tomorrow afternoon.

Died: At Mt. Gilead, Sunday morning, April 8th 1883, of consumption, Francis H. TAVENNER, in his 45th year.

Mr. Thomas CARTER, father of Dr. Shirley CARTER, of "Morven," near Leesburg, died at the residence of his son, Capt. Wm. P. CARTER, in Clarke Co, on the night of the 5th of April.

Mrs. Laura BURWELL, daughter of Maj. Chas. H. LEE is seriously ill at her home in Richmond of paralysis.

Thursday, 26 April 1883   Vol. XXVII, No. 46

Died: Monday, April 23d, 1883, Edna E., daughter of Alice and Benj. BRIDGES Jr., aged 2½ years.

Circuit Ct.: Will of Daniel WHITE admitted to probate and Jas. E. CARRUTHERS appointed Sheriff Admr. wwa. Mrs. Anna ELGIN appointed Guardian of her infant children. Thaddeus DOWELL appointed Admr. of Annie R. DOWELL, dec'd.

At Catlett's Station, Fauquier Co, on Sunday afternoon, Wallace HEFLIN was shot through the head by Calvin HEFLIN. It is said he was attacked by four brothers. HEFLIN cannot live.

Thursday, 3 May 1883   Vol. XXVII, No. 47

Married: By the Rev. J. A. MUMPOWER, April 25th 1883, at the residence of the bride's mother in Randolph Co, Mo., Rev. R. F. BEAVERS of the Missouri Conference M. E. Church, South (formerly of Loudoun Co.) to Miss Julia M. EDWARDS, of Randolph Co. Mo.

Married: At the Methodist Parsonage, in Hamilton, on Tuesday, April 24th, by Rev. J. T. WILLIAMS, Mr. Orlando M. BUSSARD, to Miss Louisa CARRUTHERS, both of this county.

Married: At Leslie Hall the residence of the bride's father, Benj. LESLIE Esq., near Hillsboro, by Rev. S. S. WARE, Mr. Harry J. KILGOUR, to Miss Florence I. LESLIE.

Married: At the Parsonage of the M. E. Church, Leesburg, April 5th 1883, by Rev. Samuel RODGERS, Geo. W. S. MOORE and Edith May MYERS.

Died: Herbert L., son of Joseph and Ellie BISSETT, on April 20th, aged 1y 4m 9d.

Died: At her residence near Mt. Hope, on Monday, March 19th inst., Mrs. Sarah J. WORTMAN, in the 76th year of her age. Member of Baptist Church. Leaves children.

Died: Suddenly, In Wilcox, Arizona, April 18th 1883, Henry, 3rd son of the late Phineas OSBURN of Loudoun Co, aged 26y 11m.

Died: On pneumonia, near Gum Spring, Apr. 24, 1883, Noble RICE, infant son of Charles W. and Carrie RICE, aged 6m 20d.

Dr. Aurelius P. BROWN, physician for many years in the village of Upperville, Fauquier co, died at his residence in that place on the 24th of April, in the 51st year of his age of typhoid pneumonia. Remains taken to Front Royal, and interred with Masonic honors, Rev. J. R. JONES, of the Episcopal church officiating at the grave.

Miss Jemima HAWLING, a daughter of the late Isaac HAWLING, died very suddenly at her home about 2 miles south of Leesburg, on Sunday last, of apoplexy. Member of Episcopal Church. Interred in Union Cemetery on Tuesday, Rev. Dr. DAVIS officiating.

Death of Mrs. Laura Lee BURWELL, in Richmond, from paralysis, on Wednesday night, April 25th. She was the wife of Mr. George W. BURWELL, of Richmond, and the only child of Maj.

Chas. H. and E. A. LEE, of this town. Interred in Hollywood Cemetery, Richmond, on Friday.

On Thursday evening a runaway couple, named Frederick N. DECK and Mary R. HARTMAN, from Loudoun Co, arrived in Washington Co, Md, and procured a marriage license. Enlisting the services of the Rev. Mr. HASLIP, of Sandy Hook, they departed to Weverton, secured a boat and proceeded to the middle of the Potomac River and were wed.

Thursday, 10 May 1883 Vol. XXVII, No. 48

Married: April 26th 1883, at the Lutheran Parsonage, Lovettsville, by Rev. P. H. MILLER, Mr. Burr H. BEANS, to Miss Mary E. HOUGH, both of Loudoun County.

Died: April 12th 1883, at Lovettsville, after a brief illness, Mrs. Alice V. DINGES, aged 28y 4m 12d.

Died: At Irvine, Ky, March 13th 1883, Emma Rose, daughter of Col. V. M. and George McVeigh JOHNSON, aged 3m 17d.

Died: In Staunton, April 30th, of scarlet fever, Eddie PARKER, 18 month old son of Ed. M. PARKER.

Departed this life in this city [Richmond], April 25, 1883, Laura Lee BURWELL, wife of George H. BURWELL, of Richmond, and only child of Charles H. and Elizabeth A. LEE, of Leesburg, Va. Funeral took place on evening of the 27th of April from the Monumental church where she was a member, Rev. Drs. ARMSTRONG and SPRING officiating.

The new Presbyterian Church at Waterford will be dedicated on Thursday, May 17th by Rev. A. W. PITZER, D.D., of Washington city.

Funeral of Mrs. Albert BLINCOE will be preached at Guilford Baptist church next Sunday, May 13th at 11 a.m. by the pastor.

On Wednesday information was given to Coroner H. O. CLAGETT, of the death at Mountain Gap, of a five days' old infant, in which foul play was suspected. Jury found death by suffocation caused by another child sitting on its head.

Washington Star: Nannie LEE, a white woman, 31 years old, from Loudoun Co., arrived here Saturday by a steamboat and at one commenced begging. She was sent to the police and stated that citizens of Loudoun Co. paid her fare on the train to Alexandria, and that police of that city gave her a pass to this city where they said she would be taken care of. She was very poor and destitute and authorities ordered her to be sent to the hospital until she is in condition to be forwarded back to Loudoun.

In Washington today is Mr. Kinchloch FAUNTLEROY, now of Louisiana, but formerly of White Post, Clarke Co., Va, and son of Dr. FAUNTLEROY, now of Leesburg. He was a wounded private soldier at the first battle of Manassas asked for and received a commission.

Patriot, published in New Lisbon, Ohio, May 3: Death of Mr. Wm. W. LONGSHORE, in the 82 year of age. Born on the 12th of September 1801 in Loudoun Co, Va, and came to Columbiana Co. in winter of 1825.

Thursday, 17 May 1883   Vol. XXVII, No. 49

Married: At the Presbyterian Manse, Leesburg, May 10th 1883, by the Rev. Jas. H. SMITH, Mr. John E. STONEBURNER and Miss Harriet P. HARPER, of Loudoun Co.

Married: At the house of F. M. TINSMAN, by Elder J. T. SKINNER, May 6th 1883, Mr. Ludwell L. SLACK and Miss Martha J. GRIMES, both of Loudoun.

Married: Near Guilford, on the 14th May 1883, by Elder A. T. M. HANDY, Mr. Boyd S. KIDWELL and Miss Irene SOLOMON, all of Loudoun.

Died: Near Guilford, of typhoid pneumonia, May 2d, Sarah C. Webster, wife of J. G. WEBSTER.

Died: Near Catoctin of typhoid pneumonia, May 9th, Manly B., son of Geo. R. and Patience DONALDSON, in the 20th year of age.

Died: Of pneumonia, near Leesburg, Miss Amanda KETTLE, in the 49th year of age. Member of M. E. Church for over 20 years.

May Ct.: Wills of Jemima HAWLING and F. H. TAVENER admitted to probate. Administration granted on the estate of Saml. L. STEER. Jas. T. MOTIN, col'd, licensed to celebrate rites of matrimony.

Thursday, 24 May 1883   Vol. XXVII, No. 50

Died: Near Gum Spring, on Wed. May 15, 1883, Mrs. Mollie RYAN.

Died: Suddenly, in Washington City, DC, on Friday, 18 May 1883, Dr. Frank A. ASHFORD. As a Confederate Soldier he bore the scar of battle. A devoted follower of Stonewall Jackson.

Died: At Mongolia Mills, the residence of her nephew, John W. DAILY, on Friday morning, May 4th 1883, Mrs. Ann REILEY [also as RIELEY] at an advanced age. Member of M. E. Church for many years.

Mrs. Annie FRED, wife of Mr. Frank L. FRED, of Anadarko, Indian Territory, died at the late home of her father, Geo. W. SMITH dec'd., in this county, on Monday afternoon last, of puerperal convulsions. Remains laid beside those of her parents in Union Cemetery on Wed.

Thursday, 31 May 1883   Vol. XXVII, No. 51

Died: On Tuesday, 15th of May, Ula KEEN, infant daughter of Benjamin B. and Annie KEEN, of this county, aged 9m 2d.

Washington City Sunday Herald of 27th: Wedding of Miss Sallie D. MILLER, of this city, and Dr. W. V. GIDDINGS, of Loudoun County, is announced for Wednesday evening, June 6.

Thursday, 7 June 1883   Vol. XXVII, No. 52

Died: Mrs. Mollie M. WILLISS, wife of Rev. R. G. WILLISS, and dau. of the late Thos. ROGERS, of this county, died on the 29th of May, at her home in Clarke Co, after a protracted illness.

Died on the 21st May 1883, at Locust Grove, Loudoun Co, the residence of her late father, Geo. D. SMITH, Esq., Mrs. Annie P. FRED, wife of Mr. Frank L. FRED, of Anadarko I. T., formerly of Loudoun County. A little more than 12 months ago she was married. About six weeks ago she left her new home to visit the home of her childhood, expecting and hoping to become a mother, but purperal convulsions set in. Member of Episcopal Church for 8 years. Interred Union Cemetery, Leesburg beside her mother, father and brother.

Invitations are out for the marriage of Clara L., daughter of Wm. H. BROWN, of this county, and John F. HATCHER, of Iowa. Ceremony will be performed to Friends custom, at Goose Creek Meeting House, on the 14th inst.

Mrs. Fannie B. MEADE died aboard the steamer Excelsior on her trip from Norfolk to Washington Tuesday night last. Remains will be carried to Clarke Co for interment in the old family burying ground. She had been visiting her daughter and was returning to Washington, where she was an inmate of the Louise home. Mrs. MEADE was the widow of the late Philip MEADE Esq., son of Bishop MEADE, of the Protestant Episcopal Church.

Mrs. F. M. RHETT died at her home in New York on Friday morning last. She was the widow of the late Col. RHETT, who was on Gen. LEE's staff during the late war, and subsequently attached to the Khedive's army in Egypt. She was a sister of Dr. J. F. MASON of this county.

On Wed., Dr. N. G. WEST, assisted by Dr. R. H. EDWARDS, removed from the neck of the colored woman, Sarah

JACKSON, living with Mr. H. C. GIST, a large cancerous tumor that he been growing for several years.

Thursday, 14 June 1883 Vol. XXVIII, No. 1

Married: May 29th 1883, at the Lutheran Church, near Lovettsville, by Rev. P. H. MILLER, Mr. Philip FRY to Miss Elizabeth C. ARNOLD.

Married: On the 6th inst., at the M. E. Parsonage, by Rev. J. S. WICKLINE, Mr. William WILSON and Miss Mary M. LAY, both of Hillsboro, Loudoun Co.

Married: At Helmswood, near Hamilton, on Tuesday, the 12th of June, by the Rev. Joseph HELM, Rev. Nelson HEAD, D.D., of the Baltimore Conference, M. E. Church, South, to Miss Fannie A. MEAD, all of Loudoun Co.

George SURVICK, Sr., father of Geo. W. SURVICK, of this town, died on Friday last in about the 65th year of his age. He had been a great sufferer for several years. Interred in Union Cemetery on Saturday.

At saw mill of Mr. Jas. CARTER, near Rectortown, last Wednesday, the 6th of June. Jas. Priest SMITH, little 10 year old son of Mr. Horace SMITH, in company with a little son of Mr. CARTER was playing about the mill. Mr. CARTER notified the children that he was about to start the mill, they were several feet in the rear behind Mr. CARTER. In an instant his attention was attracted by the mangled body of the child striking him in the side. In an unexplained way the child came in contact with the saw, and was disembowelled, yet survived about three hours, entirely conscious and asking to be carried home. He was the only son of his parents. His mother was a sister of Mr. John H. PRIEST, of Middleburg.

June Ct.: Jos. A. HUTCHISON qualified as Admr. of Lydia TORRYSON dec'd. Will of Jonah OSBURN admitted to probate. Estate of Silas COPELAND committed to Sheriff.

Thursday, 21 June 1883 Vol. XXVIII, No. 2

Married: At Goose Creek Meeting House, on Thursday, June 14th 1883, by Friends Cemetery, Mr. John F. HATCHER, of Iowa, and Miss Clara L., dau. of Mr. Wm. H. BROWN, of Loudoun.

Mr. Henry PLASTER died at his home near Unison, on Thursday morning last, in his 91st year. He was the father of Dr. Geo. E. PLASTER, rep. of this county in the last Legislature.

Rev. Jesse PORTER died at the residence of his son-in-law, Mr. Benj. BEAVERS, in Jefferson Co, W. Va., on Tuesday of last week, at an advanced age. His remains were brought to Loudoun for interment.

Mrs. Elizabeth A., wife of Major J. Harrison KELLEY, died in Fredericksburg, on Wednesday morning, after long illness and protracted suffering. Remains were taken to Charlestown, Jefferson County, her native place, for interment.

Thursday, 28 June 1883   Vol. XXVIII, No. 3

Died: At 177 Hoffman St., Baltimore, Mrs. Eliza YOUNG, in her 77th year. Eldest sister of John ALDRIDGE of this county and during the late war made her home at "The Glebe," For many years previous to her death an invalid. Died Saturday, June 23d 1883.

Mr. John STEVENS, a son of the late Edwin O. STEVENS, of Castle Point, Hoboken, and Miss Mary Marshall McGUIRE, of Va, will be married to morrow morning at Berryville, Va. The groom is about 27 years old and is said to possess $6M.

Thursday, 5 July 1883   Vol. XXVIII, No. 4

Married: On June 27th 1883, at the Methodist Episcopal Parsonage, in Leesburg, by Rev. J. S. WICKLINE, Mr. Frank P. LEWIS and Miss Mary J. VIRTS, both of Leesburg.

Married, in Burlington, Iowa, 27th inst., by the Rev. M. A. JOHNSON, C. F. SKOLD to Julia C., daughter of the late Major J. M. WAMPLER, C. S. A.

Berryville, Clarke Co., on Monday morning the wedding of Mary Marshall McGUIRE, daughter of the late D. McGUIRE, of Clarke Co, and Mr. John STEVENS, of Castle Point, Hoboken, the eldest son of the late Commodore Edwin A. STEVENS the builder and owner of the famous yachts Julia and America, and the no less famous iron ram Danderberg. Groom is 27 years old. ... Ceremony took place in Grace Protestant Episcopal church at 9:30 by Rev. P. P. PHILLIPS, rector of the church and Rev. Mr. HOUGHTON, rector of the church of Holy Innocents in Hoboken. They will reside at Castle Point, Hoboken.

Thursday, 12 July 1883   Vol. XXVIII, No. 5

Died: Francis H. JANNEY, in the 52d year of his age, of diabetes.

Died: In Shelby Co, Illinois, June 30th 1883, of consumption, Florence R. WRIGHT, daughter of John Wade BARRETT formerly of this county, in the 24th year of age.

Co. Ct.: Samuel L. MOORE qualified as Admr. dbn wwa of Saml. MOORE dec'd.; Geo. E. PLASTER as Admr. of Henry PLASTER; Cornelius SHAWEN as Guardian of E. S. HOUGH. Estates of John VANSICKLER, Geo. W. CALLAHAN, Mary TOWZER, and Jonah OSBURN, committed to Sheriff.

Burial last Thursday afternoon in Union Cemetery of Mrs. Lucy SMITH, wife of Mr. Henry SMITH, residing near Guilford, who died on Tuesday evening, very suddenly of heart disease. Leaves a husband and three children.

Death of James H. CHAMBLIN, Esq., after several years of mental and bodily suffering, died at his residence in Leesburg on Friday morning last, in his 74th year. In early life was deputy sheriff of this county, treasurer for the corp. of Leesburg, and for nearly 30 years up to the breaking out of the late war, an officer in the Branch of the Valley Bank at this place.

Thursday, 19 July 1883   Vol. XXVIII, No. 6

Died: Near Willtown, July 6, 1883, Mr. Wm. BEATTY, in his 73rd year.

Died: Near Lovettsville, July 6th 1883, Charles Henry SHAFER, in his 23rd year. Was ill for some weeks. Member of Lutheran Church.

Died: At the Infirmary in Baltimore on July 6th 1883, of Spino Meningitis, Jonie, eldest daughter of Samuel D. and Martha A. LESLIE, aged 9y 10m.

Death of Mr. J. W. DEAR at his residence in Hamilton on Saturday evening last, in about the 40th year of age. In early life associated in the editorial management of the Warrenton *Sentinel*, then removed to the Western Territories to engage in business enterprises. Interred in Union Cemetery, Leesburg, on Monday afternoon.

Wedding performed July 10th 1883, at the residence of W. T. MOUNT (formerly of Loudoun County) at No. 1623 Capitol Ave., by Rev. W. J. HARSHA, of daughter of Mr. and Mrs. MOUNT and Mr. McEWAN, junior member of the firm of Welshans & McEwan, of this city. ...

Thursday, 26 July 1883   Vol. XXVIII, No. 7

Married: On the 12th inst., in Frederick City, Md, by Rev. Dr. DASHIELL, David W. SPRING to Alice L. HICKMAN, both of Loudoun County.

Mr. Jas. M. M. DAVIS, member of Richmond bar, died on Monday, at the residence of his father, Mr. Eugene DAVIS, near Charlottesville, of consumption in the 35th year of his age. He was a nephew of Rev. R. T. DAVIS, of this town.

ON Sunday last, Geo. POTTER, a colored man living with Maj. B. S. WHITE, near this town, was murdered by a colored boy named Flave GUY. On Sunday night POTTER went to the house of a colored woman, Catherine GUY, who lived just back of Birkby's coach factory, and remained there until quite late. While he was still in the house, Flave, her son, who had been sleeping in an upper room, came downstairs and seeing POTTER sitting in his mother's room, began abusing him and struck a blow between the eyes with a brick. POTTER was about 60 or 65 years of age, he was an old family servant of Maj. WHITE's, had accompanied the Major through the 4 years of the late war, and had lived in Major W's family ever since. Flave GUY is a dusky mulatto, 21 or 23 years of age.

Mrs. Mary WOODS, widow of the late Geo. M. WOODS, died at her home near Guilford, in this county, one day last week.

Thursday, 2 August 1883   Vol. XXVIII, No. 8

Died: In Leesburg, on Thurs. morning, July 26th, Aileen, infant daughter of Judge J. B. and Ella McCABE, aged 10m 28d.

Died: Near Farmwell on July 11th 1883, Gaythie, son of Washington and Mollie JENKINS, aged 11y 1m 6d.

Died: At her home near Taylortown, July 22nd, 1883, in the 52nd year of age. Wife of Samuel SNOOTS and daughter of Isreal WILLIAMS. Victim of cancer. Funeral was preached at the Taylortown Church, by the Rev. P. H. MILLER.

Col. Wm. B. THOMPSON, late of Missouri, died at Purcellville on Saturday last after a brief illness of 4 or 5 days, in about his 65th year. Son of the late Col. Merriwether THOMPSON, was born, we believe, in Culpeper, and in early life was a lawyer in Jefferson Co, W. Va. Later removed to Missouri, where his wife, a daughter of the late Dr. STRIBLING, of Staunton, died several years ago. Was a brother of Gen. Jeff THOMPSON, of Confederate fame. His son reached his bedside Saturday morning shortly after his death.

Thursday, 9 August 1883   Vol. XXVIII, No. 9

Died: Mrs. Emily MERCHANT at the residence of her son-in-law, Mr. James BALDWIN, near Mt. Gilead, on the 30th of July 1883, in the 69th year of age.

Died: At the residence of his son, near Taylortown, on July 30th 1883, Samuel SHIPMAN, aged 82y 10m 21d.

Mrs. R. M. GEORGE, widow of the late Col. John GEORGE, died at her residence, near Lovettsville, on Friday, the 27th ult., in the 71st year of age.

Flave GUY, who killed George POTTER (both colored) in Leesburg, some ten days ago, was captured in Harrisburg, Penn., last Wednesday.

Thursday, 16 August 1883   Vol. XXVIII, No. 10

Married: On August 8th 1883, by the Rev. T. G. DASHIELL, at the residence of the bride's father, No. 608 North 9th St., Richmond, Mr. H. R. BERKELEY, of Orange Co., Va, to Miss

Nannie L. BERKELEY, daughter of L. C. BERKELEY, of Richmond, Va.

Died: Suddenly, on Saturday, August 11, 1883, in Ashe Co, North Carolina, Mary Lizzie KEPLER, aged 19 years, wife of Frank WALTER and only child of Kate V. and the late Dr. Samuel KEPLER.

Died: Near Gumspring, of paralysis, August 7th 1883, Mrs. Elizabeth M. GOLDEN, wife of John W. GOLDEN, in the 57th year of age.

In Memoriam: At his residence of Hamilton, on July 14th 1883, J. Wm. DEAR, in the 39th year of age. Born and reared in Loudoun. He served in company D of MOSBY's Battalion from its organization until its disbanding in 1863. After war he engaged in the publication of the *Sentinel* at Warrenton. Later he spent years in Dacotah and the far frontier. In Spring of 1868 he returned to his native county to marry.

Aug. Ct.: Administrations granted on estates of Sanford COCKRELL dec'd., Emily MERCHANT dec'd., Chas. B. BALL dec'd., J. W. DEAR dec'd., Sarah HARRIS dec'd., Jesse RICHARDS dec'd. and Wm. BEATTY dec'd. Sarah J. CLARK appointed guardian of J. Hannah MARTIN. E. A. TYLER appointed guardian of Caroline FRAZIER. Will of Rosanna M. GEORGE dec'd. admitted to probate.

Last Thursday at Purcellville depot, Mr. Franklin NICHOLS, son of Mr. Thornton NICHOLS, living near that place, while passing between the cars of a shifting train, was caught by the bumpers and fatally crushed. He was about 21 years of age and a student at Vanderbilt College, Tenn. [see next issue]

Col. J. W. WARE, for many years a citizen of Clarke County, died at his home near Berryville, on Monday, the 13th instant, in the 81st year of his age. He was the father of Rev. S. S. WARE, of Hamilton, in this county.

Sheriff Jas. E. CARUTHERS left Wednesday morning for Richmond having in charge Dennis LAWSON, sentenced to five year for an assault with intent to kill. As this is his second season at that penitentiary, he will probably have an additional five years added to the length of his present sojourn.

Martha Washington Lodge, I.O.G.T., No. 134: tribute to Mrs. Amanda B. WHITLOCK who died 28th July '83.

Thursday, 23 August 1883 Vol. XXVIII, No. 11

Married: In Snickersville, at the residence of Octavius OSBORNE, Aug. 7th, by the Rev. C. F. JAMES, Mr. Maurice NICHOLS to Miss Eliza, daughter of the late Robert JAMES of Loudoun.

Married: by the Rev. John WOOLF at the residence of the bride's father, on the 11th of August, Mr. Niels POULSON to Miss Mary A. LUNSFORD.

Died: In Hamilton, on Friday morning, August 17th 1883, Mrs. Mary T. BAKER, wife of Mr. J. R. BAKER, druggist in her 25th? year.

Died: At her home near Leesburg on Sunday afternoon, August 19th 1883, after a brief illness, Miss Margaret THOMAS, sister of Judge H. W. THOMAS.

Died: At his residence (Annington) near Poolesville, Montgomery Co, Md, on the morning of August 19th 1883, Robert W. SMOOT, in the 61st year of age.

Mr. Frank NICHOLS, the young man who was so seriously injured a fortnight ago, by being caught between the cars at Purcellville, still lives, though is in very precarious condition. Last week gangreen developed itself in the foot requiring amputation of the right leg between the hip and knee.

Mrs. Ellen E. SMITH, relict of the late Daniel G. SMITH, formerly of Leesburg, died at "Morven," in Albemarle Co, on Sunday the 19th inst.

Thursday, 30 August 1883   Vol. XXVIII, No. 12

Died: At his residence in Centreville, Fairfax County, on Friday, August 24, 1883, Mr. G. W. DEAR in the 67th year of his age. Interred in Middleburg, on Sunday evening, August 26rd?

Died: Friday, August 17th, S. R., son of Geo. W. and A. M. SURVICK, aged 17 months.

Lucullus HOSPITAL died at his residence near Falls Church, Va, on the 19th inst., at age 77 years. He lived for many years in this county, removed about 4 years ago to Fairfax Co. Funeral near Bloomfield on Tuesday.

Thursday, 6 September 1883   Vol. XXVIII, No. 13

Capt. John AVIS, of Charlestown, died in that town on Monday in the 65th year of his age. He was a volunteer Lt. in the Mexican war, and a Capt. for 4 years in the Confederate army. Prior to the war he was Deputy Sheriff and jailor of Jefferson Co, and as such had charge of John BROWN.

Died: June 29th, near Amitville, La Fayette Co., Mo, of congestion of heart and lungs, Alfred Campbell BELT, in his 67th year.

Died: At her late residence near Guilford, on the morning of the 1st of September 1883, Mrs. Martha HUMMER, wife of Alpheus B. HUMMER, and daughter of Albert BLINCOE, in her 36th year, of consumption. Member of Baptist Church.

Died: At her mother's residence near Northfork on the 21st of August 1883, Eliza, daughter of Samuel SIMPSON dec'd., in the 27th year of age.

Died: On Tuesday August 28th 1883, John William, infant son of Nelson and Ella HIXSON, aged 8 days.

Gen. A. M. WINN died at his home in Sonoma Co, California, on the 26th ult, at the age of 73 years. Born in Loudoun Co, but at the time of the discovery of gold in California he was living in Vicksburg, Miss. He went to Cal. early in 1849 and was the first mayor of Sacramento.

[MISSING ISSUE]

Thursday, 20 September 1883   Vol. XXVIII, No. 15

A ten year old son of Mr. J. P. ANDERSON, of Warrenton, while out shooting bullballs last Sat. evening was fatally shot in the back by a young companion named FOLY.

Married: In Baltimore, on June 21st 1883, by Rev. Chas. PARKER, Albert MITCHEL and Mamie TOWNSEND, both of Fairfax Co.

Married: At Reamer's Hotel, by Rev. Samuel RODGERS, Sept. 19, 1883, Mr. Duncan MANUEL and Miss Ida E. TAVENNER.

Died: On Wednesday, August 29th 1883, near Goresville, Sarah C., wife of Samuel MONEY, aged 40y 4m 14d.

Died: August 30th 1883, at her home in Hillsboro, Mrs. E. DAVISSON, widow of the late Dr. DAVISSON, in her 71st year. Over 50 years a member of Methodist Church.

Died: At Oakley, her late residence on Wed. September 12th 1883, of consumption, Mrs. Eliza A. POTTS, wife of the late E. D. POTTS and daughter of James and Nancy THOMPSON, in the 74th year of age.

Died: At his home in Cussein, Ala., on Monday, September 11th, Chas. W. GIST in the 71st year of age, formerly of Loudoun Co, Va, but for many years a resident of Ala.

Mr. Frank NICHOLS, who was injured at Purcellville a few weeks ago, died at his father's residence last Thursday. He was in about the 21st year of age. [see previous issues]

Thursday, 27 September 1883   Vol. XXVIII, No. 15

Married: Sept. 20th 1883, at the Parsonage of the M. E. Church, South, by Rev. Samuel RODGERS, Mr. J. S. THOMAS and Miss Josephine MYERS.

On Thursday evening last a colored man, named Julius SIMS, from near Waterford, attempted to board a moving train at the depot of the W. O & W. R. R. in this placed and missing his footing was thrown between the cars and both feet horribly mangled. On Saturday he died.

Dr. T. M. LYNN, a native and former resident of Loudoun County, has been nominated by the Democracy of Grundy Co, Iowa as a candidate for the next Legislature of that state.

Thursday, 4 October 1883   Vol. XXVIII, No. 17

Married: Sept. 26, 1883, at Woodlawn, Rappahannock Co., Va, by Elder Thos. F. GRIMSLEY, Mr. E. H. BENTON, of Loudoun Co, and Miss Lilian ROBERTS, dau. of Mr. William ROBERTS.

Married: On Tuesday the 18th inst., by Elder Benjamin BRIDGES, at the home of the bride, Mr. Samuel E. EDWARDS, of Washington, to Miss Sarah F. KEENE, daughter of Col. Newton KEENE, of Loudoun.

Died: On Tuesday night, the 25th ult., at the residence of Mrs. M. V. TURBERVILLE, near Centreville, Fairfax County, Mrs. Ann MILLAN, relict of the late Capt. George MILLAN, in the 101st year of her age.

Died: Ida C. MATTHEW, aged 13 years, died at the residence of her parents, in this county, on Wednesday September 19th. Youngest daughter of Edgar E. and Fanny MATTHEW.

Died suddenly on the morning of September 27th 1883, at the residence of her brother, Dr. N. S. WHITE, Dawsonville, Montgomery County, Md, Mrs. Emily W., wife of John SAUNDERS, Esq., of Montgomery County, Md, in her 52nd year. Member of New School Baptist church.

Death of Mr. Jesse NICHOLS (father of Mr. Ed. NICHOLS, of this town) which occurred at his home near Pursellville, on Monday last, in 69th year of age. Interred at the Friends burying ground at Lincoln on Wednesday.

Thursday, 11 October 1883   Vol. XXVIII, No. 18

Died: At his home near Gum Spring, on Monday October 1st, 1883 Mr. Isaac DAVIS, in the 73d year of age.

Oct. Ct.: A. DAVISSON qualified as Exor. of Elizabeth DAVISSON dec'd.; John I. DAVIS as Admr. of Isaac F. DAVIS dec'd.; Edward NICHOLS as Exor. of Jesse NICHOLS dec'd.; Harrison OSBORN as Exor. of Eliza POTTS dec'd.; Samuel T. NICHOLS as Admr. of Francis E. NICHOLS dec'd.; Harriet A. DANIEL as Admr. of John T. DANIEL dec'd.; Harriet A. DANIEL as Guardian of John O. DANIEL; Walter W. CHAMBLIN as Admr. of Jas. H. CHAMBLIN; D. H. BIRDSALL and David H. BROWN as Exors. of D. B. BIRDSALL.

Mr. H. B. MICHIE, formerly a member of the Staunton bar, but lately living in Loudoun Co, has purchased that Charlottesville "Chronicle," and will take possession on Oct. 15th.

Thursday, 18 October 1883   Vol. XXVIII, No. 19

Benj. R. LACEY, M. D., departed this life October 6th 1883, in his 82nd year. He lived for a time in Snickersville and ending his days on his farm near Bloomfield. He had been troubled with pulmonary affection for years. Member of Methodist Church for more than 30 years. Funeral on 8th of October, interred in old Ebenezer Cemetery near Bloomfield. Leaves a son and daughter, the son with a family of children, and the daughter a widow without family.

Death of Thos. N. LATHAM, Esq. occurred at the residence of his sister-in-law, Mrs. Robt. W. LATHAM, in New Brunswick, N.J., on Saturday last, Oct. 13, 1883, in his 72nd year. He was a lawyer by profession. For several years represented Fauquier Co in the Legislature of Va. Interred beside those of his brother in the cemetery at New Brunswick on Tuesday afternoon.

Thursday, 25 October 1883   Vol. XXVIII, No. 20

Married: At the Lutheran Parsonage near Lovettsville, Sunday morning, Oct. 14, 1883, by Rev. P. H. MILLER, Mr. Joseph M. BEAMER to Miss Mary E. COOPER, both of Loudoun Co.

Died: At Anchorage, Kentucky, after a long illness, about noon, on Tuesday the 6th inst., Richard William, infant son of Dr. Chas. G. and Ida A. EDWARDS, age 8m 20d.

On the 17th of Oct. 1833, Mr. James HOGE and Philah HOLMES were united in matrimony, and on the 17th of Oct 1883 they celebrated their golden wedding at their home near Hughesville.

Beardstown, Ill, Democrat – Funeral of late Lewis F. SANDERS, held at the congregational church last Sabbath, conducted by Rev. DICKINSON and Rev. SHAW. Buried in Oak Grove cemetery, north of town. born July 23, 1809, and died September 27, 1883. He came to Beardstown in 1845 and with the exception of 7 or 8 years spent in Virginia city, county seat of Cass Co, as circuit clerk. He was a brother of Major Wilson C. SANDERS, of this county.

Thursday, 1 November 1883   Vol. XXVIII, No. 21

Married: At the residence of the bride's mother, near Guilford, on Wed. afternoon, October 24, 1883, by Rev. R. T. DAVIS, B. F. NOLAND, M.D., and Katie, second daughter of the late Robt. BENTLY, all of Loudoun.

Married: In Loudoun Co, at "Locust Hill," home of the bride's parents, on Wednesday, October 24th 1883, by Rev. Dr. Isaac LAKE, Mr. James N. GALLEHER, of Charlestown, Jefferson Co, W. Va., and Miss Achsah W. LAKE, only daughter of Mr. T. Sherman LAKE.

Married: At the home of the bride's father, near Bloomfield, on the 3d of October 1883, by Rev. J. B. LAKE, Mr. John CHAMBLIN to Miss Cattie FURR, dau. of Mr. Wm. G. FURR.

Died: October 11th 1883, at the residence of Sydnor BENNETT, Esq., near Taylortown, Jane A. SILCOTT, in her 63d year.

Died: On Thursday night, the 24th ult, at her residence, near Gum Spring, Mrs. Margaret LEE, aged 58.

Mrs. Margaret A. LEE, widow of the late Matthew P. LEE, and mother of John F. RYAN, Esq., the Democratic candidate for the House of Delegates, died at her home near Arcola, on Thursday night, October 25th 1883, in her 58th year.

Thursday, 8 November 1883   Vol. XXVIII, No. 22

Married: In Leesburg, on Wed. morning, Nov. 7th 1883, by Rev. Dr. R. T. DAVIS, Mr. F. E. CONRAD and Miss Daisy HARRISON, daughter of the late Henry T. HARRISON, all of Loudoun.

Married: In Baltimore, Md, on Sat. Nov. 3d 1883, by Rev. Dr HAMMOND of the Presbyterian Church, Mr. S. J. JOHNSTON, of Leesburg, to Miss Louise BAYNE, of Baltimore, Md.

Married: On the 27th of Sept. 1883, at the residence of the bride's parents, by the Rev. B. F. ENTYLER, Mr. Robert PEARSON of Fairfax, to Miss Mattie N. HUMMER, formerly of Loudoun.

Married: At the Lutheran Church, near Lovettsville, Oct. 24th 1883, by Rev. P. H. MILLER, Mr. John Allen LINK, of Jefferson Co, W. Va. to Miss Eleanor A. HICKMAN, of Loudoun Co.

Married: At the Presbyterian Manse, Leesburg, October 24th 1883, by the Rev. James H. SMITH, Mr. James S. KELLEY to Miss Virginia MATTHERS, both of Loudoun Co.

Died: At Snickersville, Friday October 26th, after a protracted illness, Mrs. Sarah C. JOHNSTON, wife of Armstead JOHNSTON, Esq. in the 61st year of age.

Died: At the residence of Wm. H. RICE, near Darnestown, Md. on Friday night, November 2nd 1883, Miss Mary Ellen SHEPHERD, formerly of this place, in the 64th year of age.

Died: Near Silcott Springs, on Friday October 26th 1883, after a long and painful illness, Willie A. SIMPSON, youngest son of J. T. and R. A. SIMPSON, age 11y 10m 23d.

Mr. H. N. GALLAHER, senior editor and proprietor of the *Virginia Free Press*, published at Charlestown, W. Va., died at his residence in that place Saturday morning last, after an illness of about one year, aged 76 years.

Thursday, 15 November 1883   Vol. XXVIII, No. 23

Married: November 1, 1883, at the Lutheran Parsonage, near Lovettsville, by Rev. P. H. MILLER, Mr. Edwin M. GOVER to Miss Jane McNEALEY, both of Loudoun.

Married: At the Lutheran Parsonage, November 5th 1883, by Rev. P. H. MILLER, Mr. Wesley HOGANS to Miss Amy Ann THOMPSON, both of Loudoun.

Died: Mrs. Malinda WARNER, wife of Israel WARNER, was born April 12, 1801 and died October 25, 1883.

Died: At Jeffersonton, Culpeper Co, Va, on the 5th inst., James ROGERS, late and for many years a citizen of Fauquier Co., aged 79. His home near Salem, was the abode of elegance.

Nov. Ct.: J. A. COCKRILLE qualified as Admr. of Eliza SIMPSON dec'd.; Lewis TAYLOR AS Admr. of Wm. H. WILEY dec'd.; Jos. W. PAYNE as Admr. of Jos. H. PAYNE dec'd.; R. C. CHAMBLIN as Guardian of Oscar E. and Eva Ellen HAWS. Will of Dr. Benj. R. LACY admitted to probate, Jos. B. LACY Exor. Will of John TAVENNER admitted to probate, D. J. HOGE and J. A. TAVENER Exors.

Thursday, 22 November 1883 Vol. XXVIII, No. 24

Married: On evening of 12th of November, at the City Hotel, Frederick, Md, by Rev. Dr. DASHIELL, Mr. Robert L. JENKINS and Miss Rosa A. MOORE, both of Loudoun County.

Married: At Middleburg, November 14, 1883, by the Rev. W. F. DUNAWAY, Mr. Wm. A. JOHNSON and Miss Elizabeth GRIFFITH, both of Loudoun.

Married: November 20, 1883, at Baptist Parsonage, Middleburg, by Rev. W. F. DUNAWAY, Mr. Alpheus F. JOHNSON and Miss Bessie LICKEY, of Loudoun.

Died: November 8, 1883, Mrs. Margaret E. CHANCELLOR, daughter of Hugh and Elizabeth SMITH, and wife of Col. Lorman CHANCELLOR, of Middleburg. Member of Catholic Church since early in life. In September she visited her daughter in Baltimore, where she remained two months. From there she went to home of her brother, Lloyd T. SMITH, Esq. in Northumberland co., Interred on the 12th of November at Middleburg, Rev. Father McCALL of Md officiating.

Mr. Enos PURSEL died at his home near Pursellville, on Wednesday morning, November 21st in his 87th year.

Marriage license issued in Washington city last Sat. to Wm. R. GALLEHER and Miss Martha WEBB, both of Leesburg.

Thursday, 29 November 1883 Vol. XXVIII, No. 25

Married: November 21 at the residence of Mrs. ISH, by Rev. W. F. DUNAWAY, Dr. Jesse EWELL Jr., of Greene Co, and Miss Mollie J. ISH, of Loudoun.

Married: On Wednesday, Nov. 14, at the residence of the bride's father, by Rev. Samuel RODGERS, D.D., B. S. JOHNSON to Lizzie, eldest daughter of Mr. J. M. HALL, Esq., all of Loudoun.

Married: At the Parsonage of the Mt. Vernon M. E. Church, Washington DC, by Rev. Dr. COX, Mr. Wm. R. GALLEHER to Miss Martha J. WEBB, both of Leesburg.

Married: On Wednesday November 21, at Pleasant Valley, by the Rev. L. B. TURNBULL, John B. STRASBURGER, of Chicago, to Frederica P. HOGE of Loudoun County.

Married: On the 22d inst., at the M. E. Parsonage, in Leesburg, by Rev J. S. WICKLINE, Mr. Richard W. FRY and Miss Helen MOSSBURG, both of Loudoun Co.

Married: At the residence of the bride's father at Hughesville, on Thursday November 16th by Friend's ceremony, Mr. Charles KEEN to Miss Lizzie HOGE, both of Loudoun.

Died: At Middleburg, on the 9th of November 1883, George LEE Jr., son of George and Laura LEE, of Brooklyn, N. Y., aged 20 years last October.

Died: On Nov. 12 at the residence of her brother-in-law, Wm. STROUD, at Lincoln, Sarah P. LLOYD, in her 52nd year.

Death of Mr. Isaiah B. BEANS occurred at his home near Woodgrove, on the 23d inst., in the 93d year of age.

Mr. Edward WRIGHT, for several years a resident of this town, left Leesburg last week with his family to make his future home in Marysville, Yuba Co, California. He is a skillful mechanic.

Thursday, 6 December 1883   Vol. XXVIII, No. 26

Married: At the Lutheran Parsonage, near Lovettsville, November 22, 1883, by Rev. P. H. MILLER, Mr. William SCOTT and Miss Nancy TIMBERS.

Married: On Tuesday evening, 20th November at the residence of the bride's father, near Guilford, by Rev. A. T. M. HANDY, Mr. Charles H. NICHOLS and Miss Emma BLUNDELL, all of Loudoun.

Died: At his residence in Washington DC, on Sunday, December 2nd 1883, John W. GALLEHER, in the 57th year of age.

Died: Franklin FRITTS, formerly a residence of Loudoun County, at his home near Charlestown, W. Va, on the 19th inst., in his 28th year.

Died: On 22d instant, of diphtheria, Lelia, aged 5 years, daughter of Martha J. and Thomas F. LEE.

Two funeral processions, one immediately following the other – Mr. John W. GALLEHER, and Mrs. Fannie W. JOHNSTON, an adopted daughter of the late Burgess LONG, both brought on the train this morning from Washington city.

Mr. Thos. E. HATCHER died at his home near Purcellville, on Saturday morning last, in the 80th year of his age.

Mr. John W. GALLEHER, for several years Commissioner of the Revenue in Leesburg District, died at his home in Washington city, on Sunday night last, in the 57th year of his age. A few weeks ago removed with his family to Washington, where he died. Remains brought to Leesburg on Tuesday and interred in Union Cemetery.

Mr. NEVILLE, of Fauquier County, has received news of the death of Mr. Thomas NEVILLE, a relative who lived in Ireland, and who leaves him a fortune.

Thursday, 13 December 1883   Vol. XXVIII, No. 27

Married: At the residence of the bride's father, near Warrenton, on Thursday, December 6th 1883, by Rev. Mr. BADGER, W. W. KERSEY, Esq., of Leesburg, and Miss Fannie MOREHEAD, daughter of P. W. MOREHEAD, of Fauquier.

Married: At the residence of Robt. NEWTON, near Guilford, on Thursday, December 6, 1883, by Elder A. T. M. HANDY, Mr. James F. NICHOLS and Miss Annie E. NEWTON.

Married: At the Westminster manse, on the 6th of December, 1883, by Rev. Dr. BITTINGER, Mr. John T. MILLSTEAD, and Miss Mary J. THOMAS, both of Loudoun Co.

Married: In Leesburg, by Rev. James McDONOUGH, December 6th 1883, Daniel HARPER and Eliza A. SHACKELFORD, both of Loudoun County.

Died: Wednesday, December 5th, 1883, at 12 p.m., Rufus SMITH, formerly of Loudoun, but for the last 14 years a resident of Washington, in the 63d year of age.

Died: At Oatlands, on the 10th of December 1883, of aneurism of the heart, D. Randolph POWELL, late of St. Louis, Mo., and eldest son of Geo. Cuthbert POWELL, late of Middleburg, in about the 52d year of age.

Last Friday, December 7th, Mr. Housen L. HOOE died at his home in Hillsboro, at the age of 83 years.

Flave GUY tried for murder of Geo. POTTER was found guilty and sentenced to 17 years in prison. He is about 20 years of age.

Dec. Ct.: Wm. P. STROUD qualified as Admr. of Sarah P. LLOYD; John H. ORRISON as Admr. of Samuel ORRISON. Will of Elizabeth ARNOLD admitted to probate, L. H. POTTERFIELD Exor. Will of Emma A. TAVENNER admitted to probate, F. M. CARTER Exor. Will of Amanda WHITLOCK admitted to probate, Henry WHITLOCK Admr. wwa. Will of Enos PURSELL admitted to probate, N. S. PURSELL Exor. Octavis FURR qualified as guardian of Walter T. FURR, Edgar FURR and Minnie FURR. Will of Israel B. BEANS admitted to probate.

Thursday, 20 December 1883   Vol. XXVIII, No. 28

Married: At the residence of the bride's father, in this county, on Wednesday morning, Dec. 12th 1883, by Elder E. V. WHITE, Mr. Abner E. HUMPHREY to Miss Emma H. SILCOTT.

Married: At the Parsonage in Leesburg, December 18, 1883, by Rev. Samuel RODGERS, Mr. Jno. CAYTON and Miss Sallie J. HEATH.

Died: At the residence of D. F. FAUNTLEROY, near Mountsville, on Tuesday morning, November 27th, 1883, Mrs. Emma A. TAVENNER, widow of the late Jonathan TAVENNER, in the 70th year of age.

A little son of Logan OSBURN Jr., (and grandson of Henry W. CASTLEMAN) at Kabletown, W. Va., aged 6 or 7 years, was thrown from a hose on Sunday and seriously, if not fatally, injured, the skull being crushed so as to expose the brain.

Mr. Claiborn KENDALL died at his home near Upperville, on Saturday the 15th of December, of paralysis, in his 64th year.

One day last week, a little colored child, the daughter of Mary HEADLY, was so severely burned by her clothes taking fire that she died the next morning, after 24 hours intense suffering.

Marriage license issued in Washington to Alonzo DANIEL, of Loudoun, and Francis SYNCOX, of Pr. William County.

Dr. Townsend HEATON died at Hamilton on Sunday morning last, after a brief illness. He was the eldest son of the late Dr. Decatur HEATON. When a youth joined the confederate army and fought for four years. At end of war after he studied medicine, moved to Marquette, Michigan, where part of the time he was with his uncle, the late Dr. Abram HEATON in practice. A few years ago he returned to Loudoun. Age 37 years. Leaves a wife and one child. Interred to Short Hill burying ground on Tues. with Masonic honors.

Delaplane, Fauquier County: Mr. Robert NEVILLE received letters fro Ireland on the death of his uncle, Thomas NEVILLE. He inherits a landed estate in Ireland valued at from $5,000 to $7,000 per annum.

Thursday, 27 December 1883 Vol. XXVIII, No. 29

Married: At the Lutheran Parsonage, near Lovettsville, December 12th 1883, by Rev. P. H. MILLER, Mr. Thomas J. BALL to Miss Annie M. KEYS, both of Loudoun.

Married: On Thursday, November 22, at the Rectory, Leesburg, by the Rev. R. T. DAVIS, Clarence C. HERRELL to Miss Annie L. BRADY, all of Loudoun.

Married: On the 20th of December 1883, at Church, in Middleburg, by Rev. W. F. DUNAWAY, Dr. J. G. DOWDELL and Miss Rosalie SMITH.

Married: At the residence of the bride's father, Jno. W. LANHAM, Mr. Samuel G. HURST, of Fauquier and Miss Tacy E.

LANHAM, of Loudoun, were married by Rev. J. T. SKINNER, December 20, 1883.

Mrs. Adaline B. GALLEHER, widow of the late H. N. GALLEHER, of the Charlestown, W. Va. *Free Press*, died at her home in that town, last week, aged 73y 9m 29d. Survived her partner exactly six weeks, the latter dying on Saturday morning, November 3d, and the former on Saturday morning Dec. 15th.

Thursday, 3 January 1884   Vol. XXVIII, No. 30

Married: By the Rev. John WOLF, at the residence of the bride's father, on the 26th of Dec., Mr. William McDONOUGH to Mary B. MERCIER.

Married: By the Rev. John WOLF, at the residence of Mr. Thomas BROWN, on the 26th of December, Mr. William TAVENNER to Miss Sallie A. CUMMINS.

Married: December 5th at Mr. W. BRADFORD's by Elder Benj. BRIDGES, Mr. Stephen HEFFNER to Miss Mary C. WELLS.

Married: December 20th at the residence of the bride's mother, by Elder Benjamin BRIDGES, Mr. Samuel L. JENKINS to Miss Medra V. TAVENER, all of Loudoun.

Married: On Thursday, December 27th 1883, by Rev. J. T. SKINNER, Mr. Albert C. THOMAS, of Loudoun, and Miss Bettie A. SHAFER of Clarke Co.

Died: At the home of her parents, in Richmond, Va, on Friday morning, December 21, 1883, at 9 o'clock, of consumption of the bowels, Cordelia Kerngood, oldest daughter of Edward Mason and Sarah M. HOUGH, aged 1y 10m 5d.

Died: On Sunday 23d December, at his ancestral home near Taylortown, Mr. Samuel Henry FRASIER, in his 49th year. An Elder in the Presbyterian Church at Lovettsville, and farmer.

Death of Mr. James HEATON, eldest brother of Senator Henry HEATON, died at his home at Woodgrove, in this county last Thursday morning, December 27th in his 66th year, of disease of the heart. He was a surveyor and Justice of the Peace. Buried in Short Hill burying ground, on Friday, the Rev. Dr. DAVIS, of Leesburg, officiating.

Death of Beverly C. SANDERS, at his residence in Newark, J. J., Christmas morning. He expired unexpectedly in the arms of his son. Born in Loudoun Co and graduated from Univ. of Va. Confederate officer. In 1850 he was collector of the port at San Francisco. Member of the California Pioneers. When the New York 7th Regiment raided Baltimore, he was captured while enjoying a glass of punch at the Md. Club House, but was released immediately. Leaves a wife and four children. Brother of Major Wilson C. SANDERS, of this county.

Fauquier: William WHITE, colored, who killed Webby JOHNSON, colored, on Christmas Day, near Paris, by shooting him three times while JOHNSON was removing his coat to engage in a fight with him, was placed in jail last night.

Robert STRIBLING, whose throat was cut at Markham, Fauquier Co, on Thursday night, by J. E. GLADSTONE, died this morning. GLADSTONE is in jail here.

Fauquier: Tonight Robert FORD, a colored barber, shot John HANSBOROUGH, the son of a well known saddler here, through the head. He died in 20 minutes. FORD gave himself up.

Thursday, 10 January 1884   Vol. XXVIII, No. 31

Married: On the 3rd inst., at the M. E. Parsonage in Leesburg, by Rev. J. S. WICKLINE, Mr. John W. SNOOTS and Miss Ella E. FRY, both of Loudoun.

Married: At the residence of the bride's mother, Dec. 18, '83, by Rev. J. T. WILLIAMS, Mr. W. T. MARTIN and Miss Cornelia JANNEY.

Married: At White's Ferry, Jan. 8th 1884, by Rev. Saml. RODGERS, Mr. Douglas H. REDMAN and Miss Mary E. HALL.

Died: William VICKERS, near Morrisonville, on December 26th, 1883, aged 76y 10m 6d.

Died: At her home, In Culpeper Co., on December 28, 1883, in her 70th year, Mrs. Margaret B. ALLEN, wife of Edmund ALLEN, Esqr.

Death of Mr. Jos. L. RATHIE, of Leesburg, at the residence of his brother-in-law, Mr. Thos. W. BIRKBY, in this town, on Thursday last, in his 73d year. For the last 4 or 5 years been bed-ridden paralytic.

Mr. Geo. CRANWELL, died in Baltimore, Md, on Saturday December 29th. He was a resident of this town many years ago.

Major Luther GIDDINGS, of Anne Arundel Co, Md., died Saturday at his residence on "Horse Shoe Farm," in that county. In feeble health for some time, but ill only a week with typhoid fever. Native of Western Maryland, where his parents of English birth had settled in the early part of the century. ... He was a brother of Col. William GIDDINGS, County Superintendent of Schools in Loudoun.

Thursday, 17 January 1884   Vol. XXVIII, No. 32

Married: On Wednesday January 9th 1884, by Rev. J. S. WARE, at St. Paul's Episcopal Church, Hamilton, Mr. Edgar McCRAY to Miss Ella JANNEY, all of this county.

Married: January 1st, 1884, at the Lutheran Parsonage, near Lovettsville, by Rev. P. H. MILLER, Mr. J. Franklin COOPER to Miss Sallie E. MASON, both of Loudoun.

Married: At the residence of the bride's parents, Belmont, Loudoun Co, on the 10th of January 1884, by Rev. A. T. M. HANDY, Mr. James E. FLAHERTY and Miss Ann V. POWER.

Died: At Hardy, Montague Co., Texas, Alfred H. POWELL, in his 44th year. Youngest son of the late Dr. W. L. POWELL of Alexandria, Va. and a brother of Capt. E. B. POWELL, of this town.

Died: Joseph A. ALDER, at Snickersville, on January 4th, aged nearly 80 years.

Died: Lucretia V. GRAHAM, at her home in Hamilton, on December 30th 1883, aged 45 years.

Died: Near Dranesville, Fairfax County, Va, January 7th 1884, of consumption, Julia E. COLEMAN, in her 17th year.

Gen. James H. CARSON, for many years a citizen of Frederick County, Va, died at his boarding house in Leesburg on Sunday evening last, after a somewhat protracted and painful illness. Born on 11th of Feb 1808 and at age of 18 became an assistant teacher at the Academy in this town, where he subsequently married. Had he lived until the 11th of Feb next, he would have been 76 years old. Remains conveyed to Stevensburg, in Frederick Co, to be laid in the family burying ground at that place.

Jan. Ct.: M. M. WILLIS estate committed to Sheriff. Wm. H. FRASIER qualified as Admr. of Saml. H. FRASIER dec'd.

Cards are out for the marriage of Mr. John T. COX, of Alexandria and Miss A. C. DONOHOE, of Loudoun County. Takes place next Thursday after (today) at St. James P. E. Church, Leesburg.

Pensioners residing in this county [most receive $8/month, one receives $24/month]: Mary K. TYLER widow 1812; John WORNAL surv. 1812; William DIVINE surv. 1812; Rachel WHITMORE widow 1813; Sarah WORTMAN widow 1813; Jane LYON widow 1813; Elizab'h A. ELLMORE widow 1813; Harriet ANKINS widow 1813; Mary McCUTCHEN mother; Susan E. SHACKELFORD mother; Sarah FULTON widow 1812; Catharine UMBAUGH widow 1812; Cassandria DAVIS widow 1812; David CARR surv. 1812; Thad. W. FRANKLIN chr. rheum.; Charles BASCUE surv. 1812; Margaret ALLEN mother; Eliza NEER widow 1812; Susan SCHAFFER widow 1812; Jane COPELAND widow 1812; Ann M. SCATHERDAY widow 1812; Sarah A. STONE widow 1812; Henrietta BENEDICT widow; Jane RHODES widow 1812; Sarah HITAFFER widow 1812; Frances HAWLING widow 1812; Henry T. HARRISON surv. 1812; Mary Ann McNEALY mother; William J. FORSYTH inj. r. leg; Eliza H. BRISCOE widow 1812; Elizabeth ELGIN widow 1812; Jane D. WILDMAN widow 1812; Eliz'b'th A. ORRISON widow 1812; Catherine JONES widow 1812; Francis T. DRAKE surv. 1812; William H. OLIVER wd. r. ankle; Peter COMPHER surv. 1812; Susan Ann VIRTS mother; Jacob E. BORGER wd. r. thigh; George W. BAKER wd. l. shoulder; William H. BOOTH wd. l. shoulder; John ROOF surv. 1812; Mary SPRING widow 1812; Susannah STREAM widow 1812; Sarah SHUMAKER widow 1812; William BENTON surv. 1812; Emily MERCHANT mother; Susannah DERRY widow 1812; Jane TILLETT widow 1812; Euphemia GAINES widow 1812;

Harriet B. TAYLOR widow 1812; Julia A. HUMMER widow 1812; Wm. SIPPY ampt. r. leg; Mary Ann MINOR widow 1812; Elizabeth SPRING widow 1812; Catherine E. WIRE widow 1812; Mahala BURKE widow 1812; Robt. W. HOUGH wd. f. arm & r. hip; Louisa J. RUSSELL widow 1812; Virginia C. SILCOTT widow; John W. VIRTS minors; Margaret SHELL widow 1812; Mary A. RIDGEWAY widow 1812; Mary A. NIXON widow 1812; Elizabeth LOVELESS widow 1812; Lydia A. COX widow.

Memorial of Dr. Townsend HEATON, who died of consumption at his home in Hamilton, at 12:30 p.m. on Sunday, December 16th 1883. Interred at Catoctin Baptist Church. Born in Loudoun on 1st Sept. 1846 and was second son of Dr. Decatur HEATON. Lost his father by death in 1859. At 17 volunteered in the partizan battalion commanded by Col. John S. MOSBY. In 1866 went to Michigan and began studying medicine. ... [long article]

Thursday, 24 January 1884   Vol. XXVIII, No. 33

Married: On Wednesday January 9th at the residence of the bride's parents by the Rev. R. T. DAVIS, James W. McFARLAND, to Maggie, second daughter of Geo. M. FRY, Esq. all of Loudoun.

Married: January 16th by Rev. Saml. RODGERS, Mr. E. J. TROTTER and Miss Fannie A. DAILY.

Married: At Long Branch Church, January 15th, 1884, by Rev. W. F. DUNAWAY, Mr. O. Fleet DOWNS and Miss Lizzie J. CREEL, both of Loudoun.

Died: Near Lovettsville January 7th, 1884, very suddenly, Mrs. Anna J. LEWIS, aged 25y 6m 4d. She was buried just 2 days previous to the first anniversary of her marriage.

Died: January 13, 1884, at the residence of his father, in Centreville, Fairfax Co, Va, Adrian W. SWART, son of Henry and Elizabeth SWART, aged 26y 7m 6d.

Died: On Monday evening last, at the residence of her father, James B. HAVENER, in Leesburg, Cattie P. HAVENER, in her 20th year.

Died: At his father's residence, near Waterford, on Monday January 21st, Mr. Thos. B. VIRTZ, in about the 30th year of his age.

Dr. Magnus M. LEWIS died at his home in Alexandria on Saturday night last, aged 59 years. Native of Jefferson Co, W Va. He was with the famous 17th Reg. as surgeon, but was rapidly promoted until he became a Division Surgeon in the Army of Northern Va. After the close of the war he returned to Alexandria.

In Grace, the Parish Church of Silver Spring Parish, Md at 2 p.m. on Wednesday, the 9th inst., by the bride's uncle, Rev. A. T. PINDELL, assisted by the Rector Rev. James B. AVIRETT, Wm. M. CANBY, of Montgomery Co, Md, was married to Sallie J. RUST, daughter of Col. George RUST, formerly of Loudoun.

Thursday, 31 January 1884   Vol. XXVIII, No. 34

Mr. John T. COX, of this city, and Miss A. C. DONOHOE, of Loudoun Co, were married in St. James Episcopal church, in Leesburg, Thursday afternoon. They repaired to the residence of the groom on King Street near Patrick. *Alexandria Cor. of Washington Post*

Miss Nettie, daughter of Rev. Jno. S. MARTIN, died at her father's residence in Winchester, last Wednesday, of typhoid fever.

Dr. Arthur CALDWELL, son of the late S. B. T. CALDWELL, and a brother of Mrs. Wm. MATTHEW, of this town, died at his home in Marysville, California, on Monday last, January 21st 1884.

Marriage license issued in Washington on Tuesday, was one to Mr. Arthur T. TOLKS [TALKS?], of Washington, and Miss Sallie E. CRISSEY, of Leesburg.

Jan. Circuit Ct.: Estate of Sarah C. MONEY committed to Sheriff for administration. E. Florence HEATON (widow) appointed curator of the estate of Dr. Townsend HEATON dec'd., pending the proper proof of the attestation of decendent's will. John W. GIBSON qualified as Admr. of Claiborne KENDALL dec'd., bond of $14000. Will of James HEATON admitted to probate, H. HEATON qualified as Admr. wwa.

Mr. Lewis HAWLING, prosperous farmer of this county, died at his home near Oatlands, on Tuesday night last, in the 69th year of his age. Remains will be interred in Union Cemetery, Leesburg this Thursday afternoon at 2 o'clock.

Thursday, 31 January 1884   Vol. XXVIII, No. 34

Married: January 23d 1884, at the Lutheran Parsonage, near Lovettsville, by Rev. P. H. MILLER, Mr. John E. MASON to Miss Emma FILLINGANE, both of Loudoun.

Married: At the residence of the bride's parents, Lovettsville, January 23d, 1884, by Rev. P. H. MILLER, Mr. Joseph L. GRUBB to Miss Sallie V. WIRE.

Married: On the 17th inst., at the Reformed Church, Lovettsville by the Rev. H. St. J. RINKER, Mr. George REILY to Miss Emily V. SPEAKS, all of this county.

Died: On the morning of the 20th inst. Mrs. Elizabeth WIRE, aged 85y 10m 22d.

Died: Near Leesburg on the 13th of December 1883, Robert Franklin, infant son of Charles W. and Annie HOPE, aged 2m 16d.

Died: Near Middleburg on January 10th, Melissa Belle, only daughter of Jos. H. and Virginia LOWE.

Cards are out for the marriage of Miss Mary Thornton MARYE, and Mr. J. S. B. THOMPSON, assistant general passenger agent of the Va Midland Railroad, both of Alexandria. Takes place at St. Paul's church in that city on the evening of Feb. 5th.

Circuit Ct.: Will of Alexander BARRETT admitted to probate, Exor. named declined, estate was committed to Sheriff for Admr. wwa.

Estates of Edwin ROGERS, Victoria KING and Gustavus KING committed to Sheriff for administration.

Thursday, 7 February 1884   Vol. XXVIII, No. 35

Married: By Rev. Saml. RODGERS, at the Parsonage, Leesburg, January 30th, Mr. Philip KEYS and Miss Mollie CORNELL.

Married: January 30, 1884, at Baptist parsonage, Middleburg, by Rev. W. F. DUNAWAY, Mr. David A. PETIT and Miss Susan C. JOHNSON, both of Loudoun County.

Death of Mr. Thomas HATCHER, occurred at his home near Hamilton on Thursday the 24th of January.

After a protracted illness of much suffering, Dr. John Fouche FAUNTLEROY died at his residence in Leesburg at 8:30 p.m. on Monday, February 4th 1884. Born in Frederick, now Clarke Co, in 1809. A brother of the late Gen. T. T. FAUNTLEROY, who died in this town a few month ago, and was the youngest and last survivor of his immediate family of eight brothers and one sister. Before the war he practiced his profession at White Post, in Clarke Co. Entered Confederacy and was at battle of Corinth and siege of Vicksburg. ... Member of Olive Branch Lodge of this town. Interred in Middleburg Thursday where repose the remains of several of his children.

Aldie: Dr. R. D. LEITH is about to leave Aldie and locate in Langley.

Aldie: Mr. Joseph TAYLOR who lived near this place, died a few days ago. He had lived his three score and ten years.

Mt. Gilead, Ohio Register: Death of Mr. C. O. Van HORN occurred there on the 25th of January, in the 75th year of his age. Born in Loudoun Co Va. He was married in that state to Mary EMERSON, in 1834, the year in which he came to Mt. Gilead. He retired from business pursuits in 1873.

Thursday, 14 February 1884   Vol. XXVIII, No. 36

Married: In Hamilton, February 6th 1884, at the residence of the bride's father, James H. MUSE, Mr. James W. F. HORSEMAN, of Farmwell, to Miss Sue J. MUSE; Rev. Samuel BROWN officiating.

Married: On Thursday, January 31 at the residence of the bride's father, B. Wm. GARRETT Esq. by the Rev. S. W. HADDAWAY, Mr. Fillmore CROSON to Miss Virginia Brook GARRETT, all of Loudoun.

Married: In Washington City, Jan. 29th 1884, by Rev. Dr. EDWARDS, Walter S. CASTLE and Miss Mary CRIM, both of Leesburg.

Married: In St. Paul's. Church, Alexandria, February 5, 1884, by Rev. George H. NORTON, D.D. the rector, Mr. J. S. B. THOMPSON, Asst. Gen. Passenger Agent of the Va Midland Railways, and Miss Mary Thornton MARYE, daughter of Col. Morton MARYE, Auditor of the State of Virginia.

Died: In Leesburg, on Saturday last, of pneumonia, Mr. James T. FRANKLIN, in about the 49th year of his age.

Died: At Adamstown, Md, January 22nd 1884, Sarah A. SNOOTS, in her 26th year.

Died: January 9th, at the residence of her brother-in-law, F. A. BEAVERS, after a very short illness, Martha J., eldest daughter of Wm. P. THOMAS, in the 43rd year of her age.

Died. In Philadelphia, 2d month 5th, Sadie, infant daughter of Thomas and Ray JANNEY, aged 5m 25d.

Died: At his residence near Neersville, on January 21st, Armstead TITUS, advanced in age.

Died: At the residence of her son, near Neersville, on Jan. 22d, Mrs. Susie DERRY, widow of the late Christian DERRY, aged 87 years.

Died: At the residence of his son-in-law, near Lovettsville, January 21st 1884, Robert Sylvester OOME, in his 73d year.

Died: In Waterford, January 28th, 1884, of consumption, Louis N. B. LOVE, in the 22d year of his age.

Died: At the residence of her uncle, R. C. LITTLETON, Esq. near Bloomfield, on Thursday, Feb. 7th 1884, Annie P. BROWN, daughter of the late Dr. A. P. BROWN, of Upperville, aged 19 years.

In Memoriam: On the 22d ultimo, Mr. Lewis HAWLING died at his residence near Oatlands, in the 69th year of his age, leaving a wife and eight children.

Feb. Ct.: Wills of Wm. TATE dec'd., Thos. Ellwood HATCHER dec'd. admitted to probate. D. F. NEILL appointed guardian for Mary E., Maggie J. and Julia E. NEILL. C. C. GAVER qualified as Admr. of Franklin F. FRITTS dec'd.; C. C. GAVER as Admr. of Jonathan PAINTER dec'd. Estate of Edward WILLIAMS dec'd. committed to Sheriff. On Wednesday the will of the late Lewis HAWLING was admitted to probate with C. T. HAWLING, Wm. HAWLING and R. L. WYSONG as Exors.

Aldie: Marriage of Jas. W. FERGUSON and Miss Flora MAGEATH was celebrated in Union Church of this place, on last Wednesday morning, Rev. Mr. HADDAWAY officiating.

Thursday, 21 February 1884   Vol. XXVIII, No. 37

Mr. Thomas BURCH Sr., of this county, died at "Exeter," his home, near Leesburg, on Thursday night last, in the 65th year of his age. Interred in Union Cemetery on Saturday.

Mr. John H. THOMPSON died at his home near Hillsboro, on Thursday night last in the 72d year of his age. Buried on Saturday at the Potts' family burying ground near Hillsboro.

Engagement of Miss Lizzie FAIRFAX, daughter of Col. Jno. W. FAIRFAX, formerly of Loudoun, and Lt. Chas. G. AYRES, of the 10th Cavalry, son of Gen. R. B. AYRES, at present commanding at Washington Barracks, is announced.

Littleton JACKSON (colored) of Warrenton entered suit in Fauquier Co. Ct. against Clerk of the County Court for $10,000 damages for issuing a marriage license without consent required by law.

Married: On the 6th inst., in Church at Aldie, by the Rev. Mr. HADDAWAY, Mr. Jas. H. FERGUSON and Miss Flora MEGEATH, of Loudoun County.

Married: On the 7th inst., at the Reformed Church, Lovettsville by the Rev. H. St. J. RINKER, Mr. H. H. BEANS to Miss Lucie V. CORDELL, all of Loudoun County.

Married: At Fairfax C. H., on Wed. last, by Rev. D. F. EUSTLER, Mr. Morris KEPHART, of Loudoun, to Miss Jennie JOHNSON, of the former place.

Departed this life, near Arcola, January 20th 1884, John A. WILSON, in the 56th year of his age.

Died: January 9th, near Aldie, of scarlet fever, Lillie, only daughter of Rufus and Mary E. TEELE, in the 7th year of her age.

Died: On February 1st, of the same disease, Clarence, only son of the above, in the 5th year of his age.

Died: Near Bloomfield, February 7, 1884, at the residence of her uncle, R. C. LITTLETON, of a lingering illness, Amelia BROWN, daughter of the late Dr. Aurelius P. BROWN of Upperville, in her 19th year.

Died: On the 28th ulto, at her residence at Culpeper C. H., Va., Mrs. Kitty M. LATHAM, in her 76th year. Widow of the late Jno. F. LATHAM, for many years superintendent of transportation of the V. M. R. R. Only surviving sister of the late Fayette MANZY, clerk of Co. Ct. of Culpeper. Eldest son is Prof. R. P. LATHAM, victim of disease in early stages of war. Second son, a lawyer. Third, Lt. John F. LATHAM, member of Maj. KIRKPATRICK's battery and died in battle at Winchester. Fourth is a chief engineer in Central America. Was the grandmother of the wife of S. J. JOHNSTON, of Leesburg.

Thursday, 28 February 1884   Vol. XXVIII, No. 38

Married: At the residence of the bride's mother, on Tuesday, February 25, 1884, by Elder E. V. WHITE, Geo. W. BRADSHAW and Sallie A. MIDDLETON, all of Loudoun.

Died: On Monday evening, January 21, 1884, at Roseville, Nathan SKINNER, with consumption, aged 79y 10m 6d.

Died: In the city of Richmond, on the night of January 8th 1884, Norman BUDD, son of America and late Isaac D. BUDD, and grandson of Townsend McVEIGH dec'd. of "Valley View," Loudoun County.

Mrs. Margaret SHOAFF, widow of late Rev. Mr. SHOAFF, of the M. E. Church, South, died at the residence of her daughter, Mrs. C. W. PERRY, in Frederick county, Va, last week. Mrs. S. resided in this town several years ago with her late husband.

Gov. CAMERON on Monday granted a pardon to Joseph H. MANN, convicted in the circuit court of Loudoun, at the April term, 1878, of murder in the second degree, and sentenced to 18 years. MANN, was married in Frederick city, Md, in the fall of 1877, and returned with his bride to the residence of his mother near Lovettsville. A few nights thereafter a "Rattle-band," serenaded the paid. MANN's shot was lodged in the back of the neck of John BRISLIN, captain of the band, who died about 12 hours later. Trial took place in April 1878.

Marriage licenses issued in Washington, on Monday, was one to Marshal B. PERRY, of Leesburg, and Emma V. SEAL, of that city.

Thursday, 6 March 1884   Vol. XXVIII, No. 39

Married: In Washington city, February 25th 1884, by Rev. W. S. EDWARDS, Marshal B. PERRY, of Leesburg, and Miss Emma V. SEAL, of Washington DC.

Married: At the residence of Mr. John CONRAD, by Rev. J. S. WICKLINE, Mr. Daniel LINK, of Jefferson County, W. Va. and Miss Emma K. DEMORY, of Loudoun County.

Married: On Tuesday, March 4th 1884, at the residence of Jas. B. CLIPP, by Rev. S. BOYD, Miss Emily C. BASCUE of Loudoun County, to Mr. Jacob FREE of Amlikon, Switzerland.

Died: In Leesburg on February 27, at the residence of her son-in-law, J. J. STANSBURY, Elizabeth CROWTHER, consort of the late John CROWTHER, of Baltimore, Md.

Died: At "Raspberry Plains," the old family homestead, near Leesburg, on Saturday morning, March 1st, 1884, Miss Henrietta HOFFMAN.

Died: At the residence of her relative, Mrs. Ann S. WOOD, in Leesburg, on Saturday morning last, Miss Ann YERBY.

Died: At the residence of his parents, on the night of the 27th of January, little Ray, youngest child of Mary J. and James W. WHALEY, aged 3y 8m 17d.

Died: Mollie, eldest daughter of Levi WHITE, Esq. near Hughesville, Va, passed away on the morning of the 19th of February 1884.

Died: At his residence, near Unison, 23d of February, William CHAMBLIN, aged 77 years.

Died: At Chipola Farm, near Dalton, Georgia, on Saturday, Feb. 9th, 1884, Owen HAMILTON, formerly of Loudoun Co, in his 62d year.

Died: Monday evening, February 18th 1884, near Corner Hall, Curtis Osborn SMITH, youngest son of William H. and Rhoda SMITH, aged 4y 8m 26d.

Letter from Samuel P. HAMILTON, of Savannah, Ga, informs us of the death of Mr. Owen HAMILTON, formerly of Loudoun, which occurred at "Chipola Farm," near Dalton, Ga, on Saturday, Feb. 9th 1884, in his 62d year. Removed from this county a year or two ago.

Delaplane, Fauquier Co, March 3: John GLASSCOCK yesterday morning, while in a fit of passion by jealousy, murdered his wife and three small children, and after setting fire to his house, proceeded to a woods about ½ mile distant and shot himself through the heart.

John GLASCOCK was the second and youngest son of Thos. A. GLASCOCK one of the wealthiest land owners in this section. Mr. GLASCOCK was a farmer residing near Rectortown. He was about 30 years of age. In 1876 he married a Miss FRASIER, of this county, daughter of the late Herod FRAZIER. Three children were born, the youngest an infant only a few months old. The mother was in about the 28th year of her age. ... Buried in cemetery at Middleburg.

Samuel C. MEANS, formerly of this county, died at Queenstown, D. C., on Sunday last, in the 57th year of his age. In late war a captain of a company of Federal Scouts, known as "Means' Command" whose operations were mainly confined to Loudoun County.

Thursday, 13 March 1884   Vol. XXVIII, No. 40

Married: By Rev. Samuel RODGERS, March 4th 1884, Mr. Charles T. FLING and Miss Willie A. LOWE.

Co. Ct.: Administrations of the estate of Geo. BAKER, Thos. BURCH, Mary J. WENNER, Peter DERRY, and Jos. EVERHART granted. Will of John H. THOMPSON admitted to probate. Samuel ORRISON qualified as Guardian of Nora, Carrie and Mary B. SURVICK.

On Thursday morning the 6th inst., Miss Helen EWELL, of Pr. William Co, daughter of John S. EWELL Esq. and Mr. Greer GULICK, of this place, were married at the residence of the bride's father, by Rev. Arthur GRAY. They will reside in Washington Territory.

Waterford: Mrs. Mollie D. ORRISON, wife of G. D. ORRISON, died at the residence of her father, Wm. RUCKER, of this village, yesterday morning.

Thursday, 20 March 1884   Vol. XXVIII, No. 41

Tribute of respect from South Fork Grange, No. 376, Unison – on death of Bro. Wm. CHAMBLIN, of paralysis, which occurred at his home on the 23rd Feb 1884 after a painful illness of about 12 months.

Married: At Christ Church, Goresville, Wednesday, March 19, 1884, by Rev. R. T. DAVIS, Albert D. VANDEVANTER to Emma, youngest daughter of Jno. H. WHITMORE, all of this county.

Married: On the 11th of March, 1884, by Rev. W. F. DUNNAWAY, in Middleburg, Mr. Wm. C. FLEMING and Miss Mary Belle THOMPSON.

Died: At the residence, between Clark's Gap and Waterford, on Monday, March 17th, 1884, Mrs. Hattie FOX, widow of the late Parkison FOX, in about the 81st year of her age.

Died: At Clifton Station, March 5th, 1884, of heart disease, Mrs. Mary J., wife of Mr. W. T. GOODWIN, in the 36th year of her age.

Marriage license issued in Washington, on Tuesday, for W. H. McKENNEY, of that city, and Mollie M. JOHNSON, of Leesburg.

Thursday, 27 March 1884   Vol. XXVIII, No. 42

Married: At the Lutheran Church, near Lovettsville, March 13th, 1884, by Rev. P. H. MILLER, Mr. Maberry F. SMITH to Miss Katie C. VIRTS, both of Loudoun.

Married: In Hamilton, on the 21st inst. by Rev. S. S. WARE, Mr. John T. SHUEY and Miss Cora JANNEY.

Married: On March 20, 1884, at the residence of the bride's parents, R. Griffin JOHNSON, Esq., of South Carolina, to Emma SCHOOLEY, of Baltimore, Md.

Died: In Washington DC, on the 21st of March, Mrs. Catharine JACOBS, in the 83d year of her age, relict of William H. JACOBS, of Bolington, Loudoun Co.

Died: Near Waterford, March 15th, Mrs. Elizabeth CURRY, wife of John CURRY, in the 79th year of her age.

Died: At Farmwell, Va., March 23d, Mrs. Nettie D. HARDING, wife of H. Clay HARDING, in the 34th year of her age.

Died: At Silcott's Spring, Tuesday, March 18, 1884, Harvey, son of G. D. HULFISH, in the 9th year of his age.

Died: March 5th [or 15th] 1884, of measles and pneumonia, Florence M., youngest daughter of Harrison P. WILEY, in the 13th year of her age.

Mary Sevenia OBRISON was born in Waterford January 26, 1857 and died at the same place, March 5, 1884. Member of Methodist Episcopal Church for several years.

Died: Suddenly at her home, near Purcellville, January 24th 1884, Mrs. Rosannah REED, wife of Harmon REED, aged 57 years.

Aldie: Mrs. Elizabeth SKINNER died of paralysis, at the residence of her son Williamson SKINNER, Esqr. on the 23d inst., at 90 years of age. Interred in Middleburg Cemetery today.

Aldie: Eli THOMAS, colored, died on Wed. last, said to be 83 years old.

Thursday, 3 April 1884   Vol. XXVIII, No. 43

Delaplane, April 1: Mrs. Lucy SETTLE, wife of Dr. Thomas L. SETTLE, physician in this section, died at her home, in Paris, Fauquier County, this morning at 8 o'clock, of diphtheria, after a week's illness. She leaves five children.

Died: Mrs. Mary C. LOY, wife of Joseph F. LOY, very suddenly at her home, 4 miles north of Goresville, Sunday afternoon, 23d ult, in the 34th year of her age.

Died: Mrs. Jane GARDNER, wife of Mr. Wm. GARDNER, very suddenly on Saturday morning 22d ult, 57 years old.

Died: At the residence of his son, ear Taylortown, on Friday, March 28th 1884, James M. DOWNEY, in the 75th year of his age.

Wm. DIVINE, died at the residence of his son-in-law, John GAVER, Esq. near Bloomfield, in this county, on the 27th of March, aged 92y years. He was a soldier in the war of 1812-14.

Death on Friday last, of J. Madison DOWNEY, of this county. He was speaker of the Va House of Delegates under the PIERPOINT government, about the close of the war.

Cards are out for the marriage of Mr. Jno. L. RODGERS, son of Rev. Dr. RODGERS, of this town, and Miss Ella V. MAGRUDER, of Baltimore. Takes place Wednesday evening the 9th inst., at Trinity M. E. Church, South, Baltimore.

Remains of the late Beverley C. SANDERS, who died at his home in New Jersey, on the 25th of December last, were brought to this town on Wednesday and interred in Union Cemetery.

Warrenton: Trial of William WHITE, colored, for killing Welby JOHNSON, colored, on the 25th of December last, near Paris, verdict of murder in the second degree, sentenced to 18 years.

Thursday, 10 April 1884   Vol. XXVIII, No. 44

Married: On 26th ult., at the M. E. Parsonage, in Frederick city, by the Rev. Dr. DASHIELL, J. T. SPRIGG, of Loudoun County, Va, to Miss Mary E. SNOOTS, of Frederick Co, Va.

Married: At the residence of the bride's parents, (Ditchley, Northumberland Co, Va.) March 20, 1884, by Rev. Henry L. DERBY, Mr. Robert Conway SANFORD, of Westmoreland County, to Miss Nannie Lee, daughter of James F. and Maria L. BALL.

Died: In Washington city, on Sunday, April 6th, 1884, Kate Almyra, only child of B. W. and Virginia W. TREW, (and granddaughter of Maj. J. F. DIVINE of this town,) aged 11m 17d.

The funeral of the late George KUHN, step-son of Mr. J. B. WILSON, of Guilford, Va, (who was caught by a machine and killed at the URICH place, Herndon Va,) took place on Saturday March 29th, from his uncle's (Henry ABBERS) residence, Washington DC. Service at Grace Chapel, interment at Glenwood Cemetery.

Mrs. WHITMORE died at the residence of her son-in-law, Mr. John MULLEN, near Waterford, Sunday night at the advanced age of 87 years.

Mr. Uriah BEANS died at his home near Wheatland, on the 31st ult, in the 77th years of his age.

Mr. Jas. SILCOTT Jr. has followed many of old Virginia's sons, and has selected Arkansas for his future home.

Robert FORD the colored barber of Warrenton Va tried in Fauquier last week for killing the young white man, HANSBOROUGH, found guilty of manslaughter and sent to penitentiary for five years.

George CARDWELL was killed last Friday on the farm of Dr. W. F. BLAND, in King William County, by being struck with a plow drawn by three runaway horses.

Thursday, 17 April 1884 Vol. XXVIII, No. 45

Married: At Trinity M. E. Church, South, in Baltimore, on Wednesday evening, April 9th 1884, by the Rev. Samuel RODGERS of Leesburg, Mr. John L. RODGERS and Miss Ella V. MAGRUDE, both of Baltimore.

Died: On Sunday, the 13th inst., of pneumonia, Mary J, infant daughter of Geo. H. and Hattie NIXON.

Died: On Tuesday the 15th last of scarlet fever, Sina, daughter of the late Thos. HUTCHINSON, in about 40th year of her age.

Died: On Tuesday night, the 25th of March, at her residence near Hickory Grove, Prince William Co, Mrs. Kate, the wife of Mr. Chas. AYRES, in the 27th year of her age.

Died: Near Waterford, March 31st, Mrs. Rachel WHITMORE, in the 87th year of her age.

Died: In Raleigh, NC, April 3d, of consumption, Dr. W. W. JERMAN, formerly of Waterford.

Died: Mrs. Eveline SILCOTT, wife of Washington SILCOTT Esq., at her residence in Hamilton, on Thursday, April 10th 1884.

Thos. JONES Esq. died at the residence of his son-in-law Geo. YOUNG, near North Fork, on Tuesday, 15th inst., in his 83rd year.

Died: Near Aldie, March 18th 1884, of dropsy of the heart brought on by scarlet fever, Mary Annie eldest daughter of J. T. and S. C. DAWSON, in the 7th year of her age.

Mr. John F. ALLEN, wealthy farmer of this county, died at his home near Gum Spring, on Friday last, of heart disease. He was in about the 65th year of his age.

Co. Ct.: Wills of Uriah BEANS dec'd., John H. WILEY dec'd., Eveline SILCOTT dec'd., Jas. W. DANIEL dec'd. and John F. ALLEN dec'd. admitted to record. Sarah A. MARSHALL qualified as Committee of Martha E. HESSER; C. C. GAVER as Admr. of Elizabeth R. GRAHAM. Estate of Elsie THOMAS and Asenath GREGG committed to Sheriff. Wm. T. SMITH qualified as Guardian of A. M. SMITH.

William TATE, who died at his residence in this county, January last, left an estate of about $20,000 - $1,000 to be applied to the education of the colored children of this county.

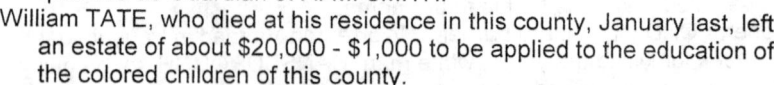

Thursday, 24 April 1884 Vol. XXVIII, No. 46

Married: April 17th 1884, at the parsonage M. E. Church, South, in Charlestown, by Rev. J. L. SHIPLEY, Mr. William P. EASTERDAY and Minnie B. ROBERTS, both of this place.

Married: At the residence of the bride's father, Mr. Joseph WEST, in Martinsburg, April 10th 1884, by Rev. R. H. PITT, Mr. Chas. W. RINKER of Waterford to Miss Josephine WEST.

Marriage of Lt. Charles G. AYRES, of the U.S.A., and Miss Mary Elizabeth FAIRFAX, daughter of Col. J. W. FAIRFAX, formerly of this county, took place at St. John's Episcopal Church, in that city on the 16th of April. ... Bride is daughter of Mr. John W. FAIRFAX of Loudoun County. Groom is son of Maj. Gen. Romeyn B. AYRES, commanding the Washington barracks. Ushers followed by Messrs. Henry, H. R., LINDSAY, and J. W. FAIRFAX Jr., brother of the bride; lastly came bride, attired in white satin, en traine, with heavy beaded front and skirt trimmed with lilies of the valley, a bridal veil of rare old lace, and carrying white rosebuds. Her ornaments were diamonds. She leaned on the arm of her father. Performed by Rev. Dr. John S. LINDSAY, of St. John's Church, Georgetown, and chaplain to the House of Representatives. ...

Cumberland, April 17 – Wedding celebrated here last night at Emmanuel Episcopal Church by Rev. P. N. MEADE, pastor, assisted by Rev. A. S. JOHNS, of Middleburg. [creased page] ___ of Middleburg and Miss Louisa A. THURSTON, a daughter of Mrs. G. A. THURSTON, of this city.

Thursday, 1 May 1884   Vol. XXVIII, No. 47

Married: At the M. E. Parsonage, in Leesburg, by Rev. J. S. WICKLINE, Mr. Thomas E. LAY and Miss Mary M. RILEY, both of Loudoun Co.

Married: At Greeley, Colorado, April 15th 1884, by Rev. J. H. MERETT, John R. HOLLAND to Miss Sallie A. BUTLER, of Washington DC, formerly of Loudoun County.

Married: In Washington DC, March 12th 1884, by Rev. Richard NORRIS, Mr. William H. McKENNEY to Miss Mollie W. JOHNSON, of Leesburg.

Died: On the 15th instant, at his residence near Bethel, Mr. Julius HARPER, in his 62d year. Member of M. E. Church for 40 years.

Died: On Sunday morning, the 20th inst., at his residence near Mt. Olivet, Mr. George W. WOLFORD, in the 83d year of his age. He was converted 7 years ago and connected with M. E. Church.

Daniel SHREVE, Esq. died at his home near Goresville, on Friday last, in the 73d year of his age. For many years prior to the war a Justice of the Peace. The last of several brothers. He was the father of Mrs. Wm. E. GARRETT, of Leesburg. Interred in the old family burying ground a few miles south of this place, on Saturday.

Mr. John V. SCHLEIF died at his home in Leesburg, on Friday last, in his 65th year. Interred in Union Cemetery on Sunday afternoon.

Mr. Geo. W. WOLFORD, of this county, died on the 20th of April, in the 83d year of his age.

Co. Ct.: Will of Dr. Townsend HEATON dec'd. proved and letters of Admr. wwa granted to E. Florence HEATON, his wife. Will of Lydia S. JANNEY dec'd. admitted to probate with Edward NICHOLS Exor. Will of Wm. CHAMBLIN admitted to probate [codicil not proved] with Albert G. CHAMBLIN and A. Franklin OSBURN Exor.

Thursday, 8 May 1884   Vol. XXVIII, No. 48

Married: On the 24th of April, at the residence of Mr. John B. EVERHART, the bride's father, by Rev. J. S. WICKLINE, Mr. Frederick H. ABLE and Miss Bettie E. EVERHART, both of Loudoun.

Married: On the 29th of April, at the M. E. Parsonage, in Leesburg, by Rev. J. S. WICKLINE, Mr. Charles W. LAY, of Hillsboro, and Miss Sarah E. WORKING, of Purcellville, Loudoun County.

John SANDERS, farmer of Montgomery Co, died suddenly Saturday afternoon while traveling in his buggy with a lady fro this place to his home near Cabin John. He was in the 65th year of his age. Priminent granter, twice elected county commissioner. Native of Loudoun, but a citizen of Maryland for a number of years.

Mr. Samuel A. JANNEY, of Sandy Springs, Md, died in Manchester, England, last Wednesday. Member of Society of Friends. He was 51 years of age.

Dr. Armstead Randolph MOTT, son of Dr. A. R. MOTT, of Leesburg, died at Riverside Hospital, New York, of typhus fever, at 11:30 on Tuesday morning, May 6th 1884, in the 27th year of his age. ....

Trial of John E. GLADSTONE for the killing of Robert M. STRIBLING, December 27, 1883, at Markham Station, Virginia commenced on Wednesday. Found not guilty.

Thursday, 15 May 1884   Vol. XXVIII, No. 49

Married: On the 1st of May, in Leesburg, Mr. John J. ALEXANDER to Miss Bell WYNCOOP, dau. of Wm. WYNCOOP, Esq. by the Rev. C. W. POPKINS, all of Loudoun.

Died: At his home, Spring Valley, near Hamilton, at 11 p.m. Friday, May 9, 1884, David CARR, aged 88y 9m 14d.

Died: At her home near Hamilton on Thursday, May 8th, 1884, of consumption, Mrs. Sarah SMITH, wife of Joshua SMITH.

Died: In Alexandria, on Saturday night, May 10th at 9 o'clock, Jno. H. PARROTT, in the 75th year of his age.

Died: Rose May CARTER, youngest child of James W. and Elizabeth CARTER died April 29, 1884, aged 2y 10m 4d.

Co. Ct.: Jos. R. WILSON qualified as Admr. of Geo. F. KUHN dec'd.; Cornelius SHAWEN as Admr. of Nath'l. BACON; T. H. CARTER as Guardian of R. E. KING. Estates of John A. WILSON and Evelina B. SILCOTT committed to Sheriff. Will of J. Thomas HATCHER dec'd. admitted to probate.

Remains of Dr. Randolph MOTT, who died at Riverside Hospital, New York, on the 6th inst. were brought to this town on Thursday and interred in Union Cemetery.

Mr. David CARR died at his home near Hamilton, on Friday afternoon last, aged 88y 9m 14d. For several years quite feeble. He lost his wife 2 or 3 years ago, with whom he had lived for upwards of 60 years. Member of M. E. Church. Interred in Union Cemetery, Leesburg, on Sunday.

Marriage license granted in Washington last week to B. G. CARTER Jr. and Rosa A. REEVES, both of this county.

Little child of Mr. George KAUFMAN, living at Woodgrove, died on Sunday last. There was nobody home during the day but the mother and her 2 year old babe. Mother gave it a few drops of laudanum, after which she set the vial down within reach of the child, who getting hold of it drank a considerable quantity and fell asleep before the mischief was discovered. Died in about six hours.

Rev. Mr. J. N. BADGER of this place and Miss Margaret HUNTON, married on Wednesday last, at the residence of the bride's mother, Fauquier County.

Mr. John H. PARROTT, suffering for some time with heart disease, died at his late residence, on Cameron St., Saturday night. Born in Matthews County, Virginia, Oct. 27, 1809, and was in his 75th year. Took up residence in this city 30 years ago. *Alex. Gazette.* Mr. PARROTT was the father of Mrs. Robert HARPER of this vicinity.

Thursday, 22 May 1884   Vol. XXVIII, No. 50

Mrs. F. H. SMITH, wife of Gen. Francis H. SMITH, superintendent of the Va. Military Institute, died at Lexington, Va on Sunday morning, at an advance age. She was the mother of Rev Jas. H. SMITH, pastor of the Presbyterian Church in this town.

Thursday, 29 May 1884   Vol. XXVIII, No. 51

Died: At his home, near Mt. Gilead, on Saturday, March 22d, 1884, of kidney disease, Mr. James W. DANIEL, aged about 57 years.

Died: On the 26th of April, in Leesburg, after a long and painful illness, John V. SCHLEIF, in the 56th year of his age.

Died: May 12th, near Waterford, Jacob MANN in his 89th year.

Died: At Short Hill, May 10, 1884, Michael COOPER, in his 86th year.

Died: At his home, Monday night, May 19th 1884, at 11:10, Alex. W. JOHNSON, in about the 64th year of his age. Poem by his children.

Died: At Goosepond, Caroline Co. Va, April 21, 1884, Rush CHAMBLIN, only son of Brook and Annie CHAMBLIN, aged 3y 4m 15d, from a severe fall he received nine days previous.

12 m. on Tuesday, May 20th, Zion Church, Fairfax C. H., marriage of Miss Susie L. MOORE, daughter of Thos. MOORE, Esq. to S.

Roszell DONOHOE, editor of the *Fairfax Herald*. Bride on arm of father, her little sister Maggie in front ....

Columbus, Ga Times of May 23d: Early yesterday morning the suicide of Mr. Thomas J. HINES, of Atlanta, at the Western Union telegraph office by slitting his throat several times with a pocket knife. He died within a few minutes. Remains taken to the residence of his brother, Mr. Randolph HINES and in afternoon to residence of Mr. T. B. HOWARD. .... He was the son of Mr. T. Jeff HINES, planter of Stewart Co, Ga. He was about 39 years of age. Served in army of Va. in late war when only 16 years old in the 31st Ga. Regt. under Col. C. A. EVANS. Discharged from Army of Va and served in Capt. W. A. LITTLE's Cavalry Co. in lower Ga. and Fl.

Thursday, 5 June 1884   Vol. XXVIII, No. 52

Married: At the Methodist parsonage in Warrenton, May 27th by Rev. I. W. CANTER, Wm. T. CUNNINGHAM, of Loudoun County, and Miss Fannie P. HEFLIN, of Fauquier County.

Departed this life at the residence of Christian NISEWARNER, near Lovettsville, Hester Ann RADLEY, aged 49y 2m 3d.

Thursday, 12 June 1884   Vol. XXIX, No. 1

June Ct.: Wm. D. VINCEL appointed Admr. of Alice M. M. VINCEL dec'd.; Virginia HARPER Admx. of Chas. J. HARPER dec'd. Will of David CARR admitted to probate. Estate of Edward TITUS dec'd. and Henry CARTER dec'd. committed to Sheriff for administration.

Thursday, 19 June 1884   Vol. XXIX, No. 2

Died: In Petersburg, Va, on Wednesday evening, June 4th 1883, Walter Kepler, infant son of T. R. and Helen MOORE, and grandson of the late James H. CHAMBLIN, of Leesburg.

Died: At Hilldale, Fauquier County, on Friday, June 6, 1884, Mary Catharine FURR, wife of M. B. FURR, and mother of Mrs. E. B. FADELY, of Washington DC in the 48th year of her age. Buried at Glenwood Cemetery, Washington DC.

Thursday, 26 June 1884   Vol. XXIX, No. 3

Married: At the residence of T. Sidney TITUS, in this county, on Sunday, the 15th of June, 1884, by Elder E. V. WHITE, Henry J. FAWLEY and Sarah W. FAWLEY, all of Loudoun County.

Married: At the home of bride, in Hamilton on the 11th inst. by the Rev. S. S. WARE, Mr. Clark MILBOURN to Miss Mollie WILEY, daughter of the late John H. WILEY.

Died: At his home near Philomont, on June 5th 1884, John NICHOLS, aged 82 years.

Peggy JACKSON, venerable colored woman died in this town on Friday last, at an advanced age. Safe to say that she was not far from 100 years old, while not a few claim that she was several years beyond that. She was buried on Saturday.

Marriage licenses granted in Washington DC on Thursday last to E. L. DODD and Minnie C. GRUBB, both of this county. Also one to Chas. H. ALLISON, of Prince William and Fanny D. POLAND, of Loudoun.

Dr. ALLBRIGHT of this place was wed to Miss Julia WILSON, of Rockbridge Co., Va. on Thursday the 12th instant.

Major John Fitzerald LEE, formerly Judge Advocate of the U.S. Army died in St. Louis. Born May 5, 1813, a grandson of Richard Henry LEE. .... [long article]

Thursday, 3 July 1884   Vol. XXIX, No. 4

Married: June 5th 1884, at the residence of the bride's father, Dr. LAMBERT, by Rev. J. H. DULANY, Mr. Willis KANNER to Miss M. B. LAMBERT, all of Loudoun County.

Thursday, 10 July 1884   Vol. XXIX, No. 5

Married: In Washington DC, on Saturday the 5th inst., at the residence of the bride's father, by Rev. Father RYON, Mr. Frank B. LLOYD, of Chester, S.C., to Miss Eolia ROLLINS, formerly of Leesburg. Groom is a brother-in-law of Judge MACKEY of S.C.

Mr. Peter ETCHER, of this county, died at the residence of his son, near Leesburg, on Monday night last, in the 87th year of his age.

And on the same night, Mrs. HOPE, wife of Mr. W. A. HOPE, living near Leesburg died in about the 76th year of her age.

Marriage licence issued in Washington on Saturday to Francis B. LLOYD, of Chester SC, and Eolia ROLLINS, daughter of John H. ROLLINS, formerly of Leesburg.

Alexander BECKHAM on Friday evening, at Nokesville Station, Va, Midland Railway, threw himself before the Louisville express and was ground into an unrecognizable mass of flesh and bones. He was a drug clerk in Washington and at time of death residing at Nokesville with his father. He has a brother who is conductor of the Va Midland. Witnesses said purely accidental. Interment in family burying ground at Warrenton.

Thursday, 17 July 1884   Vol. XXIX, No. 6

Married: On the 9th inst., at the M. E. Parsonage, in Leesburg, by Rev. J. S. WICKLINE, Mr. Joseph SHUGARS and Miss Mattie SHIPMAN, both of Loudoun County.

Died: Mrs. Jas. D. BEACH, at her home in Camargo, Illinois, June 24, wife of Jas. D. BEACH, formerly of Leesburg and daughter of Chas. PRESTON of Hamilton. She was 31 years of age and leaves a husband and 3 children.

Died: At his home, near Lovettsville, on July 5th, John W. SANBOWER, in the 61st year of his age.

Died: At the residence of her father, Mr. J. W. SOMMERS, July 2d, Sallie S. SOMMERS, aged 16y 7m 22d.

Died: In Leesburg, on Wednesday July 9th 1884, Mrs. Catharine JONES, in the 82nd year of her age.

Mr. William FAWLEY died at his residence near Taylortown, on Wednesday last, at an advanced age.

Maj. J. W. CARTER, son of B. F. CARTER, soldier in the Lost Cause, and for a time before he was 20 years of age Major commanding CHEW's battery, is visiting in Loudoun. He removed to California in 1867 and practices law. His first visit since he left 16 years ago.

Co. Ct.: C. C. GAVER qualified as Admr. of Margaret ALLEN dec'd.; George P. HUNTER as Admr. of M. COOPER; Christian NISEWARNER as Admr. of Hester Ann RADLEY.

Thursday, 24 July 1884   Vol. XXIX, No. 7

Married: In New York City, on Saturday, July 12th, by Rev. James HOADLEY, Henry S. SMITH, of Loudoun County, to Anna J. GUSTIN, of Newton, NJ.

Married: On the 14th inst., at the residence of the bride's mother, by Rev. J. S. WICKLINE, Mr. B. D. BUXTON, of Montgomery County, Maryland, and Miss Mollie J. TITUS, of Loudoun County.

Married: On the 17th inst., at the Methodist Episcopal Parsonage in Leesburg, by Rev. J. S. WICKLINE, Mr. George W. ALLEN and Miss Virginia THOMPSON, both of Loudoun County.

Died: On July 17th near Lovettsville, Miss Euphemia GREEN, in the 85th year of her age. Member of the Presbyterian church.

Died: At the residence of his son-in-law, John B. DAVIS, July 2d, Abner H. HIXSON in his 72nd year. He died with Bright's disease. One by one his children were called home until only two are left behind. Poem by Cecil DAVIS.

Mrs. Mary ROGERS, widow of the late Hamilton ROGERS, of this county, died at the residence of her son, near Middleburg, on Monday last, in about the 75th year of her age. Interred in cemetery at Middleburg on Wednesday.

Mrs. Olivia Caroline WOOTTON, mother of Dr. Edward WOOTTON, of the firm of White & Wootton, died at the residence of her son-in-law, in Montgomery Co. Md on the 17th inst., in her 78th year.

Thursday, 31 July 1884   Vol. XXIX, No. 8

Married: On July 23d 1884, by Rev. W. F. DUNAWAY, Mr. John S. H. RUSK and Miss Mary C. JOHNSON.

Died: At the Parsonage, Ridley Parish, Culpeper Co., Va, June 30th 1884, Virginia Beverley, sixth child of Rev. John and Virginia McGILL.

Died: At the residence of his grandfather, J. W. HAMMERLY in Leesburg, on Friday, July 18th 1884, Charles Paxton, son of Thos. E. and Hellen A. BURCH, aged 11m 7d.

Died: At the residence of her husband, Mrs. Susanna SKINNER, wife of Rev. J. S. SKINNER, of Loudoun Co, in the 54th year of her age.

Marriage license granted in Washington on Monday, to D. W. COLE and Sarah E. DARNES, both of Loudoun. James M. BROWN, Esq. of Jefferson Co., for many years the Co. Surveyor, and for 50 years member of M. E. Church, died last week at his home near Charlestown, in the 84th year of his age.

Warrenton, July 29: Herbert LEITH was committed to jail here today, charged with shooting John RAWLINGS, at Upperville, last night. LEITH lost both feet during the war by frostbite. He and RAWLINGS were brothers-in-law. While drinking RAWLINGS insisted upon the loan of all LEITH's money and attempted to take it, LEITH shot him in the head. Little hope of RAWLING's recovery.

Aldie Memorial Church dedicated by Rev. S. K. COX, D.D. The name was suggested in memory of the late Mrs. Henry WHITLOCK, who originated the idea before her death.

Thursday, 7 August 1884   Vol. XXIX, No. 9

Died: At her home, Shenandoah Junction, Jefferson Co., W. Va, July 22d, 1884, of cancer, Mrs. Hattie V. JACOBS, wife of Wm. W. JACOBS, formerly of Loudoun co, and daughter of the late Thomas GALLEHER, of Prince William County, Virginia.

Died: Near Wheatland, July 23d, 1884, Carl Winfield, infant son of Hector and Josephine PEACOCK.

Died: At his home, near Silcott's Springs, on Sunday, August 3d, 1884, Thompson PANCOAST in about the 40th year of his age.

Postal from Berryville informs us of the death, near that place, on the 4th of August, of Mr. Cornelius VANDEVANTER, in the 56th year of his age. Native of this town.

Rev. Samuel KEPPLER, of the M. E. Church, died Friday evening last at his residence in Baltimore, of general prostration, in the 80th year of his age. Married three times, but leaves no family except a widow. Interred in Loudoun Park Cemetery. *Balt. Sun.* He was a brother of Mrs. Jas. H. CHAMBLIN, of this town.

John RAWLINGS, who was shot at Upperville in the early part of last week by Herbert LEITH, is dead.

Thursday, 14 August 1884   Vol. XXIX, No. 10

Mr. John Thos. PERRY, of this town, died at the residence of his son, Mr. P. P. PERRY, on Sunday morning, 10th inst., in his 64th year. In January last he fell on the icy sidewalk and severely injured in the hip.

Mr. John LOWE died at his home, near Leesburg, on the 6th inst., in the 63rd year of his age.

Mr. Augustus McDANIEL died last Wednesday in about the 69th year of his age.

Aug. Ct.: Will of Benjamin WILLIAMS admitted to probate. Administrations granted on estate of John M. RAWLINGS and John NICHOLS. Timothy W. T. NOLAND licensed to celebrate the rites of matrimony. S. E. CARRUTHERS, Sheriff appointed Admr. dbn wwa of Abraham SKILLMAN dec'd.

Thursday, 21 August 1884   Vol. XXIX, No. 11

Married: On the 12th inst., at the Methodist Episcopal Parsonage, in Leesburg, by Rev. J. S. WICKLINE, Mr. Jerome DOWNS, of Prince William County, and Miss Rosie POLAND, of Loudoun County.

Died: In Leesburg, on Friday morning, August 15th 1884, Walter, infant son of Benj. F. and Belle HEAD, aged about 15 months.

Died: Nathaniel S. ODEN, in his 27th year, son of the late Dr. J. B. ODEN, of hemorrhage, in Louisa Co, Va, on the 16th inst.

Aldie: Death of Arthur LEWIS, of consumption, at his father's residence near this place on the 15th inst.

Christopher C. McINTYRE, Esq. died at his home in Savannah, Georgia, about the first of July last, in the 83d year of his age. He was a native and one represented in the Legislature of Virginia. Editor of the *Washingtonian* up to 1850.

Thursday, 28 August 1884   Vol. XXIX, No. 12

Married: On the 10th instant, at the residence of the bride's mother, in Guilford, by Elder Benjamin BRIDGES, Mr. George H. CAYLOR to Miss Annie A. SEXTON, both of Loudoun.

Married: Frederick BEACH and Alcinda SUTHERLAND, both of Fairfax County, by Elder J. T. SKINNER, of Loudoun County.

Died: At the residence of E. L. BENNETT at Clark's Gap, on Wednesday, August 20th, John CARRUTHERS, age 71y 6m 12d.

Mr. John CARRUTHERS, father of the Sheriff of Loudoun Co., died in this county, on Wednesday evening last, at an advanced age.

Death of Nathaniel S. ODEN, in Louisa County, formerly of this place.

W. B. C. SOWERS, farmer residing near Berryville, Clarke Co., fell dead one day last week of heart disease. He was 62 years of age.

Cards are out for the marriage of Mr. Wm. H. SAUNDERS, of Loudoun, and Miss Golda C. NORRIS, daughter of H. D. B. NORRIS, which takes place at Trinity Church, Marshall, Fauquier Co., on Sept. 3d.

Thursday, 4 September 1884 Vol. XXIX, No. 13

Married: On Monday, August 25th, by the Rev. Henry BRANCH, at his residence, Mr. John W. SELLMAN to Miss L. MERCHANT, both of Hamilton.

Died: On August 29th 1884, at the residence of her grandfather David WILLIAMS in Alexandria, Va. Mary Virginia, infant daughter of Wm. LEATHERLAND, aged 11 months.

Died: At the residence of her son-in-law, William TROXELL, in Celd [Cold] Spring township, Phelps Co, Mo. July 17th 1884, Mrs. Vashti, wife of Judge R. W. WADE, aged 58y 6m 22d.

Marriage license granted in Washington on Monday last to Mary G. DENSMORE of Waterford, and Wm. H. STEADMAN, of Leesburg.

Dr. Grafton TYLER, physician of District, died Tuesday week, at his residence in Georgetown, after a long illness. He was 73 years of age.

Monday afternoon Mr. LYNN, who resides on the farm of Mrs. Hattie B. GLASSCOCK, near Snickersville, sent one of his hands to a field not far from the house to clean up some briars, who was attracted by the crying of a child in a strip of woods in one corner of the field. Found a white female child, about 2 months old, entombed among the rocks, robed in its ordinary clothing, with a hankerchief around its neck. Supposed that it had been drugged with laudanum, but had vomited.

Thursday, 11 September 1884 Vol. XXIX, No. 14

Married: At Marshall, Fauquier Co, on the 3d inst. by the Rev. Mr. GRAMMER, Prof. Wm. H. SAUNDERS, of Loudoun County, to Miss Golda Calhoun, daughter of H. D. NORRIS.

Married: In Washington, on Sunday, August 31St 1884, by the Rev. J. H. RYLAND, Wm. H. STEADMAN and Miss Mary G. DINSMORE, both of Loudoun County.

Married: On the 27th of August, at the residence of the bride's father, by Rev. J. S. WICKLINE, Mr. Franklin A. SHRY and Miss Mollie MYERS, both of Loudoun County.

Married: On the 3d inst., at the M. E. Parsonage, in Leesburg, by Rev. J. S. WICKLINE, Mr. Edgar G. HOUGH and Miss Ida B. BEANS, of Loudoun County.

Married: On August 21st, 1884 at the M. E. Church, South, in Bloomfield, by Rev. A. A. P. NEAL, Lewis L. NORTHUP, of Falls Church, to Miss Nettie W. GAVER, of Loudoun.

Died: At Fairfax C. H., on Tuesday, Sept. 2d, 1884, of cholera infantum, Charles, son of C. M. and Willie NEWTON, aged about 17 months.

Died: June 21st, 1884, at St. Louis, Mo., of typhoid fever, Jos. L. MANKIN, son of Chas. L. and Mary L. MANKIN, of this county, in the 22d year of his age.

Died: On Saturday, September 6, 1884, at Leesburg, Hattie, infant daughter of Obed and Rosa COOKSEY.

Sept. Ct.: Mary E. SWANK qualified as Admx. of Aaron SWANK dec'd.; Fannie E. SANBOWER qualified as Admx. of Jno. W. SANBOWER dec'd. Wm. P. THOMAS appointed Guardian of Mary PINKETT. Jos. H. PANCOAST qualified as Admr. of Samuel T. PANCOAST dec'd.

Marriage of W. H. SAUNDERS, Esq., Prof. of Elocution, of Loudoun Co. and Miss Golda C. NORRIS, eldest daughter of Mr. H. DeButts NORRIS, of "Barrymore," took place on Wednesday the 3d inst., at Trinity Church, Marshall. Performed by Rev. James GRAMMER. Bride attired in a rich white corded silk, en train, with tablier of white lace tulle veil, fastened with a diamond star. Bridesmaids: Miss Maria NORRIS, sister of the bride; Miss Frances FEBIGER, daughter of Rear Adm. FEBIGER of the Navy, and Miss Lula FOSTER. Best man was brother of the groom. ....

Thursday, 18 September 1884   Vol. XXIX, No. 15

Married: August 6, 1884, at the residence of the bride's father in Jefferson, Iowa, Prof. W. H. SKINNER, of Loudoun County, and Miss Ella Child.

Died: In Bryan Texas, August 29th, 1884, Wyndham, infant son of Geo. W. and Annie SMITH, aged 18 months.

Died: At Oatlands, the residence of Geo. CARTER, on Sept. 3d about midnight, of cholera infantum, Roberta Randolph, daughter of Charles and Virginia MINNIGERODE, aged 8½ months.

A little more than 12 months ago, Capt. John GRAY, then of the Dry Goods firm of Hough & Gray, developed consumption. He died at his home in this town last Friday night, in his 41st year. In 1861, he joined the 8th Va regiment. The war ended, Capt. GRAY engaged in mercantile pursuits. He was a vestryman in St. James Episcopal Church. Last Sunday he was laid to rest in Union Cemetery.

Miss Julia HOFFMAN, another one of the few survivors of her family, in this county, died at "Raspberry Plains," near Leesburg, on Tuesday evening last, and buried on Wednesday.

Sudden death of Mahlon TAVENNER occurred at his home, near Hamilton, on Wednesday morning. In about his 60th year.

Marriage license granted in Washington on Tuesday to J. Forrest MANNING, of Leesburg, and Florence L. GRAHAM, of Washington.

Accident at Cameron Mills crossing at Alexandria and Fredericksburg Ry, about noon today by which R. F. ROBERTS, owner of Cameron Mills near this city was instantly killed. ... Mr. J. R. ROBERTS, son of deceased was first to hasten to the scene. He was over 70 years of age, born April 9, 1814. Member of Society of Friends. He leaves a wife and several children, nearly all married. He was a brother-in-law of Jas. M. WALKER, of this county.

Thursday, 25 September 1884   Vol. XXIX, No. 16

Married: In Leesburg on the 15th of September 1884, by Rev. James McDONOUGH, Edgar S. BARNHOUSE to Miss Estelle G. STOCKS, both of Loudoun Co.

Married: At Harpers Ferry W Va, on the 16th inst., by Rev. Jas. M. STEPHENSON, Wm. A. REED, of Loudoun County, to Miss Mary V. REED, of Jefferson County, W Va.

Thursday, 2 October 1884   Vol. XXIX, No. 17

Accident Friday afternoon near Hillsboro, Mrs. Sarah J. DANIEL, with her sister, Mrs. John PRICE, and her mother, Mrs. Jane COPELAND (the latter in the 92d year of her age) left Hillsboro for her home a mile or two distant, in a one horse carriage. Horses took fright, all cut and bruised.

Dwelling house of Mr. Thos. MUSE, living near Belmont, was consumed by fire on Monday afternoon, and a little child perished in the flames. The father was absent from home attending his daily employment and mother went to the spring. The older children dragged the cradle as far as the door, but being unable to get it out, it was soon enveloped in flames. Child was aged 7 months. Three remaining children, a girl aged 7 and two boys 5 and 2½ have only thin working clothes left.

Col. C. D. GRAY dropped dead of heart disease at Collicello, the home of Mrs. LUPTON in this place at about 8:30. He had gone from his home at Capt. F. A. DAINGERFIELD's to visit his daughter, Mrs. McCOY, who was boarding at Mrs. LUPTON's. He took his little grandchildren to his brother's, R. A. GRAY Esq. during the evening. At time of death he was Clerk of the U. S. Court here. He was in his 67th year. *Rockingham Va Register, Sept. 25.* He had a number of relatives in Loudoun.

Murder Trial in Fauquier – Case of Commonwealth vs Herbert LEITH for the murder of John RAWLINGS at Upperville on the 8th of July, was called last Wednesday. ... Found not guilty on Saturday morning.

Dr. R. S. PAYNE, oldest physician of Lynchburg, Va, died of paralysis on Sunday last. Dr. P. was a brother of Mrs. Isaac VANDEVANTER, of this town.

Thursday, 9 October 1884   Vol. XXIX, No. 18

Married: At Aldie, Oct. 1st, by Rev. W. F. DUNAWAY, Mr. George H. SMITH and Miss Mamie F. SOWERS.

Married: On Sept. 25th, 1884, by the Rev. John WOLF, at his residence, Mr. Geo. H. LEMON and Miss Fanny SEATON, all of Loudoun.

Married: September 24th 1884, at the Lutheran Church, near Lovettsville, Edward WOLFORD and Miss Sarah E. FILLER, Rev. P. H. MILLER officiating.

Died: At her home near Pursellville, on Thursday, September 18th 1884, Miss Hannah PURSELL, in the 87th year of her age.

Died: Friday evening, October 3, in Baltimore, Martha J. HOOFF, widow of the late John HOOFF, cashier of the old Exchange Bank of Alexandria, Virginia.

Died: At Powellton, on the 18th Sept. 1884, John Leven, infant son of Lucien W. and Nannie F. POWELL, aged 5m 18d.

Mr. William BERRY, of Hamilton, whose serious injury from the accidental discharge of a gun in the hands of a friend, died on Friday from the effect of his wounds. In about the 65th year of his age.

Tablet to be placed in main entrance of Hospital on North Brother's Island: In Memory of Armistead Randolph MOTT, Jr., Md. Born May 23d, 1857 at Leesburg, Va, Died May 5th, 1884, at Riverside Hospital of typhus fever, contracted in the discharge of his duty as Resident Physician.

On Wednesday, October 1st, Miss May F. SOWERS and Mr. Geo. H. SMITH, of Fauquier county, were married in the M. E. Church, South, by Rev. Mr. DUNAWAY.

Mrs. Mary K. TYLER, relict of Edmund TYLER, Esq. died on Tuesday the 7th inst. at her home, "Smithfield," near this place, in her 81st year.

Thursday, 16 October 1884   Vol. XXIX, No. 19

Married: At Herndon, Fairfax County, on the 2nd inst., Mr. C. D. CHOATE, of Washington DC, to Miss Ella V. BITZER, of Herndon, by Rev. S. Scollay MOORE.

Married: On September 29th, 1884, at Berryville, Clarke County, by Rev. Julian BROADDUS, E. P. B. CARTER to Miss Orra MILBOURN, both of Loudoun County.

Married: On the 7th inst., at the Reformed parsonage, by Dr. E. R. ESCHBACH, Robert W. SHUMAKER and Evelyn A. COOPER, both of Loudoun County.

Married: On October 12th at the residence of the bride's mother by Rev. Jas. M. STEPHENSON, Mr. Robt. A. WEBB to Miss Barbara A. EDWARDS, both of Loudoun County.

Died: At Smithfield, near Aldie, on Tuesday, October 7th 1884, Mrs. Mary K. TYLER, widow of the late Edmund TYLER, of this county, in the 81st year of her age.

Co. Ct.: Will of Mary K. TYLER admitted to probate. Martin L. MANN qualified as Admr. of Jacob MANN dec'd.; Jno. J. WILLIAMS as Admr. of John GRAY dec'd. Jas. BAUGHMAN appointed committee of Charlotte SHORTS.

Mrs. Sarah GORE, relict of the late Thomas GORE, of Loudoun, died at the residence of her daughter, Mrs. TAYLOR, at Belfontaine, Ohio, on Sunday, the 28th of September, in her 91st year, and at her

The Mirror
Thursday, 23 October 1884   Vol. XXIX, No. 20

request her remains were interred at Belfontaine, the home of her daughter, with whom she had spent the last 8 or 10 years of her life.
Ezekiel POTTS, of Hillsboro, died at the residence of R. P. W. JONES, on the 12th inst., in the 87th year of his age.
Mr. Willie GIBSON (eldest son of Mr. John M. GIBSON, clerk of court) died rather suddenly last Sat. evening at Roanoke, where he was employed in one of the railroad workshops. Attacked with convulsions and died in a half hour.

Thursday, 23 October 1884   Vol. XXIX, No. 20

Col. H. W. WILLIAMSON died in Lexington, Va last Friday. He graduated at the Va. Military Institute July 1845, was by profession a civil engineer, served in the Mexican war, entered the Confederate army as a Lt, and promoted to Lt. Col. of 6th Va Infantry, was wounded four times in battle. For years past he has been State librarian at VMI. Col. W. was a brother of Col. Thos. WILLIAMSON, of the VMI, and an uncle of Mr. Thomas WILLIAMSON, of Leesburg.

[MISSING ISSUE]

Thursday, 6 November 1884   Vol. XXIX, No. 22

B. D. UTTERBACK, of Centreville, Fairfax County, was here on Wednesday. He is 80 years of age, and spent the greater part of the late war in a Federal prison. When they came to send the last batch of prisoners out of Fort Delaware I had been a prisoner so long that all record of my name and charges against me had been lost. *Warrenton Virginian.*
Cards are out for the marriage of Eppa HUNTON Jr. and Miss Erva Winston PAYNE, daughter of Gen. W. H. PAYNE, on the 18th, at St. James' P. E. Church, at Warrenton.

Thursday, 13 November 1884   Vol. XXIX, No. 23

Married: On Tuesday, October 28th, 1884, by Rev. H. T. SHARP, at the residence of the bride's mother, William G. HODGKIN, of Warrenton, to Miss Mollie THORNTON, daughter of the late W. H. THORNTON, and granddaughter of Dr. W. B. DAY, of Dranesville.
Co. Ct.: Wills of Mahlon TAVENNER and Sarah W. EVANS admitted to probate. Annie W. BALDWIN qualified as Guardian of Eleanor H. CARTER and Robt. C. CARTER. Estates of Thos. CLARKSON and Geo. A. GEASLIN dec'd. committed to Sheriff.
Cards are out for the marriage on the 12th instant of Miss Mariana FOSTER, daughter of Major Thos. R. FOSTER, of Marshall, Fauquier County, to Mr. Samuel B. WITT, Commonwealth's Attorney of Richmond. Took place yesterday, Wednesday, November 12th. Bride is a sister of Capt. J. W. FOSTER, of this town.

Daniel REDMAN, about 17 years, and who for a year or so has driven the wagon carrying the mail between this town and Point of Rocks disappeared last Monday evening week and has not since been heard of. He drove his wagon up to the P. O. here, put out the mail, and went off leaving the wagon standing in the street.

Body of Mrs. REED, as supposed to have been murdered by her husband by administering poison, was last Friday exhumed in the burying ground near Hillsborough, where it had lain for about five months. Husband is in jail awaiting trial.

Thursday, 20 November 1884   Vol. XXIX, No. 24

Married: At the residence of the bride's parents, in Hamilton, by the Rev. S. S. WARE, on November 4th, Mr. J. B. WHEELER, of Missouri, to Miss Jenevieve THOMAS, daughter of R. W. THOMAS.

Married: At the home of the bride's mother, near Waterford, on November 12th, by the Rev. Curtis GRUBB, assisted by Rev. Carter PAGE, Mr. Joseph F. GRUBB to Miss Kate F. SCHOOLEY, daughter of the late Jonas P. SCHOOLEY.

Mr. Frank T. GRADY, formerly of Loudoun, and son of the late Dr. Frank GRADY, who lived near Snickersville, died in Baltimore on last Saturday week.

Letter from Mr. John T. MEAD, now resident at Wallula, Walla Walla Co., Washington Territory Nov. 10: Democratic candidate for Delegate to Congress from this Territory is son of Hon. D. W. VOORHEES. Umatilla Co, Oregon, near us, sends a Loudoun Co. boy to the Legislature – L. B. COX (nephew of Col. N. BERKELEY).

Marshall, November 12: Marriage of Mrs. Samuel B. WITT and Mariana FOSTER at 1:30 p.m. Bride is yet in her teens. ... Performed by Rev. William E. HATCHER, of Richmond.

Marriage on Tuesday of Miss Sadie R. TYLER, daughter of Mr. Nathaniel TYLER at "Belmont" near Alexandria, to William C. MARSHALL, of Warrenton, editor of the *Virginian*. Performed by Rev. Dr. TOWNSEND of the Church of the Incarnation, Washington. ... *Alex. Gazette* of the 13th.

Miss Erva Winston PAYNE, daughter of Gen. Wm. H. PAYNE, and Eppa HUNTON Jr., son of Gen. Eppa HUNTON, were married in the Episcopal Church in Warrenton on Tuesday night last.

Thursday, 27 November 1884   Vol. XXIX, No. 25

Married: Nov. 17th 1884, at the house of the bride, by Rev. J. T. WILLIAMS, John F. McCLANAHAN and Annie C. MOSSBURG.

Married: By Rev. James McDONOUGH, November 18th 1883 [1884], in Leesburg, George W. UMBAUGH to Miss Mary A. HARPER, all of Loudoun.

Married: On Nov. 12th, 1884, at the residence of the bride's parents, in Frederick City, by the Rev. Osborne INGLE, Allen B. MONTZ, of Shenandoah Co, to Miss Belle W. McGILL, dau. of Dr. T. J. McGILL.

Married: On Wednesday, November 19, at the residence of the bride's father, in Richmond, by Rev. Wm. H. CHRISTIAN, Barton Haxall GRUNDY and Miriam, daughter of Mr. Thomas BRANCH.

Married: At. St. Paul's Lutheran Church, Loudoun County, by Rev. E. H. HENRY, on November 20th, 1884, John W. EVERHART and Emma D. POTTS.

Benjamin Franklin TAYLOR died at the residence of his son-in-law, Mr. OTLEY, near Unison, on Wednesday of last week, of heart disease, in the 80th year of his age. Justice of Peace for many years. Principal for a long time of a male school at Hughesville.

Small dwelling house on Short Hill, near Hillsboro, was destroyed by fire last Friday afternoon and four children consumed in the flames. House was occupied by Henry JACKSON and Robt. FURR, colored men and their families. Men were at work and wives went to Hillsboro to make some purchases, leaving four children from one to six years locked up in the house. Fire of unknown cause broke out. The following day $75 to $100 had been collected for the families.

Geo. F. SHAW, of Washington city, and grandson of Maj. Jas. F. DIVINE, of this town, has been designated as asst. mail messenger from Washington city P.O., at $840 per annum.

Decatur, Ill. Republican of November 20th: Death of Capt. David L. ALLEN, in the 79th year of his age. Located in that city as early as 1828, before the county was organized. He was born in Loudoun Co, Va in 1806, and removed thence to Kentucky and Tennessee, coming to Decatur in 1828. Member of Baptist church.

On the 5th inst. at Methodist Church in Middleburg, marriage of Mr. S. R. FRED and Miss K. C. BROWN, by Rev. C. L. DAMARON assisted by Rev Jacob HOPKINS. Couple proceeded by Miss Lizzie CARTER, of Mountsville, Miss Mollie HOUGH, of Leesburg, Miss BAYNOR, of Baltimore and Misses Fannie CARTER, Nannie STEVENS and Viva HAYNES, of Middleburg as attendants. Immediately after the ceremony they started to the Indian Territory where he is engaged in business. ...

On the 20th inst. at the Baptist Church in Middleburg, marriage of Mr. E. W. SKINNER and Miss Kate, daughter of Mr. A. M. SMITH. On this occasion Mr. D. K. SMITH and Robert COCKRAN were masters of ceremony. Attendants were Mr. S. SKINNER and Miss Nellie SWARTS, Mr. C. SMITH and Miss A. Lee FRANCES, Mr. JONES, of Front Royal and Miss FOSTER, of Marshall, and Mr. C. WHITACRE and Miss Ella, bride's sister. Rev. W. F. DUNAWAY performed the ceremony.

Thursday, 4 December 1884   Vol. XXIX, No. 26

Married: In Leesburg, November 27th by Rev. Saml. RODGERS, Saml. A. B. MOSSBURG and Ida V. SKINNER, daughter of Quincy A. and Annie E. SKINNER, all of Loudoun County.

Thursday, 11 December 1884   Vol. XXIX, No. 27

Married: At Waterford, in the Presbyterian Manse, November 26th, by Rev. L. B. TURNBULL, Bartlow COOPER to Miss Sallie EVERHART, both of Loudoun.

Married: At the residence of Mr. Wm. HAVENER, by Rev. G. W. POPKINS, on December 3, 1884, Mr. L. H. HAVENER and Miss Alice CROWSON. All of Loudoun.

Died: At the residence of her son-in-law, Mr. Thos. J. CARTER, near Philomont, on Sunday, October 12, 1884, Mrs. Susan CONNER, in the 75th year of her age.

At her home in this town, at 4 o'clock Saturday morning, December 6th, 1884, of inflammation of the stomach, Mrs. Margaret A. CLINE, wife of Mr. William CLINE, in the 61st year of her age. Member of M. E. Church, South for 43 years. Bed-ridden for five months. Funeral took place on Monday morning, Rev. Dr ROGERS, assisted by Revs. J. S. GARDNER, R. T. DAVIS and Jas. H. SMITH officiating. Interred in Union Cemetery.

Hugh S. THOMPSON, Esq. died at his home near Hillsboro on Tuesday morning last, of typhoid fever, in about the 65th year of his age.

G. R. HATCHER, of Upper Fauquier, died at his residence near Rectortown, Wednesday, November 26th, in his 75th year.

Dec. Ct.: Wills of Michael SANBOWER dec'd. and Susan CONNER dec'd. admitted to probate. Henry H. TAVENNER appointed Guardian of Carroll A. TAVENNER; John T. HURST as Admr. of Samuel S. HURST dec'd. C. W. DOWNEY qualified as Guardian of Vitas C. and Zula S. DOWNEY.

Moses WARING, one of Mobile's (Alabama) wealthiest citizens, died Monday night, aged 76 years. He was a native of Connecticut. He went to Mobile in 1822. He leaves a son and three daughters One of the latter is the wife of Dr. Alfred H. POWELL (formerly of Leesburg) and another is the wife of Capt. Thomas HARRISON, of Mobile.

On the 2d inst. at the home of Mr. James DILLON, near Philomont, marriage of his eldest daughter, Rosie, to Mr. James F. HAMPTON. Bride was equipped in a jaunty travelling suit of brown. Attendants were Mr. Will PANCOST and Miss Jennie NICHOLS, Mr. Frank FENTON and Miss Maggie NICHOLS, Mr. Isaac PIGGOTT and Miss Mary FENTON. Performed by Rev. NEAL, of the M. E. Church. ...

Thursday, 18 December 1884   Vol. XXIX, No. 28

Married: At Middleburg, Dec. 16, by Rev. W. F. DUNNAWAY, Mr. Wm. H. KEPHART and Miss Annie SKILLMAN.

Married: On the 4th inst., at 921 N. Broad St., Philadelphia, under the care of the Monthly Meeting of Friends, of Philadelphia, Robert M. JANNEY (formerly of Loudoun) to Emily B. SMITH, daughter of Wm. C. SMITH.

Married: On Thursday, the 11th inst. in the parlors of Warren Green hotel, by Rev. Mr. F. B. BOSTON, Mr. Marshall D. CREEL to Miss Nettie A. GAINES, both of Upper Fauquier.

Married: In Washington DC, Dec. 10, by Rev. D. W. FAUNCE, Mr. W. S. DOWELL and Miss Matilda HOLDEN, both of Fauquier Co. Va.

Mr. Peter W. JOHNSON, of this town, died very suddenly on Friday last, in his 72d year. He ate his dinner and a half hour later was found in an adjoining room rigid in death, of apoplexy. Funeral took place on Sunday, Rev. J. H. SMITH officiating. Interred in Union Cemetery.

Mr. Michael SANBOWER died at his residence near Lovettsville on the 28th of Nov., aged 86y 9m 13d. Born and raised in this county.

In Union Church of this place, on Tuesday, Miss Gertrude LYNN and Mr. Beverley ADAMS, attended by Misses ADAMS and Miss CHAMBLIN, Messrs. ADAMS and Mr. TURNER, were married by Rev. Mr. JOHNS.

On Thursday last, Mr. Lucian CARTER of this place was married to Miss Alice CARTER, of Mountsville, by the Rev. Mr. BAGER.

Fredericksburg on the 11th, wedding of former citizen of Leesburg: Marriage last night of Mr. Samuel W. TIMMS, of Washington DC to Miss Susie French TURNER of this place, performed by Rev. Dr. MURDAUGH, at Trinity Episcopal Church. Bride, a blond, attired in travelling costume.

Thursday, 25 December 1884   Vol. XXIX, No. 29

Married: At the Valley Meeting House, December 17th 1884, by Elder E. V. WHITE, Mr. John B. WHITE to Miss Annie KIDWELL, both of Loudoun County.

Married: At the Manse, Leesburg, December 18, 1884, by the Rev. J. H. SMITH, Mr. Chas. W. MYERS and Miss Bettie MULLEN, both of Loudoun County.

Married: On the 11th inst., at Mt. Olivet M. E. Church, by Rev. J. S. WICKLINE, Mr. John REED and Miss Ida V. ORRISON, both of Loudoun County.

Married: At the residence of Thomas HAVENNER, near Leesburg, December 16th 1884, by Rev. C. T. HERNDON, Mr. W. Clayton HAVENNER and Miss Laura T. HAVENNER, all of Loudoun.

Married: At Mt. Hope Baptist Church, on the 17th inst., by Rev. G. W. POPKINS, Mr. John W. THOMPSON and Miss Susan V. MOFFETT, all of Loudoun.

Married: In the Congregational Church, Herndon, Va, December 16th by Rev. L. B. TURNBULL, assisted by Rev. Jno. McKEAN, Jas. B. GOULD and Miss Clara DOWNING, both of Fairfax County.

Married: At Leesburg, Dec. 18th by the Rev. James H. SMITH, Mr. Geo. E. ROLLISON and Miss Jeannette CLARKSON, both of Loudoun.

Married: At Belmont Chapel, December 18, 1884, by the Rev. R. T. DAVIS, Mr. Isaac GREENLEASE to Miss Ida, eldest daughter of the late R. E. FURR, all of Loudoun County.

Died: At the residence of her father, William G. FURR, near Bloomfield, December 14th, 1884, Mrs. Catherine CHAMBLIN, wife of John CHAMBLIN, in her 29th year. She was a member of the Ebenezer Baptist Church. Funeral services by her pastor Dr. J. B. Lake.

Died: In Loudoun Co, October 4th 1884, Annie M. POTTS, aged 30y 4m 10d, wife of Walter POTTS and daughter of Annie C. SHRIVER, after a protracted illness of typhoid fever.

Charles Fenton MERCER, colored, well known in Baltimore for the past 8 years as steward of the Md Jockey Club, died at 2 o'clock yesterday afternoon at his residence, No. 152 Cathedral Street. He was born in Leesburg and came to Baltimore many years ago.

Thursday, 1 January 1885   Vol. XXIX, No. 30

Married: At Mt. Hope Church, on the 23d inst. by Rev. G. W. POPKINS, Mr. Bernard THOMPSON and Miss Lizzie MUNDAY, all of Loudoun County.

Married: At the house of the bride's brother, Mr. E. E. THOMPSON, Leesburg, December 23d 1884, by Rev. James H. SMITH, Mr. Fitzhugh KERNS, of Loudoun County, and Miss Josephine THOMPSON, of Leesburg.

Married: On the 23d inst., at "River Bend," Fairfax Co. by Rev. Dr. DULANY, Mr. Chas. J. PRESGRAVES to Miss Laura L., youngest daughter of Charles W. HENDERSON, Esq.

Married: At the residence of the bride's mother, near Woodgrove, December 23d, by Rev. J. T. WILLIAMS, Mr. Robert WYNKOOP to Miss Mollie WYNKOOP, both of Loudoun.

Married: On Tuesday last, at the residence of the bride's father, by Friends' Ceremony, Mr. J. Walter SMITH to Miss Ella, youngest daughter of Thomas BROWN, all of Loudoun.

Died: At her home, near Unison, on Dec. 8, 1884, Mrs. Catherine CRAIN. Three score and ten years. Wife of Dr. P. H. CRAIN.

Thursday, 8 January 1885   Vol. XXIX, No. 31

Married: At the residence of the bride's parents, near Goresville on Tuesday morning, January 6th 1885, by Rev. Carter PAGE, Mr. Geo. F. LEWIS, of Washington, formerly of this county, and Lula, youngest daughter of Dr. N. G. WEST.

Married: At the M. E. Parsonage, on the 1st day of January 1885, by Rev. J. S. WICKLINE, Mr. Eli P. HOUSE and Miss Ella M. UNDERWOOD, of Hillsboro.

Married: At the New Jerusalem E. Lutheran Church, December 18th 1884, by Rev. P. H. MILLER, Mr. Benj. M. COOPER and Miss Maggie E. FILLINGANE.

Married: Dec. 25th 1884, by Rev. P. H. MILLER, at the New Jerusalem E. Lutheran Church, Mr. John F. SMITH and Miss Sarah V. FRY.

Married: At Reamer's Hotel, Leesburg, December 31st, by Rev. Samuel RODGERS, Mr. John DUNN and Miss Minnie ALLISON, all of Loudoun.

Died: Alexander Henry, son of Alexander and Ada SPINKS, born June 28th 1884, died about 12 p.m. December 31st 1884.

Mrs. Emily LAYCOCK, wife of Mr. Joseph LAYCOCK, died at her home a few miles from Leesburg on Sunday morning December 28th 1884, in about the 81st year of her age. Member of M. E. Church, South. Interred in burying ground at Grove Church on Monday. Her husband is now in his 86th year.

Thursday, 15 January 1885   Vol. XXIX, No. 32

Married: On Thursday, January 8th 1885, in St. Louis, by the Rev. Father POWER, Henry HARRISON, Esq. of Loudoun County, to Ann, daughter of the late Maj. John F. LEE, of Washington DC.

Married: At the Parsonage, January 8th by Rev. Samuel RODGERS, Mr. Wm. LEWIS and Miss Susannah LOWE, all of Loudoun.

Married: At the Parsonage, January 8th by Rev. Samuel RODGERS, Mr. Jesse A. POOLE and Miss Mollie SWEEDY, all of Loudoun.

Married: At the residence of the bride's parents, near Aldie, on the 18th of December 1884, by Elder Joseph BADGER, Mr. William J. SWART, of Fauquier Co. to Miss Bertie HIXSON, of Loudoun.

Died: Suddenly, at Milwaukee, Wis., on the 26th Dec. 1884, Arthur Robert FAUNTLEROY (formerly of U.S. Coast and Geodetic Survey) son of the late Robert Henry and Jane Dale FAUNTLEROY.

Co. Ct.: Wm. D. THOMPSON and Jno. A. THOMPSON qualified as Admrs. of Hugh S. THOMPSON; Wm. G. JENKINS as Admr. of Wm. S. JENKINS dec'd. Estates of E. Stanley HOUGH and Chas. LEWIS committed to Sheriff. Rev. Father Thos. J. WILSON licensed to celebrate the rites of matrimony. Geo. W. CHICK qualified as Guardian of Chas. E. CHICK.

Description of house of Henry HARRISON, Esq. just built on ten acre lot at north end of King St., Leesburg. [long, detailed article]

Mr. Lawrence P. BAYNE, formerly of this city, died at his residence in New York, on Thursday, in his 71st year, was a native of Westmoreland Co, and in his early life engaged in business in this city. Afterwards had a store at Middleburg, and removed to Baltimore. ... Member of Baptist Church. Wife, a daughter of the late Dr. Bushrod RUST, of Loudoun, survives him. Leaves 3 sons and 2 daughters Two of his brothers reside in Baltimore – Messrs. Wm. and Patterson BAYNE. Interred in Baltimore.

Mr. Chas. E. F. PAYNE, head of the banking house of Payne & Co., of Warrenton, and a brother of Gen. Wm. H. PAYNE, died at his home in Warrenton on Thursday night after a somewhat protracted illness. Leaves a wife and several small children.

Thursday, 22 January 1885   Vol. XXIX, No. 33

Married: At the Parsonage of the M. E. Church in Hamilton by Rev. J. T. WILLIAMS, on January 20th 1885, Mr. J. P. ORRISON and Miss Lillie B., daughter of Jonah NIXON Esq., both of Loudoun.

Married: In Hamilton at the home of Mrs. Margaret JANNEY, on Wednesday, January 11th by the Rev. L. B. TURNBULL, Mr. Charles L. CLARKE, of Covington Va, to Miss Josephine M. THOMPSON, of Loudoun County.

Died: In Hamilton on Monday January 12th of consumption, Miss Nettie BARTLETT, in the 20th year of her age.

Died: In Hamilton, on Wednesday, January 14th, Mrs. Catherine H. TAVENNER, wife of Mr. E. H. TAVENNER, in her 34th year.

Died: Near Philomont, on Saturday, the 10th of January 1885, Mrs. Jane E. DODD, wife of Ashton DODD, in her 73rd year. Funeral by her pastor, Rev. W. F. DUNNAWAY. Interment in cemetery at Middleburg.

Departed this life, on the 13th inst., in Washington City DC, at the residence of his son-in-law, Josiah MILLARD, after a brief illness, Sir [L]ancerlot KARNER, in his 86th year. Born and reared in Massachusetts and moved his family to Loudoun County 29 years ago. He purchased a farm adjoining Gum Spring.

From Clarkesville, *Texas Times* – In this city, January 5th 1885, at the residence of the bride's uncle, J. P. DALE, by Rev. Mr. WILLETT, Mr. Mayo JAMES (formerly of Loudoun County) to Miss Addie DEW, both of this city.

Col. R. C. HOLYDAY, ex secretary of State of Maryland, died Sunday at half past 5 o'clock at his home near Easton. He leaves a widow and a son and a daughter. He was a brother-in-law of Hon. J. R. TUCKER, both gentlemen having married daughters of the late Col. Humphrey POWELL, of this county.

Thursday, 29 January 1885   Vol. XXIX, No. 34

Married: In the Presbyterian church, LaPorte, November 19, by Rev. J. F. KENDALL, D.D., Mr. Carlton SHAFER, of Frederick City, Md, (formerly of Leesburg) and Miss Sarah Louise ANDREW, daughter of Dr. and Mrs. Geo. L. ANDREW, LaPorte, Indiana.

Married: At Christ's Episcopal Church, Goresville, morning of 27th inst., by the Rev. Carter PAGE, Mr. Mansfield WHITE, of Montgomery County. Md, to Ella, daughter of Jno. H. WHITMORE, Esq.

Mr. Landon O. MERCHANT, residing near Waterford, visited Leesburg last Thursday on business and left for home between 4 and 5 o'clock in the afternoon. He reached the top of the mountain, 2 miles from town, he fell from his horse, and sustained a severe cut on the head. Mr. SHUGARS, who witnessed the fall, assisted him to remount, and when next seen, about 11 o'clock that night, his body was found in the road a short distance beyond Mr. T. M. C. PAXSON's, his horse standing a short distance from him. He was unconscious and died about noon on Saturday, at the house of Mr. HARDING, where he was carried Thursday night. It is supposed that he was overcome by the intense cold, fell from exhaustion, again receiving a severe cut about the head. He was about 65 years of age, of temperate habits and rather delicate health, the result of a slight paralytic stroke sometime ago. Interred at Rehobeth on Sunday.

Sudden and peculiar death of Freddie, aged about five years, son of Isaac C. and Minnie HOGE, occurred about 2 o'clock last Wed. morning. On Tuesday he came into the house from the wagon house and told his mother that he had hurt himself while lifting the sleigh runner. Dr. WELTY was summoned, as he had abdomen pain and difficulty of breathing. Death by some internal injury.

Thursday, 5 February 1885   Vol. XXIX, No. 35

Married: At the residence of the bride's parents, near Taylortown, January 22, 1885, by Rev. P. H. MILLER, Mr. Chas. C. MOCK and Miss Laura J. COMPHER.

Married: On the 25th inst., at Berlin Ferry, by the Rev. H. St. J. RINKER, Mr. George T. BEAN to Miss Ella L. DAVRAL, all of Loudoun Co.

Died at the residence of A. R. JACOBS her son-in-law, on Wednesday 28th January at 1 a.m. in her 85th year, Mrs. Ann H. MURPHEY, widow of James MURPHEY, caused by cancer in her breast. Member of M. E. Church for 50 years. Interred in Ebenezer burying ground, funeral conducted by Rev. John WOOLF.

Death of Mrs. Mary B. GRAY, widow of the late Robt. W. GRAY, died on Monday morning after a brief illness of nine days, in the 66th year of her age, of pneumonia. Funeral Thursday at 2 p.m. from the Episcopal church, laid to rest in Union Cemetery.

Vicinity of Round Hill on Tuesday night Mr. Townsend BEANS and Miss DORRELL left and elopement was followed on the next night by Mr. Jno. MARCUS and Miss TRENARY who also left there hastily. Both couples were on marriage intent, but what direction they took could not be ascertained.

Thursday, 12 February 1885   Vol. XXIX, No. 36

Married: In St. James Episcopal Church, Leesburg at 2 p.m., on Wednesday, February 11th 1885, by Rev. R. T. DAVIS, Geo. O. FERGUSON and Sallie James, only daughter of the late Dr. Wm. CROSS, all of Leesburg.

Married: In Winchester, on the 28th of Jan., by Dr. J. S. MARTIN, Mr. B. J. HALL, of Loudoun Co., to Miss M. M. HESS, dau. of L. D. HESS.

Married: At New Jerusalem Evangelical Lutheran Church, January 28th 1885, by Rev. P. H. MILLER, Mr. Newton P. EVANS and Miss Mollie E. BOWERS.

Died: Suddenly, of meningitis, at the residence of S. G. ROSZEL, 54 Jefferson Place, Baltimore, on the 9th of Feb 1885, Rose A. ALDRIDGE, youngest child of John ALDRIDGE, of this county.

Died: On the night of February 7th, 1885, in Washington of scarlet fever, Robert Chew BARNES, son of Harriet P. and the late Dr. Joseph D. BARNES, in the 6th year of his age.

Died: On the morning of the 4th inst., in Philadelphia, of scarlet fever, Helen Macpherson, daughter of James W. and Lucy N. JANNEY, aged 2y 9m.

Died: February 4th at the residence of Mr. James B. HAVENNER, Leesburg, Mrs. Harriet A. PEACOCK, age 54. She had been for 18 years a member of the Baptist Church.

Died suddenly of heart disease, at the residence of her niece, Mrs. Samuel SMITH, on Thursday, February 5th 1885, Miss Eleanor H. HOUGH, in the 83rd year of her age.

Died: Mrs. Mary C. HAVENER, wife of Thomas A. HAVENER, died at her home near Belmont, Va, February 8th 1885, aged 58 years.

Co. Ct.: M. F. CHAMBLIN qualified as Guardian of John L. and Minor FURR. Estate of Susan REDD committed to Sheriff. A. W. MERCHANT qualified as Guardian of Leroy MERCHANT. Wills of A. T. BATSON and Wm. VIRTS admitted to probate. A. W. MERCHANT qualified as Admr. of Landon O. MERCHANT dec'd. Armida E. LOVE qualified as guardian of E. Dilley LOVE.

Mrs. Rose ALDRIDGE, youngest daughter of Mr. John ALDRIDGE, of this county, died in Baltimore City on Monday night last, whither she had been sent a few days before for medical treatment. Remains reached Leesburg at noon on Wednesday and were conveyed directly from the depot to Union Cemetery.

Thursday, 19 February 1885   Vol. XXIX, No. 37

Married: On February 3rd at Tenth Baptist Church, Philadelphia, by Rev. Dr. ROLAND, of Baltimore, Arthur L. CLINE, of Baltimore (formerly of Leesburg) to Anna F. OAKMAN, of Philadelphia.

Mr. Jacob HOUSER died at his residence near Gilead, January 23rd 1885 with pneumonia, aged 68 years. Leaves a wife with one son.

Miss Anna McGILL died suddenly at the residence of Dr. J. A. WILLIAMSON, in Frederick City, Md, on the 10th inst., of apoplexy. In her 78th year. An aunt of Dr. Samuel McGILL of Leesburg.

Letter from Upperville in *Warrenton Index* of Saturday says Mr. Albert FLETCHER, living near here, will be married on Wednesday week, the 18th to a Miss BROWN, of Loudoun County, and as she and her parents are members of the Society of Friends the ceremony will be at the meeting house at Lincoln in that county.

Marriage of Miss Josephine SCOTT daughter of the late Robt. E. SCOTT, of Fauquier, to Mr. Tazewell ELLETT, came off Thursday last at St. James Church, Richmond. Ceremony performed by Bishop WHITTLE, assisted by Rev. Dr. PETERKIN.

Thursday, 25 February 1885   Vol. XXIX, No. 38

Mrs. Ann PYOTT, mother of Mr. Jonah NIXON, died at her son's residence a few miles from Leesburg, on Sunday afternoon last, in her 96th year. Member of the M. E. Church. On Tuesday her remains were laid to rest in the old family burying ground at "Woodburn."

Mrs. Katie HIXSON (nee RUSE) formerly of this county, died at her home, near Leesburg, Highland Co., Ohio, on Saturday morning, February 14th 1885. Born on 5 February 1783, aged 102y 9d. There were several members of the family, all now dead, except one, each of whom had passed his or her four score years. Her youngest brother, Mr. Solomon RUSE, living near Hamilton, in this county, and the only member of the family, is now in his 87th year.

Dedication of Washington monument, on Saturday – among civilians to arrive was Ebenezer Burgess BALL, of Loudoun Co., who said his grandmother was George WASHINGTON's niece and his grandfather of the family of Washington's mother. Mr. BALL is a brother of the late Judge C. B. BALL, of this county.

Thursday, 5 March 1885   Vol. XXIX, No. 39

Married: In Leesburg, February 26th, by Rev. Saml. RODGERS, Mr. Joseph A. SHUGARS and Miss Mary A. WALLACE.

Died: On Tuesday, March 3rd 1885 at his home, "Springwood," Loudoun Co, Francis A. LUTZ, in his 66th year. Services at the M. E. Church, South, Leesburg, Thursday 1 p.m. Funeral from the residence of his son, F. A. LUTZ Jr., 335 C St., Washington, Friday morning at 11 a.m.

Died: At his residence near Arcola, on the 25th of February 1885, Mr. Alex G. SMITH, in the 82d year of his age.

Died: At the residence of her son, Mr. Jonah NIXON, on February 22, 1885, Mrs. Ann PYOTT. She was born in Hampshire Co W Va May 24, 1790. She was twice married, her maiden name being SLANE. Her first husband was Jonah NIXON, of W. Va., and her last one John PYOTT, of Loudoun Co., both of whom she survived. After her second marriage she emigrated to Tennessee, where she lived for a number of years, and returned here in 1864 where she lived until her decease. She was the mother of six children, three of whom survive her, she also left 22 grandchildren and 61 great grandchildren. She was a member of the Methodist church for over 60 years. Funeral services were preached by Rev. J. T. WILLIAMS.

Death of Mr. F. A. LUTZ, at "Springwood," his residence two miles from this town, at three o'clock on Tuesday afternoon last in his 66th year. After an attack of bronchitis, erysipelas came on. He was a native of the District of Columbia. Some 13 years ago he purchased "Springwood" estate. Member of the M. E. Church.

Mrs. Ruth THOMPSON, widow of the late Hugh S. THOMPSON, died at her residence near Hillsborough on Friday morning last in about the 58th year of her age. Her funeral took place on Sunday morning. She was the mother of Mr. Ashby THOMPSON formerly a teacher in the Academy in this town.

Philomont last week: Mrs. Delilah BEAVERS, old lady of our vicinity a few days since, while holding her little grandchild was suddenly attacked with a giddiness which caused her to fall in the fire. The child was rescued but the grandmother was seriously burned. Owing to her advanced age, recovery is considered doubtful.

Mr. John SNEDEN died at his residence, in New York City, on Monday, February 23rd, 1885, in the 72d year of his age. Mr. SNEDEN was the father of Mrs. Dr. QUINBY, of "Oak Hill," in this county.

Mr. James N. GALLAHER, a publisher of the Virginia Free Press, Charlestown, W Va., died February 25th of consumption, aged about 44 years, leaving a wife and infant child. Soldier in the 12th Va Cavalry, Confederate States army. He was a son of the late H. N. GALLAHER, veteran editor of the *Free Press*, who celebrated his golden wedding about three years ago. Shortly after this celebration, Mr. J. Shannon GALLAHER, one of the sons, died of consumption; less than a year ago Mr. H. N. GALLAHER and his wife died within a few weeks of each other; in January last Mr. Edward F. GALLAHER, youngest son, died of consumption and now Mr. James N. GALLAHER. Two sons and a daughter still survive.

Thursday, 12 March 1885   Vol. XXIX, No. 40

Married: In Leesburg, March 9, 1885, by Rev. Samuel RODGERS, Mr. J. W. HAMILTON, of Georgia, and Miss Ida MOXLEY, of Loudoun.

Died: At Centreville, Fairfax Co, Va, February 20, 1885, Sallie E. SWART, youngest daughter of Henry S. and Elizabeth J. SWART, in the 20th year of her age.

Died: On the morning of the 27th of February, at his son-in-law's near Woodburn, Va, of a protracted illness of over 2 years, of Bright's disease, Mr. David ALEXANDER, in the 69th year of his age. For 25 years a member of the Baptist Church at North Fork.

Died: At her residence, near Clarke's Gap, on the 8th of January, of consumption, Mrs. Mary Jane MYERS, wife of Mahlon Henry MYERS, in the 26th year of her age. She leaves a husband and 2 small children.

Died: In Waterford, on February 23, 1885, at 8 p.m., suddenly with apoplexy, while approaching his schoolmates who were coasting,

Chas. Courtney VIRTS, the eldest son of Chas. W. and Tracey V. VIRTS, aged 13y 6m 4d.

Died: Near Woodgrove, Friday, February 27th, Edgar Hampton, son of Edgar W. and Mollie E. WARNER, aged 2y 4m 2d.

Sheriff Jas. E. CARRUTHERS received a few days ago fro the Eastern Lunatic Asylum at Williamsburg, Va, a letter announcing the death there at 9 a.m. March 5th 1885, of Miss Rachel BEAMER, of Loudoun County, who was committed to the Asylum on the 26th of Sept, 1882. Her remains were interred in the Asylum Cemetery on Friday, the 6th.

On Wednesday evening the 4th instant, Mr. Avery DULANY, son of Mr. Daniel DULANY, of this county, attempted to cross the creek between Purcellville and Wheatland at a point near the residence of Mr. Levi JAMES. He either fell or was thrown from his horse and was drowned. Mr. DULANY was a cripple.

Mr. Wm. J. THOMAS, of Baltimore, died on Monday evening last in that city, of typhoid fever, in the 32d year of his age. He was the principal of the graded school in this town '83-84.

March Ct.: Chester C. GAVER qualified as Admr. of Mary POTTS dec'd.; Adelade S. FRY as Admx. of Danl. N. FRY. Will of Alexander G. SMITH admitted to probate. Chas. P. JANNEY qualified as Admr. of Mary E. GRAY; Chas. P. JANNEY as Admr. dbn wwa R. W. GRAY.

Thursday, 19 March 1885   Vol. XXIX, No. 41

Married: At Woburn, Mass., Jan. 20th 1885, by Rev. ___, Jno. M. WALLACE of Leesburg to Miss Mamie DAVIS, of Woburn, Mass.

Died: On March 2d 1885, at the residence of Mr. A. L. WITHERS, near Summit Point, in Jefferson Co., W Va, Miss Keturah LITTLETON, daughter of the late Richard LITTLETON, of Loudoun Co, Va.

Died: On Wednesday, March 4th 1885, at the residence of her nephew, Charles C. MAFFETT, near Gum Spring, Loudoun County, Miss Mary A. CRAVEN, in her 47th year.

Died: Near Guilford, Loudoun Co., March 6th 1885, Forest L. HUMMER, son of Alpheus P. and Martha B. HUMMER, aged 3y 5m 17d.

Miss Addie ROSS, at the residence of her father, Jno. T. ROSS, near Trappe, March 11th.

Alexander CARTER, much respected old colored man, died at his home, near Goose Creek bridge, on Wednesday last, in his 93d year. For many years a faithful servant in the Saunders' family. He has been living for many years in a house near the Goose Creek Bridge, bought for him by Mr. Henry SAUNDERS. He was blind for several years before he died.

Card from the Va penitentiary states that Wilson ELGIN, colored, sent to the penitentiary from Loudoun in 1884, for 14 years, died in the hospital of that institution on the 11th.

Mr. Anthony LAWSON, father of Mr. R. M. LAWSON, of this city, and of Mr. R. B. LAWSON, of Loudoun County, died at his home, near Wytheville, last night, aged about 73 years. He owned a valuable estate in "Burkes Garden," the finest grass region in the southwestern part of the State. His son, Mr. R. M. LAWSON, was with him at the time of his death.

Thursday, 26 March 1885   Vol. XXIX, No. 42

Married: On November 14th 1884, by the Right Rev. J. J. KEANE, of Richmond, Va, Robert Powell FAUNTLEROY, of Leesburg, and Mary Loretto CAIN, of Washington.

Married: At the Baptist parsonage in Middleburg, March 19th 1885, by Rev. W. A. DUNAWAY, Mr. Wm. F. PRESGRAVES and Miss Mary L. NICHOLS.

Married: On March 19, 1885, by Rev. Isaac LAKE, Mr. W. W. SMALLWOOD to Miss Ida D. BALLARD, both of this county.

Died: February 20th near Hughesville, at the residence of his brother, Elder Jos. FURR, Charles FURR, aged 85 years.

Miss Margaret D. WHITE, formerly of Middleburg, in this county, died at her residence near Luray, Page County, on the 10th instant, in the 81st year of her age.

Mr. Geo. W. ADAMS for many years a merchant in Middleburg, and an extensive farmer, died at his residence there on the 14th inst., in the 67th year of his age.

Mr. Peter COMPHER died suddenly at his residence near Hillsboro, on Wednesday night last, at an advanced age.

Thursday, 2 April 1885   Vol. XXIX, No. 43

Married: At the residence of the bride's father, Josiah FURGUSON, Mr. Armstead JOHNSON to Miss Lucy E. FURGUSON, both of Loudoun, Rev. Mr. WOLF officiating.

Married: At "Marengo," the residence of the bride's parents, March 11, 1885, by Rev. Wm. A. BAYNHAM, assisted by Rev. A. BROADUS, D.D., Dr. J. T. HARRIS, of Hedgesville, W. Va. to Miss Ruth Lewis MARTIN, second dau. of John Y. MARTIN, Esq. of Caroline Co. Va.

Died: In Leesburg, on Tuesday evening, March 31st 1885, Maggie W., second daughter of Clarence and Maggie HEAD, aged 6y 6m.

Mr. John MALONE, one of the richest men in Fairfax County, died at his home, near the Court House Sunday morning. He was father-in-law of R. R. FARR, State Sup. of Public Instruction.

Death of Bernard TAYLOR at 1:15 Wed. morning at the residence of his son-in-law, Dr. I. S. STONE, of Lincoln, aged 82 years. Last of four brothers who, within the past half century were most prominent in Lincoln community. Life long member of Goose Creek Meeting of Friends. Interred Thursday afternoon in their burying ground.

Mr. C. W. DOWNEY died at his residence, Downey's Mills, near Taylortown, on Thursday last, of consumption. Interred at Lovettsville on Saturday.

Mrs. Ann M. LOWE, formerly of this county, died in Washington city on the 24th of March, in the 75th year of her age. Remains interred at Dranesville.

Thursday, 9 April 1885   Vol. XXIX, No. 44

Married: On February 18, 1885, at Goose Creek Meeting House, Lincoln, by Friends' ceremony, Albert H. FLETCHER, of Fauquier County to Hannah M. BROWN, dau. of W. H. BROWN, Esq.

Married: On March 26, at the residence of Mr. Chas. BROWN, near Lovettsville, by Rev. J. S. WICKLINE, Mr. D. J. CARNES and Miss Ella V. GROSS, both of Loudoun.

Married: On March 30th, at the M. E. Parsonage, in Leesburg, by Rev. J. S. WICKLINE, Mr. Geo. W. BAGENT and Miss Sydid J. BARTLETT, both of Loudoun County.

Married: March 24th 1884, by Elder Benj. BRIDGES, at his residence, Mr. E. E. OLIVER and Miss M. REED, all of Fairfax county.

Married: on March 24, 1885, by Rev. J. H. DULANEY, Mr. Jos. J. CAYLOR, and Miss Edith COCKERILLE, all of Fairfax.

Died: At her home near Hillsboro on February 27 after a long and painful illness, Mrs. Ruth H. THOMPSON, widow of the late Hugh S. THOMPSON, in the 58th year of her age.

Died: At Fairfax C. H. Va on the morning of March 28, 1885, Hettie Marvin JOHNSON, youngest daughter of Wm. H. and Frances C. D. JOHNSON, aged 5y 1m 24d.

Thursday, 16 April 1885   Vol. XXIX, No. 45

Married: On the evening of the 9th inst., at the M. E. Church, in Waterford, by Rev. J. S. WICKLINE, Edgar E. JAMES and Miss Lizzie A. HOUGH, both of Waterford, Va.

Married: By Rev. W. F. DUNNAWAY, at the parsonage in Middleburg, on the 8th of April 1885, Mr. Charles C. KERRICK and Miss Laura BATTAILE.

Married: On the 30th of March 1885, at Yorkville, S.C. by Rev. E. P. HARRISON, Lt. Sydney B. WILLIAMSON, son of Gen. T. H. WILLIAMSON, of the Va Military Institute, and Miss Cora V. BANTON.

Died: Near Belmont, on April 12th 1885, Annie E., daughter of Henry and Lizzie ELLIOTT, aged 17y 6m.

Died: At his residence near Snickersville, on March 27, Jonah THOMAS, in his 67th year. He been ill for some time past.

Died: Agnes, daughter of H. C. and Emmet BENNETT, in Waterford, on Wednesday morning at 1 o'clock, aged 17m 3d.

Thursday, 23 April 1885   Vol. XXIX, No. 46

Died: Mrs. Amanda ROSS, wife of John T. ROSS, departed this life at her home near the Trappe, March 30, 1885, in her 53d year.

Died: At his residence, near Middleburg, March 28, 1885, Mr. Eli H. NICHOLS, in the 63rd year of his age. Of Quaker descent though not actually connected with that or any other church.

April Ct.: Wills of Jonah THOMAS and Geo. W. ADAMS admitted to probate. F. L. NICHOLS and C. W. NICHOLS qualified as Admrs. of Eli NICHOLS dec'd.; C. C. GAVER and Wm. COMPHER as Admrs. of Peter COMPHER dec'd.; Jno. T. CUMMINS as Guardian of Levi and Edgar F. CUMMINS. Will of Francis A. LUTZ admitted to probate. Wm. GAINES appointed curator of Estate of Albert JACKSON. Jacob HOWSER's estate committed to Sheriff. W. D. THOMPSON qualified as Guardian of Irving P. THOMPSON; J. A. THOMPSON as Guardian of J. Harry THOMPSON; W. D. THOMPSON as Admr. of Ruth H. THOMPSON dec'd. Carter PAGE licensed to celebrate rites of matrimony.

Tribute of respect from town council on death of Thos. W. BIRKBY.

Septimus N. TUSTIN, a grandson of the late Rev. Septimus TUSTIN, died in Philadelphia a few days ago in the 32d year of his age.

David OGDEN, 14 years of age, son of R. K. OGDEN of Berryville, Va last week died from lockjaw, caused by running a nail into his foot about a week previous.

Thursday, 23 April 1885   Vol. XXIX, No. 46

Married: April 15, 1885, by Rev J. B. LAKE, Miss Lillie E. BALDWIN, daughter of Joseph BALDWIN, near Union, Loudoun County to Mr. James D. PRATT, Smyth County, Va.

Died: At Snickersville, March 18th, of paralysis, Mrs. Sarah STONE, in her 78th year.

Died: In Washington, on Saturday morning, April 18th 1885, Frank A., son of Jacob VEIHMEYER, in his 28th year. Funeral took place Monday morning from St. Dominic's church.

Mr. Floyd HUGHES, son of Judge Robert W. HUGHES, was married in Norfolk Va, last week, to Miss Nannie RICKS of that city.

Warrenton April 17 – Dr John WARD died here this morning in the 58th year of his age. He was surgeon in the U.S. Navy who resigned and came South in 1861. He was for some time in charge of the military hospital at Danville.

Thursday, 30 April 1885   Vol. XXIX, No. 47

Two children of Mr. Wentwor[th] ZEVERLEY, of this county, died last week, aged 6m and 2½ years. Both were buried together in Goose Creek burying ground on Thursday.

Mrs. Lavinia DOWELL, wife of Mr. John T. DOWELL, formerly of this county, died at her home near Rome, Georgia, on the 16th inst. Her remains were brought to Loudoun for interment.

Mr. Thomas W. MUSE died at his home near Farmwell, on the 22d of April, in the 63d year of his age.

Mr. James HOGE died at his residence near Hughesville on Tuesday last, in the 73d year of his age. Funeral will take place at Friends Meeting House, Lincoln, this Thursday morning at 10 o'clock.

Thursday, 7 May 1885   Vol. XXIX, No. 48

The HIXSON will, contest over validity – David HIXSON Esq. just after the close of the war made his home in the family of John W. NIXON (both father and son) where he remained until his death of pneumonia on 13 Feb 1883 (18 years). Appraisers found paper in unsealed envelope dated 10 February 1883. Gives to nephews John HUGHES, James CUTHBERT, and M. M. RODGERS and sister Amanda CLIPSTINE. A. J. BRADFIELD as Exor. $1000 each to children of Jno. W. NIXON. Capt. J. W. FOSTER for contestants noted spelling of RODGERS for ROGERS, omission of middle names, spelling his sister's name CLIPSTINE instead of KLIPSTEIN. [long article] Trial continued.

Married: April 28th 1885, by Elder A. B. FRANCIS, Mr. Joshua M. HUTCHISON of Fairfax County, and Miss Mattie M. MANKIN, of Loudoun County.

Died: On Friday morning, May 1st 1885, at her home near Leesburg, Mrs. Mollie CARR, wife of Mr. Jno. C. CARR, in about her 29th year.

Rev. C. L. TORREYSON, pastor of the Methodist Episcopal Church, South, at Fairfield, Rockbridge County, died last week of typhoid pneumonia. Native of Loudoun County, and entered the ministry of the Methodist Church in 1858.

Thursday, 14 May 1885   Vol. XXIX, No. 49

Another long article [continued from last week] on will of bachelor and former Sheriff David HIXSON. Jury pronounced will a forgery.

Married: At the residence of Mr. J. H. ALEXANDER, May 12th 1885, by Rev. C. T. HERNDON, Mr. Ellis W. LACEY to Miss S. Anne CORBIN, both of Loudoun.

Died: At her home in this town, on Saturday morning last, May 9th 1885, Mrs. Belle HEAD, wife of Mr. Benj. F. HEAD, in her 41st year.

Alice EDMUNDS, young colored girl died very suddenly at her home in this town one evening last week. She had gone to a neighbor's house where she ate some partially cooked potatoes.

May Ct.: Jno. W. GARRETT qualified as committee of Catharine BOWMAN; Chas. W. HAGAN as Guardian of Lucy M., Earnest R. and Sallie E. HAGAN. Jas. R. BRIDGES licensed to celebrate rites of matrimony. Wills of James HOGE and T. W. MUSE admitted to probate. A. J. BRADFIELD's powers as Exor. of David HIXSON revoked. Jonah HIXON qualified as Admr. of Ann PYOTT dec'd. Levan C. GRUBB qualified as Admr. of Wm. H. BOGAN dec'd.

Barn on Clover Hill farm, near Marshall, Fauquier Co. belonging to Major Thos. R. FOSTER burned to the ground on Thursday night. Maj. F. is the father of Capt. J. W. FOSTER of this town.

[MISSING ISSUE]

Thursday, 4 June 1885   Vol. XXIX, No. 52

Rev. R. T. STAUTON, of Washington DC, a passenger in the steamship Nevada en route for England, died on ship board, May 28th and was buried at sea.

Married: May 20th, at Herndon, by Rev. W. T. SCHOOLEY, Mr. Walter G. WILEY, of Loudoun, and Miss Mattie WRENN, of Fairfax.

Married: At the Lutheran Church near Lovettsville, May 21st 1885, Mr. Jefferson J. RITCHIE and Miss Ella V. WILLIAMS, Rev. P. H. MILLER officiating.

Died: Jane A. BROWN, after an illness of some week, passed away, in the 80y 5m 23d of her age, at her home in Harmony, Kansas, on Friday, April 1st 1885, at 11:30 a.m.

Died: On May 24th 1885 at her residence, 906 D Street, NW at 11:20 a.m. of consumption, Mattie H., beloved wife of Jas. RUTHERFORD, aged 31 years.

On Wednesday Wm. DAVIS and W. D. SMITH, young gentlemen of Leesburg left to seek their fortunes in Missouri.

[MISSING ISSUES]

Thursday, 18 June 1885   Vol. XXX, No. 2

Died: At her home near Farmwell, on the 10th of June 1885, Mrs. Mary S. DANA, relict of the late Anderson DANA, of Wilkesbarre, Penn, in about her 65th year. Interred in cemetery at Leesburg on Friday last.

Death of Mrs. Anna J. SMITH, wife of Mr. Henry S. SMITH, of Guilford in this county, occurred at her husband's residence on Sunday night last, the 14th instant. She was a Miss GUSTIN, of Newton, N.J. and came to this county less then one year ago a bride. Interred in cemetery at Leesburg on Tuesday.

Among cadets at West Point of second class who will enter first class 1885-96 is T. Bentley MOTT son of Dr. A. R. MOTT of Leesburg.

Mr. R. Carter SCOTT, son of Maj. R. Taylor SCOTT, of Warrenton, has been appointed to a position in the revenue office at Richmond.

Rev. Frederick PAGE, pastor of Olivet Chapel, Fairfax County, was married at Fairfax C. H. on Wednesday last to Miss Caroline HARVEY of Cambridgeshire, England, Rev. Frank PAGE, of the Episcopal Church, performing the ceremony.

Thursday, 25 June 1885   Vol. XXX, No. 3

Married: On Wednesday evening, June 17th 1885, at the residence of the bride's mother in Leesburg, by Rev. Dr. R. T. DAVIS, Mr. Clinton M. HOSKINSON and Linnie, youngest daughter of the late Thos. BURCH, all of this county.

Married: At residence of the bride's parents, near Aldie, on Wed., June 17th 1885, by Elder S. B. FRANCIS, Mr. John Frank GULICK, and Miss Gertrude F., daughter of Mr. A. W. SAFFER, all of Loudoun.

Married: At Luckett's Cross Roads, June 17th, by Rev. L. B. TURNBULL, Geo. R. KIDWELL to Maria J. LUCKETT.

Married: In Leesburg, June 17th, by Rev. J. T. WILLIAMS, Mr. Lewis T. CARTER to Miss Willietta DICKEY.

Departed this life on the 21st of May 1885, Hannah McCARTY widow of the late W. T. McCARTY of Fauquier County, aged 80 years.

Died: June 15, 1885, at Fairfax Ct. House, Mrs. Sarah SEWELL, in her 93d year, for many years a member of the Methodist Church.

Cards are out for the marriage at the Metropolitan Church, Washington DC, on the 30th inst., of Mr. Chas. B. HANFORD, formerly of this county, to Miss Mariella BEAR, of that city.

The residence of Mr. W. T. SAFFER near Aldie was on Wednesday last the scene of the marriage of his daughter Gertrude F. to Mr. John F. GULICK, of this county. Ceremony performed by Elder S. B. FRANCIS. A few minutes past 11 o'clock bridal party entered: Mr. Wm. SILCOTT with Miss Addie CHAMBLIN, Mr. R. L. POWELL with Miss Sallie GULICK, Mr. Carroll CHANCELLOR with Miss Minnie LAMBERT, Mr. E. B. WHITE with Miss Rose SAFFER, the bride and groom. ...

Death of Henry W. CASTLEMAN at his home in Jefferson Co W Va on Wednesday last, in about the 63d year of his age, on 17th of June. He was a son-in-law of Mr. James SINCLAIR, a former clerk of the Circuit Ct. of Loudoun.

Mr. Mark Catesby JONES, son of the late Commodore Ap Catesby JONES, U.S.N., died suddenly at his residence at Lewinsville, Fairfax Co., on the 16th inst. of heart disease, in about his 48th year.

Thursday, 2 July 1885   Vol. XXX, No. 4

Wife of Mr. Hugh L. POWELL, of Staunton, died at the residence of her mother, in that city, on Sunday. Mr. POWELL is a son of Mr. Alex POWELL, former cashier of the Valley Bank in Leesburg.

Died: Sarah SHOEMAKER, widow of the late Naylor SHOEMAKER, at Silcott Springs, May 30th, aged 83y 6m 25d.

Mr. Gilbert SCOTT, father of Rev. R. A. SCOTT of the Va Conference, M. E. Church, died on Saturday evening, May 3d. Born and brought up in St. Mary's Co, Md. He was married to Miss Mary A. WOLFORD, of Loudoun Co. He was 80 years old. Joined the

Methodist Episcopal Church at Rehobeth 52 years ago. Leaves an aged widow, 2 sons and 3 daughters.

About 9 o'clock this morning, Mr. Bolling W. HAXALL, of Richmond died at his late residence, No. 107 east Franklin St, after an illness of considerable duration. He was 71 years of age. .... He was the father of Bolling W. HAXALL Jr., of Middleburg.

Mr. John WYSONG, of Jefferson Co., died at his home near Shepherdstown on Monday last at the age of 85y 6m 2d.

[MISSING ISSUE]

Thursday, 16 July 1885   Vol. XXX, No. 6

Died: July 2d, 1885, of acute rheumatism of the heart, William Arthur, son of Thomas and Melinda DAILEY, at the residence of his grandfather, F. W. SHAFER, in Leesburg, in his 16th year.

Died: In Leesburg, July 7th 1885, Mary, infant daughter of Benj. F. and Belle F. HEAD.

Died: On Sunday evening, July 12, 1885, at 5:30 p.m., Charles Robert, only son of Arthur T. and Salle E. TALKS, aged 4m 20d.

Died: In West Washington, on July 12, 1885, Washington Fayett DARNE, in the 58th year of his age.

Died: At the residence of Mr. E. G. CAUFMAN, near Goresville, on Tuesday morning last, after several weeks intense suffering from a fatal attack of spinal menengitis, Katie BENTLEY, youngest daughter of the late Edgar L. BENTLEY, in about her 22d year. On Wednesday afternoon interred in Union Cemetery, services in Chapel of the Immaculate Conception, Father WILSON officiating.

In Memoriam: Virginia Lee, daughter of Dr. B. F. and Kate Bentley NOLAND, died at Farmwell, Wed. morning, July 8th 1885, aged 11m.

Died: At her old home, near Evergreen Mills, May 18, 1885, Miss Lydia M. SKINNER, in the 46th year of her age, of rheumatism.

Mr. Craven A. COPELAND died at his residence near Hillsboro, on the 10th instant, at the advanced age of 86 years.

July Ct.: Minor F. CHAMBLIN executed new bond as Guardian for John L. FURR and Minor FURR. Wm. T. WHITACRE qualified as Admr. of Lydia HUMPHREY dec'd.; John T. SHRYOCK as Admr. of Geo. W. SHRYOCK dec'd.; T. H. CARTER as Admr. of Augustus KING dec'd. Daniel COLE appointed Guardian for Sarah E. COLE. Will of Mrs. E. L. HENDERSON admitted to probate. Estate of Wm. SWANK dec'd. committed to sheriff for administration.

Edward GREEN alias Edward ROBINSON is a native of Loudoun Co. and is considered by the officers of the prison to be the most desperate character in the prison. He was convicted Feb 20th 1881 of stealing a valuable mare from Washington HAYNES, of Loudoun.

Mr. George T. JOHNSTON and Miss Minnie C. JONES, of this town, were married by Rev. H. W. KINZER at 5 o'clock in the M. E.

Church. Attendants were Mr. E. D. POULTON and Miss Ella TROUT, Mr. John MORGAN and Miss Annie MILLER, and Mr. W. P. KING and Miss Etta BOYD. Mr. Arthur W. POULTON and A. L. WARTHEN as ushers. ... *Front Royal Sentinel of Friday*. Best man is a native of this town, a younger brother of Mr. S. J. JOHNSTON.

Mr. W. Fayette DARNE, of Georgetown DC, died on Sunday in that place from the effects of drinking ice water while overheated, causing congestion of the stomach.

An Independence Mo. special say Christopher MANN, aged 111 years, died here on the 12th. He was born in Va in 1774 and came to this place in 1838.

[MISSING ISSUE]

Thursday, 30 July 1885   Vol. XXX, No. 8

Died: At her residence near Lovettsville, on the 13th inst., Mrs. Elizabeth SANBOWER, aged 84y 9m. Member of the German Reform Church.

Died: At his home in Philadelphia, on Tuesday, the 21st instant, James MATHESON, a native of Scotland, in the 57th year of his age.

Mrs. Mary W. ELLMORE died at the residence of her son, Mr. C. A. ELLMORE, in this town, on Wednesday last, aged 74. She was a member of the Old School Baptist Church for 39 years. Her funeral took place Thursday afternoon, Elder E. V. WHITE officiating, interment in Union Cemetery.

Wm. CARN, 78 years old, was kicked in the stomach by a bull on the farm of his daughter near Lovettsville, on Saturday the 18th instant, and died the next day from the injury.

Herbert COLE, colored, was last week convicted of stealing 18 chickens from Mr. David F. DANIEL and sent to jail for six months. Wife who brought the fowls to market was also found guilty and paid $9 (cost of chickens) and set free.

Death of Mr. Thos. G. GLASSCOCK, which occurred at his home near Rectortown, Fauquier County, on Thursday evening last. He died suddenly, while conversing with his son. One of the richest men in Virginia, upwards of $500,000. He was about 70 years of age and leaves one son, Mr. Bedford GLASSCOCK.

Mrs. Lillie GRAY, wife of Mr. R. Bently GRAY, of St. Louis, and daughter of Mrs. Jane A. PANCOAST, died at the residence of her mother in this town, at 10:30, Wednesday morning, July 29th 1885. He leaves a husband and a little daughter.

Marriage license issued in Washington on Tuesday to John H. MISKELL and Lily Maud MORAN, of Loudoun.

Thursday, 6 August 1885   Vol. XXX, No. 9

Married: In Saluda, Va, on July 15th 1885, by Rev. Mr. WYATT, Geo. L. BLACKBURN, of Middlesex Co., to Hattie A. SHUMAN, of Loudoun.

The Mirror
Thursday, 13 August 1885   Vol. XXX, No. 10

Married: At Fayettesville, Ark., July 14th, at the residence of Col. O. C. GRAY, Rev. S. W. DAVIES, officiating, Prof. Cuthbert P. CONRAD, late of Winchester, Va, and Miss Sarah E. HARRIS.

Died: Mrs. Fanny NICHOLS, at the residence of Thos. J. NICHOLS, near Silcott's Springs, July 22d, in the 88th year of her age.

After several months sickness, Mr. George W. SHRYOCK died near Farmwell Station, Loudoun Co., on the 5th of July 1885. He was born in this county Oct 5th 1845, of pious Methodist parents. He leaves an aged father and mother, and wife.

Mrs. Adelaide WALLACE, wife of Mr. James M. WALLACE, formerly of this town, died suddenly of heart disease, at 11:30 last Sunday morning, at the residence of her daughter, in Woburn, Massachusetts, in the 69th year of her age. Body brought to Leesburg on Wednesday evening train and interred in family burying ground in Union cemetery.

About 9 o'clock Monday night Aug 3rd 1885, death of Mrs. Rose JOHNSON, wife of Mr. Wm. A. JOHNSON and dau. of Capt. Geo. R. HEAD. From childhood a member of the M. E. Church, South. Leaves a husband and 3 little children, one scarce 3 months old.

Death of Dr. J. J. WENNER, physician of Lovettsville, found dead in his bed on Saturday night, supposed from an affection of the heart. His wife awoke about 1 o'clock and found her husband's head resting upon her breast, and he was dead. He was in about his 38th year.

Mr. Alexander MARBURY died at his home near Hamilton in this county, on Monday. He was formerly of Georgetown DC.

Prof. Robt. J. FULTON and wife, of Kansas city, arrived in Leesburg on Monday to visit relative, Mr. Henry SAUNDERS near town, where the Prof.'s brother, Dr. Wm. FULTON, still lies critically ill.

Mrs. Mary STRIBLING, widow of Dr. Taliaferro STRIBLING, of Virginia, died at the residence of her grandson, M. S. THOMPSON, in Washington, on Friday last, in the 93rd year of her age. Remains taken to Berryville, Va for interment.

Mrs. Richard Henry CARTER, of "Glen Welby," died at the residence of her son-in-law, Mr. John WASHINGTON, at The Plains, Fauquier County on Thursday evening last. She leaves a large family of sons and daughters.

Thursday, 13 August 1885   Vol. XXX, No. 10

Death of Mr. A. T. HESSER occurred at his home near Silcott's Springs, in this county, one day last week. In about his 49th year of age.

Will of Thos. GLASSCOCK admitted to probate in Ct. on Monday, son Bedford GLASSCOCK as Exor. Provision for widow during her lifetime, is devised to Tacy FLETCHER, a little grand-daughter of the testator, and his son, Bedford.

Co. Ct.: Bedford GLASSCOCK qualified as Exor. of Thos. GLASSCOCK dec'd.; C. P. COPELAND as Exor. of Craven A.

COPELAND dec'd. Anna M. ADAMS as Admx wwa of Geo. W. ADAMS; J. F. HAMPTON as Admr. wwa of Fanny NICHOLS. S. P. FISHER (colored) minister Baptist Church, licensed to celebrate rites of matrimony. Emmett W. SKINNER qualified as Guardian of Willis H. and Mary C. SKINNER. Estates of Wm. F. BARRETT and Elizabeth Y. SIDEBOTTAMS committed to Sheriff to Administration. Will of Abner H. HIXSON admitted to probate, estate committed to Sheriff. Sanford THORNTON (col) relieved from payment of capitation tax. John MARBURY Jr. qualified as Admr. of Alexander MARBURY dec'd. Estate of R. C. BOWMAN committed to Sheriff.

[MISSING ISSUES]

Thursday, 3 September 1885   Vol. XXX, No. 13

Married: On Tuesday evening, September 1st 1885, at the residence of the bride's father, by Rev. R. T. DAVIS, Mr. Albert G. ORRISON, of Alexandria, and Katie, daughter of Matthew McPHERSON of Loudoun County.

Married: In Washington Co Md, on the 24th of August, by the Rev. Jas. M. STEPHENSON, Mr. James B. MARCUS to Miss Ida TRENARY, both of Loudoun County, Virginia.

Died: On Saturday the 22d of August, near the Great Falls, Fairfax Co., Va, from the effects of billious diarrhea, Annie Estelle, only child of Thomas J. and Katie V. MYERS, aged 1y 11m 17d.

Died: At her home, Oak Hill, Prince William Co., Mrs. Emsey GLASCOCK, the wife of Burr GLASCOCK, in her 69th year.

Died: John M. ADAM, formerly of Loudoun Co., died at the residence of his nephew, Wm. F. ADAM, in Louisa Co., on Tuesday, August 25th, in the 74th year of his age.

On Tuesday, the 25th of August, Wm. Thomas SCHAFFER, a little son of Mr. John SCHAFFER, near Hamilton, was riding on a wagon being loaded with sand, lost his balance and the hind wheel passed over his side, crushing the thigh, fracturing the pelvis. He died on Friday following, aged 6y 6m 13d.

Mr. Webb HUTCHISON, of Broad Run District, passed through Leesburg, Monday, en route for Warren Co., to be united in matrimony with a Miss PAGE, of that county.

Thursday, 10 September 1885   Vol. XXX, No. 14

Died: Mr. Frank J. PADGETT, after a brief illness, died at his residence near Union, Loudoun Co., August 22d 1885. He was a skillful mechanic.

Died: Near Purcellville, on Friday, September 4th 1885, at the residence of her son-in-law, Octavius OSBORNE, Mrs. Winifred JAMES, relict of the late Robert JAMES, in 72nd year of her age.

Mr. Clayton PAXSON, son of Mr. Jno. C. PAXSON, died after an illness of about two weeks, at his father's residence near Bunker Hill in this county, of typhoid fever, on Tuesday morning last in about his 28th year. In employ of Messrs. Albert Bros., of Baltimore. Interred at Short Hills burying ground on yesterday (Wednesday) morning.

Mr. Chas. M. BALL, successor of Haskins & Ball, Druggists, is well known in this county. He is a native of this county, a son of Mr. Wm. BALL, who, after familiarizing himself with the drug business under Dr. A. R. MOTT, left here a few years ago and settled in Colorado.

Charles BLAND died at the residence of Mr. N. D. OFFUTT, in this town, on Thursday morning last after being confined to he bed for several weeks with typhoid fever, aged 20 years. He was a nephew of Mrs. OFFUTT and been living with her for the last year. *Rockville (Md.) Sentinel of the 4th.* He was a grand-son of the late Dr. Charles G. EDWARDS, of this county and remembered from school boy days in Leesburg.

A letter from Palmyra, Mo informs us that Mr. Thos. H. JAMES, wife and daughter, of Texas, and Mrs. Susan ROGERS, of Virginia, are visiting their cousin, Mrs. Granville KELLER of that place. Also Mrs. Samuel WITHERS and 2 youngest children.

Nuptials of Mr. George A. ORRISON of Alexandria and Miss Katie McPHERSON of Loudoun took place at the residence of her father, some 5 miles from this town, on Tuesday night last. Rev. Dr. DAVIS, pastor of the P. E. Church, of Leesburg, tied the marriage knot. Miss Lucy McPHERSON, Inez ORRISON, Nora ELGIN, Annie SPRING, of Loudoun, and Miss Minnie RILEY, of Washington appeared as attendants of the bride. Mr. J. C. ROSS, of Alexandria, was best man, accompanied by Messrs. John McPHERSON and John DOWNS, of Loudoun, and Messrs Arthur M. ORRISON and Gus T. RILEY, of Washington. They will reside by the Potomac, in Alexandria.

[MISSING ISSUE]

Thursday, 24 September 1885   Vol. XXX, No. 16

Married: In Hancock, Md, on Thursday, September 17th 1885, by Rev. George BUCKLE, assisted by Rev. Dr. W. T. THOMPSON and Rev. P. D. STEVENSON, Rev. J. R. BRIDGES (pastor of the Presbyterian Church, Leesburg) to Miss Nannie BRIDGES, daughter of Robt. BRIDGES, of Hancock.

Married: September 16th 1885, by Rev. I. W. CANTER, in Leesburg, Wm. TALLY and Sarah S. C. WATERS, both of Loudoun County.

Married: At the Lutheran parsonage, near Lovettsville, September 9th, 1885, by Rev. P. H. MILLER, Mr. George H. HARRISON and Miss Alberta R. ROLLER.

Married: At the residence of Mrs. A. A. MOORE, September 17th 1885, by Rev. C. T. HERNDON, Mr. Jos. R. JANNEY to Miss Josie N. ORRISON, both of Loudoun.

On Tuesday evening, Sept. 2d 1885, at the residence of F. A. COCHRAN, at Welltown, by Friends' ceremony, Samuel R. BALDWIN, of Loudoun County and Miss Rebecca T. WRIGHT, of Rest, Frederick County.

Died: On September 15th, at Bellefield, Mrs. E. O. CARTER, in her 89th year, wife of Geo. CARTER, dec'd., of Oatlands, Loudoun County.

Death of Mrs. Elizabeth O. CARTER, relict of late George CARTER, of Oatlands in this county, one of the wealthiest citizens of Loudoun. Her maiden name was GRAYSON and her first husband, Joseph LEWIS, for several years represented this district in the Congress of U.S. She was a communicant of the Protestant Episcopal Church. She died after having reached her 4-score and ten years. She leaves two children – Messrs. George and B. G. CARTER. Remains laid at rest in family vault at Oatlands, on Thursday.

A son of Mr. Thos. KIDWELL, was killed on Sunday week, by the explosion of a shell. He had found the shell in the mountain, near by. His father resides near the foot of the mountain, about two miles from Lovettsville.

Commodore Alexander A. SEMMES, commandant of the Washington navy yard, died suddenly at Hamilton yesterday afternoon, of peritonitis, after an illness of a few days. He was connected with the navy yard for about seven years, first as executive officer, and since 1883, when he was promoted to commodore, as commandant. His family were with him at Hamilton. Death result of suicide.

Marriage licences were issued in Washington on Monday last to Fernando DANIEL, of Loudoun County, and Mollie REILEY of Prince William County. Also to J. Wade BARRETT, of Shelbyville, Illinois, and Mrs. Sarah GORE, of Loudoun County.

Thursday, 1 October 1885   Vol. XXX, No. 17

[top part of article cut out]

Married: On September 15th 1885, at the residence of Mr. Chas. G. WALTER, in Frederick, by the Rev. Osborne INGLE, Scott W. MISKELL to Miss Lydia APPEL, both of Loudoun County.

Married: On the 30th of September, at the M. E. Parsonage in Leesburg, Mr. Samuel SNOOTS and Mrs. Annie STOUTS, both of Taylortown, Loudoun County.

Died: Mrs. Sallie RUSSELL, the widow of Wm. RUSSELL dec'd., formerly of Loudoun County, died at the residence of her son, Thomas J. RUSSELL, Hillsboro, Montgomery County, Ill., August 27, 1885, aged 75y 2m 18d.

Died: At his home near Leesburg, September 28th 1885, Thomas COATS, in the 45th year of his age.

Died: On the 22d inst., suddenly, at her home in the Trappe, in this county, Mrs. Sarah E. FRASIER, wife of Townsend FRASIER, aged 63y 2m 23d. Member of the Methodist Church. She was taken short of breath in returning from the school house nearby and died a few minutes after she reached her house. A husband and 8 children, the youngest child being eighteen survive.

Died: Mrs. Sopronia BEANS, wife of Isaiah BEANS Esq., died at the home of her son-in-law, Mr. Jonathan MATTHEW, in Hillsboro, after a brief illness, on the 16th of September, aged 69y 5m 24dy and in the 49th year of her married life.

Letter to Editor from E. TINSMAN from Clarksburg, W Va, September 27, 1885: I was born at the Trappe, in the house now owned and occupied by Townsend FRASIER, in the year 1824, and left my native home on 5 July 1847, and landed in Clarksburg on 12th of same month. ...

Cards are out for the marriage, in Washington DC, on the evening of October 8th 1885, of Mary, daughter of Mrs. M. B. and the late Thos. SAUNDERS, of this county, to Richard McALLISTER Jr., of Washington.

Mrs. S. DICE, wife of Rev. J. C. DICE, of the M. E. Church, South, died at her home in Staunton, last Wednesday, September 23d.

Mr. Clement A. PECK died at his residence at Tenleytown yesterday morning, at the age of 62 years from an affection of the spine, which he suffered for a year or more past. At the time of his death he was engaged in teaching. Funeral will take place tomorrow afternoon, interment at Oak Hill. *Wash. Star of Saturday last.* He was a native of Loudoun.

Sheriff of Loudoun passed through Alexandria en route to Staunton, having in charge Mr. C. F. CASTLEMAN, a teach in Leesburg public schools, adjudged a lunatice and placed in the Western Lunatic Asylum.

Fauquier: Mrs. Robert HOLTZCLAW, 80 years old, died Thursday.

Thursday, 22 October 1885   Vol. XXX, No. 20

Commonwealth vs. William A. REED, charged with the murder of his wife in May, 1884, with strychnine. ... He was a school teacher residing at Neersville. Shortly after the funeral it became apparent that the accused was paying attention to a lady for whom he had shown a decided partiality before the death of his wife. Friends of his first wife were also suspicious. Court found not guilty.

Married: On Sept. 14, 1885, by the Rev. John FORSYTHE, of Herndon, Va., W. G. COLLINS, to Brittie ROLLINS, both of Washington City.

Married: On October 15, 1885, at the residence of the bride's brother, Tenleytown, by the Rev. D. HASKELL, Harry C. DEAN, of Tenleytown, to Lilly M. BEACH, daughter of Philip BEACH, of Loudoun County.

Married: At the residence of the bride's mother on the 6th of October 1885, by Elder Joseph FURR, Mr. Newton MADDEN, of Pa to Miss Henrietta WILLIAMS, second daughter of John WILLIAMS dec'd., of Loudoun County.

Married: At the residence of the bride's father, T. M. OSBURN, Esq., in Snickersville, Wednesday, October 14th 1885, by Rev. A. C. HOPKINS, D.D., Dr. Charles B. TURNER to Miss Mattie V. OSBURN, both of Loudoun County.

Married: At the Reform Parsonage in Frederick, Md, on October 14th, 1885, by the Rev. Dr. E. R. ESCHBACH, Charles E. SPRING to Miss Sousan E. SOUDER, both of Loudoun County.

Married: On the 12th inst., in Rockville, Md., Mr. Charles H. M. PEYTON, of Loudoun Co., and Miss Delia E. EVERHART, of Montgomery Co.

Married: October 14th at the parsonage in Hamilton, by Rev. J. T. WILLIAMS, Robert L. MYERS and Bettie COPELAND, all of Loudoun County.

Married: Near Farmwell by Rev. G. W. POPKINS, on the 15th, Mr. H. T. MORAN to Miss Alice PAXTON, all of Loudoun.

Married: At Washington DC, October 1st, by Rev. S. K. COX, D.D., Mr. Jefferson D. LAMBERT to Miss Sarah P. WEADON, all of Loudoun.

Died: On Monday October 12th 1885, at his father's residence, Mr. William F. DOWELL Jr., in the 37th year of his age. Interment in cemetery at Middleburg.

Tribute of Respect: In memory of Mrs. Martha G. RODGERS, organizer and superintendent of the Leesburg Mission Bank, M. E. Church, South.

Thursday, 29 October 1885   Vol. XXX, No. 21

Married: At St. James' Episcopal Church, Leesburg, at 2 o'clock Wed. afternoon, Oct 28th 1885, by Rev. Dr. R. T. DAVIS, Richard H. TEBBS, Esq., member of Loudoun bar, and Lillian, dau. of Capt. Wm. B. LYNCH, editor of the *Washingtonian*, all of Leesburg.

Married: In the M. E. Church, South, at Hamilton, October 21, 1885, by Rev. L. H. CRENSHAW, Mr. James A. WYNKOOP to Miss E. Gertie SHRIVER, both of Hamilton.

Married: At the residence of the bride's grandfather, Mr. Michael WIARD, near Lovettsville, October 30th 1885, Mr. George C. WIRE to Miss Leah M. SMITH, Rev. P. H. MILLER officiating.

Married: At Shelbourne, on the 20th inst., Mr. Tarlton THOMAS, of Prince William and Miss Mary N. HUTCHISON of Loudoun Co.

Married: At St. James church by Rev. Joshua PETERKIN, D.D. on Tuesday, 20th of Oct.1885, Rev. S. Scollay MOORE, of Herndon, Fairfax Co, to Annie E., daughter of Mr. Wm. B. ISAACS.

Married: October 21, 1885, in the Methodist Church, at Union, by Rev. I. B. LAKE, Mr. John L. GILL to Miss Sudie V. LEITH, daughter of the late Dr. Theo. LEITH, of Bloomfield.

Co. Ct.: Francis M. KENDALL appointed Guardian for Margaret L. KENDALL. Naturalization papers granted to William STALLARD, of England.

Wm. H. T. LEWIS qualified as Admr. of Fisher A. LEWIS dec'd. Estate of Vincent LEWIS committed to Sheriff.

St. James' Episcopal Church last Wednesday afternoon, marriage of R. H. TEBBS, Esq. and Miss Lillian LYNCH, daughter of Capt. W. B. LYNCH, editor of the *Washingtonian*. Rev. R. T. DAVIS performed the ceremony.

Marriage of Miss Sudie V. LEITH to Mr. J. C. GILL, both of Loudoun, at the Methodist church in Unison on the 21st inst. Attended by Messrs. G. Earnest LEITH, brother of the bride, and Julia BALDWIN. Rev. Dr. LAKE of Baptist Church performed the ceremony. Wedding march arranged by bride's cousin, Mrs. Lulu Lloyd BARNUM, of Louisville Ky.

Thursday, 5 November 1885   Vol. XXX, No. 22

Died: On the 17th of October, 1885, near the Valley Meeting house at her mother's residence, Sallie A. UMBAUGH, daughter of George and Catharine UMBAUGH, aged 15y 7m 2d.

Died: Near Aldie, October 23th, 1885, Mrs. Susannah RITICOR, wife of Charles RITICOR dec'd., in her 71st year. For nearly 10 years she has suffered from shortness of breath.

[MISSING ISSUES]

Thursday, 17 December 1885   Vol. XXX, No. 28

Married: On December 1, 1885, at the Lutheran Church, Frederick City, Md, by the Rev. Dr. DIEHL, Thomas H. SMITH, to Miss Florence TROTER, both of Loudoun County.

Passed away December 10th, 1885, infant son of Joseph and Rose HOWELL aged 3m 28d.

Died: Near Gum Spring, Va, November 27th 1885, Daniel Alpheus, eldest son of Lawson E. and Lydia A. JOHNSON, in his 16th year.

Died in Petersburg, Va, on the 10th inst., Helen, little daughter of Thomas R. and Helen MOORE, granddaughter of the late Jas. H. CHAMBLIN, of Leesburg.

Family of Dr. Samuel J. COCKERILLE, of Washington DC (formerly of this town), his son, Stanard, aged about 21 years, and a student at the Baltimore Medical College, died at 8 o'clock Tuesday evening Dec 8th of diptheria. His younger brother, Dufour, about 17 years of age, died the next day, Wednesday, and on Thursday they were both buried in the same grave.

Mr. J. H. INGRAHAM, newly elected Judge of the Hustings Court of Manchester, is a grandson of the late John P. SMART of Leesburg.

Thursday, 24 December 1885 Vol. XXX, No. 29

Married: At Unison, November 18, 1885, by Rev. A. A. P. NEILL, Mr. C. H. L. OSBURNE, formerly of Shepherdstown, and Miss Ella TAYLOR, of Unison.

Died: Oct. 24th 1885, near Wheatland, at the residence of his brother-in-law, F. J. CRIM, after a brief illness of typhoid fever, Samuel L., youngest son of Jonas and Sarah C. HARVEY, aged 22 years.

Died: At his home near Gumspring, in this county, James W. HANCOCK, on the 11th inst. in the 47th year of his age. He was the son of Samuel G. and Jane T. L. HANCOCK.

Died: At Carson City, Colorado, at 4 a.m., Dec. 15, from injuries received from an accident in the Thornton Mine, Ashby H. GULICK, youngest son of the late James H. and Ann V. GULICK of this county, in the 24th year of his age.

Mr. Geo. W. DORRELL died at his home near Daysville, on Saturday last, of cancer, in about the 76th year of his age. Interred in Union Cemetery, Leesburg, on Sunday.

Miss Mollie TOWNER, daughter of late John TOWNER, of this town, died very suddenly in Washington one day last week, at the house of a neighbor upon whom she had gone to make a call, by the bursting of a blood vessel in the head. She was in the 29th year of her age and lived in Washington a good many years.

Miss Ida Oswald MASON died at her home in Alexandria last Wednesday, after a protracted illness. She was the youngest daughter of the late James M. MASON, U. S. Senator from Va.

Death of Mrs. Ann Maria POWELL, of this town, in Alexandria last Sunday in the 86th year of her age. Daughter of Hon. Cuthbert POWELL, a former rep. from this District in the U. S. Congress. Mother of Capt. E. B. POWELL, lately of Leesburg. Funeral took place from Christ Church, Alexandria, Monday afternoon.

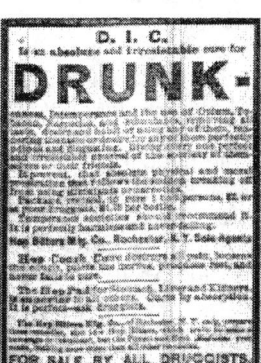

Twilight wedding took place on November 25th 1885 at the Howard House, Washington DC, of Laura A., eldest daughter of S. H. WILSON, Silcott's Springs, Va, to Mr. J. T. CORNWELL, of Fauquier Co, by Rev. J. A. PRICE of that city. Attendants were Mr. Willie CORNWELL and the bride's sister. They will reside in Delaplane.

Tribute of respect: death of James W. HANCOCK which occurred at his sister's home in Loudoun County

[MISSING ISSUE]

Thursday, 7 January 1886   Vol. XXX, No. 31

Married: At the residence of the bride's father, near Leesburg, on Wednesday, January 6th 1886, by Rev. R. T. DAVIS, Richard M. GREEN, Esq., of New York, and Miss Sarah V., daughter of Christian T. HEMPSTONE, Esq. of Loudoun.

Married: At the residence of the bride's parents, on December 10, 1885, by Rev. Henry BRANCH, Wm. H. FRAZIER Esq., and Miss Mollie F. HICKMAN, both of Loudoun County.

Married: December 29th 1885, at the residence of Mr. RATCLIFFE, uncle of the bride, near North Fork, by Elder B. BRIDGES, Mr. Cornelius C. SEATON to Miss Sarah V. BARNES, all of Loudoun.

Married; December 23d 1885, at the residence of Mr. G. JENKINS, near Guilford, by Elder Benjamin BRIDGES, Mr. James ETCHER to Miss Eugene A. HOUSER, both of Loudoun.

Married: December 24th 1825 [1885], at the Lutheran Church, near Lovettsville, Mr. J. W. FRY to Miss Maggie C. BOGER, Rev. P. H. MILLER, officiating.

Died: suddenly in Aldie, of heart disease, December 30, 1885, Mrs. Sarah J. SANFORD, wife of W. L. SANFORD, Esq., late of Rapides Parish, La, aged 59 years.

Died: Near Evergreen Mills, on Christmas Eve, Mary Jane, fourth child of Rector and Mary E. LOWE, aged 5y 1m 10d.

Died: On December 26th 1885, at her residence near Leesburg, of Mrs. Matilda LAYCOCK, relict of the late Samuel LAYCOCK, in the 76th year of her age.

On Wednesday last, December 30th, Mrs. Sarah J. SANFORD, wife of Mr. Wm. L. SANFORD, of this county, arose in the morning in her usual health and after breakfast drove into Aldie. For a short time, she was taken suddenly ill with heart disease, and carried to house of Mr. J. H. GREEN, where she expired. In her 59th year. Leaves a husband and several children. On the first day of the new year her remains were laide at rest in the cemetery in this town.

On Tuesday, 5th instant, at Mrs. Mahlon THOMAS', marriage of her daughter, Mattie to Mr. Samuel R. JAMES. Bride attended by Miss SMITH, of Culpeper, and Misses Annie THOMAS, Celia JAMES and Tamar THOMAS, of Loudoun. Groom attended by Messrs. Owen THOMAS Jr., Arthur NICHOLS, Tom LITTLETON and Scott PAXSON, of Loudoun. Ceremony by Dr. I. B. LAKE. Refreshments at residence of groom's father, Mr. Craven JAMES.

Thursday, 14 January 1886   Vol. XXX, No. 32

Married: On Thursday afternoon, Jan. 7th 1886, near Mt. Gilead, by Rev. J. R. BRIDGES, Charles E. WHITE to Miss Edmonia WILLIAMS.

Married: In Leesburg, January 4th 1886, by Rev. I. W. CANTER, Miss Belle THOMPSON, of Leesburg, and Mr. Wm. E. WILEY, of Montgomery County. Md.

Married: At the Baptist church, in Luray, on the morning of December 31st, by Rev. A. C. BARROR, of Baltimore, assisted by Rev. L. R. MILBOURNE, of Luray, Lillie, daughter of D. H. SNYDER, of the latter place, to Howard H. McVEIGH, of Baltimore, son of the late Dr. Wm. H. McVEIGH, of Loudoun County.
Mr. Thomas GREEN died at the residence of his son-in-law, in the lower part of Loudoun on Tuesday night last. He was about 93 years old. Interred at the cemetery in this town today, Thursday.
Marriage license issued in Washington, on Tuesday of last week, to C. W. POWELL and Carrie HEFFNER, both of Loudoun.
Miss Eliza RANDOLPH, dau. of Bishop A. M. RANDOLPH, was married in Richmond on Tuesday, to Mr. James M. AMBLER, of Baltimore, the bride's father officiating, assisted by Rev. Dr. MINNEGRODE.
Co. Ct.: Estates of Jos. LEWIS and Saml. P. SWANK committed to Sheriff. J. W. FOSTER qualified as Guardian of Arthur J. EVANS.

[MISSING ISSUES]

Thursday, 18 February 1886   Vol. XXX, No. 37

To the memory of Henry C. JOHNSON who died February 3rd near Hughesville, Va, aged 32 years after an illness of four years. Interred in Leesburg Cemetery, February 5th 1886.
Marriage licence granted in Washington DC on Tuesday to Thos. E. SILCOTT and Kate M. DOWNS, both of this county.

[MISSING ISSUES]

Thursday, 4 March 1886   Vol. XXX, No. 39

Married: At Lovettsville, on February 23rd 1886, by Rev. J. H. MILLER, Mr. Robert W. OFFUTT, of Montgomery County, Md, and Miss Edna M. GRUBB, of Loudoun County.
Died: At the residence of her parents, in Waterford, on Thursday, February 25th 1886, of brain fever, Mabel Heaton, daughter of Dr. R. W. and Emma L. JANNEY, aged 1y 5m. Her remains brought to Leesburg on Saturday and laid to rest in Union Cemetery.
Died: At the residence of her parents near Aldie, February 25th 1886, Viola D., youngest daughter of W. T. and Emma R. SAFFER, aged 1y 10m 25d.
Marriage of Mr. Joshua FLETCHER Jr., of Fauquier County, and Miss Lula FOSTER, of Marshall, took place Wednesday. She is the daughter of Maj. Thomas R. FOSTER and sister of Capt. J. W. FOSTER of Leesburg.
The same day Miss Mamie SHEPHERD, daughter of Capt. Ham SHEPHERD, U.S. Collector of Revenue, married W. B. WILLIAMSON, commission merchant of Warrenton. Ceremony

performed at St. James Episcopal Church by Rev. George W. NELSON.

[MISSING ISSUE]

Thursday, 18 March 1886   Vol. XXX, No. 41

Married: At the Lutheran Church near Lovettsville, March 4th 1886, by Rev. P. H. MILLER, Mr. Wm. A. VIRTZ and Miss Sallie B. EVERHART.

Died: Sarah POTTS, wife of Thomas POTTS, at her home in Hillsboro, on Sunday February 21st, in the 72d year of her age.

Died: John R. WHITE, at his home in Hillsboro, March 5th of bronchial affection, in the 76th year of his age.

Died: At her home, near Farmwell, on March 3d, 1886, Miss Mary R. LEFEVER, in the 24th year of her age. She was the second daughter of Mr. John LEFEVER.

Two grown daughters of Mr. Peter L. BIGGS, living near Guilford, died, one on Wed. the other on Thurs. of last week of pneumonia.

Peter COMPHER, soldier of the war of 1812-14, died at his home near Lovettsville, on the 3d inst., at the age of 93 years. He was a private in the 57th Reg. of Va militia, commanded by Col. A. T. MASON, which marched from Leesburg in August 1814, to the defence of Baltimore. He was a member of the Lutheran church.

Martin CAVANAUGH, member of the Catholic Church, died at his home near Ball's Mill, Friday night. Interred in Union Cemetery on Sunday, the funeral taking place from the Chapel of the Immaculate Conception, Father WILSON officiating.

On Tuesday morning last, of pneumonia, Miss Minnie, daughter of Mr. John V. TAVENNER, aged about 18 years. Miss Maggie TAVENNER, sister of the deceased is very sick at this time.

Miss Martha D. LYNCH, sister of the editor of the *Washingtonian*, of this town, died at the residence of her brother, Judge John A. LYNCH, in Frederick City, Md, last Wednesday afternoon, in her 56th year.

[MISSING ISSUES]

Thursday, 15 April 1886   Vol. XXX, No. 45

Died: March 20th 1886, at Salem Va, Thomas STOCKS, of Loudoun County, aged 47y 3m 14d. He was a soldier in the confederate arm, leaves a wife and four children.

Died: In Baltimore, on Sunday, April 4th, Walter Dulaney, aged 11y 8m, youngest son of W. D. and Mary G. ADDISON, and grandson of the late Henry KEPLAR, Richmond, Va.

Died: At his residence, near Lincoln, March 5, 1786 [1886], Benjamin F. STEVENS in about the 80th year of his age.

Peyton DAVIS, of this county, died one day last week at his home near Snickersville, at an advance age.

April Ct.: Wills of Danl. N. WELLS dec'd., Philip VANSICKLER dec'd. and Peyton DAVIS dec'd., admitted to probate. Wm. H. GAINES (col'd) license to celebrate rites of matrimony.

At 5 o'clock last evening at the residence of Mrs. Mary KLEIN, on Locust street, the marriage of Mr. G. J. BRADFIELD, formerly State attorney and a lawyer of Delta, La, now practicing law at Lebanon, Mo, to Mrs. Annie E. WARE, of this city. Rev. Mr. WOODWARD officiating.

Virginia N., little daughter of Dr. R. C. POWELL, of Alexandria, died in that city a few days ago of spinal menegitis.

[MISSING ISSUES]

Thursday, 6 May 1886   Vol. XXX, No. 48

Married: April 22d 1886, at the residence of the bride's parents, near Harper's Ferry, Mr. Arthur W. BUTTS and Miss Mary E. EVERHART, Rev. P. H. MILLER officiating.

Married: In the M. E. Church, South, Upperville, Fauquier County, on the 28th of April, by the Rev. Dr. Samuel RODGERS, the Rev. John N. McCORMICK, of Baltimore, and Miss Maud L., daughter of Mr. Washington RICHARDS, of Loudoun County.

Married: In the Chapel of the Protestant Episcopal Theological, Seminary, near Alexandria, Va, Wednesday, April 28th 1886, by the Rev. William F. GARDNER, assisted by the Rt. Rev. George W. PETERKIN, D.D., J. Thompson COLE, of the Japan Mission, and Annie E. LEE, youngest daughter of Cassius F. LEE, Esq., of Fairfax county.

Died: At Farmwell, April 24, 1886, Sarah Dana, child of George and Elizabeth C. HAY, aged 1y 2m 8d.

Marriage on Wednesday Morning of last week, in the M. E. Church, South, Upperville, of Miss Maud H. RICHARDS, daughter of Mr. W. L. RICHARDS of this county, to Rev. Jno. N. McCORMICK, of the Methodist Church, by Rev. Dr. RODGERS, presiding Elder of this district. No bridesmaids or ushers – Rev. D. M. JAMES, Rev. F. J. PRETTYMAN, Mr. C. PORTER and Mr. G. Earnest LEITH. They will reside in Baltimore.

Mr. Hirst MILHOLLEN died at his home at Philomont on Saturday.

Miss Mary DeWITT and Mr. William H. ADAMS were married in St. Paul's Church to day at 10 o'clock, Rev. Dr. MINNIGERODE officiating. ... He is a son of Mr. Samuel ADAMS, formerly of this county.

R. Hirst MILHOLLEN, Junior member of the firm of Milhollen Bros. of Philomont, died after a short illness at the residence of his mother, on Saturday night last, in about the 25th year of his age. Funeral on

Tuesday with masonic brethren. Services by the mystic order, assisted by Rev. Mr. Light, Rev. A. A. P. NEALE, of M. E. Church, South. Interred in South Fork beside her father.

Cards are out for the marriage of Miss Maggie HARMON, daughter of Allen C. HARMON, of this city, and Mr. Henry W. BROWN, of Georgetown, which will take place at the residence of the bride's parents, on south Royal street, on Thursday next. *Alexandria Gazette of Tuesday.* Mr. BROWN for years was proprietor of the Bookstore in this town.

Thursday, 20 May 1886   Vol. XXX, No. 50

Died: In Charlestown, on Monday morning, May 10th 1886, Mrs. Mary E. WOODDY, widow of the late Samuel H. WOODDY, in the 74th year of her age. She was a member of the Methodist Church.

In Canton, Mo, May 10th 1886, of paralysis, Alfred POULTON, aged 84y 2m 9d. Born in Loudoun Co, March 1st, 1802, was married and removed to Columbianna Co, Ohio, in 1825; removed thence to Marion Co, Mo, in 1857, and resided near Palmyra until 1868, when he removed to Canton, where he resided until his death. Stricken with paralysis March 15th 1882 and cared for by a son and daughter.

Mr. H. C. LYNN, formerly of Snickersville, has located in Richmond as a member of the firm of Boxley & Lynn, stove and tinware business, plumbing, gas-fitting &c.

Mr. Thomas PRESTON, aged 80 years, died at his residence near Hamilton on the 4th instant. He fell in his yard with paralysis and never rallied.

Jim BROOKINS, colored man of this town, was stricken with paralysis last Tuesday evening and died that night.

Death of William MATTHEW, Esq. between 5 and 6 o'clock last Thursday morning, from suicide. He resided until a few years ago in Hillsboro. Lost his father while yet a child. [long article]

Marriage license issued in Washington on Monday, to Chas. T. ATTWELL, of Loudoun, of Katie DAVOIR.

Thursday, 27 May 1886   Vol. XXX, No. 51

Married: At the Lutheran Church, Jefferson, Md, May 12th 1886, Mr. Charles T. HUGHES and Miss Emma C. CULLER, Rev. P. H. MILLER, officiating.

Died: At her home at North Fork, on April 25th, Jane HICKS, in the 75th year of her age.

Died: On April 31st, at the residence of her cousin (John STEANSON), Maria GUIDER.

Death of George MUSE, who died after a few days illness, in Bell-View Hospital NY, aged 32 years. Remains were brought on by his brother-in-law, C. W. PALMER and interred in Herndon Cemetery.

During a thunder storm last Saturday night, Mr. Fayette FINK, residing on the farm of Mr. Jonathan MATTHEW, about 3 miles from Hillsboro, was struck and killed by lightning. He leaves a wife and two children.

Thursday, 3 June 1886 Vol. XXX, No. 52

Married: At the Parsonage, Lovettsville, May 20th 1886, Mr. George W. CASE and Miss Rosa B. SNOOTS, Rev. P. H. MILLER officiating.

Married: At the residence of the bride's mother, near Rehobeth church, by Rev. D. C. HEDRICK, John H. PEACOCK, of Missouri, to Margaret J. WOLFORD, of Loudoun.

Married: At the residence of the bride's parents, near Hillsboro, on May 12th 1886, by the Rev. J. R. VANHORN, Mr. Samuel E. NICHOLS to Miss Ella M. STOCKS, daughter of Mahlon STOCKS, Esq.

Mr. James B. WHITE, formerly of Hillsboro, died at the residence of Mr. John MILTON, in Hamilton, on Sunday last, in his 77th year.

Hon. Emory DORSEY, member of Congress from Nebraska, spent Monday night in Leesburg. He is a son of the late Hamilton DORSEY, of Waterford, in this county, where the son was born, and lived until a few years before the war.

Mr. John W. OTLEY, formerly of Loudoun, was elected Alderman in Monroe Ward, Richmond city.

Jesse W. JONES, one of the oldest citizens of Charlottesville died there at noon on Monday, after he fell two weeks ago down his stairway. He was father-in-law of Mr. J. W. EDWARDS, formerly of this town.

Thursday, 10 June 1886 Vol. XXXI, No. 1

Married: On May 26th 1886, at the Lutheran parsonage, in Frederick city, by the Rev. Dr. DIEHL, Edward R. TRIDAPOE to Miss Ada M. CORDELL, both of Loudoun County.

Died: Near Guilford, May 4th 1886, after a few days illness, Thomas E. HUMMER, son of G. W. and L. J. HUMMER, aged 24y 6m 7d.

Died: Mrs. Sallie C. WILSON (widow of James B. WILSON dec'd) at her home near Middleburg, May 26th, in her 84th year. For several years a cripple caused by a fall, and 3 months ago had a stroke of paralysis.

Dr. Thomas J. McGILL, of Frederick City, Md, died at his residence in that city on Wednesday last, after a protracted illness. He was a member of the Episcopal Church. Interment in the Frederick cemetery. He was the father of Dr. Saml. McGILL, of this town.

Rev. Dr. Kinlock NELSON for several years Professor of Pastoral Theology, Church History and canon Law at the Virginia Theological Seminary at Alexandria, has been elected Bishop of the Dioceses of Easton. He was born in Clarke Co. in 1840, was a gallant soldier. He is a brother of Mrs. Thos. WILLIAMSON, late of this town.

Mrs. Catharine SCHOOLEY, wife of Mr. Milton SCHOOLEY, of Waterford, died at her home in that place, on Thursday evening last. Confederates killed and wounded in the 8th Va Reg, as taken from the Mirror 30 Oct 1861: Co. A – killed – F. A. OSBURN, 2nd corporal; private John E. REEDER. Wounded – Z. F. MILBURN, severely in right shoulder; Flavius B. HAINES, seriously in right leg, since amputated; Wm. F. JANNEY, seriously in right arm, and slightly in abdomen; Jno. W. SCHAEFFER, slightly in the face. Co. D – wounded – J. H. HUTCHISON, mortally shot through lungs since dead; J. GRUBB, wounded by bayonet on head. Co. E – wounded – Capt. Manly HAMPTON in left heel slightly; Lt. J. A. TAVENNER in left leg; privates Samuel WYNKOOP in left leg slightly, Chas. JONES in left leg slightly, John STEPHENS slightly on the arm, Benj. TAVENNER in the forehead slightly, Hugh KILPATRICK slightly in the leg, J. S. HAWS slightly, D. PEARCE slightly in the hip. Co. F – killed – Sgt. T. C. L. HATCHER; Corp. George A. DONOHOE; private, Joseph CASTILLO. Wounded – Lt. C. PETIT shot in the hip and badly wounded, private Wm. C. FURR mortally wounded since died, private Joseph W. BROWN wounded in the head but not dangerously. Co. G – killed – Private Jas. BALLENGER. Wounded – Corp. H. I. O'BANNON, in the arm badly, private Thomas TEMPLAR shot through the shoulder badly, private John HUTCHISON shot in the leg slightly, missing, and supposed to have been taken prisoner, 1st Lt. J. Owens BERRY. Co. J. – wounded – Lt. B. G. CARTER in the hand slightly, private Chas. G. TAYLOR flesh wound in the thigh, private Joel SMOOT flesh would in the shoulder, private John SKILLMAN slightly in the shoulder, private John RUSH badly bruised being ridden over by horsemen. Co. K. – wounded – private Erasmus FLETCHER shot through the right lung, Jos. FURR badly wounded in the left side, Wm. E. RECTOR leg broken, Silas B. HANBACK badly wounded in the ankle, J. S. SIDALLE, shot through the leg since dead, W. G. SWAIN in the foot slightly, J. S. COOK in the hand.

Thursday, 17 June 1886   Vol. XXXI, No. 2

Died: Mr. Thomas J. GARDNER, son of James L. and Susan GARDNER, departed this life June 7, 1886. He would have been 21y the 22nd of June.

Died: At his home near Fairfax C. H., on Monday, June 7th 1886, of consumption, John A. SIEBER, in the 55th year of his age. He had been an invalid for a long time.

June Ct.: Geo. F. EAMICH qualified as Guardian of Wm. L. and Ellen BARTLETT; C. C. GAVER as Admr. of Lafayette FINK; Jonah NIXON as committee of Mary A. NIXON; John J. TYLER as Guardian of Cely TOLIVER; J. L. BELT as Admr. of Alfred BELT; Sarah C. CARTER as Admr. of Oswall CARTER; John MEAD as

Admr. of Zitha COLBERT. Jas. B. PEUGH as Admr. of Susan A. TAVENNER.

Last Tuesday morning the people of Hamilton were shocked by the report that Mr. E. M. DUNBAR, of the merchantile firm of McVeigh & Dunbar, was found dead in his bed, dying between 4 and 6 o'clock.

Thursday, 24 June 1886   Vol. XXXI, No. 3

Married: On the 16th inst., at the residence of the bride's parents, by the Rev. Dr. Nelson HEAD, Mr. William H. LACOCK to Miss Lucy B. THOMAS, all of Loudoun.

Married: June 17, 1886, at Zion P. E. Church, Fairfax Court House, by the Rev. Frank PAGE, Alfred H. TAYLOR, of Washington DC to Miss Gertrude MOORE, of Fairfax, Va.

Married: on the 15th of June, at Mt. Hope Church, Mr. R. W. A. POWER and Miss Ada BODINE, by Rev. G. W. POPKINS, assisted by the Rev. Mr. BAILY.

Mr. Benjamin MOFFETT, who resides in Buckeystown District, was paralyzed at the City Hotel, in this city, on Wednesday afternoon last. *Frederick Md Citizen of Friday.* He died at 6 o'clock Friday evening. Native of Loudoun, having moved to Maryland a few years ago. He was visiting his daughters in Frederick. He was in the 64th year of his age. On Sunday afternoon his remains were laid beside his wife in Union Cemetery, Leesburg, Rev. Dr. DAVIS officiating.

Little 7 year old grandson of Mrs. Margaret M. KILGOUR, of Potomac, Braden VANDEVANTER (son of Mr. Chas. O. VANDEVANTER, of this county) was bitten badly by a dog in Saturday.

Dr. A. M. FAUNTLEROY died suddenly at his home in Staunton last Saturday evening, and was buried in Winchester on Monday. His brother, Capt. Chas. M. FAUNTLEROY, of this town, was summoned. Dr. FAUNTLEROY was until recently Superintendent of the Western Lunatic Asylum. Hemorrhage of the bowels was the immediate cause of his death. He leaves a wife (sister of Mr. F. E. CONRAD, of this town) and a large family of children.

Marriage license issued by the clerk of the Washington city court on Monday to R. E. CLOWE and A. E. WORTS, of Loudoun county.

Prof. William B. BEAMER, leader of vocal music throughout this section, died Friday.

Thursday, 1 July 1886   Vol. XXXI, No. 4

Married: On Thursday, 24th instant, at the residence of the bride's father, by the Rev. C. M. BROWN, Mr. Wm. CLOUD and Miss Minnie Bell GARRETT, daughter of Mr. B. W. GARRETT, all of Loudoun Co.

Married: June 23d, 1886, at the Short Hill, near Morrisonville, by Rev. P. H. MILLER, Mr. John W. L. JACOBS and Miss Mary M. E. WILT.

Died: At the Short Hill near Lovettsville, June 13th 1866 [1886], Nellie Myrtle, infant daughter of William L. and Flora E. SLATER, aged 1y 5m 19d.

Died: At the Short Hill, near Lovettsville, June 22d, 1886, Ellen BUTTS, aged 62y 8m 23d. Funeral services were held at Mt. Olivet M. E. Church by Rev. P. H. MILLER.

Died on the 26th ult., near Mountsville, Mrs. Sallie C. WILSON, in her 81st year, widow of James B. WILSON. She joined the Presbyterian Church a few weeks since. Mother of 13 children, only five of whom survive her, 4 daughters. and 1 son. Left a widow 31 years ago.

George Prentiss BUTLER, son of William Allen BUTLER, was married in Yonkers at noon yesterday to Miss Ellen MUDGE, daughter of Daniel C. MUDGE, at the First Presbyterian Church. Bridesmaids were Miss Mary CURRIE of Pamrapo, N.J. and Miss Margaret C. BUTLER, sister of the groom. Best man was John M. HARLAN, of Washington. Ceremony performed by Rev. John REID, pastor of the church, assisted by the Rev. Richard D. HARLAN, pastor of the First Presbyterian Church of this city. *N. Y. Sun of Friday.*

Late Dr. A. M. FAUNTLEROY was born in Warrenton, Fauquier County, July 8th 1836. His father was the late Gen. T. T. FAUNTLEROY, former Colonel of the 1st U. S. Dragoons. On his mother's side he was grandson of Col. Chas. MAGIL, of Winchester, an officer of the Rev. War. His brothers surviving him, are Col. Chas. M. FAUNTLEROY, who resigned his commission in the navy of U.S. and served in defence of the South, and Judge T. T. FAUNTLEROY, of Supreme Court of Appeals of Va. ...

Warrenton: Leeman SCOTT, a white boy ten years of age, was brought from Landmark charged with killing with a shotgun his cousin, Wm. Henry DAWSON, 9 years old. He is the son of Robert SCOTT living near Landmark. DAWSON stopped at SCOTT's father's to see his grandmother who is an aged invalid. DAWSON's mother died 6 weeks ago and there had been bad feeling between her and SCOTT's mother.

Thursday, 8 July 1886   Vol. XXXI, No. 5

Died: At his residence, near Amwell, on June 19th 1886, of consumption, Samuel S. GEASLIN, in the 45th year of his age.

Mr. and Mrs. Samuel RECTOR, of Middleburg, are visiting their daughter, Mrs. Judge W. A. HUDSON [Staunton, Va]

[MISSING ISSUES]

Thursday, 22 July 1886   Vol. XXXI, No. 7

Died: On Saturday 17th July 1886, at the residence of his brother-in-law, Stirling MURRAY, in this county, Thos. Jesup MILLER, of Washington City, DC, aged 41 years, son of the late Dr. Thomas

MILLER, of that city. He was a lawyer. [article on another page] He was a native of this city [Washington] born in 1845. Funeral will take place at Rock Creek cemetery this afternoon.

Mr. Jesse J. STANSBURY died at his home in this town, on Monday afternoon last, in the 57th year of his age. He was a native of Baltimore city, but for the last 35 years has been a resident of Leesburg in the jewelry business. He was recording steward of the M. E. Church, South. He leaves a wife and three children. Funeral took place from the M. E. Church, South, at 5 o'clock Tuesday afternoon, by Rev. I. W. CANTER, assisted by Rev. Dr. HEAD and Rev. Dr. ARMSTRONG, of Baltimore. Interred Union Cemetery, Messrs. W. B. LYNCH, W. W. ATHEY, B. F. HEAD, Ed. LITTLETON, Wm. H. THOMAS and Jos. L. NORRIS as pallbearers. Member of Olive Branch Lodge, A. F. & A. Masons.

[MISSING ISSUES]

Thursday, 19 August 1886   Vol. XXXI, No. 11

Died: In Washington on Sunday August 15, 1886, at 6 a.m. after a brief illness of typhoid fever, L. Maud TOWNSEND, daughter of Mrs. Jane J. TOWNSEND, aged 21 years.

Died: In Harper's Ferry, on the 13th inst., Mr. Israel RUSSELL, aged 74 years. He was an old merchant of that place.

Died: At her residence in Wichita, Kansas, July 27th, of typhoid fever after an illness of one week, Mrs. America MARTIN, wife of W. A. MARTIN and daughter of the late Col. John LESLIE, of Loudoun.

Died: Henry Hamilton FRED, son of Mr. Frank L. FRED, of Indian Territory, died in Middleburg, July 28th, at the home of his brother, Saml. R. FRED, in the 30th year of his age. He had been away in Atlanta and Indian Territory for six years and returned to native Loudoun a few weeks ago when he was attacked with typhoid fever and died in nine days. He was borne to Middleburg cemetery, funeral conducted by Rev. C. M. BROWN of the Methodist Church.

Mrs. Nancy ROGERS died at Mt. Airy, the residence of her husband, Richard L. ROGERS at 5 a.m. Aug 10th in her 70th year. Daughter of the late Jesse McVEIGH, and leaves brothers and sisters.

Thursday, 26 August 1886   Vol. XXXI, No. 12

Married: At the residence of Mr. J. W. McFARLAND, near Rockville, Md, on Wednesday, August 18th, by Rev. R. T. BROWN, Mr. Jas. R. DOVE and Miss Nora L. BURCH, of Loudoun County.

Married: In Washington, on August 11th 1886, at the residence of Rev. C. C. MEADER, R. S. HUTCHINSON, of Loudoun county, to Miss Annie M. CHARLTON, of Baltimore Md.

Married: On August 10, 1886, at the Lutheran Parsonage, in Frederick city, Md, by the Rev. Dr. DIEHL, Robert S. CROMWELL to Miss Margaret F. FILLER, both of Loudoun County.

Married: At the residence of the officiating minister, in Leesburg, on Tuesday, August 24th 1886, by Rev. Dr. HEAD, Mr. John R. WADDLE and Mary A. GRIMES, all of Loudoun.

Married: On August 14th, 1886, in Frederick city, Md, by the Rev. J. KNOTT, Wm. J. MITCHELMORE to Miss M. E. DUVALL, both of Loudoun county.

Died: At his home in Muskingum Co., Ohio, August 14th 1886, Mahlon WHITE, formerly of this county, in about his 77th year.

Departed this life on the 3d August 1886, after a protracted and painful illness at Clifton, the residence of her son, Thomas Lee WORSLEY, near Leesburg, in her 66th year, Mrs. Virginia G. WORSLEY, relict of Wm. WORSLEY dec'd., and daughter of the late Dr. Charles G. EDWARDS, formerly a physician of Loudoun County. She was a member of the Episcopal Church.

Mrs. America Leslie MARTIN, wife of W. A. MARTIN, and daughter of Col. John LESLIE, dec'd., of Loudoun Co, died at her residence in Wachita, Kan., July 27, of typhoid fever. She emigrated to Kansas with her husband in 1874, grasshopper year.

Mr. Justus KUHLMAN died at his home near Hamilton, on Tuesday the 24th inst., in about the 65th year of his age. He was a thrifty farmer and died after an illness of about ten days.

On Saturday evening last, over the marriage of Mr. Wm. E. CRIM and Miss Mary MOSS, performed at the Old School Baptist Parsonage, Rev. Mr. BADGER officiating.

The *Baltimore Sun* referring to the death of Mrs. Elizabeth SAUNDERS, who died at her home in Newark, N. J. on the 17th inst., and was buried beside her husband in Union Cemetery Leesburg last Thursday says she was 71 years of age. She was a native of Baltimore, daughter of the late Thos. HILLEN, sister of the late Col. Solomon HILLEN, at one time the mayor of this city. She leaves 2 sons and 2 daughters who reside in Newark. Mr. Beverley C. SANDERS, her husband was a Virginia and formerly resided in Baltimore. He was once collector of the port of san Francisco and died several years ago. She was the last of the children of Mrs. Thos. HILLEN to pass away.

[MISSING ISSUES]

Thursday, 16 September 1886   Vol. XXXI, No. 15

Died: On Sunday, Sept. 6, 1886, of spinal menengitis, Ashford Elwood Leslie, son of J. H. and Parilla LYNN, aged 4y 10m 28d.

Died: September 6th 1886, Lillie Pearl ORRISON, daughter of John P. and Lillie B. ORRISON, aged 4 days.

Died: Near Hillsboro, at the residence of his mother, Saturday, August 14th, 1886, of consumption, Willie O. CORDER, aged 24y 7d.

Sept. Ct.: Administrations of estates of Abram WARFORD dec'd., Sarah A. SANBOWER dec'd. and Isaiah BEANS dec'd. granted. Wills of Sallie A. FRANCIS dec'd., Justice KUHLMAN dec'd., Saml. ROPP dec'd., Isaiah B. BEANS dec'd., Jno. J. CURRELL dec'd. and Alfred CLINE dec'd. admitted to probate.

One day last week, at the boarding house of Mr. John HAMPTON, near Snickersville, the little 5 year old son of Mr. GAUTER, of Washington, whose family has been spending the summer at Mr. HAMPTON's fell, and the hind wheel passed over his breast, he died in a few minutes. His remains were taken to Washington Thursday morning.

Mrs. Col. Wm. KILGOUR died last Friday morning at Rockville, Md, after a short but severe illness in the 52 year of her age. She leaves a husband and daughter.

Thursday, 30 September 1886   Vol. XXXI, No. 17

Married: On Thursday evening, September 16, 1886, at Stumptown, Loudoun County, by Rev. Carter PAGE, Mr. Millard FRY to Miss Teressa AYRES, daughter of William AYRES Esq. of Stumptown.

Married: On Tuesday evening, 14th September 1886, at Lucket's Cross Roads, Loudoun County, by the Rev. Carter PAGE, Mr. James KIDWELL to Miss Sallie LUCKETT, daughter of the late William LUCKETT Esq.

Died: Cora D. FRY, of congestion of the brain, after a lingering illness. she lay in sleep for nine days, only opening her eyes a few moments to close them in death. Aged 14y 8m 17d, daughter of Peter W. and Mary E. FRY.

[MISSING ISSUE]

Thursday, 14 October 1886   Vol. XXXI, No. 19

Married: October 5th 1886, at the residence of the bride's parents, Charlestown, W. Va., Mr. Geo. W. COMPHER of Taylortown, to Miss Abbie E. WATSON.

Married: On October 6th at Christ Church, Chantilly, Fairfax County, by Rev. Frank PAGE, Mr. Thomas J. REED, of Loudoun, and Miss Lizzie, daughter of Wm. F. LEE, of Fairfax.

Married: At the Lutheran parsonage near Lovettsville October 6th 1886, Mr. Russell PRICE to Miss Lizzie A. BEANS, Rev. P. H. MILLER officiating.

Married: On July 17th at the residence of the groom's father in Leesburg, by Rev. D. C. HEDRICK, Mr. David SKINNER and Miss Mary AYERS, all of Loudoun.

Married: Near Mt. Hope, October 6, 1886, by the Rev. G. W. POPKINS, Mr. Richard LOW to Miss Sallie R. HOSKINSON, all of Loudoun.

Married: At the residence of the bride's father in Leesburg by Rev. D. C. [page creased and rest hidden]

Died: [page creased and rest hidden] 1886, Joseph M. CONARD, aged 62y 9m 18d.

Died: At his residence in Fauquier County, near Rector's Cross Roads, on the 21st of September 1886, Mr. Wm. FLETCHER Sr., in the 83d year of his age.

Died: On Friday, September 24th, 1886, Joseph Heaton, youngest son of Albert and Emma VANDEVANTER, aged 7m 18d.

Mrs. Louisa S. BUSSARD, wife of Mr. O. M. BUSSARD, Deputy Sheriff of this county, died of consumption at her home near Woodburn, on Thursday last, in about the 33rd year of her age. She was buried in Union Cemetery on Saturday.

Ernest MYERS, son of Mr. George MYERS, died at the residence of his father, about 2 miles east of Leesburg, on Thursday night last, of diphtheria, in his 15th year. Buried in Union Cemetery, Leesburg, on Saturday. Mr. MYERS younger child has the same disease.

Co. Ct.: Wills of Cath. A. R. CARSON dec'd., and Jos. M. CONARD dec'd. admitted to probate. Mary C. VIRTZ qualified as Admx. of Peter T. VIRTS dec'd.

Mrs. Susan J. CANTER, mother of Rev. Isaac W. CANTER, of Leesburg Va, died at her home near Stephens City, the 27th ult. of heart disease. She was about 73 years of age. She and her husband, who survives her, married about 54 years ago and moved to the homestead where she died. She was the mother of 10 children, 9 of whom are living; two of her sons are members of the Baltimore Conference and one of her daughters is the wife of Rev. W. N. WAGNER, of Covington, Va.

Mr. David STEADMAN of this town died on Sunday evening, at the residence of his son-in-law, Mr. Thomas W. MYERS, near Waterford, in the 76th year of his age. Born in Leesburg and residing here almost continuously. Interred in the Cemetery of the M. E. Church, of this town, on Tuesday.

On Thursday last three colored boys, Oscar JACKSON and two others, living near Guilford, went out gunning. Later the two boys returned bringing JACKSON's gun saying nothing. JACKSON's body was found in the woods not far from his home, almost the whole side of his head was torn away. The close discharge of the gun had ignited his clothes and consumed his body. Thought to be an accidental discharge of the gun.

Thursday, 21 October 1886   Vol. XXXI, No. 20

Married: On Tuesday, October 12th 1886, near Lovettsville, by Rev. D. C. HEDRICK, Mr. Jacob Z. RINKER of Edinburg, Va, and Miss Girta D. KALB, of Loudoun, daughter of Silas D. KALB, Esq.

Married: At the parsonage of the M. E. Church South, in Leesburg, on October 14th, 1886, by Rev. Isaac W. CANTER, Mr. Welby S. ARNETT and Miss Kate V. SIMMONS, both of Loudoun.

Died: In Richmond, October 12, 1886, in her 53d year, Mrs. Sarah J. SCHLEIF, widow of the late John V. SCHLEIF, formerly of this town.

Died: Earnest L., 4th son of G. W. and L. E. MYERS, died October. 7, 1886, of diphtheria, aged 16y 11m 2d.

Died: On Sunday morning, October 17th, at the home of her parents, Mabel Moore, infant daughter of Charles M. and Virginia TITUS, in the 5th year of her age.

Miss Ella PORTER, niece of the Rev. A. J. PORTER (formerly stationed in Leesburg) died at Old Point on the 6th of October, aged 18y 8m 3d. Her remains were taken to Baltimore for interment.

Sheriff CARRUTHERS left for Richmond Wednesday morning having in charge Franklin H. DOVE, colored, sentenced to 8 years in penitentiary.

Mr. and Mrs. James K. SKINKER, of Huntley, Fauquier Co., Wednesday last celebrated the 50th anniversary of their marriage. He was 73 and she 70 years old. Children attending were Dr. and Mrs. J. W. McILHENNEY, of Milton Hall, Loudoun Co.; Mr. and Mrs. William K. SKINKER, of Richland, Madison Co.; Mr. Charles Bispham SKINKER, of Stonely; Mr. and Mrs. Beverly TURNER, of Roughland; Dr. and Mrs. Norman De Vere HOWARD, of Apopka, Fla.; Capt. and Mrs. John GOLDSMITH, of Bellefield, Fauquier Co., and Mrs. Lizzie Eyre SMITH, of Ripley, Va. The ages of the seven children and bride and groom amount to 397 years. Huntley, his homestead, was purchased in 1725 from Lord Fairfax by his great grandfather, Col. Sam SKINKER, and numbered 1600 acres, has been in the family continuously since.

J. Heath HUNTON, a nephew of Gen. Eppa HUNTON, died on Sunday at the residence of Maj. FOSTER, his uncle, at Marshall, Fauquier County, of consumption.

[MISSING ISSUE]

Thursday, 4 November 1886   Vol. XXXI, No. 22

Married: At the Reamer House, Leesburg, on Wednesday, October 27, 1886, by Rev. J. R. BRIDGES, Edward F. CORNELL to Miss Lilly Jane HAWS.

Died: On Sunday evening, in Loudoun Valley, October 19th, Mrs. Amanda BAGENT, wife of Jos. D. BAGENT, in her 46th year.

Died: On Monday, September 27th 1886, at his parent's residence in Loudoun Valley, John F. EDWARDS, son of S. R. and Annie V. EDWARDS, in his 10th year.

Departed this life on the 21st inst. at the residence of her nephew Isaac C. HOGE, Loudoun Co., Ann N. SCOFIELD, in her 71st year.

Died: Near Sudley Springs, on Monday, November 4th, 1886, Miss Charlotte T. SMITH, daughter of the late Patrick K. and Edmonia SMITH dec'd. of Loudoun.

Mr. Fenton M. HENDERSON, commissioner in chancery here for several years, died in the asylum at Staunton, on the 19th inst., in his 69th year. A vestryman of St. James Episcopal Church. During the war he was a member of Loudoun Guard. His death makes 3 members of the company who have died within the last 3 weeks.

At the residence of Mr. Joel BEALES, in Hamilton, on Tuesday last, the Rev. Mr. ARMSTRONG, of the M. E. Church, South, officiating, Mr. James M. WALLACE of this town was married to Mrs. Mary Ann WHITE, of the former place. They were aged 77 and 74 years.

At "Old Stone Church" of Augusta Co, on Wednesday morning October 20th, the marriage of Mr. John T. HIRST, to Miss Jennie BITZER, both of Purcellville, Loudoun County. Rev. Geo. L. BITZER, cousin of the bride performed the ceremony.

Cards are out for the marriage on the 11th inst., in the West St. Presbyterian Church, Georgetown, DC, of Miss Margaret LEETCH of that place, and Mr. George J. EASTERDAY, of this town.

Rev. Frank Montgomery STROTHER, of the M. E. Church, South, died last week at Markham Va. His last charge was at Fincastle, Botetourt Co.

A. M. KITZMILLER, Esq. for many years clerk in the National Armory at Harper's Ferry and former resident of Leesburg, died at the residence of his son in Washington city in the 75th year of his age.

Engagement of Mr. Hamilton R. FAIRFAX is announced to Miss Eleanor C. Van RENSSELAER, of New York. She is the daughter of the late William P. Van RENSSELAER, a son of the late Stephen Van RANSSELAER, the Patroon of Albany. The name is identified with the early history of this country, and since the year 1620 when the manor of Albany and Rensselaer counties was granted to the family by the Staates-General of Holand, the Van RENSSELAERS have been honored. Mr. FAIRFAX is a native of this county, a son of Col. J. W. FAIRFAX, and now resides in New York.

In the chapel of Washington and Lee University, Lexington, Va. a marble tablet – in memory of William C. LYNCH, of Loudoun Co. Va, drowned in an heroic effort to save the life of a fellow student on Christmas Day 1878.

Thursday, 11 November 1886　　Vol. XXXI, No. 23

Marriage license issued in Washington last week to George E. KERCHEVAL and Texana SWAIN, both of Loudoun Co.

Married: By the Rev. John WOLF, on the 26th ult, at the residence of the bride's father, in Wood Grove, Mr. William E. MATTHEW to Miss Jennie HAMMERLY.

Co. Ct.: Will of Charlotte T. SMITH admitted to record.

In memoriam by Leesburg and Hillsboro Circuit, M. E. Church, held at Bethel on 30 Oct 1886 for death on 13 Sept 1886 of Joseph M. CONARD (member for the past 30 years.)

Thursday, 18 November 1886　　Vol. XXXI, No. 24

Died: In St. Mary's Co., Md., November 3d 1886, Stuart Lomax, son of Rev. Theodore and Kate Lomas REED, aged 2y 8m.

Died: On Nov. 5th 1886, at Rosemont, near Goresville, of diphtheria, Lillie SMITH, daughter of Gunnell and Mary F. SMITH, aged 12y 8m.

Mrs. __ SHUMATE, widow of the late Murphy SHUMATE, and mother of L. M. SHUMATE, Co. Superintendent of Public Schools, died at her son's residence, Near Leesburg, on Friday night last, in her 84th year. She was a member of the M. E. Church, South. Interred in Union Cemetery on Sunday, conducted by Rev. Dr. HEAD.

F. M. WEADON, a former resident of this town, died at his home in Alexandria, Va last Saturday morning in the 73d year of his age.

Mr. George J. EASTERDAY, of Washington, formerly of this town, was on Thursday evening, November 11th in the West Street Presbyterian Church, Georgetown, married to Miss Margaret LEETCH, of the latter place, Rev. Dr. FULLERTON officiating.

In Memoriam from Hamilton Lodge No. 37, A. F. & A. M., on 5 October, resolution on death of William Virginius GIDDINGS which occurred at his home in this county on 16 September 1886.

[MISSING ISSUES]

Thursday, 16 December 1886　　Vol. XXXI, No. 28

Married: In Baltimore, on Thursday, November 24th 1886, by Rev. Henry SCHEIB, at the parsonage, Herman LOCK of Baltimore, and Gussie WHEELER, formerly of Leesburg.

Died: Near Leesburg, Lena Elleanor, infant of William H. and Annie E. GREENLEASE, died of brain affection, December 7, 1886, aged 5m 3w 4d.

In Memoriam: Dr. J. W. ALBRIGHT, aged 41 years.

Co. Ct.: George W. HUBBLE qualified as Guardian of Calvin ATKINSON; Phebe A. GREGG as Admx. of Martha A. GREGG dec'd. M. H. AUSTIN, minister of the Baptist Church, authorized to celebrate rites of matrimony. J. W. FRY appointed Guardian of John E. BOGER. Thos. E. HOUGH qualified as Admr. of Wm. HOUGH. J.

E. CARRUTHERS, Sheriff, appointed curator of the estate of Wm. E. KEYES dec'd.

Wednesday morning wedding at Ketoctin Baptist Church of Jas. E. CARRUTHERS, Esq. Sheriff of Loudoun County, and Miss Lutie GREGG, daughter of Mr. G. G. GREGG, of Round Hill, by Rev. Dr. I. B. LAKE.

Thursday, 23 December 1886   Vol. XXXI, No. 29

Married: At the residence of Chas. L. CLARKE, Covington, Va., Wednesday, December 8th, by the Rev. W. E. HILL, Mr. John THOMSON, of Atianta, Ga, to Miss Belle JANNEY, of Loudoun.

Married: On December 9th 1886, in New Brittain, Pa, by Rev. Mr. FETTER, Mr. Harvey BISHOP to Miss Edna Earl McNEALY, formerly of Leesburg.

Married: On the 16th of December 1886, in La Crosse, Wisconsin, at the residence of the bride's brother, Mr. Wm. Skeffington JAMESON, by the Rev. C. [damaged] DAUCETT, Mr. Richard B. DEAR, of Duluth, Minn. (formerly of Va) to Miss R??ie [damaged] L., youngest daughter of the late M. M. JAMESSON Esq. of Fairfax County.

Married: December 21, 1886, at the residence of the bride's parents [damaged] west of Lovettsville, Mr. Joseph C., son of Mr. John P. and Mrs. Janey E. DERRY to Miss Nettie E., daughter of Mr. John J. and Mrs. Mary E. STEVENS, the Rev. D. C. HEDRICK, officiating.

Died: Dr. Charles Edward NICOL, born June 1st 1805, at Goslar, Germany, died Nov. 24th 1886 at Leesburg Va.

Miss Catherine GARNER an aged maiden lady, died at her home in this town on Sunday, the 12th inst., and was buried on Tuesday 14th inst., in the old Presbyterian burying ground.

Thursday, 30 December 1886   Vol. XXXI, No. 30

Married: At the St. John's Evangelical Lutheran Church, Lovettsville, Thursday, December 16th 1886, Mr. George R. ROBERTS, of Balto. County, Md, and Miss Florence BARTLETT, of Loudoun Co., Rev. P. H. MILLER officiating. Mr. William ROBERTS, a brother of the groom and Mr. Edward CROMER acted as ushers. they will reside in Balto. County, Md.

Married: On Thursday, December 16, 1885 [1886] by the Rev. Dr. NEWMAN, Mr. Augustus D. WRIGHT, of Natchitoches, La., to Miss Lauretta V. NEWLON, of Loudoun County.

Married: On Tuesday evening the 21st inst. at the residence of Cornelius WARD, Esq. near Hawkinstown, by Rev. A. ROBEY, Mr. Charles E. PHILLIPS to Miss Laura E. ORTH, both of Shenandoah Co. Va.

Died: On the 19th inst. at her home near Harper's Ferry, in Loudoun County, Mrs. Elizabeth VIRTS, in the 95th year of her age. She was a member of the M. E. Church for 74 years.

Died: December 4th 1886, America M. CONRAD, daughter of David and Annie B. CONRAD, aged 1y 11m 14d. Leaves parents, grandmother and 6 other children.

Died: Near Lovettsville November 1886, after a lingering illness from internal cancer, Mr. Jno. G. R. KALB.

Died: December 7th 1886, John THOMAS, in the 78th year of his age, from something like typhoid pneumonia.

Died: At his home near Bethel, Loudoun County, of typhoid fever, Isaiah Nicholas STOCKS, aged 17y 2m 6d.

Died: At his residence near Aldie, on December 17th 1886, Mr. Edward THOMPSON, aged 83y 10m 11d.

Died: On December 6th 1886, Loretta, eldest daughter of C. Frank and Sarah McKIMMEY, aged 5y 24d.

Rev. L. B. TURNBULL received a telegram on Tuesday announcing the death in Massachusetts of his wife's only brother.

L. C. YOUNG Esq. formerly of Montgomery Co. Md, and Miss Hattie ODEN, dau. of Mr. Jas. S. ODEN, formerly of Loudoun were married at the residence of the bride's father in Washington, on Wednesday evening, Dec. 22, 1886, the Rev. S. K. COX, of Baltimore officiating.

Thursday, 6 January 1887   Vol. XXXI, No. 30 [31]

Married: On Wednesday evening, December 15th 1886, at the residence of T. H. SIMPSON, Logansport, Ind., by the Rev. Stephen H. GREENE, of St. John's Church, St. Louis, Mo., L. L. BOOKER, of Las Vegas, Hot Springs, New Mexico, formerly of Va, to Miss Bessie D. G. ARMSTRONG, daughter of the late Capt. James Welby ARMSTRONG, and granddaughter of the late Wm. A. STEPHENSON, Esq. of Upperville, Fauquier County.

Married: At Midwood, Fluvanna County, December 15th 1886, by the Rev. T. E. LOCKE, Edgar JACKSON, of Leesburg, to Miss Evelyn A. PLEASANTS, daughter of the late T. S. PLEASANTS.

Married: On December 22d, 1886, at the residence of Chas. HENDERSON Sr., Fairfax County, by Rev. W. T. SCHOOLEY, Mr. John R. HENDERSON, formerly of Loudoun County, to Miss Emma V. MILSTEAD, of Fairfax County.

Married: On December 29th by the Rev. John WOLF, at the residence of Mr. Wm. McDONALD, Mr. John MOURLAND to Miss Caroline JENKINS.

Married: December 8th 1886, at Mirador, near Greenwood Depot, Albemarle Co., Va by Rev. J. B. FUNSTEN, assisted by Rev. Geo. SOMERVILLE, Rev. Robert Allen CASTLEMAN to Fannie S. FUNSTEN, daughter of Col. Oliver R. and Mary FUNSTEN, of Clarke Co., Va.

Died: At her residence on the 28th of 12th month, 1886, Sarah Alis, widow of the late Asa M. BOND, and the last of the children of Bernard TAYLOR dec'd.

Died: At her home near Aldie, on Saturday, December 18th 1886, Mrs. Harrison LEWIS after months of suffering from consumption. Member of M. E. Church for more than 30 years.

Cards are out for the marriage of Elijah B. WHITE, son of Col. E. V. WHITE, and Rosa L., youngest daughter of Mrs. Jane A. PANCOAST. Takes place on the 12th inst. at St. James' Episcopal Church in this town.

Mr. Wm. L. ROYALL and Miss Page AYLETT were to have been married in St. Paul's Church, Richmond, Wednesday night.

Mrs. Isabel MADDUX, widow of Dr. T. Clay MADDUX, of Baltimore, who was killed in November 1881, at Odenton, Anne Arundel Co., Md, during a political riot, was married last Friday in Georgetown DC, to Mr. George MARTIN, an editor of the *Atlanta Sunday Avalanche*. Her maiden name was Isabel BETTS and she was born in Va. She is about 27 years old.

Mrs. Elizabeth Stockton SHEPHERD, daughter of the Hon. Alexander R. BOTELER, died at her residence near Shepherdstown, W. Va. Friday last.

Thursday, 13 January 1887   Vol. XXXI, No. 31

Married: At the Presbyterian Manse, by Rev. J. R. BRIDGES, Thursday Jan. 7, 1887, L. F. MYERS to Laura B. ELLMORE, both of Loudoun.

Married: January 5th 1887, by Rev. W. F. DUNNAWAY, Mr. Frederick ELLISON and Laura J. WHITE.

Died: At the residence of his father, Wm. H. GRIMES, in Leesburg, on December 9th 1886, Wm. Henry GRIMES, aged 1y 1m.

Died: Mrs. Harrison LEWIS on 18th December 1886. Member of M. E. Church for over 30 years.

Marriage license issued in Washington DC last week to E. H. BERRY and Edna SHUEY, of Waterford.

Co. Ct.: Andrew ROBEY's resignation as Guardian of Ella V. BOGER accepted and H. H. RUSSELL qualified as her Guardian. John T. THOMPSON qualified as Guardian of Mary C. MAFFETT, John L. MAFFETT, Chas. H. MAFFETT, Gracie A. MAFFETT. J. Howard KEYES qualified as Admr. of Wm. E. KEYES. Will of Edgar THOMPSON admitted to probate. Chas. H. DODD qualified as Guardian of his infant child; Ann C. BENTLEY as Guardian of Margaret BENEDICT.

Mr. William HOLMES died at his home near Lincoln, on Saturday night at the advanced age of 94 years.

St. James Episcopal Church, Leesburg, at 1:30 p.m. Wednesday, wedding of Mr. Elijah B. WHITE of the firm of E. B. White & Bro. and Miss Rosa L., only daughter of Mrs. Jane A. PANCOAST, of this town. Ushers were Thos. SWANN, G. Mason CHICHESTER, Robt. B. WILDMAN and C. L. POLLOCK. Bridesmaids and groomsmen in pairs were Misses Laura DeLONEY and Flora FOX, A. B. DOWELL and Benj. V. WHITE; Misses Gracie CARTER and Jane HOFFMAN; W. W. CHAMBLIN and Bolling ROBERTSON; Misses Kate WILDMAN and Annie BENTLEY, E. B. HARRISON and Arthur SHEETZ. Episcopal ceremony performed by Rev. Dr. DAVIS. Senator Henry HEATON gave away the bride.

Thursday, 20 January 1887   Vol. XXXI, No. 32

Married: By the Rev. John WOLF, on the 6th inst., at the residence of Mr. Thomas PASTON, Miss Virginia PASTON to Mr. J. C. MARCH.

Married: At the same time and place, by the same, Miss Joannah C. MARCH to Mr. James ASHBY.

Married: At the residence of Mr. Wm. A. JOHNSON on January 5th 1887, by the Rev. G. W. POPKINS, Mr. James POOL and Miss M. V. LEFEVER, all of Loudoun.

Married: At the Lutheran church near Lovettsville, January 13, 1887, by Rev. P. H. MILLER, Mr. John T. MERCHANT and Miss Annie A. MOCK.

Died: At his residence near Mountsville, in this county, on the evening of the 12th inst., of consumption, Sidnor B. FRANCIS in his 39th year.

Died: At her residence, December 31st 1886, near Mt. Hope, Mrs. Henrietta C. PAXSON, in the 70th year of her age. Member of the church for 40 years. Leaves an aged husband and six children.

Circuit Ct.: Naturalization papers granted Patrick SCANLON and James J. BYRNE, former subjects of the Queen.

Robert L. DADE, who in the beginning of the late war enlisted in Co. B. of Col. E. V. White's command, died at his residence in Carson, Iowa, on January 7th. Only brother of L. M. DADE, of this county.

Edwin BOOTH is playing this week at the Holliday St. Theatre in Baltimore. He was formerly a resident of Guilford.

First day of last Sept. in Pursellville, as people were leaving a public ball a pistol shot was fired into the head of Charles, the 12 or 14 year old son of Mr. Jno. E. BENEDUM, killing him instantly. The next day Mr. Chas. A. NEWLON of the neighborhood was arrested. Found guilty of voluntary manslaughter and given 3y 6m.

In Memoriam: William HOUGH, who died 25 Nov. 1886, age 77 years.

At home of Mr. Nathan MAYNARD, of this county (Frederick, Md,) residing near New London, wedding of Miss Fannie, eldest daughter of Mr. MAYNARD to Mr. Barney Taylor NOLAND, of Loudoun County, at 8 o'clock by Rev. T. W. T. NOLAND, brother of the groom. They will reside in Loudoun.

[MISSING ISSUES]

Thursday, 24 March 1887   Vol. XXXI, No. 41

Last week the will of the late Samuel H. JANNEY was admitted to probate in Alexandria. Disposes of $30,000 worth of property to children of Mahlon H. JANNEY. Provision made for his sister, Miss Elizabeth JANNEY, of Loudoun County. Messr. Phineas JANNEY of Loudoun and Edw. S. LEADBEATER are Exors.

Married: On the 17th inst., by the Rev. John WOOLF, in the church at Snickersville, Mrs. Sarah A. TRUSSELL to Mr. Thos. R. BRACKETT.

Died: At the residence of Lucien POWELL in Loudoun County, on the morning of March 16, 1887, Eva Louisa Bronaugh LUCKETT, eldest daughter of the late Ludwell LUCKETT.

Died: At Hoysville, March 7, 1887, at age 59y 4m 22d, Mr. T. M. EDWARDS, after a lingering illness from dyspepsia and bronchitis. He died spending 40 years in service of Jesus.

Died: On the 18th inst. of pneumonia, in Hamilton, Mrs. Elizabeth JACOBS, aged 76y 1m 18d. Her home, for some time, had been with her daughter, Mrs. Alverna THOMAS, who recently moved from her farm near the Trappe to Hamilton. She joined the Methodist Church in Hillsboro years ago.

Mrs. Rebecca SIMPSON, widow of Samuel SIMPSON, and last survivor of the children of the late Benj. SHREVE, died suddenly at her residence near North Fork, on Saturday morning, March 19th, in the 66th year of her age. Funeral on Monday by Rev. W. F. DUNNAWAY at the church at North Fork, interred in the cemetery at that place.

[MISSING ISSUE]

Thursday, 7 April 1887   Vol. XXXI, No. 43

Died: At Arcola, on Friday March 4th 1887, of pneumonia, Mrs. Ann LEE, wife of Matthew P. LEE, Esq. in the 79th year of her age.

Died: At his home, "Declade," March 5th 1887, at the age of 63 years, Mr. Jos. S. REED, after a lingering illness.

Died: Mrs. Annie E. FRANCIS, widow of the late Wm. H. FRANCIS, in Howard Co., Md. at the residence of her daughter-in-law, Mrs. H. C. DORSEY, aged 61 years. Interred at Middleburg.

Died: At her parents' near Farmwell Church, on March 18th 1887, Odie, daughter of John W. and M. Pleasant ELLMORE, in the 6th year of her age, of whooping cough.

Died: On March 22d 1887, at her home near Snickersville, in her 75th year, Mrs. Hannah JAMES, widow of the late Mason JAMES.

Mr. Chas. W. POWELL, young farmer living near Dry Mill, died on Thursday last, after a short illness, of typhoid pneumonia, in the 20th year of his age. Son of Mr. Chas. E. POWELL, leaves a wife and one young child. Funeral took place Saturday morning, Elder E. V. WHITE officiating. Interred at North Fork burying ground.

Mr. Jonah HATCHER died at his home near Pursellville on Friday last, in the 77th year of his age. For 40 years a member of Baptist

Church. One year ago he lost his aged partner, childless. Interred in Short Hill burying ground, Rev. I. B. LAKE officiating.

T. Rolling ROBERTSON, Esq. formerly of Alexandria, citizen of Fauquier County, died at his home near Broad Run last Thursday. At one time represented in both branches of the Council and also in the House of Delegates. He was a brother-in-law of Col. Jno. W. FAIRFAX, formerly of Loudoun.

Thursday, 14 April 1887 Vol. XXXI, No. 44

Married: At Washington DC, on April 6, 1887, by Rev. Mr. ADAMS, Littleton F. BYRNES to Minnie J. LAMBERT, third daughter of Dr. Francis LAMBERT, all of Gum Springs.

Died: March 19, 1887, Mrs. Rebecca SIMPSON, widow of the late Saml. SIMPSON, in the 66th year of her age. Member of North Fork Baptist Church.

Departed this life, March 31st, 1887, Charles W. POWELL, in the 29th year of his age.

Co. Ct.: Wills of Henry M. JACKSON dec'd.; Hannah JAMES dec'd.; Tacie BLEAKLEY dec'd.; Jonah HATCHER dec'd.; Mary PIGGOTT dec'd. admitted to probate. Estate of John HOPE dec'd. committed to Sheriff.

The M. E. Church, South, at Bloomfield having been entirely remodelled was on Sunday last, rededicated.

Jonah HATCHER died at his residence near Purselville on the 1st of April 1887, nearly 77 years old.

Thursday, 21 April 1887 Vol. XXXI, No. 45

Married: On March 9th 1887, at the parsonage of Whatcoat M. E. Church, by Rev. Wm. F. WARD, Willard W. GREENE, of Baltimore and Miss Ella, daughter of Mr. Jos. ABBOTT, formerly of Leesburg.

Married: At the residence of G. W. POPKINS on the 18th, Mr. G. B. FLETCHER and Miss Lucy V. HAVENER, by the Rev. G. W. POPKINS, all of Loudoun.

Died: April 6th 1887, of pneumonia, Joseph P., eldest son of Thomas L. POWELL, in the 25th year of his age.

Marriage of Miss Mamie PHILLIPS, of Fredericksburg, to Mr. B. H. WARNER, wealthy real estate agent of Washington DC is announced for 2nd of June. She is a grand-daughter of the late Col. Hamilton ROGERS, of Loudoun.

Death of Col. Leven W. SHEPHERD, son of the late Chas. and E. SHEPHERD, of Leesburg, was born in this town in 1836, and died at his home in Springfield, Illinois, a few weeks ago, in the 51st year of his age. He left Loudoun in 1858. Funeral from First Methodist Episcopal Church, service by the Masonic Grand Lodge.

Thursday, 28 April 1887   Vol. XXXI, No. 46

Married: At the residence of Mr. Samuel GRIMES, in Leesburg, on Tuesday, April 26th 1887, by Rev. Dr. HEAD, Charles C. CRIDLER, of W. Va, and Miss Mollie T. WILSON, of Montgomery Co., Va.

Died: At Luckett's old store, Jacob R. RODERICK, aged 65y 3m 17d.

Circuit Ct.: Administration of the estate of Mrs. Rebecca M. SIMPSON dec'd. was granted to Saml. SIMPSON Admr.

Aldie: Mrs. Lemuel SKILLMAN died on Thursday last.

Mr. E. P. PHELPS, minister of the Baltimore Conference of the M. E. Church, died last evening at his lodgings, No. 402 6th street, of heart disease. Born in Frederick Co Va, March 28, 1815. ... Funeral took place from the Metropolitan M. E. Church on Wednesday morning at 10 o'clock.

Thursday, 5 May 1887   Vol. XXXI, No. 47

Married: April 27, 1887, at Hamline M. E. Church, by Rev. H. R. NAYLOR, J. W. DAVIS and Virginia I. BOPP, both of Washington DC. Bride is daughter of Mr. Wm. G. BOPP, formerly of this town.

Died: At her home, near Aldie, Mrs. Catherine J. SKILLMAN, in the 44th year of her age. Survived by mother and husband.

Died: At her residence near Snickersville, on the 23rd inst., Mrs. Margaret BEAVERS, wife of Morgan BEAVERS, in her 45th year, of consumption. Sermon by her pastor, Rev. J. R. Van HORN.

Died: Of consumption, near Gum Spring, April 29th 1887, Leroy M. HUTCHISON, in his 37th year. Sermon by Rev. Mr. CUSHING.

Circuit Ct.: Will of Justus KUHLMAN dec'd. annulled and declared void. Will of Mary L. KERSEY dec'd. admitted to probate. Estate of Charles BINGHAM dec'd. committed to Sheriff for administration.

Mrs. Julia KEITH, widow of the late Isham KEITH, of Fauquier, and mother of Judge Jas. KEITH, died at her home in that county, on 25th of April in the 88th year of her age.

Thursday, 12 May 1887   Vol. XXXI, No. 48

Married: On Thursday, May 5th 1887, at the residence of B. H. HAMMERLY, Hillsboro, by Rev. J. R. Van HORN, Mr. J. Ashby GALLEHER, of Washington DC, formerly of Leesburg, and Miss Sallie PRESTON, of Loudoun.

Died: On May 2d 1887, Elenor Hope DUNLOP, daughter of G. T. and E. R. DUNLOP, aged 5y 4m.

Died: At Locust Hill, near Aldie, Loudoun Co, April 20th 1887, Catharine J. SKILMAN, aged 43y 9m, wife of Mr. Lemuel F. SKILMAN and daughter of the late Samuel A. and Caroline C. TILLETT. She leaves a husband and mother.

May Ct.: John W. SILCOTT qualified as Guardian of Mary SILCOTT. Administrations of estates of Henry BRONAUGH and Eva B. L.

LUCKETT granted. Will of Nelson HALL partly proved and continued. Saml. E. ROGERS qualified as Guardian of Edw. McV. DUNBAR.

Mr. Jacob RODERICK, eldest son of the late Lewis RODERICK, of Catoctin Switch, this county, died on Thursday evening of last week, at his home, near Luckett's Store, or Taylortown, Va, aged 63 years. He married Hester STOCK, of this vicinity. Interred in the Reformed Cemetery near Lovettsville on Saturday last.

Thursday, 19 May 1887   Vol. XXXI, No. 49

Died: In Waterford, May 14th, William CONNER, in his 75th year.

Died: In Waterford, May 16th, Jacob LEMON, in his 81st year.

Died: Near Morrisonville, May 4th, Mrs. Charlotte Elizabeth SHIELDS, 20y 2m.

Death of Miss Lucy McINTYRE occurred at her home in Leesburg, about 10 o'clock Thursday night, May 12th. She was a sister of the late C. C. McINTYRE for many years editor of the *Washingtonian*, and we believe the last survivor of her family. She finished 4 score years on earth. Funeral took place Saturday afternoon, Rev. Dr. DAVIS officiating, assisted by Rev. Dr. HEAD.

Cards are out for the marriage on June 1st 1887, of Miss Eleanor C., daughter of Mrs. Wm. P. Van RENSSELLAER, and Mr. Hamilton R. FAIRFAX, formerly of this county. Ceremony will take place in the Presbyterian church, Rye, New York.

Cards are out for the marriage of Miss Bettie HAWLING, of this town, and Thos. B. M. PERKINS, Esq. of Nelson Co Va, the ceremony to take place in Episcopal Church, on Wednesday May 25th.

Mr. Samuel E. VIERS, young farmer residing about 3 miles from this place, met with a sudden death on Sunday morning last. While tending cattle, his wife found him with his head submerged in the water in a trough. He had been subject to epileptic fits. He was in the 39th year of his age and a member of the Baptist church at this place for several years. *Rockville Md. Sentinel of the 13th*. Mr. VIERS was a nephew of Col. E. V. WHITE, of this county.

Thursday, 26 May 1887   Vol. XXXI, No. 50

Ex-Governor William SMITH died at his home in Warrenton on Wednesday morning May 18th 1887, in his 90th year. Born in King George Co. Va on 6 Sep 1797....Two sons and a daughter survive. Elder son, Col. Thos. SMITH, is U.S. district attorney for New Mexico. Capt. Fred'k. SMITH, the other son, is a prominent citizen of Arizona Territory. A sister, Mrs. Anna Maria JOHNSON, wife of the chaplain of Hampton Brigade, died in S. C. ... Remains deposited in the family vault at Hollywood, burial service of the Episcopal Church only being read. Regular funeral services were held at Warrenton.

St. James Episcopal Church, Leesburg at 1 o'clock yesterday (Wednesday) marriage of Thos. B. M. PERKINS Esq. of Nelson Co. Va, and Miss Bettie HAWLING, daughter of the late Lewis HAWLING, of this county, by Rev. Dr. R. T. DAVIS. Mr. Henry SAUNDERS gave the bride away, Messrs. W. W. CHAMBLIN, Thos. W. EDWARDS Jr., Dr. R. B. FISHBURNE and S. Carroll CHANCELLOR acted as ushers.

[MISSING ISSUES]

Thursday, 16 June 1887 Vol. XXXII, No. 1

Married: In the Presbyterian Church, at Rye, New York, on Wed. June 1st 1887, by Rev. Dr. E. D. G. PRIME, Mr. Hamilton R. FAIRFAX (formerly of Loudoun Co.) and Miss Eleanor Van RENSSELAER, daughter of Mrs. Wm. P. Van RENSSELAER, all of New York.
Died: Near Lovettsville, on June 4th 1887, of diphtheria, John Wise, infant son of John and Lizzie SMITH, aged 7y 10m 10d.
Died: On June 7th 1887, Mr. Arthur ORRISON, at an advance age.
Died: On June 2d at her late home near Lovettsville, after a long period of suffering and pain, Mrs. Margaret Elizabeth RUST in her 52^d year.
Co. Ct.: Wills of Wm. CONNER, Marietta B. GRUBB, Lucy McINTYRE and Alfred CRAVEN admitted to probate. Geo. P. HUNTER qualified as Admr. of J. R. RODRICK dec'd. Estate of Jas. E. SILCOTT committed to Sheriff. Susan F. PAXSON executed new bond as Guardian of her infant children.

Thursday, 23 June 1887 Vol. XXXII, No. 2

Married: At the residence of Mr. John B. WILLIAMS, near Oatlands, by Rev. C. T. HERNDON, June 16th 1887, Mr. Thos. M. CARLISLE to Miss M. C. WILLIAMS.
Died: At his home near Hamilton (where he had resided for 53 years) at 4 p.m. Wednesday, June 15th, Mr. Israel WARNER, in his 92nd year.
Died: On May 17th 1887, Charles W. HENDERSON, aged 64 years.
On Wednesday, June 15th 1887, Mr. Israel WARNER died at his home about six miles from Leesburg, in his 92nd year. Funeral on Friday at Catoctin Church, Rev. C. T. HERNDON officiating.
Cards are out for the marriage on Tuesday the 28th inst. at Powhatan, Belmont Co., Ohio, of Dr. S. S. REAMER, formerly of Leesburg, and Miss Myrta A. McMURRY, of the former place.
Mr. Hector DULANY, formerly of Loudoun, was last week married in St. Louis, to Miss Carrie FULTON, of that city.

Thursday, 30 June 1887 Vol. XXXII, No. 3

Married: At Unison, Va, June 14, 1887, by Rev J. H. LIGHT, Mr. Geo. W. DOLWICK, of Martinsburg W. Va., and Miss Rena MONROE, of Loudoun County.

Married: In St. Anne's Church, Annapolis, Md, by the Rector of the Parish, June 22d, Armistead RUST, U.S.N. and Miss Annie Weems RIDOUT, of Annapolis.

Died: In Washington, On Monday, June 20th 1887, at 9:40 p.m., Arthur Irving, only son of Arthur T. and Sallie E. TALKS, aged 7m 1d.

Died: At the residence of Mary L. Van SICKLE, in Peru, Marrow County, Ohio, on the 12th of June 1887, Mrs. Hannah L. SMITH aged 79y 4m 2d. She was born in Loudoun County Feb 10th 1811, her maiden name was Hannah L. DANIEL.

Died: In Louisville, Ky, June 10th 1887, Flavius Alfred, infant son of James M. and Willa OSBURN, aged 7 months.

Mr. Emanuel WENNER, of Lovettsville district, died at his residence on Wednesday last, in the 74th year of his age. He was the father-in-law of Mr. J. L. McINTOSH, Treasurer of Loudoun County.

Mr. Armistead RUST, of the U. S. Navy (a son of Col. A. T. M. RUST of this county) was married in St. Annie Protestant Episcopal church, Annapolis, Md, on Wednesday evening June 22d 1887, by Rev. Mr. SOUTHGATE, to Miss Nannie W. RIDOUT, of Annapolis. Weems RIDOUT, of Annapolis, cousin of the bride, gave her away.

[MISSING ISSUE]

Thursday, 14 July 1887   Vol. XXXII, No. 5

Married: On the 30th of June, 1887, at the Lutheran Church in Lovettsville by Rev. H. St. J. RINKER, Mr. George W. LEITCH, of Chicago, Ill, to Miss Rose W. FILLER, daughter of A. T. M. FILLER, Esq., of Loudoun County.

Died: At his home, near Hillsboro, June 29th, after a lingering illness, Samuel CLENDENING.

Died: Charles Luther, infant son and only child of John W. and Mary V. HAMMERLY, of cholera infantum, aged 7 months.

Died: At the residence of her son-in-law, Rev. P. H. MILLER, in Lovettsville, Mrs. ___ REX. Funeral on Tuesday, 5th inst.

Died: In Richmond, Va, July 3d 1887, America BUDD, widow of the late S. D. BUDD, and daughter of the late Townsend McVEIGH of this county.

Died: At his residence near Silcott Springs, Loudoun County, June 27th, 1887, Mr. Joseph WILDMAN, aged 72 years. He leaves a widow and son.

On Saturday morning last, James SMALLWOOD departed this life in the 31st year of his age. Funeral took place on Sunday afternoon, conducted by Rev. Mr. J. H. LIGHT (Methodist Episcopal Church of Unison), interred Bethsaida [??] Cemetery.

Circuit Ct.: Wills of Israel WARNER dec'd., Saml. CLENDENING dec'd., and Rosa A. DARR dec'd. admitted to probate. Administrations granted on estates of John CARTER Jr. dec'd. and Justus KUHLMAN dec'd.

The remains of Harvey C. BALL, whose death at his home in Kansas we noticed last week, did not reach Point of Rocks until Friday evening. Interred in Union Cemetery, Leesburg, on Saturday, Rev. Carter PAGE officiating.

On Thursday June 30th at 4 p.m., Miss Rose W. FILLER was married to Mr. Geo. W. LEITCH, of Chicago, performed by Rev. Jno. RINKER, at St. Johns' Church in Lovettsville. She is daughter of Col. A. T. M. FILLER. Groom is of Chicago, and engaged in mercantile pursuits in that city. Bridesmaids were Misses Kate WISSLER, Ada BOND and Misses Ella, Lillian, Nanie and Lizzie Lee FILLER, sisters of the bride. ...

Thursday, 21 July 1887   Vol. XXXII, No. 6

Married: At Canton, Montana, on Tuesday March 15th 1887, by Rev Mr. ___, Mr. Thos. KINNEY, of White Sulphur Springs, Montana, and Miss Bettie D. KEENE, formerly of Loudoun County.

Died: At the residence of her son-in-law John SKIRVING, in Washington DC, on Tuesday morning last, Mrs. Sarah R. TOWNER, widow of the late Jacob C. TOWNER, of Leesburg, in her 78th year. Funeral will take place from the depot in Leesburg this Thursday morning immediately upon the arrival of the 11 o'clock train.

Died: At his residence near Waterford, on the 19th inst., John CURRY, in the 87th year of his age.

Died: At Union Bridge, Md, July 7th, Susan G. BROWN, relict of the late John H. BROWN, of this county, aged 73y 11d. Her body was embalmed and shipped to the house of her son-in-law, J. W. GARRETT, of this county, then buried in the Lincoln Cemetery on the 11th, preached by Elder Jos. N. BADGER.

Mr. Philip BROOKS, of the firm of P. Brooks & Son, Grocers, in Leesburg, died at his residence on Cornwall Street, on Thursday last, in the 65th year of his age. He had lived in Leesburg since 1866. Funeral took place at 5 o'clock Friday afternoon, Rev. R. T. DAVIS officiating. Interred in Union Cemetery.

Wm. H. GILL Esq, of Bloomfield, died on the 8th inst., from the effects of cancer. Funeral took place on Sunday the 10th, the Rev. J. C. DICE officiating. Interred in South Fork burying ground.

Death of William H. COCKRAN at his home near Leesburg on Friday night last, in about the 47th year of his age. During the late war he was a member of the Loudoun Guards, 17th Va. Regiment from spring of 1861 till the end in April 1865. Sunday morning, Rev. I. W. CANTER officiating, his remains were interred in Union Cemetery. He leaves a widow and several little children.

A three year old son of Mr. John EMERICK (and grandchild of Mr. Lewis TAYLOR) living near Purcellville, one day this week accidently fell into a pail of boiling water and was scalded, and is in critical condition.

Col. Armistead T. M. RUST died at his residence, "Rockland," on Sunday morning last, in his 68th year. Son of Gen. Geo. RUST, formerly of "Exeter," who died in 1857. Graduated from West Point about 1842. Married first, a Miss LAWRENCE, of Brooklyn, N. Y. and afterward Miss LEE, daughter of the late Edmund I. LEE, of W. Va, who survives him. One son of the first marriage is a Professor in Kenyan College, Ohio. Of the last marriage he left many, of whom the eldest son is now an officer in the U.S. Navy. At the outbreak of the war he entered the Confederate service and was Col. of the 19th Reg. of Va Vols. since the war he has resided at his place, "Rockland," some 4 miles from Leesburg. Remains were taken to the Episcopal Church, services by Rev. R. T. DAVIS. At the setting of the sun last Monday he was laid by his father's grave in the Cemetery. Member and Vestry of the St. James Church, Leesburg.

Dr. Jno. H. MOORE, formerly of Waterford, but latterly of San Antonio, Texas with his wife is visiting old friends in Loudoun.

Mr. J. Wilmer HUGHES, formerly of Loudoun, but for several years past a lawyer in Texas united in matrimony with Miss Olive HUDSON, of Gainesville. They will reside in San Diego, California.

Thursday, 28 July 1887   Vol. XXXII, No. 7

Died: On Sunday morning, Bessie Estelle, daughter of J. T. and B. E. WAMPLER.

Died: On Sunday afternoon, July 17, 1887, by drowning, near Catoctin Switch, Frederick County, Md, Mr. Thos. C. RITCHIE, son of George and Catherine E. RITCHIE, Taylortown, Va, aged 25y 7m 11d.

Died: On Sunday, July 10, 1887, in Des Moines, Iowa, at the residence of her sister, Mrs. S. N. GRAYSON, Miss Kate Gedney RHODES, daughter of the late Lt. H. H. RHODES, U.S. Navy, and formerly of Leesburg.

Died: On the 12th of July 1886, near sunset, Chas. R. P. BAUGHMAN, son of John and Ella BAUGHMAN, of Leesburg, aged 1y 6m.

Died: At Corning NY, on Tuesday, July 19th 1887, in the 52d year of her age, Mrs. Elizabeth BOOTH, wife of W. H. BOOTH, of that place, and daughter of Mrs. Catherine JONES, of Leesburg.

Lynchburg July 20th: Mr. James T. WILLIAMS, merchant of this city, was married today at noon to Mrs. Mary H. MARTIN, at the residence of Mrs. Judge HENRY, on Court St., Rev. T. H. EARLY performing the service. Mr. Williams was formerly in business in Richmond. Mrs. MARTIN, was a Miss HANVEY, formerly of Leesburg.

Thursday, 4 August 1887   Vol. XXXII, No. 8

Married: At the residence of Mr. Westwood HUTCHINSON, Prince William County, Va, July 27th 1887, by Rev. T. A. HALL, Mr. Chas.

E. SKINNER and Miss Laura M. ISH, the former of Loudoun and the latter of Prince William County, Va.

Died: At his home, in Georgia, on July 26th 1887, after a brief illness, J. Sheridan PALMER, formerly of this county, in his 62d year.

Died: In Staunton, Va, July 25th, of meningitis, Elizabeth Dunbar, infant child of Frank R. and Kate Jones BEAR, aged 3m 25d.

Died: Charles Theodore, infant son of Charles and Florence PAGE, born March 27, 1887, aged 3m 23d.

About noon, on Wednesday, August 3d, 1887, at the home of the bride's parents, near Leesburg, Mr. N. S. PURSEL (of the Drug firm of Mott & Pursel, of Leesburg) married with Helen J., daughter of Isaac VANDEVANTER Esq., Rev. J. R. BRIDGES officiating.

At the Naval Hospital, Boston, at 6 a.m. Saturday, July 30th 1887, after a short illness, of consumption, Dr. Joseph SHAFER, Assistant Surgeon U.S. Navy, and son of F. W. SHAFER, of this town, in the 26th year of his age. ... Remains reached Leesburg on the evening train Sunday and Monday evening at 5 o'clock his funeral took place from his father's residence, Rev. Dr. DAVIS officiating, assisted by Rev. J. R. BRIDGES.

Mrs. Eliza B. THOMPSON, wife of Mr. George G. THOMPSON, and sister of Hon. John S. BARBOUR, died at her home at Culpeper C. H. yesterday evening, after an illness of some duration. *Alex. Gaz. of Monday.*

A negro girl, Ida MANLEY, 18 years of age, left her home on the farm of Thornton SAFFER on Tuesday with her little brother, six years old. She returned without him, and today his body was found in the woods, near the house, showing that he had been killed by beating over the head with a stone. The girl was arrested and committed.

Thursday, 11 August 1887   Vol. XXXII, No. 9

Married: In Charlestown, W. Va., Aug. 3d, 1887, by Rev. Dallas TUCKER, Dr. W. F. LIPPITT, Jr., to Miss Mary CRAIGHILL, daughter of Col. W. P. CRAIGHILL.

Died: Miss Fanny E. McVEIGH, died at Mt. Airy, near Middleburg, Friday, August 5th. Suffered from consumption for ten years. Baptised by Elder GRIMSLEY of Long Branch church, and she in 1847 united fifteen persons in the constitution of the Baptist Church of Middleburg.

Ida MANLEY, 18 year old colored girl, arrested and charged with the murder of her six year old half-brother, near Aldie, was lodged in jail last night awaiting trial.

On Monday afternoon last, Mr. D. M. BEANS and Miss Bettie ROLES, both of this county, were wed, the Rev. Chas. T. HERNDON officiating.

Aug. Ct.: Daniel M. BEANS, seduction, under promise of marriage. Chas. JONES for attempt to rape. Ida MANLY for murder. Wm. H.

McKENNA for attempt to murder. Wills of Danl. N. WINE and A. T. M. RUST admitted to probate. J. J. RODERICK qualified as Admr. of Margaret E. RUST.; C. C. & Robt. WENNER as Admr. of Emanuel WENNER; Andrew G. CURRY as Admr. of John CURRY; John H. STREAM as guardian of Nannie H. STREAM.

James F. TRAYHERN of Baltimore bar, died Saturday after a brief illness, in his 63d year. Native of Loudoun County. At breaking out of war he joined Southern army and was at the battle of Manassas.

Thursday, 18 August 1887 Vol. XXXII, No. 10

Died: On Friday morning, August 12th 1887, at the residence of her son, Mr. Chas. H. ELGIN, near Leesburg, Mrs. Elizabeth ELGIN, widow of the late Gustavus ELGIN, of this county, having nearly reached her four-score years and ten.

Drowned on Saturday August 6th 1887, at 9 p.m. off the steamer Lady of the Lake, Thomas Lee, eldest son of Thomas and Annie V. STILES, aged 23y 4m 21d.

Died: At "Clifton" of typhoid fever, July 27th, Henry ROGERS, second son of Hugh and Rosalie ROGERS, in the 33d year of his age.

Died: At the home of her son-in-law, John C. PAXSON, August 15th 1887, Rachel NICHOLS, in the 88th year of her age.

Died: At her home, in Leesburg, on Thursday last, August 11th 1887, after a short illness, Miss Isabella KAIGHN, daughter of the late Dr. John H. KAIGHN, of this town.

Died: July 26th, in Defiance, Ohio, at the residence of her son-in-law, R. A. NEFF, Mrs. Caroline E. CRAIG and daughter of the late Wm. H. and E. H. BRISCOE.

Died: In Leesburg, August 11th 1887, at the residence of her brother, Jas. S. HARRIS, Mrs. Eliza H. BRISCOE, in her 90th year.

Death of Mrs. Maria V. HIXSON occurred at her home near Dover in this county, Aug. 6th, aged 71y 5m. Had been in delicate for years.

Mr. H. Franklin TURNER, brother of Mr. Richard TURNER, and Mrs. J. L. NIXON, of Leesburg, and who formerly resided and was in business here, died in Hickman Co, Kentucky, on August 1st. A carriage accident cause a partial paralysis and finally his death. He was about 66 years of age.

Died: At his home, in Delphi, Indiana, of sunstroke, on Sunday morning, Aug. 7, 1887, Dr. Stacy T. NOLAND formerly of this county, and son of George W. NOLAND, and brother of Dr. NOLAND, of Farmwell.

Mrs. M. L. PENDLETON, wife of Dr. E. Boyd PENDLETON, died at Berkeley Springs Sunday night. She was the daughter of the late Col. Charles Pendleton TUTT, of Loudoun County.

Thursday, 25 August 1887   Vol. XXXII, No. 11

Married: On August 4th 1887, at the Lutheran Parsonage, in Frederick City, Md, by the Rev. Dr. DIEHL, James W. ATTWELL to Miss Cora V. ELLMORE, both of Loudoun County.

Died: In Leesburg, August 23d 1887, at the residence of her son, Mr. Walter CASTLE, Mrs. Rowena EVANS, in about her 63d year.

Died: At Hamilton, Va, August 14, Melicent Jarvis, infant daughter of Rev. Henry and M. M. BRANCH.

Died: August 21st 1887, at the residence of C. F. OTLEY Esq., Thomas YOUNG, in the 71st year of his age.

Died: At her residence, near Aldie, on July 8th 1887, of consumption, Mrs. Maria V. HIXSON, youngest daughter of Capt. Joseph B. LYNN, of Pr. William County, Va, in the 71st year of her age. She leaves a husband, 5 daughters and 1 son.

Died: Dr. Stacy T. NOLAND, son of George W. and Ruth H. NOLAND, of Loudoun Co, died from the effects of sun prostration at his residence in Delphi, Indiana, Sunday, 9:35 a.m. August 7th 1887, in the 43d year of his age. Born in Loudoun County. .... In April 1874 he married Miss Isabella LYON, eldest daughter of Mr. John L. LYON, by which union there were born 2 daughters, Anna and Edith. Member of I. O. O. F. Funeral from his late residence on Monday afternoon at 3 o'clock, Rev. S. R. SCAWRIGHT officiating. Member of Ketoctin Baptist Church and Delphi Baptist Church.

Mrs. Mary J. ATTWELL, wife of Mr. Ewell ATTWELL, of this town, died unexpectedly about 10 o'clock Saturday morning. She had been an invalid for some time. She leaves a husband, two sons and two daughters. Funeral took place at 5 o'clock Sunday afternoon, Rev. I. W. CANTER officiating, interred in Union Cemetery.

Mr. Zeller B. HAMMERLY, son of Mr. J. A. HAMMERLY, formerly of Leesburg, but now of this city, died yesterday at his father's residence on Queen street, from erysipelas. he was 18 years of age. *Alex. Gazette of Monday.*

Thursday, 1 September 1887   Vol. XXXII, No. 12

Died: At Flint Hill, Rappahannock County, Va, on August 8th 1887, of Bright's disease, Mr. Thos. J. DODD, in his 77th year.

Died: At "Springdale," Loudoun Co., August 19th 1887, of consumption, Mary A. CHAMBLIN, wife of J. L. CHAMBLIN, aged 73 years.

Died: On Saturday, August 20th 1887, at her home, near Leesburg, Mrs. Mary J. ATTWELL, wife of Mr. Ewell B. ATTWELL. An invalid for many weeks.

Died: At Mt. Stirling, Loudoun Co., Aug. 22d 1887, Hazel Leola WILEY, aged 18m 5d, only daughter of Mr. and Mrs. Walter S. WILEY.

Marriage is announced for the 13th of September of Mr. Jno. M. JOHNSON, attorney of Alexandria, and Miss Constance C. BEACH, daughter of S. F. BEACH, of the same city.

B. LITTLEPAGE, of Virginia, appointed as consul of St. Thomas, Ontario. ... He married a daughter of the late Henry W. CASTLEMAN, of Jefferson County, W. Va., and grand-daughter of James SINCLAIR, Esq. formerly of Loudoun.

Thursday, 8 September 1887 Vol. XXXII, No. 13

Died: At the residence of Mr. Robert W. GRUBB, near Hillsboro, on August 26th 1887, Irim THOMPSON, son of the late Hugh THOMPSON, in the 19th year of his age.

Dr. Chas. G. EDWARDS, of Louisville, Ky, spent a day or two in Leesburg, with his father, Dr. R. H. EDWARDS.

Marriage license issued in Washington on Monday to James THORNTON and Mary J. KODY?, both of Loudoun.

Marriage licenses issued in Washington last week, to John T. HARDY and Minnie MATTHEWS, both of Loudoun County.

Thursday, 15 September 1887 Vol. XXXII, No. 14

Married: At the residence of the bride's mother, in Hamilton, on Thursday, September 8, 1887, by Rev. Father WILSON, Mr. W. F. NORMAN and Miss Fannie MENARD, both of Loudoun.

Married: September 8th 1887, at Rozzell Chapel, Loudoun County, by Rev. J. H. LIGHT, Arthur S. HOUGH and Isadora HUTCHINSON, all of Loudoun.

Died: Nathaniel, infant son of Natalie and Rev. Jas. H. SMITH, former pastor of the Leesburg Presbyterian Church, died in Lexington, Va, September 3d, at the residence of Gen. F. H. SMITH.

Died: On Thursday morning, September 8, 1887, after a brief illness at the home of his parents, Charles E. and Elizabeth POWELL, near Leesburg, Robert L. POWELL, in the 5th year of his age. Funeral took place fro his father's residence, preached by Elder BADGER. Interred in the old church yard at North Fork.

Co. Ct.: Administration granted on the estates of Rachel NICHOLS dec'd., Cal. SPALDING dec'd., Jos. H. ROSS dec'd. and Wm. H. GILL dec'd. Will of Margaret EBERT dec'd. admitted to probate.

Thursday, 22 September 1887 Vol. XXXII, No. 15

Married: In Washington DC, on September 7th 1887, by Rev. W. E. PARSON, of the Lutheran Church, Mr. Rodney W. GRAY, of Loudoun Co., to Miss Ida L. STIPE, of Jefferson Co., W. Va.

Married: On Tuesday, September 13, 1887, at the residence of the bride's father, by the Rev. Henderson SUTER, rector of Christ Church, John M. JOHNSON to Constance C. BEACH, eldest daughter of S. Ferguson BEACH, all of Alexandria, Va.

Col. M. D. BALL, formerly editor of the *Alexandria Sentinel*, and District Attorney of Alaska, died in Alaska, Sept. 13, in his 51st year.

Gen. Asa ROGERS of this county died at his daughter-in-law's, Mrs. A. L. ROGERS, near Middleburg, on Tuesday afternoon, in his 86th year. Born in Loudoun Co. 24 June 1802. He was placed in a country store at the early age of 12 years, where he remained for six years, when he qualified as Deputy Sheriff. ... Married Ellen ORR, daughter of Dr. John D. ORR, of Frederick County. Active as a merchant, milling and farming, Justice of the Peace. When war came he refused to take the oath and was imprisoned at Washington and in Fort Delaware. He later removed to Richmond and in Dec 1886 [??] was elected Second Auditor by the Legislature. Gen. ROGERS was a communicant in the Episcopal Church, confirmed by Bishop MEAD in 1858. Buried in Sharon Cemetery, Middleburg this Thursday morning at 11 o'clock.

Thursday, 29 September 1887   Vol. XXXII, No. 16

Married: At the residence of the bride's father, near Milltown, September 15, 1887, by Rev. C. F. BEALES, Mr. Samuel R. RIDGEWAY and Miss Virginia L. STEWART, both of Loudoun County.

Died: At his residence, in Washington DC, on September 19th 1887, James W. STEADMAN, formerly of Leesburg, in his 66th year.

Departed this life, Wednesday morning Sept. 26th, Wm. B. WYNKOOP, aged 75 years. Member of North Fork Church for over 40 years.

Maj. J. Lawrence HOOFF, of Jefferson County, W. Va., and President of the County Court, died on Saturday.

Middleburg: Mr. S. L. COCHRAN will leave our community on the 1st of October to take charge at the Industrial School at Keams Cavern, Arizona.

The remains of the late Col. M. D. BALL, who died recently in Alaska, were conveyed to Falls Church for interment in the old family burying ground.

Thursday, 6 October 1887   Vol. XXXII, No. 17

Married: At "Forrest Glen," the residence of the bride, on Tuesday, October 4, 1887, by Rev. H. M. WHITE, J. R. SMITH of Loudoun County and Miss Mary V. WOOD, of Clarke County, Va.

Married: At the residence of the bride's father, T. Sherman LAKE, Esq., on Sept. 26th, by the Rev. B. W. BOND, Mr. Louis M. SMITH and Mrs. Achsah W. GALLEHER. They will reside in Washington.

Married: September 29, 1887, by Rev. W. F. DUNAWAY, Mr. Edward B. GOODE and Miss Eliza G. ELLYSON.

Married: Near Purcellville, September 29th 1887, by the Rev. L. R. TURNBULL, R. Allison BAKER to Mary D. CROESDALE.

Married on Tuesday morning, October 4th, 1887, at "Forest Glen," home of the bride, Mr. Jno. R. SMITH of the firm of Hirst & Smith, of Pursellville, in this county, to Miss Mary V. WOOD, of Clarke County, Rev. H. M. WHITE officiating.

Mr. Frank G. ODENHEIMER, of Philadelphia, cousin of the late P. E. Bishop ODENHEIMER, of New Jersey and Miss Cordellia Sothron POWELL, daughter of Capt. E. B. POWELL (formerly of Leesburg), sister of W. S. POWELL of this city, were married Wednesday morning at St. Paul's Protestant Episcopal church by Rev. J. S. B. HODGES, rector. Wedding was very quiet on account of the illness of Capt. POWELL, who is at his son's home, Mt. Washington. The bride was given away by W. S. POWELL, her brother. Mr. B. M. LARZELEAR, of Philadelphia, was best man. They will reside in Philadelphia. ...

Thursday, 13 October 1887   Vol. XXXII, No. 18

Married: On the 5th inst., at the residence of Mr. Frank OSBURNE, in Snickersville, by the Rev. J. R. VanHORN, Mr. J. Frank PALMER to Miss Mary Ellen CHAMBLIN, all of this county.

Died: At Waterford, Va, on Saturday morning, Sept. 24th 1887, Lloyd Lester, infant son of Oscar C. and Sue F. JAMES, aged 7 months.

Co. Ct.: Wills of Fannie E. McVEIGH dec'd., Joseph WILDMAN dec'd., and John Q. EVERHART dec'd. admitted to probate.

Death of Chas. L. MANKIN, of Broad Run District, at his home near Gum Spring on Thursday October 6th, in about his 56th year. He was a husband and father. Remains were laid beside those of his parents in the old family burying ground a few hundred yards from where he died, Elder E. V. WHITE officiating at the funeral.

Geo. D. WILLIAMSON, brother-in-law of the mayor's secretary, Col. Wm. H. LOVE, died Monday at Williamsport Md, where he was a teacher in the public school. He was a bookkeeper for a canning firm in Baltimore some years ago. He was in the Mexican war as a member of the First Mississippi Reg., under Jefferson DAVIS and served in the Confederate army. He married a sister of Col. LOVE, and was a graduate of Princeton College. *Balt. Sun.* For several years immediately preceding the war, he was proprietor of the old Loudoun Hotel.

The old colonial homestead, "Oatlands," in Loudoun Co, belonging to Mrs. Geo. W. CARTER, formerly Miss Kate Custis POWELL, will shortly pass out of the family who have possessed of for over 200 years. This once royal estate was ceded to the great-grandfather of the present proprietor by King George.

Marriage license issued in Washington DC, on Monday to John T. SMITH and Minnie G. TINSMAN, both of Loudoun.

Thursday, 20 October 1887   Vol. XXXII, No. 19

Miss Meta HOLLIDAY, a granddaughter of the late Humphrey B. POWELL, of Middleburg, and daughter of the late Richard HOLLIDAY, of Easton Md, was married on Wed. of last week in Christ Church, Easton, to Mr. W. Perry SEMPLE, of Louisville, Ky.

Married: On Wednesday, October 12, 1887, at the residence of the groom's brother, by Rev. J. C. HUMMER, uncle of the bride, Matthew PURCELL, of New York, and Lavinia B. HUMMER, of Langley, Fairfax County, Va.

Married: On Wednesday, October 12th 1887, Rev. Carter PAGE, of Christ Church, Goresville, Mr. Frank L. FRED, of Loudoun, and Miss Jennie SMITH, daughter of the late Geo. D. SMITH, of this county. They will reside at the present home of the groom, at Anadarko, Indian Territory.

Circuit Ct.: F. A. NICOL's declaration to become a citizen. A. K. MANKIN qualified as Admr. of C. L. MANKIN dec'd.

Mr. Jessee T. HIGGINS, a merchant at Poolesville, Md and at the time of his death a citizen of Baltimore and member of the firm of Higgins and Waters. He was stricken with paralysis on Wednesday and died Friday, in the 74th year of his age.

Marshall Missouri Daily News: Marriage of Miss Sallie GOODWIN of that place, and Mr. R. E. L. SMITH, son of Capt. Wm. P. SMITH, of Leesburg, last evening at the Presbyterian Church. She is the daughter of James W. GOODWIN, of that city. He is of Kansas City, where they will make their home. Ceremony performed by Rev. L. P. BOWEN, pastor of the church. ...

Thursday, 27 October 1887   Vol. XXXII, No. 20

Died: At the Plains, Loudoun County, on Sunday morning, the 23d instant, Gertrude Lee, infant daughter of Beverly and Gertrude ADAMS, aged 7m 5d.

Ida MANLY, colored, tried in Circuit Court of Loudoun last week, for the murder in August last near Mt. Zion Church, in this county, of her 7 year old brother, was found guilty of murder in the 2nd degree and given 18 years in the penitentiary.

John VINCEL, aged 69 years, died early yesterday morning, of an affection of the bladder, at the Md University Hospital. His home is in Taylorstown, Loudoun County.

Thursday, 3 November 1887   Vol. XXXII, No. 21

Married: At Round Hill, October 20th 1887, by Rev. I. B. LAKE, Miss F. Anna LODGE, daughter of Mr. Harmon LODGE, to Mr. R. Scott PAXSON, of Loudoun County.

Married: At the residence of W. F. LYNN, near Snickersville, October 27th 1887, by Rev. I. B. LAKE, Miss Evie FURR, daughter of Wm. Gilmore FURR to Wm. Greer BONHAM, of Texas.

Married: By Elder E. V. WHITE, at the residence of the bride's father on Wednesday October 26th 1887, Mr. John T. RITICOR to Miss Jennie E. HIGDON, both of Loudoun.

Married: On Oct. 20, 1887, at Grace M. E. Church, South, Capitol Hill, by Rev. J. C. JONES, assisted by Rev. G. D. WHITE, Mr. Percy C.

BOWEN, of Hyattsville, Md, and Miss Laura L., daughter of Mr. James H. DODD, of Washington, formerly of Loudoun County.

Married: At the Lutheran parsonage, Lovettsville, October 25, 1887, by Rev. P. H. MILLER, Mr. M. F. JANNEY and Miss Anna B. McGAVACK.

Death of my grandmother, Mrs. Jane WHITE occurred at her son-in-law, Samuel C. CROSEN's near Lincoln, October 11, 1887, aged 70 years. Signed Jennie.

Died: On Tuesday, October 25, 1887, at the residence of her son-in-law, Joseph CROWN, 166 Fourteenth St, NW, Washington DC, Mrs. B. A. GRUBB, wife of the late Curtis GRUBB, of Loudoun County, aged 69 years. Interment Loudoun County.

Died: In Leesburg, on Monday, October 31, 1887, Ethel Boyd, daughter of C. B. and F. A. HESS, aged 5y 2m 27d.

Died: In Berryville, Clarke County, on Monday, October 31st 1887, Virginia Powell, widow of Lawrence B. TAYLOR, aged 66 years.

Mr. and Mrs. Walter J. HARRISON celebrated their 10th wedding anniversary last Thursday evening.

John GOODIN, an aged man, died at his home near Purcellville, on the 19th inst.

At home of Mrs. Adelaid ADAMS near Aldie, marriage on Wednesday evening of her daughter Rose, to Harry B. BADGER, son of Rev. J. K. BADGER, performed at 8 o'clock by Rev. Arthur JOHNS.

In Lovettsville, Loudoun Co. on Thursday last, Mr. Julius J. PRUFER, a former attache of the Vindicator, and now of the job printing firm of Stoneburner & Prufer, in this city, married Miss Eliza G. MOORE, daughter of the late Edw. G. MOORE, of Richmond, took place in the parsonage of the Rev. P. H. MILLER, the Lutheran pastor, who is an uncle of the bride and performed the ceremony at 9 a.m., assisted by the Rev. W. H. SETTLEMYER, late pastor of the Staunton Lutheran Church. Miss Emma E. PRUFER, a sister of the groom accompanied them on the train to Staunton. They will reside at 710 Frederick St., just erected by the groom.

Chief Judge John RITCHIE, of the Frederick and Montgomery, Md judicial district, died at his home in Frederick City last Thursday. He was buried on Saturday.

Thursday, 10 November 1887   Vol. XXXII, No. 22

Died: At the Reamer House, in Leesburg, on the morning of Nov. 6th 1887, Frank Thorne ANDREWS, in his 26th year. Funeral took place from St. Ignatius Church, Baltimore, Md, Tuesday, Nov. 8th.

Died: In Kaufman Co, Texas, on Saturday, October 29th 1887, H. W. HUGHES, son of D. L. and M. T. HUGHES, in the 38th year of his age, formerly of Loudoun County.

Died: Near Hamilton, September 23d 1887, Daissy Caral THOMPSON, grandson of R. A. THOMPSON.

Died: On the 28th proximo, at "Auburn," the residence of S. A. BUCKNER, Loudoun County, E. Jaqueline SMITH, in his 70th year.

Died: Ethel Boyd, child of Chas. B. and E. A. HESS, was born August 4th 1882, and died October 31, 1887, aged 5y 2m 27d.

Died: Chas. Bertram, son of Chas. B. and F. A. HESS, was born January 21st, 1884 and died November 3d 1887, aged 3y 9m 13d.

Died: Nannie Blanche, youngest daughter of Wm. and R. E. TAVENNER, at her aunt's, Mrs. Thomas BROWN, near Round Hill, October 20, 1887, of typhoid pneumonia, in the 15th year of her age. She leaves father, sisters, and brothers. Her funeral was preached at the M. E. Church, Unison, by Rev. J. H. LIGHT. Interred at the family burying ground, Bethesda.

Died: On Saturday morning, October 29th, at the residence of his father, near Leesburg, Clarence J. MYERS, the infant son of E. Franklin and Florence H. MYERS, age 14m 17d.

Mr. Phineas Janney STEER, for many years a leading tailor of this city, died Saturday morning at his residence, No. 914 I St NW, in his 80th year. He learned the business of tailoring in West Washington. Member of Methodist Protestant Church. *Wash. Star of Monday.*

Thursday, 17 November 1887   Vol. XXXII, No. 23

Married: On November 10th 1887, at the residence of the bride, near Leesburg, by the Rev. J. R. BRIDGES, Mr. James W. THOMAS to Mrs. Elizabeth A. BARRETT.

Married: At the parsonage of the M. E. Church, South, in Leesburg, November 1st 1887, by Rev. Isaac W. CANTER, Mr. Edward ASTON and Miss Laura GRAHAM, both of Loudoun County.

Married: At Sycolin, November 3d, 1887, by Rev. Isaac W. CANTER, Mr. Jas. E. FLAHERTY and Miss Eliza E. COOKSEY, both of Loudoun County.

Circuit Ct.: Louisa BEANS qualified as Guardian of Norra Arthur, Alice BEANS and Annie BEANS. Will of Isabella G. KAIGHN admitted to probate. C. C. GAVER qualified as Admr. of Philip WILTSHIRE dec'd.

"Prosperwell," farm belonging to estate of the late Mrs. C. A. R. CARSON, on Pt. of Rocks road about 5 miles from Leesburg, containing 229 acres of land was sold to Jno. H. WHITMORE.

Died at Widows' Home, St. Louis, Mo, on the 1st inst., Mrs. Helen C. ANNAN, aged 85 years. In her youth she taught school in Leesburg, where her father lived. Her hip was broken by a fall and she died suddenly.

The engagement is just announced of Miss Ann CARTER, second daughter of Col. Thos. H. CARTER, of "Pampatike," Virginia to Mr. Rozier DULANY, of Fauquier.

Thursday, 24 November 1887   Vol. XXXII, No. 24

Married: At the residence of the bride's mother, November 16, 1887, by Rev. I. W. CANTER, Mr. James Hammond LAWSON and Miss Cordace S. EVERHART, all of Loudoun county.

Died: Mrs. Charlotte WILDMAN, widow of the late Jos. WILDMAN, near Silcott's Springs, Loudoun County, died suddenly on Saturday morning last, at the residence of her son, No. 1215 Wyly St., Washington DC.

Mrs. Fannie PLASTER, widow of Henry PLASTER dec'd., celebrated her 97th birthday not long since. She retains her mental faculties and is unusually active for her age. She is the mother of Dr. Geo. E. and David H. PLASTER, of this county.

Mr. Henry S. SMITH, of Guilford, Loudoun Co, was married on the 15th inst., Tuesday last, to Miss Ella SEYMOUR, of Little Falls, New York.

Death at Rupert, Pa, on Monday, the 15th of November of Mrs. Catherine PAXTON, widow of the late Col. Jos. T. PAXTON of Pa and mother of Chas. R. PAXTON, of Leesburg. Had she survived until next Christmas day she would have been 101 years old. She is said to have been quite active up to her death and possessed unimpaired mental faculties to the last.

Marriage license issued in Washington last week to Jno. McPHERSON and Gertrude MYERS, both of Loudoun.

Thursday, 1 December 1887   Vol. XXXII, No. 25

Mrs. Veturia LEITH, widow of the late Dr. Theodoric LEITH, of this county, died at her home in Unison, on Saturday November 19th. Her funeral took place from the Methodist Church, preached by her pastor, Rev. J. C. DICE.

Thursday, 8 December 1887   Vol. XXXII, No. 26

Married: At the residence of Rev. I. W. CANTER, in Leesburg, November 26th, Mr. Mortimer WHITE and Miss Cecelia WARNER, daughter of Chas. E. WARNER Esqr.

Married: At the residence of Thos. MYERS, Esq., November 30, 1887, by the Rev. B. W. BOND, Mr. Monroe FLIPPO to Miss Mattie COLE, both of Loudoun.

Married: Nov. 24th 1887, at the home of the bride, near Purcellville, Mr. Chas. W. HUDSON, of Culpeper, to Miss Annie SHOEMAKER.

Died: In Middleburg, on Thursday morning, December 1st 1887, Mrs. G. W. SHUMAN, in about the 70th year of her age. She was a daughter of the late James SURGHNOR, of Middleburg.

Died: In Waterford, November 5th 1887, Raymond Lester, youngest child of Joseph and Kate SCHOOLEY, aged 1y 6m 7d.

Mr. Claude N. WISE, son of Mr. George WISE, of Alexandria, and a nephew of Mr. Wm. N. WISE, of Leesburg, died of typhoid fever in Alexandria last week.

Marriage in the old Monumental Church of Richmond last Thursday night of Mr. ___ CARTER a son of Major Thomas H. CARTER, of King William County, and the daughter of Mr. Peter H. MAYO, of Richmond. Bridal party included Ann CARTER (sister of the groom) Sallie MAYO (sister of the bride) and Miss Juliet CARTER (sister of the groom.) Performed by Rev. Dr. J. B. NEWTON and Rev. Robert A. MAYO (cousin of the bride) of Baltimore. Mr. CARTER is a law partner of his cousin, Mr. Thomas Nelson PAGE. Groom is a nephew of Dr. C. S. CARTER, of this county.

Thursday, 15 December 1887   Vol. XXXII, No. 27

Married: In Waterford at the Presbyterian Church, December 7th, 1887, by the Rev. L. B. TURNBULL, Joseph H. RUSSELL and Julia S. BENNETT.

Married: On 25th November 1887, in Leesburg, by Rev. I. W. CANTER, Joseph A. SHUGARS and Annie E. BRECKENRIDGE, all of Loudoun.

Married: On December 12th 1887, in Leesburg, by Rev. I. W. CANTER, Chas. C. BROWN and Martha J. STEWARD, all of Loudoun.

Died December 6th 1887, in the 51st year of his age, at his home, near Hillsboro, Norval, second son of Reuben JENKINS, of this county. In the late war he enlisted, first in the 8th infantry and afterwards in WHITE's Battalion. Death caused by dropsy of the heart.

Mr. Thomas SWANN, stepson of Mayor LATROBE, and grandson of the late Thomas SWANN, is to be married on the 31st inst., at Wormley's Hotel, in Washington, to Miss Carita MASON, daughter of Dr. J. Frank MASON, of Loudoun County. They will reside in Baltimore.

Death of Joseph CARR Esq. at his home 3 miles S of Leesburg on Sunday night last, after an illness of several weeks. For many years President of the Board of Supervisors of Loudoun. Member of M. E. Church south. Born on the 15th of December 1813, and had he lived until today, December 15th, 1887, he would have been 74 years old. After a married life of more than 50 years, we believe his is the first death in his own immediate family. An aged widow, 4 sons and 3 daughters and a large number of grandchildren survive. On Tuesday his remains were interred in Union Cemetery, Leesburg, Rev. Dr. HEAD officiating at the funeral.

Dec. Ct.: Jos. H. JENKINS qualified as Admr. of Norval JENKINS dec'd.; Jno. W. SOUDER as Admr. of Emeline SOUDER dec'd.; G. Ernest LEITH as Admr. of Veturia A. LEITH dec'd. Estate of W. C. McG. GREEN committed to Sheriff.

Mr. Wm. HIBBS, an old citizen of this county, died on Sunday morning last, at an advanced age. During the late war he was a member of MOSBY's command, in which he won the sobriquet of "Major," and in service was wounded, the painful effects of which he carried with him to the grave.

Thursday, 22 December 1887 Vol. XXXII, No. 28

Married: In Leesburg, at the residence of the bride's uncle, Mr. A. DIBREL, on Wednesday morning, December 21st, 1887, by Rev. R. T. DAVIS, Dr. A. L. PENUEL and Miss Estelle, daughter of the late Dr. McARTHUR, of Petersburg.

Married: On November 30, 1887, Edw. N. KINNAHAN and Maggie E. BOPP, by the Rev. Father SULLIVAN, both of Washington.

Married: On December 7, 1887, at Sunnyside, Loudoun County, by Rev. S. S. WARE, Jos. N. FIFIELD, of Washington DC, to Miss Sallie F. COOKSEY, of Loudoun.

Married: December 14th, 1887, on Sycolin, by Rev. Isaac W. CANTER, John G. EVERHART and Sarah C. HARNSBOROUGH, all of Loudoun County.

Married: On the 27th of October 1887, at the Baptist Church, in the City of Delphi, Ind., by the Rev. T. Wm. T. NOLAND (brother of the groom) assisted by the Rev. S. R. SEAWRIGHT, Mr. Geo. A. NOLAND, son of Maj. Geo. W. NOLAND, of Loudoun County, and Miss Margarette R. WEBBER, youngest daughter of the late Dr. Robert WEBBER, of Indiana.

Died: At his residence near Hillsboro, December 6th, 1887, Norval JENKINS, aged 50y 1m 22d.

Died: In Waterford, December 9th, 1887, George H. DIVINE, in the 69th year of his age.

Died: At the residence of son, Chas. A. SMITH, Middleburg, on the morning of the 16th of December 1887, in the 77th year of her age, Mrs. Ann M. SMITH, wife of the late Augustus G. SMITH and last surviving daughter of the late John and Mary JOHNSTON, of Alexandria, Va. Member of M. E. Church for 35 years.

Miss Eliza FLETCHER, of "Sherland Hall," near Middleburg, died last Thursday at her home and was buried in the old burial ground near Rectortown.

Death of Henry C. GIST, partially paralyzed on Sunday morning, December 11, he lingered until 12:23 Thursday night, passed away in the 59th year of his age. Member of the M. E. Church South for nearly 40 years. On Saturday his remains were interred in Union Cemetery, Revs. I. W. CANTER, Nelson HEAD and R. T. DAVIC [DAVIS] officiating at the obsequies.

Death of Mrs. H. H. KENNEDY, wife of Rev. H. H. KENNEDY, pastor of St. Paul's M. E. Church, Jacksonville, Fla, died in that city, Dec. 10th 1887. She leaves husband and 5 children, youngest boy of 3 years.

Willie T. CARRUTHERS, formerly of this county, recently died at the home of his sister in Girard, Kansas, of pneumonia. He had been living in Texas for the past five years, but returned to the home of his sister a few months ago.

Col. John W. FAIRFAX, of Prince William Co, was in town on Saturday last searching the records in the clerk's office, his object being to tract the genealogy of the Maryland branch of his family. He is examining the church records of Durham Parish, found recorded the birth and baptism of several members of this branch of his family, the parents of whom resided at the time in the parish. Col. FAIRFAX is a younger brother of the Virginia planter, who can at any time cross the ocean and assume the title of Lord Fairfax, and occupy the seat in the House of Lords, in the British Parliament, but being a native born American he prefers the simplicity, and the laws of his native land, to that of law-maker for a country for which his only admiration is that it gave birth to his ancestors. *Port Tobacco (Md) Independent.*

Cards are out for the marriage at 3:30 Saturday afternoon, Dec. 31st 1887, at Wormley's Hotel, Washington DC, of Mr. Thos. SWANN and Miss Carita, daughter of Dr. J. F. MASON, of this county.

Thursday, 29 December 1887   Vol. XXXII, No. 29

At "Round Hill Side," the home of Maj. Geo. W. NOLAND, was on Wed. evening, December 21st 1887, the scene of the 50th anniversary of the marriage of Maj. George W. NOLAND and his wife Ruth. Speaking were John C. ODELL, Esq. of Indiana, who married the eldest daughter who presented a gold headed cane in the name of the widow of the late Dr. S. T. NOLAND, himself and wife, Rev. T. W. T. NOLAND presented the pair with gold dollars.

Married: By the Rev. John WOLF, at his residence on the 15th inst., Mr. Samuel E. HINDMAN to Miss Mollie L. HOWELL, all of Loudoun.

Married: On Wed., Dec. 21, 1887, at Mt. Hope Baptist church, Miss Annie D. LEFEVER, and Mr. Frank S. JENKINS, all of Loudoun.

Married: At the residence of the bride's father, Mr. Geo. BEANER, on the 22d inst., by Rev. D. C. HEDRICK, Mr. Thos. W. HICKMAN and Miss Mollie C. BEAMER.

Died: At the residence of her father, in Rhea Co, Tennessee, on Thursday, December 15th 1887, after a long illness, Mollie, wife of Mr. John L. BALL, formerly of Loudoun, in the 32d year of her age. She leaves a husband and 5 children, and aged parents.

M. Virginia Robertson BLAIR, wife of Jas. E. BLAIR, Esq. of Richmond, died at her home in that city, last Friday morning, and her funeral took place from the Second Presbyterian Church (Dr. HOGE,) on

Saturday. She was a sister of Rev. J. R. BRIDGES, pastor of the Presbyterian Church, in Leesburg.

Veterans of the Army of Northern Virginia residing in Loudoun County are requested to meet in Leesburg on February 13, 1888: E. V. WHITE, H. O. CLAGETT, C. M. FAUNTLEROY, Wm. B. LYNCH, W. E. GARRETT, S. McGILL, Edgar LITTLETON, E. L. BENNETT, Geo. R. HEAD, W. W. ATHEY, J. M. ORR, J. W. FOSTER, W. N. WISE, S. FOUCHE, J. B. FRANKLIN, John H. ALEXANDER, John GRAY, Ewell ATTWELL, Herbert OSBURN, R. S. BURKE, J. R. BEUCHLER, W. W. DIVINE Jr., J. F. BRAWNER, S. E. FOX, Wm. GRIMES, P. F. SHROFF, Geo. W. SURVICK, Thos. B. NORRIS, Jno. Y. BASSELL, Jno. H. INZER.

Death of Mr. H. Clay RYON, of consumption, at his mother's residence, Leesburg, on Thursday morning, in the 45th year of his age. Confederate soldier - he joined WHITE's Battalion.

Thursday, 5 January 1888 Vol. XXXII, No. 30

Married: At the residence of the bride's parents, by Rev. L. B. TURNBULL, on December 29th 1887, T. Frank VIRTZ and Effie Ann EVERHARD.

Married: At Unison, December 14th 1887, by Rev. J. H. LIGHT, Jno. T. ROSS and Mrs. Susan A. HOGE, all of Loudoun.

Married: At the Presbyterian Manse, Waterford, by the Rev. L. B. TURNBULL, January 2d 1888, Thomas E. EDWARDS and Mary W. CARTER.

Died: At Lovettsville, on December 13th 1887, Miss Sarah Ann HODGE, in the 83rd year of her age.

Died: Sunday, December 18th 1887, Henry B. MORIARITY, very suddenly, from convulsion, age 2y 3m 17d. Son of John H. and Sarah J. MORIARITY.

Cards are out for the marriage of Mr. Bedford GLASSCOCK, of Fauquier, and Miss Lulu Cochran RICHARDS, daughter of Burr H. RICHARDS, of Baltimore, but formerly of Loudoun.

Si WILLIAMS, colored, for many years a grave-digger in Middleburg, was found dead in his bed Monday morning.

Saturday afternoon while the snow was falling fast, Mr. Thomas SWANN and Miss Carita MASON were married in the red parlor at Wormley's Hotel. The groom is a grandson of the late Gov. SWANN, of Maryland, and a stepson of Mayor LATROBE, of Baltimore. The bride is the daughter of Dr. J. F. MASON, of Loudoun County. ... The bride was attired in a traveling dress of stone gray cloth with a side panel of striped plush. She carried a bouquet of niphetos roses and hyacinths. Best man was groom's brother, Mr. Sherlock SWANN. Service of the Catholic Church was performed by Rev. Father WILSON, who came from Harper's Ferry to officiate. ...

The *Alexandria Gazette* of December 30th states that the engagement of Mr. E. GOLDSMITH and Miss Ida E. BRAGER, both of that city, is announce.

Shepherdstown, December 31: Wedding occurred at the Carter House, in Charlestown, W. Va. today, Mr. A. H. MARTIN, of Brooklyn, N.Y., came to attend the KELLER-HOMRICHOUSE wedding on the 27th inst. He became fascinated with Miss Fannie POFFENBERGER, of this place, and they went to Charlestown, where they were married. The ceremony was performed by Rev. E. G. EGGLESTON. They will reside in Brooklyn, N. Y.

Thursday, 12 January 1888   Vol. XXXII, No. 31

Married: On Jan. 4, 1888, at the Presbyterian Church, Waterford, by the Rev. L. B. TURNBULL, LeRoy B. CALLOW, of Baltimore City, son of the late Wm. CALLOW, to Miss Adele LOW, of Loudoun Co., only daughter of the late Capt. Aaron LOW, U.S.A., Poughkeepsie, N. Y.

Married: On January 4, 1888, at New Windsor, Md., by the Rev. T. D. VALLANT, W. O. SHAW, of Washington, to Miss Maude H. DIVINE, of Waterford.

Married: At Bethel Church, on Tuesday, December 11, 1887, by Rev. Carter PAGE, James W. MULLEN and Emma D. FRY, daughter of George FRY, all of Loudoun.

Married: On the 6th inst., at the M. E. Parsonage, by Rev. D. C. HEDRICK, Mr. Geo. R. MYERS and Miss Emma JENKINS, all of Loudoun.

Married: On Dec. 27th, at Fork Church, Hanover Co, Va, by the Rev. J. Green SHACKELFORD, of Trinity church, Fredericksburg. Mr. Abel J. NORWOOD, of New Orleans, La, and Miss Emelina JONES, daughter of Major Horace JONES, of Hanover Academy, Va.

Died: In Purcellville, Jan. 5th, 1888, Mrs. Julia V. FRAME, aged 38y 9d.

Died: Mrs. Maggie E. PEACOCK, wife of James W. PEACOCK, January 4th in her 31st year. Elder E. V. WHITE preached the funeral.

Mr. Joseph H. RUSSELL, of this county, at one time teacher of public schools near Harper's Ferry, died after a very short illness on Wednesday. He had been married about one month to Miss Julia L. BENNETT. *Wash.*

Death of Mrs. Florence E. VASS, wife of Mr. R. C. VASS, of Culpeper C. H., occurred at her home there on Sunday last, January 8, 1888, of pneumonia. Her little daughter, Mary, has the same disease. Mrs. V. was a daughter of Mr. Robt. HARPER, of this community.

Marriage license issued in Washington last week to Benj. F. BROWN and Frances ROGERS, both of Loudoun.

Circuit Ct.: Frank P. GIST and Edgar F. BURCH qualified as Admrs. of Henry C. GIST dec'd.; Thos. C. HUMPHREY as Guardian of Wilmer D. HUMPHREY; George E. PLASTER as Admr. of Henry JACKSON dec'd.; Jas. W. CARR and Jno. C. CARR as Admrs. of Josephus CARR dec'd. Will of Uriah FRENCH dec'd. admitted to probate.

Wedding last night (Thursday) at Central M. E. Church, South, at the corner of Edmundson Ave. and Stricker St. Parties were Mr. Bedford GLASSCOCK, of Rectortown, Va, and Miss Lulu RICHARDS, daughter of Mr. Burr RICHARDS, of the firm Stoneburner & Richards. The groom's party consisted of Miss Gertie CRENSHAW, of Rectortown; Miss May GLASSCOCK, of Leesburg; Miss S. A. GLASSCOCK, of Rectortown; Miss M. S. HOUGH, of Leesburg, and Mr. C. LEACH, of Upperville, Va. Ushers were C. A. CRENSHAW and James M. LAKE, of Rectortown; Mr. S. Carroll CHANCELLOR, of Leesburg, and Mr. STONEBURNER, of this city. Performed by Rev. Mr. WILLIAMS, pastor of the church.

Dr. Wm. H. CRIM, of Baltimore, formerly of Loudoun, was married on Saturday last to Mrs. Ella G. HAZLETON, at the house of Mr. John ALBURGER, Germantown, Pa, Rev. Dr. Samuel UPJOHN officiating. Bride is the widow of the late William B. HAZLETON, a Baltimore journalist.

About 15 years ago, Rhoda FEWELL, a native of Manassas, Prince William Co. obtained entrance in the jail of Brentsville, where one James CLARKE, then editor of a paper at Millwood, Clarke Co., was confined for eloping with his sister, and shot CLARKE dead. FEWELL, under the force of public opinion, was acquitted. Now FEWELL is confined in New Mexico, charged with murdering several persons. His trial will occur at Fort Smith, Arkansas.

Thursday, 19 January 1888   Vol. XXXII, No. 32

Married: On Dec. 14, 1887, by Rev. Dr. J. P. NEWMAN, J. Herbert ATHEY, of Leesburg, to Nannie B. McALLISTER, of Baltimore, Md,

Married: At Misses Luptons Boarding House, Winchester, Dec. 21st, Jas. B. HARRISON, of Bedford Co., and Miss Virginia LUPTON, of Frederick Co., daughter of the late Jonah LUPTON dec'd.

Married: By J. Q. RHODES, at Madison C. H., Va., January 12, 1888, Mr. E. Hays NICHOLS, of Loudoun County, and Miss Emma C. HAWKINS, of Warren County.

Married: At the residence of bride's father, Ebenezer CONARD, near Hillsboro, on the 11th inst., by Rev. J. R. VANHORN, Mr. Wm. COMPHER and Miss Rose CONARD.

Married: At the home of the bride on the 11th inst., by Rev. J. R. VANHORN, John COCKERELL and Mrs. Jane KIDWELL.

Married: At the residence of Mr. James GAYNOR, on the 11th inst., by Rev. J. R. VANHORN, Mr. G. H. LONGERBEAM and Miss Rachael SCHELL.

Died: In Washington DC, January 14th 1888, of consumption, William L. WILLIAMS, in the 38th year of his age.

Died: January 11, at the residence of his parents, No. 1322 S St. NW, Washington DC, of pneumonia, Hardin B. LITTLEPAGE, son of Capt. E. B. and Emilie C. LITTLEPAGE, aged 3y 8d.

Circuit Ct.: John W. HALL appointed Guardian of Jas. L. TAVENNER and others under will of Danl. WHITE dec'd.

Mr. W. W. THOMPSON, Mayor of Hamilton, died suddenly at his home in that town last Monday morning. Member of the Masonic fraternity, by the members of which he was buried on Wednesday.

Death of Mrs. Florence E. VASS, daughter of Mr. Robt. HARPER, of this place, chronicled in *Culpeper Exponent*: Funeral took place at the Episcopal Church on Monday, the rector, Rev. W. T. ROBERTS officiating.

Mrs. Margaret KINZER, of Alexandria, died at her home in that city, last Wednesday night from the effects of a fall from a chair a short time ago. Relict of the late I. Louis KINZER, member of the Alexandria bar who died in 1863, and daughter of the late George P. WISE. Mrs. K. was an aunt of Mr. W. N. WISE, of this town.

Thursday, 26 January 1888   Vol. XXXII, No. 33

Married: In Leesburg, by Rev. Dr. HEAD, on the 18th of January 1888, John W. BENTON and Nannie T. MOORE, all of Loudoun.

Died: Frank REAMER, infant son of Christian and Emma REAMER, died at the Reamer House, Tuesday, Jan. 17th 1888, aged 14m 19d.

Died: At her residence, near Snickersville, December 28th, 1887, Kesiah, wife of Isaac STANTINYERS [SANTMYER], in the 40th year of her age, of consumption. Funeral preached by the Rev. John WOOLF, interred in Ebenezer burying ground.

Death of Abner C. TRUNDLE, last Saturday, at the residence of Mr. John HEFFNER, at the mouth of the Monocacy, Md, of paralysis. He was the eldest son of the late Horatio TRUNDLE, at one time owner of Exeter estate, near Leesburg. Shortly after the death of the father, Mr. TRUNDLE became involved, and lost the whole of what was at one time a handsome fortune. He was about 55 years of age.

Circuit Ct.: Decree entered granting absolute divorce to Maria L. COE from her husband Aurelius COE.

Thursday, 2 February 1888   Vol. XXXII, No. 34

Married: January 30, 1888, by Rev. J. R. BRIDGES, at the home of the bride's parents, Samuel THRIFT to Lucy E. McPHERSON, daughter of M. E. McPHERSON, of Loudoun County.

In memoriam: Death of Annie May TAVENNER, daughter of Mr. Alpheus and Mrs. Emma TAVENNER, Jan. 19, 1888, aged 6y 10m.

Death of Dr. Thos. F. TEBBS, at his home near Haymarket, in Prince William County, on Friday morning last, January 27th 1888, after a short illness of pneumonia. Native of this county, and was uncle of Judge R. H. TEBBS. He served throughout the late war as a surgeon in the Confederate Army, a good portion of his time with the 8th Va regiment. He was in the 60th year of his age.

Miss Henrietta E. CHILTON, sister of the late Hon. Samuel CHILTON, of Fauquier, died near Vermont, Mo., on January 9th, aged 84 years. She was born in Fauquier Co, and removed with her father in Missouri in 1830.

Capt. Chas. G. MINNIGERODE committed suicide about 5:30 yesterday afternoon by shooting himself in the head at his late residence on Washington Street [Alexandria]. ... About 42 years of age, a son of Rev. Dr. MINNIGERODE, Episcopal divine of Richmond. He was a Confederate soldier, and served on Gen. Fitzhugh LEE's staff. In the fighting preceeding the final surrender at Appomattox C. H., he was struck in the breast by a bullett, thrown from his horse, and to all appeared killed. Gen. LEE took him for dead. His father and other members of the family arrived here today and this afternoon the remains were taken to "Oatlands," Loudoun Co., where they will be interred in the family burying ground. Funeral took place on Friday.

Thursday, 9 February 1888   Vol. XXXII, No. 35

Died: January 27th 1888, Mrs. Margaret J. BENTON, widow of the late B. H. BENTON, in the 71st year of her age.

Marriage license issued last week in Washington DC, to John D. CONNER and Miss ___ SMITH, both of Loudoun County.

Thursday, 16 February 1888   Vol. XXXII, No. 36

Married: At the M. E. Church, South, Leesburg, on Thursday, February 9th, 1888, by the Rev. Dr. Nelson HEAD, grandfather of the bride, Mr. Adin W. LAYCOCK (of the dry goods firm of Wildman & Co.) to Miss Margaret M. KENT, all of Leesburg.

Married: At the residence of Mr. Cuthbert B. ROGERS, February 9th, Mr. Beverly HUTCHISON, of Texas, and Miss Mary L. ROGERS, daughter of C. B. ROGERS.

Married: At his residence by the Rev. John WOOLF, on the 2d inst., Mr. James E. BALLENGER to Miss Mary C. POLEN.

Married: By the Rev. G. W. POPKINS, on the 8th of Feb., in Washington DC, Mr. John E. LOVELESS to Miss Cornella GOODRICK.

Married: By the Rev. John T. ALEXANDER near Daysville, Mr. Robert W. ALEXANDER to Miss Ada PALMER, all of Loudoun.

Died: In Herndon, On Friday, February 3d, 1888, Ferderie, infant son of Charles H. and Annie REED.

Died: At "Glenmore," Loudoun Co., on Dec. 29th 1887, Miss Rachel MOORE. Member of the Old School Baptist Church at Ebenezer.

Mr. Amos SEATON departed this life Sunday, February 12th '88, in his 83d year. He was buried at Northfork burying ground.

Death of Elder Joseph FURR, for many years a minister in the Old School Baptist Church, at his home near Hughesville, on Monday night last, at the advanced age of nearly four score years. Today (Thursday) interred in the burying ground near the Old Valley Meeting House, Elder E. V. WHITE officiating.

Co. Ct.: W. W. THOMPSON's will admitted to probate. Morgan BEAVERS qualified as Guardian of Lewis W., Kate E. and Agnes BEAVERS. Wm. GAINES qualified as Admr. of Joseph WOOD dec'd. F. W. SHAFER qualified as Admr. of Joseph SHAFER dec'd. Estate of Littleton EDMUNDS Jr. committed to Sheriff. Geo. W. PIERSON qualified as Admr. of Wm. HIBBS dec'd.

Marriage license issued in Washington DC to Mr. John E. LOVELESS, of Loudoun, and Miss Cornelia GOODRICK, of Washington.

Col. John E. BOYD, of Martinsburg, W. Va, died on Sunday last, of paralysis of the heart. He was a son of Elisha BOYD, a brother-in-law of the late C. J. FAULKNER, and an uncle of the present C. J. FAULKNER, the newly elected Senator from that State. He was 76 years of age.

Colored man Levi PROCTOR, who lived near Upperville, died not long since at the age of 91 years, and was well known in that portion of Fauquier. His children, grand children and great grand children number 160.

Thursday, 23 February 1888   Vol. XXXII, No. 37

Married: At Mt. Vernon Place, M. E. Church, South, Washington DC, on Wed. Feb. 15, 1888, by the Rev. G. Dorsey WHITE, assisted by Revs. HADDAWAY and KENNARD, Dr. Luther A. BROWN, of Leesburg, and Miss Viola McCHESNEY, of Prince George Co. Md.

Married: At Little River Baptist Church, Loudoun Co., by Rev. T. A. HALL, the pastor, February 14th 1888, Mr. James SOWERS to Miss Mary J. SPRIGG, both of Loudoun Co., Va.

Died: At the residence of Dr. N. B. NEVITT, Accotink, Fairfax Co., on Ash Wednesday, February 15th in her 79th year, Mrs. Sally M. LEE, widow of Dr. George LEE, late of Leesburg.

Death of Mrs. Sallie M. LEE, of Leesburg, occurred suddenly on Thursday last, at the residence of her niece, Mrs. Dr. NEVITT, near Accotinck, Va. Widow of the late Dr. Geo. LEE, a daughter of the late Richard HENDERSON, an eminent lawyer, and sister of the late Fenton M. HENDERSON, all of this place. Member of the Episcopal Church. Funeral at 11 o'clock Saturday morning, laid to rest in the same grave with her departed husband, Rev. Dr. DAVIS, assisted by Rev. Mr. WALLACE, of Fairfax, officiating.

Mrs. Rurhea Ann PIERPOINT, relict of the late Joseph PIERPOINT, died last Friday morning at her home, near Hamilton, in this county, aged 79 years.

Thursday, 1 March 1888   Vol. XXXII, No. 38

Married: At the parsonage of the M. E. Church, South, in Leesburg, February 16th, 1888, by Rev. Isaac W. CANTER, Thos. HAWS and Fannie ELLMORE, both of Loudoun County.

Married: At the parsonage of the M. E. Church, South, in Leesburg, February 23d, 1888, by Rev. Isaac W. CANTER, William ANTSWORTH and Mary POTTS, both of Loudoun County.

Married: On the 22d of Feb. 1888, by the Rev. H. St. John RINKER, Mr. James H. WHITE to Miss L. Annie GRUBB, all of Loudoun Co.

Married: In Rockville, Md, on the 20th of February, by Rev. S. R. WHITE, Mr. Charles L. AHALT, of Virginia, to Miss Lillie B. BEAN, of Montgomery County.

Died: At her home, near Philomont, 2nd month, 19th, 1888, in the 25th year of her age, Emma W. GREGG, daughter of Wm. and Elizabeth GREGG.

Sudden death of Robt. E. DIVINE, of stout build and picture of health, on Saturday about 4:30 of apoplectic stroke. For many years he engaged in the grocery business on King St., Leesburg. Member of the Presbyterian Church. In his 63d year, and leaves a widow and one son, with large family connection. Funeral took place from his late residence at 2 o'clock Monday afternoon, conducted by Rev. J. R. BRIDGES, assisted by Rev. Dr. N. HEAD, Rev. R. T. DAVIS, and Rev. D. C. HEAD. He was a member of Loudoun Lodge, I. O. O. F., and an officer of Olive Branch Lodge, A. F. & a. Masons.

Mrs. Mary CARR, widow of the late Thos. CARR, of this county, died in Leesburg, on Monday morning last, at the residence of her son-in-law, Mr. Thos. B. NORRIS. Buried in Union Cemetery Tuesday afternoon, Revs. I. W. CANTER, Dr. N. HEAD and Mr. BRIDGES officiating.

At her home, in Leesburg, on Thursday night, February 23d, Mrs. Michael HOURIHANE died after a brief illness. She was the mother of Dr. M. HOURIHANE and of Mr. John HOURIHANE, in the Clothing Store of C. W. LITTLEJOHN. Member of the Catholic Church, from the Chapel of which in this town her funeral took place on Friday, Father WILSON officiating.

Mr. David MERCHANT, of Leesburg, where he had passed more than 50 years of his life, died in this town on Thursday morning last, after a short illness, in his 79th year. Interred in Union Cemetery of Friday afternoon, with ceremony by Order of Good Templars.

Mr. Nicholas HOGAN died at the residence of his brother, Mr. Patrick HOGAN, near Aldie, on Sunday last at an advanced age. Funeral took place from the Chapel of Immaculate Conception in this town, on Tuesday afternoon, Father WILSON officiating. Interred in Union Cemetery.

Mrs. Mary Ellen HATCHER, wife of Mr. Joshua HATCHER, near Lincoln, in this county, died on Monday last at an advance age.

Mr. Mayo BROWN, son of Burr BROWN, died on the 18th inst., of typho-malario, in the 31st year of his age. On Tuesday he was buried in the Friends' burying ground at Lincoln.

On Sunday night, 19th inst., Mrs. Hannah SHRIGLEY, died at her home in Hamilton, in the 48th year of her age. Her husband, who was a soldier in the Confederate army, was killed and buried on the battle field of Gettysburg.

On Wednesday, at his home in Hamilton, T. Sherman LAKE, after a few days' illness, died of congestive chills. On Thursday he was buried with Masonic honors by Hamilton lodge, of which he was a member.

Mr. Leroy SQUIRES, died on Sunday, January 1st, at Dover, and just six weeks after, on Sunday, the 12th of February, died his wife, Mrs. Eliza SQUIRES, At Mr. MATHER's near Farmwell. He was nearly 88 years old and she was nearly 80, and they had been married for over 50 years.

Tom OLDEN, alias Thomas JACKSON (col'd) was arrested Saturday at Fox Mountain ore bank, in Rockingham Co, on the charge of killing Wm. BROYLES (col'd) near Middleburg, Loudoun County, in the Spring of 1886. He was seen and recognized by a colored resident of Milnes, who formerly lived in Loudoun County.

Thursday, 8 March 1888   Vol. XXXII, No. 39

Married: By Rev J. R. BRIDGES, at the Presbyterian Manse, Leesburg, Feb. 29th, 1888, Mr. John T. SEWELL to Miss Susan B. SHUGARS.

Married: On the 29th ult., near Lovettsville, by the Rev. H. St. John RINKER, Mr. Robert J. GARDNER to Miss Mary ROLLER, all of Loudoun County.

Died: Rue A. PIERPOINT, the widow of Joseph PIERPOINT, died of paralysis, 2d month, 17th, 1888, aged 78y 11m 20d.

Mrs. J. D. HOSPITAL died at her home in Falls church, last Sunday morning, aged 40 years. Had the measles, which ran into pneumonia, of which she died. She was a Miss MONROE of Loudoun. Her 6 week's old child died about two weeks ago, and at her death the child was disinterred, and the remains taken to Loudoun with her on Monday, for burial. Before the train had gotten ten miles from Falls Church, her son, about 19 years old, who had the measles also died. His remains were also taken to Loudoun. A ten year old daughter is now sick. The three were buried from the Bloomfield M. E. Church South at Ebenezer Cemetery, on Wednesday last.

Colored woman, Maria HARRIS, wife of Phil. HARRIS, while attending to ordinary household duties last Saturday morning, suddenly fell and died in a few minutes. She had been an invalid for some time past. She was buried on Monday by the order of Good Samaritans, of which she was a member.

Mrs. Louisa MINOR, widow of the late John W. MINOR, of this county, died on Saturday, February 4th 1888, at Providence Hospital, in Washington City, where she was under treatment for gangrene. She was in her 72d year. Buried in Mt. Olivet Cemetery.

Dr. D. W. MYERS, Dentist of this county, and a few years ago, a resident of this town, died at the home of his father, near Hughesville, on Wed. morning, March 7th 1888, of consumption.

[MISSING ISSUE]

Thursday, 22 March 1888   Vol. XXXII, No. 41

Died: At the residence of her son, in Washington city, March 18, 1888, at 9:45 p.m., Mrs. Ann E. KITZMILLER, widow of the late A. M. KITZMILLER, in the 74th year of her age.

Died: Near Sterling, February 29, 1888, after a few days illness, Andrew COLE, son of William and Harriet COLE, in his 18th year.

In Memoriam: Lina A. JONES, at her home, in Aldie, on the 11th inst., of consumption. Funeral preached by her pastor, Rev. Mr. BROWN of the M. E. Church, and her remains taken to Alexandria for burial. Leaves brother and sister.

Thursday, 29 March 1888   Vol. XXXII, No. 42

Mrs. Ellen MOORE, wife of Maj. S. J. C. MOORE, and daughter of the late Dr. Randolph KOWNSLAR, died in Berryville last Saturday of paralysis.

Died: At his mother's residence near Hamilton, on the 18th of March, 1888, Edward M. THOMPSON, age 24y 9m 9d.

Died: March 15th 1888, Mrs. Elizabeth FRY, widow of William FRY, aged 79y 4m 14d.

Died: In Washington city, March 25th 1888, at 10:30 a.m., Mrs. M. E. CARROLL (wife of Andrew CARROLL) in the 60th year of her age.

Died: From an attack of meningitis, Henry Howison RATCLIFFE, son of Mr. James and Mrs. Susie RATCLIFFE, of North Fork, on March 18th 1888, age 11y 3m 14d. Funeral by Elder Benjamin BRIDGES.

Thursday, 5 April 1888   Vol. XXXII, No. 43

Married: At the residence of Mr. Robert FRENCH, March 29th, by Rev. C. T. HERNDON, Mr. Thos. F. ATTWELL and Miss Capitola FRENCH, all of Loudoun.

Married: At the M. E. Parsonage, Frederick city, Md, by Dr. Geo. V. LEECH, of the Baltimore Annual Conference, Mr. Joseph Franklin LOY, of Loudoun, late of Montgomery Co., Md, and Miss Catharine R. McCOY, of Loudoun Co., March 22d, 1888.

Died: In Leesburg, on Thursday, March 29th 1888, Mr. Robert J. WEBB, formerly of Frederick Co., Md, in the 79th year of his age.

Died: At Oatland, on Tuesday morning, March 27th, Annie May, daughter of James E. and Mollie J. TAVENNER, aged 3y 3m 27d.

Last Thursday, Mr. Robt. J. WEBB died at his home in Leesburg, at the age of 79 years. For several years afflicted with partial blindness and more recently with paralysis. Laid to rest on Saturday.

On the same day, Mrs. Annie E. WIARD, wife of Mr. Jacob S. WIARD, died of cancer, after several years of suffering. She was a daughter of the late Henry C. WILDER and member of Presbyterian Church. Laid to rest on Saturday.

Marriage license issued in Washington city last week to Warren F. SILCOTT, of Dover, in this county, and Lillie B. SAFFER, of Aldie.

Wm. D. Bowie McKENZIE died in Baltimore on Tuesday, in the 30th year of his age.

The wife of John R. TURNER, clerk of the Circuit Court of Fauquier Co., died last Monday.

Dr. J. G. DOWELL, of Middleburg, at the home of his father-in-law, Mr. James A. SMITH, near Middleburg, in presence of his wife and two little children, died on Thursday March 29th 1888. He was buried in Middleburg on Saturday, and on Friday afternoon his brother, Capt. W. F. DOWDELL, left him home, at Woodburn, to attend the funeral. Late in the evening he passed the Pot House, intending to spend the night with his sister, at Rector's X Road. Between 7 and 8 o'clock Saturday, Capt. DOWDELL's dead body was found lying in the public road, some 3 miles from the Pot House. Supposed he died of heart disease. On Sunday his remains were interred beside his brother in Middleburg Cemetery. During the late war, Capt. DOWDELL commanded Co. B, WHITE's Battalion. He leaves a wife and several children. He was in about the 53d year of his age.

Mr. Champ SHEPHERD of Clarke Co, died last Friday.

J. Howard SMITH, brother of Prof. F. H. SMITH, of University of Va, and a son of the late Daniel G. SMITH, for many years a citizen of Leesburg, died at his home in Albemarle Co., on Wednesday, March 28th of pneumonia.

Gen. Thomas H. WILLIAMSON, Prof. of topographical drawing at Va. Military Institute, died last Saturday, aged about 78. He was a native of Norfolk. He was the father of Mr. Thomas WILLIAMSON, formerly a resident of this town.

Thursday, 12 April 1888   Vol. XXXII, No. 44

Died: At Norris Farm, Bureau Co., Ill., on March 2d, 1888, Elizabeth Dunnick, eldest child of Clarkson and Margaretta H. NORRIS, aged 5y 7m.

Died: At Norris Farm, March 10th '88, Josephine Hoge, second child of Clarkson and Margarette H. NORRIS, aged 4 years.

Died: At the residence of his parents, in Hamilton, March 5th 1888, George T. LEWIS, aged 19 years.

Mr. John RITICOR, of this county, died at his home near Aldie, on Sunday, March 18, 1888, at the age of 85 years. Interred in Mt. Zion burying ground, on Tuesday March 20th.

At the residence of the bride's father, in Richmond, last week, Miss Sarah POWELL, eldest daughter of Jno. H. POWELL, Esq., was married to Mr. R. Logan COLEMAN, of Pittsylvania Co., Va. Rev. Joshua PETERKIN, rector of St. James Episcopal Church, officiating. Bride is niece of Mr. Louis H. POWELL, of Leesburg, and Edward F. POWELL, Druggist, of Middleburg.

Mrs. Martha L. ISLER, relict of the late Jacob ISLER, died at her home near Berryville, on Saturday last, after having reached the age of 91 years. Her late husband was a soldier in the war of 1812, and she was a pensioner. Surviving her are 2 daughters, 21 grandchildren and 51 great grandchildren, and 3 great great grandchildren.

Co. Ct.: Wills of Mary E. H. BASCUE dec'd., John RITICOR dec'd. and Jas. G. DOWDELL dec'd. admitted to probate. Samuel R. SEATON qualified as Admr. of Edward JOHNSON dec'd.; Roxanna HOUSEHOLDER as Admx. of Silas A. HOUSEHOLDER dec'd.; Wm. GAINES as Admr. of S. C. RIDDLE dec'd. Gabriel V. WARNER appointed committee for John H. STOCKS. Oscar S. BRADEN qualified as guardian of Cabell Y. PEYTON; Burr W. PRESGRAVES as Admr. of Wm. W. PRESGRAVES dec'd. Estates of Mary CARR dec'd. and Wyatt THOMPSON dec'd. committed to sheriff.

Thursday, 19 April 1888   Vol. XXXII, No. 45

Married: At the residence of the bride's father, Mr. C. T. HEMPSTONE, on Thursday, April 12, 1888, by the Rev. R. T. DAVIS, Mr. Charles L. HAWKS, of New York, to Miss Mary HEMPSTONE, of Leesburg.

Married: At the Reamer House, in Leesburg, at 8 o'clock Tuesday evening, April 17th 1888, by Rev. D. C. HEDRICK, Mr. Leven H. McDONOUGH, of Leesburg, and Miss Annie E. CLARK, of Manitoba, Canada.

Died: At her home near Leesburg, on Thursday morning, April 12th 1888, Mrs. Mary HEMPSTONE, wife of Mr. C. T. HEMPSTONE, in the 73d year of her age.

Died: Mrs. Louisa VINSELL, near Lovettsville, on March 26th 1888, in the 80th year of her age.

Died: L. P. CLARK, at his home in Purcellville, on April 9th, of consumption of the bowels, aged about 39 years.

Died: Thomas POTTS, at his home in Hillsboro, April 4th, in the 80th year of his age.

Died: March 25th 1888, Jane COPELAND, widow of Andrew COPELAND, aged 95y 2m 17d. Over 33 years a widow. Mechanicsville.

Died: April 13th 1888, of typhoid pneumonia, Martha F. MORAN, 3rd daughter of H. T. MORAN, in the 10th year of her age.

Died: John F. REEVES, at his residence, at Mountain Gap, on Saturday, April 14th 1888, in the 48th year of his age. He leaves a wife and nine children.

Mr. Richard TIMBERLAKE, of Jefferson Co. W. Va., was paralyzed Monday morning and died at his residence in Charlestown at 4 o'clock. He was in the 81st year of his age. He served on the jury in 1859 that convicted John BROWN.

Mr. John REEVES, of this county, died at his home at Mountain Gap, last Saturday, after a long and painful illness. During the late war he was a soldier in the 8th Va. Regiment.

Dr. Americus COCKERILLE died at his residence in Alexandria, Louisiana, on Thursday morning last, 12th inst. He was an uncle of Judge R. H. TEBBS, of Leesburg, and brother of Judge COCKERILLE, of Fairfax county.

Mrs. Mary HEMPSTONE, wife of Mr. C. T. HEMPSTONE, residing near Leesburg, died suddenly last Thursday morning. For some time past she was somewhat of an invalid, she died of appoplexy. In about her 73d year, for more than 50 years a wife. Services of the Episcopal Church, by Rev. Dr. DAVIS, interred in Union Cemetery. Thursday last, at noon, was the appointed hour for the marriage of Miss Mary HEMPSTONE, daughter of C. T. and Mary HEMPSTONE, to Mr. Chas. L. HAWKS, of New York. Despite the death of Mrs. HEMPSTONE, the marriage ceremony was performed.

Community shocked last Thursday morning by a telegram received by his brother-in-law, C. P. JANNEY, Esq. announcing the sudden death in Warrenton the night before of Charles Lee POLLOCK Esq., a member of the law firm of Pollock & Garrett, of Leesburg. Son of the Rev. A. D. POLLOCK and wife Elizabeth, and grandson on the mother's side of Charles LEE, Attorney General of the U.S. under WASHINGTON. Died at residence of his parents, "Leeton Forest," near Warrenton on Thursday the 12th of April 1888, aged 37 years.

Miss Helen JEWETT, eldest daughter of Mr. Hugh J. JEWETT, former president of the Erie Railroad, was married in New York Saturday to Mr. Thomas HUNT, son of Judge Wm. HUNT, ex-minister to Russia. She is a niece of Mr. Jos. H. JEWETT of this county.

Wedding took place in the parlors of the Reamer House, Leesburg, last Tuesday evening, of Mr. Leven H. McDONOUGH, of Leesburg, and Miss Annie E. CLARKE, of Manitoba, Canada. About 12 months ago, a few simple lines published in the matrimonial columns of a northern journal attracted the attention of the groom and they corresponded. Last Monday they met for the first time. Ceremony performed by Rev. D. C. HEDRICK of the M. E. Church.

Charlestown W. Va.: Maj. John S. RUDD was found in his room at the Montgomery Hotel, Coal Valley, about 5 o'clock Sunday, suffering from an over dose of chloroform, and died 20 minutes later. He was a soldier in the Confederate Army being a staff officer of Gen. LONGSTREET. Of late he had threatened suicide.

Thursday, 26 April 1888   Vol. XXXII, No. 46

Died: In Washington city, on Sunday April 22d, 1888, Virginia Nelson, only child of George and Lulie F. LEWIS, aged 9m 16d. Funeral took place from the residence of the grand-mother, Mrs. LEWIS, in Leesburg, on Tuesday.

Mr. James H. ROGERS, only son of Mr. Wm. H. ROGERS, died at his home near Dover, in this county, on Wednesday morning, after a few days illness of pneumonia. He was in about the 60th year of his age. Funeral will take place at 11 o'clock Friday morning.

Last Friday morning, Mrs. Susannah SHAFER, wife of Mr. F. W. SHAFER, of this town, and mother of a large family of children, among them Carlton SHAFER, Esq., Clerk of the Md House of Delegates, and the late Dr. Joseph SHAFER, U.S.N. whose unexpected death was recorded less than one year ago. Funeral took place Sunday afternoon, Revs. Mr. BRIDGES and Dr. DAVIS officiating. Interred in Union Cemetery.

Death of A. Campbell MASON, youngest son of Dr. J. F. MASON, of this county, occurred in Washington city on Wednesday, April 12, 1888, of pneumonia. Funeral took place from Christ church, Alexandria, on Friday afternoon.

Death of Mrs. Ella SMITH, wife of Mr. Henry S. SMITH, near Guilford, occurred at her home on Sunday evening last, of heart disease. Her husband was absent from the house at the time.

J. W. WORKS, of this county, died at his home near Farmwell last Thursday. He died in a few hours. Leave a wife and several small children.

Flave GUY, colored youth sent some five years ago to the penitentiary for a term of 17 years for killing an old negro named Geo. POTTER, returned to Leesburg one day last week having been pardoned.

Resolution by the Loudoun bar on the death of Charles Lee POLLOCK.

Thursday, 3 May 1888   Vol. XXXII, No. 47

Died: At his residence near Unison, on Friday morning, April 27th, after a protracted illness from paralysis, Dr. Philo R. CRAIN, in the 77th year of his age.

Died: At Mt. Gilead, Apr. 21st 1888, Miss Ginevra H., only daughter of John W. and Virginia C. DENNIS, of consumption, in the 28th year of her age. Member of North Fork Baptist church for 12 years.

Wilkesbarre Pa Leader of Apr. 26th: Miss Lillian COOLBAUGH was last evening wed to Dr. Alexander HODGDON of Virginia, performed at the residence of the bride's parents on Academy St. by Rev. Dr. HODGE, of the First Presbyterian Church. ... The groom is a physician of Farmwell, but will not be making Loudoun their permanent home.

On Friday morning last, about 4 o'clock, the mother of Mr. Brooke CHAMBLIN, who had her home near Bloomfield, died very suddenly at an advanced age, opinion that it was paralysis of the heart. Funeral took place on Saturday afternoon, by Rev. Jno. C. DICE.

Francis FELLOWES, lawyer of Hartford, Conn, died there last night, aged 85 years. ... He married a lady, formerly of Leesburg, and was the plaintiff in the suit of FELLOWES vs Town of Leesburg disposed of in the Circuit Ct. of this county last week.

Marriage license issued in Washington on Monday, to Geo. W. PETTITT, of Fairfax Co., and Alice C. GARNETT, of Loudoun Co.

[MISSING ISSUE]

Thursday, 17 May 1888   Vol. XXXII, No. 49

Died: At Norris Farm, Illinois, on the 9th inst., Margaretta R. Hoge NORRIS, wife of Clark NORRIS, and daughter of the late Isaac and Rachel N. HOGE, of Loudoun Co.

Death of R. Stretchley CHINN occurred at his home near Middleburg, on Friday last, from the effects of injuries received a short time ago by his team running away.

Co. Ct.: Wills of Philo. R. CRAIN dec'd.; Ellen C. SMITH dec'd.; Ann C. ABEL dec'd.; George COOPER dec'd.; Peter WIRE dec'd. and Henry H. GREGG dec'd. were admitted to probate. C. C. GAVER qualified as Admr. of Nancy COCKRILL dec'd.; Wm. G. JENKINS as Admr. of Thos. J. SMITH dec'd.; Jno. HUTCHISON as Admr. of Margaret J. BURTON dec'd. Estate of Mary CARR dec'd. committed to Sheriff for Admr. C. E. MOUNT appointed committee of Geo. B. McCARTY.

Jas. H. MOORE, of Jefferson Co, W. Va. died Saturday, sick but a few days, and was in his 98th year. His brother, Wm. H. MOORE, aged 75, died one week ago.

Thursday, 24 May 1888   Vol. XXXII, No. 50

Dr. Jonah NICHOLS, of Snickersville, left Loudoun the first of the week for Central California to practice the healing art. He is brother of Dr. F. M. NICHOLS, of Round Hill.

Thursday, 31 May 1888   Vol. XXXII, No. 51

Married: On May 15th 1888, at the Lutheran Parsonage, in Frederick city, Md, by the Rev. Luther KUHLMAN, Julius McLYNN to Miss Roberta L. CORDELL, both of Lovettsville.

Died: Friday, May 18th 1888, of whooping cough and bronchitis, Wm. Berkeley MOORE, infant son of Alexander B. and Lucy B. MOORE, aged 3m 12d.

Died: At his residence near Mountsville, May 20th, G. B. McCARTY, in the 76th year of his age.

Died: On Tuesday, May 22, 1888, in Washington DC, of consumption, John T. HOLROYD, youngest child of Sarah E. and the late John HOLROYD, aged 38y 9m.

Died: In Washington on Thursday, May 24th, Charles Rowland WATKINS, aged 22m 3w.

Jesse PEARSON, colored boy formerly of this town, but who held a position in the Washington post office, died in that city last week and was brought here for burial.

Near Raveswood, W. Va., on Monday, Mr. and Mrs. Wm. POWELL were killed by lightning while sitting in their home. At Charleston, W. Va., Mrs. Robert SHANNON was killed by a falling tree.

Thursday, 7 June 1888   Vol. XXXII, No. 52

Judge N. B. MEADE, of the Corp. Court of Alexandria, died at Marshall, Fauquier Co., Tuesday night, May 29th, of disease of the heart. He was on his way to his country home. He was a native of Clarke Co, and a nephew of Bishop MEADE.

Mrs. POULTON, wife of Mr. Wm POULTON, and mother of Frank and Reed B. POULTON, of this town, died last Monday night at an advanced age.

Hannah J. TAYLOR, relict of the late Henry S. TAYLOR, died at the residence of her daughter, Susan C. GORE, Hamilton, May 27th 1888, aged 82y 16d. On May 11, 1806 she was born at the place where now resides William F. MERCER, near Hamilton depot, about a mile from the place where she died. On May 30, 1829 she married Henry S. TAYLOR, at Friends Meeting House, in Waterford, where she was a member. The funeral took place on her wedding anniversary. On Wednesday morning, Rev. B. W. BOND of the Methodist Church, read, followed by Rev. S. S. WARE, of the Episcopal Church. Body conveyed to Friends Meeting House at Lincoln. Jesse HOGE and D. J. HOGE, son-in-law of the deceased, and Phineas J. NICHOLS, spoke. Two nieces also spoke. Mrs. TAYLOR was the mother of Thos. E. TAYLOR, of Lincoln.

Thursday, 14 June 1888   Vol. XXXIII, No. 1

Married: At "Boydville," Martinsburg, W. Va., June 6th, by Rev. L. B. TURNBULL, Rev. C. D. PRICE, of Richmond, Va. and Miss Ella BOCOCK, daughter of Hon. Thos. M. BOCOCK.

Died: At the residence of her brother, Mr. L. T. NICHOLS, near Middleburg, on Wednesday, May 14th, 1888 after a long and painful illness, Miss Annie V. NICHOLS, aged 29y 2m.

Mrs. Duanna CHAMBLIN, widow of the late Mason CHAMBLIN, of this county, and mother of H. C. and John CHAMBLIN, of Richmond, died at her home in Hamilton, on Monday morning last at the advanced age of 88 years. She was buried Wednesday at Short Hill, Rev. C. T. HERNDON officiating.

Mr. Erastus C. BENEDICT, residing near Round Hill, was found dead in his bed last Monday morning. He was in about the 36th year of his age. He leaves a wife (daughter of the late R. M. BENTLEY) and one child. Interred Tuesday afternoon in Union Cemetery.

Marriage license issued in Washington last week to Charles E. BERKELEY, of Loudoun, and Mary F. MOORE, of that city.

On night of 3d of April 1886, Thos. OLDEN assaulted colored man Wm. BRIERLY, who died the next day. OLDEN fled and assumed the name of Thos. JACKSON. He was arrested and has been sentenced to the penitentiary for 18 years.

June Ct.: Will of R. S. CHINN admitted to probate. Chas. E. MOUNT qualified as Admr. of Geo. B. McCARTY dec'd.; Chas. A. FRAME as Admr. of Jane FRAME dec'd. Estate of Elizabeth A. METZGER committed to sheriff.

Marriage license issued in Washington on Monday to Jos. B. PITCHER, of Anacostia, DC, and Rosie L. COPELAND, of Leesburg.

Mrs. KLEIN, wife of the late Dr. John A. KLEIN, and mother of Dr. John KLEIN, died at her residence near Snickersville on Monday last at an advanced age.

Thursday, 21 June 1888   Vol. XXXIII, No. 2

Died: June 7th 1888, at the residence of George GRIMES, Madison GRIMES, aged about 76 years.

Mr. R. H. RECTOR, of Fauquier, died on Saturday 9th inst., after a long illness. Interred in the village cemetery at Middleburg.

Thursday, 28 June 1888   Vol. XXXIII, No. 3

Married: Near the Valley Church, Loudoun Co, June 18th 1888, by Rev. James McDONOUGH, James Edgar NEWTON to Miss Sarah C. COOPER, all of Loudoun.

Married: On the 18th inst., at the Reformed Church near Lovettsville, by the Rev. H. St. John RINKER, Mr. Wm. B. SHUMAKER to Miss Christina SPEAKS, all of Loudoun County.

Died: In Leesburg, June 14th 1888, Harry Edward CURRY, infant son of Charles E. and Rebecca E. CURRY, aged 12m 21d.

Mrs. Frances HAMMOND, wife of Rev. C. W. HAMMOND of the Baltimore Conference M. E. Church South, and a sister of Mr. P. W. CARPER, of this county, died in Buffalo, N. Y. (where she had gone for treatment of cancer) on June 19, 1888. Interred in Union Cemetery, Leesburg, on Thursday, Revs. Dr. HEAD and DAVIS officiating.

Mrs. Lydia TIMMS, wife of the late Jas. F. TIMMS, of Leesburg, died at the residence of her son in Washington, on Sunday last, at an advanced age.

Washington Wedding of a former citizen of Loudoun – Mr. T. Wirton MATTHEWS, of "Creedmoor," Fauquier Co., was married yesterday morning to Miss May Renshaw GULICK, daughter of the late James H. GULICK, of Pennsylvania, at 25 Lafayette square at 9:30, by Rev. Dr. W. A. LEONARD. Mr. James H. GULICK, of Pa, gave his sister in marriage. ... They will go for the summer to the Forest Glen House.

James LAWSON, 74 years of age, fell from the top of a cherry tree near the Plains, Fauquier Co., last Thursday and was instantly killed.

Thursday, 5 July 1888   Vol. XXXIII, No. 4

Married: On Monday, July 2, 1888, in Baltimore Md, at the residence of his cousin, C. De Forrest Van SCHAICK, Esq. by the Rev. J. P. FUGETTE, Benj. B. BRADFORD, of Washington DC, to Miss Nellie Irene HARVEY, of Marshall, Mo., daughter of the late Dr. Granville HARVEY.

died: On Friday morning, June 29th 1888, at the residence of her mother, Mrs. Elizabeth D. DeLANCEY, at West Brighton, Staten Island, N.Y., Annie Hunter DeLANCEY.

Cards are out for the marriage of Mr. Emanuel GOLDSMITH, formerly of this town, to Miss Ida BRAGER, of Alexandria. The ceremony is to take place in the Synagogue in that city, on Wednesday afternoon, July the 18th, at 5 o'clock p.m.

Mrs. Lydia CHICHESTER, wife of Washington CHICHESTER, died suddenly of heart disease at her home near Olney, in Montgomery Co, Monday evening, in the 49th year of her age. She was a sister in law of Capt. A. M. CHICHESTER, of this county.

Marriage license issued in Washington this week, to Mr. M. B. YOUNG, of Loudoun, and Miss M. L. ATKINSON [rest torn off]

Thursday, 12 July 1888   Vol. XXXIII, No. 5

Married: At the residence of Jno. H. Alexander, by Rev. C. T. HERNDON, Mr. E. L. LEWIS and Miss S. F. KILPATRICK, all of Loudoun.

Married: July 10th 1888, at the residence of Benjamin MATTHERS, Esq. by the Rev. J. R. BRIDGES, Noah MATTHERS to Miss Laura THOMAS, both of Loudoun.

Married: On Tuesday, June 19, at St. Paul's Church, Richmond, by the Rev. Chas. MINNIGERODE, D.D., Mary Amanda, youngest daughter of Mrs. Lucy W. and the late E. B. BENTLEY, of Richmond, to Dr. Richard Heath DABNEY, Professor of History University, Indiana, Bloomington, formerly of Va.

Died: On Sunday evening, July 1st, 1888, in Leesburg, at the residence of his grandmother, Mrs. L. BURCH, Thomas Grafton, only child of Clinton and Linnie E. HOSKINSON, aged 19m 22d.

Died: [partly torn] At her home, "Hope Grove" in this county, on the 27th of June, Mrs. Marizee F. RUSK, relict of Samuel RUSK, aged 83y ??? Mother of 12 children, five of whom survive her; leaves 27 grandchildren and 22 great-grandchildren.

Circuit Ct.: Wills of Erastus C. BENEDICT and Washington MYERS admitted to probate. Estate of Jas. W. WORKS dec'd. and Julia JOHNSON dec'd. committed to Sheriff. H. C. CHAMBLIN qualified as Admr. of Dewanna CHAMBLIN dec'd.; John H. ALEXANDER as Admr. of Kate BENTLEY dec'd.; B. W. PRESGRAVES as committee of Washington KEEN.

Mrs. Catherine RITCHE, wife of Mr. George RITCHE, of Taylortown, died of paralysis, on Wednesday evening. She, her husband and daughter were hiving bees on Sunday evening and she was attacked by the swarm. An elderly lady.

Mr. James SINCLAIR, a former citizen of this county, died at the home of his daughter, Mrs. Henry W. CASTLEMAN, in Jefferson Co., W. Va., on Monday, July 2d, and was buried in Edge Hill Cemetery, Charlestown Tuesday. He was Justice of Peace in Loudoun, Mayor of Leesburg, a Commission in Chancery and Clerk of the Circuit Court. He was in the 92nd year of his age.

Thursday, 19 July 1888 Vol. XXXIII, No. 6

Died: Near Waterford, July 11th, 1888, of congestion of the brain, Duanna C., wife of Griffin W. PAXTON, in the 70th year of her age.

Died: At the residence of her mother, Mrs. Armistead TITUS, near Neersville, on Thursday, June 27th 1888, Mrs. Madora E. SMALLWOOD, in the 33th [33rd?] year of her age.

Mr. John BALL, who was born in Loudoun Co, in Nov. 1814, died at his home in Washington city last Friday, and was buried on Sunday.

Thursday, 26 July 1888 Vol. XXXIII, No. 7

Mr. Julian A. HUTCHISON, a native of this county, and for several years a member of the drug firm of Edwards & Hutchison, but for the past few years engaged in business in Atlanta, Ga. is visiting.

Thursday, 2 August 1888 Vol. XXXIII, No. 8

Married: At the house of the bride, July 25, Mr. J. D. NEWLON, of Washington, formerly of Loudoun, to Miss Gracie HERRISFORD, of Fauquier County.

Married: At the residence of her mother, in Manassas, on the 18th of July 1888, by Rev. Frazier FURR, Mr. Wood WEIR and Miss Annie Parker, daughter of the late Wm. B. KINCHELOE.

Died: In Waterford, July 22, 1888, Walter Duncan DODD, second son of J. F. and Mary C. DODD, aged 10y 8m.

Died: At Ruckersville, Green Co., Va, of cholera infantum, on July 27th and 28th, Helen and John, infant children of Jesse and Mary J. EWELL. Aged 2 months.

Wm. H. GRIMES, of the firm of Grimes Bros, of this town, died at his home on Friday last, after a long illness of consumption, in about his 46th year. In early part of 1862, Mr. G., then a youth of some 26 years, enlisted in Capt. O. S. BRADEN's Co. A, of the 6th Va. Cavalry and served until capture near the close of the war. He was then confined in a Northern prison from which he was not released until after the close of hostilities. Funeral took place Sunday afternoon at Union Cemetery, Rev. I. W. CANTER, assisted by Rev. R. T. DAVIS and Dr. N. HEAD officiating. Leaves a wife and several small children.

In Fauquier Co. last week, Chas. P. JANNEY qualified as Admr. of Chas. L. POLLOCK dec'd.

[MISSING ISSUE]

Thursday, 16 August 1888   Vol. XXXIII, No. 10

Married: At the residence of the bride's mother in Leesburg, on Wednesday morning, Aug. 15th 1888, by Rev. R. T. DAVIS, D.D., assisted by Rev. J. C. AMBLER, John MASON of Fairfax Co., and Fanny E. FOX, daughter of the late Geo. K. FOX, Jr. of this place.

Married: In Leesburg, on Monday, the 13th of August by Rev. Nelson HEAD, D.D., Samuel W. SHIPMAN and Catherine E. WENNER, all of this county.

Mr. Wm. P. HARRIS died at the residence of his brother, Mr. James S. HARRIS, in this town, on Wed. morning, August 15th, in the 87th year of his age. He was born in Leesburg and here spent the greater portion of his long life. Funeral will take place from his brother's residence this (Thurs) afternoon at 4 o'clock.

Aug. Ct.: Wills of Geo. COOPER, Lydia J. EVERHART, Wm. H. GODFREY and Wm. H. GRIMES admitted to probate. Lydia C. REEVES qualified as Admr. of John T. REEVES dec'd.; Roxanna HOUSEHOLDER as Guardian of Adam HOUSEHOLDER; Wm. GAINES as Guardian of Annie HOLLIDAY. Estate of Mary E. BASCUE and Joseph W. RUSSELL committed to Sheriff.

John MASON Esq., of Fairfax Co. and Fanny E. FOX, dau. of the late Geo. K. FOX Jr., for many years clerk of the county ct. of Loudoun, were married in Leesburg on Wed., the 15th inst. They will proceed to Prescott, Arizona Ter. where the groom is at present stationed.

Last Thursday morning, James DRUMMOND and George JACKSON, two colored men residing near Goresville started out hunting. After a few hours, JACKSON returned to the home of DRUMMOND's mother and report that DRUMMOND was dead, that he "started a rabbit and as he ran to shoot it he stumbled, fell, and his gun went off and killed him". His sisters (he had 3, one named Mary Eliza) and mother immediately went in search and found him in Mr. ARNOLD's field. Jury of inquest found JACKSON shot him and he was arrested.

Mr. Notley BALL, with his family, left Loudoun on Tuesday last to make his future home in the San Luis valley of Colorado.

Thursday, 23 August 1888   Vol. XXXIII, No. 11

Married: At the parsonage of the M. E. Church, South, Middleburg, on Thursday, August 2, 1888, by Rev. C. M. BROWN, Mr. James GRAY and Mrs. Mary COCHRELL.

Married At the parsonage of the M. E. Church, South, Middleburg, Wednesday August 8, 1888, by Rev. C. M. BROWN, Mr. Corbart O'BANNON and Miss Georgiana SMALLWOOD.

Died: At Waterford, on the 17th inst., William N. PUSEY, son of the late Joshua PUSEY, in the 79th year of his age.

On August 14th, Mr. Thos. WYNKOOP, living near Silcott Springs, sent his little boy to drive up some horses. While doing so one kicked him, both feet striking square in his stomach. He died last night.

Dr. George W. WEST, aged 85 years, physician of Frederick Co. Md, died at Ingleside, the home of his son-in-law, Mr. John W. PAGE, near Petersville, Saturday. His funeral took place from St. Mark's Church, Petersville, last Sunday. He was the father of Dr. N. G. WEST, of this town.

Thursday, 30 August 1888   Vol. XXXIII, No. 12

Married: In Washington DC, at the residence of the groom's aunt, Mrs. Margaret BALLANGER, by Rev. Dr. BROWN, Mr. S. K. BRECKENRIDGE and Miss Katie V. WRIGHT, both of Leesburg.

Married: On the 17th inst. at the residence of Mr. Edward KOOTZ, W. Fifth St., Frederick, Md, by Rev. John KANTNER, Ernest S. BUTTS to Miss Nannie L. SNOOT, all of Loudoun County.

Died: In Findley, Ohio, Aug. 24th, James Wm. HOGELAND, formerly of Loudoun County.

Died: Richard Hunton, son of J. T. and Fannie WYNKOOP, born April 16, 1875, died at his home near Silcott's Springs, Wed. Aug. 15th 1882, at 10 p.m. For thirty hours he suffered unspeakable pain.

Death of Harvey SMITH (son of Thos. R. SMITH, member of the Board of Supervisors of Loudoun) occurred at his father's residence near Lincoln, on Sunday afternoon, August 26, from the kick of a horse received the preceding Monday. ...

Marriage licenses issued in Washington this week to Jos. V. BELL, of Charlestown, W. Va, and Ella C. ARNOLD, of Lovettsville,; Minor S. LYON and Henrietta PAXSON, both of Loudoun, and to Saml. K. BRECKENRIDGE and Katie V. WRIGHT, both of Leesburg.

Funeral services of the Rev John S. LEFEVRE, minister of the Presbyterian church took place at Charlestown, W. Va. Interred at Edge Hill cemetery. Died at Rockbridge Sulphur Springs, Va., on the 22nd inst. Native of Berkeley Co, W. Va.

Mr. John T. THOMAS, of Fairfax Courthouse, died last night. He was the son of Judge H. W. THOMAS, formerly Lt.-Gov. of Va.

Thursday, 6 September 1888   Vol. XXXIII, No. 13

Died: At the residence of Erastus FLORENCE, Esq. August 11th, Miss Martha ANDERSON (sister of the late Mrs. David CONNER) in the 67th year of her age.

Died: At the residence of his parents, on the 30th of July 1888, aged 3m 29d, George W., infant son of William F. and Ellen V. FLING.

Thursday, 13 September 1888   Vol. XXXIII, No. 14

Married: On Wednesday, September 5th 1888, by Rev. W. F. DUNAWAY, Mr. Wm. E. ROBERTS, of Rappahannock, and Ciara F. BENTON, of Loudoun.

Married: On Wednesday, Sept. 5, 1888, by Rev. W. F. DUNAWAY, Mr. John E. SMITH and Miss Lizzie CARTER, both of Loudoun.

Died: In Waterford, on the evening of 21st of 8th month, Phebe M. STEER, in the 69th year of her age.

Mr. Henry GAVER, father of Justice Chester C. GAVER, died at his home near Hillsboro, on Wednesday last, in his 69th year. Mr. GAVER moved to this county from Md, about 40 years ago and engaged in woolen manufacture. Member of the M. E. Church.

Mr. C. E. KEPHART, formerly of Loudoun, died at the residence of his brother-in-law, Mr. E. W. MERCER, at Point of Rocks, Md. on Thursday August 30th. His remains were brought to Leesburg and interred in Union Cemetery on Saturday.

Sept. Ct.: Wills of Phoebe M. STEER and Portia H. SMITH admitted to probate. L. M. FRANCIS qualified as Guardian of her infant children. Estate of Maria RUST committed to Sheriff.

[MISSING ISSUE]

Thursday, 27 September 1888   Vol. XXXIII, No. 16

Married: At the residence of Mr. SOMMERS, the home of the bride, Edmund COMPTON, to Emily CHICHESTER, September 19th 1888, Rev. C. M. BROWN, of Middleburg officiating.

Married: On Sept. 23, 1888, in Leesburg, by Rev. Dr. Nelson HEAD, Mr. John M. STEADMAN and Miss L. C. MYERS, all of Loudoun.

Married: On the 23d inst., at the parsonage of the Methodist Protestant Church, in Alexandria, by Rev. L. R. DYOTT, Mr. Wm. Lee CRAVEN to Miss Gertie V. L. ROLLINS, both of Alexandria city.

Thursday, 4 October 1888   Vol. XXXIII, No. 17

Died: At her residence, near Poolesville, Md, on the 2d inst., Mrs. Phoebe R. YOUNG, formerly of Loudoun Co, and relict of the late David YOUNG, in the 92d year of her age.

Mrs. AHALT, wife of Mr. Carlton AHALT, living a few miles this side of Point of Rocks died on Monday last of typhoid fever. Interred in Union Cemetery on Wednesday.

Mrs. Phoebe YOUNG, relict of the late David YOUNG, died at her home near Poolesville, Md, on the 1st of September, in her 92d year. Member of the M. E. Church for 82 years. A niece of the late Rev. Geo. ROSZELL, and an aunt of Mr. J. C. DONOHOE of this town.

Funeral of the late Mrs. J. E. R. WOOD, who died on Monday last at the residence of her brother Arthur SHREVES, of Loudoun Co, took place this Wednesday morning. Interment made at Mt. Olivet cemetery about noon, the Rev. Dr. BRAND officiating. Pallbearers were Messrs. Zach SMITH, Henry WHITMORE, George BALL and Scott MISKELL. *Frederick News.*

At the M. E. Church at Markham, Fauquier County, September 19th 1888, marriage of Mr. Wm. H. STROTHER to Miss Nannie D. ANDERSON, both of Upper Fauquier, by the Rev. F. A. STROTHER of the Methodist Church.

Rev. W. O. ROBEY, colored minister, died at his home in Leesburg, on Friday, September 21st 1888, in his 68th year. ... At 2 o'clock Sunday afternoon his remains were taken to Zion M. E. Church, Rev. J. S. COOPER, pastor, delivered the discourse. Remains then borne to the burying ground of the Presbyterian Church.

Thursday, 4 October 1888   Vol. XXXIII, No. 17

Married: On the 20th inst., near Bethel, by the Rev. Carter PAGE, Mr. Peter COOPER and Miss Mary E. CRIM, all of Loudoun.

Mrs. Sarah R. COE died at her residence at Oatland, on Wednesday, September 16th, 1888, in the 36th year of her age.

Died: William GREGG, at his home, near Philomont, September 21st 1888, after a lingering illness of several weeks in his 65th year. Funeral on Sunday the 23d, interred Goose Creek burying ground beside a daughter who had preceded him only a few months.

Died: In Washington City, September 15th 1888, Sarah J. MORIARTY, wife of John H. MORIARTY, formerly of Loudoun County.

Died: Sept. 8th 1888, at her home near Leesburg, Ellen V. FLING, wife of Wm. E. FLING and daughter of the late Charles HENDERSON.

Thursday, 11 October 1888   Vol. XXXIII, No. 18

Died: At her home on the 26th of September, of diptheria, Bessie, youngest child of Samuel T. WYNKOOP, age 8 years, from a disease assumed its most malignant form. She was laid to rest by the side of her little brother n the Short Hill Cemetery.

Little seven year old daughter of Mr. James PEACOCK, living near Morrisonville, was burned to death on Friday last. About 7 Friday morning Mrs. PEACOCK left the house for a few minutes to attend some outdoor duties, leaving the little girl with a younger child or two in the house. The child's clothing took fire from an open fire, she was burned and death ensued in a few hours.

Cards are out for the marriage, on the 17th inst., at the residence of the bride's parents near Mountsville, of Mr. W. Frank GARRETT, son of W. E. GARRETT, of this town, and Miss Rosa, daughter of Mr. Jas. A. COX.

Co. Ct.: Marizee RUSK's estate committed to sheriff. Thos. R. SMITH qualified as Admr. of Harvey S. SMITH dec'd.; C. C. GAVER as Admr. of Henry GAVER dec'd.; L. P. BROWN as Guardian of C. E. and Preston D. BROWN. Will of Ann Eliza GUSTIN dec'd. admitted to probate.

Mr. Bushrod W. HERBERT died at his residence near Charlestown, W. Va. last Thursday, aged 78 years. His mother was a grandniece of George WASHINGTON and a niece of Judge Bushrod WASHINGTON.

Thursday, 18 October 1888   Vol. XXXIII, No. 19

Married: At the residence of the bride's parents, near Mountsville, on Wednesday morning, October 17th 1888, by Elder BADGER, W. Frank GARRETT, of Mt. Gilead, and Miss Rosa, daughter of James A. COX, Esq., all of Loudoun.

Married: At the residence of the bride's parents, in Leesburg, on Tuesday morning, October 16th 1888, by Rev. I. W. CANTER, Lemuel NORRIS, Esq., and Miss Kate E., eldest daughter of Mr. R. H. TURNER, all of this town.

Died: On the 25th of August of dysentery, at the residence of her parents, near Woodgrove, Annie Eliza, daughter of Thos. D. and Etta C. McARTOR, aged 1y 10m 27d.

Died: Mrs. Ellen V. FLING died at her home, near Leesburg, on Thursday, September 8, 1888, in the 35th year of her age. She leaves a husband and four children.

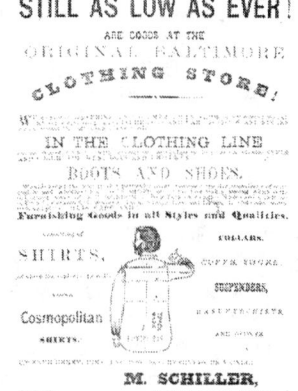

Mrs. Ann SHAWEN, widow of the late W. C. SHAWEN, of this county, died at her home, near Waterford, on Thursday, October 9th, 1888, in about the 52nd year of her age. She was buried in the Fox burying ground on Saturday, Rev. L. B. TURNBULL officiating.

Miss Caroline T. FROST died on Wednesday night at the residence of Rev. R. T. DAVIS, in Leesburg. Miss FROST was an aunt of Mrs. DAVIS. Daughter of Mr. John T. FROST, of N. Y., but who moved to Washington in 1796 when that city contained only 50 houses. He was an officer in the capitol for 55 years. In 1812 his house was burned by the British. Miss FROST was born in Washington in the second year of this century and was 86 years of age. She resided here with Dr. DAVIS for many years. funeral at the Episcopal Rectory on Friday evening at 4 o'clock. Interred in the Congressional cemetery in Washington. Member of Christ Church, Navy Yard, and then of Trinity Church, Washington DC.

Mr. Henry G. DULANEY died at his residence, near Middleburg, Sunday night last, aged 54 years. He was a brother of Col. R. H. DULANEY, who commanded the 7th Va Cavalry, Confederate States army during the late war, and an uncle of Mr. Hal DULANEY.

Mr. M. B. CAREY, of the Loudoun Hedge Fence Company, returned to Leesburg on Tuesday. His father died at his home in New York on Sunday, the 10th inst. He was in the 83rd year of his age.

Thursday, 25 October 1888   Vol. XXXIII, No. 20

Married: In St. James Episcopal Church, Leesburg, at 1 p.m. Wednesday October 24th, 1888, by Rev. R. T. DAVIS, Dr. R. B. FISHBURNE, of Leesburg, and Elizabeth Clagett ROGERS, eldest daughter of Alexander H. ROGERS, Esq. of Woodburn, Loudoun.

Married: In the M. E. Church, South, at Bloomfield, on Wed. morning, Oct. 24th 1888, by Rev. J. C. DICE, Mr. Gabriel V. BRADEN and Miss Sallie Gill FURR, dau. of the late Fenton FURR, all of Loudoun.

Died: In Leesburg, September 27th, of typhoid fever, the wife of Joseph A. SHUGARS, aged 21y 8m 5d., the daughter of Samuel T. and Nancy A. BRECKENRIDGE.

Died: At Miss Mary SHUGARS, October 7th, Samuel T. McGill, infant son of Annie and Joseph A. SHUGARS, aged 4 weeks.

At St. James Episcopal Church at 1 p.m. Wednesday, marriage of Dr. R. B. FISHBURNE, and Miss Bessie, daughter of A. H. ROGERS, Esq. Ushers were Messrs. W. W. CHAMBLIN, M. CHICHESTER, Arthur SHEETZ and R. L. SANFORD.

Marriage licenses by the clerk of the court in Washington city last Monday, one to Samuel F. WALLACE and Daisy L. GALLEHER. She is a daughter of the late John W. GALLEHER of Leesburg.

At an early hour last Wednesday morning at residence of Mr. Jas. A. COX, marriage of his daughter, Rosa, to Mr. W. Frank GARRETT, of Leesburg. Bridesmaids were Miss Julia HOLTON, Stella SKINNER, Laura COLE and Claire DODD. Groomsmen were Messrs. Ashton CLAPHAM, Ben WHITE, Arthur SHEETZ and Wm. RUSSELL. Performed by Elder J. N. BADGER of Baptist Church. Bride arrayed in a white cloth, trimmed with Moire silk, made demi train, the front being looped with orange blossoms. Bouquet of orange blossoms.

Major Wm. Deakins NUTT died at the residence of his son-in-law, Mr. Peter WISE, in Alexandria, Sat., aged 86 years. Upwards of 23 years in the office of the U.S. treasurer. Held similar position in the Confederate treasury. Native of Alexandria but had lived for several years in Loudoun Co.

Thursday, 1 November 1888   Vol. XXXIII, No. 21

Married: In Washington DC, by the Rev. Dr. COREY of Metropolitan M. E. Church, Mr. Samuel F. WALLIS, of Washington, to Miss Daisy Leland, dau. of the late John W. GALLEHER, formerly of Leesburg.

Married: At the residence of the bride's sister, Miss L. J. JANNEY, of Baltimore, October 22d, by Rev. Mr. WILLIAMS, of that same city, Capt. J. Henry WHEELER, of Leonardtown, Md, to Miss Henrietta H. JANNEY, late of Hamilton, Va.

Married: On October 18, 1888, at Grace Church, New York, by its rector, Dr. W. R. HUNTINGTON, Alexander Boteler SHEPHERD, formerly of Shepherdstown, West Virginia, but now of Mobile, Alabama, and Miriam, daughter of the late Hon. Philip Hickey MORGAN, of New Orleans, U.S. Minister to Mexico.

Died: At her home, Glen Ora, near Middleburg, October 27th 1888, Mrs. Elizabeth Winn NOLAND, the widow of the late Col. Lloyd NOLAND, in the 87th year of her age. Her only surviving child is Mrs. Ella MacKENZIE of Baltimore.

The wedding of Miss Susie BENNER to Mr. Charles EVARD of Leesburg, took place in Alexandria on Tuesday, 23d, Rev. Dr. SENTER officiating. Among those present were Mr. and Mrs. EVARD, the father and mother of the groom; Mr. and Mrs. P. WALLACH, Miss Jennie and Maud WALLACH, Miss Sarah LULLEY, Mr. Henry HOFFA, S. H. WALLACH, S. NICKARD, Mrs. GURY and son.

Thursday, 8 November 1888   Vol. XXXIII, No. 22

Married: In Frederick Md, on Wednesday, October 24th 1888, at the residence of Mr. Granville THOMAS, by the Rev. W. L. OULD, Rev. J. H. MOORE, pastor of the Presbyterian Church at Berryville, Vaiss Bessie Cunningham, of that city.

Augustine Washington BALL, third son of the late Judge Chas. B. BALL, of Loudoun, died at the residence of his grandfather, Rev. Chas. H. READ, in Richmond, on Sunday morning, the 4th of October 1888, in the 21st year of his age.

John V. TAVENNER is now engaged in business in Roanoke.

Cards are out for the marriage on the 14th inst., of Miss Virginia DOUGALL and Mr. Wm. A. LEETCH, of Georgetown, DC, at the West St., Presbyterian church in that city.

At the residence of the bride's sister, near Middleburg, on Wednesday, October 31st at 6:30 p.m. by Rev. Mr. DUNNAWAY, Miss Rebecca, daughter of Jos. CAMPBELL, of Prince Wm. Co., Va, to Mr. GREEN of Washington city.

Charlestown, W. Va., November 5: Sudden death yesterday of Mr. Nathan S. WHITE, an old attorney of this place, of apoplexy. Born in Montgomery Co, Md, in 1817, and was 71 years of age at his death. He was a graduate of Princeton College. He came to this county in 1840. Some years ago he formed a partnership with his son-in-law, Mr. Jos. TRAPNELL under the name of White & Trapnell. For 40 years a member of Zion Episcopal Church. He leaves a widow and one daughter, the wife of Mr. Joseph TRAPNELL. His only son was killed at Chancellorsville in the late war, a member of the Stonewall brigade.

Thursday, 15 November 1888   Vol. XXXIII, No. 23

Married: On November 1st, 1888, near Lovettsville, by the Rev. H. St. J. RINKER, Mr. Wm. L. BARTLETT to Miss Charlotte E. FRY, all of Loudoun County.

Married: In Washington DC, on Wednesday 7th inst., by the Rev. Dr. SUNDERLAND, Mr. Stephen DOWNS to Miss Annie E. SOLOMON, both of Loudoun County.

Died: Sunday morning, 4th instant, at the residence of his grandfather, Rev. Charles H. READ, in his 21st year, Augustine Washington BALL, third son of Mrs. Emma R. and the late Charles B. BALL. He leaves his mother, his brothers and grandparents.

Nov. Ct.: Will of Wm. GREGG dec'd. admitted to probate. Will of Caroline J. FROST dec'd. admitted to probate. Estate of Joshua EVERHART committed to Sheriff. Daniel SCHINDLER, Minister of the Gospel. Lutheran Church, licensed to celebrate rites of matrimony.

At 4:30 last Tuesday afternoon, Mrs. Laura VANDEVENTER, wife of Mr. Robt. S. VANDEVENTER, and dau. of Dr. R. H. EDWARDS, died at her home in Leesburg. Funeral will take place from her husband's residence, on Cornwall St. this Thursday afternoon, at 2:30.

Thursday, 22 November 1888   Vol. XXXIII, No. 24

Married: Wed. evening Nov. 14th 1888, at the residence of the bride's mother, in Leesburg, by Rev. Isaac W. CANTER, Mr. Nelson H. KENT and Miss Nannie E. STANSBURY, both of Leesburg.

Married: Tuesday, November 29th 1888, at the residence of the bride's father, in Leesburg, by Rev. Isaac W. CANTER, Mr. Chas. R. LOWENBACK, of Baltimore, Md, and Miss India LEWIS, of Leesburg.

Married: At the parsonage of the M. E. Church, South, in Washington, on Wed. evening, Nov. 15th 1888, by Rev. S. W. HADDAWAY, Mr.

James Decatur SMITH and Miss Annie E. BROOKS, daughter of the late Phillip W. BROOKS, both of Leesburg.

Married: Near Thoroughfare, on Thursday, the 15th inst., by Rev. A. P. BOUDE, Mr. Arthur CAMPBELL and Miss Alice FLETCHER, all of Prince William County.

Married: At the residence of the bride's father, Capt. Jno. R. CARTER, near Oatlands, on Tuesday November 20th 1888, by Rev. R. T. DAVIS D.D., Mr. Chas. F. RITICOR and Mrs. Constance ODEN, all of this county.

Died: Edmond ALLEN, an old citizen of Prince William County, died at his home at Gainesville on the 6th inst. He was a native of Loudoun and member of the Methodist Church for 55 years.

Died: At his parents' residence, near Mt. Hope, on November 12th 1888, Marvin W. POPKINS, aged 3y 10m.

Cards are out for the marriage of Miss Elizabeth, daughter of Mr. Peyton RANDOLPH, and Jno. T. HARRIS Jr., son of Hon. Jno. T. HARRIS, of Virginia, at the church of the Incarnation, Washington DC, on Wednesday evening, November 28th.

Twenty five years ago, at the battle of Crampton's Gap or South Mountain, Col. Edmund BERKELEY, then of the 8th Va Regiment but now of this city [Alexandria, Va] was shot in the leg by a minnie ball, which surgeons could not find. Last night he poulticed his leg and this morning the ball fell out.

Thursday, 29 November 1888   Vol. XXXIII, No. 25

Married: At Ball Hill, Loudoun County, October 30th, by Rev. James McDONOUGH, George W. HARPER and Mary J. KIDWELL, all of Loudoun.

Married: On Friday, November 16th in Frederick City, Md, by Rev. G. V. LEECH, of the M. E. Church, Mr. Walter A. ANDERSON, of Leesburg, to Miss Florence J. TRUSSELL, of Hamilton, in this county.

Married: On Wednesday afternoon, November 21st 1888, at the Noviate, in Frederick City, Md. by the Rev. Father O'KANE, Mr. Boyd SURVICK of Leesburg, to Miss Mollie E. MACKENZIE, of Petersville, Frederick Co Md. They will reside in Leesburg.

Married: On Wednesday November 21st at the Parsonage M. E. Church, South, Hamilton, by Rev. B. W. BOND, Mr. Press POSTON and Miss Loula F. SMITH, both of Loudoun.

Married: At the residence of the bride's father, near Wheatland, in Loudoun Co, on Thursday Nov. 22nd, 1888, by Rev. J. R. VanHORN, Mr. James D. MANOR, of New Marker, Shenandoah Co., Va., and Miss Annie A. WHITE, dau. of Mr. Josiah T. WHITE, of this county.

Died: In Leesburg, Nov. 16th 1888, Charles Marshal STEADMAN, youngest son of Wm. and Mamie STEADMAN, aged 7m 5d.

Mr. Charles G. DAWSON, son of the late Capt. Samuel DAWSON, of this county, died in Atlantic City, Iowa, on Sunday last, in the 50th year of his age. He had been engaged in the mercantile business until his health failed about a year ago.

A commission *de lunatico inquirendo* visited the jail on Tuesday to examine a feeble minded young named Wm. HARRISON, from the Lovettsville district. Recommended that he be sent to an asylum.

Mrs. Mary Eleanor MARTIN, widow of the late Dr. George T. MARTIN, of Winchester, Ky, died suddenly on the 14th of November at the residence of her son-in-law, Robt. W. TAYLOR, in Davis Co, Ky, in the 70th year of her age. Mrs. MARTIN was a sister of Dr. A. R. MORE [MOORE?] of this town.

Hillsboro: At "Fairview," the residence of Josiah T. WHITE. on Thursday November 22, Annie, second daughter of the house, was married to Mr. James MANOR of New Market, Shenandoah Co, at 8 a.m. by Rev. Mr. VANHORN. The bride was dressed in a brown traveling suit and attended by her sister, Miss Sue WHITE, with the brother of the groom ___.

Richmond Dispatch of Thursday: Governor's Mansion scene yesterday evening of marriage of H. Rozier DULANEY of Washington DC and Miss Annie Willing CARTER, a kinswoman of the Governor and youngest daughter of Col. Thos. H. CARTER, of Pampatike, King William Co. ... The bride is a niece of Dr. C. S. CARTER of "Morven," near Leesburg.

Thursday, 6 December 1888 Vol. XXXIII, No. 26

Married: At the residence of Thos. J. MOFFETT, Mr. Wm. H. FRENCH, of Washington DC, to Miss K. A. MOFFETT, of Loudoun.

Mr. Jno. T. HARRIS Jr., son of Hon. Jno. T. HARRIS, of Virginia, and Miss Elizabeth RANDOLPH, daughter of Maj. Peyton RANDOLPH, manager of the Richmond & Danville railway were married at the church of the Incarnation in Washington on Wednesday evening of last week. They will reside in Harrisonburg.

The recently build public school house between Wheatland and Clarke's Gap was destroyed by fire on Monday night of last week. Mr. Isaac WARNER, who lives nearby, has tendered a room in his dwelling house for the use of the school until other accommodations can be made.

[MISSING ISSUE]

Thursday, 20 December 1888 Vol. XXXIII, No. 28

Married: By the Rev. John WOOLF, at his residence, on the 12th inst., Mr. Samuel T. MARTS to Miss Emma GAVER, all of Loudoun.

Married: At the residence of Mr. J. H. ALEXANDER, Leesburg, by Rev. C. T. HERNDON, on Tuesday, December 18th, 1888, Mr. Wm. W. W. MOFFETT and Miss Janie S. TAVENNER.

Death of Mrs. Lalla CLAGETT, widow of the late Dr. Thos. H. CLAGETT (and daughter of the late John GRAY) died at her home in Leesburg, on Thursday morning last, of progressive paralysis, in the 69th year of her age. Member of the Episcopal Church. Funeral took place from the Episcopal Church at 3 o'clock Sunday afternoon, Rev. R. T. DAVIS officiating. Laid to rest beside her husband in the burying ground attached to the church.

Cards are out for the wedding on December 27th, of Miss Grace BRADFORD and Mr. R. Lindsey FAIRFAX, of Virginia. The groom is a son of Col. J. W. FAIRFAX, and a younger brother of Mr. Henry FAIRFAX, of "Oak Hill," in this county.

The little child of R. H. and Laura HOSKINSON, which got a grain of corn fast in its windpipe, a few weeks since, and which was removed by Dr. I. S. STONE, died at the home of its grandmother in Hamilton, Thursday. The wound where the opening was made failed to heal and resulted in death.

Just at the eastern base of the Blue Ridge, near "The Trappe", where Bro. John T. ROSS resides – at this mansion on the 31st of October was celebrated the 97th birthday of Mrs. Fanny PLASTER, widow of the late Henry PLASTER, of Unison. She makes her home with Bro. ROSS and his wife, who is her only surviving daughter. Mrs. PLASTER was born in 1791 near what is now Rectortown, Fauquier Co. Her maiden name was LLOYD. Her father lived to be 95 years of age. She joined the Methodist Church at 12 years old.

Thursday, 27 December 1888   Vol. XXXIII, No. 29

Married: At Pleasant Vale Baptist Church, near Delaplaine, Fauquier Co, December 10, 1888, by Rev. C. T. HERNDON, George M. BURKE, of this city, and Belle H. GLASCOCK, daughter of T. J. GLASCOCK, of Fauquier County.

Married: On December 19th, 1888, in Middleburg, by Rev. W. F. DUNAWAY, Mr. Samuel CREEL, of Fauquier, and Miss Julia ADAMS, of Loudoun.

Married: In Waterford, at the house of the bride, Dec. 19th, by the Rev. L. B. TURNBULL, Sydnor BENNETT to Mrs. Virginia C. SILCOTT.

Married: At the residence of the bride's father on Wednesday, Dec. 10, 1888, by Friends Ceremony, Alice HOGE, only daughter of Daniel and Sarah HOGE, to Arthur WARNER, of Loudoun County.

Married: On December 19th, Mr. Henry A. THOMPSON to Mary J. MUNDAY, near Mt. Hope, by Rev. G. W. POPKINS, all of Loudoun.

Death of Wm. ROGERS ("Uncle Billy") died at the home of his son-in-law, M. M. ROGERS, at Dover, in this county, on Saturday, December 22d, in his 89th year. He was a brother of the late Gen.

Asa and Col. Hamilton ROGERS. He owned an estate near Dover. Interred in Sharon Cemetery at Middleburg on Monday morning, Revs. HATHAWAY and HERNDON of the Baptist Church officiating.

Col. R. Welby CARTER, son of John Armistead CARTER, died at his home "Crednal," Loudoun County, early Friday morning, of a complication of diseases, aged 53 years. He was a Confederate soldier and at the battle of Manassas, at the head of his company, made the famous charge, breaking through the lines of the N. Y. Zouaves and routing the command. Only son of his aged father.

Mr. Thomas APPLE, of this county, died at his home, at Limestone Mills, a few miles north of Leesburg on Monday morning last, in about the 75th year of his age. On Wednesday, his remains were borne to Frederick City, Md, for interment.

Thursday, 3 January 1889   Vol. XXXIII, No. 30

Married: At the residence of the bride's parents, Fairfax C. H., Va. on Monday, December 24th 1888, by Rev. O. C. BEALL, Mr. George R. WOODARD, of Fairfax C. H. (formerly of Leesburg) to Miss Alice GAINES, daughter of George W. GAINES, Esq.

Married: On December 19, 1888, by the Rev. W. U. MURKLAND, Baltimore, Maryland, William C. HAMNER, of Baltimore, to Anna B. BRIDGES, of Richmond, Virginia.

Married: December 27th 1888, at the residence of the bride's father (John DAVIS Esq.) near Taylortown, Va, by Rev. D. C. HEDRICK, Mr. Wm. S. BEST and Miss Minnie B. DAVIS, all of Loudoun.

Died: In Baltimore, December 20th 1888, of spinal meningitis, Nora Lee, second daughter of Sallie and the late Benjamin D. SURVICK, in the 11th year of her age.

Last week an accident occurred at the saw mill of Col. R. H. DULANEY, at Millsville, Loudoun County, by which a colored man named Wm. RUNNER lost his life by being thrown against the saw.

Mr. John SOWERS, of Clarke County, died at his home, "Farnley," in that county, on Friday last.

Augustus ZEREGA, for over 50 years a citizen of New York, died December 22d at the home of his son-in-law, Horace BERNARD, aged 85 years. Born in Martinique, December 4, 1803, his family having emigrated from Genoa about the middle of the last century. His father, a ship owner, sent him to Europe to be educated. Returning to his West Indian home at the age of 15 he made several voyages on his father's ship and learned the art of practical navigation. When 17 years old he went to St. Thomas, bought a small schooner, and sailed between islands. When 19 years old he was ill at St. Thomas, his physician Danish nobleman John Uytendahl Baron Von BRITON saved his life. Two years later he married the doctor's daughter. He removed with his family to LaGuavra, where he rapidly acquired wealth. During the war he furnished munitions of war to the patriot army and navy and in 1831 came to the U.S. for military equipments which he sent to Bolivar. Discovering a plot in LaGuayra to accuse him of aiding the Spaniards he succeeded in escaping in a small vessel with his wife and family. Although his possessions were valued at $200,000, he was able to bring away only $1,000 in money. In 1855 he retired from business having amassed a fortune. Mr. ZEREGA's wife survives him, after 63 years of marriage. Also leaves 6 sons and 3 daughters. Some years ago Mr. ZEREGA purchased property at Aldie, formerly owned by Chas. Fenton MERCER, which was occupied by his son, Alfred B. ZEREGA.

Thursday, 10 January 1889   Vol. XXXIII, No. 31

Married: At the residence of the bride's father, Mr. T. O. WYNDHAM, on the 18th of December 1888, by Rev. J. H. MOORE, Mr. Chas. A. WILLIAMS, of Loudoun County, and Miss Annie C. WYNDHAM, of Clarke County.

Died: At "Sunny Side," the residence of her daughter, in Loudoun Co., Dec. 28, 1888, Mrs. Catharine M. COOKSEY, aged 70 years.

Died: Mrs. Lucy SKINNER, wife of the late James SKINNER, died at her home near Middleburg, November 11th 1888, in her 68th year. For about 44 years a member of the Methodist Church.

Died: At his residence, near Silcott's Springs, January 1st, 1889, Bushrod PIGGOTT, aged 43 years. Member of the Society of Friends and interred in their burial grounds at Lincoln.

Marriage license was issued in Washington last week, to Richard A. KIDWELL and Gertrude ADRIAN, both of Loudoun.

Thursday, 17 January 1889   Vol. XXXIII, No. 32

Married: December 19, 1888, by Danl. SCHINDLER, D. D., at the home of the bride, Mr. George W. MYERS to Miss Mary V. SPRING, both of Loudoun County.

Married: December 20, 1888, by Danl. SCHINDLER, D. D., at the home of the bride, Mr. W. G. BISER to Miss Lydia C. COOPER, both of Loudoun County.

Married: December 27, 1888, by Danl. SCHINDLER, D. D., at New Jerusalem Church, Mr. Luther H. BOYER to Miss Lulu B. BEATTY, both of Loudoun County.

Married: January 7, at the M. E. Parsonage, Leesburg, by Rev. D. C. HEDRICK, Mr. Charles HIGDON and Miss Sallie COOKSEY, all of Loudoun County.

Married: January 3rd 1889, at the residence of the bride's parents, Fairfax County, Va, by Rev. S. A. BALL, of Herndon, Va, Samuel M. JENKINS to Maggie V. DAILY, both of Virginia.

Married: At. St. John's Lutheran Church, Lovettsville, January 10th 1889, Mr. Newton M. STONE and Miss Ada V. RODEFFER, Rev. P. H. MILLER, of Westminster, Md., officiating.

Died: Of typhoid pneumonia, Dec. 22d, Clinton Clyde BALLENGER, son of Edgar and Dorcas O. BALLENGER, aged 13y 3m.

Mr. C. M. BALL, formerly of this county, by now a prosperous druggist in Alamosa, Colorado, arrived in Leesburg on Tuesday for a visit.

Mr. Levi NIXON, of this county (brother of Joel L. NIXON of this town) was stricken with paralysis last Friday afternoon, and died at his home near Hughesville, on Tuesday evening, in about his 60th year.

This morning the W. O. & W. R. R. brought down from Virginia, Mr. Ira C. BRADFIELD, of Loudoun County, and Miss Carrie MORELAND, of Snickersville, were married at the courthouse. Mr. CLANCY, assistant Clerk furnished the license. Rev. E. D. BAILEY married them. Four other licenses were issued within 45 minutes thereafter. *Star* of Thursday.

Lt. C. R. MILES died on board the U.S. S. Yantic, of yellow fever, on Monday. The Yantic is at quarantine station in New York harbor since her return from Port-au-Prince. Paymaster R. M. T. BALL, formerly of this town, is one of her officers.

Co. Ct.: C. J. C. MAFFETT qualified as Guardian of Lillie B. CRAVEN. Wills of Wm. T. HUNT dec'd., Smith REED dec'd., Jacob BODMER dec'd. and Lalla CLAGETT dec'd. were admitted to probate. Wm. B. POTTS qualified as Admr. of Jane E. POTTS dec'd.; A. G. CHAMBLIN as Guardian of Clara CHAMBLIN; Wm. PIGGOTT as Admr. of Bushrod PIGGOTT dec'd.; A. B. CHAMBLIN as Admr. of Eveline B. CHAMBLIN dec'd. Estates of Mrs. Louise F. MINOR and Townsend J. McVEIGH committed to Sheriff.

Thursday, 24 January 1889 Vol. XXXIII, No. 33

Married: By Rev. J. R. BRIDGES, on January 17, 1889, David BLAIR, of Clay Co., Ky, to Miss Nancy COCKRILLE, of Loudoun County.

Died: On Sunday morning, January 13th 1889, in Waterford, at the residence of her brother, William C. JAMES, Imogene May, only daughter of Wm. JAMES, of Washington City.

Remains of the late F. M. HENDERSON, who died in Staunton a year or two ago, were brought to this town last Thursday, and laid to rest in the family lot in Union Cemetery.

Miss Hallie O. WOODWARD, of Charlottesville, who teaches school in Loudoun, and who is a first cousin to President-elect Harrison and Colonel MOSBY was married in Washington city last week to Mr. S. D. HICKS Jr. of Richmond.

Thursday, 31 January 1889   Vol. XXXIII, No. 34

Married: At the Parsonage, of the M. E. Church, South, Middleburg, Va, January 9th, 1889, by Rev. C. M. BROWN, Chas. H. SMITH and Rosa J. SELBAUGH, both of Loudoun County.

Died: At his home in Hughesville, on the evening of the 18th of January 1889, after prolonged suffering, Wm. T. HUNT in his 39th year.

Died: January 22d, 1889, at her residence near Mountain Gap, Mrs. Elizabeth J. DANIEL, in the 54th year of her age.

Thursday, 7 February 1889   Vol. XXXIII, No. 35

Died: At the home of her parents near Leesburg on Friday night, Feb. 1, 1889, after an illness of one week from diphtheria, Mary Randolph, only child of Randolph and Nannie RHODES, aged 5y 7m 23d.

Died: Miss Nannie POTTS, at the home of her brother, J. O. POTTS, in Hillsboro, Jan. 24th, after a lingering illness, aged about 40 years.

Married: January 24th 1889, at the house of Mr. Ed. SPRING, near Taylortown, by Rev. D. SCHINDLER, Mr. John D. BUNTER and Miss Jeannie E. A. POTTERFIELD, both of Loudoun County.

Married: January 24th 1889, by Rev. John WOOLF, at the residence of the bride's father, Mr. James CARLISLE to Mrs. Susan SEATON, all of Loudoun.

Remains of the late James THRIFT, who died in Chicago some months ago, were brought to Leesburg on Wednesday, and interred in Union Cemetery.

Susan JACKSON, colored, died at her home in Washington, on Monday last, after 15 days illness with paralysis, in the 87th year of her age. she was formerly a slave to the CARROLLs of Carrolton, Md, and subsequently to the BENTLEYs of Leesburg.

Death of Charles Rupert PAXTON occurred at "Carlheim," his home near Leesburg, about 1 o'clock p.m. on Friday, February 1st 1889. Thursday evening he had driven to the station to meet his wife who was returning from Washington with her sister, Mrs. ADSIT and her husband. He was born on 2d March 1816 in Cattawiss, Columbia Co, Pa. and was one month short of 73 years old. As a young man he was a civil engineer on the Erie Railroad. He purchased land in Alleghany Co, NY, and later removed to Bloomsburg, Pa. About 1879 he came to Loudoun and purchased about 1200 acres, the old "Exeter" estate near Leesburg. ... Funeral took place from the late residence of the deceased at 11:30 Monday morning. Services by Rev. R. T. DAVIS D.D. of the Episcopal Church. Interred in Union Cemetery. Pall bearers were Walter J. HARRISON, Chas. H. LEE, F. P. GIST, W. B. LYNCH, Henry HARRISON, John HUTCHISON, Chas. P. JANNEY and Stirling MURRAY.

Thursday, 14 February 1889   Vol. XXXIII, No. 36

Died: Near Mt. Gilead, Loudoun Co, January 21st 1889, M. Katie, daughter of Wm. H. and F. C. D. JOHNSON, aged 17y 10m 28d.

Co. Ct.: Wills of Chas. R. PAXTON, Samuel ANKERS, and H. Clay COOPER admitted to probate. Emily A. MOXLEY qualified as Ex. of Benj. F. MOXLEY dec'd.

Divorce suit of THROCKMORTON vs THROCKMORTON argued at last term was decided by Judge KEITH in favor of the defendant.

Dr. H. W. GREGG, died on the night of January 1st, at the residence of Col. FREEMAN, in Hamilton. He came to Hamilton from Virginia, where he has a brother and two sisters, about nine years ago, and established himself as a physician. *Hamilton (Texas) Herald.* Dr. GREGG was a native of Loudoun.

Thursday, 21 February 1889   Vol. XXXIII, No. 37

Mr. Thomas N. PERCIVAL, who died a few days ago at the Potomac House, Harper's Ferry, W. Va., was an active participant of the Brown's raid. Resident of Harper's Ferry for over 40 years and a native of Vermont. He left no relatives, his wife died a few years ago.

Died: At the home of her husband, about 3 miles south of Leesburg on Friday, February 15th 1889, Mrs. Jane Francis HOGELAND, wife of Mr. John J. HOGELAND, in the 71st year of her age. Interred in Union Cemetery, Leesburg.

Died: At her home near Hillsboro, on Friday, February 8th 1889, Mrs. Matilda J. STOCKS, in the 67th year of her age.

Died: At the residence of her daughter, Mrs. M. E. JOHNSTON, at Sterling, Va., on Sunday February 17th at 3 p.m., Mrs. Mary CAMP, after an illness of two weeks in the 69th year of her age.

Died: At the residence of her aunt, in Frederick Co., Md, on 9th of Feb, Mary R., second dau. of F. M. and Maggie L. MYERS (and grand dau. of Spencer MINOR dec'd. of Loudoun) in her 18th year.

Mr. Selden M. GIBSON, who for many years before the war served first as Deputy and then as Sheriff, in Loudoun, died at his home near North Fork, on Tuesday night, February 12th at an advanced age.

Mr. Lindsay FAIRFAX was married in New York on Thursday to Miss Grace BRADFORD, of that city. He is the son of Col. John Fairfax. Ceremony took place at 3 o'clock at the bride's home, Rev. Dr. HUNTINGTON, of Grace church officiating, assisted by Rev. Dr. EATON. ... John FAIRFAX is a brother of the groom.

From the *Echo* published at La Jara, in the San Luis Valley of Colorado: recent visit to the ranch of the Ball Bros. They are natives of Loudoun (sons of Mr. Wm. BALL). Ranch is on Conejos river, 15 miles east of La Jara. John BALL is the senior brother of the firm.

Thursday, 28 February 1889   Vol. XXXIII, No. 38

Married: At the residence of the bride's parents, on Feb. 21St 1889, by Elder E. V. WHITE, Mr. Edwin L. ROE, of Muskingum Co. Ohio to Miss Louanna WHITE, dau. of Mr. Levi WHITE, of this county.

Married: Near Pleasant Valley, by the Rev. G. W. POPKINS on the 20th of February, Mr. Robert MATTOCKS to Miss Lulu TRAMMELL, all of Fairfax County.

Mrs. Maria METZGER, wife of Mr. Geo. T. METZGER (and daughter of Mr. Wm. HALL) died at her home in Leesburg about 8:30 Tuesday night, of pneumonia with heart failure. Funeral will take place from her late residence (Thursday afternoon) at 4 o'clock.

Death last night of Mrs. William BEVERLEY, of heart disease, at her home near Broad Run, Fauquier, after an illness of some months. Daughter of the late Richard Henry CARTER, of "Glen Welby," and leaves six children. Mr. J. Sprigg POOLE, of Washington city, and Miss Anna E. JONES, of Howard Co, Md, were married last Wed. at the residence of the bride's parents, Rev. H. P. HAMILL, of W. Va. performed the ceremony.

Edward BLUE (colored) was convicted and sent to jail for 30 days for stealing chickens from Mr. Townsend BELT, near town.

Robert and Franklin JOHNSON (colored) charged with robbing the store of E. W. PRESGRAVES, near Aldie, of a lot of dry goods.

John JACKSON (colored) convicted of stealing money from T. E. HOUGH, of Hillsboro, and sent up for 60 days.

Thursday, 1 March 1889   Vol. XXXIII, No. 39

John Augustine WASHINGTON: Mount Vernon estate, the home of George Washington, was devised by Augustine WASHINGTON, who died in Stafford Co, April 12, 1743, to Lawrence, the second son by his first wife, Jane BUTLER. Lawrence WASHINGTON, who gave the name of Mount Vernon to the estate in honor of Admiral VERNON, of the English Navy, died in 1752. Under the will it became the property of his half brother, George, the oldest child of Augustine and his second wife, Mary BALL. Gen. WASHINGTON, who died Dec. 14, 1799, left Mt. Vernon to his nephew Bushrod, a son of his brother John Augustine. Bushrod WASHINGTON died Nov. 26, 1829, without issue, leaving it in turn to John Augustine WASHINGTON, who soon after the death of his uncle Bushrod, removed to Mt. Vernon, where he resided until his death in June, 1832. After the death of his widow Mt. Vernon became the property of his son, John Augustine. Col. John Augustine WASHINGTON was born May 3, 1820. at "Blakely," the residence of his father, in Jefferson Co, Va, now W. Va. He married in Feb. 1842, at "Exeter," Loudoun Co, Eleanor Love, daughter of Wilson Carey SELDEN Esq. He had 2 sons and 5 daughters, all of whom are now living and all married save one daughter. He resided at Mt. Vernon until a short time prior to the last war. ...

Died: At her home near Lovettsville, on the morning of the 22d of February, 1889, Mrs. Mary A. BROWN, consort of Mr. Charles L. BROWN, in her 59th year, from a protracted sickness.

Mr. Jas. GRUBB, of this county, died at his home near Hillsboro on Friday last at an advanced age.

Mr. Clarence HEAD, of Leesburg, died at his home in this town on Saturday morning last, of typhoid pneumonia, in the 34th year of his age. He leaves a wife and 3 young children. Funeral took place Sunday afternoon, Revs. I. W. CANTER and D. C. HEDRICK officiating. Interred in Union Cemetery.

[MISSING ISSUE, 7 March issue - should be No. 40]

Thursday, 14 March 1889   Vol. XXXIII, No. 40

Married: At the residence of the bride's parents, March 12, 1889, by Rev. I. W. CANTER, Mr. L. H. SAMPSELL and Miss Clara WYNKOOP, both of Leesburg.

Married: At the residence of the bride's parents, March 12, 1889, by Rev. I. W. CANTER, Mr. J. F. WARNER and Miss Lucie E. ROLLINS, both of Loudoun County.

Married: At the home of the bride's parents, near Lovettsville, on the 5th inst., by the Rev. St. J. RINKER, Mr. Wm. B. WASHINGTON to Miss Ella M. McGAHEY, daughter of James and Mary McGAHEY, all of Loudoun County.

Married: On February 13, 1889, at Augusta, Ga., Mr. Thomas MERRIWETHER, of South Carolina, to Miss Alice B. SMITH, formerly of Loudoun County.

Died: In Leesburg, on March 11th 1889, Mrs. Carita SWANN, wife of Thomas SWANN Esq. and only daughter of Dr. J. F. and Carolina MASON, of this county, in the 23d year of her age.

Died: At the rectory at Lewisburg, W. Va., February 26, 1889, age 12y 10m, Norvell Radford, daughter of Arthur P. and Mina R. GRAY.

Died: On Friday morning, March 8th 1899 [1889] after a long illness, Louis H. POWELL, of Leesburg, in the 41st year of his age.

Died: On Saturday morning, March 9, 1889, at her home near Brookland, D.C., Mary Alice MEANS, daughter of the late Samuel C. and Rachel A. MEANS, formerly of Loudoun County.

Died: On Saturday, March 9th, 1889, at Ravenswood, Prince William Co., Mary Chesley, wife of the late William J. BRONAUGH, formerly of southwest Washington. She was originally from St. Mary's Co., Md, and her late husband from Loudoun Co.

Sudden death of Capt. Wm. P. SMITH, of Leesburg, on Thursday March 7th 1889, in the 70th year of his age, of heart trouble. He fell in front of Mrs. Annie E. JOHNSON's millinery store, on King St. and was borne to the residence of Mrs. M. A. BURKE (his mother-in-law) opposite. Member of I.O.O. Fellows. Leaves 4 sons and 1 daughter, the latter residing in this town, one of his sons, Decatur, resides in Washington, another, Chas. W., in Warrenton, a third, Robert, in Missouri, and the fourth, Burke in Indian Territory. Only Burke was at the funeral which took place Sunday afternoon, Rev. Nelson HEAD, D.D. and Rev. I. W. CANTER officiating. Interred in Union Cemetery at 2 o'clock Sunday afternoon.

Death of Louis H. POWELL, member of the Leesburg bar, died after a long illness, at 4 o'clock Friday morning, March 8th 1889, in his 41st year. He was a son of the late Dr. Frank POWELL, of Middleburg. Funeral took place from his late residence at 4 o'clock Sunday afternoon, Rev. Dr. DAVIS officiating. Interred in Union Cemetery.

Death of Mrs. Carita SWANN: A little more than one year ago, Carita, wife of Mr. Thos. SWANN, and only daughter of Dr. J. F. and Carolina MASON, of this county, stood before the altar. On Monday last, she died in the 23d year of her age, leaving an infant son, husband, and parents. Interred in Union Cemetery, funeral taking place from the chapel of Immaculate Conception, Rev. Father WILSON officiating, at 11 o'clock Wednesday morning.

Died: At Mt. Gilead, March 2, 1889, Mr. Joseph M. HOWELL, in the 39th year of his age. He leaves a wife and seven small children. Member of the Baptist Church at Short Hill.

Mr. Wm. STEVENSON, living near Aldie, committed suicide last Monday evening, March 11, by hanging himself in his own barn. He was some 70 years old and in bad health for a good many years.

Misses Rebecca and Etta BOWEN, of Delphi City, Ind. and Miss Blanche WINGER, of Washington DC, are visiting their cousin, Mrs. Geo. A. NOLAND of Round Hill.

March Ct.: Wills of James GRUBB, Elizabeth H. THRASHER, Augustus ZEREGA and Antoni WILSON admitted to probate. Letters of administration on estate of S. M. GIBSON, R. Emma GIBSON Admx.

Taylortown: Mrs. Maria WILLIAMS, wife of Stout WILLIAMS dec'd., died at the residence of her son-in-law, S. L. PORTER, on Sunday, March 10, at 2:30 p.m.

Taylortown: Mr. Samuel COOPER, father of our postmaster, landed at the home of his son in Talipoosa, Ga. last week.

Thursday, 21 March 1889   Vol. XXXIII, No. 41

Married: On Tuesday, March 5th, at the home of the bride's mother, in Baltimore, Md, by the Rev. W. T. EVANS, Miss Olivia KERN and Emory V. CHINN, Esq., junior partner of the mercantile firm of Chinn Bros., Lovettsville.

Married: At the residence of the bride's parents, on the 18th, by the Rev. G. W. POPKINS, Mr. A. M. HAYNES to Miss Annie M. THRIFT, all of Loudoun.

Married: At the residence of the bride's uncle, Mr. N. H. BARTLETT, near Lovettsville, March 14, 1889, by Rev. P. H. MILLER, of Westminster, Md., Mr. Elmer E. ARNOLD, of Washington Co Md, and Miss Rebecca H. V. BARTLETT, of Loudoun Co.

Death of Mrs. M. A. STANSBURY at her home in Leesburg on Thursday night last. She was the widow of the late J. J. STANSBURY, who died a short time ago. Funeral took place Sunday afternoon, Rev. I. W. CANTER, officiating. Interment in Union cemetery.

Washington Post of Thursday – Wedding took place on Tuesday evening at the residence of Mrs. M. J. EASTWOOD, at 515 Sixth St., Mr. J. W. JOHNSTON Jr., of Loudoun Co., and Miss Mamie J. EASTWOOD, of this city. Rev. S. GREEN officiated. Mr. JOHNSTON was formerly with the dry Goods House of W. W. Chamblin, and is now with Woodward & Lothrop, Washington.

Baltimore Sun article: Rev. Nelson HEAD, D.D. was born in Leesburg on 3 Feb 1811, and coverted at a camp meeting when 16 years of age, licensed to exhort in 1832, licensed to preach in 1838, ...[lists all his charged.] Retired in Staunton, Va, March 1886.

Died March 11th 1889, at his home near Mt. Zion Church, William STEVENSON, of Loudoun County. Billy was a philosopher and a humorist.

[MISSING ISSUE]

Thursday, 4 April 1889   Vol. XXXIII, No. 43

Married: At the residence of Maj. Chas. H. LEE, in Leesburg, at 1 o'clock Wednesday afternoon, April 3, 1889, by Rev. R. T. DAVIS, D.D., Rich'd. L. WALTON, Esq. of Norfolk, Va and Miss Laura Virginia d'LONY, of this town.

Married: At Tankerville, March 27th, by Rev. Dr. SCHINDLER, Mr. Richard T. NEWTON and Miss Mary F. KIDWELL, both of Loudoun.

Married: At the home of the bride, in Waterford, by Rev. SCHINDLER, Mr. John PAXTON and Mrs. L. Kate RICKARD, both of Loudoun Co.

Died: In Miami, Mo., March 19th, Albert HARDING, aged 71 years, formerly of Loudoun Co.

Died: George REDMAN, near Hillsboro, March, 22, 1889, of pneumonia, aged 80 years.

Died: Mrs. Olivia MYERS, wife of Thos. J. MYERS and daughter of David and Elizabeth STEADMAN, born in Leesburg, February 9th, 1842, died at the residence of her husband, near Taylortown, Va, April the 1st, 1889 in her 48th year. Funeral took place Wednesday a.m., Rev. S. P. SHIPMAN, officiating. Interred at Union Cemetery.

Mr. Henry MAFFETT died at his residence near Ball's Mill, on Thursday morning last, in the 84th year of his age. He was a successful farmer and leaves a comfortable estate.

Thursday, 11 April 1889   Vol. XXXIII, No. 44

Patrick GILL died at his home in Leesburg Monday afternoon, at an advanced age. Funeral took place Wednesday from the Chapel of the Immaculate Conception, Father WILSON officiating.

April Ct.: Wills of Henry MAFFETT, Elizabeth J. DANIEL and Louis H. POWELL admitted to probate. Administrations on estates of Emma TAVENNER and Ebenezer J. CONARD granted. Estates of Thos. APPLE and Isaac D. BUDD committed to Sheriff.

In the Upperville Methodist Church, on Tuesday, April 2d, marriage of Mr. James KINCHELOE to Miss Annie GIBSON. Bride is daughter of Mr. and Mrs. John GIBSON of Loudoun Co. Groom is native of Fauquier. Bride escorted to the altar by her uncle, Mr. Gilbert GIBSON, the groom by his best man, Mr. Willis HERNDON. Performed by Rev. J. C. DICE. Bride's maids were Misses Esther GIBSON, Ada GIBSON, Meta GIBSON, Lucy GIBSON, Annie ROGERS and Blanche KINCHELOE. Mr. KINCHELOE will start a mercantile enterprise of his own in Upperville.

Death of Andrew S. FLEMING at his home in Alexandria last Wednesday. At one time was in mercantile business with Wm. N. McVEIGH. Deacon in Second Presbyterian Church for many years.

Thursday, 18 April 1889   Vol. XXXIII, No. 46

Col. Jas. McH. HOLLINGSWORTH, who up to 1885 was superindendent of the Mt. Vernon estate, died at his home in Georgetown on Monday.

Died: Mrs. Elizabeth FAWLEY, wife of Jeremiah FAWLEY, died at her home, near Goresville, April 11th 1889, of pneumonia, aged 43y 6m 21d

The family of Mr. Thomas B. HALL, of Berry, Illinois, son of Mr. James M. HALL of Leesburg. [part creased] [note: appears that his daughter Bertha died at age 1y 20d.]

Cards are out for the marriage of Rev. Carter PAGE, rector of Christ Church, Goresville to Miss Nannie BANBURY, dau. of Col. Wm. GIDDINGS, of this county, on April 25th 1889, at Christ Church.

Mrs. Jane RHODES, widow of the late George RHODES, died at her home near the Dry Mill, in this county, on Wednesday night of last week, in her 89th year. She had been confined to her room since last August. Member of the M. E. Church. Funeral took place Friday morning, interred in Union Cemetery, Revs. B. W. BOND and Dr. N. HEAD officiating.

Aquilla JANNEY of this county, last surviving brother of the late John JANNEY, of this town died at the home of his son, Dr. Edgar

JANNEY, in Washington last Friday night, in his 83d year. Friday night he retired and the next morning he was found lying on the chamber floor, dress just as on Friday, probably from heart affection. Remains were taken to Lincoln (his old home) Saturday evening and Sunday afternoon. Interred in Friends' burying ground at that place.

Marriage of Mr. Robt. L. BENTLEY, of Baltimore, son of the late R. M. BENTLEY of this town, to Miss M. C. MYERS, is announced to take place next Wednesday, the 24th inst. at "Rosland," the residence of the bride's mother, near Pikesville, Baltimore Co., Md.

Thursday, 25 April 1889 Vol. XXXIII, No. 47

Married: At the residence of John H. ALEXANDER, Esq., of Leesburg, on Tuesday, April 23d, 1889, by Rev. C. T. HERNDON, Dr. Edward A. DUNCAN, of Washington DC, and Miss Alice W. BOND, daughter of the late Asa BOND, of Loudoun.

Married: On Thursday, April 11, 1889, at Washington DC, by the Rev. Henry BRANCH, Jas. A. DORRITEE, of Baltimore, to Miss Ellen G. ARCHER, of Loudoun County.

Married: At the residence of Jno. H. ALEXANDER, Esq., in Leesburg, on Tuesday, April 23d, 1889, by Rev. C. T. HERNDON, Mr. A. T. SHAWEN and Miss Amanda C. BERRY, all of Loudoun.

Died: In Washington City, April 18, 1889, of consumption, Daniel MORIARTY, of Loudoun County, aged 26y 7m.

Marriage of Miss Roberta MOTT, dau. of Dr. A. R. MOTT, of Leesburg, to Dr. Woodruff CHAPIN will take place today (Thursday) at the bride's home in this town. They will reside in Astoria, Long Island.

Wednesday, Apr 24th, Mr. Robt. L. BENTLEY, son of the late R. M. BENTLEY, of this town, was married at "Rosland," the residence of the bride's mother, near Baltimore, to Miss M. C. MYER.

Today, Thursday, April 25th, Rev. Carter PAGE, rector of Christ Church, Goresville, and Miss Nannie BANBURY, daughter of Col. Wm. GIDDINGS, of this county, will be united at Christ Church.

Dr. Woodruff CHAPIN, of Long Island, New York and Miss Roberta, daughter of Dr. A. R. MOTT, of this town, will be married at the residence of the bride's parents in Leesburg.

At 5:30 this afternoon, Mr. Thos. S. PURDIE will marry Emily, daughter of Mr. Jos. N. ATKINSON, of Norfolk, Va.

Miss Annie L. GARRETT died at her home near Silcott's Springs, on Tuesday night, April 23d. Funeral will take place from her late residence, at 10 o'clock, Friday morning. Interment at North Fork burying ground.

Thursday, 2 May 1889 Vol. XXXIII, No. 48

Married: At the residence of the bride's father, at Gum Spring, on Wed., April 24th 1889, by Elder E. V. WHITE, Mr. Dennis HIGGINS and Miss Mary C. PALMER, dau. of L. F. PALMER, Esq. All of Loudoun.

Married: In Carroll Hall, Baltimore, Sunday April 14th 1889, Harris LEVI, of Loudoun, to Miss Esther MILLER, of that place.

Mrs. Ellen HUTCHISON, daughter of James and Mary WHALEY, died on the 5th of January, near Gum Spring, in her 54th year.

On the 20th of February, Mrs. Fanny ROSE died and three days after her sister Mrs. BLACK, both living near Gum Spring.

Dr. R. S. MOORE died suddenly at his home in Norfolk the 19th inst. and was buried from the Presbyterian Church of Warrenton the following Sunday. He married a daughter of Rev. A. D. POLLOCK, and with his little family spent his summers at "Leeton Forest." He leaves a widow and two daughters.

Rev. L. C. MILLER, member of the M. E. Church, South, died in Harrisonburg, Va. last.

Baltimore American: Mr. Robt. L. BENTLY was married at 3:30 o'clock to Miss Constance MYER, at the residence of the bride's mother, Mrs. Thomas J. MYER, near Pikesville. Performed by Rev. Father MACALL, and Cardinal GIBBONS. ....

On Thursday, April 25, Dr. Woodruff CHAPIN, of New York, and Miss Roberta, daughter of Dr. A. R. MOTT, were married at the residence of the bride's parents in Leesburg, Rev. Alfred HARDING of Washington city, officiating. They will reside at Astoria, Long Island.

On the 25th of April, Thos. S. PURDIE, Esq., a former member of the Leesburg Bar, and Miss Emily ATKINSON, of Norfolk, Va, were married at the residence of the bride's mother in that city.

St. Luke's P. E. Church was scene yesterday of wedding of Miss Olive C. JACKSON, youngest daughter of Dr. S. K. JACKSON and Mr. Francis T. STRIBING of Staunton. Dr. JACKSON, father of the bride, was for a number of years a practitioner in Leesburg.

Charlestown, W. Va., April 30: Mr. Thos. A. MOORE, clerk of the county court of Jefferson Co., suffered an attack of apoplexy a few days ago and died this evening, in his 87th year. Born in Fairfax Co., in 1803, read law in Leesburg, and at 21 removed to Charlestown. He was a Mason. Leaves a daughter and 4 sons, the latter being Col. J. C. S. MOORE, and Rev. J. Harry MOORE, of Berryville, Va., Mr. Cleon MOORE, of this place, and Mr. B. W. MOORE, of Fayette C. H., W. Va.

Thursday, 9 May 1889   Vol. XXXIII, No. 48 [49]

Died: Near Centreville, Fairfax Co. Va., April 28th, Elizabeth T., wife of Henry SWART, in the 68th year of her age.

Died: At his home near Leesburg, Richard T. WHITE on April 27th 1889, after a long illness. Member of the M. E. Church, South.

Mr. Richard T. WHITE, died at the home of his brother, W. H. WHITE, near this town, on the 27th ult., of consumption, in the 41st year of his age. Interred in Union Cemetery. Member of M. E. Church, South.

Rev. B. W. BOND, Rev. C. T. HERNDON and Rev. W. G. EGGLESTON attended the funeral

Mr. Charles H. FADELY and Miss Anna B. WIERMAN were married Tuesday morning at ten o'clock at the residence of the bride's father, John R. WIERMAN, Esq., Edinburg, Va. Rev. O. C. BEALL of the Methodist church performed the ceremony. Bridal party attended by Dr. Geo. FADELY, brother of the groom and Miss Lelia RIDDLEBERGER, of Woodstock. ... Mr. FADELY is salesman for the hardware firm of Martin Lane & Co. of Baltimore. His father is M. M. FADELY, Esq. of Farmwell.

Thursday, 16 May 1889   Vol. XXXIII, No. 49

Married: In Salem, Va., May 8, 1889, by the Rev. J. R. BRIDGES, J. E. BLAIR, of Richmond, Va, to Mrs. A. B. VENABLE, sister of the officiating minister.

A solder of the War of 1812 – about 9 o'clock Thursday night, John McCABE, father of Chas. P. and grandfather of Judge J. B. McCABE of this town, in his 92nd year, nearly the whole passed in Leesburg. He was a soldier of the war of 1812. At 10 o'clock Saturday morning interred in Union Cemetery. Revs. B. W. BOND and Dr. N. HEAD, officiating.

May Ct.: Will of John McCABE admitted to probate. N. H. KENT qualified as Admr. wwa of Margaret A. STANSBURY dec'd. Estate of R. Y. MORAN, John KEEN and J. W. KEEN committed to Sheriff.

Maj. John N. EDWARDS, writer of Missouri, died in Kansas City on the 4th inst. He had been connected with daily papers in St. Louis, St. Joe, Sedallia and Kansas City. He was a native of Warren Co. Va., but spent a portion of his boyhood in Leesburg, where his two sisters, Misses Edmonia and Fannie EDWARDS, still reside. He was a nephew of Dr. R. H. and Thos. W. EDWARDS Esq. of this place.

Death of Mr. L. C. CHAMBLIN occurred at the family residence on Cypress Ave. yesterday afternoon after a short illness. Native of Muskingum Co., Ohio. A veteran of the late rebellion, served as a volunteer of the Third Ohio Regiment. For 12 or 14 years prior to coming to Riverside, a manager of the manufacturing establishment at Grand Haven, Michigan. Leaves a wife and brother. *Riverside (Cal.) Enterprise of April 27.* His parents, Mr. Norval CHAMBLIN and his mother, nee Miss VANDEVENTER, were natives of Loudoun Co. They moved to Ohio early in their married life.

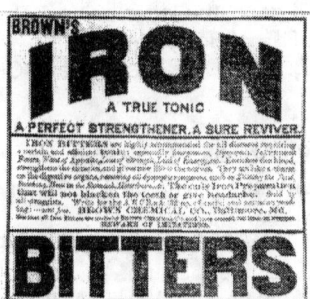

Mrs. Louisa SHEFFEY, widow of the late Judge Hugh J. SHEFFEY, of Staunton, died in that city on Monday, the 6th inst., just four weeks after her husband was laid to rest.

Thursday, 23 May 1889   Vol. XXXIII, No. 50

Married: At the Episcopal Rectory in Baltimore, on Thursday, May 16th 1889, by Rev. George A. LEAKIN, Mr. Edgar W. BIRKBY, of Leesburg, and [page creased]

Married: May 2nd 1889, at Lutheran parsonage, Lovettsville, by Dr. D. SCHINDLER, Mr. William B. FILLER and Miss Jennie HUNTER, both of Loudoun County.

Died: In Richmond, Saturday, May 18th at 1:35 p.m., Mary Amanda BENTLEY, wife of Dr. Richard Heath DABNEY, of the Univ. of Indiana, and youngest child of E. B. BENTLEY, of that city.

Died: At the home of her son, John F. KIDWELL, near Herndon station, Fairfax Co, on the morning of April the 20th 1889, Mrs. Ann KIDWELL in the 66th year of her age. She was the widow of Geo. H. KIDWELL of Loudon Co. She leaves three children. Interment at Valley Meeting House, Elder E. V. WHITE officiating.

[MISSING ISSUE]

Thursday, 6 June 1889   Vol. XXXIII, No. 52

Died: At Tankerville, Loudoun Co, Mr. Charles JONES, May 21st, in the 67th near of his age. Interment in Mt. Hope graveyard.

The little child of Mr. Henry FURR, died about a week ago of diphtheria. Another child is similarly afflicted.

Thursday, 13 June 1889   Vol. XXXIV, No. 1

Mrs. Sarah HAMTRAMCK, widow of the late Col. Jno. F. HAMTRAMCK, who commanded the Va regiment in the Mexican war, died at her home in Shepherdstown, last week, aged 78 years.

Mark[h]am, June 10: Messrs. Robert F. and E. C. TURNER Jr. called upon their brother in law, Mr. E. P. TURNER, yesterday in regard to some difference between them. Shots were fired and Robert TURNER was killed by E. P. TURNER. He leaves a widow and three children. Robert was the son of Edward C. TURNER Sr. Lt. TURNER was a son of the late Admiral TURNER and several years since, while in the U.S. Army, killed a man in Texas. R. F. TURNER's wife was Miss MEREDITH, of Fauquier. They say Lt. E. P. TURNER had been treating his wife harshly for sometime past and on Saturday it was reported he had struck her. On Sunday, while she was at church her brothers, R. F. and E. C. TURNER, went to E. P. TURNER's house. ... [long article]

Markham: Edward Palmer TURNER who was shot and killed his cousin and brother-in-law, Robert TURNER, near The Plains, Fauquier Co,

Sunday afternoon, and was in turn shot through the breast and hand by Edward C. TURNER, brother of Robert, died from his wounds at an early hour this morning. A message received Wednesday morning states that Lt. TURNER was not dead Tuesday afternoon.

Died: At Daysville, Loudoun County, May 24, 1889, Mrs. R. Virginia HAVENER, wife of B. T. HAVENER, in her 41st year. She leaves a husband, three children, father, mother and one sister.

Mrs. Margaret DULIN, widow of the late Alfred DULIN, of this county, and mother of Mr. George C. DULIN, died at Cool Springs, Md., on Monday last, in the 77th year of her age. Interred in Union Cemetery, Leesburg on Wednesday.

Co. Ct.: Alberta J. PIGGOTT qualified as Guardian of Mary E. PIGGOTT &c. Estates of Julius MASON and Maria MASON committed to Sheriff. Will of Wm. H. STEPHENSON admitted to probate. G. B. GIBSON and Jos. A. GIBSON qualified as Admr. of John N. GIBSON. Albert MILHOLLIN qualified as Admr. of B. F. BROWN dec'd.

Thursday, 20 June 1889   Vol. XXXIV, No. 2

Departed this life at Silver Springs, Montgomery Co, Md, June 9th '89, Mrs. Margaret DULIN, relict of the late Alfred DULIN, in the 78th year of her age. She was for most of her life a resident of Loudoun County and a member of the M. E. Church, South, of Leesburg.

Died: At Sterling, Loudoun County, June 14th, 1889, Goldie Rozella, daughter of W. S. and Mattie R. WILEY, aged 13m 8d.

Mrs. Hattie B. GLASCOCK, of Washington, widow of the late Capt. Alfred GLASCOCK, died at the home of her mother, Mrs. Orra M. FADELY, in this town, on Monday evening last, in about the 44th year of her age. Early last fall she had a severe attack of typhoid pneumonia. Funeral took place at 10 o'clock Wednesday morning, Rev. Dr. HEAD, of the M. E. Church, South, of which she was a member, officiating. Interred in Union Cemetery.

Martinsburg, W. Va., June 11: Mr. Wm. A. EASTERDAY, of Washington DC, formerly of Leesburg, and Miss Mollie WILEN, oldest daughter of Mr. Henry WILEN, of this city, were married this morning at Trinity M. E. Church, South, Rev. H. H. KENNEDY assisted by Rev. John LANDSTREET, performed the ceremony. Ushers were Messrs. W. C. HALDEMAN and Herbert C. EASTERDAY, of Washington, R. S. BARR and Adrian C. NADENBOUSCH, of Martinsburg. ...

Last week, Mr. Joseph HALL, of Richmond and his wife (nee Miss Sallie CHAMBLIN, of this county) sailed for Europe for the summer.

Aldie: Death Saturday morning of Mr. John L. CHINN, farmer, living near the place. About 4 o'clock his wife heard him make a slight noise and found him dead. Member of the 8th Va Regiment and was wounded in its service. In his 54th year and leaves a wife and one daughter.

Thursday, 27 June 1889   Vol. XXXIV, No. 3

Died: At the residence of Mr. James H. RYON, No. 1508 34th St., West Washington DC, June 7th 1889, at 8 p.m., George Francis, only son of Benjamin G. and Rosa B. CARTER, both of Loudoun County, grandson of John T. REEVES dec'd. of Loudoun County, died of diptheria after a week of terrible suffering, aged 4y 3m 25d. Remains were buried in Tennallytown Cemetery, about 2 miles from West Washington DC, on Saturday evening the 8th at 2:30 o'clock.

Thursday, 4 July 1889   Vol. XXXIV, No. 4

Died: On Saturday, June 22d, 1889, at Whitehall, the residence of her uncle, T. S. TITUS, of cholera infantum, Virginia, daughter of Clinton and Lennie E. HOSKINSON, aged 8m 9d.

Died: In Washington City, on Friday, June 28th 1889, at 12 o'clock, after a long and painful illness, Samuel TITUS, beloved husband of Martha A. TITUS, in the 75th year of his age.

Died: At the residence of his brother, Edwin DAVIS, near Farmwell, Loudoun County, June 19th 1889, Mr. Robert L. DAVIS, of consumption. He leaves one sister and two brothers. The last two years his home has been in Washington. He came to his brother's for his health. Col. E. V. WHITE preached on the occasion. interred in North Fork burying ground.

Mr. O. M. BUSSARD, of Woodburn, was married in the Baptist Church, of this town last Thursday, to Miss Rose, daughter of Mr. Mason LOVELACE, the Rev. C. T. HERNDON officiating. They will reside near Woodburn.

Died: Wednesday morning, July 3d, Mr. William CLINE. After retiring his daughter-in-law and grand-daughter called to him and between 1 and 2 o'clock found him unconscious. He was the senior member of the Hardware firm of Cline & Sons, of Leesburg. Member of the M. E. Church, South, in this town. He died in the 72d year of his age. Interment in Union Cemetery Friday afternoon.

On the farm of Col. J. R. BRINTON, about 1 mile south of Leesburg, last Tuesday morning. Mr. S. A. CAMPBELL and Mr. S. E. HORSEMAN, who were employed on the farm, were driving sheep into the pen. A support for the roof was knocked out and struck Mr. HORSEMAN, breaking his neck. 33 years old and leaves a wife and one child.

Major John H. CHICHESTER, died at his residence in Fairfax county yesterday evening. For many years he had been treasurer of Fairfax Co. He was about 60 years of age.

Trial of Lt. E. P. TURNER for manslaughter – verdict of acquittal.

Thursday, 11 July 1889   Vol. XXXIV, No. 5

Married: July 3d, at the residence of the officiating minister, Rev. J. W. WOLF, Mr. William A. CARLISLE to Miss Mary BROWN, all of Loudoun County.

Died: On Thursday, July 4th 1889, Morris Lee BROWN, aged 3m 6d, infant son of Dr. and Mrs. L. A. BROWN, of Leesburg.

Died: At her home in Washington DC, on the 24th of May, 1889, Mrs. Cordelia LYNN, in her 67th year, of consumption. Widow of William LYNN of lower Prince William, where she had spent all her life except the last 16 years, which had been spent in Washington. Elder CHICK officiated at her funeral, interred at family burying ground in Prince William, near Independent Hill. She leaves 5 sons.

July Ct.: Will of Wm. CLINE dec'd. admitted to probate, Chas. A. and Wm. CLINE Exors.

Thursday, 18 July 1889   Vol. XXXIV, No. 6

Married: On the Harper's Ferry bridge, June 25th 1889, by Rev. James M. STEVENSON, Mr. James D. COPELAND, of Loudoun County, to Miss Lizzie WALDOM, of Conn.

Mr. Edw. C. JORDAN, proprietor of Jordan's White Sulphur Springs, 6 miles from Winchester, died this morning of blood poisoning, caused by the bite of a pet squirrel about 8 weeks ago. About 65 years of age. He married Miss Belle EUBANKS, of Tidewater Virginia, who survived him, with children Mr. E. C. JORDAN Jr. and a daughter who was married a few weeks ago to Mr. H. H. BAKER, a merchant of Winchester.

Biography of author and journalist John N. EDWARDS by his wife Jennie EDWARDS. [see 16 May issue for death notice] He died poor.

Thursday, 25 July 1889   Vol. XXXIV, No. 7

Married: At the residence of the bride's father, near Oatlands, July 17th, 1889, by Rev. C. T. HERNDON, Miss Lillie DODD, and Mr. W. G. GIBSON, all of Loudoun.

Died: Near Leesburg, on July 16, '89, after a lingering illness of several months, Mrs. Lucy L., wife of David GAINES and daughter of the late Thomas A. and Precilla C. GAINES, near Middleburg, in the 44th year of her age.

Died: Near Snickersville, Thursday, July 11th 1889, Mary Ellen, infant son [dau.?] of John B. and Bettie SANTENYERS, aged 11d. Poem "by her sister."

Died: At "Newstard," near Bloomfield, July 19th 1889, of cholera infantum, Richard Chamblin, son of Henry and Lizzie FRASIER, aged 7m 2d.

Died: On the morning of July 19th '89, little Ella, babe of Henry and Cossie JANNEY, but a few short months old.

Death of Mrs. Kate ELLIOTT, wife of former countyman, Mr. Chas. O. VANDEVENTER, occurred in Hagerstown, Md, on Friday last, July 19th. Remains were on Sunday conveyed to Bellefonte, in Pa, the home of her maiden life, for interment.

Mrs. Mary E. LOTT, widow of the late Parkinson L. LOTT, of this town died at the residence of her sister-in-law, Mrs. Olivia SMALE, last Thursday night. She was in the 81st year of her age. She was a member of the M. E. Church. Interred in Union Cemetery Saturday afternoon, Revs. BOND and HEAD officiating.

Thursday, 1 August 1889   Vol. XXXIV, No. 8

Married: The 13th inst., by Rev. A. H. TUTTLE, H. E. ALTMAN, of Loudoun County, and Hattie MARTIN, of Fauquier County, at the parsonage of Mt. Vernon M. E. Church, Baltimore, Md.

Died: On the evening of July 26, 1889, at the residence of her uncle, A. E. HOOVER, No. 1033 North Caroline St, Jessie Herbert, aged 8m 3d, dau. of Nannie B. and the late J. Herbert ATHEY, and granddau. of W. W. ATHEY, of this town. Remains laid beside those of her father in Union Cemetery, Leesburg, at 6 o'clock Monday evening.

Death of Capt. Charles Magill FAUNTLEROY at the residence of his daughter, Mrs. Powell HARRISON, in Leesburg about 8 o'clock last Sunday night, 27th July, after a protracted and painful illness, in his 67th year. The son of the late Gen. Thomas T. FAUNTLEROY, formerly Col. of Dragoons, U.S.A. and a native of Winchester, Frederick Co Va. He entered the U.S. Navy at 16 years of age but in 1861 associated with the Southern States. ... For some years he has resided with his widowed daughter. Member of St. James P. E. Church. On Tuesday morning his remains were laid beside those of the wife he lost in early life, and by the graves of her father and mother, Thomas P. and Catherine KNOX, in the Presbyterian Church yard in this place. Services held in the Episcopal Church, Rev. Dr. DAVIS, assisted by Rev. Carter PAGE, officiating.

Probable death of Jno. T. DOWELL – highly probable that he was one who was lost and remains destroyed by fire in the recent accident on the Norfolk and Western railroad near Thaxton, Va. It is known that he left Rome, Ga. where he had resided of late years, for Washington on the day before the accident. Nothing has been heard from him. He was a native of Loudoun.

[MISSING ISSUES]

Thursday, 22 August 1889   Vol. XXXIV, No. 11

Mr. Thos. W. McCANOE, of Richmond, died at his residence in that city last Wednesday, in his 77th year. Father of Mrs. Jno. P. ROGERS.

Married: On August 9th 1889, in Frederick city, by Rev. Mr. DIEHL, John C. MOORE to Miss Katie MYERS, both of Loudoun County.

Died: Near Mt. Hope Church, July 31st, 1889, Mary Margaret, infant daughter of Burr T. and Malvina G. ALEXANDER, aged 6 months.

Clara Blanch GRUBB, infant daughter of L. M. and Maggie V. GRUBB, died at the residence of Benj. GRUBB, near Taylortown, July 13, 1889, aged 10m 21d.

Died: At his home near Middleburg, Aug. 11th 1889, Mr. F. M. COLE, aged 56 years. For about ten months he had been confined to the house and his bed. Member of the Old Baptist Church. Leaves a wife, 4 daughters and a son, 2 brothers, and an aged mother.

Mr. Samuel GEORGE, of this county, a wealthy farmer, died last Sunday morning at his home near Lovettsville, in the 70th year of his age, of cancer. Funeral took place on Tuesday.

Mr. R. P. FAUNTLEROY, formerly of this town, but for the last few years of Cincinnati, is visiting relatives in Leesburg.

Mr. Thos. OSBURN, another former citizen, but for past 6 years living in Florida, is visiting relatives.

At "Rockland," the home of the bride's mother, Mrs. Ida L. RUST, at 8 o'clock Wed. evening, August 14th 1889, by Rev. Harry B. LEE, of Culpeper, uncle of the bride, assisted by Rev. R. T. DAVIS, of Leesburg, Thos. W. EDWARDS, Esq., of the drug firm of Edwards & Son, and Miss Lillie Southgate, daughter of the late Col. A. T. M. RUST of this county. Bridesmaides and groomsmen: Miss Lizzie MICHLE of Charlottesville and Mr. George RUST; Miss Ida RUST and Mr. George ROGERS; Miss Katie GOLDSBOROUGH of Frederick, Md, and Mr. R. B. WILDMAN; Miss Lucy LEE, of Culpeper, and Mr. Eddie RUST; Miss Lizzie SMITH of Winchester, and Mr. W. F. DOUTHIRT, of Ohio; Miss Nettie RUST and Mr. E. B. HARRISON. They will reside in Leesburg.

Thursday, 29 August 1889   Vol. XXXIV, No. 12

Married: At the residence of the officiating clergyman, in Leesburg, on Wednesday morning, August 28, 1889, by Rev. Nelson HEAD, D.D., William H. TEEL and Texanna GEASLIN, all of Loudoun.

Married: On the same day, at same place, and by same minister, Walter KENT and Emily P. COLE, all of Loudoun.

Died: in Leesburg, at the residence of her grandmother, Mrs. Annie GRIMES, August 6th 1889, Nellie May, aged 7y 6m, eldest child of Henrietta and Smith McGILL.

Died: Mrs. Jane JONES, wife of Mr. Burr JONES, at Mt. Gilead, August 10th 1889, of chronic diarrhea, in the 56th year of her age.

Died: At her residence near Pleasant Valley P.O., August 23, 1889, Annie, beloved wife of Manley RUSK, in the 54th year of her age.

Mrs. Anne Triplett HAXALL, mother of Mr. Bolling HAXALL, of Middleburg, died at her home in Richmond, Va. on Sunday last. She had been sick a long time with rheumatism.

Mr. Wm. S. HARRISON, of Montgomery Co., Md, died suddenly at his home, near Potomac, on Monday afternoon last, of heart disease. He was born in Loudoun Co. on 29th Oct 1814.

Thursday, 5 September 1889   Vol. XXXIV, No. 13

Died: At the residence of her sister, Mrs. Catherine HOSPITAL, near Falls Church, on Tuesday Aug. 10th 1889, Miss Keziah ARNOLT, at an advanced age. Resided in Loudoun, a few months ago she left home to pay a visit to her sister in Fairfax, was taken sick and died.

Died: Alice Gertrude GRIFFITH, adopted daughter of Mrs. Mary E. CLARK, died at her home at Round Hill, on Thursday afternoon at 3:35 p.m., aged 2yy 5m 17d.

Died: at her residence near Cool Spring, Mrs. D. H. REDMON, in the 38th year of her age. Funeral preached by Rev. J. C. DINWIDDIE. Member of Leesburg Presbyterian.

Died: Near Sudley, August 23d, 1889, at the home of her parents, Randolph and Alice THOMPSON, Mary Lee, aged 7 years.

Charlestown W. Va. Free Press, Aug. 29th: Mrs. Margaret MYERS died at her home in this town on Wednesday, Aug. 21st, aged 78 years. Widow of the late Nathaniel MYERS and a sister of B. F. SHEETZ, editor of the *Loudoun Mirror*. Funeral took place from the Presbyterian Church on Thursday afternoon, by Rev. Dr. HOPKINS. Her name was recorded on the books of the Church in 1833. She had two sons in the Confederate army, one of them only 18 fatally wounded in the first Manassas battle; the other died after the war. A daughter, Mrs. George W. WELSH, survives her and grandchildren.

At a picnic at Lewisville, Loudoun Co, last Saturday, a child of Isaac JACKSON was killed. A horse attached to the cart in which JACKSON's wife and child and sister in law were riding upset, killing the child instantly.

Thursday, 12 September 1889   Vol. XXXIV, No. 14

Died: At her residence in Washington, D.C. on Thursday morning, September 5th, after a protracted illness, Mrs. Alice C., wife of Wesley B. BARKER, in the 58th year of her age. She was aunt of Mr. S. FOUCHE, of this town.

Died: July 25th 1889, at Bailey's X Roads, Fairfax Co, Ellen A., wife of John W. RICE, (formerly of Loudoun) in the 33d year of her age.

Died: Sept. 2, 1889, after a protracted illness, Mary Daniel, wife of Joseph P. GRUBB.

Died: At Round Hill, Loudoun County, on Thursday August 29, 1889, Alice Gertrude GRIFFITH, dau. of Charles T. and the late Matilda GRIFFITH, and adopted daughter of Mrs. Mary E. CLARKE, of this county, aged 20y 6m 27d.

Jams. McDONOUGH died on Wednesday evening, September 4th 1889, at his home in Leesburg, the place of his nativity, and where he had sojourned for nearly 85 years. He was by occupation at wheelwright, for many years minister in M. E. Church. On Thursday afternoon, Revs. Nelson HEAD and R. T. DAVIS officiating, he was laid to rest in the burying ground of the old stone church.

Sept. Ct.: Will of Samuel W. GEORGE Sr. admitted to probate. Estate of John W. STEWART dec'd. committed to Sheriff. V. V. PURSELL appointed committee of Robt. OSBURN. Estate of Mary BROWN committed to Sheriff and power of Chas. J. BROWN, Exor. revoked. Will of Achsah W. SMITH admitted to probate and estate committed to Sheriff. Geo. W. TITUS qualified as Admr. of Geo. COOPER. Case of Thom HAMILTON (colored) with assault upon another colored man with intent to kill, found guilty and given 5 years.

Death of Mr. Thos. H. GORE, of Loudoun, a member of the firm of Gore & Janney, 929 F. St., Washington, occurred in that city Sunday Morning. He leaves a widow, the daughter of the late Nathan JANNEY. Body was brought to Loudoun on Monday and in the afternoon interred beside his parents in the Friends burying ground at Lincoln, Rev. R. T. DAVIS officiating.

Thursday, 19 September 1889   Vol. XXXIV, No. 15

Died at the residence of W. E. TRABUE, in neighborhood of Farber, Mo., at 7 p.m., August 16th 1889, Mrs. Elizabeth Josephine HURST. She was a daughter of the late Stephen R. MOUNT, and a native of Clarke Co, but a long time resident of Loudoun, where she married in early life to James W. HURST, of Jefferson Co., Va. She resided in her native state a few years when with her husband she moved to Pike Co., Missouri, and in 1882 moved to Andrain Co., where she died. She had not children. Of her original family there only survive her three sisters: Mrs. J. N. KLEIN, of Vicksburg, Miss; Mrs. S. F. ANDERSON, of Washington DC. and Mrs. G. J. BRADFIELD, of Billings, Mo.

Died: At her husband's residence, near Mountsville, Mrs. Sallie M. GOCHNAUER, wife of W. L. GOUCHNAUER, departed this life Sunday, the first day of Sept. 1889, aged 50 years. Member of the Baptist Church for 30 years and was ready to go.

Marriage license issued in Washington last week to Jno. F. DOWNS and Ella ATTWELL, of Loudoun, and on Monday last to Klein WRIGHT, of Round Hill and Virginia L. HOUGH, formerly of Leesburg.

Sept. Ct.: Estate of John JANNEY and John L. JORDAN committed to Sheriff. Will of James McDONOUGH dec'd. admitted to probate.

Thursday, 26 September 1889   Vol. XXXIV, No. 16

Married: Mr. Klein WRIGHT and Miss Virginia Lee HOUGH were married at the Episcopal parsonage in Anacostia by the Rev. W. G. DAVENPORT at 3 o'clock Tuesday afternoon, September 17. The bride wore a dress of gray Henrietta cloth and was attended by Miss Mamie QUIGLEY.

Died: Near Gumspring, Va., September 11, 1889, after a short illness, William Holmes CRAVEN, in the 68th year of his age. Funeral preached at the house by Rev. G. W. POPKINS. Interred at North Fork September 13th.

Death of James M. WALLACE of Leesburg suddenly, at his home in Hamilton, about 9 o'clock Tuesday morning in the 80th year of his age. He was engaged in mercantile pursuits in this town. He leaves a widow, his second wife, a family of 7 children. A few weeks age he visited his married daughters living in Massachusetts and returned only 10 days ago. He was a first cousin of Gen. Lew. WALLACE, author of "Ben Hur." Their fathers were brothers. Interred in Union Cemetery, Leesburg about noon today (Thursday).

Mr. Nathan LOUGHBOROUGH, formerly of Fauquier Co., and father of Mr. Augustus G. LOUGHBOROUGH, of Leesburg, died in Washington city, on Sunday morning last, September 22nd, 1889, in the 76th year of his age. Funeral took place from St. Stephen's Church, at 11 a.m. on Tuesday.

Cards are out for the marriage on Tuesday last, Sept. 24th, of Mr. John L. BALL, of Colorado (formerly of Loudoun) and Miss Mary V., daughter of the late Capt. Wm. CHISWELL, of Frederick Co., Md.

Death of Mr. G. Frank KELLY, this morning at the Infirmary, at which institution he was recently taken. He had been sick for some time at the Alexandria House and a few days since removed to the Infirmary. He was a native of Loudoun and served during the war in the 8th Va regiment. After the war he was a clerk in the store of Messrs. Gould & Wilkening. Subsequently he formed a partnership with Mr. J. W. CARR. Member of Lee Camp, who escorted his remains to Fauquier Co. for Interment. He leaves a daughter 4 years of age who will inherit estate valued at $20,000.

Thursday, 3 October 1889   Vol. XXXIV, No. 17

Died: At the home near Hillsboro, July 29th, Samuel, second son of Ann and the late Thomas McARTER, in his 32nd year, from consumption.

Died: In Leesburg, on Friday night, September 20th, after a short illness of dysentery, at the residence of her grandmother, Mrs. Catharine RYAN, Katie Celestine CROSS, oldest child of William and Annie V. CROSS, aged 9y 6m 18d.

Marriage license issued in Washington on Monday to Harry EAMICH and Bertie GRUBB, both of Lovettsville in this county.

Funeral of Mrs. Mary BURCH, wife of Edgar F. BURCH, of this county, who died last Saturday, took place from St. James Episcopal church Tuesday morning, Rev. Dr. DAVIS officiating. Interred in Union Cemetery.

Dr. Geo. B. FADELEY, of Farmwell, has recently moved to Falls Church, Fairfax Co. and entered the practice of medicine.

Death of Milton M. ROGERS, Esq. occurred at his home at Dover, last Wednesday. For the last two years he was bed-ridden. Death the result of progressive paralysis, the effect of inflammatory rheumatism, contracted during his four years service in the Confederate army. He entered the Confederate service as a member of the Loudoun Guards, in April 1861; in December of that year transferred to the Loudoun Artillery. In October 1862 he was assigned to duty with Stribling's Battery, and served there until the end of the war. He was in the 50th year of his age. His wife, the daughter of the late Col. Wm. ROGERS, of Dover, survives him. Funeral will take place tomorrow (Friday).

The new Methodist church at Round Hill was formally dedicated on Sunday last.

Hearing of Marietta (BOOZE) BROOKINS, Henry FRAZIER, and John JOHNSON alias Jack BROOKINS, all colored, arrested for complicity in the fatal shooting of Mary Ellen JACKSON col'd. on the morning of August Court day, in the suburbs of this town, was held today. ... matter submitted to the next grand jury.

Thursday, 10 October 1889 Vol. XXXIV, No. 18

Married: On the 1st of October at St. James Hotel, Washington DC, Mr. G. H. HORSEMAN to Miss Eva V. MUNDAY, by the Rev. G. W. POPKINS.

Miss Frances FAUNTLEROY, dau. of the late Capt. Charles M. FAUNTLEROY, of Leesburg, was married at Oakland Plantation, Rapides Parish, La, last Wed. week, to Mr. Charles CHAFFE Jr.

Last Saturday night David BLAIR, formerly of Kentucky, and who a few months ago married a Miss COCKERILLE, daughter of the late Bailey COCKERILLE, who resided about four miles east of Leesburg, went home drunk and assaulted his wife. The wife's mother, quite an old woman, went to the daughter's rescue, when BLAIR threatened to kill her and called for his pistol. She rushed from the house crying he will kill me, soon expired, literally scared to death. BLAIR was arrested.

Mr. John SHAEFFER, a farmer, residing four miles east of Charlestown, W. Va. committed suicide at his home at 7 o'clock Monday morning, by shooting himself through the head with a pistol. He was about 45 years of age and leaves a widow and one child.

Thursday, 17 October 1889 Vol. XXXIV, No. 19

Married: On the 3d inst., at the residence of the officiating clergyman, by the Rev. Dr. Nelson HEAD, Mr. C. F. HAWLING to Miss Mollie M. BROWN, all of Loudoun.

Married: At the bride's residence, in Washington DC, on Thursday, October 10th 1889, by Rev. GREEN, Mrs. George LAYCOCK, of Hamilton, to Miss Ella G. JOHNSON, of Washington.

Died: In Leesburg, September 21st, Robert Henry, youngest child of Henrietta and Smith McGILL, aged 5y 13d.

Died: September 30th 1889, Mrs. Fannie THOMPSON, wife of Eli THOMPSON, in the 26th year of her age. she leaves four step-daughters and a babe two weeks old.

Unexpected death of Mr. C. B. HESS, Dry Goods merchant, occurred at his home in Leesburg, Monday night. He leaves a wife and one child. He was in about the 33d year of his age. Funeral took place on Wednesday morning, Rev. B. W. BOND, assisted by Rev. Dr. Nelson HEAD, officiating. Interred in Union Cemetery.

Oct. Ct.: Wills of James M. WALLACE dec'd., Jacob SCOTT dec'd., M. M. ROGERS dec'd., Wm. KOLB and Susan Ann VIRTS dec'd. admitted to probate. Estate of Abel WARFORD dec'd. committed to Sheriff.

Mr. Robert E. L. SMITH, of Marshal, Mo. with his wife and little child is visiting his grandmother, Mrs. M. A. BURKE.

Marriage licenses issued in Washington last week to Murray D. PHILLIPS and Rosie E. BROWN, both of this county.

Col. Richard S. COX died at his home in Georgetown Saturday afternoon, in the 65th year of his age. Prior to the war the deceased was Col. of the District militia and after the war resided in Loudoun.

[MISSING ISSUES]

Thursday, 14 November 1889   Vol. XXXIV, No. 23

Married: On Wed. morning, Nov. 13th 1889, at the residence of Mrs. Orra M. FADELY, grandmother of the bride, by Rev. B. W. BOND, Mr. David L. GRAYSON, of Chattanooga, Tennessee and Miss May, daughter of the late Capt. Alfred GLASCOCK, of this county.

Married: On Wednesday, November 6, by the Rev. J. P. CAMPBELL, of Faith Presbyterian Church, David A. BRECKENRIDGE, of Leesburg, to Miss Estelle E. SIMS, of Washington DC.

Married: October 9th 1889, at the parsonage of the M. E. Church, South, by Rev. B. W. BOND, James SKILLMAN and Annie POLLARD.

Married: At the parsonage of the M. E. Church, South, Leesburg, on Tuesday, November 5th 1889, by Rev. B. W. BOND, Chas. T. MORIARTY and Kate CLARK, all of Loudoun.

Died: Elma COLE, little daughter of Mr. K. B. COLE, which occurred on the 5th of November, about 1 p.m., of diphtheria. About 2:30 the following Thursday she was laid to rest by the side of her cousin Robert DAVIS, who preceded her only a few months.

Lewen T. JONES, farmer of this county, died very suddenly at his home near Waterford, on Thursday last, in about his 65th year, of apoplexy. A son of the late Philip JONES, of Winchester, and a nephew of the late Commodore Ap. Catesby JONES. Interred in Union Cemetery, Leesburg, on Saturday, Rev. H. BRANCH, officiating.

Rev. Jas. Henderson SMITH, Presbyterian minister, and son of Gen. Francis H. SMITH, Superintendant of the Va Military Institute, died at his home in Lexington, Va, last Saturday morning. He was for several years pastor of the Presbyterian church in Leesburg. He leaves a wife and several young children.

Nov. Ct.: Edgar McCRAY qualified as Admr. of Dr. R. W. JANNEY dec'd.; C. Powell NOLAND as Admr. of Susan C. NOLAND dec'd. Wills of Elizabeth SHUMAKER, Mary E. CLARK and Burr P. NOLAND admitted to probate.

Unison: Funeral sermon of Miss Susie HOSPITAL of Falls Church, Va. was preached in the Ebenezer Baptist church on Tuesday, 5th inst., by Rev. David HARRIS.

Mrs. E. T. JACOB of Philomont died on last Saturday morning after an illness of two weeks.

On Wed. evening, October 30th, 1889, a 15 year old daughter of a gentleman of this county, was returning to her home from the Academy at Hamilton, she was assaulted at a somewhat secluded point in the road, with an attempt at rape by Owen ANDERSON, a negro 19 or 20 years old. Her screams and resistance frightened her assailant who fled. She said she believed her assailant was Orion ANDERSON. ANDERSON was arrested but the girl was unable to identify him because he was disguised when the assault was made, and he was released. The next day her friends searched the ground and fund an old guano sack which was known to have been in ANDERSON's possession the day of the assault. ANDERSON confessed his guilt. Last Thursday night between 12 and 1 o'clock a group entered the jail, took ANDERSON, and hung him and shot on a derrick at the old depot now the freight depot of the Richmond & Danville Railroad in Leesburg.. Witnesses at trial were Joe BROOKINS (col.); C. F. LAYCOCK, jailor; W. R. WEBB, night police; Elizabeth HUNTON (col.); Henry JOHNSON (col.); L. W. SHEPHERD; and Wm. LAYTON (col.) The raiders were not known.

[MISSING ISSUE]

Thursday, 28 November 1889   Vol. XXXIV, No. 25

Married: In Culpeper, November 13th by Rev. C. F. JAMES, Prof. C. B. WALLACE, of Nashville, Tenn., and Miss Mary BARBOUR, second daughter of Hon. Jas. BARBOUR, and niece of Senator John S. BARBOUR.

Married: In Leesburg, on Tuesday, November 26th 1889, by Rev. N. HEAD, D.D., Mr. Arthur MULLEN and Miss Ada BROOKS, daughter of the late Philip W. BROOKS, all of this place.

Died: At her home, at Luckett's Cross Roads, on the 10th of October 1889, Mary LUCKETT, widow of the late Wm. C. LUCKETT, in the 77th year of her age.

Joseph G. RODGERS, son of Rev. Samuel RODGERS, D.D., of the M. E. Church, South, died at his father's home, in Staunton, last Thursday, in the 16th year of his age. Interred in Greenmount Cemetery, Baltimore, at 4 o'clock Saturday afternoon.

Cards are out for the marriage on Wednesday next, December 4th 1889, at 11 o'clock in Memorial church, Aldie, of Mr. [torn off, Chas. on marriage reg.] T. HAWLING and Miss Jennie, daughter of Mr. Wm. GAINES, of this county.

At new Baptist Church in Hamilton at 11:30 last Thursday morning, the first bride with marriage of Mr. Albert SCANLAND and Miss Rose CHAMBLIN, daughter of Mrs. __ and Peyton CHAMBLIN dec'd. Bridesmaids Misses Lullu WHARTON, of Washington, Miss Laura CHAMBLIN, sister to bride, and Miss Phila CRAIG. Messrs. W. W. CHAMBLIN of Leesburg, Mr. Arthur NICHOLS of Washington and Mr. HAMPTON, were groomsmen. Little maids of honor – Miss Hazel KEEN and Miss Mabel WILMARTH. Rev. C. T. HERNDON performed the ceremony.

Miss Sallie ROSS, in her 88th year, visited her niece Mrs. Thomas E. WOODWARD, near Summit Point.

Mr. Richard H. RUST died from congestion of the lungs at the residence of his son, Mr. N. A. RUST, in Luray, about 4 o'clock in Tuesday morning last, at the age of 75y 9m 19d. He was born near Leesburg, but lived the greater portion of his life in Fauquier Co., having removed to Page about 14 years ago.

Thursday, 5 December 1889   Vol. XXXIV, No. 26

Married: At the residence of John H. ALEXANDER, in Leesburg, Wednesday, November 27th 1889, by the Rev. C. T. HERNDON, Mr. D. H. TITUS and Miss Hattie V. WHITE, all of Loudoun.

Married: On the 27th inst., near Lovettsville, by the Rev. St. J. RINKER, Mr. Kenny C. CHINN and Miss Emma V. SOUDER, daughter of Mr. Geo. P. SOUDER, all of Loudoun.

Married: On Monday, Nov. 18, 1889, by Rev. A. R. REILEY, Fenelon D. HAY, of Washington DC, to Bessie E. SURVICK, of Leesburg.

Married: At the residence of the bride's father, J. T. SKINNER, Octavia, Neb., November 23, 1889, Rev. BENTLEY officiating, Prof. M. M. SMITH, formerly of Highland Co., O., to Miss Alice SKINNER, formerly of Loudoun Co. Both are leading educators of Nebraska.

Died: In Washington, on Sunday, December 1, 1889, at 7:20 p.m., Margaret A. POLAND, widow of the late Alexander POLAND. Interment at Leesburg on Thursday the 5th instant.

Died: On Sunday, December 1, 1889, Edgar COOPER, son of John W. and Sarah A. COOPER, aged 13y 5m 6d.

Died: Nov. 5, 1889, Mary Elma COLE, aged 11y 7m, the youngest dau. of Kendric and Jennie COLE.

Death on Friday last shortly before midnight of consumption, of Mr. Thomas R. MOORE. His first wife was a sister of Mr. A. DIBRELL, cashier of the Loudoun National Bank, and his second wife a daughter of the late Jas. H. CHAMBLIN of this town. He was the son of Thomas and Judith MOORE and born November 11, 1831 in county of Greenesville. He removed to Gaston N, C. at an early age and remained until 1849, when he moved to Petersburg. ...He married a daughter of the late Rev. Anthony DIBRELL of the Va Conference in 1855. After her death he married Miss Helen CHAMBLIN of Leesburg, who survives him with one son. He was connected with the Market Street Methodist Church.

Lexington Dec. 2: Major John D. ROGERS, solicitor of the Chesapeake & Ohio Railroad, son of the late Gen. Asa ROGERS, and ex-Auditor of Va, relative of Gen. R. E. LEE, chief quartermaster Gen. D. H. HILL's division, Army of Northern Va C.S.A., died Sunday from injuries received in a railroad collision at Scottsville, in August last. He was buried from the Lee Memorial Episcopal Church today.

In Aldie last Wednesday morning, 4th inst., the marriage of Mr. Chas. T. HAWLING to Miss Jennie GAINES, a handsome blonde and eldest daughter of Wm. GAINES, Esq. of Oatlands at Memorial Church in Aldie, by Rev. C. M. BROWN. Ushers were Wells A. HARPER and Ed. B. HARRISON of Leesburg. They will reside at "Wheatland," the country home of the groom.

Wedding on Thursday, Nov. 28 at 12 m. at the M. E. Church, South, in Paris, Va, of Miss Ada Warren GIBSON, dau. of Mr. H. D. GIBSON to Rev. J. C. JONES, of Washington City. Bride attired in suit of blue plush trimmed in corded Passementerie ornaments with hat to match trimmed in tips and ribbons, carried cream chrysanthemums and smilax. Ushers Mr. Herman D. GIBSON, brother of the bride; Prof. Stanhope HENRY, Rev. C. D. HARRIS and Mr. Tyson JANNEY, friends of the groom. Performed by Rev. J. C. DICE.

Thursday, 12 December 1889   Vol. XXXIV, No. 27

Judge Thomas Claiborne GREEN, Pres. of the W. Va. Ct. of Appeals, died at his home in Charlestown last week, aged 69 years. Native of Culpeper Co Va but had resided in Charlestown for nearly 40 years. For several years after the war he practised law in Loudoun.

Married: November 28th 1880 [1889] in Trinity Methodist Church, Paris, Va, by Rev. J. C. DICE, Rev. John Clay JONES, pastor of Grace m.

E. Church, South, Washington DC and Miss Ada WARREN, daughter of Douglass GIBSON, Esq.

Married: In Baltimore, November 28, 1889, by the Rev. F. T. LITTLE, W. T. HACKETT of Baltimore, Md, and Miss Ellen B. MEANS of Washington DC, formerly of Loudoun County.

Died: At the residence of her son, Mr. Thos. G. ELGIN, near Leesburg, on Tuesday night, December 10th, 1889, Mrs. Mary J. ELGIN, widow of the late Francis ELGIN, in the 85th year of her age. Funeral will take place today (Thursday) at 2 p.m.

Co. Ct.: Annie S. FRY qualified as Guardian of John T. FRY, Malinda E. FRY and Wm. B. FRY. R. W. GRUBB qualified as Admr. of Eliza JANNEY dec'd.; W. R. JONES as Admr. of Lewen T. JONES dec'd. Estate of Wm. H. STEPHENSON dec'd. committed to Sheriff.

Wills of Eliza and Mary TATE admitted to probate.

Mr. Solomon RUSE, living near here, passed quietly away last Saturday night. For several year he had been confined to his house. He had passed his 91st birthday a little over two months. A sister, living in the west, who died a few years ago, lived past a century. He was connected with the M. E. Church, South, for nearly half century. funeral at the M. E. Church last Tuesday noon by Rev. Mr. EGGLESTON, and attended by Mr. Hiram TAVENNER, 82; Mr. Joseph HELM, 84; and Mr. Samuel CROCKET, nearly 90.

Thursday, 19 December 1889   Vol. XXXIV, No. 28

Died: Mrs. Julia A., wife of Samuel SLATER, and only sister of Peter A. FRY, died at the residence of her husband, 3 miles east of Lovettsville, on Monday morning, Dec. 2nd 1889, aged 65 years.

Died: At the residence of Mr. Henry SNOOTS, near Wheatland, Va, December 5th 1889, Daniel ADAMS, in the 79th year of his age.

Died: On December 4th 1889, in Gilmore City, Iowa, of heart disease, Mary C., wife of Rev. John W. FORSYTH, in the 44th year of her age. She was born in West Newton, Penn.

Wedding at Rock Spring, near Leesburg, the home of the bride's mother, on Wed. morning, Dec. 18th 1889, of M. D. KITE, Esq. of the drug firm of Dolly, Kite and Co., of Baltimore, formerly of Orange Co, Va, and Mary G., only dau. of the late Henry C. GIST, of this county, Rev. R. T. DAVIS, D.D. officiating. They will reside in Baltimore.

Mr. R. J. C. THOMPSON died at his home in Leesburg about midnight Tuesday, in his 79th year. Resident of Leesburg for nearly 60 years, settled her in 1831. He leaves an aged widow. Funeral will take place from the one Stone Church, of which he was for years a member, at 2:30 o'clock, this Thursday afternoon, Dec. 19, 1889.

Maj. James F. DIVINE died at the residence of his dau., Mrs. TREW, in Washington city, Thursday evening, December 12th 1889, after a short illness, in his 73d year. He always voted the Democratic ticket. At the beginning of the late war, Maj. DIVINE was holding a position in the P. O. Department of the national government, but gave that up to return to Va. Remains brought to Leesburg on Saturday morning, and conveyed to M. E. Church, South, services by Rev. Nelson HEAD, D. D. Interred in Union Cemetery.

[MISSING ISSUE]

Thursday, 2 January 1890   Vol. XXXIV, No. 30

Married: In Winchester, Va, December 26, 1889, by Rev. H. M. WHITE, Mr. J. Walter SMITH, of Loudoun County, to Miss Rachel IRISH, of Frederick County.

Married: By the Rev. John WOOLF, at his residence on the 31st of Dec. 1889, Mr. Chas. E. SONGERBEAM to Miss Sarah C. REED.

Married: In Washington DC, January 2, 1889, by Rev. S. W. HADDAWAY, William L. ELGIN and Mollie T. RODGERS.

Mr. Chas. E. GARDNER departed this life the 31st December, in the 87th year of his age. Funeral conducted by Rev. G. W. POPKINS.

Died: Of typhoid fever, on Nov. 1, 1889, Edditson GALLEHER, son of T. H. and Jane D. GALLEHER, formerly of Loudoun. He was aged 25y 7m 9d. Member of Methodist Church since Feb. 1889. Funeral preached by Rev. Mr. DUFFY. Interment at cemetery at Falls Church. Having lost his father when about 16 years of age, he took on the care of his mother, six sisters and a younger brother.

Thursday, 7 January 1890   Vol. XXXIV, No. 31

Married: By Rev. Frazier FURR, at the residence of bride's parents, Mr. Walter Gray MAFFITT to Miss Estelle ELLMORE, daughter of J. Russell ELLMORE.

Died: On January 8, 1890, in Washington, Marvin Paul, son of Wm. D. and Mary E. EASTERDAY, aged 10 days.

Died: At Sterling, January 1, 1890, Eugenia, only daughter of B. A. and Sallie N. SHREVE, aged 3y 1m.

Died: At the residence of her husband, Oscar TAYLOR, at Fall River, Kansas, January 5, 1890, Mrs. Ella F. TAYLOR, daughter of the late Luther A. THRASHER of Loudoun.

Mr. John MARLOW, son of the late George MARLOW, of this county, died at his home in St. Joseph, Mo., on Wednesday the 8th of January. He resided for several your in his early life in this community. Interred in Union Cemetery, Rev. Dr. DAVIS officiating.

Mr. John PRICE died at his home at Morrisonville, on Monday, January 6th 1890, in the 81st year of his age.

Edmund H. CHAMBERS, father of Mrs. C. W. LITTLEJOHN, of this town, died at his home in Harper's Ferry, W. Va., last Monday. He had passed his 90th birthday.

The Mirror
Thursday, 23 January 1890   Vol. XXXIV, No. 33

Death of Samuel C. HOLMES, a son of the late Wm. HOLMES, of this county, died at his home in Dover, Del., last Saturday January 11th in about the 43d year of his age, of pneumonia from la grippe.

Jas. HARRIS, colored man, died at his home in Leesburg in Monday. He was an experienced and reliable nurse.

Co. Ct.: Wm. PINN (col) found guilty of burglary and sentenced to five years. Wills of Louisa H. L. HERNDON, Solomon RUSE and Elizabeth COMPHER were admitted to probate. Estates of R. L. DAVIS and Wm. T. CLENDENNING were committed to the Sheriff.

Baltimore Sun: Wedding on Thursday at noon at the bride's residence on Linden Ave., the Rev. Dr. Wm. DAME officiating. Parties were Mr. Edward T. POWELL, of Loudoun Co., and Miss Hannis Vorhees THOMPSON. Bride was attired in a traveling gown of wine-colored broadcloth and velvet, with wrap and hat. They will reside in Va.

[MISSING ISSUE]

Thursday, 23 January 1890   Vol. XXXIV, No. 33

Married: On Thursday, January 16th 1890, at the residence of the bride's father, Mr. R. B. McCORMICK, Dover, by Rev. C. T. HERNDON, Miss Mary E. McCORMICK to Dr. John F. HICKS, of Bristol, Tenn.

Mr. George W. FLING died at his residence near Woodburn on Friday morning. Dropsy with heart failure was the cause. He was about 60 years of age.

Death of Amos HUGHES: Farmer, died at his home near Lincoln, on Monday morning last, in the 66th year of his age, of pneumonia induced by la grippe. He was sick less than ten days. He had been Pres. of the Loudoun Agricultural Society. Interred on Wednesday in the Friends' burying ground at Lincoln.

Mr. Thos. W. AYRES died at his home near Aldie, on Sunday, after a lingering illness of Bright's disease, in the 66th year of his age. Interred in Union Cemetery, Leesburg, on Tuesday.

Miss Elizabeth Sherlock WHIPPLE and Mr. Pemberton Hare POWELL were married at the residence of Mr. John WHIPPLE, at Newport R. I., on the 14th of January, performed by Rev. R. B. PEET in the famous picture gallery in the villa near the Cliffs, owned and occupied by the late Governor SWANN. Bride is a granddaughter of the late Thos. SWANN, of Md, and a niece of Dr. C. S. CARTER, of Morvan, in the county.

Clarence L. CULLEN $900 clerk in the Census Office had caused a sensation in that office by marrying Miss Hettie PRYOR, a pretty type-writer with a trace of negro blood in her veins, only about 1/16th. She is between 17 or 18 years of age. She was formerly a student of Howard University, and resided with her mother at 932 E St. SW. Mr. and Mrs. CULLEN are now in Philadelphia assisting the special agent, who is collecting statistics on mines and mining. The bride was born and resided in this community until a few years ago, as the daughter of Fanny PRYOR.

Thursday, 30 January 1890   Vol. XXXIV, No. 34

Died: In Washington DC, January 23, 1890, Samuel MORRISON, aged 65 years.

Died: At Mt. Gilead, Jan. 16th 1890, John W. DENNIS, aged 53y 3m.

Died: At her parents home near Union, Jan. 23d, 1890, Rosa Myrtle, infant daughter of J. Clay and Emma JENKINS, aged 4 months.

Died: Mrs. Annie SMALLWOOD, wife of F. M. SMALLWOOD, and daughter of Wm. C. and Amelia MORGAN, of Clark Co., Va, January 14, 1890. Funeral preached by Rev. Mr. DICE, of Loudoun circuit and buried in Ebenezer cemetery.

Mrs. Delia DONOHOE, wife of Mr. John C. DONOHOE, died at her home in this town, on Saturday evening last, after one week's illness of catarrhal pneumonia in the 48th year of her age. Member of M. E. Church, South. Funeral took place on Monday, Rev. B. W. BOND, Dr. Nelson HEAD and D. C. HEDRICK officiating. Interred in Union Cemetery.

Mrs. Rebecca WILDMAN of Leesburg died on Sunday last at an advanced age. Funeral took place on Tuesday.

Cards are out for the marriage at St. James' Episcopal Church, Leesburg, at 7 p.m. Tuesday, Feb. 18th 1890 of Miss Annie, dau. of the late R. M. BENTLY and Mr. Howard SCRIBNER, of Philadelphia.

Mr. John WRIGHT, of Orleans, Fauquier Co., and Miss Loretta ORRISON, of Hamilton, were married last Wednesday

Mr. Cassius F. LEE Sr., died this morning at 11:30, after a short illness, at his home on Cameron St. For the larger part of the century he had been a citizen of Alexandria. A grandson of Richard Henry LEE and first cousin of Gen. R. E. LEE. Elder brother of Major C. H. and Col. R. H. LEE of this town. He was in the 82d year of his age.

Marriage license issued in Washington on Monday to C. W. BARTON and Ella FURR, both of Loudoun County.

Thursday, 6 February 1890   Vol. XXXIV, No. 35

Married: On the 22d inst., at Short Hill Baptist Church, by A. A. P NEEL, J. Hoover ADAMS and Mary E. JENKINS, both of this county.

Died: On Wednesday, January 29, 1890, at 9:45 a.m., Annie Almira, wife of Edgar Heston HIRST, and daughter of W. W. and Mary F. CASE, at the home of the latter, in Washington DC.

Died: At the residence of her husband, near Snickersville, January 28th 1890, Marietta, wife of James ALLDER, aged 46 years.

Died: In Atlanta, Ga, January 27th 1890, at the residence of her son, Thos. H. HOGE, Mrs. Mary A. HOGE, relict of the late Thos. HOGE, of Loudoun County.

Died: Flavius C., only son of Jno. J. OTLEY, at his home, near Silcott's Springs, in the 16th year of his age.

Three weeks ago, Herbert OSBURN, Esq., had an attack of la grippe, and last week attacked with pneumonia. He died about 11 a.m. on Tuesday, Feb. 4th 1890, in his 47th year, leaving a wife and 3 little children. Born in Unison, and in June 1861 joined the Confederate services as a private in Co A 6th Va Cavalry where he served until paroled in 1865. Later he became a teacher in the public schools and married a daughter of Mr. Jno. H. WHITMORE. ... Member of the Masonic Fraternity and M. E. Church, South. Funeral by Rev. B. W. BOND assisted by Rev. R. T. DAVIS, will take pace today (Thurs.) at 2 p.m. from St. James Episcopal Church.

Death of Mr. Frank FURR, at his home a few miles each of Leesburg, last Friday morning in about the 36th year of his age from pneumonia. Farmer, he leaves a widow and five young children. Funeral by Rev. Dr. DAVIS took place on Sunday morning. Interment in Union Cemetery. Member of Ketoctin Lodge, No. 32.

Thursday, 13 February 1890   Vol. XXXIV, No. 36

Married: At the residence of Ish Myers, February 6, 1890, by Rev. D. C. HEDRICK, Mr. Jos. W. CORDELL to Miss Amanda E. STOUT, all of Loudoun County.

Married: On the 5th inst., near North Fork, by Rev. C. T. HERNDON, Robt. WILLIAMS to Maud SPALDING, all of Loudoun.

Died: At her home near Philomont, February 5th 1890, Mrs. Delilah BEAVERS, widow of the late Thos. BEAVERS, in her 84th year.

Feb. Ct.: Administrations granted on estates of Frank N. FURR dec'd., Amos HUGHES dec'd., Geo. W. FLING dec'd., Catherine CHAMP dec'd. and Wm. SMITH dec'd. Will of Herbert OSBURN dec'd. admitted to probate. Estate of Wm. E. LUCKETT committed to Sheriff.

We notice in the Washington papers, the death in that city, on Sunday, February 9th, 1890, of Mrs. Catherine GOVER, relict of the late Robert GOVER, of Leesburg, in the 92nd year of her age.

Last Thursday, Herbert OSBURN interred in Union Cemetery.

Wm. H. GRAY died on Saturday February 8th, 1890, at the rectory, the residence of his son, Rev. Arthur P. GRAY, at Amherst C. H. Va, in his 85th year, having been born in Loudoun Co in 1805. He was a successful lawyer and Mayor of Leesburg for several years. He was the brother of Messrs. John and Joseph GRAY, of Loudoun and Rockingham Co. he married first, Miss Francis ELLZEY, dau. of Col. Wm. ELLZEY, and second, Miss Ellen D. POWELL, dau. of Hon. Cuthbert POWELL, of Llangollen, Loudoun. J. Bradshaw BEVERLEY and Robert BEVERLEY Jr., Rev. Arthur P. GRAY, of Amherst Co., and Mrs. Catherine McDONALD, wife of Prof.

McDONALD, of Berryville, Clarke Co, are among his surviving descendants. Funeral from St. James' Episcopal Church here.

Wm. DODD and his wife, residing near Mountville – Mrs. DODD died on Monday the 10th inst. and her husband died the next day, Tuesday, the 11th. Both had passed their three score and ten.

Rockville, Md.: Wedding at St. John's Church, at Olney, in that county, last Wednesday afternoon, February 5th, of Miss Margaret Bowie CHICHESTER, the eldest daughter of Washington B. CHICHESTER, Esq. and Mr. Warrington G. SMITH, of Baltimore. The bride was attired in white ottoman silk, and bridal veil fastened with diamond ornaments with lilies of the valley and Marguerite roses. Her cousin, Mr. G. Mason CHICHESTER, of Leesburg, was an usher. Guest include Mrs. PAGE, of Nashville, Tenn, and Miss Janie CHICHESTER, of Leesburg, cousins of the bride; and A. M. CHICHESTER, of Leesburg, uncle of the bride. Ceremony took place at five o'clock, Rev. Dr. HUTTON, assisted by Rev. W. H. LAIRD, officiating. They will reside in Baltimore where the groom is engaged in business as a flour merchant.

Unison: Mrs. Delilah BEAVERS died at the home of her son, Mr. O. L. BEAVERS, on Wednesday last. Rev. J. C. DICE preached, interred in the old Bethesda Grave Yard.

Thursday, 20 February 1890 Vol. XXXIV, No. 37

Married: On the 12th inst., at the residence of the bride's father, by Rev. C. T. HERNDON, Howard THOMPSON to Mary E. TRUSSELL, all of Loudoun.

Married: On January 15th 1890, at the home of the bride, by Rev. J. E. ZERGER, Flavius J. HOWELL, of Round Hill, to Miss Florence J. MICHAEL, of near Mountain Dale, Frederick Co., Md.

Died: On February 11th 1890, Charlotte E. DENHAM, daughter of L. H. DENHAM and the late Caroline DENHAM, at her late residence, 463 G St NW, Washington DC.

Died: At the home of her sister, Elizabeth GREGG, near Philomont, on the 14th of second month, Mary N. WALTERS, in her 58th year.

Last Saturday, the death of Mr. John R. CURRY, who died of pneumonia after a short illness in about his 53d year. He was a plasterer by occupation. Interred in Union Cemetery on Monday, Rev. J. C. DINWIDDIE of the Presbyterian church officiating.

Mr. Tolliver BOLYN, brother of Mr. S. BOLYN, died at his home in Purcellville last Friday.

Mrs. McCREA, wife of Mr. Wm. McCREA, near Hamilton, died on Sunday, the 9th inst., at an advanced age.

Mr. Eli HOGE, member of the Society of Friends, farmer, died at his home near Hughesville on Tuesday last in his 72d year. He was at first seized with severe vomiting and within 48 hours was a corpse.

Mr. Mahlon SCHOOLEY, a Quaker minister from Waterford, with his new wife (formerly Miss ROWZEE, of Warren Co.) were in town on Tuesday.

St. James Episcopal Church, Leesburg, last Tuesday evening, February 25th 1890, married of Mr. Howard SCRIBNER of New York and Miss Anna, youngest daughter of late R. Montgomery BENTLEY of this town. [long article] They will reside in New York.

Thursday, 27 February 1890   Vol. XXXIV, No. 38

Wedding in the Presbyterian Church, Leesburg, at 12:30 Wed. Feb 26th 1890, Rev. J. C. DINWIDDIE officiating, Mr. R. C. VASS, of Culpeper C. H. Va, and Miss Adda B., dau. of Mr. Robert HARPER, of Loudoun. Ushers were W. McDOUGAL, of Washington, W. W. CHAMBLIN of Leesburg, Robt. N. HARPER of Washington and Wells A. HARPER, of Leesburg – the last two brothers of the bride.

Mrs. Jane ORRISON died near Sterling in this county last Saturday.

Mrs. Louisa FORSYTH, wife of Mr. Wm. T. FORSYTH, of this town, died on Monday last, in the 66th year of her age.

Mr. J. Thos. STEADMAN, of this town, died at his home on Tuesday last, in about the 50th year of his age.

Died: At her parents' home near Goresville, February 18th 1890, Una Moran, infant daughter of John H. and Lillie M. MISKELL, of convulsions, aged 2m 11d.

[MISSING ISSUE]

Thursday, 13 March 1890   Vol. XXXIV, No. 40

Married: At the residence of the bride's father, on Tuesday, the 4th inst. by Rev. B. W. BOND, Mr. Robt. E. ADRAIN to Miss Melissa McPHERSON, all of Loudoun.

Died: In Macon, Georgia, March 3rd 1890, Stirling Murray, son of Sallie H. and Dr. W. R. WINCHESTER, aged 19 months.

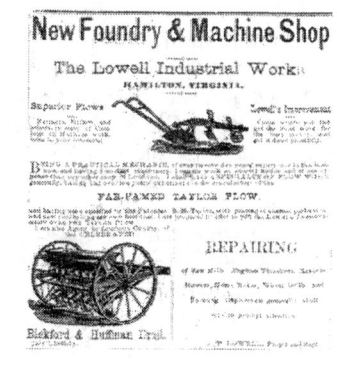

Died: On the 27th of February, at his home near Woodgrove, Reuben JENKINS departed this life in his 83rd year. He had been in ill health for several years. One of the best farmers in Loudoun. He equipped two sons for the Confederate Army. Buried at Salem M. E. Church.

Died: February 17th 1890, at his residence, near the Trappe, Loudoun Co, Carr Bayly NALLS, in his 84th year. Member for 52 years of

Methodist Church. Fifty years of his life were spent teaching school. Buried in Methodist Church yard at Upperville.

Died: At Landsdown, Prince William Co, Va March 1st 1890, Mrs. Harriet R. HIXSON, relict of Abner H. HIXSON, in the 80th year of her age. Member of the Old School Baptist Church at Mt. Zion, for 38 years. She leaves two daughters.

At Belmont, last Friday afternoon, Jesse, 6 year old son of Mr. Henry ELLIOTT was accidentally shot and killed by a discharged from a pistol in the hands of an elder brother.

Miss Jane, youngest dau. of Major E. H. JANNEY, formerly of Hamilton, in this county, died at the residence of her father, near Alexandria, on Tuesday morning last, after an illness of but a few days.

March Ct.: Wills of Reuben JENKINS, Mary J. ELGIN, Ruth H. SMITH, Thos. W. AYRES and William DODD dec'd. admitted to probate. Isaac FLETCHER qualified as Admr. of Mary E. FLETCHER dec'd. Estates of Wm. GODFREY, John CRIDLER, Peter SKINNER and James HARRIS committed to Sheriff. Geo. D. HOGE qualified as Admr. of Delilah H. BEAVERS dec'd.

Mrs. Rachael HAVENER, of Loudoun, and mother of Mr. R. H. HAVENER, of this city, died at her home near Farmwell, Tuesday morning, aged 79 years.

Thursday, 20 March 1890 Vol. XXXIV, No. 41

Married: At the Reformed Church, Lovettsville, on the 8th inst., by the Rev. H. St. J. RINKER, Mr. Charles BOOTH to Miss Fannie B. GREEN, all of Loudoun.

Died: On February 15th 1890, Mrs. Jane E. ORRISON, at the residence of her son-in-law, J. W. WHALEY, Sterling, Va.

Died: At her residence near Lovettsville, the ?? [blurred] inst., Mrs. Isaac FRY, in the 78th year of her age.

Death of Jonathan KEEN, residing near Unison, from accident last Thursday afternoon. He was thrown from his horse and fell in front of a wagon with locked wheels on a hill. He married a Miss SOWERS of Clarke Co, who with a son, survive. On Sunday the remains were taken to Berryville for interment. In his 63d year.

Rev. Andrew ROBEY, of the Baltimore Conference, died Thursday night.

Mrs. Elizabeth HOWELL died on Saturday last, at the residence of Col. E. V. WHITE, in her 91st year. Member of Col. WHITE's household for a number of years. Member of the Old Baptist Church, interred on Monday in the burial ground of the Valley Church.

Mr. Hiriam N. TAVENNER died at his home in Hamilton last Thursday morning after a short illness, in the 83d year of his age. For many years postmaster at Hamilton.

Cards are out for the marriage at Trinity Church, Washington DC, on Thursday evening, March 27th 1880 [1890] at 8 o'clock, of Mr.

Herbert C. EASTERDAY, formerly of Leesburg, and Miss Ellora EDRINGTON, dau. of Col. Samuel SIMPSON, of Washington.

Thursday, 27 March 1890   Vol. XXXIV, No. 42

Married: By the Rev. John WOOLF, at his residence, March 11th 1890, Mr. Benjamin DUKE and Miss Lena WILEY, both of Clarke Co.

Married: By the same at his residence, March 13th, Mr. John W. BEANS and Mrs. Harriet A. WYNKOOP, all of Loudoun.

Died: John Eveleth, son of John M. and L. C. STEADMAN, born February 15, 1890, died March 14th 1890, aged 28 days.

Died: March 12, 1890, in Leesburg, Clifton M. ROLLINS, son of Samuel M. and Laura ROLLINS, aged 8y 2m.

Mrs. Sarah BENEDUM, widow of the late Jas. H. BENEDUM, and daughter of the late Edward HAMMETT, of this town, died at her home in Hamilton on Thursday last, of pneumonia, in about the 68th year of her age. Remains brought to Leesburg on Saturday and interred in Union Cemetery.

Mrs. Jane McVEIGH, widow of the late Jas. N. McVEIGH, died in Alexandria last week, at the age of 83 years.

Mr. John E. GREEN died at the residence of his son in Leesburg on the morning of the 20th inst., in the 89th year of his age. Interred in Union cemetery Sunday afternoon.

In Winchester on Tuesday morning last, Mr. Bruce WORTHINGTON was married to Miss Flora HANCOCK of the same city. Groom is a son of Maj. C. E. WORTHINGTON, of this town, and is engaged in the wholesale tobacco business in Winchester.

Aldie: Mrs. John CHINN died on the 22nd inst. Services held at the house on Monday, by the Rev. Mr. TURNER, of the Episcopal Church, of which she was a member. Laid to rest in family burying ground.

Thursday, 3 April 1890   Vol. XXXIV, No. 43

Married: March 20, 1890, at New Jerusalem Church, by Rev. Dr. D. SCHENDLER, Mr. Wm. HUNTER to Miss Claretta M. FRY, both of Loudoun County.

Frederick, March 28: Mrs. Emma TYLER, wife of Dr. R. Bradley TYLER and dau. of Gen. Edward SHRIVER, of Baltimore, died at her residence, on West Third St, this city, last night, of lockjaw. She was in the 42d year of her age.

Thos. M. CARPER, of Fairfax Co., died at his home near Dranesville, last Sat. morning, after a short illness. He was a brother of Mr. Philip W. CARPER, of this county. Interred in Union Cemetery, Leesburg, on Sunday, Rev. B. W. BOND, officiating.

Wm. ELLZEY, eldest son of the late Thos. ELLZEY, died at his home near Farmwell, last Sunday morning. Sick for some time. Buried in old family burying ground, in Broad Run District, on Monday.

Mr. Wm. H. CLOWE died suddenly on Wed. at his home near Guilford, heart disease seems to be the cause. He was about 68 years of age. Interred in Union Cemetery, Leesburg, Friday afternoon, Elder E. V. WHITE officiating.

George RHODES, eldest son of the late George RHODES, of this county, died at his home in Georgetown DC, last Thursday morning, after a protracted illness in the 79th year of his age. He was a native of Loudoun, but resided in Georgetown for more than 40 years. Funeral on Saturday morning from Holy Trinity Church.

Mrs. LACEY, wife of Mr. B. F. LACEY, died at her home in this town Sunday night, of paralysis. She leaves a husband and one child. She was in about the 26th year of her age.

Mr. Lewis M. SHUMATE, business man of Dalton, Georgia, died at his home there last week, in the 24th year of his aged, after a protracted illness. He was a brother-in-law of Mr. Dorsey BRIDGES and a nephew of Mr. L. M. SHUMATE of this county.

At Hillsboro, on the 31st March 1890, by the Rev. Jas. GRUBB, of Baltimore, Nina, daughter of Thomas CAMP, of Hillsboro to N. Janney, son of J. H. PURSELL, of this county. Performed in the Methodist Church, South at 7:30 p.m. Procession: children Master Frank HOUGH and Miss Annie ERWIN carrying flowers, Messrs. Claude M. ACKLAND, of Washington, Eppa PURSELL, Albert GREGG and A. M. WHITE, Miss Nannie CAMP, sister of the bride, dressed in Orange tarleton and satin, Miss CABELL in red, Miss WHITE in blue, and Miss KILGOUR in pink. Brides dress in white silk and tulle, with lilies of the valley.

[MISSING ISSUE]

Thursday, 17 April 1890   Vol. XXXIV, No. 45

Married: In Washington DC, March 6th 1890, in the M. E. Church, South, by Rev. S. W. HADDAWAY, Mr. Charles J. GATES, of Washington, and Miss Ada CURRY, formerly of Leesburg.

Married: On the 8th inst., at the residence of Mr. Geo. W. SCHOOLEY, in Waterford, by Rev. J. S. WICKLINE, Mr. Elliott S. DONALDSON and Miss Emma J. SPURGEON, both of Loudoun.

April Ct.: Wills of Jno. PRICE, Colvin COATES, Thos. SETTLE, Eli J. HOGE, Hiram V. TAVENNER, Mary M. KERN, Rachel HAVENNER, Mary S. DANA, Henry B. HUTCHISON, and Michael WIARD admitted to probate. F. W. CHINN qualified as Admr. of Jno. L. CHINN dec'd. G. Ludwell SEATON appointed Committee of Jos. G. EACHES. Powers of V. V. PURSELL, committee of Robt. OSBURN revoked.

Miss Minnie MITCHELL, daughter of the late Rev. Jas. MITCHELL, of Mississippi and niece of Messrs. John and Thos. HUTCHISON, near Leesburg, left last Tuesday for a visit in that state.

John W. WILDMAN, senior member of dry good house of Wildman & Co., died at his home in Leesburg, at 5 p.m. on Monday April 14th 1890, in the 70th year of his age. Member of first graduating class in Va Military Institute a half century ago. ... Member of St. James Episcopal Church. Funeral by Rev. Dr. DAVIS, took place from the late residence of the deceased. Wednesday afternoon, at 4 o'clock. Interment in Union Cemetery.

Mr. T. R. TILLETT Jr. of Middleburg, left Leesburg on Monday for Roanoke, Va, where he will engage in the real estate business.

Miss Mollie B. LUCKETT, daughter of Mr. Samuel C. LUCKETT, died at her home in Waterford, Sunday, March 16, 1890.

[MISSING ISSUES]

Thursday, 8 May 1890 Vol. XXXIV, No. 48

Died: Friday, April 18th 1890, near Wheatland, Mrs. Sarah N. HOUGH, aged 72 years, wife of Mr. Wm. N. HOUGH. She was in delicate health for several years. She leaves a husband and son.

Died: Mrs. Ella STOUFFER died at her home at Point of Rocks, on the 20th of April, 1890. She was a daughter of Mrs. Ann E. HICKMAN, of Taylortown, and wife of Mr. Frank STOUFFER, of Pt. of Rocks, Md. She was in the 32d year of her age. She leaves a husband and three little children. Member of the Episcopal Church.

Died: Lewis Albert, son of E. A. and the late Wm. SMITH, died at his home near Lovettsville, Friday, April 25th 1890, after a short illness of bronchial-pneumonia, aged 19 years. Funeral from the Lutheran Church, Sunday, the 27th, Rev. Dr. SCHINDLER officiating.

Mr. Clarkson T. COLBERT and Miss B. M. HUTCHISON, both of Va, were married at Mt. Vernon Church last evening, the Rev. Mr. WEIGHTMAN officiating. Bride wore a traveling suit of blue and carried yellow roses. Bridesmaids were Miss Maggie HUTCHINSON and Miss Nannie CLEMENTS. Ushers were Mr. L. F. MATTINGLY and Mr. J. A. HUTCHISON. They will reside in Waterford.

Rev. A. D. POLLOCK, D.D., died in Warrenton, on Saturday evening last, aged 81. Presbyterian clergyman, a native of Pa and first cousin of Gov. POLLOCK, of that state. He came to Va 60 years ago and married a daughter of Charles LEE. He pastorated at Culpeper, Richmond, Wilmington, Delaware, and Warrenton. ... Father of the late Chas. L. POLLOCK, and Mrs. Chas. P. JANNEY, of Leesburg. His eldest son, Gordon POLLOCK, of Confederate army, was killed at Gettysburg.

Thursday, 15 May 1890 Vol. XXXIV, No. 49

Married: At the parsonage of the M. E. Church, South, on Thursday, May 8, 1890, by Rev. B. W. BOND, Mr. Ewell B. ATTWELL to Mrs. Maggie HEAD, both of Leesburg.

Died: Near Farmwell, May 2nd 1890, Carrie B., daughter of Charles and Alice D. MYERS, aged 1y 8m 26d.

May Ct.: Wills of Newton SETTLE dec'd. and Thornton WHITACRE dec'd. admitted to probate. Estate of Daniel PAYNE (col.) committed to Sheriff. Geo. C. LYON qualified as Admr. of Mary E. LYON dec'd.; W. S. SUMMERS as Admr. of Sanford COCKERILLE dec'd.; Summerfield BOLYN as Admr. of T. M. BOLYN dec'd.; Wm. J. STONE as Admr. of Michael WIARD dec'd. Eva R. SWANK qualified as guardian of Sarah E. and Jno. W. SWANK. A. H. DAVIS, col'd., licensed to celebrate the rite of matrimony.

The old "Dry Mill" on the road from Leesburg to Hughesville, burned last Friday afternoon. Named from fact that its water power was insufficient to keep it steadily running. Only mill in this vicinity that did not fall before the torch of war.

At Clerk's Office, Thos. POPKINS, aged 53 and Annie BROCKMAN, aged 50 were married by Rec. C. T. HERNDON.

Dr. Robt. Conrad POWELL, physician of this city (Alexandria) died at his residence on north Washington St., at 12:15 this morning after a long illness from a complication of diseases. A son of the late Dr. Wm. POWELL, physician of this place, and was born nearly 52 years ago. ... He married a daughter of the late Wm. GREGORY and leaves a widow and three children. He was a son of the late Dr. M. L. POWELL, of this town, and a brother of Capt. E. B. POWELL, formerly of Leesburg.

Rev. A. D. POLLOCK, D. D., died at his residence in Warrenton, on Saturday, May 3rd 1890, aged 83 years. ... He married with Elizabeth G. (daughter of Charles LEE, formerly Att'y Gen. of the U.S.) She with four daughters survive him. [long article]

Thursday, 22 May 1890   Vol. XXXIV, No. 50

Death of Henry HEATON, Esq., State Senator from Loudoun and Fauquier Co., occurred at his rooms in Leesburg, about midnight on Saturday, Mary 17th 1890, of apoplexy. Had been in bad health for sometime past. Youngest son of the late Dr. Jonathan HEATON, of this county. Born at Woodgrove, the old family homestead, on the 18th March 1834, age 57 years. ...Ft. Lt. in the Loudoun Artillery, at first battle of Manassas. He was a younger member of a family of ten children, only two of whom survive him, a brother Capt. N. R. HEATON and a sister, Mrs. Rodney PURCELL. On Sunday afternoon remains taken to his old home at Woodgrove, the residence of his brother. Funeral at 11:30 Tuesday morning by Rev. Dr. I. B. LAKE, of the Baptist church. Interred Short Hill Church. [very long article]

Mrs. POWERS, wife of Mr. Chas. POWERS, residing a few miles east of Leesburg, and dau. of Mr. Jas. H. MUSE, of Hamilton, was taken suddenly ill last Sunday night and died in a few minutes. Leaves an infant less than one week old. Buried at Mt. Hope on Tuesday.

Mrs. Orra M. CARTER, formerly of Hamilton, and mother of Dr. Paul CARTER of the Columbia Hospital, died at her home in Washington City last Sunday night. Interred at Oak Hill Cemetery on Tuesday.

Dr. Thos. PHILLIPS, Asst. Surgeon of the Insane Asylum at Stockton, Ca (formerly of Loudoun) and wife are visiting.

John WELSH, son of Mr. __ WELSH, of Middleburg, died at his father's house last Thursday, in about the 20th year of his age. Student at Randolph Macon College. Funeral took place on Saturday. [later memoriam gives as Jno. J. Welsh].

Death of Col. R. J. T. WHITE at his home near Hamilton, on Sunday last, in about his 68th year. He represented the county in the Senate of Virginia. At start of war he removed to Arkansas and for some time was Secretary of State. He returned to Loudoun after the war.

Thursday, 29 May 1890   Vol. XXXIV, No. 51

Married: May 15, 1890, by Rev. John WOOLF, at his residence, Mr. Jerome B. GRAY and Miss Julia GOUGH, all of Loudoun.

Married: In Leesburg, on Saturday, May 24th 1890, by Rev. B. W. BOND, Jno. RICE and Alice C. RECTOR, all of Loudoun.

Died: At the residence of her son-in-law, Mr. Phillip HOWSER, at Farmwell, Apr. 16, 1890, Mrs. Harriet HIGGINS, in her 61st year.

Rev. Samuel BROWN, a local preacher of the M. E. Church, South, died at his home at Farmwell, last Tuesday morning, in his 74th year.

John Murray FORBES died at his home in Fauquier Co, on Saturday, May 24th at the age of 73 years, a week before his 50th wedding anniversary.

Thursday, 5 June 1890   Vol. XXXIV, No. 52

Married: At the bride's residence in Florence, Alabama, on Thursday, May 1st 1890, by Rev. J. A. PRESTON, Mr. J. W. GAVER, formerly of Loudoun, to Miss Alice GRAFT, of Florence.

At the Baptist Church in Waterford, on Tuesday, June 3d 1890, Mr. Joseph A. LODGE, of Round Hill, was married to Miss Lucy W., daughter of Mr. John COMPHER, Rev. C. T. HERNDON, officiating.

At Ebenezer Baptist church, near Bloomfield, on Wednesday, June 4th, by Rev. I. B. LAKE, D.D., Mr. Arthur L. MOORE, of Round Hill, and Miss Laura J., daughter of Mr. James W. NICHOLS, all of Loudoun.

Today (Thursday) at 12 m., in the M. E. Church, South, Rev. B. W. BOND will unite Harry C. STANDSBURY and Miss Carolyn SMALE, all of Leesburg.

Death of Mr. Edgar LICKEY occurred at his father's home near Round Hill on Saturday last, of consumption, in the 29th year of his age. Interred in burying ground at Short Hill, on Monday, Rev. Dr. LAKE and Rev. C. T. HERNDON preaching.

On Tuesday morning last, Jos. A. LODGE, of Round Hill, and Miss Lucy, daughter of Mr. John CONPHER [COMPHER] of Waterford, were married in the Baptist church, at the latter place, Rev. Chas. T. HERNDON officiating, at 11:30 a.m. Bridal party of Mr. Harry CROSS with Miss Dollie GRUBB; Mr. Ashton CLAPHAM with Miss Edmonia RUSSELL; Mr. Jos. L. LODGE with Miss Ella CROSS, and Mr. William RUSSELL best man with Miss Mollie COMPHER sister of the bride. They will reside in Round Hill.

Mrs. Lucy Peachy POWELL, widow of the late Wm. A. POWELL (for many years Cashier of the old Valley Bank at Leesburg) died at the home of her son-in-law, Wm. F. BROOKES, in Alexandria at 8:30 on the morning of May 31st, in the 86th year of her age. Remains were buried beside her husband, in Hollywood Cemetery, Richmond.

Mrs. Francis TAYLOR, relict of the late Joseph TAYLOR, died at her home in Prince William on the 26th inst., at 80 years old. Funeral preached by Rev. Mr. DUNAWAY of the Baptist church, interred at Middleburg Cemetery.

[MISSING ISSUE]

Thursday, 19 June 1890   Vol. XXXV, No. 2

Rev. Dr. Philip SLAUGHTER died at his home near Mitchell's in Culpeper, last Thursday morning in his 82d year. He was a son of Capt. Philip SLAUGHTER, of the Rev. War. ...

Married: On May 28th 1890, in the M. E. Church, South, in Mt. Jackson, Shenandoah Co, Va, by Rev. J. K. GILBERT, Mr. Harvey K. ARTHUR, of Henderson, N.C., and Miss Katie L. ALLEN, of Shenandoah Co.

Married: In Hillsboro, on Wed. June 11, 1890, by Rev. J. H. DULANY, Dr. R. W. TAVENNER to Miss Orra C. HOOE, both of Loudoun.

Joseph D. BAKER, Esq., of Frederick City, Md, and Pres. of the Peoples Nat. Bank of Leesburg, was married in Baltimore last Thursday, to Miss Virginia H. MARKELL, of the latter city, at the residence of the bride's father, by the Rector of St. Peters Protestant Episcopal Church, the Rev. Dr. Julius E. GRAMMER. They will reside in Frederick City.

[MISSING ISSUE]

Thursday, 3 July 1890   Vol. XXXV, No. 4

Married: At 914 New York Ave., Washington City on Thursday, June 26th, 1890, by Rev. J. T. WIGHTMAN, pastor of Mt. Vernon Place, M. E. Church, South, Mr. Wm. HEAD, and Miss Florence M. ATTWELL (daughter of Mr. Ewell ATTWELL), both of Leesburg.

Married: At Christ Church, Goresville, on Wednesday morning, July 2d, 1890, Rev. W. G. HAMMOND, pastor of Middleburg circuit, M. E.

Church, South, and Miss Ellen R. GIDDINGS, daughter of Col. Wm. GIDDINGS, Rev. Nelson HEAD, D.D., and Rev. Carter PAGE, officiating, all of Loudoun

Died: At her home in Bloomfield, on Sunday, June 8th 1890, at the residence of her uncle, H. H. TAYLOR, little Louise, infant child of Leven T. JACOBS, aged 7m 15d.

Mr. Samuel RECTOR, of this county, died at the home of his son, Mr. Howard N. RECTOR, near Mountsville, on the 20th of June, after a brief illness, in the 86th year of his age.

Mrs. Henrietta BENEDICT, after a protracted illness, died at the residence of her son-in-law, Mr. Jno. Y. BASSELL, in Leesburg, on Thursday evening, June 26th 1890, in her 76th year. A daughter of the late John GRAY, of this town, and was the last of a family of seven children. She was the widow of the late Prof. Wm. B. BENEDICT, of the U.S. Naval Observatory, Washington DC. Born and raised in Leesburg. Member of St. James Episcopal Church. Leaves two children, Mrs. J. Y. BASSELL and Mrs. Walter J. HARRISON. Funeral took place Saturday afternoon, interred in burying ground of St. James Episcopal Church, Rev. R. T. DAVIS, D.D., officiating, assisted by Rev. Drs. Nelson HEAD and B. W. BOND, of the M. E. Church, South.

Mr. John W. HARPER, near Upperville, sister to the late Dr. A. F. BROWN, died on the 21st instant in Front Royal, Va.

Thursday, 10 July 1890   Vol. XXXV, No. 5

Mr. Silas HUME died after a long illness in his 77th year, at his home near Cliff Mills, Fauquier Co., on the 39th [29th?] of June. He had a mare about 24 years old, which a few hours before its owner's death, went into the grave yard and died on the exact spot selected by Mr. HUME for his grave.

Died: At the home of his brother, Capt. J. R. HUTCHISON, Aldie, of paralysis, Major T. B. HUTCHISON, on the 6th inst.

Died: At her home, near Hillsboro, on Thursday, July 3rd, 1890, Mrs. Ann McARTOR, in the 56th year of her age. Daughter of the late Reuben JENKINS, and widow of the late Thomas McARTOR. Leaves children and grand-children.

Died: In Leesburg, on Thursday, July 3d, 1890, Charles Lewis, aged 8m 15d, son of Charles R. and India LOWENBACH.

Death of Christian T. HEMPSTONE occurred at his home adjoining Leesburg, at an early hour on Tuesday morning, July 8th 1890. Born in Montgomery Co, Md, in Oct 1819, and was in his 80th year. Nearly 50 years ago he purchased the farm where he died. He reared a large family among them Robert, of the wholesale firm of Rouse, Hempstone & Co. of Baltimore, and Mr. W. Dade HEMPSTONE. Vestryman of St. James Episcopal Church. Funeral at 5:00 Wed.

afternoon, interred in Union Cemetery, Rev. R. T. DAVIS, D.D., officiating.

Mr. W. Selden PEACH, of Fauquier Co., died at his home near Upperville on Saturday evening last of apoplexy.

Maj. T. B. HUTCHISON died on morning of the 6th inst. In 1861 he joined the 8th Va. Regiment. Funeral on Monday conducted by Rev. W. G. HAMMOND, at the Methodist church in this place (Aldie), conveyed to Middleburg cemetery.

Aldie: Mr. Richard SKINNER, formerly of this county, but for many years a resident of Texas, is home on a visit.

Mrs. Nannie ELGIN, daughter of the late Judge H. W. THOMAS, died at the Infirmary in Alexandria, about 1 o'clock yesterday morning. Remains will be brought her today. *Fairfax Herald, July 4th.*

Thursday, 17 July 1890   Vol. XXXV, No. 6

July Ct.: Will of Adam COOPER dec'd. admitted to probate. Wm. H. LUCKETT qualified as Admr. of Mary B. LUCKETT dec'd.; H. N. RECTOR and W. J. LUCK as Admrs. of Samuel RECTOR dec'd. Estate of William CLOWE committed to Sheriff.

Mrs. Mary Ann NIXON, widow of the late George NIXON, of this county, committed suicide by hanging on Thursday last, at the residence of Mr. Ed. HAWLEY, about 3 miles S of Leesburg. She was about 75 years of age and had been twice in her lifetime an inmate of the asylum. Interred in Presbyterian churchyard, Leesburg, on Friday evening, Rev. B. W. BOND officiating.

Miss Mary E. FOSTER, of Fauquier Co., was thrown from her carriage at The Plains yesterday and died in an hour. She was a sister of Mr. T. R. FOSTER, of Fauquier, and aunt of Capt. J. W. FOSTER, of Leesburg. She leaves a large estate.

Mr. W. S. PEACH died suddenly on Saturday evening. About 7 o'clock he dismounted his horse and leaned against a fence. Two friends carried him to the house of C. C. CALVERT nearby when he expired in about ten minutes. *Warrenton Virginian.*

Thursday, 24 July 1890   Vol. XXXV, No. 7

Died: Near Morrisonville, July 4th 1890, after a brief illness, Mabel, infant daughter of Geo. W. and Rosa B. CASE, aged 11m 5d.

Departed this life, July 4th, 1890, Mrs. Christina SHRY, aged 70y 3m 24d.

Died: On Tuesday, July 7th 1890, of cholera infantum, Randolph F. MYERS, infant son of E. F. MYERS, aged 8m 28d.

Mr. Lott TAVENNER, living near Lincoln, died last week at an advance age.

Article about the Methodist Church of Leesburg, known as the Old Stone Church. Gives history of Methodist Society and present building that was built in 1790, stone furnished by John WRENN, grandfather of Mr. Jas. S. HARRIS, of Leesburg.

Aldie: Mrs. EWELL, wife of Dr. Jesse EWELL Sr., died at her home in Prince William on the 7th inst., in her 91st year. For upwards of 60 years member of Episcopal Church. Funeral by Rev Mr. TURNER, of Episcopal Church and interred in the family burying ground.

Thursday, 31 July 1890   Vol. XXXV, No. 8

Married: July 29th 1890, at the Presbyterian Manse, Leesburg, by Rev. J. C. DINWIDDIE, Mr. Lewis HOUGH to Miss Lucy PRESTON.

Died: June 22, at her home in Texas, Mrs. Tina LAMAR, age 48 Years. She was a daughter of Mr. Samuel H. PRICE of this county.

Mrs. S. Ella BEALES, wife of J. E. BEALES and daughter of Mortimer BEALES, died at her home in Hamilton, about 9 o'clock Monday evening, after an illness of about three weeks, in her 28th year.

Mr. Henry VANDEVANTER, formerly of this county, but for the past 7 or 8 years a resident of Mecklenburg Co, is visiting.

Griffith PAXTON, of this county, died at his home near Waterford, on the 21st inst., in the 81st year of his age. Interred in the burying ground at Waterford, on Wednesday of last week.

Mrs. Jno. W. MORAN, mother of W. H. W. MORAN, editor of the Hamilton Enterprise, died at her home near Farmwell, on Saturday night, July 26th, of typhoid fever, in the 46th year of her age.

Rev. Joseph HELM died at the home of his son-in-law, Mr. Lewis SHUMATE, on Friday afternoon, July 25th, in his 85th year. Born in Hagerstown, Maryland, but spent his early manhood in Georgetown, DC. In 1834 he was married to Miss Mary Ellen CARR, a sister of the late David CARR, of this county. They resided in Georgetown until his health became enfeebled. Member of Methodist Episcopal Church, South. He leaves an age widow and two children. Funeral took place from his son-in-law's residence on Saturday afternoon, Rev. Nelson HEAD, D.D, officiating assisted by Rev. W. G. EGGLESTON. Interred in Union Cemetery, Leesburg.

Death of Mrs. PEACOCK, wife of Mr. Noble B. PEACOCK, Supervisor of Jefferson district. She had been an invalid for some time. She died at her home near Wheatland on Monday, and her funeral took place at Ketoctin church on Wednesday.

Tribute of respect for Susie VANSICKLER.

[MISSING ISSUE]

Thursday, 14 August 1890   Vol. XXXV, No. 7

Aug. Ct.: Wills of Jos. HELM, Ann E. GAYNOR, Henrietta BENEDICT, Mahlon JAMES and Jas. M. WALKER admitted to probate. H. H. RUSSELL appointed curator of estate of J. R. BAKER dec'd.; Wm. PIGGOTT as Admr. of Lott TAVENNER dec'd.; E. V. WHITE as

Admr. of Wm. H. CLOWE dec'd.; John H. SHRY as Admr. of Christina SHRY dec'd.

[MISSING ISSUES]

Thursday, 11 September 1890 Vol. XXXV, No. 14

Married: In Washington City, on Tuesday, August 26th 1890, by Rev. Dr. ADDISON, Rector of Trinity Church, Mr. Jno. S. CASTLEMAN, of Jefferson Co. and Miss Eleanor BLACKBURN, Washington, eldest daughter of B. C. WASHINGTON Esq. of Charlestown.

Mrs. Olivia NICHOLS, wife of Isaac NICHOLS, died last Sunday night at an advanced age. Interred in Friends' burying ground at Lincoln on Tuesday.

Rev. Elias WELTY, at one time stationed at the M. E. Church in Leesburg (and father of Dr. WELTY, lately of Hamilton in this county) died at his home in Baltimore last Thursday, in his 70th year.

Cards are out for the marriage on Wednesday, September 24th 1890, at Mt. Vernon Place, M. E. Church, Washington DC, of Miss Katie Louise SHAW and Mr. Jos. S. CHURCH. She is a grand-daughter of the late Maj. Jas. F. DIVINE, of this town.

Sept. Ct.: Wills of Emily DIVINE, Jos. GOCHNAUER and Amy A. BEANS admitted to probate. Wm. F. COOPER qualified as committee of W. GARRETT. Robt. R. and Samuel H. LOVE qualified as Admr. of Eli A. LOVE dec'd. Estate of John MITCHELL committed to Sheriff.

Mr. Elias HUGHES, farmer of this county, died last Saturday, after a somewhat protracted illness, in about the 65th year of his age. He was a brother of the late Amos HUGHES. Funeral took place on Tuesday. Interment in Friends' burying ground at Lincoln.

Thursday, 18 September 1890 Vol. XXXV, No. 15

Rev. Wormley HUGHES sentenced at same term to five years in the penitentiary for stealing chickens, still awaiting appeal.

Mr. John H. TITUS, farmer, residing on the 'Temple Hall' farm, a few miles from Leesburg, died last Friday night after a 7 weeks' illness of typhoid fever. Belonged to the Ketoctin Lodge Knights of Pythias of this town and Baptist Church. Leaves a wife and large family of children. Funeral took place Sunday, Elder E. V. WHITE officiating. Interment in Union Cemetery.

Mrs. Rachael FRED, mother of Messrs. Frank L. and Burr P. FRED, died at the residence of her son-in-law, Mr. Hugh SWART, near Warrenton Junction, on the 4th inst., in the 94th year of her age. Member of the Baptist church for nearly half century.

Mr. Philip DERRY and Mr. Jos. SMITH, residing a few miles from Hillsboro, in this county, died at their respective homes on the 2d inst. The former was in the 71st and the latter in the 73rd year of his age.

Mr. Richard J. PAYNE, of Lynchburg, was found dead in his bed at his boarding house in Washington last Thursday morning. He was the son of the late D. B. PAYNE, of this city and a nephew of Mrs. Isaac VANDEVANTER, of Leesburg.

Bloomfield: Looking back a few years in my memory, I can recall the names of Wm. RILEY, Peyton MOORE, John GILL, John BURSON and wife, the two PLASTERS, Michael and Henry, Mrs. Jenny PLASTER, Mrs. E. B. CHAMBLIN and others who died about the age of 90. We have left, W. G. FURR, active, hale and hearty at 87. Norval SILCOTT, who says he never took a dose of medicine in his life and tends to his work on the farm regularly is 82. Mrs. M. L. POWELL is still well preserved at about the same age, and Mrs. PLASTER still in possession of her faculties must be 100. Mrs. Peyton MOORE high up in the 90's enjoys pretty good health.

Fauquier: Mrs. Henry MARSHALL died at her home near Hume on Monday last, in the 78th year of her age.

Fauquier: Mr. Parker C. WYETH, of St. Joseph, Mo. and Miss Ellen Ashton HORNER, of the county, were married in St. James church at Warrenton today.

Main Street Baptist Church in Richmond marriage of Mr. Albert NICHOLS, of Washington DC and Miss Lulu WHARTON, a daughter of Major W. J. WHARTON, also of Washington, by Rev. H. M. WHARTON, of Baltimore (uncle of the bride) assisted by Rev. J. S. WHARTON, of Crisfield, Md.

Thursday, 25 September 1890   Vol. XXXV, No. 16

Mrs. Sarah McCLELLAND died suddenly on Friday night last at her home in Lincoln, in about the 55th year of her age. Funeral took place in Lincoln on Sunday afternoon.

Thursday, 2 October 1890   Vol. XXXV, No. 17

Married: At the residence of the bride's father in Leesburg, on the 19th of September 1890, by the Rev. B. W. BOND, D.D., Miss Bertha L., daughter of Mr. Chas. A. CLINE, and Mr. Francis H. S. MORRISON, son of Col. J. H. MORRISON, of Lexington, Va, and grandson of the late Gen. F. H. SMITH, of the Va. Military Institute.

Died: At the residence of his father, Ellzey CHAMBLIN, near Mechanicsville, John CHAMBLIN on September 26th 1890, aged 44y 11m 26d, of cancer.

Died: September 11th, at the home near Lincoln, Fannie, daughter of Wm. H. and Martha FLETCHER, in the 17th year of her age.

Died: Harvey ELLMORE died at his home near Old Farmwell, September 11th, 1890, aged 15y 3m 11d.

292　　　　　　　　　　The Mirror
　　　　　Thursday, 16 October 1890　　Vol. XXXV, No. 19

Died: At his home near Centreville, Fairfax Co., Sept. 22nd 1890, Henry S. SWART, in the 70th year of his age. He leaves 1 dau. and 4 sons.

Mr. James MITCHELL, of this county, but for the past year a resident of West End, Fairfax Co, leaves in a few days for Macon, Mississippi, where he expects to make his future home.

Mr. Craven JAMES purchased a 400 acre farm in Lunenburg Co., 7 miles from Chase City, to which his son-in-law, John A. LYNCH, and family expect to move in a few days.

Dedication of the new Rozell Chapel at Philomont on last Sunday. The chapel as first built stood something of a mile or more south of Philomont, on the land then owned by Miss Phoebe ROZELL and sister. ...

[MISSING ISSUE]

Thursday, 16 October 1890   Vol. XXXV, No. 19

Married: On the 9th inst. at Lovettsville, by the Rev. H. St. J. RINKER, Mr. Charles W. WIRE, to Miss Estella C. POTTERFIELD, all of Loudoun.

Mrs. Susan RINKER, widow of the late John L. RINKER, died at her home in Leesburg Tuesday night, October 14th, in the 75th year of her age. Funeral will take place from the house this (Thursday) afternoon, at 3 o'clock.

Miss Nina RODRIGUEZ, of San Antonio, Texas, niece of Mrs. Dr. J. F. MASON, of this county, died at the residence of Dr. N. G. WEST, in this town, on Tuesday night.

Oct. Ct.: Mary E. CONARD Admx. of Jno. W. CONARD dec'd. executed new bond. R. R. WALKER qualified as Admr. dbn wwa of Jacob SCOTT dec'd. Wills of Leven RICHARDS and Elias HUGHES admitted to probate. Geo. W. SMITH qualified as Admr. of Job SMITH dec'd. Jas. Lemuel THOMAS, colored, for grand larceny, three years in penitentiary. Estates of Portia R. DORSEY and Oswell CARTER committed to Sheriff. Commodore John PAGE, of the Argentine navy, died recently near the Bolivian frontier. He was a native of Va. and had served in the U.S. and Confederate States navies. He was an uncle of Dr. J. F. MASON, of this county, having married a sister of Mrs. Betsy MASON, the doctor's mother; and father of Prof. Fred. PAGE, who married a dau. of Capt. A. M. CHICHESTER, of this county.

Jas. M. SINCLAIR, brother of the late Judge Chas. E. SINCLAIR, of Prince William Co., died of paralysis last week at his home at Manassas.

Thursday, 23 October 1890   Vol. XXXV, No. 20

Married: At St. James Church, Richmond, Wednesday October 15th by Rev Joshua PETERKIN, Miss Imogen SCOTT, daughter of the late Robt. E. SCOTT, of Fauquier Co., and sister of Hon. R. Taylor SCOTT, Attorney Gen. of Va., to Dr. Armistead L. WELLFORD.

Mr. William HALL, father of Mrs. A. J. BRADFIELD, died at his home in Leesburg about 8 o'clock last Monday night in the 81st year of his age. He had spent the greater portion of his life in this town. He had been an almost helpless invalid for many years, and almost blind. Interred Wednesday morning in the Presbyterian burying ground, Rev. Mr. DINWIDDIE officiating.

Atlanta: Wedding of Miss Maud Deleplaine CRICHTON, daughter of Dr. John CRICHTON, to Dr. Charles Glenville GIDDINGS, yesterday afternoon at St. Luke's Cathedral. ... Dr. GIDDINGS came from Va to make Atlanta his home several years ago.

Circuit Ct.: On Monday S. T. TITUS qualified as Admr. of John H. TITUS dec'd. Estate of L. W. S. HOUGH dec'd. committed to Sheriff.

[MISSING ISSUE]

Thursday, 6 November 1890   Vol. XXXV, No. 22

Married: In Harper's Ferry, at the residence of the bride's parents, on Tuesday evening, October 21st 1890, by the Rev. Wm. HARRIS, Mr. Walter POTTS, of Ohio, to Miss Ida MANUEL.

Dr. I. H. THOMAS, late of Aldie, has located in Savannah.

Union: Mrs. Henry PLASTER, formerly of this town, celebrated her 99th anniversary on last Friday.

Mr. and Mrs. H. C. WALLACE have issued cards for the marriage of their daughter, Essie Courtland, to Mr. Eugene F. ROBINSON son of Mr. Bushrod ROBINSON, of Washington DC. Ceremony will take place at 12 o'clock on Tuesday, November 11th 1890 in the M. E. Church, South, this town.

Mr. Robt. DAWSON died yesterday (Wednesday) morning at the residence of his parents in this town, of consumption, in about the 23rd year of his age. He was a printer by trade.

Mr. Hugh Glover DIVINE, resident of Georgetown, died last week. A resident of Georgetown for fifty years, having been born at Leesburg 72 years ago. He was a brother of the late Maj. Jas. F. and William DIVINE, of this town.

Death of Mr. T. Walter FRED, son of Mr. Frank L. FRED, last Wednesday morning in Indian Territory, where he was engaged in business with his father.

A pension was on Monday granted to Alcinda, widow of Septimus POTTERFIELD, of Neersville, in this county.

Thursday, 13 November 1890   Vol. XXXV, No. 29 [23]

Married: Nov. 5th at the house of Mr. Amos BEANS, near Round Hill, by Rev. J. C. DINWIDDIE, Charles Spring, Esq. to Miss Alice BEANS.

Died in Hamilton, Nov. 2, 1890, of meningitis, Helena Noland MORAN, youngest dau. of W. H. W. and Bessie MORAN, aged 2y 11m 11d.

Nov. Ct.: L. H. POTTERFIELD qualified as Admr. of Thos. SANDBOWER dec'd. Estates of J. D. GIBSON dec'd. and Nancy T. BENTON dec'd. committed to Sheriff. A. J. BRADFIELD qualified as guardian of Maria H. and W. A. METZER.

Divorce suit of HAMPTON vs HAMPTON from the Circuit Ct. of Loudoun was argued before the Court of Appeals in Richmond last Friday.

Marriage license issued in Washington on Saturday, to Robt. G. JOHNSON and Ella E. GEORGE, both of Loudoun county.

M. E. Church, South wedding at high noon on Tuesday, Mr. Eugene F. ROBINSON, of Washington DC and Miss Essie Courtland, only daughter of Mr. H. C. WALLACE, of Leesburg. ... No bridesmaids, ushers were Messrs. B. M. BRIDGET, of Washington DC, Frank WALLACE, brother of the bride, T. J. BROOKE, Clarence U. WEBSTER, Wm. A. GEISKING and W. C. DOUGLASS of Washington. Bride wore a gown of dark blue cloth with hat to match and carried violets. She is daughter of Mr. H. Clay WALLACE. He is son of Mr. Bushrod ROBINSON, of Robinson, Parker & Co., Washington.

Death of Hal Grafton DULANY died at "Welbourne," the residence of his father, Col. R. H. DULANY, at 8 o'clock Saturday morning, November 8th 1890, in his 37th year. ... Through his mother he inherited the estate of Lady HUNTER, of England, and was worth a million and a half dollars. He leaves a father and one brother, Mr. Richard H. DULANEY, and 2 sisters, Mrs. Robert NEVILLE, of Fauquier, and Mrs. J. S. LEMMON of Baltimore. Part of estate to eldest son of his brother. Private funeral took place Sunday evening, by Rev. E. S. HINKS of Episcopal Church. Pall bearers were first cousins – Messrs. R. H. DULANY, Guy WHITING, R. W. WHITING, J. P. DeBUTTS, G. A. ROSZELL and R. D. ROSZELLE.

Thursday, 20 November 1890   Vol. XXXV, No. 30

Died: In Leesburg, after a long and wasting sickness, on Saturday November 15, 1890, Mrs. Mary Ann McNEALY, aged 80 years.

Little Mary, 5 year old dau. of Alexander and Ada SPINKS, of this town, died on Monday night, Nov. 17th 1890, of membranous croup.

Cards are out for the marriage of Miss Ella LOWENBACH to Mr. Isa MONHEIMER, on Tuesday, November 25th, at Standard Club, Chicago. She is a cousin of Chas. R. LOWENBACH, of this town.

Wm. POPE, an aged citizen of Washington, who had been a clerk in the Third Auditor's Office for many years, died suddenly at the Treasury Department last Thursday morning, of heart trouble. He was the father in law of Mr. George T. GALLEHER, formerly of this town.

Thursday, 27 November 1890   Vol. XXXV, No. 31

Married: November 25th at the Presbyterian Manse, Leesburg, by Rev. J. C. DINWIDDIE, Mr. Harvey N. FRY to Miss Mary E. CHICK.

Died: Near Mechanicsville, of typhoid fever, on Nov. 4th 1890, Joseph P. DERRY, son of the late L. W. and Virginia DERRY, aged 27y 28d.

Dr. L. F. HOUGH, of Hamilton, and Miss Nannie GORE, were married at the house of the bride's parents (Mr. and Mrs. Albert GORE) on Wednesday November 19th, by Rev. C. T. HERNDON.

In Loudoun Co. home of Rev. John S. CHESTER, a clergyman who several years ago was a missionary to the west coast of Africa, lives an African girl named Nellie. She was treated as a member of the family. Now 15 years old, she can speak French and English. A month ago received a letter from her parents that the King wished to claim his bride. CHESTER refused unless the girl was to be the King's only Queen (tribe is polygamous). In a few months she will return to Africa to wed a man many years her senior and whom she has not seen since she was a very small child.

[MISSING ISSUE]

Thursday, 11 December 1890   Vol. XXXV, No. 33

Married: On the 4th instant, in Washington, Rev. A. G. APPELL married Miss Ida M. LESLIE, of Loudoun County, and Dr. George T. SHOWER, of Baltimore.

Died: In Washington on Friday December 5th at 10 p.m., Jennings KITZMILLER, husband of Mollie E. and son of A. M. and A. KITZMILLER, formerly of Harper's Ferry, Va.

Died: At her home in Waterford, Nov. 29, 1889 [1890] of paralysis, Ida A., wife of Robt W. HOUGH, after an illness of several weeks. Member of M. E. Church. She leaves a husband and one little girl.

Dec. Ct.: Wills of H. Grafton DULANY dec'd., Basil W. SHUMAKER dec'd. and Susan TAVENNER dec'd. admitted to probates. S. T. NICHOLS and H. W. DAVIS qualified as Admrs. of Isaac NICHOLS dec'd. Estate of J. R. BAKER committed to Sheriff. A. B. MOORE qualified as Admr. wwa of James H. ROGERS dec'd. Mr. E. McLINN, minister of Lutheran Church, licensed to celebrate rites of matrimony.

Miss Eliza MILLER, sister of the late Francis MILLER of Md, died in Washington last Saturday.

Aldie: Mr. A. L. B. ZEREGA, Mrs. Gussie ZEREGA, and the Misses ZEREGA started for New York on Monday last to attend the marriage of their cousin, Miss Dot ZEREGA, who is to wed Sir Frederick FRANKLIN.

[MISSING ISSUE]

Thursday, 25 December 1890   Vol. XXXV, No. 36 [35]

Married: By the Rev. G. W. POPKINS, on the 18th inst. at Mt. Hope Baptist Church, Mr. H. C. ELLIOT to Miss Emma W. SIMPSON, all of Loudoun.

Married: At the residence of R. B. NIXON, Esq., Washington DC, at 8:30 p.m. Wednesday, December 10, 1890, by Rev. Samuel DOMER, D.D., of St. Paul's Lutheran Church, D. McCarty RAMSEY, of Alexandria and Miss Fannie B. MANKIN, of Loudoun.

Died: Mrs. Mary Ann CARLISLE, widow of the late David CARLISLE, died at the residence of Morgan BEAVERS, near Snickersville, where she had made her home for a few years past, on Sunday, December 21st in the 84th year of her age.

Died: At her home in Lovettsville, December 16th, Minerva SCOTT, of consumption. Member of M. E. Church for 15 or 20 years.

Died: At her home near Taylortown, Amanda E. CORDELL, born July 15, 1867, died December 19, 1890.

Mr. Samuel O. BROWN died last week of typhoid fever in Georgetown, where he was engaged in business. Interred in Friends Burying Ground at Lincoln on Monday.

Mr. Ross CRAVENS and Miss Gracie HOGE, daughter of Jesse HOGE, were married last Wednesday at the residence of the bride's parents near Hughesville.

On Thursday, Mr. Orland CHAMBLIN and Miss Lula, daughter of Mr. J. B. VANSICKLER, of Philomont, were married, Rev. J. C. DICE officiating.

Same day Mr. Will ROGERS, of Barnesville, Ohio, and Miss Annie Lee THOMAS, daughter of Owen THOMAS Esq. of Round Hill were married and left at one for Ohio, home of the groom.

Same day Mr. Chas. R. NORRIS and Miss Rata DIVINE were married in Leesburg, Rev. B. W. BOND officiating.

Marriage license issued in Washington last week to W. B. McCULLOCH and Hattie B. JENKINS, both of Loudoun county.

On Monday, Francis, 8 year old son of Mr. R. M. PRESTON, died at his father's home in this town, of membranous croup. Interred in Union Cemetery on Tuesday afternoon, Rev. J. C. DINWIDDIE officiating.

Dr. Chas. E. HARPER, formerly of Leesburg, but for the past 2-3 years practicing dentistry in Danville, is home for a visit.

Thursday afternoon "at home" wedding at residence of Mr. and Mrs. W. W. DIVINE, of their daughter Rata to Mr. Chas. R. NORRIS, son of Jos. L. NORRIS, of this town. ... Attended by Mr. Luther DIVINE, brother of the bride and Mr. Frank J. NORRIS, brother of the groom. Ceremony by Rev. B. W. BOND. Bride carried smilax and roses and wore gown of fawn colored broadcloth with trimmings of black and gold. They will make their home for the present with the groom's parents.

Roszell Chapel, at Philomont, marriage on Wednesday of last week, Miss Lulu VANSICKLER and Mr. O. CHAMBLIN, of above named place, were married by the Rev. Mr. DICE. Attendants were Miss C. DILLON, Mr. G. LYNN, Miss E. CHAMBLIN, Mr. CHAMBLIN, Miss L. ORRISON, Mr. J. C. CHAMBLIN, Miss D. BROWN and W. CHAMBLIN. Bride wore a traveling dress.

Wedding on Wednesday, December 17, 1890, at the residence of the bride's parents, Mr. Edgar WOOLF and Miss Jennie M. RECTOR, daughter of Mr. and Mrs. W. A. RECTOR, of Rectortown, Fauquier Co., by Rev. Henry WOOLF, of Md, a brother of the groom. Bridesmaids were Miss Carrie RECTOR and Miss Bessie WOOLF, sisters of the bride and groom; Miss Annie RAWLINGS and Miss Janie SMITH. Ushers were Messrs. Chas. M. WOOLF, of Washington, a brother of the groom; Fred. YOUNG, of Washington, and C. H. OSBURN and Frank FENTON, both of Loudoun. ...

Marriage of Miss Ethel JANNEY to Mr. Paul ANDREWS, of Boston, will take place early in February.

Carrollton, Mo News: Dr. James French SIMPSON died at his residence in this city on Saturday morning last at 6:20 o'clock. He was born in Culpeper Co, Va., Oct. 10, 1814. Nov. 19, 1834 he came to Medora, Macoupin Co, Illinois where he finished his medical course. In 1837 he came to Carrollton. ... In January 1838 he married Harriet C. MILLER, who died in 1841. In 1844 he married Miss Jane E. HOPKINS who survives him. During the war Dr. SIMPSON was a Republican and called into the army as a supply surgeon of the 14th Illinois regiment. In later years he became a prohibitionist.

INDEX

___, Danny, 69
___, Nellie, 295
ABBERS
　Henry, 133
ABBOTT
　Ella, 197
　Jos., 197
　Joseph, 21
　Mary, 21
　Mary E., 21
ABEL
　Ann C., 230
ABLE
　Frederick H., 136
ACKLAND
　Claude M., 282
ADAM
　John M., 169
　Wm. F., 169
ADAMS
　___, 151
　Adelaid, 211
　Anna M., 169
　Beverley, 151
　Beverly, 210
　Daniel, 273
　Geo. W., 160, 162, 169
　Georgie B., 8
　Gertrude, 210
　Gertrude L., 210
　J. Hoover, 276
　John J., 62
　John Q., 9
　Julia, 245
　Miss, 151
　Rose, 211
　Sallie J., 10
　Samuel, 179
　W. H., 64, 92
　William H., 179
ADDISON
　Mary G., 178
　W. D., 178
　Walter D., 178
ADIE
　Fannie A., 57
ADRAIN
　Robt. E., 279
ADRIAN
　Gertrude, 247
ADSIT
　Mrs., 249
AGUILLA
　Samuel, 78
AHALT
　C. E., 70
　Calrton, 238
　Charles L., 223
AISQUITH
　Margaret, 79
ALBAUGH
　Christian, 62
　Albert Bros., 170
ALBRIGHT
　J. W., 191
ALBURGER
　John, 219
ALDER
　Joseph A., 124
　Joseph F., 4
　Meshach, 4
　Sallie M., 4
ALDRIDGE
　Eliza, 109
　Hattie, 12
　John, 12, 109, 156
　Rose, 156
　Rose A., 156
ALEXANDER
　Anna E., 12
　Annie E., 10
　B. T., 65
　Burr T., 264
　David, 158
　H. C., 67
　Hannah, 33
　J. H., 163, 245
　James, 50
　Jno. H., 233, 256
　John H., 217, 234, 256, 271
　John J., 136
　John T., 100
　M. J., 90
　Malvina G., 264
　Mary M., 264
　Robert W., 221
ALLBRIGHT
　Dr., 139
ALLDER
　James, 276
　Marietta, 276
ALLEN
　David L., 149
　Edmond, 243
　Edmund, 123
　George W., 140
　John F., 134
　Katie L., 286
　Margaret, 124, 140
　Margaret B., 123
ALLISON
　Chas. H., 139
　Mary M., 32
　Minnie, 153
ALTMAN
　H. E., 263
AMBLER
　J. C., 235
　James M., 177
AMES
　Annie R., 82
　Charlie N., 82
　Wm. H., 82
AMOS
　Margaret C., 82
ANDERSON
　Dora E., 37
　George B., 1
　Ira I., 63
　J. P., 114
　Martha, 237
　Mary, 36
　Nannie D., 238
　Orion, 270
　Owen, 270
　S. F., 266
　Walter A., 243
ANDREW
　Geo. L., 154
　Sarah L., 154
ANDREWS
　Frank T., 211
　Paul, 297
ANKERS
　Harriet, 41
　Samuel, 250
ANKINS

The Mirror
INDEX

Harriet, 124
ANNAN
  Hattie, 22
  Helen C., 212
  Roberdean, 22
ANTSWORTH
  William, 223
APPEL
  Lydia, 171
APPELL
  A. G., 295
APPLE
  Thomas, 246
  Thos., 255
ARCHER
  Ellen G., 256
ARMSTRONG
  Bessie D. G., 193
  James W., 193
ARNETT
  John, 6
  Mahlon T., 88
  Mary V., 75
  Ruthanna, 6
  Welby S., 189
ARNOLD
  Annie S., 64
  Chas., 80
  E. Sheldon, 38
  Elizabeth, 120
  Elizabeth C., 108
  Ella C., 236
  Elmer E., 254
  Mr., 236
  Saml. S., 9
ARNOLT
  Keziah, 265
ARTHUR
  Harvey K., 286
ARUNDELL
  Joseph, 41
ASHBY
  Edwin T., 96
  Estelle V., 93
  James, 195
  L. T., 8
  N. T., 8
  Ned, 96
  Samuel T., 93
ASHFORD
  Frank A., 106
ASHTON

Gennie L., 21
Geo. D., 21
ASTON
  Edward, 212
ATHEY
  J. Herbert, 219, 263
  Jessie H., 263
  John, 13
  Nannie B., 263
  Thos. B., 13
  W. W., 13, 185, 217, 263
ATKINSON
  Calvin, 191
  Emily, 256, 257
  Jos. N., 256
  M. L., 233
ATTWELL
  Chas. T., 180
  Ella, 266
  Ewell, 206, 217, 286
  Ewell B., 206, 283
  Florence M., 286
  James W., 206
  Mary J., 206
  Thos. F., 225
ATWELL
  Bettie, 91
  Hattie, 60
  Jared, 2
  Thos., 60
AUSHERMAN
  Martha E., 55
AUSTIN
  M. H., 191
AVIS
  John, 113
AXLINE
  John W., 58
AYERS
  Mary, 187
AYLETT
  Page, 194
AYRES
  Charles G., 135
  Chas., 134
  Chas. G., 128
  Kate, 134
  R. B., 128
  Romeyn B., 135
  Teressa, 187
  Thos. W., 275, 280

William, 187
BACON
  Nath'l., 136
BADGER
  Harry B., 211
  J. K., 211
  J. N., 137
BAGEANT
  Geo. W., 46
  Wm., 46
BAGENT
  Amanda, 189
  Geo. W., 161
  Jos. D., 189
BAKER
  Alexander M., 79
  Ann E., 43
  Curtis J., 67
  Geo., 131
  George D., 23
  George W., 124
  H. H., 262
  J. R., 113, 289, 295
  James A., 16
  Joseph D., 286
  Mary T., 113
  Mary V., 67
  R. Allison, 208
BALDWIN
  Adrian, 26
  Anna, 26, 67
  Annie M., 67
  Annie W., 147
  Emma, 26
  James, 111
  John B., 24
  Joseph, 162
  Julia, 174
  Julian, 26
  Lillie E., 162
  M. K., 44, 46, 67
  Mary E., 24, 46, 67
  Orion, 46
  Samuel R., 171
BALL
  Augustine W., 241, 242
  Burgess, 32
  C. B., 157
  C. M., 248
  C. W., 94

The Mirror
INDEX

Catharine, 94
Charles, 68
Charles B., 103, 242
Chas. B., 72, 112, 241
Chas. M., 170
Ebenezer B., 157
Ella J., 68
Emma R., 242
Geo. A., 83
Geo. W., 20, 32
George, 238
George A., 7
Harvey C., 202
James F., 133
Janie E., 68
John, 234, 250
John L., 216, 267
M. D., 57, 207, 208
Maria L., 133
Mary, 251
Mary R., 32
Mollie, 216
Nannie L., 133
Notley, 26, 236
R. M. T., 248
Richard T. M., 20
S. A., 94
Samuel, 3, 94
Samuel H., 83
Thomas J., 121
Virginia A., 83
Wm., 170, 250
Wm. T., 83
Ball Bros., 250
BALLANGER
  Margaret, 236
BALLARD
  Ida D., 160
BALLENGER
  Clinton C., 248
  Dorcas O., 248
  Edgar, 248
  James E., 221
  Jas., 182
BANBURY
  Nannie, 255, 256
BANTON
  Cora V., 161
BARBOUR
  Eliza B., 204
  Jas., 270

John S., 204, 270
Mary, 270
BARHAM
  Wm. B., 43
BARKER
  Alice C., 265
  Jno., 88
  Lula M., 88
  Marian, 88
  Wesley B., 265
BARLEY
  Claiborne, 3
Barley, Beatty & Co., 24
BARNES
  Harriet P., 156
  Joseph D., 74, 156
  Joseph K., 74
  Robert C., 156
  Sarah V., 176
BARNHOUSE
  Catharine, 37
  Edgar S., 145
  John R., 4, 36
BARNUM
  Lulu L., 174
BARR
  R. S., 260
BARRETT
  Alexander, 126
  C. Boyd, 16
  Elizabeth A., 212
  Florence R., 109
  J. Wade, 171
  John W., 109
  Wm. F., 169
BARTAMOSS
  Robert, 76
BARTELS
  H., 52
BARTLETT
  Alice P., 55
  Burgess D., 24, 47
  Ellen, 182
  Florence, 192
  John W., 55
  Myrtle, 55
  N. H., 254
  Nettie, 154
  Rebecca H. V., 254
  Sydid J., 161
  Wm. L., 182, 242
BARTON

Benjamin, 33
C. W., 276
M. A. E., 33
BASCUE
  Charles, 21, 124
  Emily C., 130
  Mary E., 235
  Mary E. H., 227
BASSELL
  Farian, 86
  J. Y., 287
  Jno. Y., 217, 287
  John Y., 86
  Rebecca, 86
Bassell & Ferguson, 55
BATSON
  A. T., 156
BATTAILE
  Laura, 161
BATTS
  Theresa A., 67
BAUGHMAN
  Charles H., 63
  Chas. R. P., 203
  Ella, 203
  James A., 73
  Jas., 146
  John, 203
  John W., 73
  Neta, 63
BAYNE
  Lawrence P., 153
  Louise, 117
  Patterson, 153
  Wm., 153
BAYNOR
  Miss, 149
BEACH
  Albert D., 5
  Constance C., 206, 207
  Frederick, 142
  Jas. D., 139
  Lilly M., 172
  Philip, 172
  S. F., 206
  S. Ferguson, 207
BEALE
  M. J., 86
BEALES
  Amos A., 83
  Benjamin B., 50

INDEX

C. F., 82
Edgar T., 50
Ella, 75
J. E., 289
James E., 75
Joel, 102, 190
John D., 50
Luther, 86
Mortimer, 289
Rodney, 18
S. Ella, 289
William R., 50
BEAMER
  Elizabeth, 46
  George H. T., 58
  Joseph M., 116
  M. A. V., 60
  Mollie c., 216
  Rachael, 83
  Rachel, 159
  Rachel A., 3
  William B., 183
  William F., 40
BEAN
  George T., 155
  Lillie B., 223
BEANER
  Geo., 216
  Wm., 81, 94, 95, 101
BEANS
  Alice, 294
  Allice, 212
  Amos, 69, 294
  Amy A., 290
  Annie, 212
  Burr H., 105
  D. M., 204
  Daniel M., 204
  Ellwood H., 69
  Florence, 69
  Florence E., 69
  Florence V., 69
  H. H., 129
  Ida B., 143
  Isaiah, 172, 187
  Isaiah B., 119, 187
  Israel B., 120
  John W., 281
  Lizzie, 60
  Lizzie A., 187
  Louisa, 69, 212
  Norra A., 212
  Sopronia, 172
  Thos., 40
  Townsend, 155
  Uriah, 133, 134
BEAR
  Elizabeth D., 204
  Frank R., 204
  Kate J., 204
  Mariella, 165
BEARD
  Martin L., 20
BEATTY
  Charles H., 24
  Lulu B., 247
  Susan, 59
  Wm., 110, 112
BEATY
  John, 69
  Wm., 41
BEAVER
  John A., 87
BEAVERS
  Agnes, 222
  Benj., 108
  Benjamin, 68
  Delilah, 84, 158, 277, 278
  Delilah H., 280
  F. A., 128
  Fannie, 4
  John W., 19
  Kate E., 222
  Lewis W., 222
  Margaret, 198
  Miss, 52
  Morgan, 198, 222, 296
  O. L., 278
  Oscar, 89, 90
  R. F., 104
  Saml., 52
  Samuel, 54
  Thomas, 37
  Thomas B., 19
  Thos., 277
  Washington, 4, 83, 84, 87
BECKHAM
  Alexander, 139
BeCRAFT
  Annie E., 102
BELL
  Jos. V., 236
  William S., 11
BELT
  Alfred, 182
  Alfred C., 113
  Harry S., 28
  J. L., 182
  Townsend, 251
BENEDICT
  Erastus C., 232, 234
  Henrietta, 124, 287, 289
  Margaret, 194
  Wm. B., 287
BENEDUM
  Eliza, 13
  Jas. H., 281
  Jno. E., 195
  John E., 13
  Sarah, 281
BENNER
  Susie, 241
BENNETT
  Ada E., 5
  Agnes, 161
  E. L., 142, 217
  Emmet, 161
  H. C., 91, 161
  Julia L., 218
  Julia S., 214
  Rev., 66
  Sydnor, 117, 245
BENTLEY
  ___, 249
  Ann C., 194
  Anna, 279
  Annie, 195
  Bessie, 87
  E. B., 233, 259
  Edgar L., 166
  Kate, 234
  Katie, 166
  Lucy W., 233
  Mary A., 233, 259
  R. M., 87, 232, 256
  R. Montgomery, 279
  Robt. L., 256
  Rosa, 53
BENTLY
  Annie, 276
  Katie, 116
  R. L., 27

R. M., 276
Robt., 116
Robt. L., 27, 257
BENTON
  B. H., 221
  Ciara F., 237
  E. H., 115
  James M., 86, 89
  John W., 220
  Maggie, 89
  Maggie C., 90
  Margaret J., 221
  Nancy T., 294
  William, 124
  Wm., 49, 51, 89
  Wm. H., 90
BERKELEY
  Charles E., 232
  Edmund, 43, 243
  Fannie, 43
  H. R., 111
  L. C., 112
  Lucy B., 37
  Mary M., 47
  N., 148
  Nannie L., 112
  Wm. N., 37
BERLIN
  B. R., 40
BERNARD
  Horace, 246
BERRY
  Amanda C., 256
  E. H., 194
  J. Owens, 182
  William, 146
BEST
  Arabelia V., 81
  Jas., 82
  Wm. S., 246
BETTS
  Isabel, 194
  Isabel O., 18
BEUCHLER
  Alice V., 21
  George T., 21
  Gertrude A., 21
  J. R., 217
BEVERLEY
  Fannie, 20
  Fannie W., 22
  J. Bradshaw, 277

J. H. C., 42
Jane, 79
Robert, 79, 277
Robt. A., 43
William, 251
Willie, 95
Wm., 20, 43
Wm. G., 22
BEVERLY
  Robert, 30
BIGGS
  Peter L., 178
BIGHAM
  M. M., 48
BINGHAM
  Charles, 198
BIRD
  M. Dora, 27
BIRDSALL
  D. B., 115
  D. H., 115
BIRKBY
  ___, 110
  Edgar W., 259
  Joseph W., 75
  Lucy, 82
  Mary, 75
  Thos., 82
  Thos. W., 123, 162
BIRKETT
  Wm., 7
BISER
  W. G., 247
BISHOP
  Harvey, 192
BISSETT
  Ellie, 104
  Herbert L., 104
  Joseph, 104
BITZER
  Amanda C., 77
  C. C., 46
  Ella V., 146
  Geo. L., 190
  Harmon, 73
  Jennie, 190
  John, 77
  John W., 33
BLACK
  Mrs., 257
BLACKBURN
  Eleanor, 290

Geo. L., 167
BLADEN
  James, 50
BLAIR
  David, 248, 268
  J. E., 258
  Jas. E., 216
  Virginia R., 216
BLAND
  Charles, 170
  W. F., 133
BLEAKLEY
  Tacie, 197
BLINCOE
  Adeline, 49
  Albert, 49, 105, 113
  Martha, 113
  Mary, 49
BLUE
  Edward, 251
BLUNDELL
  Emma, 119
BOCOCK
  Ella, 231
  Thos. M., 231
BODINE
  Ada, 183
  Margret E., 55
  Martha J., 67
  Melvina, 65
BODMER
  Jacob, 248
BOGAN
  Wm. H., 163
BOGER
  Ella V., 194
  John E., 191
  Maggie C., 176
  Mary E., 39
BOLEN
  Ellen, 37
BOLYN
  Mary, 25
  S., 278
  Sarah, 25
  Somerfield, 25
  Summerfield, 284
  T. M., 284
  Thos.M., 82
  Tolliver, 278
BOND
  Alice W., 256

The Mirror
INDEX

Asa, 202, 256
Asa M., 193
Dr., 76
Sarah A., 193
Thos. H., 70
BONHAM
  Wm. G., 210
BOOKER
  L. L., 193
BOOTH
  Barbara L., 1
  Charles, 280
  Edwin, 195
  Elizabeth, 203
  Geo. G., 1
  W. H., 203
  William H., 124
BOOZE
  Marietta, 268
BOPMER
  George W., 75
BOPP
  Maggie E., 215
  Virginia I., 198
  Wm. G., 198
BORGER
  Jacob E., 124
BOTELER
  Alexander R., 194
  Elizabeth S., 194
  Genevieve, 4
BOWEN
  Etta, 253
  L.P., 210
  Percy C., 211
  Rebecca, 253
BOWERS
  H. G., 20
  Jno. H., 10
  John H., 92
  Mattie S., 20
  Mollie E., 156
BOWIE
  Julia A., 47
  R. G., 41
  Robt. G., 47
BOWLEN
  Ellen, 23
BOWLEY
  Cyrus W., 90
BOWMAN
  Catharine, 163

Geo. W., 65
R. C., 169
Boxley & Lynn, 180
BOYD
  Elisha, 222
  Etta, 167
  John E., 222
BOYER
  Luther H., 247
BOYNTON
  Henry S., 63
  Jane L., 63
BRABHAM
  Sue F., 88
BRACKETT
  Thos. R., 196
BRADEN
  Carrie E., 21
  G. V., 21, 22
  Gabriel V., 240
  Oscar S., 227
  W. F., 25
BRADFIELD
  A. J., 44, 103, 163, 293, 294
  Edna J., 67
  Elizabeth L., 44
  G. J., 179, 266
  Ira C., 248
  Rose, 97
BRADFORD
  Benj. B., 233
  Grace, 245, 250
  W., 122
BRADNER
  A. H., 98
BRADSHAW
  Geo. W., 129
  Romulus, 68
BRADY
  Annie L., 121
  Thomas, 88
BRAGER
  Ida, 233
  Ida E., 218
BRANCH
  Henry, 206
  M. M., 206
  Melicent J., 206
  Miriam, 149
  Thomas, 149
BRAUSFORD

Bettie J., 66
BRAWNER
  J. F., 217
  Jas. W., 86
  Laura, 86
  Mollie T., 84
BRECKENRIDGE
  Annie E., 214
  David A., 269
  Lemuel W., 6
  Nancy A., 240
  S. K., 236
  Saml. K., 236
  Samuel T., 240
BRENNER
  Jennie, 39
  John E., 39
  Lillian, 39
BRENT
  A. M., 31
BRIDGES
  Alice, 103
  Anna B., 246
  Benj., 15, 19, 103
  Benjamin, 115
  Dorsey, 282
  Edna E., 103
  Hardage, 60
  J. R., 170, 217
  Jas. R., 163
  Mollie E., 60
  Nannie, 170
  R. D., 57
  Robt., 170
  Virginia R., 217
BRIDGET
  B. M., 294
BRIERLY
  Wm., 232
BRINTON
  J. R., 261
BRISCOE
  Caroline E., 205
  E. H., 205
  Eliza H., 124, 205
  Wm. H., 205
BRISLIN
  John, 130
BROCKMAN
  Annie, 284
BRODERS
  Jos., 33

INDEX

BRONAUGH
  Henry, 198
  J. W., 66
  Jos. W., 92
  Mary C., 252
  William J., 252
BROOKE
  T. J., 294
BROOKES
  Wm. F., 286
BROOKHIZER
  Rosa, 63
BROOKINS
  Jack, 268
  Jim, 180
  Joe, 270
  Marietta, 268
BROOKS
  Ada, 271
  Annie E., 82, 243
  Chauncey, 17
  Philip, 82, 202
  Philip W., 271
  Phillip W., 243
  Richards, 82
  Samuel W., 54
  Westley, 56
Brooks, P. & Son, 202
BROWN
  A. F., 287
  A. P., 128
  Amelia, 129
  Annie P., 128
  Aurelius P., 104, 129
  B. F., 260
  Benj. F., 218
  Bettie L., 38
  Braxton, 43
  Burr, 224
  C. E., 239
  Charles L., 252
  Chas., 161
  Chas. C., 214
  Chas. J., 266
  Clara E., 39
  Clara L., 107, 108
  D., 297
  David H., 115
  Ella, 152
  Geo. N., 33
  Hannah M., 161
  Henry C., 8

  Henry W., 180
  Hiram D., 71
  J. Isaac, 1
  James M., 141
  Jane A., 164
  John, 113, 228
  John H., 202
  Jonathan, 73
  Joseph W., 182
  Julia A., 33
  K. C., 149
  L. A., 262
  L. P., 239
  Lelia A. E., 66
  Luther A., 222
  M. T., 55
  Martha, 43
  Mary, 262, 266
  Mary A., 252
  Mattie, 32
  Mayo, 224
  Miss, 156
  Mollie M., 268
  Morris L., 262
  Parmelia, 38
  Parmelia A., 38
  Preston D., 239
  Richard H., 88
  Rosie E., 269
  Samuel, 38, 285
  Samuel O., 296
  Son R., 23
  Susan G., 202
  T. N., 89
  Thomas, 122, 152, 212
  Thos., 37
  W. H., 161
  William, 51
  Wm. H., 107, 108
  Wm. T., 41
  Yardly T., 16
BROYLES
  Wm., 224
BRYNE
  Fannie, 35
BUCK
  Marcus B., 57
BUCKLEY
  T. C. T., 18
BUCKNER
  Peter, 68

  S. A., 212
  Willa, 89
BUDD
  America, 201
  Isaac D., 129, 255
  Norman, 129
  S. D., 201
BUFFINGTON
  Armstead, 83
BUNTER
  John D., 249
BURCH
  Charles P., 141
  Edgar F., 218, 267
  Helen A., 2
  Hellen A., 141
  L., 234
  Linnie, 165
  Mary, 267
  Nora L., 185
  Ridie, 2
  Thomas, 128
  Thomas F., 2
  Thos., 131, 165
  Thos. E., 141
BURGESS
  Penelope, 53
  W. F., 53
  William, 11
  Wm., 12
BURKE
  Clara, 54
  George M., 245
  M. A., 253, 269
  Mahala, 125
  R. S., 217
  Wm., 54
BURSON
  John, 291
BURTON
  Margaret J., 230
BURWELL
  George H., 105
  George W., 104
  Laura, 103
  Laura L., 104, 105
  Mary, 32
  Nathaniel, 32
BUSSARD
  Annie R., 45
  C. A., 76
  Louisa S., 188

INDEX

O. M., 45, 188, 261
Orlando M., 104
BUSY
  Ezra F., 17
BUTLER
  George P., 184
  Jane, 251
  Margaret C., 184
  Millie, 11
  Mollie, 10
  Sallie A., 135
  William A., 184
BUTTS
  Annie E., 102
  Arthur W., 179
  Ellen, 184
  Ernest S., 236
  Oliver G., 102
  Sweringer, 100
BUXTON
  B. D., 140
  Clara, 76
  Clara J., 76
BYARD
  Lavenia, 86
  Thompson C., 86
BYRD
  John, 53
BYRNE
  Ann L., 61
  George M., 61
  Henry M., 61
  James J., 195
  Sydnor B., 61
  Thomas W., 61
  Uriah E., 61
  Virginia M., 61
BYRNES
  Elizabeth T., 10
  Littleton F., 197

CABELL
  Miss, 282
CAIN
  Mary L., 160
CALDWELL
  Arthur, 126
  George W., 100
  S. B. T., 48, 97, 100, 126
CALLAHAN
  Geo. W., 109

CALLOW
  LeRoy B., 218
  Wm., 218
CALVER
  Jos. C., 51
CALVERT
  C. C., 288
  David, 7
CAMP
  Mary, 250
  Nannie, 282
  Nina, 282
  Thomas, 282
CAMPBELL
  Arthur, 243
  Benjamin F., 28
  Jos., 242
  Rebecca, 242
  Ruth A., 91
  S. A., 261
  Samuel, 71
CANADA
  Clem, 27
CANBY
  Wm. M., 125
CANNON
  J. F., 8
  John F., 9
CANTER
  Isaac W., 188
  Susan J., 188
CARDWELL
  George, 133
CAREY
  M. B., 240
CARLISLE
  David, 296
  Emily E., 68
  James, 249
  Jas., 68
  Mary A., 296
  Sallie E., 32
  Thos. M., 200
  William A., 262
CARN
  Wm., 167
CARNEAL
  C. N., 70
CARNES
  D. J., 161
  Ida V., 36
  Samuel L., 40

CARPENTER
  B. Frank, 16
  L. F., 16
  M. B., 16
CARPER
  Frances, 232
  P. W., 232
  Philip W., 281
  Thos. M., 281
CARR
  David, 22, 51, 84, 124, 136, 137, 138, 289
  Isaac, 76, 77
  J. C., 84
  J. W., 267
  Jas. W., 219
  Jno. C., 163, 219
  Joseph, 214
  Josephus, 219
  Lewis M., 57
  Mary, 223, 227, 230
  Mary E., 289
  Mollie, 163
  Saml., 37
  Samuel, 30
  Susan B., 51
  Thos., 223
  William, 84
  William P., 97
CARRINGTON
  W. F., 8
CARROLL
  ___, 249
  Andrew, 225
  Charles, 28
  M. E., 225
CARRUTHERS
  ___, 189
  Anne G., 90
  Carrie M., 90
  J. E., 68, 192
  Jas. E., 104, 159, 192
  John, 142
  Louisa, 104
  S. E., 142
  Thos., 88
  Thos. N., 87, 90
  Virginia L., 87
  Willie T., 215
CARSON

The Mirror
INDEX

C. A. R., 212
Cath. A. R., 188
J. W., 4
James H., 124
Wm., 50
CARTER
  A. B., 1
  Alexander, 159
  Alice, 151
  Ann, 75, 212, 214
  Annie W., 244
  B. F., 140
  B. G., 137, 171, 182
  Benjamin G., 261
  C. S., 214, 244, 275
  Constance, 44
  E. O., 171
  E. P. B., 146
  Eleanor H., 147
  Elizabeth, 136
  Elizabeth O., 171
  Emily, 81
  Emily M., 71, 81
  F. M., 120
  Fannie, 149
  Francis M., 75
  Geo., 144, 171
  Geo. W., 97, 209
  George, 171
  George F., 261
  Georgie O., 97
  Gracie, 195
  Henry, 100, 138
  J. W., 140
  James S., 80
  James W., 136
  Jas., 108
  Jno. R., 243
  John, 71, 81, 202
  John A., 246
  John M., 96
  John R., 44
  Juliet, 214
  Lewis T., 165
  Lizzie, 149, 237
  Louise S., 21
  Lucian, 151
  Maria B., 1
  Mary A., 75
  Mary E., 64
  Mary W., 217
  Orra M., 285
  Oswall, 182
  Oswell, 292
  Paul, 285
  Phebe H., 43
  R. Welby, 246
  Richard, 76
  Richard H., 168, 251
  Robt. C., 147
  Rosa B., 261
  Rose M., 136
  Sarah C., 182
  Shirley, 21, 103
  T. H., 136, 166
  T. J., 43
  Tamar, 43
  Thomas, 103
  Thomas H., 214
  Thos. A., 100
  Thos. H., 212, 244
  Thos. J., 150
  Willie C., 43
  Wm. P., 103
CARUTHERS
  J. E., 47
  Jas. E., 112
CASE
  Geo. W., 288
  George W., 181
  Mabel, 288
  Mary F., 276
  Rosa B., 288
  W. W., 276
CASTILLO
  Joseph, 182
CASTLE
  Hattie F., 34
  Walter, 206
  Walter S., 127
CASTLEMAN
  C. F., 172
  Estelle S., 39
  Henry W., 39, 83, 121, 165, 207, 234
  Jno. S., 290
  Robert A., 193
CAUFMAN
  E. G., 32, 65, 166
CAVANAUGH
  Martin, 178
CAYLOR
  George H., 142
  Jos. J., 161
CAYTON
  Jno., 121
CHAFFE
  Charles, 268
CHAMBERS
  Edmund H., 274
  Wilford C., 60
CHAMBLIN
  A. B., 248
  A. G., 11, 63, 103, 248
  A. M., 56
  Addie, 165
  Albert G., 136
  Anna L., 102
  Annie, 100, 137
  B. A., 43
  Brook, 137
  Brooke, 230
  Burr P., 12
  Catherine, 152
  Clara, 248
  Dewanna, 234
  Duanna, 232
  E., 297
  E. B., 291
  Ellzey, 291
  Eva A., 58
  Eveline B., 248
  Fannie, 50
  Geo. W., 37
  H. C., 232, 234
  Helen, 272
  Henry W., 50
  Humphrey R., 103
  J. C., 297
  J. L., 206
  James H., 46, 110, 138
  Jared, 19
  Jas. H., 115, 141, 174, 272
  Jno. B., 103
  John, 116, 152, 232, 291
  L. C., 258
  Laura, 271
  Levin P., 58
  Lillian, 58
  Luther L., 58
  M. F., 156
  Mary A., 206

Mary E., 209
Mary V., 43
Mason, 232
Minor F., 166
Miss, 151
Norval, 258
O., 297
O. J. C., 51
Olivia C., 43
Orland, 296
Peyton, 271
Philip H., 50
R. C., 100, 118
Richard C., 102
Rose, 271
Rush, 137
Sallie, 260
Sarah T., 11
W., 297
W. W., 195, 200, 240, 271, 279
Walter W., 115
William, 130
Wm., 43, 131, 136
CHAMP
  Catherine, 277
CHANCELLOR
  Carroll, 165
  Lizzie P., 22
  Lorman, 22, 118
  Margaret E., 118
  Melzi, 97
  S. Carroll, 200, 219
  Susie, 97
CHAPIN
  Woodruff, 256, 257
CHARLTON
  Annie M., 185
CHATHAM
  James, 50
CHESTER
  John S., 295
CHEW
  Aldridge, 39
  Robert S., 74
CHICHESTER
  A. M., 27, 233, 278, 292
  Emily, 237
  G. Mason, 194, 278
  Janie, 278
  John, 57

John H., 261
Lydia, 233
M., 240
Margaret B., 278
Nannie L., 1
Richard M., 1
Sadie B., 27
Sallie B., 3
Washington, 233
Washington B., 278
CHICK
  Chas. E., 153
  Geo. W., 70, 153
  George W., 69
  M. W., 66
  Mary E., 295
CHILTON
  Henrietta E., 221
  Samuel, 221
CHINN
  Emory V., 253
  F. W., 282
  J. S., 86
  Jno. L., 282
  John, 281
  John L., 260
  Kenny C., 271
  R. S., 8, 232
  R. Stretchley, 230
  S. J., 87
  W. R., 8
Chinn Bros., 253
CHISWELL
  Joseph N., 4
  Mary V., 267
  Rachie, 4
  Wm., 267
CHOATE
  C. D., 146
CHRISTIAN
  Charles P., 47
  May, 55
CHURCH
  Jos. S., 290
  Church dedication
  M. E. Church South, 197
  Waterford Presbyterian, 105
CHURCHILL
  John, 7
  S. E., 7

CLAGETT
  Christiana H., 45
  H. O., 105, 217
  Lalla, 245, 248
  Thomas H., 45
  Thos. H., 29, 45, 245
  W. B., 42
  Wm. B., 29
CLAGGETT
  H. O., 42
CLAIR
  John S., 38
CLANCY
  Mr., 248
CLAPHAM
  Ashton, 240, 286
  Hannah W., 20, 22
  Josiah, 20
CLARK
  Annie E., 227
  Kate, 269
  L. P., 227
  Mary E., 265, 270
  Sarah J., 112
CLARKE
  Annie E., 228
  Charles L., 154
  Chas. L., 192
  James, 219
  Mary E., 265
  Mrs., 59
CLARKSON
  Jeannette, 152
  Thomas, 100
  Thos., 147
CLEMENTS
  Henry, 7
  Nannie, 283
CLENDENING
  Saml., 201
  Samuel, 201
CLENDENNING
  Saml., 93
  William, 95
  Wm. T., 275
CLINE
  Alfred, 187
  Arthur L., 156
  Bertha L., 291
  Chas. A., 262, 291
  Jeannette, 57
  Margaret A., 56, 150

INDEX

William, 150, 261
Wm., 57, 262
CLIPP
  Jas. B., 130
CLIPSTINE
  Amanda, 163
CLOUD
  Wm., 183
CLOWE
  R. E., 183
  William, 288
  Wm. H., 58, 272, 290
COATES
  Colvin, 282
COATS
  Thomas, 171
COCHRAN
  Ann, 97
  Annie, 3
  F. A., 171
  John J., 18
  Mary F., 3
  S. L., 208
  Wm. J., 3
COCHRELL
  Mary, 236
COCKERELL
  John, 219
COCKERILL
  Samuel, 81
COCKERILLE
  America, 4
  Americus, 228
  Bailey, 268
  Dufour, 174
  Edith, 161
  H. W., 4
  James, 4
  James C., 4
  James F., 52
  Jas., 10
  Jno., 15
  John, 14, 19
  Lucinda, 4
  Miss, 268
  Nannie L., 1
  R. H., 1, 4
  Samuel J., 174
  Sanford, 284
  Stanard, 174
COCKRAN
  Robert, 149

William H., 202
COCKRELL
  Sanford, 112
COCKRILL
  Jane A., 38
  Joseph, 80
  Nancy, 230
COCKRILLE
  J. A., 118
  Nancy, 248
COE
  Aurelius, 220
  Lillie V., 26
  Maria L., 220
  Sarah R., 238
COGLIN
  Michael, 11
COLBERT
  Clarkson T., 283
  Zitha, 183
COLE
  Andrew, 225
  D. W., 141
  Daniel, 166
  Elma, 269
  Emily P., 264
  F. M., 264
  Harriet, 225
  Herbert, 167
  J. Thompson, 179
  Jennie, 272
  K. B., 269
  Kendric, 272
  Laura, 240
  Mary E., 272
  Mattie, 213
  Peter, 100
  Sarah E., 166
  William, 225
COLEMAN
  David J., 3
  Fannie, 62
  Florence S., 79
  J. C., 29, 62
  J. Cleveland, 79
  James, 96
  Jane, 79
  John C., 79
  Julia E., 124
  R. Logan, 227
  Richard, 96
COLLINS

Cebella A., 32
Ella E., 58
Flora E., 5
W. G., 172
COLT
  Chester M., 32
COMBS
  Leslie, 12
COMPHER
  Annie M., 16
  Burr O., 2
  Elizabeth, 275
  Geo. W., 187
  Hannah A., 41
  John, 285, 286
  Laura J., 155
  Lucy, 286
  Lucy W., 285
  Mollie, 286
  Peter, 124, 160, 162, 178
  Saml., 103
  Wm., 162, 219
COMPTON
  Edmund, 237
CONARD
  Ebenezer, 219
  Ebenezer J., 255
  Jno. W., 292
  Jos. M., 188
  Joseph M., 188, 191
  Mary E., 292
  Rose, 219
CONDRY
  Ella A., 62
CONNER
  David, 45, 237
  Elizabeth F., 45
  Jas. W., 81
  John D., 221
  Martha, 237
  Mary V., 81
  Robert, 30
  Susan, 150
  Susan A., 60
  William, 199
  Wm., 200
CONRAD
  A., 2
  America M., 193
  Annie B., 193
  B. F., 35, 87

Cuthbert P., 168
David, 193
F. E., 117, 183
John, 11, 130
John W., 86
Jos. M., 95
Lizzie, 35
CONSTABLE
  John T., 84
CONWAY
  Nannie S., 35
COOK
  Amelia, 43
  David, 43
  J. S., 182
  Mattie, 43
COOKSEY
  Catharine M., 247
  Decatur W., 99
  Eliza E., 212
  Hannah R., 55
  Hattie, 144
  Obed, 144
  Rosa, 144
  Sallie, 247
  Sallie F., 215
COOKSIE
  Mary, 102
  Obed, 54
COOLBAUGH
  Lillian, 229
COOPER
  Adam, 288
  Alvery A., 76
  Bartlow, 150
  Benj. M., 153
  Columbus, 76
  Cordelia J., 76
  Edgar, 272
  Emeline, 59
  Evelyn A., 146
  Geo., 235, 266
  George, 230
  H. Clay, 250
  J. Franklin, 123
  Lucy, 12
  Lydia C., 247
  M., 140
  Mary E., 116
  Michael, 137
  Noah, 1, 10
  Peter, 238

Samuel, 253
Sarah A., 272
Sarah C., 232
Wilfred L., 89
Wm. F., 290
COPELAND
  Andrew, 227
  Bettie, 173
  C. P., 168
  Craven A., 166, 169
  J. E., 39
  James D., 262
  Jane, 124, 145, 227
  Rosie L., 232
  Silas, 108
CORBETT
  Libbie S., 8
CORBIN
  S. Anne, 163
CORDELL
  Ada M., 181
  Amanda E., 296
  Jos. W., 277
  Lucie V., 129
  Roberta L., 230
CORDER
  ___, 5
  Miss, 4
  Willie O., 187
CORNELL
  Edward F., 189
  Geo., 93
  Mollie, 127
CORNWELL
  J. T., 175
  Willie, 175
COX
  Caroline, 61
  James A., 239
  Jas. A., 239, 240
  John T., 124, 126
  L. B., 148
  Lydia A., 125
  Richard S., 269
  Rosa, 239
  S. K., 17, 141
CRAIG
  Caroline E., 205
  Henry, 85
  John, 47
  John A., 100
  John F., 100

Phila, 271
Rose, 33
CRAIGHILL
  Mary, 204
  W. P., 204
CRAIN
  Catherine, 152
  P. H., 152
  Philo R., 229
  Philo. R., 230
CRANE
  J. C., 79
  N. L., 79
  Smith, 66
  Theodore H., 79
CRANWELL
  Geo., 123
CRAVEN
  Alfred, 200
  G. G., 103
  Giles T., 103
  Lillie B., 248
  Mary A., 159
  William H., 267
  Wm. L., 237
CRAVENS
  Ross, 296
CREEL
  Lizzie J., 125
  Marshall D., 151
  Samuel, 245
CRENSHAW
  Annie, 2
  C. A., 219
  Gertie, 219
  L. H., 2
  Repps B., 2
CRICHTON
  John, 293
  Maud D., 293
CRIDLER
  Charles C., 198
  John, 280
  Missouri C., 48
CRIM
  F. J., 175
  Mary, 127
  Mary E., 238
  Wm. E., 186
  Wm. H., 219
CRISSEY
  Bertie, 95

The Mirror
INDEX

James B., 95
Johnnie W., 95
Sallie E., 126
CROCKET
  Samuel, 273
CROESDALE
  Mary D., 208
CROMER
  Edward, 192
CROMWELL
  Robert S., 186
CROSEN
  Samuel C., 211
CROSON
  Fillmore, 127
CROSS
  Annie V., 267
  Ella, 286
  Harry, 286
  James, 26
  Katie C., 267
  Sallie J., 155
  William, 267
  Wm., 155
CROUCH
  California, 2
CROWN
  Joseph, 15, 211
CROWSON
  Alice, 150
CROWTHER
  Elizabeth, 130
  John, 130
CRUPPER
  A. B., 90
  Elizabeth, 90
CRUZEN
  Mary E., 25
CULLEN
  Clarence L., 275
CULLER
  Emma C., 180
CUMMINS
  Edgar F., 162
  J. W., 68
  Jno. T., 162
  Levi, 162
  Sallie A., 122
  Thomas, 10, 11
CUNNINGHAM
  Wm. T., 138
CURRELL

Jno. J., 187
CURRIE
  E. A., 62
  Mary, 184
CURRY
  Ada, 282
  Andrew G., 205
  Annie, 68
  Charles E., 232
  Elizabeth, 132
  Harry E, 232
  John, 132, 202, 205
  John R., 278
  Katie, 88
  Rebecca E., 232
CUTHBERT
  James, 163

DABNEY
  Mary A., 259
  Richard H., 233, 259
DADE
  L. M., 195
  Lee M., 86
  Maurice, 4
  Medora, 86
  Robert L., 195
  Sarah E., 86
DAILEY
  Melinda, 166
  Thomas, 166
  William A., 166
DAILY
  Aaron T., 39
  Fannie A., 125
  John W., 106
  Maggie V., 247
  Wm. H., 53
DAINGERFIELD
  F. A., 145
DALE
  J. P., 154
DANA
  Anderson, 164
  Mary S., 164, 282
DANIEL
  Alonzo, 121
  David F., 167
  Elizabeth J., 249, 255
  Fernando, 171
  Hannah L., 201
  Harriet A., 115

James W., 137
Jas. W., 134
John O., 115
John T., 115
Sarah J., 145
DARBY
  Agnes M., 58
  Nickolas R., 58
DARNE
  W. Fayette, 167
  Washington F., 166
DARNES
  John W., 5
  Sarah E., 141
DARR
  Alpheus R. L., 96
  E. W., 38
  M. A., 38
  Mary E., 38
  Rosa A., 201
DAVENPORT
  W. G., 266
DAVIS
  A. H., 284
  Anna P., 57
  Arthur, 59
  Benjamin, 75, 82
  Cassandria, 124
  Cecil, 140
  Chas. E., 2
  Edwin, 261
  Eugene, 110
  Geo. F., 82
  H. W., 295
  Henry J., 22
  Isaac, 115
  Isaac F., 115
  J. W., 198
  Jane P., 22
  Jas. M. M., 110
  John, 61, 246
  John B., 140
  John I., 115
  Jos. L., 24
  Mamie, 159
  Martha A., 33
  Mary F., 8
  Mary J., 12
  Mary M., 75
  Minnie B., 246
  Peyton, 179
  R. L., 275

INDEX

Robert, 269
Robert L., 261
R. T., 110, 240
Richard T., 57
Wm., 164
DAVISSON
  A., 115
  E., 114
  Elizabeth, 115
DAVOIR
  Katie, 180
DAVRAL
  Ella L., 155
DAWSON
  Charles G., 244
  Elizabeth, 47
  J. T., 134
  M. K., 46
  Mary A., 134
  R. T., 46
  Robt., 293
  Rodger T., 46
  S. C., 134
  Samuel, 244
  Wm. H., 184
DAY
  W. B., 147
DAYMUDE
  Elizabeth, 54
DEAN
  Harry C., 172
DEAR
  G. W., 113
  J. W., 110, 112
  J. Will., 20
  J. Wm., 112
  Richard B., 192
DeBUTTS
  J. P., 294
  Mrs., 72
DECK
  Frederick N., 105
DEGRANGE
  Martha C., 92
DeLANCEY
  Annie H., 233
  Elizabet D., 233
DELANEY
  Nora, 29
DELANY
  Evelyn, 91
  Thos. J., 91

DeLONEY
  Laura, 194
DEMORY
  Emma K., 130
  Ophilia F., 11
DENHAM
  Caroline, 278
  Charlotte E., 278
  L. H., 278
DENNIS
  Ginevra H., 229
  John W., 229, 276
  Virginia C., 229
  Wm. A., 71
DENSMORE
  Mary G., 143
DERRY
  Christian, 128
  Emma L., 12
  G. W., 46
  Ida F., 46
  Janey E., 192
  John P., 192
  Joseph C., 192
  Joseph P., 295
  L. W., 78, 295
  Peter, 131
  Philip, 290
  Susannah, 124
  Susie, 128
  Virginia, 295
DEW
  Addie, 154
DeWITT
  Mary, 179
DIBREL
  A., 215
DIBRELL
  A., 272
  Anthony, 272
DICE
  J. C., 172
  S., 172
DICKEY
  Willietta, 165
DIEDERICK
  Clara V., 102
DILLON
  Anna E., 19
  C., 297
  J. W., 80
  James, 150

John J., 19
DINGES
  Alice V., 105
DINSMORE
  Mary G., 143
DISHMAN
  E. Virginia, 86
  Jams W., 86
  Joseph L., 26
  Margaret B., 86
DISHMOND
  Thos. E., 41
DIVINE
  C. N., 10, 12
  Emily, 290
  George H., 215
  Hugh G., 83, 293
  J. F., 133
  James F., 273
  Jas. F., 70, 149, 290, 293
  Luther, 297
  Mary A., 83
  Maude H., 218
  Rata, 296, 297
  Robt. E., 223
  Virginia W., 70
  W. W., 217, 297
  William, 124, 293
  Wm., 132
DIXON
  Collins, 11
d'LONY
  Laura V., 254
DODD
  Ashton, 154
  Chas. H., 194
  Claire, 240
  E. L., 139
  Henry, 84
  J. F., 235
  James H., 211
  Jane E., 154
  Laura A., 38
  Laura L., 211
  Lillie, 262
  Mary C., 235
  Mattie T., 34
  Thos. J., 206
  Walter D., 235
  William, 34, 280
  Wm., 278

The Mirror
INDEX

Dolly, Kite & Co., 273
DOLWICK
  Geo. W., 200
DONAHUE
  Ann, 42
  Fanny C., 42
  Thos. C., 29
  Wm., 42
DONALDSON
  Elliott S., 282
  Geo. R., 106
  Manly B., 106
  Patience, 106
DONOHOE
  A. C., 124, 126
  Delia, 276
  George A., 182
  Heloise E., 19
  J. C., 60, 238
  John C., 276
  Rebecca, 101
  S. R., 19
  S. Roszell, 138
DONOHUE
  Emily, 99
DORRELL
  Geo. A., 94
  Geo. W., 175
  Miss, 155
DORRITEE
  Jas. A., 256
DORSEY
  Emory, 181
  Geo. W., 51
  H. C., 196
  Hamilton, 181
  Portia R., 292
DOUGALL
  Virginia, 241
DOUGLAS
  J. E., 64
DOUGLASS
  W. C., 294
DOUTHIRT
  W. F., 264
DOVE
  Franklin H., 189
  Jas. R., 185
  Sallie E., 10
  Thomas, 10
DOWDELL
  J. G., 121

Jas. G., 227
  W. F., 226
DOWELL
  A. B., 194
  Annie R., 104
  J. G., 226
  Jno. T., 263
  John T., 162
  Lavinia, 162
  Lulah O., 32
  Lulie, 32
  Thaddeus, 104
  W. S., 151
  William F., 173
DOWNEY
  C. W., 31, 150, 161
  J. Madison, 133
  James M., 132
  Laura V., 31
  Vitas C., 150
  Zula S., 150
DOWNING
  Clara, 151
DOWNS
  Jerome, 142
  Jno. F., 266
  John, 90, 170
  Kate M., 177
  O. Fleet, 125
  Stephen, 242
  Thos. J., 85
DRAKE
  Francis T., 124
DRISH
  John H., 48
  William D., 11
  Wm. D., 48, 54
DRUMMOND
  James, 235
  Mary E., 236
  Dry Mill, 284
DUKE
  Benjamin, 281
  J. F., 82
DULANEY
  H. Rozier, 244
  Hal, 240
  Henry G., 42, 240
  Henry S., 25
  R. H., 240, 246
  Rebecca, 42
  Richard H., 294

Tim, 56
DULANY
  Avery, 159
  Daniel, 28, 159
  H. Grafton, 295
  Hal G., 294
  Heath, 57
  Hector, 200
  Henry G., 28
  John P., 72
  Marietta, 28
  R. H., 28, 294
  Rozier, 212
DULENY
  W. T., 57
DULIN
  Alfred, 42, 260
  George C., 260
  Margaret, 260
  T. C., 74
DUNAHUE
  T. C., 77
DUNBAR
  E. M., 183
  Edw. McV., 199
DUNCAN
  Edward A., 256
DUNLAP
  Joseph M., 62
DUNLOP
  E. R., 198
  Elenor H., 198
  G. T., 198
DUNN
  John, 153
  John W., 32
DUTTON
  John B., 62
  Lizzie S., 62
DUVALL
  Julia, 43
  M. E., 186

EACHES
  Jos. G., 282
EAMICH
  Geo. F., 182
  Harry, 267
EASTERDAY
  George J., 190, 191
  Herbert C., 260, 281
  Marvin P., 274

Mary E., 274
William P., 134
Wm. A., 260
Wm. D., 17, 274
Wm. P., 17
EASTWOOD
  M. J., 254
  Mamie J., 254
EBERT
  Margaret, 207
EDMONDS
  Adaline, 31
  E. G., 31
  Elias, 31
EDMUNDS
  Alice, 163
  Littleton, 222
EDRINGTON
  Ellora, 281
EDWARDS
  Alpheus L., 51
  Annie V., 190
  Barbara A., 146
  Charles G., 170, 186
  Chas. G., 116, 207
  Edmonia, 258
  Fannie, 258
  Ida A., 116
  J. W., 181
  James R., 59
  Jennie, 262
  John F., 190
  John N., 258, 262
  Julia M., 104
  Laura, 242
  R. H., 54, 55, 107, 207, 242, 258
  Richard W., 116
  S. R., 190
  Samuel E., 115
  T. M., 196
  Thomas E., 217
  Thos. W., 200, 258, 264
Edwards & Hutchison, 20, 234
Edwards & Son, 264
EGGLESTON
  W. G., 289
ELGIN
  Anna, 104
  Chas. H., 205

Elizabeth, 124, 205
Francis, 273
Gustavus, 205
John F., 70, 71
Mary J., 273, 280
Nannie, 288
Nora, 170
Thos. G., 273
William L., 274
Wilson, 159
ELKIN
  Sarah A., 56
ELLETT
  Tazewell, 157
ELLIOT
  H. C., 296
ELLIOTT
  Annie E., 161
  Henry, 161, 280
  Jared L., 42
  Jesse, 280
  Kate, 263
  Lizzie, 161
ELLISON
  Frederick, 194
  Wm. E., 30
ELLMORE
  C. A., 167
  Chas. A., 63
  Cora V., 206
  Elizab'h A., 124
  Estelle, 274
  Fannie, 223
  Harvey, 291
  J. Russell, 274
  John W., 196
  Laura B., 194
  M. Pleasant, 196
  Martha S., 82
  Mary W., 167
  Odie, 196
ELLYSON
  Eliza G., 208
ELLZEY
  Francis, 277
  Thos., 281
  Wm., 277, 281
ELWOOD
  R. P., 99
EMERICK
  John, 202
  John H., 102

EMERSON
  Mary, 127
EMMONS
  Douglas W., 59
ENGLISH
  Chester, 65
  Florence S., 29
ERWIN
  Annie, 282
ETCHER
  Ann, 28
  James, 176
  Peter, 28, 139
EUBANK
  Annie, 8
  Joseph C., 19
  Thomas P., 8
EUBANKS
  Belle, 262
EVANS
  Arthur J., 177
  C. A., 138
  Newton P., 156
  Rowena, 206
  Sarah W., 147
EVARD
  Charles, 241
  Charles E., 46
  Mary E., 21
EVART
  Chas. E., 21
EVERHARD
  Effie A., 217
EVERHART
  Bettie E., 136
  Calvin L., 102
  Cordace S., 213
  Delia E., 173
  George O., 56
  John, 3
  John B., 136
  John G., 215
  John Q., 209
  John W., 149
  Jos., 131
  Joseph, 86
  Joshua, 242
  Lydia J., 235
  Mary E., 179
  Rachel, 71
  Sallie, 150
  Sallie B., 178

The Mirror
INDEX

Tilghman, 2
EVERSON
  Ellen V., 102
EWELL
  Helen, 131
  Hellen, 235
  Jesse, 118, 235, 289
  John, 235
  John S., 131
  Mary J., 235

FADELEY
  Edward A., 36
  Edward B., 36
  Geo. B., 268
  Mary A., 36
FADELY
  C. F., 36
  Charles H., 258
  E. B., 36, 138
  Edward B., 35
  Geo., 258
  Henry J., 70
  M. M., 258
  Mary A., 35
  Mary L., 35
  Orra M., 260, 269
FAIR
  Enoch, 25
FAIRFAX
  Archibald B., 64
  Arthur P., 64
  Hamilton, 199
  Hamilton R., 190, 200
  Henry, 245
  J. W., 135, 190, 245
  Jno. W., 128, 197
  John, 250
  John W., 135, 216
  Lindsay, 250
  Lizzie, 128
  Mary E., 135
  Orland, 61
  R. Linsdey, 245
FANLEY
  John H., 41
FARR
  Enoch, 23
  Georgie L., 94
  R. R., 160
FAULKNER
  C. J., 222

FAUNTLEROY
  A. M., 183, 184
  Arthur R., 153
  C. M., 217
  Charles M., 263, 268
  Chas. M., 74, 183, 184
  D. F., 121
  Frances, 268
  J. H., 27
  Jane D., 153
  John F., 127
  Kinchloch, 105
  Minna, 27
  Minnie, 27
  R. P., 264
  Robert H., 153
  Robert P., 160
  T. T., 127, 184
  Thomas T., 263
FAWLEY
  Elizabeth, 255
  Geo. W., 36
  Henry J., 138
  Jeremiah, 255
  Sarah W., 138
  William, 140
FEASTER
  D. W., 76
  Kate E., 49
  Wm. F., 23
FEBIGER
  Frances, 144
FEBREY
  Annie, 36
FEICHSTER
  Edward T., 79
FELLOWES
  Francis, 230
FENTON
  Enoch, 67, 68
  Frank, 150, 297
  Hester, 67
  Laura J., 55
  Mary, 150
  Ruth E., 68
FERGUSON
  Bertha T., 61
  Geo. O., 61, 155
  George O., 55
  Hattie F., 61
  J. S., 12

Jas. H., 129
Jas. W., 128
Mattie T., 55
FEWELL
  Kate, 93
  Rhoda, 219
  Wm. S., 93
FIELD
  Edmonia, 9
  Samuel, 9
  Sarah V., 9
FIELDS
  EmoryJ., 93
  Geo., 12
  Jas., 84
  Mary V., 40
FIERY
  B. F., 56
  Mollie, 56
FIFIELD
  Jos. N., 215
FILLER
  A. T. M., 1, 39, 201, 202
  C. W., 1
  Ella, 202
  Jas. H., 21
  Lillian, 202
  Lizzie L., 202
  Margaret F., 186
  Maud, 39
  Nanie, 202
  Robert B., 1, 10
  Rose W., 201, 202
  Sarah E., 145
  William B., 259
FILLINGANE
  Emma, 126
  Maggie E., 153
FINCH
  Ella, 47
FINK
  Fayette, 181
  Lafayette, 182
FISHBURNE
  R. B., 200, 240
FISHER
  Nelson, 74
  S. P., 169
FITZGERALD
  Johanah, 46
  Peter, 46

FITZHUGH
  Matilda W., 48
  Nannie, 26
  Wm. C., 48
FLAHERTY
  James E., 123
  Jas. E., 212
FLEMING
  Andrew S., 255
  Wm. C., 131
FLETCHER
  Albert, 156
  Albert H., 161
  Alice, 243
  Eliza, 215
  Erasmus, 182
  Fannie, 291
  G. B., 197
  Isaac, 280
  Joshua, 177
  Julia, 68
  Martha, 291
  Mary E., 280
  Tacy, 168
  Wm., 188
  Wm. E., 32
  Wm. H., 291
FLING
  Alice, 13
  Charles T., 131
  Edward, 13
  Ellen V., 237, 238, 239
  Geo. W., 75, 97, 277
  George W., 237, 275
  James L., 44
  Josephine, 13
  Sarah E., 31
  Susan, 75
  William F., 237
  Wm. E., 238
FLIPPO
  Monroe, 213
FLORENCE
  Erastus, 237
FOLEY
  Margaret J., 80
  William, 11
FOLLANSBEE
  Josie M., 40
FORBES
  John M., 52, 285

FORD
  Geo. T., 53
  Robert, 123, 133
FORSYTH
  Geo. R., 60
  John W., 273
  Louisa, 279
  Mary C., 273
  William J., 124
  Wm. T., 279
FORTNEY
  James B., 46
FOSTER
  J. W., 12, 13, 147, 163, 164, 177, 217, 288
  John H., 46
  Lula, 144, 177
  Maj., 189
  Mariana, 147, 148
  Mary E., 288
  Miss, 149
  T. R., 288
  Thomas R., 177
  Thos. R., 147, 164
FOUCHE
  G. W., 49
  S., 217, 265
FOUSCHE
  D. T., 33
FOX
  Charles E., 92
  Fanny E., 235
  Flora, 194
  Geo. K., 235
  Hattie, 131
  Hettie, 51
  Parkison, 131
  S. E., 217
  Wm., 82
FRAME
  Chas. A., 232
  Jane, 232
  Julia V., 218
  Wm. H., 6
FRANCES
  A. Lee, 149
  Wm. H., 31
FRANCIS
  A. B., 163
  Annie E., 196
  Ella C., 41, 47, 51

  Henry, 3
  J. E., 51
  L. M., 237
  Rebecca, 3
  Sallie A., 187
  Sidnor B., 195
  Susie E., 90
  Thomas, 41
  Virginia S., 61
  Wm. H., 196
FRANKLIN
  Alice C., 24
  C. D., 24
  Chas. D., 14
  Frederick, 296
  J. B., 217
  James T., 127
  Thad. W., 124
FRASIER
  Henry, 262
  Lizzie, 262
  Miss, 131
  Richard C., 262
  Saml. H., 124
  Samuel H., 122
  Sarah E., 172
  Townsend, 172
  Wm. H., 124
FRAZIER
  Caroline, 112
  Henry, 268
  Herod, 131
  J. W., 39
  Rush C., 39
  Wm. H., 176
FRED
  Annie, 107
  Annie P., 107
  Burr P., 62, 290
  Frank L., 55, 107, 185, 210, 290, 293
  Hamilton, 185
  Rachael, 290
  Rebecca J., 62
  S. R., 149
  Saml. R., 185
  T. Walter, 293
FREE
  Jacob, 130
FREEMAN
  Annie L., 84, 85
  Col., 250

The Mirror
INDEX

Hattie L., 84
John McG., 85
Lewis H., 84
FRENCH
  Capitola, 225
  Robert, 225
  Uriah, 219
  Wm. H., 244
FRERE
  Mary C., 6
FREY
  J. Cost, 30
  Laura J., 102
  Saml. L., 102
FRIEND
  Annie, 81
FRITTS
  Franklin, 119
  Franklin F., 128
  Frederick H., 7
FROST
  Caroline J., 242
  Caroline T., 240
  John T., 240
FRY
  Adelade S., 159
  Annie J., 95
  Annie S., 273
  Butler, 71
  Charlotte E., 242
  Claretta M., 281
  Cora D., 187
  Danl. N., 159
  Elizabeth, 225
  Ella E., 123
  Emma D., 218
  Emma J., 39
  Geo. M., 125
  George, 218
  George W., 39
  Harvey N., 295
  Isaac, 280
  J. W., 176, 191
  James W., 67
  John T., 273
  Julius F., 40
  Lucinda, 13, 22
  Lydia E., 98
  Maggie, 125
  Malinda E., 273
  Martha, 92
  Mary A., 36

Mary E., 40, 187
Mary F., 23
Millard, 187
Peter A., 273
Peter W., 187
Philip, 108
Richard W., 119
Sarah V., 153
William, 225
Wm. B., 273
FULTON
  Carrie, 200
  D. C., 22
  Jno. E., 10
  R. I., 76
  Robert I., 76
  Robt. J., 168
  Sarah, 124
  Wm., 168
FUNK
  Fayette, 12
FUNSTEN
  Fannie S., 193
  Mary, 193
  Oliver R., 193
FURGUSON
  George O., 34
  Janie F., 88
  Josiah, 160
  Lucy E., 160
  Romulus, 88
FURR
  Cattie, 116
  Charles, 160
  Edgar, 120
  Edward, 37
  Ella, 46, 72, 276
  Evie, 210
  Fannie, 80
  Fenton, 48, 72, 240
  Frank, 80, 277
  Frank N., 7, 277
  Harry E., 41
  Henry, 259
  Ida, 152
  John L., 156, 166
  Johnson, 12
  Jos., 160, 182
  Joseph, 221
  Joseph P., 41
  Kemp B., 46
  M. B., 138

Mary C., 138
Maude W., 80
Minnie, 120
Minor, 156, 166
Mollie T., 41
Octavis, 120
Pleasant, 99
R. E., 99, 152
Richard E., 80, 97, 100
Robt., 149
Sallie G., 240
Townsend C., 75
W. G., 291
Walter T., 120
William G., 152
Wm. C., 182
Wm. G., 116, 210

GAINES
  Alice, 246
  David, 262
  Euphemia, 51, 53, 124
  George W., 246
  Jennie, 271, 272
  Lucy L., 262
  Mary B., 24
  Nettie A., 151
  Precilla, 262
  Thomas A., 262
  Wm., 162, 222, 227, 235, 271, 272
  Wm. H., 179
GALLAHER
  Edward F., 158
  H. N., 117, 158
  J. Shannon, 158
  James N., 158
GALLEHER
  Achsah W., 208
  Adaline B., 122
  Daisy L., 240, 241
  Edditson, 274
  George T., 295
  H. N., 122
  J. Ashby, 198
  James N., 116
  Jane D., 274
  John W., 119, 240, 241
  T. H., 274

INDEX

Thomas, 141
Turner H., 34
Wm. R., 118
GARDEN
  Annie B., 89
GARDNER
  Chas. E., 274
  James L., 182
  Jane, 132
  Jas., 37
  Jas. L., 30
  Jennie H., 38
  R. E., 38
  Robert J., 224
  Susan, 182
  Thomas J., 182
  Wm., 132
GARNER
  Catherine, 192
GARNETT
  Alice C., 230
GARRETT
  Annie L., 256
  B. W., 183
  B. Wm., 127
  H. H., 61
  J. W., 202
  Jno. W., 163
  John W., 46
  Minnie B., 183
  Robert L., 54
  Rosa, 240
  Virginia B., 127
  W., 290
  W. E., 217, 239
  W. Frank, 239, 240
  Wm. E., 135
GARRISON
  B. T., 34
  Mary E., 34
GATES
  Charles J., 282
GAUTER
  Mr., 187
GAVER
  C. .C., 230
  C. C., 78, 128, 134, 140, 162, 182, 212, 239
  Chester C., 159, 237
  Emma, 244
  Henry, 237, 239

J. W., 285
John, 132
Mamie W., 77
Nettie W., 143
Roy, 77
T. F., 77
GAYNOR
  Ann E., 289
  James, 219
GEASLIN
  Geo. A., 147
  Samuel S., 184
  Texanna, 264
GEISKING
  Wm. A., 294
GEORGE
  Ella E., 294
  James, 76
  John, 111
  R. M., 111
  Rosanna M., 112
  Samuel, 264
  Samuel W., 266
GERMAN
  Smith, 79
GIBSON
  Ada, 255
  Ada W., 272
  Annie, 255
  Douglass, 273
  Esther, 255
  G. B., 260
  Gilbert, 255
  H. D., 272
  Herman D., 272
  J. D., 294
  John, 255
  John M., 147
  John N., 260
  John W., 126
  Jos. A., 260
  Lucy, 255
  Meta, 255
  R. Emma, 253
  S. M., 253
  Selden M., 250
  W. G., 262
  Willie, 147
GIDDINGS
  Charles G., 293
  Ellen R., 287
  Luther, 123

Nannie, 255
W. V., 107
William, 123
William V., 191
Wm., 255, 256, 287
GILKESON
  J. Smith, 79
  Jennie, 79
GILL
  Catharine L., 101
  Charles H., 101
  J. C., 174
  John, 291
  John L., 173
  Patrick, 255
  Sarah R. C., 101
  Wm. H., 202, 207
GILLINGHAM
  Chalkey, 35
GILMOR
  Harry, 100
GINGRICH
  Cyrus M., 32
GIST
  Bettie, 25
  Chas. W., 114
  F. P., 249
  Frank P., 218
  H. C., 108
  Henry C., 215, 218, 273
  Mary G., 273
GLADSTONE
  J. E., 123
  John E., 136
GLASCOCK
  Agnes, 6
  Alfred, 36, 260, 269
  Belle H., 245
  Burr, 169
  Emsey, 169
  Hattie B., 36, 260
  Henry V., 6
  John S., 6
  May, 269
  T. J., 245
  Thos. A., 131
GLASSCOCK
  Alfred, 31, 33, 36, 51
  Bedford, 167, 168, 217, 219
  H. B., 33

Hattie, 51
Hattie B., 143
John, 130
May, 219
S. A., 219
Thos., 168
Thos.G., 167
GOCHNAUER
　Jos., 290
　Sallie M., 266
GODFREY
　Wm., 280
　Wm. H., 235
GOLDEN
　Elizabeth M., 112
　John W., 112
GOLDSBOROUGH
　Katie, 264
GOLDSMITH
　E., 218
　Emanuel, 233
　John, 189
GOOD
　John B., 67
GOODE
　Edward B., 208
GOODHART
　Leonoro, 33
　Sarah, 62
GOODHEART
　Roberta, 30
GOODIN
　John, 211
GOODRICK
　Cornelia, 222
　Cornella, 221
GOODWIN
　James W., 210
　Mary J., 131
　Sallie, 210
　W. T., 131
GORDON
　Arthur, 4
　George W., 90
　Lemuel C., 27
　Nannie B., 90
GORE
　Albert, 295
　Nannie, 295
　Sarah, 146, 171
　Susan C., 231
　Thomas, 146

Thos. H., 266
Tilghman, 19
Gore & Janney, 266
GORUM
　Arthur, 23
GOUCHNAUER
　W. L., 266
GOUGH
　Julia, 285
GOULD
　Jas. B., 151
Gould & Wilkening, 267
GOULDIN
　John W., 74
GOUVERNEUR
　Samuel L., 12
GOVER
　Alice C., 14
　Catherine, 277
　Edwin M., 117
　Edwin R., 83
　Jane, 67
　John B., 67
　Lizzie, 86
　Mrs., 51
　Robert, 277
GRADY
　Frank, 148
　Frank T., 148
GRAFT
　Alice, 285
GRAHAM
　Elizabeth R., 134
　Florence L., 144
　Herbert, 6
　Laura, 212
　Lucretia V., 124
GRAY
　A. P., 53
　Arthur P., 252, 277
　Asher W., 18, 41
　C. D., 145
　Chas. S., 1
　Henrietta, 287
　James, 236
　Jerome B., 285
　John, 94, 144, 146,
　　217, 245, 277, 287
　Joseph, 277
　Lalla, 245
　Laura L., 45
　Lillie, 167

Mary B., 155
Mary E., 159
Mina R., 252
Norvell R., 252
O. C., 168
R. A., 145
R. Bently, 167
R. W., 20, 159
Rebecca, 94
Robt. W., 155
Rodney W., 207
Wm. H., 277
GRAYSON
　David L., 269
　Elizabeth O., 171
　S. N., 203
GREEN
　Edward, 166
　Euphemia, 140
　Fannie B., 280
　Henry, 84
　J. H., 176
　James, 61
　John E., 22, 281
　L. R., 14
　Maggie, 61
　Mary F., 53
　Mary J., 22
　Mr., 242
　Richard M., 176
　Theodosia S., 84
　Thomas, 177
　Thomas C., 272
　W. C. McG., 214
GREENE
　Chas., 65
　Emma A., 6
　J. Frank, 7
　Willard W., 197
GREENLEASE
　Annie E., 191
　Isaac, 152
　Lena E., 191
　William H., 191
GREGG
　Albert, 282
　Alice G., 87
　Asenath, 134
　Elizabeth, 223, 278
　Emma W., 223
　G. G., 192
　H. W., 250

Henry H., 230
Lutie, 192
Martha A., 191
Phebe A., 191
William, 238
Wm., 47, 223, 242
GREGORY
Wm., 284
GRIDLEY
Lucius E., 7
GRIFFITH
Alice G., 265
Benj. F., 24
Charles T., 265
Elizabeth, 118
Matilda, 265
GRIGSBY
William, 44
GRIMES
Annie, 264
Bradshaw, 55
Geo. W., 33
George, 232
Henrietta J., 53
John T., 32, 33
Madison, 232
Martha J., 106
Mary A., 186
Miranda, 55
Samuel, 198
Wm., 217
Wm. H., 55, 194, 235
Grimes Bros., 235
GROSS
Ella V., 161
John W., 98
GRUBB
B. A., 211
Benj., 264
Bertie, 267
Clara B., 264
Curtis, 65, 211
Dollie, 286
Edna M., 177
Fannie, 15
J., 182
J. T., 80
J. W., 54
James, 253
Jas., 252, 282
Joseph F., 148
Joseph L., 126

Joseph P., 265
L. Annie, 223
L. M., 264
Laban C., 39
Levan C., 163
Maggie V., 264
Marietta B., 200
Mary D., 265
Minnie C., 139
R. W., 273
Robert W., 12, 207
GRUNDY
Barton H., 149
GUIDER
Maria, 180
Nimrod, 20
GULICK
Ann, 72
Ann V., 175
Ashby H., 175
Emoretta H., 58
Francis, 58
Georgie, 94
Greer, 131
James H., 175, 233
John F., 165
May R., 233
Nancey, 58
Sallie, 165
GUNNELL
Chas. T., 69
GURY
Mrs., 241
GUSTIN
Ann E., 239
Anna J., 140, 164
GUY
Catherine, 110
Flave, 110, 111, 120, 229

HACKETT
W. T., 273
HAGAN
Chas. W., 163
Earnest R., 163
Lucy M., 163
Sallie E., 163
HAIGHT
Alexander, 18
HAINES
Edward, 12

Flavius B., 182
Joseph A., 9, 10, 12
Washington, 65
HALDEMAN
W. C., 260
HALEY
Mary D., 60
HALL
B. J., 156
Bertha, 255
E. Goldsborough, 62
J. M., 25, 118
James M., 255
John W., 220
Joseph, 260
Lizzie, 118
Maria, 251
Martha E., 25
Mary E., 123
Nelson, 199
Sallie, 260
Thomas B., 255
William, 293
Wm., 251
HALLACK
Geo., 83
HALLAN
Armilda, 23
HALLER
Isaac, 63
HALLEY
Fannie V., 39
S. N., 39
HAMILTON
Burr, 29
J. W., 158
Lydia J., 61
O. A., 14
Owen, 130
Samuel P., 130
Sarah, 73
Sarah T., 68
Thom, 266
HAMMERLY
B. H., 198
Charles L., 201
J. A., 206
J. W., 141
Jennie, 191
John, 57, 59, 65
John W., 2, 201
Jos. A., 68

Mary E., 68
Mary V., 201
Zeller B., 206
HAMMETT
  Edward, 281
  Sarah, 281
HAMMON
  ___, 13
HAMMOND
  C.W., 232
  Frances, 232
  O. W., 97
HAMNER
  William C., 246
HAMPTON
  ___, 271, 294
  George H., 79
  J. A., 3
  J. F., 169
  James F., 150
  John, 187
  Manly, 90, 182
  Mary E., 62
  Rosie, 150
HAMTRAMCK
  Jno. F., 259
  Sarah, 259
HANBACK
  Silas B., 182
HANCOCK
  Edwin A., 58
  Flora, 281
  James W., 175
  Jane T. L., 175
  Samuel G., 175
HANES
  Sarah, 101
HANFORD
  Chas. B., 165
HANNEWINCLE
  Meta A., 92
HANNON
  Nannie D., 50
HANSBOROUGH
  ___, 133
  John, 123
HANVEY
  Dorcas H., 55
  Jas. D., 55
  Mary, 203
HARDEN
  Alfred, 15

HARDING
  ___, 155
  Albert, 254
  Alfred, 257
  Elizabeth, 78, 80
  H. Clay, 132
  Lucy C., 32
  Margaret J., 39
  Nettie D., 132
HARDY
  Alvarrado, 60
  Harrison K., 78, 79
  Hattie A., 74
  Henry, 79
  Howard, 74, 79
  Indiana, 23
  John T, 207
  Magaret, 79
  Margaret, 74
  Robt., 79
HARLAN
  John M., 184
HARMON
  Allen C., 180
  Maggie, 180
HARNSBOROUGH
  Sarah C., 215
HARPER
  Adda B., 279
  Bertie A., 31
  Chas. E., 296
  Chas. J., 138
  Daniel, 120
  Florence E., 218, 220
  Florence N., 91
  George W., 243
  Harriet P., 106
  Ida, 78
  J. C., 78
  J. Newton, 31
  John W., 287
  Julius, 135
  Mary A., 148
  Robert, 91, 137, 279
  Robt., 220
  Robt N., 279
  Robt., 42, 218
  Sarah E., 29
  Virginia, 138
  Wells A., 272, 279
HARRIS
  C. D., 272

Edward, 10
Eliza, 205
J. T., 160
James, 280
James S., 235
Jas., 275
Jas. S., 205, 289
Jno. T., 243, 244
Maria, 224
Phil., 224
Robert C., 96
Sarah, 112
Sarah E., 168
Wm. P., 235
HARRISON
  Annie, 71
  Daisy, 117
  E. B., 195, 264
  Ed. B., 272
  George H., 170
  Henry, 153, 249
  Henry T., 46, 47, 117, 124
  Jas. B., 219
  Kate, 96
  Lizzie C., 88
  Powell, 263
  T. W., 68
  Thomas, 150
  W. P., 96
  Walter J., 211, 249, 287
  Wm., 244
  Wm. S., 265
Harrison & Powell, 18
HARTGROVE
  J. F., 60
HARTMAN
  Mary R., 105
  Mollie, 2
HARVEY
  Caroline, 164
  Granville, 233
  Jonas, 175
  Nellie I., 233
  Samuel L., 175
  Sarah C., 175
Haskins & Ball, 170
HATCHER
  Ella, 26
  Elma, 70
  G. R., 150

INDEX

J. Thomas, 136
John F., 107, 108
Jonah, 196, 197
Joshua, 70, 223
Lizzie, 38
Mary E., 223
T. C. L., 182
Thomas, 127
Thos. E., 119, 128
HAVENER
　Annie E., 95
　B. T., 260
　Benjamin, 83
　Cattie P., 125
　Dora L., 95
　Edgar B., 95
　James B., 125
　L. H., 150
　Lucy V., 197
　Marion I., 93
　Mary C., 156
　R. H., 56, 280
　R. Virginia, 260
　Rachael, 280
　Thomas A., 156
　Wm., 150
HAVENNER
　clayton, 151
　Ida J., 5
　James B., 156
　Laura T., 151
　Lucinda E., 39
　Rachel, 282
　Thomas, 151
HAWKINS
　Charles, 24
　Emma C., 219
　Molie, 24
HAWKS
　Charles L., 227
　Chas. L., 228
HAWLEY
　Ed., 288
HAWLING
　Bettie, 199, 200
　C. F., 268
　C. T., 128
　Chas. T., 271, 272
　Frances, 19, 124
　Isaac, 19, 104
　Jemima, 104, 106

Lewis, 26, 126, 128, 200
Mary L., 26
Wm., 128
HAWS
　Eva E., 118
　J. S., 182
　Lilly J., 189
　Mary J., 91
　Minnie J., 91
　Oscar E., 118
　Thos., 223
　William A., 91
HAXALL
　Anne T., 264
　Bolling, 264
　Bolling W., 166
HAY
　Elizabeth C., 179
　Fenelon D., 271
　George, 179
　Sarah D., 179
HAYES
　Frederick B., 37
HAYNES
　A. M., 254
　J. A., 11, 59
　Viva, 149
　Washington, 166
HAZLETON
　Ella G., 219
　William B., 219
HEAD
　B. F., 185
　Belle, 142, 163
　Belle F., 166
　Benj. F., 142, 163, 166
　Benjamin F., 23
　Clarence, 160, 252
　D. C., 223
　Geo. R., 18, 50, 168, 217
　George R., 49
　James M., 1
　Maggie, 160, 283
　Maggie W., 160
　Margaret, 73
　Mary, 166
　Nelson, 73, 108, 221, 254
　Rev., 46

Rosa, 18
Walter, 142
Wm., 286
HEADLY
　Mary, 121
HEATH
　Sallie J., 121
HEATON
　Abram, 121
　Abram S., 78
　Decatur, 121, 125
　E. Florence, 126, 136
　H., 126
　Henry, 25, 66, 78, 86, 122, 195, 284
　James, 122, 126
　Jonathan, 78, 284
　N. R., 284
　Town., 71
　Townsend, 121, 125, 126, 136
HEFFNER
　Carrie, 177
　George, 41
　John, 42, 220
　Stephen, 122
HEFLIN
　Calvin, 104
　Fannie P., 138
　Wallace, 104
HEISKEL
　J. Monroe, 73
HEISKELL
　Esther F., 84
　J. Monroe, 84
　Teackle W., 84
HEISS
　Washington, 63
HELM
　Jos., 289
　Joseph, 71, 273, 289
　Lewis C., 35
　Sophia, 71
HEMPSTONE
　C. T., 37, 227, 228
　Christian T., 176, 287
　Ida L., 37
　Mary, 227, 228
　Robert, 287
　Sarah V., 176
　W. Dade, 287
Hempstone & Perry, 93

The Mirror
INDEX

HENDERSON
  Annie, 96
  Annie B., 28
  Charles, 238
  Charles W., 28, 152, 200
  Chas., 193
  E. L., 166
  Ellen V., 238
  F. M., 2, 96, 248
  Fenton M., 190, 222
  John R., 193
  Laura L., 152
  Martha, 20
  Richard, 222
  Richard H., 20
  William H., 92
  Willie, 20
HENRY
  ___, 98
  Stanhope, 272
HERBERT
  Bushrod W., 239
HERNDON
  C. T., 271
  Chas. T., 56
  Louisa H. L., 275
  Willis, 255
HERRELL
  Clarence C., 121
HERRISFORD
  Gracie, 234
HESS
  C. B., 211, 269
  Chas. B., 212
  E. A., 212
  Ethel B., 211, 212
  F. A., 211, 212
  L. D., 156
  M. M., 156
HESSER
  A. T., 168
  Alcinda R., 68
  Elizabeth, 72
  Elizabeth H., 73
  Martha E., 134
HEWETT
  Abraham, 10
  Isabella, 10
HIBBS
  Mary J., 65
  Wm., 214, 222

HICKMAN
  Alice L., 110
  Ann E., 102, 283
  Bessie M., 65
  Eleanor A., 117
  G. L. H., 65
  Jas. B., 80
  Laura J., 102
  Mollie F., 176
  Rosie M., 65
  Thos. W., 216
  Wm., 102
HICKS
  Catherine W., 97
  Emma F., 76
  Jane, 180
  John F., 275
  S.D., 248
HIGDON
  Charles, 247
  James L., 21
  Jennie E., 210
  Mollie M., 91
  Sallie A., 75
HIGGINS
  Dennis, 256
  Harriet, 285
  Jesse T., 210
  Higgins and Waters, 210
HILL
  D. H., 272
HILLEARY
  W. P., 77
HILLEN
  Elizabeth, 186
  Solomon, 186
  Thos., 186
HILLIARY
  H. C., 70
HINDMAN
  Robert, 92
  Samuel E., 216
HINES
  Randolph, 138
  T. Jeff, 138
  Thomas J., 138
HIRST
  Annie A., 276
  Edgar H., 276
  John T., 190
  Hirst & Smith, 208

HITAFFER
  John, 54
  Sarah, 54, 59, 124
HITZ
  Anna, 100
  Jno., 100
HIXON
  Jonah, 163
HIXSON
  Abner H., 140, 169, 280
  Bertie, 153
  David, 97, 98, 99, 100, 103, 163
  Ella, 114
  Emily, 99
  Harriet R., 280
  John, 99
  John W., 114
  Joseph, 99
  Katie, 98, 99, 157
  Maria V., 205, 206
  Nancy, 99
  Nelson, 114
  Noah, 99
  Polly, 99
  Samuel, 99
  Taylor, 99
  William, 99
HODGDON
  Alexander, 229
HODGE
  Sarah A., 217
HODGKIN
  William G., 147
HODGSON
  Sarah J., 44
  William, 44
HOFFA
  Henry, 241
HOFFMAN
  Henrietta, 130
  Jane, 195
  Julia, 144
  Otterbein, 87
  Peter E., 8
HOGAN
  James, 85
  Nicholas, 223
  Patrick, 223
HOGANS
  Wesley, 117

INDEX

HOGE
  Alice, 245
  D. J., 118, 231
  Daniel, 245
  Eli, 278
  Eli J., 282
  Frederica P., 119
  Geo. D., 280
  Gracie, 296
  Isaac, 25, 230
  Isaac C., 155, 190
  J.M., 16
  James, 116, 163
  Jesse, 231, 296
  John B., 64
  Lizzie, 119
  Maggie, 25
  Margaretta R., 25
  Mary A., 276
  Minnie, 155
  Nancy H., 64
  Rachel N., 25, 230
  Rebecca N., 16
  Sarah, 245
  Susan A., 217
  Thos., 276
  Thos. H., 276
HOGELAND
  Henry St. L., 83
  James W., 236
  Jane F., 250
  John J., 250
HOLDEN
  Matilda, 151
HOLLAND
  John R., 135
HOLLIDAY
  Annie, 235
  Meta, 209
  Richard, 209
HOLLINGSWORTH
  Eleanor E., 16
  Jas. McH., 255
HOLMES
  Ann, 28
  Emily, 68
  Lot, 9
  Philah, 116
  S. E., 94
  Samuel C., 275
  William, 194
  Wm., 275

HOLROYD
  John, 231
  John T., 231
  Sarah E., 231
HOLTON
  Julia, 240
HOLTZCLAW
  Robert, 172
HOLYDAY
  R. C., 154
HOMRICHOUSE
  ___, 218
HOOE
  Housen L., 120
  Nancy, 59
  Orra C., 286
HOOFF
  C. R., 86
  John, 146
  J. Lawrence, 208
  Martha J., 146
  Rebecca, 86
HOOVER
  A. E., 263
HOPE
  Alice R., 68
  Annie, 126
  Charles W., 126
  Jno., 68
  John, 197
  Lydia, 68
  Robert F., 126
  W. A., 139
HOPKINS
  Betsy, 7
  Jane E., 297
  Josephine E., 93
  Louis N., 93
HOPPER
  Milton J., 6
HORNER
  Chas. W., 70
  Ellen A., 291
  Sarah, 70
HORSEMAN
  G. H., 268
  James W. F., 127
  Martha A., 4
  S. E., 261
HOSKINSON
  Clinton, 234, 261
  Clinton M., 46, 165

  Laura, 245
  Lennie E., 261
  Linnie E., 234
  R. H., 245
  R. W., 46
  Sallie R., 188
  Thomas G., 234
HOSPITAL
  Catherine, 265
  J. D., 224
  Lucullus, 113
  Susie, 270
HOSTLER
  W. R., 46
HOUGH
  Anna, 67, 68
  Arthur S., 207
  Bernard, 19
  Cordelia K., 122
  E. M., 47
  E. S., 109
  E. Stanley, 153
  Edgar G., 143
  Edgar P., 11, 69, 70
  Edward M., 122
  Eleanor H., 156
  Elizabeth, 37
  Frank, 282
  Ida A., 295
  Jonah, 67, 68
  Joseph, 91
  L. F., 295
  L. W. S., 3, 33, 293
  Lewis, 289
  Lizzie A., 161
  M. S., 219
  Mary, 33
  Mary E., 105
  Mary F., 44
  Mollie, 149
  Neal, 5
  Robt. W., 125, 295
  Sarah M., 122
  Sarah N., 283
  Slias F., 50
  T. E., 251
  Thos. E., 191
  Virginia L., 266
  William, 5, 195
  Wm., 191
  Wm. N., 283
  Hough & Gray, 144

INDEX

HOURIHANE
  John, 223
  M., 223
  Michael, 223
HOUSE
  Eli C. H., 70
  Eli H. C., 69
  Eli P., 152
HOUSEHOLDER
  Adam, 82, 84, 235
  Roxanna, 227, 235
  Silas A., 227
HOUSER
  Christopher, 91
  Eugene A., 176
  Jacob, 156
  James R., 88
  M. T., 81
HOWARD
  Norman DeV., 189
  T. B., 138
HOWELL
  Elizabeth, 280
  Flavius J., 278
  Joseph, 174
  Joseph M., 62, 253
  Mollie L., 216
  Rose, 174
HOWSER
  Jacob, 162
  Philip, 285
HUBBLE
  George W., 191
HUDSON
  Chas. W., 213
  Olive, 203
  W. A., 184
HUGHES
  Amos, 275, 277, 290
  Annie, 2
  Carrie V., 77
  Charles T., 180
  D. L., 211
  Elias, 2, 290, 292
  Floyd, 162
  H. W., 211
  J. Wilmer, 203
  James, 163
  Louise K., 77
  M. T., 211
  Robert W., 162
  Virginia, 2
  Willis, 84, 87
  Wm., 77
  Wormley, 290
HULFISH
  G. D., 132
  Harvey, 132
HUME
  Silas, 287
HUMMER
  Alpheus B., 113
  Alpheus P., 159
  David, 103
  Forest L., 159
  G. W., 181
  Julia A., 125
  L. J., 181
  Lavinia B., 210
  Martha, 113
  Martha B., 159
  Martina, 103
  Mattie H., 117
  Thomas E., 181
  Walter V., 60
HUMPHREY
  Abner E., 120
  Lydia, 166
  Margaret, 100
  Margaret A., 63, 70
  Thos. C., 218
  Thos. L., 13
  Wilmer D., 218
HUNSICKER
  Ursula, 26
HUNT
  Geo. A., 81, 94
  George A., 102
  Thomas, 228
  Wm., 228
  Wm. T., 248, 249
HUNTER
  Geo. P., 200
  George P., 140
  Jennie, 259
  Lady, 294
  Wm., 281
HUNTON
  Elizabeth, 270
  Eppa, 147, 148, 189
  J. Heaton, 189
  Margaret, 137
HURST
  Elizabeth J., 266
  James W., 266
  John T., 150
  Samuel G., 121
  Samuel S., 150
HUTCHINSON
  Catharine, 49
  Isadora, 207
  Lemuel, 49
  Maggie, 283
  R. S., 185
  Sina, 134
  T. B., 49
  Thos., 134
  Westwood, 203
HUTCHISON
  A. M., 77
  Annie, 59
  Athelia, 75
  B. M., 283
  Beverly, 221
  Charles L., 63
  Cuthbert, 45
  Ellen, 257
  Franklin, 77
  Henry B., 282
  J. A., 283
  J. H., 182
  J. R., 287
  Jno., 230
  John, 182, 249, 282
  John R., 86
  Jos. A., 108
  Joshua M., 163
  Julian A., 20, 234
  L. E., 98
  Leah, 40
  Leeah, 34
  Leroy M., 198
  Lucy W., 45
  Maria, 45
  Maria L., 77
  Mary E., 77
  Mary N., 173
  Redding, 98
  Reuben, 40
  T. B., 287, 288
  Thos., 57, 282
  Webb, 169
INGLE
  Osborne, 95
  Rev., 62

INGRAHAM
  J. H., 174
INGRAM
  Eliza, 101
  S. L., 101
INZER
  Jno. H., 217
IRISH
  Rachel, 274
ISAACS
  Annie E., 173
  Wm. B., 173
ISH
  Jacob, 40
  Laura M., 204
  Mollie J., 118
ISLER
  Jacob, 227
  Martha L., 227

JACKSON
  Albert, 162
  Edgar, 71, 193
  Geo., 60
  George, 235
  George W., 23
  H. Melville, 14
  Henry, 149, 218
  Henry M., 197
  Isaac, 265
  John, 251
  Littleton, 129
  Mary E., 268
  Olive C., 257
  Oscar, 188
  Peggy, 139
  S. K., 257
  Sarah, 108
  Susan, 249
  Thomas, 224
  Thos., 232
  Wm. B., 35, 37
JACOB
  E. T., 270
JACOBS
  A. R., 155
  Annie, 28
  Catharine, 132
  Catharine A., 41
  Elizabeth, 196
  Hampton, 40
  Hattie V., 141
  James W., 41
  John W. L., 183
  Leven T., 28, 287
  Louise, 287
  Robert C., 41
  Sarah E., 59
  Turner A., 28
  William H., 132
  Wm. W., 141
JAMES
  Benton, 102
  Celia, 176
  Chas. E., 33
  Craven, 176, 292
  D. M., 179
  Edgar E., 161
  Elijah, 22, 24
  Eliza, 96, 112
  Eliza P., 102
  Hannah, 196, 197
  Imogene M., 248
  Joseph, 33
  Levi, 159
  Lloyd L., 209
  Mahlon, 289
  Mason, 96, 196
  Mayo, 154
  Mollie L., 53
  Oscar C., 88, 209
  Robert, 112, 169
  Rose, 56
  Samuel R., 176
  Sarah, 33
  Sue F., 209
  Thos. H., 170
  Will, 56
  William C., 248
  Winifred, 169
  Wm., 248
  Wm. M., 33
JAMESON
  Wm. S., 192
JAMESSON
  M. M., 192
  William, 67
JANNER
  Mahlon H., 67
  Willie H., 67
JANNEY
  Abijah, 15
  Alice, 34
  Alice S., 42
  Anna M., 47
  Aquilla, 255
  Asa M., 26
  Belle, 192
  C. P., 34, 42, 228
  Chas. P., 159, 235, 249, 283
  Cora, 132
  Cornelia, 123
  Cossie, 262
  E. H., 280
  Edgar, 256
  Edwin L., 94
  Eliza, 273
  Elizabeth, 196
  Ella, 123, 262
  Emma L., 177
  Ethel, 297
  Francis H., 109
  George W., 7
  Helen M., 156
  Henrietta H., 241
  Henry, 262
  J. C., 8
  James W., 156
  Jane, 280
  Jas. C., 47
  Jeffie, 29
  John, 7, 34, 255, 266
  John C., 10
  Jos. R., 171
  L. J., 241
  Lizzie, 26
  Lucy N., 156
  Lydia S., 136
  M. F., 211
  Mabel H., 177
  Mahlon H., 82, 196
  Margaret, 154
  Nathan, 266
  Phineas, 196
  Pleasant, 73
  R. W., 177, 270
  Ray, 128
  Robert M., 151
  Sadie, 128
  Saml. M., 15
  Samuel A., 136
  Samuel H., 15, 82, 195
  Thomas, 128
  Tyson, 272

The Mirror
INDEX

Wm. F., 182
Janney & Cogden, 94
JARVIS
  Chas. F., 74
  Josephine, 74
Jeffras, Seeley & Co., 78
JEFFRIES
  E. M., 58
JENKINS
  Ann, 287
  Caroline, 193
  Charles, 38
  Charles W., 69
  Chas. T., 74
  E., 33
  E. V., 4
  Elijah V., 66
  Elizabeth, 74
  Emma, 218, 276
  Frank S., 216
  G., 176
  Gaythie, 111
  Harry S., 101
  Hattie B., 296
  Herbert, 91
  J. Clay, 276
  James C., 58
  Jos. H., 214
  Mary E., 276
  Mary F., 33
  Mollie, 111
  Norval, 214, 215
  Reuben, 214, 279, 280, 287
  Robert L., 118
  Rosa M., 276
  Samuel, 50
  Samuel L., 122
  Samuel M., 247
  Washington, 111
  Wm. G., 153, 230
  Wm. S., 153
JERMAN
  W. W., 134
JEWETT
  Annie, 17
  Edward H., 17
  Helen, 228
  Hugh J., 17, 228
  Isaac, 17
  Isaac W., 18

  James J., 17
  John, 17
  Jos. H., 17, 228
  Joseph H., 17
  Joshua, 17
  Susannah, 17
  Thomas L., 17
JOHN
  Annie, 17
  Stephen S., 17
JOHNS
  Annie W., 17
JOHNSON
  Alex. W., 137
  Alexander, 71, 72, 73
  Alpheus F., 118
  Anna M., 199
  Annie E., 252
  Araminta, 19
  Armstead, 160
  B. S., 118
  Charles W., 35
  D. I., 93
  Daniel A., 174
  Edward, 227
  Ella G., 269
  Emma R., 105
  F. C. D., 250
  Frances C. D., 161
  Franklin, 251
  George McV., 105
  Gertrude, 2
  Henry, 270
  Henry C., 177
  Hettie M., 161
  Jennie, 129
  Jno. M., 206
  John, 268
  John M., 207
  John N., 58
  John S., 89
  Julia, 234
  Lawson E., 174
  Louisa, 89
  Lydia A., 174
  M. Katie, 250
  Mary C., 141
  Mary E., 70
  Mollie M., 131
  Mollie W., 135
  Nancy, 99
  Peter W., 151

  R. Griffin, 132
  Robert, 251
  Robt. G., 294
  Rose, 168
  Susan C., 127
  V. M., 105
  Webby, 123
  Welby, 133
  Wm. A., 118, 168, 195
  Wm. H., 18, 161, 250
JOHNSTON
  Armstead, 117
  Fannie W., 119
  George, 87
  George T., 166
  J. W., 254
  John, 215
  M. E., 250
  Mary, 215
  S. J., 117, 129, 167
  Sallie J., 6
  Sarah C., 117
JONES
  ___, 149
  A. Catesby, 270
  Anna E., 251
  Ap C., 165
  Burr, 264
  Catharine, 140
  Catherine, 124, 203
  Charles, 259
  Chas., 182, 204
  Claggett B., 14
  Emelina, 218
  Horace, 218
  J. C., 272
  J. H. C., 14
  Jane, 264
  Jesse W., 181
  John C., 272
  John E., 25
  Jos. H., 2
  Lewen T., 269, 273
  Lina A., 225
  Lucinda, 75
  Mark C., 165
  Minnie C., 166
  Philip, 270
  R. P. W., 147
  T. Marshall, 20
  Thos., 134

The Mirror
INDEX
327

W. R., 273
JORDAN
 Arthur, 5
 Belle, 262
 Bessie, 48
 E. C., 262
 Edw. C., 262
 John L., 48, 266
 Julia, 48, 80

KAIGHN
 Isabella, 205
 Isabella G., 212
 John H., 77, 205
 Mary E., 77
KALB
 Alice O., 33
 Floretta D., 2
 Girta D., 189
 Jno. G. R., 193
 Nettie M., 54
 Silas D., 189
KANNER
 Willis, 139
KARNER
 Lancerlot, 154
KAUFMAN
 Geo. W., 3
 George, 137
KEEN
 Amanda S., 74
 Annie, 107
 Benjamin B., 107
 Charles, 119
 Dr., 80
 Geo., 75
 Hazel, 271
 J. W., 258
 John, 65, 68, 258
 Jonathan, 74, 280
 Ula, 107
 Washington, 234
 Willie S., 74
KEENE
 Bettie D., 202
 Newton, 12, 115
 Sarah F., 115
KEIM
 Susie, 9
KEITH
 Isham, 85, 198
 Jas., 198

Judge, 250
 Julia, 198
 Margaret, 85
KELLER
 ___, 218
 Granville, 170
KELLEY
 Elizabeth A., 109
 J. Harrison, 109
 James S., 117
 Mary E., 85
 Robert, 45
 Samuel D., 45
KELLY
 G. Frank, 267
KEMPER
 David S., 32
KENDALL
 Claiborn, 121
 Claiborne, 126
 Francis M., 174
 Margaret L., 174
KENDRICK
 Louisa E., 81
 Wm. L. H., 81
KENNEDY
 C. Estelle, 25
 H. H., 215
KENT
 Laura, 38
 Margaret M., 221
 N. H., 258
 Nelson H., 242
 Walter, 264
KENTER
 Kate, 93
KEPHART
 C. E., 237
 Chas. C., 92
 Geo., 44
 John W., 64
 Julius E., 44
 Morris, 129
 Wm. H., 150
KEPLAR
 Henry, 178
KEPLER
 H. S., 25
 Kate V., 112
 Mary L., 112
 Samuel, 112
KEPPLER

Samuel, 141
KERCHEVAL
 Geo. E., 68
 George E., 191
 J. R., 58
 James R., 58
KERN
 John A., 96
 Kate, 96
 Mary M., 282
 Olivia, 253
KERNS
 Fitzhugh, 152
KERRICK
 Charles C., 161
KERSEY
 Mary L., 198
 W. W., 120
KETTLE
 Amanda, 106
KEYES
 J. Howard, 194
 Wm. E., 192, 194
KEYS
 Annie M., 121
 Jane E., 19
 Philip, 127
KIDWELL
 Ann, 259
 Annie, 151
 Boyd S., 106
 Eliza J., 100
 Geo. H., 259
 Geo. R., 165
 James, 187
 Jane, 219
 Jas., 76
 John F., 33, 100, 259
 Mary E., 76
 Mary F., 254
 Mary J., 243
 Richard A., 247
 Samuel, 16
 Susan M., 100
 Thos., 171
 Zedekiah, 16
KILGOUR
 Harry J., 104
 Margaret M., 183
 Miss, 282
 Wm., 187
KILPATRICK

Hugh, 182
S. F., 233
KINCHELOE
  Annie P., 234
  Blanche, 255
  James, 255
  Wm. B., 234
KING
  Augustus, 166
  Gustavus, 127
  R. E., 136
  Victoria, 127
  W. P., 167
KINNAHAN
  Edw. N., 215
KINNEY
  Thos., 202
KINSER
  Sarah F., 85
KINTZ
  Jacob, 28
KINZER
  I. Louis, 220
  Margaret, 220
KIRKMAN
  Mrs., 93
KITE
  M. D., 273
KITZMILLER
  A., 295
  A. M., 190, 225, 295
  Ann E., 225
  Jennings, 295
  Mollie E., 295
KLEIN
  J. N., 266
  John, 232
  John A., 232
  Mary, 179
KLICE
  Thomas, 93
KLIPSTEIN
  John H., 60
KNIGHT
  Julia, 68
  Wm., 68
KNOX
  Catherine, 263
  Thomas P., 263
KODY
  Mary J., 207
KOLB

Wm., 269
KOOTZ
  Edward, 236
KOWNSLAR
  Ellen, 225
  Randolph, 225
KUHLMAN
  Caroline, 37
  Justice, 37, 187
  Justus, 186, 198, 202
  Mary M., 37
KUHN
  Geo. F., 136
  George, 133
  Lulle, 64

LACEY
  B. F., 282
  Benj. R., 115
  Ellis W., 163
  M. H., 16
LACK
  Mary, 43
  Wm., 43
LACOCK
  William H., 183
LACY
  Benj. R., 118
  Jos. B., 118
LAKE
  Achsah W., 116
  Charles R., 59
  F. Marion, 38
  James M., 219
  Susan, 71
  T. Sherman, 116, 208, 224
LAMAR
  Tina, 289
LAMBERT
  Francis, 197
  Jefferson D., 173
  M. B., 139
  Minnie, 165
  Minnie J., 197
  Mort., 30
LANE
  Amanda L., 69
  Beverly H., 97
  M. Florence, 97
LANHAM
  Annie, 56

Jno. W., 121
Lizzie, 1
Tacy E., 122
LANSDALE
  Alice, 2
  B. F., 2
  H. N., 2
LARZELEAR
  B. M., 209
LATANE
  James A., 14
  Julia, 14
LATHAM
  Humphrey N., 32
  Jno. F., 129
  John F., 129
  Kitty M., 129
  R. P., 129
  Robt. W., 116
  Thos. N., 116
LATROBE
  Mayor, 214, 217
LAUCK
  Wm. C., 61
LAUMAN
  Maugrate E., 69
LAWRENCE
  Miss, 203
LAWSON
  Anthony, 160
  Dennis, 112
  James, 233
  James H., 213
  R. B., 160
  R. M., 97, 160
LAY
  Charles W., 136
  Mary M., 108
  Thomas E., 135
LAYCOCK
  Adin W., 221
  C. F., 270
  Emily, 153
  George, 269
  James, 97
  Joseph, 153
  Mary J., 97
  Matilda, 176
  Samuel, 75, 176
LAYTON
  Wm., 270
LEACH

INDEX

C., 219
LEADBEATER
　Edw. S., 196
LEATHERLAND
　Mary V., 143
　Wm., 143
LEATHERMAN
　Eli, 58
LEE
　Ann, 153, 196
　Annie E., 179
　C. F., 98
　C. H., 276
　Cassius F., 179, 276
　Charles, 228, 283, 284
　Charles H., 105
　Chas. H., 103, 105, 249, 254
　David I., 27
　David J., 62
　E. A., 105
　Edmund I., 65, 203
　Elizabeth A., 105
　Elizabeth G., 284
　Evelyn, 91
　Fitzhugh, 221
　Geo., 222
　George, 119, 222
　John F., 139, 153
　Laura, 103, 105, 119
　Laura M., 13
　Lelia, 119
　Lily P., 13
　Lizzie, 187
　Lucy, 264
　Margaret, 117
　Margaret A., 117
　Martha J., 119
　Matthew P., 27, 117, 196
　Miss, 203
　Nannie, 105
　R. E., 272, 276
　R. H., 276
　Rebecca L. R., 65
　Richard H., 139, 276
　Sallie M., 222
　Sally M., 222
　Thomas F., 119
　Wm. F., 187
LEETCH

　Margaret, 190, 191
　Wm. A., 241
LEFEVER
　Annie D., 216
　John, 178
　M. V., 195
　Mary R., 178
LEFEVRE
　John S., 237
　Theresa, 92
LEIDY
　Amos, 79
　Isabella M., 79
LEITCH
　Geo. W., 202
　George W., 201
LEITH
　B. F., 66
　Chris., 32
　Christian, 37
　G. Earnest, 174, 179
　G. Ernest, 214
　Herbert, 141, 145
　James, 24
　Mary S., 66
　Mollie, 24
　R. D., 88, 127
　Sudie V., 173
　Sudith V., 174
　Theo., 173
　Theodore H., 72
　Theodoric, 213
　Thomas, 66
　Veturia, 213
　Veturia A., 214
　Wm., 32
LEMMON
　J. S., 294
LEMON
　Chas. W., 50
　Geo. H., 145
　John, 199
LENT
　Abram, 34
　Casper, 30, 34
　Sam., 30
　Samuel E., 34
LESLIE
　Benj., 104
　Ethel V., 66
　Florence I., 104
　Ida M., 295

　John, 185, 186
　Jonie, 110
　Martha A., 110
　Samuel D., 110
LEVI
　Harris, 257
LEWIS
　___, 70
　Anna J., 125
　Arthur, 142
　Chas., 153
　D. W., 58
　E. L., 233
　Elizabeth O., 171
　Fisher A., 174
　Frank P., 109
　Geo. F., 152
　George, 229
　George T., 226
　Harrison, 194
　India, 242
　Jas., 89
　John H., 95
　Jos., 177
　Joseph, 171
　Lulie F., 229
　Magnus M., 125
　Margaret L., 89
　Thos. M., 31
　Vincent, 174
　Virginia N., 229
　Wm., 153
　Wm. H. T., 174
LICKEY
　Bessie, 118
　Edgar, 285
LINDSAY
　H. R., 135
　Henry, 135
LINK
　Daniel, 130
　John A., 117
LIPPINCOT
　Howard W., 47
LIPPITT
　W. F., 204
LIPSCOMB
　William C., 26
LITTLE
　W. A., 138
LITTLEJOHN
　C. W., 223, 274

INDEX

LITTLEPAGE
  B., 207
  E. B., 220
  Emilie C., 220
  Hardin B., 220
  Henry C., 83
  Mary, 83
LITTLETON
  Ed., 185
  Edgar, 71, 217
  Emily, 73
  Jessie, 93
  Keturah, 159
  Oscar, 93
  R. C., 128, 129
  Richard, 159
  Tom, 176
LLOYD
  Charles, 56
  Fanny, 245
  Francis B., 139
  Frank B., 139
  Mamie, 51
  Richard, 98
  Sarah P., 119, 120
LOCK
  Herman, 191
LOCKWOOD
  Geo. R., 57
LODGE
  F. Anna, 210
  Harmon, 210
  Jos. A., 286
  Jos. L., 286
  Joseph A., 285
LOGAN
  Annie, 46
  John, 28
LONG
  Burgess, 119
  E. C., 31
  Mary, 74
  William, 19
  Wm., 74
LONGERBEAM
  G. H., 219
LONGSHORE
  Wm. W., 106
LOTT
  Mary E., 263
  Parkinson L., 263
LOUGHBOROUGH

  Augustine, 27
  Augustus G., 267
  Nathan, 267
LOVE
  Armida E., 156
  David W., 48
  E. Dilley, 156
  Eli A., 290
  Eli N., 82
  Fenton M., 75
  J. C., 78
  Louis N. B., 128
  Luther A., 80
  Robt. R., 290
  Samuel H., 290
  Wm. H., 209
LOVELACE
  Mason, 261
  Rose, 261
LOVELESS
  Alcinda, 56
  Elizabeth, 4, 125
  John E., 221, 222
  John R., 56
  John W., 56
LOVELL
  J. T., 58
LOVETT
  Caroline, 30
  Tazewell, 30
LOW
  Aaron, 218
  Adele, 218
  Annie A., 95
  Florence E., 95
  Joseph, 95
  Richard, 188
LOWE
  Ann M., 161
  Catharine T., 9
  John, 142
  Jos. H., 126
  Mary E., 176
  Mary J., 176
  Melissa B., 126
  Rector, 176
  Susannah, 153
  Virginia, 126
  Willie A., 131
LOWELL
  Charles I., 62
  Jas. P., 62

  Kate, 62
LOWENBACH
  Charles L., 287
  Charles R., 287
  Chas. R., 295
  Ella, 295
  India, 287
LOWENBACK
  Chas. R., 242
LOY
  Adam, 5
  Joseph F., 132, 225
  Mary C., 132
  Sallie, 2
  Sarah, 5
  Thomas J., 6
LUCAS
  Ruth, 80
LUCK
  W. J., 288
LUCKETT
  Eva B. L., 199
  Eva L. B., 196
  Horace, 62
  J. C., 15
  Ludwell, 196
  Maria J., 165
  Mary, 271
  Mary B., 288
  Mollie B., 283
  Mollie F., 15
  Sallie, 187
  Samuel C., 283
  William, 187
  Wm. C., 271
  Wm. E., 277
  Wm. H., 288
LULLEY
  Sarah, 241
LUNSFORD
  Mary A., 113
  T. R., 70
LUPTON
  J. W., 8, 9
  Jonah, 219
  Mary, 8
  Mary H., 9
  Mrs., 145
  Virginia, 219
LUTZ
  F. A., 158
  Francis A., 157, 162

INDEX

LYNCH
 J. A., 43
 John A., 178, 292
 Lillian, 174
 Martha D., 178
 W. B., 174, 185, 249
 William C., 190
 Wm. B., 19, 173, 217
LYNN
 ___, 143
 Ashford E. L., 186
 Cordelia, 262
 G., 297
 Gertrude, 151
 H. C., 180
 H. Clay, 38
 H. F., 94
 J. H., 186
 Joseph B., 206
 Maria V., 206
 Minerva A., 100
 Parilla, 186
 T. M., 114
 W. F., 210
 William, 262
LYON
 Alexander, 27
 Eliza J., 75
 Geo. C., 284
 Isabella, 206
 Jane, 27, 124
 John L., 206
 Mary E., 284
 Minor S., 236

MACGILL
 Eddie, 55
 L. T., 55
 R. E., 55
MACKENZIE
 Ella, 241
 Mollie E., 243
MACKEY
 Judge, 139
MADDEN
 Newton, 173
MADDUX
 Isabel, 194
 T. Clay, 18, 194
MAFFETT
 C. J. C., 248
 Charles C., 159

Chas. H., 194
Gracie A., 194
Henry, 255
James, 36
John L., 194
L. Chris., 73
Levin C., 75
Linnie J., 36
Mary C., 194
MAFFITT
 Walter G., 274
MAGAHA
 Armistead, 3
MAGEATH
 Flora, 128
MAGIL
 chas., 184
MAGILL
 Lloyd T., 54
 Rachel, 54
 Richard E., 54
MAGRUDE
 Ella V., 134
MAGRUDER
 Ella V., 133
MALONE
 John, 160
MANKIN
 A. K., 210
 C. L., 210
 Chas. L., 143
 Fannie B., 296
 Jos. L., 143
 Mary L., 143
 Mattie M., 163
 Mollie L., 63
MANKIN
 Chas. L., 209
MANLEY
 Ida, 204
MANLY
 Ida, 204, 210
MANN
 Christopher, 167
 Jacob, 137, 146
 Joseph H., 129
 Martin L., 45, 146
MANNING
 J. Forrest, 144
MANOR
 James, 244
 James D., 243

MANUEL
 Duncan, 114
 Ida, 293
MANZY
 Fayette, 129
MARBURY
 Alexander, 168, 169
 John, 169
MARCH
 J. C., 195
 Joannah C., 195
MARCUS
 James B., 169
 Jno., 155
MARDERS
 Ida E., 93
 Kate E., 93
MARKELL
 Virginia H., 286
MARLOW
 George, 274
 John, 274
 Thomas, 67
MARMADUKE
 Sampson, 34
MARMION
 Nicholas, 69
MARSHALL
 Elizabeth C., 10
 Henry, 291
 Sarah A., 134
 W. B., 10
 William C., 148
MARSTELLA
 H. M., 46
MARTIN
 A. H., 218
 Addie, 97
 America, 185
 America L., 186
 George, 194
 George T., 244
 Hattie, 263
 J. Hannah, 112
 Jno. S., 97, 126
 John Y., 160
 Leslie R., 66
 Mary E., 244
 Mary H., 203
 Nettie, 126
 Ruth L., 160
 W. A., 185, 186

The Mirror
INDEX

W. T., 123
Martin Lane & Co., 258
MARTS
  Samuel T., 244
  Sarah E., 67
MARYE
  Mary T., 126, 127
  Morton, 127
MASON
  A. Campbell, 229
  A. T., 178
  Betsy, 292
  Carita, 214, 216, 217, 252, 253
  Carolina, 252, 253
  Eugene W., 93
  George, 52
  Ida O., 175
  J. F., 23, 107, 216, 217, 229, 252, 253, 292
  J. Frank, 214
  James M., 175
  John, 35, 235
  John E., 126
  John Y., 52
  Julius, 260
  Maria, 260
  Mary A., 14
  Sallie E., 123
  Temple C., 60
MATHER
  Mr., 224
MATHERS
  Margaret, 90
MATHESON
  James, 167
MATTHERS
  Benjamin, 233
  Noah, 233
  Virginia, 117
MATTHEW
  Edgar E., 115
  Fanny, 115
  Ida C., 115
  Jonathan, 172, 181
  William, 180
  William E., 191
  Wm., 100, 126
MATTHEWS
  Georgietta, 63
  Minnie, 207

T. Wirton, 233
MATTINGLY
  L. F., 283
MATTOCKS
  Robert, 251
MAYNARD
  Fannie, 195
  Nathan, 195
MAYO
  Peter H., 214
  Sallie, 214
McALISTER
  Mary C., 42
McALLISTER
  Nannie B., 219
  Richard, 172
McARTER
  Ann, 267
  Samuel, 267
  Thomas, 267
McARTHUR
  Estelle, 215
McARTOR
  Ann, 287
  Annie E., 239
  Etta C., 239
  Thomas, 287
  Thos. D., 239
McBURNEY
  Agnes, 56
  Geo., 56
McCABE
  Aileen, 111
  Chas. P., 258
  Ella, 111
  J. B., 111, 258
  Jas. B., 59
  Jas. E., 92
  John, 258
McCANOE
  Thos. W., 263
McCARTY
  G. B., 230
  Geo. B., 230, 232
  Hannah, 165
  W. T., 165
McCARVIN
  William, 40
McCHESNEY
  Viola, 222
McCLANAHAN
  John F., 148

McCLELLAND
  Sarah, 291
McCORMICK
  Edward, 16
  Elvira, 16
  John N., 179
  Mary E., 275
  R. B., 275
McCOY
  Catharine R., 225
  Mrs., 145
McCRAY
  Edgar, 123, 270
McCREA
  Wm., 278
McCULLOCH
  W. B., 296
McCUTCHEN
  Mary, 124
McDANIEL
  Annie, 26
  Augustus, 142
  James, 26
  John, 16, 19
  Matilda, 98
  Wm., 98
McDONALD
  Catherine, 277
  Julia A., 1
  Wm., 193
McDONOUGH
  James, 265, 266
  Leven H., 227, 228
  William, 122
McDOUGAL
  W., 279
McEWAN
  Mr., 110
McFARLAND
  Annie, 87
  J. W., 185
  James W., 125
  Jos. W., 74
  Maurice, 87
McGAHEY
  Ella M., 252
  James, 252
  Mary, 252
McGARTER
  Jennie, 80
McGAVACK
  Anna B., 211

S. Alice, 52
McGILL
  Anna, 156
  Belle W., 149
  Henrietta, 264, 269
  James, 30
  John, 141
  Nelie M., 264
  Robert H., 269
  S., 217
  Saml., 181
  Samuel, 30, 156
  Smith, 53, 264, 269
  T. J., 149
  Thomas J., 181
  Virginia, 141
  Virginia B., 141
McGUIRE
  D., 109
  Mary M., 109
  Wm. P., 3
McILHENNEY
  J. W., 189
McILLHANY
  Ann, 77
  Milton, 77
McINTIRE
  C. C., 52
  Ed S., 52
  Harriet E., 52
McINTOSH
  Arabella F., 23
  David, 39
  Geo. W., 75
  J. L., 201
  Mary J., 39
McINTYRE
  C. C., 199
  Christopher C., 142
  Lucy, 199, 200
McKENNA
  Wm. H., 205
McKENNEY
  W. H., 131
  William H., 135
McKENZIE
  Wm. D. B., 226
McKIMMEY
  C. Frank, 193
  Sarah, 193
McKIMMY
  Addison G., 52

McLINN
  E., 295
McLYNN
  Julius, 230
McMURRY
  Myrta A., 200
McNEALEY
  Jane, 117
  L. Virginia, 102
McNEALY
  Edna E., 192
  Mary A., 124, 294
McNELLY
  John S., 47
McPHERSON
  Henry, 24
  Jno., 213
  John, 170
  Katie, 169, 170
  Lucy, 170
  Lucy E., 220
  M. E., 220
  Matthew, 169
  Melissa, 279
McQUIN
  Patrick, 65
McQUINN
  Patrick, 93
McVEIGH
  Fannie E., 209
  Fanny E., 204
  Hiram, 37
  Howard H., 177
  James M., 37
  Jane, 281
  Jas. N., 281
  Jesse, 185
  Mary E., 37
  Nancy, 185
  Townsend, 129, 201
  Townsend J., 248
  Wm. H., 177
  Wm. N., 255
  McVeigh & Dunbar, 183
McWALKER
  Katie, 99
MEAD
  Fannie A., 108
  John, 182
  John T., 148
  Mary A., 42
MEADE

  Fannie B., 107
  N. B., 231
  Philip, 107
MEADER
  C. D., 78
  Miriam E., 78
MEANS
  Ellen B., 273
  Mary A., 252
  Rachel A., 252
  Samuel C., 131, 252
MEGEATH
  Blanch, 12
  Flora, 129
  H. G., 76
  Joseph P., 1
  Lelia A., 12
  Marietta F., 1
MENARD
  Ella D., 85
  Fannie, 207
  John B., 85
MERCER
  Charles F., 152, 247
  E. W., 237
  Silas, 14
  William F., 231
MERCHANT
  A. W., 156
  David, 223
  Emily, 111, 112, 124
  John T., 195
  L., 143
  Landon O., 154, 156
  Leroy, 156
MERCIER
  Mary B., 122
  W. F., 22
MEREDITH
  Miss, 259
MERRIWETHER
  Thomas, 252
METZER
  Maria H., 294
  W. A., 294
METZGER
  Elizabeth A., 232
  Geo. T., 251
  Maria, 251
MICHAEL
  Florence J., 278
MICHIE

INDEX

H. B., 115
MICHLE
  Lizzie, 264
MIDDLETON
  Campbell, 1
  Sallie A., 129
MILBOURN
  A. J., 77
  Alice, 53
  Blanch, 80
  Clark, 138
  Jefferson, 75
  Orra, 80, 146
MILBURN
  Sallie C., 2
  Z. F., 182
MILES
  C. R., 248
MILHOLLEN
  John, 50
  Hirst, 179
  R. Hirst, 179
Milhollen Bros., 179
MILHOLLIN
  Albert, 260
MILLAN
  Ann, 115
  Annie H., 96
  George, 115
  L., 96
MILLARD
  Josiah, 154
MILLER
  Annie, 167
  Armistead M., 51
  Eliza, 296
  Ella V., 3
  Esther, 257
  Francis, 296
  George F., 3
  H. Clay, 21
  Harriet C., 297
  L. C., 257
  Lizzie M., 38
  P. H., 201
  Sallie D., 107
  Thomas, 185
  Thos. J., 184
Miller & Co., 21
MILLS
  Francis R., 67
  Harrison, 67

MILLSTEAD
  John T., 120
MILSTEAD
  Emma V., 193
MILTON
  Jno., 3
  John, 181
Minister
  ADAMS, ___, 197
  ADDISON, ___, 290
  ALEXANDER, John T., 100, 221
  ALRICH, W. A., 43
  AQUILLA, Samuel, 78
  ARMSTRONG, ___, 105, 185, 190
  ATHEY, S. M., 86, 87
  AUSHERMAN, D., 34
  AUSTIN, M. H., 191
  AVIRETT, James B., 125
  BADGER, ___, 12, 120, 186, 207, 239
  BADGER, J. N., 240
  BADGER, Jos. N., 202
  BADGER, Joseph, 58, 153
  BADGER, Joseph N., 31
  BAER, ___, 23
  BAER, R. N., 75
  BAGER, ___, 151
  BAILEY, E. D., 248
  BAILY, ___, 183
  BALDWIN, ___, 32
  BALL, B. F., 36
  BALL, S. A., 84, 247
  BARROR, A, C., 177
  BAYNHAM, Wm. A., 160
  BEALES, C. F., 82, 208
  BEALL, O. C., 29, 246, 258
  BEAVERS, R. F., 19
  BENTLEY, ___, 271
  BITTINGER, ___, 120
  BITZER, Geo. L., 190
  BOBST, Isaac W., 2

BOND, ___, 263
BOND, B. W., 208, 213, 231, 243, 255, 258, 269, 276, 277, 279, 281, 283, 285, 287, 288, 291, 296, 297
BOSTON, F. B., 151
BOUDE, A. P., 243
BOYD, S., 130
BOYLE, W. K., 1, 47, 54, 57, 59
BRANCH, ___, 26
BRANCH, H., 270
BRANCH, Henry, 12, 14, 25, 68, 143, 176, 256
BRAND, ___, 238
BRIDGES, ___, 223, 229
BRIDGES, B., 176
BRIDGES, Benj., 122, 161
BRIDGES, Benjamin, 4, 60, 66, 122, 142, 176, 225
BRIDGES, J. R., 176, 189, 194, 204, 212, 220, 223, 224, 233, 248, 258
BRIDGES, Jas. R., 163
BROADDUS, Julian, 146
BROADUS, A., 160
BROWN, ___, 225, 236
BROWN, A. G., 45
BROWN, B. F., 80
BROWN, C. M., 183, 185, 236, 237, 249, 272
BROWN, R. T., 185
BROWN, Saml., 6, 67
BROWN, Samuel, 12, 32, 127
BUCKLE, George, 170
BUHRMAN, E., 2
BUTTE, ___, 21

The Mirror
INDEX

CAIVIN, F. N., 76
CAMPBELL, C. C., 29
CAMPBELL, J. P., 269
CANNON, J. F., 2, 14, 21, 23, 28, 33, 39
CANNON, J. P., 28
CANTER, I. W., 138, 170, 176, 185, 202, 206, 213, 214, 215, 223, 235, 239, 252, 253, 254
CANTER, Isaac W., 189, 212, 215, 223, 242
CARSON, Thomas E., 72
CHAMBERS, J. H., 58
CHESIRE, ___, 24
CHICK, ___, 262
CHRISTIAN, Wm. H., 149
CLAFLIN, Jehiel, 76
COLE, ___, 19
COOPER, J. S., 238
COREY, ___, 241
COX, ___, 73, 118
COX, S. K., 54, 173, 193
CRENSHAW, L. H., 7, 9, 173
CURTIS, ___, 4
CUSHING, ___, 198
DAMARON, C. L., 149
DAME, Wm., 43, 275
DASHIELL, ___, 110, 118, 133
DASHIELL, T. G., 111
DAUCETT, C., 192
DAVID, ___, 263
DAVIES, S. W., 168
DAVIS, ___, 19, 27, 73, 104, 122, 170, 183, 195, 199, 204, 222, 228, 229, 232, 253, 267, 274, 283
DAVIS, R. T., 27, 37, 42, 44, 87, 88, 116, 117, 121, 125, 131, 150, 152, 155, 165, 169, 173, 174, 176, 200, 202, 203, 215, 223, 227, 235, 240, 243, 245, 249, 254, 264, 266, 273, 277, 287, 288
DERBY, H. L., 62
DERBY, Henry L., 133
DICE, ___, 276, 297
DICE, J. C., 202, 213, 240, 255, 272, 278, 296
DICE, Jno. C., 230
DICKINSON, ___, 116
DIEHL, ___, 56, 174, 181, 186, 206, 263
DINWIDDIE, ___, 293
DINWIDDIE, J. C., 265, 278, 279, 289, 294, 295, 296
DOMER, Samuel, 296
DONOHO, ___, 20
DUFFY, ___, 274
DULANEY, J. H., 161
DULANY, ___, 152
DULANY, J. H., 139, 286
DULIN, B. P., 49
DUNAWAY, ___, 146, 286
DUNAWAY, W. A., 160
DUNAWAY, W. F., 56, 64, 118, 121, 125, 127, 141, 145, 149, 208, 237, 245
DUNNAVON, A. M., 61
DUNNAWAY, ___, 242
DUNNAWAY, W. F., 91, 131, 150, 154, 161, 194, 196
DYOTT, L. R., 237
EARLY, T. H., 203
EATON, ___, 250
EDWARDS, ___, 127
EDWARDS, Jonathan, 78
EDWARDS, W. S., 130
Eggleston W. G., 258
EGGLESTON, ___, 273
EGGLESTON, E. G., 218
ENTYLER, B. F., 117
ESCHBACH, ___, 92
ESCHBACH, E. R., 146, 173
EUSTLER, D. F., 129
EVANS, W. T., 253
FAUNCE, D. W., 84, 151
FETTER, ___, 192
FLIPPO, O., 55
FOLEY, ___, 101
FOLLANSBEE, ___, 40
FORREST, Douglas P., 64
FORSYTH, W. H., 5, 6, 11
FORSYTHE, John, 172
FRANCIS, A. B., 90
FRANCIS, S. B., 165
FUGETTE, J. P., 233
FULLERTON, ___, 191
FUNSTEN, J. B., 193
FURR, Frazier, 234, 274
FURR, Joseph, 10, 44, 87, 173
FURR, Joseph L., 7
G. W., 268
GARDNER, ___, 19, 23

INDEX

GARDNER, J. S., 16, 31, 38, 150
GARDNER, William F., 179
GIBBONS, ___, 257
GIBSON, Robt. A., 52
GILBERT, J. K., 286
GRAMMAR, ___, 79
GRAMMER, ___, 143
GRAMMER, James, 144
GRAMMER, Julius E., 286
GRAY, Arthur, 131
GRAY, Arthur P., 47, 93
GREEN, ___, 26, 269
GREEN, S., 254
GREENE, Samuel H., 86
GREENE, Stephen H., 193
GRIMSLEY, ___, 204
GRIMSLEY, Thos. F., 115
GRUBB, Curtis, 148
HADAWAY, W. F., 75
HADDAWAY, ___, 64, 88, 89, 90, 94, 128, 129, 222
HADDAWAY, S. W., 79, 127, 242, 274, 282
HALL, T. A., 203, 222
HAMILL, H. P., 251
HAMMOND, ___, 117
HAMMOND, C. W., 232
HAMMOND, W. G., 8, 47, 286, 288
HANCKEL, ___, 36
HANCKEL, J. C., 57
HANDY, ___, 82
HANDY, A. T. M., 10, 19, 29, 47, 48, 63, 69, 83, 106, 119, 120, 123
HARLAN, Richard D., 184
HARRIS, David, 270

HARRIS, Wm., 293
HARRISON, ___, 1
HARRISON, E. P., 161
HARSHA, W. J., 110
HASKELL, D., 172
HASLIP, ___, 105
HATCHER, William E., 148
HATHAWAY, ___, 246
HAYNES, ___, 8
HAYNES, J. A., 1
HEAD, ___, 18, 64, 75, 85, 97, 185, 186, 191, 198, 199, 214, 220, 223, 232, 235, 260, 263
HEAD, N., 223, 255, 258, 271
HEAD, Nelson, 97, 183, 215, 221, 235, 237, 253, 264, 266, 268, 269, 274, 276, 287, 289
HEDRICK, D. C., 181, 187, 189, 192, 216, 218, 227, 228, 246, 247, 252, 276, 277
HEIRONIMUS, R. S. D., 58
HELM, Joseph, 108
HENRY, ___, 97
HENRY, E. H., 149
HERNDON, ___, 246
HERNDON, C. T., 151, 163, 171, 200, 225, 232, 233, 245, 256, 258, 261, 262, 271, 275, 277, 278, 284, 285
HERNDON, Chas. T., 204, 286
HERNDON, Thaddeus, 15
HILL, W. E., 192
HINKS, E. S., 294

HOADLEY, James, 140
HODGE, ___, 229
HODGES, J. S. B., 209
HOGE, ___, 216
HOGE, Moses, 89
HOPKINS, ___, 265
HOPKINS, A. C., 173
HOPKINS, Jacob, 149
HOUGH, ___, 86
HOUGHTON, ___, 109
HUBARD, ___, 1
HUBARD, J. R., 79
HUBBARD, E. W., 53
HUBBARD, J. P., 13
HUMMER, J. C., 210
HUNTINGTON, ___, 55, 250
HUNTINGTON, W. R., 241
HUTTON, ___, 278
INGERSOL, ___, 19
INGLE, Osborne, 149, 171
J. C., 272
JAMES, C. F., 58, 112, 270
JAMES, T. H., 53
JANSSENS, ___, 22
JOHNS, ___, 34, 151
JOHNS, A. S., 135
JOHNS, Arthur, 211
JOHNS, John, 42
JOHNSON, ___, 48
JOHNSON, M. A., 109
JONES, ___, 58
JONES, J. C., 210
JONES, J. R., 104
KANTNER, John, 236
KEANE, J. J., 160
KELLER, Joseph T., 70
KENDALL, J. F., 154
KENNARD, ___, 222
KENNEDY, H. H., 6, 9, 25, 260
KINZER, H. W., 166

The Mirror
INDEX
337

KINZER, Hamilton W., 75
KNOTT, J., 186
KUHLMAN, Luther, 230
LAIANE, J. A., 25
LAIRD, W. H., 278
LAKE, ___, 174, 285
LAKE, I. B., 1, 6, 102, 173, 176, 192, 197, 210, 284, 285
LAKE, Isaac, 116, 160
LAKE, J. B., 38, 59, 76, 116, 162
LAKE, J. H., 42
LANDSTREET, John, 260
LAWRENCE, ___, 85
LEAKIN, George A., 259
LEE, ___, 46
LEE, Harry B., 264
LEECH, G. V., 243
LEECH, Geo. V., 225
LEECH, S. V., 16
LEEDS, ___, 18
LEFEVRE, John S., 237
LEONARD, ___, 8
LEONARD, W. A., 233
LIGHT, J. H., 200, 201, 207, 212, 217
LINDSAY, John S., 135
LINDSEY, ___, 13
LINDSEY, J. S., 12
LITTLE, F. T., 273
LOCKE, T. E., 193
LOVE, J. C., 78
LYLE, L. M., 32
LYLE, Lee M., 39
MACALL, ___, 257
MARTIN, J. S., 156
MARTIN, Jno. S., 97
MAYO, Robert A., 214
McBRYDE, ___, 35
McBRYDE, R. J., 85
McCALL, ___, 118

McCORMICK, Jno. N., 179
McDONOUGH, James, 24, 49, 120, 145, 148, 232, 243
McGILL, John, 93
McKEAN, Jno., 151
MEAD, ___, 208
MEADE, P.N., 135
MEADER, C. C., 185
MEADOR, C. C., 37
MERETT, J. H., 135
MILBOURNE, L. R., 177
MILLER, J. H., 177
MILLER, L. C., 3
MILLER, P. H., 2, 5, 8, 9, 10, 12, 14, 20, 30, 31, 33, 38, 39, 40, 41, 43, 45, 46, 52, 54, 55, 58, 60, 64, 67, 69, 71, 92, 95, 96, 102, 105, 108, 111, 116, 117, 119, 121, 123, 126, 132, 145, 153, 155, 156, 164, 170, 173, 176, 178, 179, 180, 181, 183, 184, 187, 192, 195, 211, 248, 254
MILLER, R. H., 88
MINNEGRODE, ___, 177
MINNIGERODE, ___, 179
MINNIGERODE, Chas., 233
MOORE, J. H., 247
MOORE, S. Scollay, 146
MORGAN, J. A., 96
MOTIN, Jas. T., 106
MUMPOWER, J. A., 104
MURDAUGH, ___, 151
MURKLAND, W. U., 246

NAYLOR, H. R., 198
NEAL, ___, 150
NEAL, A. A. P., 143
NEALE, A. A. P., 180
NEEL, A. A. P., 1, 26, 28, 33
NEELE, A. A. P., 276
NEILL, A. A. P., 175
NELSON, G. W., 85
NELSON, George W., 178
NEWMAN T. W., 58
NEWMAN, ___, 192
NEWMAN, J. P., 219
NEWMAN, T. W., 32, 59
NEWTON, J. B., 214
NOLAND, T. W. T., 195
NOLAND, T. Wm. T., 215
NOLAND, Timothy W. T., 142
NORRIS, Richard, 135
NORTON, ___, 56
NORTON, George H., 127
ODENHEIMER, ___, 209
O'KANE, ___, 243
O'REILLY, J. B., 84, 85
O'REILY, J. B., 63
OULD, W. L., 241
PAGE, Carter, 148, 152, 154, 162, 187, 202, 210, 218, 238, 263, 287
PAGE, Frank, 96, 164, 183, 187
PAGE, Frederick, 164
PARET, ___, 39
PARKER, Chas., 114
PARKER, J., 38
PARSON, W. E., 207
PEARSON, C. C., 25
PEET, R. B., 275
PENICK, ___, 5, 38
PENICK, W. S., 72
PETERKIN, ___, 157

The Mirror
INDEX

PETERKIN, George W., 179
PETERKIN, Joshua, 173, 227, 293
PHILLIPS, ___, 39
PHILLIPS, P. P., 16, 109
PINDELL, A. T., 125
PIRKEY, John, 46
PITT, R. H., 135
PITZER, A. W., 105
POPKINS G. W., 72
POPKINS, C. W., 136
POPKINS, G. W., 9, 31, 65, 83, 100, 150, 151, 152, 173, 183, 188, 195, 197, 221, 245, 251, 254, 267, 274, 296
POPKINS, Geo. W., 36, 53, 91
PORTER, A. J., 13, 29, 36, 38, 46, 53, 62, 63, 78, 88, 91, 98, 102
POULTON, J. F., 31
POULTON, Jno. F., 32
POWER, ___, 153
POWERS, ___, 70
PRATT, ___, 89
PRESTON, J. A., 285
PRICE, J. A., 175
PRIME, E. D. G., 200
RAWLINGS, Jas., 14
REID, John, 184
REILEY, A. R., 271
RETTLEMYER, W. H., 92
RICHARDS, ___, 15
RINKER, H. St. J., 9, 23, 25, 53, 64, 71, 126, 129, 155, 201, 242, 280, 292
RINKER, H. St. Jno., 2
RINKER, H. St. John, 53, 67, 223, 224, 232

RINKER, Jno., 202
RINKER, St. J., 252, 271
RINKER, St. John, 30
ROBERT, Isaac W., 11
ROBERTS, W. T., 220
ROBEY, A., 192
ROBEY, Andrew, 9
RODGERS, ___, 179
RODGERS, Saml., 123, 125, 127, 150, 157
RODGERS, Samuel, 70, 81, 82, 98, 104, 114, 118, 121, 131, 134, 153, 158, 179
ROGERS, ___, 14, 150
ROLAND, ___, 156
RYLAND, J. H., 143
RYON, ___, 139
SCAWRIGHT, S. R., 206
SCHEIB, Henry, 191
SCHENDLER, D., 281
SCHINDLER, ___, 254, 283
SCHINDLER, D., 249, 259
SCHINDLER, Danl., 247
SCHOFIELD, M., 70
SCHOOLEY, W. T., 82, 164, 193
SCOTT, W. R., 38
SEAWRIGHT, S. R., 215
SENTER, ___, 241
SETTLEMYER, W. H., 2, 211
SHACKELFORD, J. Green, 218
SHAFFEREY, J. J., 23
SHARP, H. T., 147
SHARP, Henry T., 47
SHAW, ___, 116
SHEPHERD, ___, 76

SHIPLEY, J. L., 134
SHIPMAN, S. P., 254
SHREVE, B. A., 5, 6, 39, 54, 55, 64, 66
SIMONS, V. M., 16
SKINNER, J. T., 106, 122
SMITH, ___, 60
SMITH, J. H., 89, 151
SMITH, James H., 63, 69, 117, 152
SMITH, Jas. H., 88, 90, 92, 106, 150
SMITH, R., 68
SOMERVILLE, Geo., 193
SOUTHGATE, ___, 201
SPRING, ___, 105
STEEL, A. Floridus, 7
STEELE, L. R., 96
STEPHENSON, James M., 60
STEPHENSON, Jas. M., 145, 146, 169
STEPHENSON, P. D., 170
STEVENSON, James M., 262
STINESPRING, C. W., 28
STRINGER, W. R., 4, 5, 25, 67
STROTHER, F. A., 35, 90, 238
SULLIVAN, ___, 215
SUNDERLAND, ___, 93, 242
SUTER, H., 31
SUTER, Henderson, 207
TEMPLE, J. H., 44
THOMPSON, W. T., 170
TIERNAN, ___, 31
TOWNSEND, ___, 148
TRAPNELL, ___, 4, 15
TUCKER, Dallas, 204
TURNBULL, L. B., 39, 67, 92, 99,

INDEX

119, 150, 151,
154, 165, 214,
217, 218, 231,
239, 245
TURNBULL, L. R., 208
TURNER, ___, 281, 289
TURPIN, John B., 90
TUTTLE, A. H., 263
TYLER, George, 14
UPJOHN, Samuel, 219
VALLANT, T. D., 218
Van DeVIVER, ___, 32
Van HORN, J. R., 198
VANHORN, ___, 244
VanHORN, J. R., 209, 243
VANHORN, J. R., 181, 219
WALKER, Louis, 68
WALLACE, ___, 96, 222
WARD, W. F., 74
WARD, Wm. F., 197
WARE, J. S., 123
WARE, S. S., 7, 14, 15, 26, 55, 67, 104, 132, 138, 148, 215, 231
WARREN, ___, 51
WARREN, F. T., 48
WARREN, P. F., 33
WARREN, P. P., 15
WARREN, P. T., 44, 50, 52, 55, 56, 62, 64, 71, 72, 75, 79, 83, 85, 87, 88, 90, 91
WEIGHTMAN, ___, 283
WHARTON, H. M., 26, 291
WHARTON, J. S., 291
WHITE, E. V., 6, 10, 23, 36, 40, 52, 120, 129, 138, 151, 167, 196,
209, 210, 218, 222, 251, 256, 259, 261, 282, 290
WHITE, G. D., 210
WHITE, G. Dorsey, 222
WHITE, H. M., 208, 274
WHITE, S. R., 223
WHITTLE, ___, 157
WHITTLE, F. M., 14
WICKLINE, J. S., 108, 109, 119, 123, 130, 135, 136, 139, 140, 142, 143, 151, 152, 161
WIGHTMAN, J. T., 286
WILLETT, ___, 154
WILLIAMS, ___, 219, 241
WILLIAMS, J. T., 57, 81, 104, 123, 148, 152, 154, 157, 165, 173
WILSON, ___, 166, 178, 207, 217, 223, 253, 255
WILSON, Thos. J., 153
WOLF, ___, 160
WOLF, J. W., 262
WOLF, John, 10, 122, 145, 191, 193, 195, 216
WOODWARD, ___, 179
WOODWARD, B. F., 66
WOOLF, Henry, 297
WOOLF, John, 4, 6, 10, 11, 32, 55, 66, 67, 75, 92, 113, 155, 196, 220, 221, 244, 249, 274, 281, 285
WYATT, ___, 167
WYER, H. H., 1, 31, 60
YATES, ___, 47
ZERGER, J. E., 278
MINNIGERODE
  Charles, 144
  Chas. G., 221
  Roberta R., 144
  Virginia, 144
MINOR
  Fairfax C., 70
  John W., 225
  Kitty, 85
  Launcelot, 85
  Louisa, 225
  Louise F., 248
  Mary A., 125
  Spencer, 250
MISKELL
  John H., 167, 279
  Lillie M., 279
  Scott, 238
  Scott W., 171
  Una M., 279
  W. A., 25
MITCHEL
  Albert, 114
  Mitchell, F. & Bro., 1
MITCHELL
  James, 292
  Jas., 282
  John, 290
  Mamie, 12
  Mary, 13
  Minnie, 282
MITCHELMORE
  Wm. J., 186
MOCK
  Annie A., 195
  Chas. C., 155
  Evert, 41
  Isaac H., 6
  John T., 62
  Joseph, 69
  Josephine, 69
  Rosetta, 92
MOFFETT
  Benj., 80
  Benjamin, 183
  Drucilla T., 80
  John W., 28
  K. A., 244
  Marcellus, 31
  Susan V., 151
  Thos. J., 244
  Wm. W. W., 245

MONCURE
  Hallie E., 35
  R. C. L., 35
MONEY
  Samuel, 114
  Sarah C., 114, 126
MONHEIMER
  Isa, 295
MONROE
  Lizzie O., 54
  Miss, 224
  Rena, 200
  Wm. R., 54
MONTAGUE
  A. P., 55
MONTZ
  Allen B., 149
MOORE
  A. A., 171
  A. B., 295
  Alex. B., 36
  Alexander B., 230
  Arthur L., 285
  B. W., 257
  Bartholomew, 11
  Cato, 59, 79
  Cleon, 257
  Edw. G., 211
  Edwin L., 59
  Eliza G., 211
  Ellen, 225
  Emma R., 36
  Florence, 28
  Geo. L., 67, 68
  Geo. W. S., 104
  Gertrude, 183
  Harrison D., 47
  Helen, 138, 174
  J. C. S., 257
  J. H., 241
  J. Harry, 257
  Jas. M., 230
  Jno. H., 203
  John C., 263
  Judith, 272
  Kate, 29
  Lee S., 29
  Lucy B., 230
  Maggie, 137
  Margaret, 79
  Mary F., 232
  Nanie T., 220

Oscar N., 33
Peyton, 291
R. S., 257
Rachel, 221
Rosa A., 118
S. J. C., 225
S. Scollay, 173
Saml., 109
Samuel L., 68, 109
Samuel S., 16
Susie L., 137
T. R., 138
Thomas, 83, 272
Thomas R., 174, 272
Thos., 137
Thos. A., 257
Walter K., 138
Walter S., 29
Wm. B., 230
Wm. H., 230
MORALLEE
  T. C., 78
  W. Yale, 78
MORAN
  Bessie, 294
  H. T., 173, 227
  Helena N., 294
  Jno. M., 14
  Jno. W., 289
  Joshua, 100
  Lily M., 167
  Martha F., 227
  Mary J., 100
  Norah, 100
  R. Y., 258
  W. H. W., 91, 289, 294
MORE
  A. R., 244
  Mary E., 244
MOREHEAD
  Fannie, 120
  P. W., 120
MORELAND
  Carrie, 248
MORGAN
  Amelia, 276
  B. F., 97
  Harriet E., 97
  John, 167
  Lillie M., 97
  Miriam, 241

Philip H., 241
Wm. C., 276
MORIARTY
  Chas. T., 269
  Daniel, 256
  Henry B., 217
  James W., 1
  Jane E., 77
  John, 80
  John H., 77, 217, 238
  Sarah, 80
  Sarah E., 80
  Sarah J., 217, 238
MORISSEY
  Julia A., 38
MORMAN
  Mary, 6
MORRIS
  Jno., 65
MORRISON
  Francis H. S., 291
  J. H., 291
  Polly, 99
  Samuel, 276
MORROW
  B. J., 10
  Judith W., 10
MORTON
  John B., 46
MOSBY
  Col., 248
  John S., 125
MOSS
  Fannie, 23
  Mary, 186
MOSSBURG
  Annie C., 148
  Helen, 119
  Saml. A. B., 150
MOTIN
  Jas. T., 106
MOTT
  A. R., 101, 136, 164, 170, 256, 257
  Armistead R., 146
  Armistead R., 136
  Katie L., 101
  Randolph, 137
  Roberta, 256, 257
  T. Bentley, 164
Mott & Pursel, 70, 204
MOUNT

INDEX

C. E., 230
Chas., 65
Chas. E., 10, 232
Stephen R., 266
W. T., 110
William T., 68
MOUNTJOY
  Thornton, 9
MOURLAND
  John, 193
MOXLEY
  Benj. F., 250
  Emily A., 250
  Ida, 158
MUDGE
  D. C., 52
  Daniel C., 184
  Ellen, 184
  Emma C., 52
MULLEN
  Arthur, 271
  Bettie, 151
  James W., 218
  John, 133
  Lydia A., 21
  Saml., 21
  Samuel, 6
  Samuel P., 23
MUNDAY
  Eva V., 268
  Lizzie, 152
  Mary J., 245
  Thos., 103
MURPHEY
  Ann H., 155
  James, 155
MURRAY
  Elizabeth, 63
  Nellie W., 63
  Stirling, 184, 249
  William, 63
MURRY
  John, 68
MUSE
  Chas. F., 5
  George, 180
  George E., 56
  James H., 30, 78, 127
  Jas. H., 67, 284
  Mary E., 30
  Mollie F., 78

Sue J., 127
T. W., 163
Thomas W., 163
Thos., 145
Thos. T., 78
MUSSELLEER
  ___, 62
MYER
  Constance, 257
  M. C., 256
  Thomas J., 257
MYERS
  Alice D., 284
  Annie E., 169
  Carrie B., 284
  Charles, 284
  Chas. W., 100, 151
  Clarence J., 212
  D. W., 225
  E. F., 288
  E. Franklin, 212
  Earnest, 189
  Edith M., 104
  Elizabeth A., 24
  Ernest, 188
  F. M., 250
  Florence H., 212
  G. W., 189
  Geo. R., 218
  George, 188
  George W., 247
  Gertrude, 213
  Henry C., 100
  Jane, 158
  Jno. F., 100
  John H., 28
  Jonathan W., 100
  Josephine, 114
  Katie, 263
  Katie V., 169
  L. C., 237
  L. E., 189
  L. F., 194
  Luther R., 29
  M. C., 256
  Maggie L., 250
  Mahlon H., 158
  Malinda, 97, 100
  Margaret, 265
  Margaret E., 88
  Mary, 63
  Mary E., 66

Mary R., 250
Minnie M., 100
Mollie, 143
Nathaniel, 265
Olivia, 254
Randolph F., 288
Robert L., 173
Robt. L., 100
T. Jefferson, 88
Thomas J., 169
Thomas W., 188
Thos., 213
Thos. J., 254
Washington, 234

NADENBOUSCH
  Adrian C., 260
NALLS
  Carr B., 279
NEAL
  Delma, 54
  Williard H., 54
NEER
  Eliza, 124
NEFF
  R. A., 205
Negro
  Ramsey's Lewis, 6
  Roger's Dick, 6
NEILL
  D. F., 128
  Julia E., 128
  Maggie J., 128
  Mary E., 128
NELSON
  Kinlock, 181
  Robert W., 85
NESMITH
  Edmonia, 33
NEVILLE
  Robert, 121, 294
  Thomas, 120, 121
NEVITT
  N. B., 222
  Napoleon B., 96
  Sallie M., 222
NEWLON
  Chas. A., 195
  J. D., 234
  Lauretta V., 192
NEWMAN
  Geo. A., 71

INDEX

John T., 91
NEWTON
  Alexander, 11, 21
  Annie E., 120
  C. M., 143
  Charles, 143
  James E., 232
  John, 40
  Judith, 40
  Martha A., 21
  Mary A., 40, 41, 47
  Richard T., 254
  Robt., 120
  Willie, 143
NICEWARNER
  Henry M., 91
NICHOLS
  Albert, 291
  Annie J., 89
  Annie V., 231
  Arthur, 176, 271
  C. W., 162
  Charles, 55
  Charles H., 119
  E. Hays, 219
  Ed., 115
  Edward, 115, 136
  Eli, 162
  Eli H., 162
  Eli J., 66
  F. L., 162
  F. M., 230
  Fanny, 168, 169
  Francis E., 115
  Frank, 113, 114
  Franklin, 112
  Geo. W., 61
  Harriet, 13
  Hattie C., 49
  Isaac, 290, 295
  James F., 120
  James W., 285
  Jennie, 150
  Jesse, 115
  John, 14, 138, 142
  Jonah, 230
  L. T., 231
  Laura J., 285
  Lydia, 66
  Maggie, 150
  Martha E., 5
  Mary L., 160

  Maurice, 112
  Mollie E., 49, 89
  Olivia, 290
  Phineas J., 231
  Rachel, 205, 207
  Rosa E., 85
  S. T., 295
  Sallie B., 14
  Samuel, 42
  Samuel E., 49, 89, 181
  Samuel J., 66
  Samuel T., 115
  Thornton, 112
  Thos. J., 168
  Walter, 97
NICKARD
  S., 241
NICKENS
  C. F., 26
NICOL
  Charles E., 192
  F. A., 86, 210
NISEWARNER
  Christian, 138, 140
NIXON
  Blanche E., 83
  Blanche V., 83
  Geo. H., 75, 80, 134
  George, 288
  Hattie, 134
  J. L., 205
  Jno. W., 163
  Joel L., 248
  John W., 97, 163
  Jonah, 24, 154, 157, 182
  Levi, 248
  Lillie B., 154
  Mary A., 125, 182, 288
  Mary J., 134
  R. B., 296
  S. J., 83
NOLAND
  Anna, 206
  B. F., 116, 166
  Barney T., 195
  Burr P., 270
  C. Powell, 270
  Edith, 206
  Elizabeth W., 241

  Ella, 7
  Geo. A., 215, 253
  Geo. W., 7, 215, 216
  George W., 205, 206, 216
  Kate, 166
  Lloyd, 241
  Ruth, 216
  Ruth H., 7, 206
  S. T., 216
  Stacy T., 205, 206
  Susan C., 270
  T. W. T., 216
  T. Wm. T., 215
  Timothy W. T., 142
  Virginia L., 166
NORMAN
  Chas. E., 94
  W. F., 207
NORRIS
  Chas. R., 296, 297
  Clark, 25, 230
  Clarkson, 226
  Elizabeth D., 226
  Ella, 59
  Frank J., 297
  Golda C., 142, 143, 144
  H. D., 143
  H. D. B., 142
  H. DeB., 144
  Jos. L., 59, 100, 185, 297
  Joseph L., 101
  Josephine H., 226
  Lemuel, 239
  Margaretta H., 226
  Margarette H., 226
  Maria, 144
  R. Hoge, 230
  Thos. B., 217, 223
NORTHUP
  Lewis L., 143
NORTON
  ___, 63
NORWOOD
  Abel J., 218
NUTT
  Samuel, 19
  Wm. D., 241

OAKMAN

Anna F., 156
O'BANNON
  Annie, 79
  Corbart, 236
  H. I., 182
OBRISON
  Mary S., 132
ODELL,
  John C., 216
ODEN
  Constance, 243
  Frank A., 44
  Hattie, 193
  Huldah, 72, 75, 90
  J. B., 142
  Jas. S., 193
  Nathaniel, 142
  Nathaniel J., 72
  Nathaniel S., 142
  Thomas, 63
ODENHEIMER
  Frank G., 209
OEHLRICH
  Herman, 81
OFFUTT
  N. D., 170
  Robert W., 177
OGDEN
  David, 162
  R. K., 162
OGILVIE
  John, 60
  Margaret E., 60
OLDEN
  Thos., 232
  Tom, 224
OLIVER
  E. E., 161
  Susan A., 59
  William H., 124
OOME
  Robert S., 128
OREAR
  Maria L., 10
O'REILLY
  J. B., 84
OREM
  Edward, 19
ORR
  Ellen, 208
  J. W., 217
  John D., 208

ORRISON
  Albert G., 169
  Arthur, 200
  Arthur M., 170
  Eliz'b'th A., 124
  G. D., 131
  George A., 170
  Ida V., 151
  Inez, 170
  Isaac A., 40
  J. P., 154
  Jane, 279
  Jane E., 280
  John H., 120
  John P., 186
  Josie N., 171
  L., 297
  Lillie B., 186
  Lillie P., 186
  Loretta, 276
  Mollie D., 131
  Samuel, 46, 120, 131
ORTH
  Laura E., 192
OSBORN
  Harrison, 115
  Phineas, 93
OSBORNE
  Ocatvius, 169
  Octavius, 112
OSBURN
  A. Franklin, 136
  Bushrod, 95
  C. H., 297
  Edward C., 10
  Emily J., 60
  F. A., 182
  Flavius A., 201
  Henry, 104
  Herbert, 217, 277
  James M., 89, 201
  Joab, 60, 89
  John J., 7
  Jonah, 102, 108, 109
  Logan, 121
  Mary, 7
  Mattie V., 173
  Maurice, 61, 95
  Mortimer, 7
  Olivia, 95
  Phineas, 104
  Robt., 266, 282

  T. M., 173
  Thos., 264
  W. Edmund, 2
  Walter C., 77
  Willa, 201
  William B., 77
  Wm. B., 77
OSBURNE
  C. H. L., 175
  Frank, 209
OTLEY
  ___, 149
  C. F., 72, 206
  Flavius C., 277
  Jno. J., 277
  John W., 181
  Wm. H., 44
OWENS
  Mary O., 90

PACE
  James B., 14
  Violet L., 14
PACKARD
  Joseph, 92
PADGETT
  Frank J., 169
PAGE
  Carter, 162, 255, 256
  Charles, 204
  Charles T., 204
  F. M., 27
  Florence, 204
  Fred, 292
  Frederick, 164
  John, 292
  John W., 236
  Miss, 169
  Mrs., 278
  Thomas N., 214
PAINTER
  Jonathan, 128
  Samuel R., 38
PALMER
  Ada, 221
  Alice V., 15
  Ann E., 43
  C. W., 180
  J. Frank, 209
  Jas. F., 81
  Johnson S., 43
  L. F., 256

INDEX

Mary C., 256
Sallie A., 56
Sheridan, 204
PANCOAST
  Bertha, 61
  Jane, 61
  Jane A., 167, 194
  Jos. H., 144
  Rosa L., 194
  Samuel T., 144
  Thompson, 141
PANCOST
  Will, 150
PANGLE
  Annie M., 75
  Virginia B., 6
PARKER
  E. M., 41
  Ed. M., 105
  Eddie, 105
  Ida M., 41
  N. E., 41
PARKS
  John W., 89
PARROTT
  Elizabeth E., 42
  Jno. H., 136
  John A., 42
  John H., 137
PASTON
  Thomas, 195
  Virginia, 195
PAXSON
  C. W., 32, 88
  Clara, 65
  Clayton, 170
  Henrietta, 236
  Henrietta C., 195
  Jno. C., 170
  John C., 205
  John S., 102
  Lillian, 14
  R. Scott, 210
  Rose, 32
  Sarah F., 103
  Scott, 176
  Susan F., 200
  T. M. C., 155
  Westwood F., 37, 38
PAXTON
  Alice, 173
  Catherine, 213

Chas. R., 47, 213, 250
Duanna C., 234
Griffin W., 234
Griffith, 289
John, 254
Jos. T., 213
Rupert, 249
PAYNE
  Bessie, 20
  Chas. E. F., 154
  D. B., 291
  Daniel, 284
  Erva W., 147, 148
  Ida C., 1
  James F., 64
  Jos. H., 118
  Jos. W., 118
  Laura, 32
  R. S., 145
  Rice W., 20
  Richard J., 291
  W. H., 147
  Wm. H., 148, 154
  Payne & Co., 154
PEACH
  W. S., 288
  W. Selden, 288
PEACOCK
  Carl W., 141
  Harriet A., 156
  Hector, 69, 141
  James, 239
  James W., 55, 218
  John H., 181
  Josephine, 141
  Maggie E., 218
  Noble B., 289
  Sarah C., 63
PEARCE
  D., 182
  Wm., 32
PEARSON
  Barnett C., 91
  Jesse, 231
  Robert, 117
PECK
  Clement A., 172
PENDLETON
  E. Boyd, 205
  M. L., 205
  Philip, 78

PENUEL
  A. L., 215
PEPPER
  Susan E., 103
  W. W., 103
PERCIVAL
  Thomas N., 250
PERKINS
  Sarah A., 82
  Thos. B. M., 199, 200
PERRY
  Augustus, 93
  C. W., 129
  Charles, 93
  John T., 142
  Marshal B., 130
  P. P., 42, 142
  R. Ross, 93
PETIT
  C., 182
  David A., 127
PETTITT
  Geo. W., 230
PEUGH
  J. B., 34
  Jas. B., 183
PEYTON
  Cabell Y., 227
  Charles H. M., 173
  Henry E., 42
PHELPS
  E. P., 198
PHILIP
  Dr., 70
PHILIPS
  Mary, 57
PHILLIPS
  Charles E., 192
  Mamie, 197
  Murray D., 269
  Thos., 285
PICKETT
  Lucelia, 39, 44
PIERCE
  Mary E., 9
PIERPOINT
  James, 74
  John R., 29
  Jonathan, 35
  Joseph, 222, 224
  L. T., 74
  O. J., 74

The Mirror
INDEX
345

Obed, 35
Rue A., 224
Rurhea A., 222
PIERSON
  Ella, 31
  Geo. W., 222
PIGGOTT
  Alberta J., 260
  Bushrod, 85, 247, 248
  Hannah J., 3
  Isaac, 85, 150
  Mary, 197
  Mary E., 260
  Wm., 248, 289
PINKETT
  Mary, 93, 144
PINKHAM
  Richard, 47
PINN
  Wm., 275
PITCHER
  Jos. B., 232
PLASTER
  David h., 213
  Fannie, 213
  Fanny, 245
  Geo. E., 66, 108, 109, 213
  George E., 218
  Henry, 108, 109, 213, 245, 291, 293
  Jenny, 291
  Michael, 291
PLEASANTS
  Evelyn A., 193
  T. S., 193
POFFENBERGER
  Fannie, 218
POISAL
  John, 76
POLAND
  Alexander, 272
  Fanny D., 139
  Margaret A., 272
  Rosie, 142
POLEN
  Mary C., 221
POLLARD
  Annie, 269
POLLOCK

A. D., 228, 257, 283, 284
C. L., 194
Charles L., 228, 229
Chas. L., 235, 283
Elizabeth, 228
Elizabeth G., 284
Gordon, 283
Pollock & Garrett, 228
POOL
  James, 195
  John, 92
  Lucretia, 83
  Rose E., 66
POOLE
  J. Sprigg, 251
  Jesse, 70
  Jesse A., 153
POPE
  Wm., 295
POPKINS
  G. W., 68
  James H., 68
  Marvin W., 243
  Thos., 284
PORTER
  A. J., 189
  C., 179
  Ella, 189
  Jesse, 68, 108
  Mary E., 103
  S. L., 253
  Willie, 103
POSTON
  John H., 81
  Press, 243
POTTER
  Geo., 110, 120, 229
  George, 111
POTTERFIELD
  Alcinda, 294
  Estella C., 292
  Jeannie E. A., 249
  L. H., 120, 294
  Septimus, 294
POTTS
  Annie M., 152
  E. D., 114
  Eliza, 115
  Eliza A., 114
  Emma D., 149
  Ezekiel, 95, 147

Henry C., 60
J. O., 249
Jane E., 248
Mary, 159, 223
Nancy, 95
Nannie, 249
Sarah, 178
Thomas, 178, 227
Walter, 152, 293
Wm. B., 248
POULSON
  Niels, 113
POULTON
  Alfred, 180
  Arthur W., 167
  E. D., 167
  Eva R., 42
  Frank, 231
  J. F., 42
  Reed B., 231
  Wm., 231
POWELL
  Alex, 165
  Alfred H., 124, 150
  Ann M., 175
  C. W., 177
  Charles E., 207
  Charles W., 197
  Chas. E., 196
  Chas. W., 196
  Cordelia S., 21, 209
  Cuthbert, 175, 277
  E. B., 65, 124, 175, 209, 284
  Edward B., 21
  Edward F., 227
  Edward T., 275
  Elizabeth, 207
  Ellen D., 277
  Frank, 253
  Geo. C., 120
  Hugh L., 165
  Humphrey, 154
  Humphrey B., 209
  Jno. H., 227
  John H., 85
  John L., 146
  Joseph P., 197
  Kate C., 209
  Llewellyn, 21
  Louis H., 18, 85, 227, 252, 253, 255

Lucian, 26
Lucien, 196
Lucien W., 146
Lucy P., 286
M. L., 284, 291
Nannie F., 146
P. P., 95, 97
Pemberton H., 275
R. C., 179
R. L., 165
Randolph, 120
Robert L., 207
Robt. C., 284
Sarah, 227
Thomas L., 85, 197
Virginia N., 179
W. L., 65, 124
W. S., 209
William L., 65
Wm., 231, 284
Wm. A., 286
POWER
  Ann V., 123
  Joseph T., 49
  R. W. A., 183
  Robert, 56
POWERS
  ___, 8
  Chas., 284
  J. S., 39
  Robt., 61
PRATHER
  Hattie L., 100
  Joseph, 100
  Martha J., 100
PRATT
  James D., 162
PRESGRAVES
  B. W., 234
  Burr W., 227
  Chas. J., 152
  E. W., 251
  Ida F., 68
  W. W., 50
  Wm. F., 160
  Wm. W., 227
PRESTON
  Chas., 139
  Francis, 296
  Jas., 30
  John, 60
  John F., 65

Lucy, 289
R. M., 12, 296
Sallie, 198
T. L., 57
Thomas, 180
William M., 9
PRETTYMAN
  F. J., 179
PRICE
  C. D., 231
  Jno., 282
  John, 145, 274
  Russell, 7, 187
  S. E., 7
  Samuel H., 289
PRIEST
  John H., 108
PRITCHETT
  Wm. H., 96
PROCTOR
  Levi, 222
PRUFER
  Emma E., 211
  Julius J., 211
PRYOR
  Fanny, 276
  Hettie, 275
PURCEL
  Samuel, 70
PURCELL
  Mahlon, 39
  Matthew, 210
  Rodney, 284
PURDIE
  Thos. S., 89, 256, 257
PURSEL
  Enos, 118
  N. S., 204
PURSELL
  Enos, 120
  Eppa, 282
  Hannah, 146
  J. H., 282
  N. Janney, 282
  N. S., 120
  V. V., 266, 282
PUSEY
  Joshua, 236
  William N., 236
PYOTT
  Ann, 157, 163

John, 157

QUICK
  Vanderbilt, 9
  Vanderbuilt, 9
QUIGLEY
  Mamie, 267
QUINBY
  Mrs., 158

RADFORD
  Annie N., 53
  Mina M., 53
  Winston, 53
RADLEY
  Hester A., 138, 140
RAMSAY
  Jonathan B., 16
RAMSEY
  D. McCarty, 296
RANDOLPH
  A. M., 177
  Eliza, 177
  Elizabeth, 243, 244
  J. Innes, 98
  Mary P., 98
  Peyton, 243, 244
RANSON
  James M., 24
  Mary E., 24
RATCLIFFE
  Henry H., 225
  James, 225
  Mr., 176
  Susie, 225
RATHIE
  Benjamin D., 82
  Jos. L., 123
  Nannie D., 82
RAWLINGS
  Annie, 297
  John, 141, 145
  John M., 142
REACH
  Mollie E., 92
READ
  C. H., 103
  Charles H., 242
  Chas. H., 72, 241
  Zachariah, 24
REAMER
  Christian, 220

INDEX

Emma, 220
Frank, 220
S. S., 200
W. S., 51
Wm. S., 28
RECKLEY
  Q. S. J., 62
RECTOR
  Alice C., 285
  Asa H., 31
  Carrie, 297
  Edward W., 36
  H. N., 288
  Howard N., 287
  Jennie M., 297
  R. H., 232
  Samuel, 184, 287, 288
  W. A., 297
  Wm. E., 182
REDD
  Andrew J., 51, 61
  Susan, 156
REDMAN
  Daniel, 148
  Douglas H., 123
  George, 254
REDMON
  D. H., 265
REED
  Annie, 221
  Bettie R., 53
  Beverly L., 16
  Charles H., 221
  Chas. A., 25
  Ferderie, 221
  Harmon, 132
  Henry, 3
  J. Milton, 53
  J. V., 53
  John, 31, 151
  John H., 2
  Jos. S., 51, 196
  Kate L., 191
  M., 161
  Mary V., 145
  Mrs., 148
  R. F., 68
  Rosannah, 132
  Sarah A., 53
  Sarah C., 274
  Smith, 32, 248

Stuart L., 191
Theodore, 16, 191
Thomas J., 187
William, 172
Wm. A., 145
REEDER
  John E., 182
REEVES
  John, 228
  John F., 228
  John T., 235, 261
  Lydia C., 235
  Rosa A., 137
  Roxanna, 63
REGESTER
  Annie E., 8
  Samuel, 8, 54
REID
  Charley, 51
  Jennie, 51
REILEY
  Ann, 106
  Mollie, 171
REILY
  George, 126
Residences
  Appleton, 80
  Arlosta, 83
  Auburn, 212
  Avon, 1
  Barrymore, 144
  Belmont, 148
  Blakely, 251
  Boydville, 231
  Bramilton, 45
  Brierley, 103
  Briery Knowe, 85
  Burkes Garden, 160
  Carlheim, 47, 249
  Carrara, 97
  Carter Hall, 32
  Chipola Farm, 130
  Clifton, 186, 205
  Collicello, 145
  Corner Hall, 130
  Crednal, 246
  Creedmoor, 233
  Declade, 196
  Dresden, 53
  Evergreen, 47
  Exeter, 128, 203, 220, 249, 251

  Fairview, 244
  Farnley, 246
  Forest Glen, 208
  Glebeland, 12
  Glen Welby, 168, 251
  Glenmore, 221
  Govers' Hill, 86
  Green Valley, 43
  Greyfields, 54
  Groveton, 75
  Hartlands, 46
  Helmwood, 73, 108
  Hope Grove, 234
  Horse Shoe Farm, 123
  Laurel Hill, 16
  Leeton Forest, 228, 257
  Leslie Hall, 104
  Locust Grove, 107
  Locust Hill, 57, 116, 198
  Marengo, 160
  Montsylva, 53
  Morven, 21, 103, 113, 244
  Mountain View, 87
  Mt. Airy, 185
  Nestling, 19
  Newstart, 262
  Oak Hill, 158, 245
  Oak Level, 28
  Oakley, 28, 42, 114
  Oatlands, 144, 209, 221
  Pampatike, 212
  Powellton, 146
  Prosperwell, 212
  Raspberry Plains, 8, 87, 130, 144
  River Bend, 152
  Rockhill, 63
  Rockland, 203, 264
  Rokeby, 21
  Rosemont, 75
  Rosland, 256
  Round Hill Side, 216
  Salome, 22
  Selma, 20, 50
  Sherland Hall, 215
  Smithfield, 146
  Soldier's Rest, 85

The Mirror
INDEX

Spring Valley, 51
Springdale, 206
Springwood, 157, 158
Sugarland View, 4
Sunny Side, 247
Temple Hall, 290
The Glebe, 109
The Groves, 45
Valley View, 129
Walnut Hill, 54
Welbourne, 294
Welbourne Mills, 53
Wheatland, 272
Whitehall, 19
Woodburn, 29, 157
Woodlawn, 35
Woodside, 66
REX
  Benj. L., 2
  Mrs., 201
RHETT
  F. M., 107
RHINES
  Annie L., 58
RHODES
  George, 255, 282
  H. H., 203
  J. Q., 219
  Jane, 124, 255
  Joseph, 34
  Joseph R., 31
  Kate G., 203
  Katie, 34
  Mary R., 249
  Nannie, 249
  Randolph, 249
RICE
  Carrie, 104
  Charles W., 104
  Ellen A., 265
  Jno., 285
  John W., 265
  Noble, 104
  Wm. H., 117
RICHARDS
  A. E., 64, 78
  Burr, 219
  Burr H., 217
  Jesse, 112
  Leven, 292
  Lulu, 219

  Lulu C., 217
  Maud H., 179
  Maud L., 179
  W. L., 179
  Washington, 179
RICKARD
  L. Kate, 254
RICKS
  Nannie, 162
RIDDLE
  S. C., 227
RIDDLEBERGER
  Lelia, 258
RIDGEWAY
  Annie M., 45
  Mary A., 125
  Samuel R., 208
RIDOUT
  Annie W., 201
  Nannie W., 201
  Weems, 201
RILEY
  Gus T., 170
  Jennie D., 3
  Mary M., 135
  Minnie, 170
  Wm., 291
RINKER
  Chas. W., 135
  Jacob Z., 189
  John L., 292
  Susan, 292
RIPPON
  William, 66
RISLER
  John T., 90
RITCHE
  Catherine, 234
  George, 234
RITCHIE
  Catherine E., 203
  George, 203
  Jefferson J., 164
  John, 211
  Thos. C., 203
RITICOR
  Charles, 174
  Chas. F., 243
  John, 227
  John T., 210
  Malinda, 77
  Susannah, 174

RIXEY
  B. F., 59
  Florence V., 59
  Samuel R., 95
ROADS
  William, 99
ROBERTS
  Carrie B., 30
  George R., 192
  J. R., 144
  James, 6
  Jas. W., 93
  Lillian, 115
  Minnie B., 134
  R. F., 144
  William, 115, 192
  Wm. E., 237
ROBERTSON
  Bolling, 195
  Carrie B., 30
  Norville R., 30
  T. Rolling, 197
ROBEY
  Andrew, 80, 194, 280
  Clara J., 2
  F. E., 51, 53
  Julia A., 9
  W. O., 238
ROBINSON
  Bushrod, 293, 294
  Edward, 166
  Eugene F., 293, 294
  George, 9
  Meredith, 78
  Sam., 101
  Saml., 6
  Samuel, 11
  Robinson, Adams & Co., 45
  Robinson, Parker & Co., 294
RODEFFER
  Ada V., 248
  Geoerge W., 9
  Kate, 9
  M., 15
  M. M., 9
RODERICK
  Hester, 199
  J. J., 205
  Jacob, 199
  Jacob R., 198

Lewis, 199
W. L., 44
RODGERS
  Jno. L., 133
  John D., 85
  John L., 134
  Joseph G., 271
  M. M., 163
  Martha G., 173
  Mollie T., 274
  Samuel, 23, 271
  Wm. B., 23
RODRICK
  J. R., 200
RODRIGUEZ
  Nina, 292
ROE
  Edwin L., 251
ROESER
  Carl, 96
  Thehla, 96
ROGERS
  A. E., 55
  A. H., 240
  A. L., 208
  Alexander H., 240
  Annie, 255
  Asa, 45, 77, 208, 246, 272
  Besse, 240
  C. B., 221
  Cuthbert B., 221
  Edmonia S., 68
  Edwin, 127
  Elizabeth C., 240
  Ellen, 208
  Frances, 218
  George, 264
  Hamilton, 48, 77, 81, 140, 197, 246
  Henry, 205
  Hugh, 205
  J. Pendleton, 45
  James, 118
  James H., 229, 295
  James P., 101
  Jno. P., 263
  John D., 272
  John L., 48
  M. M., 245, 269
  Mary, 140
  Mary L., 221
  Milton M., 268
  Mollie M., 107
  Nancy, 185
  Richard L., 185
  Rosalie, 205
  S. S., 72
  Saml. E., 199
  Susan, 170
  Thos., 107
  W. H., 45
  W. T., 87
  Will, 296
  Wm., 245, 268
  Wm. H., 101, 229
  Rogers, J. P. & Co., 45
ROLES
  Bettie, 204
ROLLER
  Alberta R., 170
  Mary, 224
ROLLINS
  Brittie, 172
  Clifton M., 281
  Eolia, 139
  Gertie V. L., 237
  Jas. H., 54
  John H., 139
  John L., 49
  Laura, 281
  Lucie E., 252
  M. Virginia, 52
  Margaret M., 46
  Samuel M., 281
  V. G. L., 46
ROLLISON
  Geo. E., 152
ROOF
  John, 124
ROPP
  Saml., 187
ROSE
  Fanny, 257
  Lavenia, 86
  T. H., 2
ROSS
  Addie, 159
  Amanda, 162
  J. C., 170
  Jno. T., 159, 217
  John T., 162, 245
  Jos. H., 207
  Sallie, 271
  Susan E., 103
ROSSER
  Leo., 93
  Lulu, 93
ROSZEL
  S. G., 156
ROSZELL
  G. A., 294
  Geo., 238
  Stephen G., 72
ROSZELLE
  R. D., 294
ROTCHFORD
  Annie, 1
Rouse, Hempstone & Co., 287
ROWZEE
  Miss, 279
ROYALL
  Wm. L., 194
ROZELL
  Phoebe, 292
RUCKER
  Wm., 131
RUDD
  John S., 228
  Katie D., 5
RUNNER
  Wm., 246
RUPP
  G. W., 82
RUSE
  cora, 85
  Eli T., 79
  Elizabeth, 98
  Ella, 79
  Katie, 98, 99, 157
  Michael, 98
  Solomon, 99, 157, 273, 275
RUSH
  John, 182
RUSK
  Annie, 264
  Carrie A., 64
  John, 90
  John S. H., 141
  John T., 64
  Manley, 264
  Marizee, 239
  Marizee F., 234
  Marizee H., 32

The Mirror
INDEX

Samuel, 32, 40, 234
Susan C., 32
RUSSELL
  Alice J., 102
  Blaine G., 102
  Edmonia, 286
  Geo. R., 102
  H. H., 83, 194, 289
  Henry W., 33
  Ida, 11
  Israel, 185
  Joseph H., 214, 218
  Joseph W., 235
  Louisa J., 125
  Lucy, 18
  Sallie, 171
  Thomas J., 171
  William, 286
  Wm., 171, 240
RUST
  A. T. M., 22, 65, 201, 205, 264
  Armistead, 201
  Armistead T. M., 203
  Bushrod, 153
  Eddie, 264
  Geo., 203
  Geo. T., 50
  George, 125, 264
  Ida, 264
  Ida L., 264
  Lillie S., 264
  Margaret E., 200, 205
  Maria, 237
  N. A., 271
  Nettie, 264
  Rebecca L., 65
  Richard H., 271
  Sallie J., 125
RUTHERFORD
  Jas., 164
  Mattie H., 164
RUTTER
  Mollie, 10
  Mrs., 59
RYAN
  Catharine, 267
  John, 3
  John F., 117
  Mollie, 106
  Susan A., 3
RYON

Ann, 3
H. Clay, 217
James H., 261
John, 3
Millard F., 96

SAFFER
  A. W., 165
  B. F., 80
  Emma R., 177
  Franklin E., 38
  Gertrude F., 165
  Lillie, 26
  Lillie B., 226
  Pocahontas D., 80
  Rose, 165
  Thornton, 204
  Viola D., 177
  W. T., 165, 177
  Wm. T., 10
SAFFLE
  Hannah E., 55
SAMPSELL
  L. H., 252
SANBOWER
  Elizabeth, 167
  Fannie E., 144
  Jno. W., 144
  John W., 140
  Michael, 150, 151
  Sarah A., 187
SANDBOWER
  Thos., 294
SANDERS
  Beverley C., 133, 186
  Beverly C., 122
  John, 136
  Lewis F., 116
  Wilson C., 116, 122
SANFORD
  R. L., 240
  Robert C., 133
  Sarah J., 176
  W. L., 176
  Wm. L., 176
SANGSTER
  Edward, 66
  James, 66
SANTENYER
  Bettie, 262
SANTENYERS
  John B., 262

Mary E., 262
SANTMYER
  Eva L., 56
  Isaac F., 56
  Kesiah, 220
  Kesiah F., 56
SAUNDERS
  A. L., 49
  Benj., 47
  Edith, 60
  Elizabeth, 186
  Emily W., 115
  Henry, 159, 168, 200
  John, 21, 22, 115
  M. B., 172
  Mary, 172
  Philips V., 52
  Sarah M., 47
  Sarah R., 58
  Thos., 172
  W. H., 144
  Wm. H., 61, 142, 143
SCANLAND
  Albert, 271
SCANLON
  Patrick, 195
SCATHERDAY
  Ann M., 124
SCHAEFFER
  Jno. W., 182
SCHAFFER
  John, 169
  Susan, 124
  Wm. T., 169
SCHELL
  Rachael, 219
SCHINDLER
  Daniel, 242
SCHLEIF
  Geo. W., 45
  John V., 60, 81, 135, 137, 189
  Reta, 81
  Sarah J., 189
  Theresa W., 60
SCHOOLEY
  Catharine, 182
  Emma, 132
  Emma N., 82
  Geo. W., 282
  Jonas P., 148
  Joseph, 213

INDEX

Kate, 213
Kate F., 148
Mahlon, 279
Milton, 182
Raymond L., 213
Thos. A., 82
SCIPIO
  John, 93
SCOFIELD
  Ann N., 190
SCOTT
  Caroline, 52
  Gilbert, 165
  H. A., 84
  Imogen, 293
  Jacob, 269, 292
  John, 34, 87
  Josephine, 157
  Leeman, 184
  Mary A., 165
  Minerva, 296
  Oliver D., 52
  R. A., 165
  R. Carter, 164
  R. Taylor, 87, 164, 293
  Robert, 184
  Robert E., 34
  Robt. E., 87, 157, 293
  William, 119
  Wm. E., 52
SCRIBNER
  Howard, 276, 279
SEAL
  Emma V., 130
SEATON
  Amos, 221
  Cornelius C., 176
  Fanny, 145
  G. Ludwell, 282
  Hiram K., 60
  Mary P., 98
  Samuel R., 227
  Susan, 249
  Townsend D., 98
SEIBER
  Rosa, 54
SEITZ
  Amanda, 100
SELBAUGH
  Rosa J., 249

SELDEN
  Eleanor L., 251
  Wilson C., 251
SELLMAN
  John W., 143
SEMMES
  Alexander A., 171
SEMPLE
  Perry, 209
SESSON
  Charlotte D., 55
SETTLE
  Ida E., 86, 87
  Lucy, 132
  Newton, 284
  Thomas L., 132
  Thos., 282
SEWELL
  James, 91
  John T., 224
  Sarah, 165
SEXTON
  Annie A., 142
  M. E., 81
SEYMOUR
  Ella, 213
SHACKELFORD
  Eliza A., 120
  Susan E., 124
SHAEFFER
  John, 268
SHAFER
  Bettie A., 122
  Carlton, 154, 229
  Charles H., 110
  Emma V., 16
  F. W., 70, 166, 204, 222, 229
  Jos., 70
  Joseph, 204, 222, 229
  Susannah, 229
SHANNON
  Robert, 231
SHAW
  Geo. F., 149
  Katie L., 290
  W. O., 218
SHAWEN
  A. T., 256
  Ann, 239

Cornelius, 61, 109, 136
W. C., 239
Wm. C., 20, 21
SHEETZ
  Arthur, 195, 240
  B. F., 265
SHEFFEY
  Hugh J., 259
  Louisa, 259
SHELHORN
  Antoine, 50
  Godfrey, 50
SHELL
  Margaret, 125
SHEPHERD
  Alexander B., 241
  Champ, 226
  Chas., 197
  E., 197
  Elizabeth S., 194
  Fanny, 3
  Ham, 177
  L. W., 270
  Leven W., 197
  Mamie, 177
  Mary E., 117
SHIELDS
  Charlotte E., 199
SHIPMAN
  Mattie, 139
  Samuel, 111
  Samuel W., 235
  Stephen P., 55
SHOAFF
  Margaret, 129
SHOEMAKER
  Annie, 213
  Naylor, 165
  Sarah, 165
  Wm., 24
SHORTS
  Charlotte, 146
SHOWER
  George T., 295
SHREVE
  Arthur, 67
  Arthur B., 67
  B. A., 52, 274
  Benj., 196
  Daniel, 135
  Eugenia, 274

J. Frank, 36
Matilda C., 52
S. N., 52
Sallie N., 274
SHREVES
  Arthur, 238
SHRIGLEY
  Hannah, 224
SHRIVER
  Annie C., 152
  Annie M., 152
  E. Gertie, 173
  Edward, 281
  Emma, 281
SHROFF
  P. F., 217
SHRY
  Alberta, 6
  Andrew F., 63
  Christina, 288, 290
  Elizabeth, 87, 89
  Franklin A., 143
  John H., 290
  Margaret A., 13
SHRYOCK
  Ann M., 30
  Geo. W., 166
  George W., 168
  John T., 166
SHUEY
  Edna, 194
  John T., 132
SHUGARS
  ___, 155
  Annie, 240
  Joseph, 139
  Joseph A., 157, 240, 241
  Mary, 240
  Samuel T. McG., 240
  Susan B., 224
SHUGART
  Joseph, 47
SHUMAKER
  Alice, 53
  Basil W., 295
  Jas. S., 41
  Maggie E., 41
  Margaret, 80
  Margaret T., 58
  Marie E., 67
  Robert W., 146

Sarah, 124
Sarah P., 28
Susan C., 270
Wm. B., 232
SHUMAN
  G. W., 213
  Hattie A., 167
SHUMATE
  J. E., 57
  L. M., 191, 282
  Lewis, 96, 289
  Lewis M., 96, 97, 282
  M. C., 100
  Mary T., 96
  Mollie, 57
  Murphy, 97, 191
  W. J., 31
  William, 31
SHUPP
  Chas., 4
SIDALLE
  J. S., 182
SIDEBOTTAMS
  Elizabeth Y., 169
SIEBER
  John A., 182
SILCOTT
  Armistead, 95
  Emma H., 120
  Evelina B., 136
  Eveline, 134
  Howard, 48
  Jane A., 117
  Jas., 133
  Jas. E., 200
  John W., 198
  Landon C., 103
  Mary, 198
  Norval, 291
  Thos. E., 177
  Virginia C., 125, 245
  Warren F., 226
  Washington, 134
  Wm., 165
SILLCOTT
  Norval, 7
SIMMONS
  Kate V., 189
SIMPSON
  Eliza, 113, 118
  Emma W., 296
  J. T., 117

James F., 297
James H., 8
Lillie, 96
Mary V., 99
Mollie L., 88
R. A., 117
Rebecca, 196, 197
Rebecca M., 198
Saml., 197, 198
Samuel, 26, 94, 97, 113, 196, 281
T. H., 193
Virginia, 25
W. A., 13
Willie A., 117
SIMS
  Estelle E., 269
  Julius, 114
SINCLAIR
  Chas. E., 293
  James, 165, 207, 234
  Jas. M., 293
SIPPY
  Wm., 125
SKILLMAN
  Abraham, 142
  Annie, 150
  Catherine J., 198
  James, 269
  John, 182
  Lemuel, 198
SKILMAN
  Catharine J., 198
  Lemuel F., 198
SKINKER
  Charles B., 189
  James K., 189
  Sam, 189
  William K., 189
SKINNER
  Alice, 271
  Annie E., 150
  Chas. E., 204
  David, 187
  E. W., 149
  Elizabeth, 132
  Emma F., 88
  Emmett W., 169
  H. W., 64
  Ida V., 150
  J. S., 141
  J. T., 10, 142, 271

INDEX

James, 88, 247
Lucy, 247
Lydia M., 166
Marion, 64
Mary C., 169
Mary E., 88
N. J., 12
Nathan, 129
Octavia, 271
Peter, 280
Quincy A., 150
Richard, 288
S., 149
Samuel, 53, 87
Stella, 240
Susanna, 141
Truman, 87
W. H., 144
Williamson, 132
Willis H., 169
SKIRVING
  Carrie, 37
  Carrie T., 38
  John, 202
SKOLD
  C. F., 109
SLACK
  Lillie M., 93
  Ludwell L., 106
SLANE
  Ann, 157
SLATER
  Flora E., 184
  Julia A., 273
  Nellie M., 184
  Samuel, 273
  William L., 184
  Wm. L., 5
SLAUGHTER
  Philip, 286
SLAYMAKER
  H. C., 9
SLENTZ
  Annie J., 40
SLOANE
  John, 79
SMALE
  Carolyn, 285
  Olivia, 263
SMALLWOOD
  Annie, 276
  Augusta M., 1

F. M., 276
Georgiana, 236
James, 201
John T., 56
Madora E., 234
W. W., 160
SMART
  John P., 101, 174
SMITH
  A. M., 134, 149
  Achsah W., 266
  Alex G., 157
  Alexander G., 159
  Alice B., 252
  Ann M., 215
  Anna J., 164
  Anna P., 55
  Annie, 101, 107, 144
  Augustus G., 215
  Burke, 252
  C., 149
  Charlie, 89
  Charlotte T., 190, 191
  Chas. A., 215
  Chas. H., 249
  Chas. W., 252
  Curtis O., 130
  D. K., 149
  Daniel G., 113, 226
  Decatur, 252
  Dr., 63
  E. Jaqueline, 212
  Edgar L., 43
  Edmonia, 30, 190
  Elizabeth, 61, 118
  Ella, 149, 229
  Ellen C., 230
  Ellen E., 113
  Emily B., 151
  F. H., 137, 207, 226, 291
  Francis H., 137, 270
  Fred'k., 199
  Geo. D., 41, 43, 55, 107, 210
  Geo. H., 146
  Geo. W., 107, 144, 292
  George H., 145
  Gunnell, 191
  Hannah L., 201
  Harvey, 236

  Harvey S., 239
  Henry, 61, 110
  Henry S., 140, 164, 213, 229
  Horace, 108
  Hugh, 118
  J. H., 73
  J. Howard, 226
  J. R., 208
  J. W., 64
  J. Walter, 152, 274
  James A., 226
  James D., 243
  James H., 89
  Janie, 297
  Jas. H., 81, 137, 207, 270
  Jas. P., 108
  Jennie, 210
  Jno. R., 208
  Job, 292
  John, 200
  John E., 237
  John F., 153
  John R., 26, 101
  John T., 209
  John W., 200
  Jos., 290
  Joshua, 136
  Kate, 149
  Lavinia J., 2
  Leah M., 173
  Lewis A., 283
  Lillie, 191
  Lizzie, 200, 264
  Lizzie E., 189
  Lloyd T., 118
  Louis M., 208
  Loula F., 243
  Lucy, 110
  M. M., 271
  Maberry F., 132
  Margaret E., 118
  Martha S., 61
  Mary F., 191
  Mary L., 19
  Miss, 176, 221
  Natalie, 207
  Nathaniel, 207
  P. H., 28, 30, 37
  Patrick K., 190
  Portia H., 237

R. E. L., 210
Rhoda, 73, 130
Robert, 252
Robert E. L., 269
Rosalie, 121
Rufus, 120
Ruth H., 280
Samuel, 156
Sarah, 136
Thomas, 13
Thomas H., 174
Thos., 199
Thos. J., 230
Thos. R., 236, 239
W. D., 164
Warrington G., 278
William, 199
William H., 130
William T., 98
Wm., 42, 277, 283
Wm. C., 151
Wm. E., 56
Wm. H., 73
Wm. N. R., 73
Wm. P., 210, 252
Wm. T., 134
Wyndham, 144
Zach, 238
SMOOT
  Joel, 182
  Robert W., 113
SNAPP
  Eugene D., 89
  Rose V., 88, 89
SNEDEN
  John, 158
SNIDER
  Marion F., 47
  Peter, 98
SNOOT
  Nannie L., 236
SNOOTS
  Henry, 273
  John, 22
  John W., 123
  Margaret O., 2
  Mary E., 133
  Rosa B., 181
  Samuel, 111, 171
  Sarah A., 128
SNOWDEN
  Edgar, 31

Jennie, 31
SNYDER
  D. H., 177
  Elizabeth C., 102
  Lillie, 177
SOLOMON
  Annie E., 242
  Irene, 106
  Sarah F., 2
SOMERS
  John, 89
SOMMERS
  J. W., 140
  Mr., 237
  Sallie S., 140
SONGERBEAM
  Chas. E., 274
SOUDER
  Emeline, 214
  Emma V., 271
  Geo. P., 271
  Jno. W., 214
  Mary M., 15
  Sousan E., 173
SOWERS
  Annie, 76
  James, 222
  John, 246
  Mamie F., 145
  May F., 146
  Miss, 280
  W. B. C., 142
SPALDING
  Cal., 207
  Maud, 277
SPEAKS
  Christina, 232
  Emily V., 126
SPILMAN
  John A., 90
SPINKS
  Ada, 153, 294
  Alexander, 153, 294
  Alexander H., 153
  Mary, 294
SPOTSWOOD
  Alexander, 64
SPRIGG
  J. T., 133
  Mary J., 222
SPRING
  Annie, 170

Charles E., 173
David W., 110
Ed., 249
Elizabeth, 125
Fannie V., 56
Mary, 124
Mary V., 247
SPURGEON
  Emma J., 282
SQUIRES
  Eliza, 224
  Leroy, 224
STALEY
  Cora, 63
STALLARD
  William, 174
STANDLEY
  James S., 88
STANDSBURY
  Harry C., 285
STANLEY
  Ida, 63
STANSBURY
  C. F., 15, 80
  J. J., 80, 130, 254
  Jesse J., 185
  Laura, 15
  M. A., 254
  Margaret A., 258
  Nannie E., 242
STANTINYERS
  Kesiah, 220
STAUTON
  R. T., 164
STEADMAN
  Charles M., 243
  David, 188, 254
  Elizabeth, 254
  J. Thos., 279
  James W., 208
  John E., 281
  John M., 237, 281
  L. C., 281
  Mamie, 243
  Marshal B., 73
  Olivia, 254
  Susan, 78
  Wm., 243
  Wm. H., 143
STEANSON
  John, 180
STEER

Edward B., 60
Phebe M., 237
Phineas J., 212
Phoebe M., 237
Saml. L., 106
Samuel J., 103
Wm. B., 61
STEPHENS
John, 182
Joseph M., 58
STEPHENSON
Wm. A., 193
Wm. H., 260, 273
STEVENS
Benjamin F., 178
Edwin A., 109
Edwin O., 109
James A., 9
John, 109
John H., 58
John J., 192
Jos. M., 69
Mary E., 192
Nannie, 149
Nettie E., 192
STEVENSON
Amanda F., 29
William, 254
Wm., 253
STEWARD
Martha J., 214
STEWART
John W., 266
Virginia L., 208
STICKLES
Gertrude, 11
STICKLEY
E. E., 73
Sophia, 71
Sophia H., 73
STICKLY
E. E., 71
STICKNEY
Mary K., 86
STILES
Annie V., 205
Thomas, 205
Thomas L., 205
STINEMETZ
Irene D., 74
STIPE
Ida L., 207

STOCK
Hester, 199
STOCKS
Ella M., 181
Estelle G., 145
Isaac L., 36
Isaiah N., 193
John H., 227
Jos. H., 23
Mahlon, 181
Matilda J., 250
Thomas, 178
STONE
I. S., 160, 245
Newton M., 248
Samuel, 10
Sarah, 162
Sarah A., 124
William J., 39
Wm. J., 284
STONEBURNER
___, 219
Armstead McG., 58
C., 56
John E., 106
M. V., 58
S. G., 58
Stoneburner & Prufer, 211
Stoneburner & Richards, 219
STONESTREET
Addie, 14
E. E., 14
STOTT
John E., 21
STOUFFER
Ella, 283
Frank, 283
STOUT
Amanda E., 277
STOUTS
Annie, 171
STOUTSENBERGER
Clara, 10
Margaret, 57
STOVER
Solomon, 17
STRASBURGER
John B., 119
STREAM
Janie, 88

John H., 205
Nannie H., 205
Susannah, 124
STRETCH
Emma, 99
John, 99
Polly, 99
STRIBING
Francis T., 257
STRIBLING
Dr., 111
J. B., 4
Lizzie, 46
M. C., 46
Mary, 168
Robert, 123
Robert M., 136
Taliaferro, 168
STRINGER
W. R., 66
STROTHER
A. W., 35
Frank M., 190
Wm. H., 238
STROUD
Wm., 119
Wm. P., 120
SUMMERS
Daniel, 86
G. W., 3
Geo. W., 92
Matilda, 86
R. H., 70
Richard H., 75
W. S., 284
Wm. S., 3
SURGHNOR
James, 213
Lloyd W., 101
V. H., 24
SURVICK
A. M., 113
Benjamin, 24
Benjamin D., 246
Bessie E., 271
Boyd, 243
Carrie, 131
Geo. W., 108, 113, 217
George, 108
Mary B., 131
Nora, 131

INDEX

Nora L., 246
S. R., 113
Sallie, 246
SUTHERLAND
  Alcinda, 142
SWAIN
  Texana, 191
  W. G., 182
SWANK
  Aaron, 144
  Eva R., 284
  Jno. W., 284
  Mary E., 144
  Saml. P., 177
  Sarah E., 284
  Wm., 166
SWANN
  Carita, 252, 253
  Governor, 275
  Sherlock, 217
  Thomas, 214, 217, 252
  Thos., 194, 216, 253, 275
SWART
  Adrian W., 125
  Elizabeth, 39, 125
  Elizabeth J., 158
  Elizabeth T., 257
  Henry, 125, 257
  Henry S., 158, 292
  Hugh, 290
  Sallie E., 158
  William J., 153
  Wm. R., 39
SWARTS
  Elizabeth, 43
  Nellie, 149
SWEEDY
  Mollie, 153
SYNCOX
  Francis, 121

TALKS
  Arthur I., 201
  Arthur T., 126, 166, 201
  Charles R., 166
  Sallie E., 166, 201
TALLY
  Maggie, 50
  Wm., 170

TARLETON
  William H., 25
TATE
  Eliza, 273
  Mary, 273
  William, 134
  Wm., 128
TAVENER
  F. H., 106
  George W., 85
  J. A., 118
  Medra V., 122
TAVENNER
  ___, 60
  Alpheus, 220
  Anna, 92
  Annie M., 220, 226
  Benj., 182
  Benjamin, 64
  Carroll A., 150
  Catherine H., 154
  E. H., 154
  Emma, 220, 255
  Emma A., 120, 121
  Estell, 5
  Fielding, 37, 40
  Francis H., 103
  Henry, 92
  Henry H., 150
  Hiram, 273
  Hiram V., 282
  Hiriam N., 280
  Ida E., 114
  J. A., 182
  James E., 226
  Janie S., 245
  Jas. L., 220
  John, 118
  John V., 178, 241
  Jonathan, 121
  Lott, 288, 289
  Maggie, 178
  Mahlon, 16, 144, 147
  Minnie, 178
  Mollie A., 69
  Mollie J., 226
  Nannie B., 212
  R. E., 212
  R. W., 286
  Richardetta, 44
  Sarah W., 1
  Susan, 295

Susan A., 183
W. W., 5
William, 69, 122
Wm., 44, 75, 212
TAYLOR
  Alfred H., 183
  Annie, 52
  Benj. F., 44
  Benjamin F., 149
  Bernard, 160, 193
  Carrie, 102
  Chas. G., 182
  Daingerfield, 52
  Ella, 175
  Ella F., 274
  Francis, 286
  H. H., 287
  Hannah, 5, 12
  Hannah J., 231
  Harriet B., 61, 72, 125
  Henry S., 231
  Jane, 21
  Jane M., 44
  Joseph, 127, 286
  Lawrence B., 211
  Lewis, 102, 118, 202
  Lewis R., 86
  Mary E. N., 52
  Mary P., 61
  Mrs., 146
  Oliver, 89
  Oscar, 274
  Robt. W., 244
  Sarah A., 193
  Snowden W., 31
  Thomas E., 61
  Thos. E., 231
  Timothy, 72, 80
  Virginia P., 211
  William H., 52
  Wm. H., 52
  Yardley, 5
TEBBS
  R. H., 3, 174, 220, 228
  Richard H., 173
  Thos. F., 220
TEEL
  William H., 264
TEELE
  Clarence, 129

INDEX

Lillie, 129
Mary E., 129
Rufus, 129
TEMPLAR
  Thomas, 182
TERRELL
  Susannah, 99
TERRY
  F. S., 90
THAYER
  Hiram, 98
THELL
  Sarah, 19
  Stephen D., 19
THOMAS
  Addie, 77
  Adelaide, 75
  Albert C., 122
  Alverna, 196
  Alvernon, 71
  Annie, 176
  Annie L., 296
  Edward, 5, 11
  Eli, 132
  Elsie, 134
  Emma L., 16
  Granville, 241
  H. W., 113, 237, 288
  Henry, 33, 73
  Herod, 77
  I. H., 293
  J. S., 114
  James, 80
  James W., 212
  Jas. L., 292
  Jeff C., 93
  Jenevieve, 148
  John, 193
  John T., 237
  Jonah, 161, 162
  Jos., 61
  Joseph, 71
  Laura, 233
  Lucy B., 183
  Mahlon, 43, 93, 176
  Margaret, 113
  Martha J., 128
  Mary J., 120
  Mattie, 176
  Nannie, 288
  Owen, 176, 296
  R. W., 148

Tamar, 176
Tarlton, 173
W. S. O., 10
Wm. H., 185
Wm. J., 159
Wm. P., 128, 144
THOMPSON
  Alice, 265
  Amy A., 117
  Ashby, 158
  Belle, 80, 176
  Bernard, 152
  Daissy C., 211
  E. E., 152
  Edgar, 194
  Edward, 101, 193
  Edward M., 225
  Eli, 269
  Eliza A., 114
  Eliza B., 204
  Fannie, 269
  George G., 204
  Hannis V., 275
  Harriet, 78
  Henry, 245
  Howard, 278
  Hugh, 207
  Hugh S., 150, 153, 158, 161
  Irim, 207
  Irving P., 162
  Israel B., 94
  J. A., 162
  J. Harry, 162
  J. S. B., 126, 127
  James, 114
  Jeff, 111
  Jno. A., 153
  John, 13
  John H., 128, 131
  John T., 194
  John W., 151
  Josephine, 152
  Josephine M., 154
  M. S., 168
  Mary B., 131
  Mary L., 265
  Merriwether, 111
  Nancy, 114
  R. A., 211
  R. J. C., 273
  Randolph, 265

Rebecca, 22
Ruth, 158
Ruth H., 161, 162
Sallie M. B., 12
Saml., 13
Samuel, 13
Susie B., 33
Virginia, 140
W. D., 162
W. W., 80, 220, 222
Wm. B., 111
Wm. D., 153
Wyatt, 227
THOMSON
  Israel B., 100
  John, 192
THORNTON
  James, 207
  Mollie, 147
  Sanford, 169
  Thomas, 93
  W. H., 147
THRASHER
  Elizabeth H., 253
  L. A., 56
  Luther A., 274
  T. E., 56
THRIFT
  Annie M., 254
  James, 249
  Martha, 57
  Mary B., 33
  Samuel, 220
THROCKMORTON
  ___, 250
THROCMORTON
  J. B., 56
THURMAN
  Senator, 12, 13
THURSTON
  G. A., 135
  Louisa A., 135
TIFFANY
  Hugh A., 28
  Mollie, 28
  Wallace, 28
TILLETT
  Caroline C., 198
  Catharine J., 198
  Jane, 12, 124
  Samuel A., 198
  Samuel C., 71

T. R., 283
Thomas R., 76
TIMBERLAKE
  Richard, 228
TIMBERS
  Nancy, 119
TIMMS
  James F., 91
  Jas. F., 233
  Lydia, 233
  Samuel W., 151
  Wm. L., 77
TINSMAN
  E., 172
  Elizabeth A., 49
  Enoch, 49
  F. M., 106
  Minnie G., 209
TITUS
  Armistead, 234
  Armstead, 128
  Charles M., 189
  D. H., 271
  Edward, 138
  Geo. W., 266
  John H., 290, 293
  Laura W., 81
  Lovisa, 81
  Mabel M., 189
  Martha A., 261
  Mollie J., 140
  S. T., 293
  Samuel, 261
  T. S., 81, 261
  T. Sidney, 138
  Virginia, 189
TOLIVER
  Cely, 182
TOLKS
  Arthur T., 126
TOPPIN
  Henry, 44
TOPPING
  Henry, 46
  John, 46, 73
  John H., 72
TORREYSON
  C. L., 163
TORRYSON
  Lydia, 108
TOWNER
  Jacob C., 202

John, 175
John L., 57
Mollie, 175
Sarah R., 202
TOWNSEND
  Jane J., 185
  L. Maud, 185
  Mamie, 114
TOWZER
  Mary, 109
TRABUE
  W. E., 266
TRAMMELL
  Lulu, 251
  Rosa, 66
TRAPNELL
  Joseph, 242
TRAVERS
  Capt., 17
TRAYHERN
  James F., 205
TRENARY
  Hannah F., 92
  Ida, 169
  Miss, 155
TREW
  B. W., 133
  Bushrod W., 70
  Kate A., 133
  Mrs., 273
  Virginia W., 133
TRICKETT
  William, 4
TRIDAPOE
  Edward R., 181
TRIPLETT
  Margaret, 80
  William, 59
TRIPLETTS
  Leonidas, 59
TROTER
  Florence, 174
TROTTER
  E. J., 125
TROUT
  Ella, 167
TROXELL
  William, 143
TRUITT
  G. E., 51
TRUNDLE
  Abner C., 220

Horatio, 220
TRUSSELL
  Florence J., 243
  Mary E., 278
  Sarah A., 196
TUCKER
  J. R., 154
TURBERVILLE
  M. V., 115
TURNBULL
  L.B., 193
TURNER
  ___, 151
  Admiral, 27
  Beverly, 189
  Charles B., 173
  E. C., 259
  E. P., 259, 261
  Edward C., 25, 259, 260
  Edward P., 25, 259
  H. Franklin, 205
  Henry C., 34
  Jno., 77
  John R., 226
  Kate E., 239
  Martha E., 77
  Mary, 37
  Mary B., 25
  Mary E., 87
  R. H., 239
  Richard, 205
  Robert, 259
  Robert F., 259
  Samuel, 87
  Susie F., 151
TUSTIN
  Septimus, 162
  Septimus N., 162
TUTT
  Ann M., 78
  Charles P., 78, 205
  M. L., 205
TYLER
  E. A., 112
  Edmund, 146
  Emma, 281
  G. W., 95
  Grafton, 143
  John J., 1, 182
  John W., 95
  Mary K., 124, 146

INDEX

Nathaniel, 148
R. Bradley, 281
Sadie R., 148

UMBAUGH
Catharine, 124, 174
Catherine, 64
Catherine V., 63
George, 174
George W., 148
John W., 64
Mary E., 6
Sallie A., 174
Silas H., 98
UNDERWOOD
Alice, 96
Ella M., 152
URICH
___, 133
UTTERBACK
B. D., 147

Van HORN
C. O., 127
Van RANSSELAER
Stephen, 190
Van RENSSELAER
Eleanor, 200
Eleanor C., 190
William P., 190
Wm. P., 200
Van RENSSELLAER
Eleanor C., 199
Wm. P., 199
Van SCHAICK
C. DeF., 233
Van SICK
Mary L., 201
VANDERHOFF
Wm. H., 65
VANDERHOOF
William H., 62
VANDEVANTER
Addison, 14
Albert, 188
Albert D., 131
Braden, 183
C. O., 39
Carrie E., 21
Chas. O., 38, 64, 183
Cornelius, 141
D. H., 83

Emma, 188
Helen J., 204
Henry, 289
Isaac, 64, 145, 204, 291
Joseph H., 188
Patience, 14
Washington, 21, 22
VANDEVENTER
Chas. O., 263
Laura, 242
Miss, 258
Robt. S., 242
VANSICKLER
Emanuel, 64
J. B., 296
John, 109
John A., 71
Lula, 296
Lulu, 297
Mahala, 45
Margaret, 82
Orra L., 71
Philip, 45, 179
Rose B., 64
Susie, 289
VASS
Douglas, 65
Florence E., 218, 220
R. C., 91, 218, 279
Rosslyn C., 91
VEIHMEYER
Frank A., 162
Jacob, 162
VENABLE
A. B., 258
VERMILLION
Mary T., 64
VERTS
J. L., 69
Oda L., 69
VICKERS
William, 123
VIERS
Samuel E., 199
VILLARD
Andre J., 29
VINCEL
Alice M., 66
Alice M. M., 138
John, 210
Wm. D., 138

VINSELL
Louisa, 227
VIRTS
Bessie, 30
Chas. C., 159
Chas. W., 159
Conard, 58
Cornelius O., 41
Elizabeth, 192
Fannie B., 7
Henry, 7, 77
John W., 125
Katie C., 132
Mary J., 109
Peter T., 188
Rose A., 91
Susan A., 124, 269
Tracey V., 159
Virginia, 89
Virginia L., 88
Wm., 156
VIRTZ
Abraham, 30
Florida, 30
John T., 102
Mary C., 188
Mary V., 6
Susan A., 46
T. Frank, 217
Thos. B., 125
Wm. A., 178
Wm. W., 53
Von BRITON
John U. B., 246
VOORHEES
D. W., 148
Nelson, 74
VYE
Fred. W., 16

WADDLE
John R., 186
WADE
R. W., 143
Vashi, 143
WAGNER
W. N., 188
WALDOM
Lizzie, 262
WALKER
___, 5
Edith A., 7

INDEX

Elisha H., 12
Jas. M., 144, 289
John W., 37
R. R., 292
WALLACE
  Adelaide, 168
  Amanda F., 31
  Elizabeth, 22
  Essie C., 293, 294
  Frank, 294
  H. C., 293, 294
  H. Clay, 294
  James M., 168, 190, 267, 269
  Jno. M., 159
  Lew., 267
  Lillian M., 42
  Lizzie S., 16
  Mary A., 157
  P. B., 270
  Page, 6, 7
  Samuel F., 240
  Thomas, 35
WALLACH
  Jennie, 241
  Maud, 241
  P., 241
  S. H., 241
WALLIS
  Samuel F., 241
WALTER
  Chas. G., 171
  Frank, 112
WALTERS
  Mary N., 278
WALTMAN
  A. C., 42
WALTON
  Rich'd. L., 254
WAMPLER
  B. E., 203
  Bessie E., 203
  Carrie, 24
  J. M., 109
  J. Morris, 24
  J. T., 24, 203
  Julia C., 109
  Kate R., 24
WARD
  Cornelius, 192
  John, 162
WARE

  ___, 97
  Annie E., 179
  J. W., 112
  S. S., 112
WARFORD
  Abel, 269
  Abram, 187
WARING
  Moses, 150
WARNER
  Arthur, 245
  B. H., 197
  Cecelia, 213
  Chas. E., 213
  Edgar H., 159
  Edgar W., 62, 159
  Gabriel V., 227
  Isaac, 244
  Israel, 118, 200, 201
  J. F., 252
  Malinda, 118
  Mollie E., 159
WARREN
  Ada, 273
WARTHEN
  A. L., 167
WASHINGTON
  Augustine, 251
  B. C., 290
  Bushrod, 239, 251
  Bushrod C., 33
  Eleanor L., 251
  George, 157, 239, 251
  Jane B., 251
  John, 168
  John A., 251
  Lawrance, 251
  Wm. B., 252
WATERS
  Hugh, 55
  Mary E., 39
  Mattie, 84
  Sarah S. C., 170
  Wm., 84
WATKINS
  Charles R., 231
WATSON
  Abbie E., 187
  Annie M., 49
  Jacob B., 49
  Lemuel, 82

  Lucy, 82
WEADON
  Charles D., 37
  F. M., 191
  G. W., 4
  Lizzie, 90
  Mary M., 37
  Sarah P., 173
  T. W., 90
WEBB
  Martha, 118
  Martha J., 118
  Mary A., 98
  Richard, 70
  Robert J., 225
  Robt J., 226
  Robt. A., 146
  W. R., 270
WEBBER
  Margarette R., 215
  Robert, 215
WEBSTER
  Clarence U., 294
  J. G., 106
  Sarah C., 106
WEEDON
  Robert, 60
WEEKS
  Sallie, 37
  Sally, 31
WEIR
  Wood, 234
WELCH
  Fayette, 26
WELLFORD
  Armistead L., 293
WELLS
  Danl. N., 179
  Mary C., 122
WELSH
  George W., 265
  John, 285
  Welshans & McEwan, 110
WELTY
  Dr., 155
  Elias, 290
WENNER
  C. C., 34, 67, 205
  Carrie V., 9
  Catherine E., 235
  Emanuel, 201, 205

INDEX

Geo. W., 16, 21
George F., 64
J. J., 21, 168
J. W., 10
Mary J., 131
Orra B., 64
Robert, 33
Robt., 205
WEST
  George W., 236
  Joseph, 135
  Josephine, 135
  Lula, 152
  N. G., 107, 152, 236, 292
  Roberta L., 70
WHALEY
  Ellen, 257
  J. W., 280
  James, 257
  James W., 130
  Lydia, 53
  Mary, 257
  Mary A., 51
  Mary J., 130
  Ray, 130
WHARTON
  Lullu, 271
  Lulu, 291
  W. J., 291
WHEELER
  Gussie, 191
  J. B., 148
  J. Henry, 241
WHIPPLE
  Elizabeth S., 275
  John, 275
WHITACRE
  C., 149
  Samuel J., 54
  Thornton, 284
  Wm.T., 166
WHITE
  A. M., 282
  Annie, 244
  Annie A., 243
  B. S., 110
  Ben, 240
  Benj. V., 195
  Charles E., 176
  Daniel, 96, 104
  Danl., 24, 220
  E. B., 165
  E. V., 36, 194, 199, 217, 280, 289
  Elijah B., 194
  Hattie V., 271
  James B., 181
  James H., 223
  Jane, 211
  John B., 151
  John R., 178
  Josiah T., 243, 244
  Laura B., 90
  Laura J., 194
  Levi, 130, 251
  Louanna, 251
  Mahlon, 186
  Maj., 111
  Mansfield, 154
  Margaret D., 160
  Mary A., 190
  Mary E., 91
  Miss, 282
  Mollie, 130
  Mortimer, 213
  N. S., 115
  Nathan S., 242
  R. J. T., 285
  Richard T., 257
  Sue, 244
  W. H., 257
  William, 123, 133
White & Trapnell, 242
White & Wootton, 140
White, E. B. & Bro., 194
WHITING
  Frank, 32
  Guy, 294
  Mary B., 32
  R. W., 294
WHITLOCK
  Amanda, 120
  Amanda B., 112
  Henry, 120, 141
  Robt., 90
WHITMORE
  Annie, 7
  Ella, 154
  Emma, 131
  Henry, 238
  Jno. H., 131, 154, 212, 277
  John H., 7
  Michael T., 16
  Mrs., 133
  Rachel, 124, 134
WIARD
  Annie E., 226
  Jacob S., 226
  Maria, 69, 75
  Michael, 173, 282, 284
  Stephen, 71
WIERMAN
  Anna B., 258
  John R., 258
WIGGINGTON
  W. H., 53
WILCOXEN
  J. W., 93
WILDER
  Annie E., 226
  Henry C., 226
WILDMAN
  Charlotte, 213
  Jane D., 23, 124
  John W., 283
  Jos., 213
  Joseph, 201, 209
  Kate, 195
  R. B., 264
  Rebecca, 276
  Robt. B., 194
Wildman & Co., 221, 283
WILEN
  Henry, 260
  Mollie, 260
WILES
  Henry G., 25
WILEY
  Eliza J., 100
  Florence M., 11, 132
  Goldie R., 260
  H. G., 100
  Harrison P., 132
  Hazel L., 206
  J. H., 11
  John G., 29
  John H., 134, 138
  Laura, 15
  Lena, 96, 281
  Mattie R., 260
  Mollie, 138
  W. S., 260

The Mirror
INDEX

Walter G., 164
Walter S., 206
Wm. E., 176
Wm. H., 118
WILLIAMS
  Benjamin, 142
  Chas. A., 247
  David, 143
  Edmonia, 176
  Edward, 128
  Ella V., 164
  George S., 43
  Henrietta, 173
  Israel, 111
  James T., 203
  Jno. J., 146
  John, 36, 88, 173
  John B., 200
  John H., 32
  Joseph J., 41
  M. C., 200
  Maria, 253
  Mary E., 88
  Minerva, 36
  Robt., 277
  Si, 217
  Stout, 253
  William L., 219
WILLIAMSON
  Geo. D., 209
  H. W., 147
  J. A., 156
  Sydney B., 161
  T. H., 161
  Thomas, 147, 226
  Thomas H., 226
  Thos., 181
  W. B., 177
WILLINER
  Alfred, 64
WILLIS
  ___, 49
  M. M., 124
WILLISS
  Mollie M., 107
  R. G., 107
WILMARTH
  Mabel, 271
WILSON
  Antoni, 253
  J. B., 133
  James B., 181, 184

John A., 129, 136
Jos. R., 136
Julia, 139
Laura A., 175
Mary A., 83
Mollie T., 198
S. H., 175
Sallie C., 181, 184
Thos. J., 153
William, 108
WILT
  Mary M. E., 183
WILTSHIRE
  Philip, 212
WINCHESTER
  Matthew H., 72
  S. H., 72
  Sallie H., 279
  Stirling M., 279
  W. R., 72, 279
WINE
  Danl.N., 205
WINGER
  Blanche, 253
WINN
  A. M., 114
WIRE
  Catherine E., 125
  Charles W., 292
  Elizabeth, 126
  George C., 173
  John, 55, 56
  Peter, 230
  Sallie V., 126
WISE
  Claude N., 213
  George, 213
  George P., 220
  Peter, 241
  W. N., 217, 220
  Wm. N., 213
WISSLER
  Kate, 202
WITHERS
  A. L., 159
  R. W., 54
  Robt. E., 54
  Samuel, 170
WITMAN
  Harry W., 52
WITT
  Samuel B., 147, 148

WOLFORD
  Catharine, 92
  Chas., 103
  Edward, 145
  Geo. W., 135
  George W., 135
  John, 48
  Margaret J., 181
  Mary A., 165
WOOD
  Ann S., 130
  J. E. R., 238
  Jno. W., 77
  Joseph, 222
  Mary V., 208
WOODARD
  Edgar T., 22
  George R., 246
WOODDY
  Mary E., 180
  Samuel H., 180
WOODS
  Geo. M., 111
  Mary, 111
WOODSON
  B. L., 29
WOODWARD
  Hallie O., 248
  Thomas E., 271
  Woodward & Lothrop, 254
WOOLF
  Andrew, 75
  Bessie, 297
  Chas. M., 297
  Edgar, 297
  Gertrude T., 75
  Henry, 297
WOOTTON
  Edward, 140
  Olivia C., 140
WORKING
  Sarah E., 136
WORKS
  Alfred, 33
  Alfred P., 82
  Betsy, 33
  Helen E., 48
  J. W., 229
  James, 82
  Jas. W., 234
  Mary F., 4, 33

INDEX

WORNAL
  John, 124
WORSLEY
  Thomas L., 186
  Virginia G., 186
  Wm., 186
WORTHINGTON
  Bruce, 281
  C. E., 281
WORTMAN
  Joseph W., 36
  Peyton S., 39
  Sarah, 124
  Sarah J., 104
WORTS
  A. E., 183
WRENN
  John, 289
  Mattie, 164
WRIGHT
  Alfred, 30
  Anna, 30
  Augustus D., 192
  Bennett, 96, 97
  Beverley O., 100
  Edward, 119
  Edwin, 85
  Florence R., 109
  Jno. E., 91
  John, 276
  John E., 92
  Joseph E., 100
  Katie V., 236
  Klein, 266
  Lillie, 85
  Rebecca T., 171
  Samuel J., 64
  Samuel T., 100
  Sarah J., 41
  Silas W., 30
WYCKOFF
  A. Cornelius, 1
  Emily V., 52
  Irene M., 40
  James W., 40
  Willie A., 40
WYETH
  Parker C., 291
WYNCOOP
  Bell, 136
  Wm., 136
WYNDHAM
  Annie C., 247
  T. O., 247
WYNKOOP
  Adeline, 83
  Ann A., 14
  Bessie, 238
  Clara, 252
  Fannie, 236
  Geo., 47
  George W., 101
  Harriet A., 281
  J. T., 236
  James A., 173
  John, 102
  Luther, 88
  Mary, 102
  Mollie, 152
  Richard H., 236
  Robert, 152
  Samuel, 182
  Samuel T., 88, 98, 238
  Thos., 236
  Wm. B., 208
WYSONG
  John, 166
  R. L., 128
  Robert W., 26

YELLOTT
  A. R., 22
  Emily M., 71
  Florence, 22
  John J., 71
  R. E. L., 22
  Sarah J., 71
YERBY
  Ann, 130
  Susan, 48
YOUELL
  A. J., 2
YOUMANS
  Cornelia M., 28
  Miss, 51
YOUNG
  Campbell H., 19
  David, 238
  Eliza, 109
  Fred., 297
  Geo., 134
  Jane L., 18
  L. C., 193
  M. B., 233
  Phoebe, 238
  Phoebe R., 238
  Thomas, 206
YULEE
  D. L., 72
  Margaret C., 72

ZEREGA
  A. L. B., 296
  Alfred B., 247
  Augustus, 246, 253
  Dot, 296
  Gussie, 296
ZEVERLEY
  Wentworth, 162
ZRUNDELLO
  Joseph, 40

Other Heritage Books by Patricia B. Duncan:

1850 Fairfax County and Loudoun County, Virginia Slave Schedule

1850 Fauquier County, Virginia Slave Schedule

1860 Loudoun County, Virginia Slave Schedule

*Clarke County, Virginia Will Book Abstracts:
Books A-I (1836-1904) and 1A-3C (1841-1913)*

Fauquier County, Virginia, Birth Register, 1853-1880

Fauquier County, Virginia, Birth Register, 1881-1896

Fauquier County, Virginia, Marriage Register, 1854-1882

Fauquier County, Virginia, Marriage Register, 1883-1906

Fauquier County, Virginia Death Register, 1853-1896

Hunterdon County, New Jersey 1895 State Census, Part I: Alexandria-Junction

Hunterdon County, New Jersey 1895 State Census, Part II: Kingwood-West Amwell

Genealogical Abstracts from The Lambertville Press, *Lambertville, New Jersey:
4 November 1858 (Vol. 1, Number 1) to 30 October 1861 (Vol. 3, Number 155)*

Genealogical Abstracts from The Democratic Mirror *and*
The Mirror, *1857-1879, Loudoun County, Virginia*

Genealogical Abstracts from The Mirror, *1880-1890, Loudoun County, Virginia*

Genealogical Abstracts from The Mirror, *1891-1899, Loudoun County, Virginia*

Genealogical Abstracts from The Mirror, *1900-1919, Loudoun County, Virginia*

Jefferson County, Virginia/West Virginia Death Records, 1853-1880

Jefferson County, West Virginia Death Records, 1881-1903

Jefferson County, Virginia 1802-1813 Personal Property Tax Lists

Jefferson County, Virginia 1814-1824 Personal Property Tax Lists

Jefferson County, Virginia 1825-1841 Personal Property Tax Lists

1810-1840 Loudoun County, Virginia Federal Population Census Index

1860 Loudoun County, Virginia Federal Population Census Index

1870 Loudoun County, Virginia Federal Population Census Index

Abstracts from Loudoun County, Virginia Guardian Accounts: Books A-H, 1759-1904

Abstracts of Loudoun County, Virginia Register of Free Negroes, 1844-1861

Index to Loudoun County, Virginia Land Deed Books A-Z, 1757-1800

Index to Loudoun County, Virginia Land Deed Books 2A-2M, 1800-1810

Index to Loudoun County, Virginia Land Deed Books 2N-2U, 1811-1817

Index to Loudoun County, Virginia Land Deed Books 2V-3D, 1817-1822

Index to Loudoun County, Virginia Land Deed Books 3E-3M, 1822-1826

Index to Loudoun County, Virginia Land Deed Books 3N-3V, 1826-1831

Index to Loudoun County, Virginia Land Deed Books 3W-4D, 1831-1835

Index to Loudoun County, Virginia Land Deed Books 4E-4N, 1835-1840

Index to Loudoun County, Virginia Land Deed Books 4O-4V, 1840-1846

Loudoun County, Virginia Birth Register, 1853-1879

Loudoun County, Virginia Birth Register, 1880-1896

Loudoun County, Virginia Clerks Probate Records Book 1 (1904-1921) and Book 2 (1922-1938)

(With Elizabeth R. Frain) *Loudoun County, Virginia Marriages after 1850, Volume 1, 1851-1880*

Loudoun County, Virginia 1800-1810 Personal Property Taxes

Loudoun County, Virginia 1826-1834 Personal Property Taxes

Loudoun County, Virginia Will Book Abstracts, Books A-Z, Dec. 1757-Jun. 1841

Loudoun County, Virginia Will Book Abstracts, Books 2A-3C, Jun. 1841-Dec. 1879 and Superior Court Books A and B, 1810-1888

Loudoun County, Virginia Will Book Index, 1757-1946

Genealogical Abstracts from The Brunswick Herald, *Brunswick, Maryland: Mar. 6 1891-Dec. 28 1894*

Genealogical Abstracts from The Brunswick Herald, *Brunswick, Maryland: Jan. 4 1895-Dec. 30 1898*

Genealogical Abstracts from The Brunswick Herald, *Brunswick, Maryland: Jan. 6 1899-Dec. 26 1902*

Genealogical Abstracts from The Brunswick Herald, *Brunswick, Maryland: Jan. 2 1903-June 29 1906*

Genealogical Abstracts from The Brunswick Herald, *Brunswick, Maryland: July 6 1906-Feb. 25 1910*

CD: *Loudoun County, Virginia Personal Property Tax List, 1782-1850*

www.ingramcontent.com/pod-product-compliance
Lightning Source LLC
Chambersburg PA
CBHW071952220426
43662CB00009B/1095